The Jesup North Pacific Expedition

Edited by FRANZ BOAS

VOL. 11

AMS PRESS

NEW YORK

The Jesup North Pacific Expedition

Edited by FRANZ BOAS

Memoir of the American Museum

of

Natural History

NEW YORK

VOL. XI

CRANIOLOGY OF THE NORTH PACIFIC COAST

BY

BRUNO OETTEKING

LEIDEN	NEW YORK
E. J. BRILL Ltd	G. E. STECHERT
Printers & Publishers	American Agents
1930	1930

Library of Congress Cataloging in Publication Data

Oetteking, Bruno, 1871-
    Craniology of the North Pacific coast.

    Reprint of the 1930 ed. published by E. J. Brill, Leiden, and G. E. Stechert, New York, which was issued as v. 15, pt. 1 of the Memoirs of the American Museum of Natural History, and as v. 11, pt. 1 of the Publications of the Jesup North Pacific Expedition.
    1. Indians of North America—Northwest coast of North America—Craniology. 2. Craniology—Northwest coast of North America. I. Title. II. Series: American Museum of Natural History, New York. Memoirs ; v. 15, pt. 1. III. Series: The Jesup North Pacific Expedition. Publications ; v. 11, pt. 1.
E78.N78035   573'.7   73-3533
ISBN 0-404-58111-0

Reprinted, with permission, from a volume in the collections of the University of Idaho Library.

Reprinted from the edition of 1930, Leiden and New York
First AMS edition published, 1975
Manufactured in the United States of America

International Standard Book Number:
Complete Set: 0-404-58100-5
Volume 11:   0-404-58111-0

AMS PRESS, INC.
New York, N.Y. 10003

PART I — CRANIOMETRY

CONTENTS.

	Page
Introduction	1
Material	4

Part I: CRANIOMETRY

	Page
Technique	9
Deformation of the head	12
1. Nature of deformation and general distribution	12
2. Tribal methods of deformation and metrical interpretation	16
Orientation	24
1. General remarks	24
2. Angular relation between ear-eye and glabella-lambda planes	25
3. Klaatsch's "central angle" (Zentralwinkel)	26
4. Angle of basion-bregma height line and ear-eye plane	29
Cranial capacity	33
Principal diameters and indices of skulls	34
1. Maximum length	34
2. Maximum breadth	35
3. Basion-bregma height	36
4. Comparative aspect of principal diameters of skulls	36
5. Length-breadth index	38
6. Length-height index	41
7. Breadth-height index	42
Median-sagittal arc	44
1. Median-sagittal arc	44
2. Divisions of median-sagittal arc	45
3. Participation of frontal, parietal and occipital divisions in median-sagittal arc	47
4. Percental ratio between frontal and parietal arcs	49
Os frontale	51
1. Minimum frontal breadth	51
2. Maximum frontal breadth	51
3. Transverse frontal index	52
4. Transverse fronto-parietal index	53
5. Median-sagittal frontal arc	54
6. Median-sagittal frontal chord	54
7. Sagittal frontal index	55
8. Frontal angle	57
Os parietale	59
1. Median-sagittal parietal arc	59
2. Median-sagittal parietal chord	60
3. Sagittal parietal index	60
4. Parietal angle	62

CONTENTS.

	Page
Os occipitale	64
1. Median-sagittal occipital arc	64
2. Median-sagittal occipital chord	64
3. Sagittal occipital index	65
4. Occipital angle	66
5. Interoccipital angle	70
Cranial base	72
1. Length of cranial base (nasion-basion)	72
2. Angular relation between cranial base and ear-eye plane	73
3. Length of cranial base in relation to other metrical quantities of skull	74
Foramen magnum	76
1. Length of foramen magnum	76
2. Width of foramen magnum	76
3. Foramen magnum index	77
4. Angular relation between foramen magnum and ear-eye planes	78
5. Angular relation between cranial base and foramen magnum plane	80
Face	82
1. Upper facial height	82
2. Bizygomatic breadth	83
3. Upper facial index	83
4. Facial lenght	85
5. Facial triangle	86
6. Profilation	87
a. Profile angle of upper face	87
b. Profile angle of middle face	89
c. Profile angle of pars alveolaris	90
Cranio-facial proportions	92
1. Transverse cranio-facial index	92
2. Jugo-frontal index	93
3. Jugo-mandibular index	94
4. Cranio-facial angle	95
Upper jaw	97
1. Maxillo-alveolar length	97
2. Maxillo-alveolar breadth	97
3. Maxillo-alveolar index	98
4. Palatal length	100
5. Palatal width	100
6. Palatal index	101
7. Maxillo-cranial correlations	102
Nose	105
1. Nasal height	105
2. Nasal width	106
3. Nasal index	106
Orbit	109
1. Orbital height	109
2. Orbital width	109
3. Orbital index	112
4. Anterior interorbital breadth	114
5. Sagittal declination of orbit	115
Mandible	117

CONTENTS.

	Page
1. Bicondylar breadth	117
2. Bigonial breadth	118
3. Breadth index	119
4. Height of ramus	119
5. Minimum breadth of ramus	120
6. Ramus index	121
7. Height of chin	122
8. Angular relations	123
a. Between alveolar plane and ramus tangent (ramus angle)	123
b. Between ramus and basal tangents ("postero-basal" angle)	125
c. Between chin vertical and basal tangent ("antero-basal" angle)	127
d. Between alveolar plane and condylocoronoid line ("condylocoronoid" angle)	127
Summary to Part I: Craniometry	130
1. Comparative aspect of the four series (divisions)	130
a. Cerebral cranium	131
b. Facial cranium	134
c. Intracranial correlations	135
d. Lower jaw	136
2. The non-deforming tribal elements	136
a. Cerebral cranium	136
b. Facial cranium	139
c. Intracranial correlations	140
d. Lower jaw	141
3. Mongolo-mongoloid differentiation	141
a. Cerebral cranium	142
b. Facial cranium	142
c. Lillooet affinities	145
4. Mongolo-mongoloideo-caucasid differentiation	146
a. Cerebral cranium	146
b. Facial cranium	146
5. Cranio-typological differentiation	148
Summary	155
Deformed skulls	155
Undeformed skulls	156

Part II: CRANIOSCOPY

General remarks	157
Norma verticalis	159
1. Cranial contour	159
2. Pathological cranial forms	160
3. Postorbital constriction	162
4. Foramina parietalia	163
5. Os bregmaticum	166
6. Vertical aspect of arcus zygomaticus	167
Norma basilaris	170
1. Foramen magnum	170
a. Shape	170
b. Anterior border	172
c. Posterior border	173
d. "Manifestation of the occipital vertebra" (Kollmann)	175
e. Assimilation of atlas	177

CONTENTS.

	Page
f. Ankylosis atlantis	179
2. Regio occipitalis lateralis	180
a. Condyli occipitales	180
b. Fossa et canalis condyloideus	181
c. Canalis hypoglossi	185
d. Foramen jugulare	186
e. Processus paracondyloideus (s. paramastoideus)	189
f. Incisura mastoidea	193
g. Fossa mandibularis (glenoidalis)	193
3. Regio occipitalis posterior	194
a. Processus retromastoideus (Waldeyer)	194
b. Fossa vermiana (Albrecht)	194
4. Regio occipitalis anterior	195
a. Tuberculum pharyngeum	195
b. Fossa pharyngea	198
5. Regio pterygoidea	201
a. Processus pterygoideus	201
b. Foramen pterygospinosum (Civinini) incl. foramina ovale and spinosum	202
6. Regio maxillaris	204
a. Dental arch	204
b. Sutura palatina mediana	208
c. Sutura palatina transversa	208
d. Sutura incisiva (Goethei)	211
e. Foramen incisivum	213
f. Torus palatinus	213
g. Spina nasalis posterior	217
h. Foramina palatina majora et minora	219
Norma lateralis	221
1. Cranial contour	221
2. Lineae temporales	222
3. Squama temporalis	225
a. Form and size	225
b. Sutura squamosa	225
c. Processus parietalis	226
d. Incisura parietalis	227
e. Crista supramastoidea	232
f. Tuberculum mastoideum anterius (Waldeyer)	234
g. Sutura sphenosquamosa	234
h. Processus frontalis (squamae temporalis)	235
4. Regio mastoidea	236
a. Processus mastoideus	236
b. Sutura mastoideosquamosa	239
c. Sulcus supramastoideus (Waldeyer)	240
d. Tuberculum supramastoideum posterius (Waldeyer)	240
e. Processus asteriacus (Haferland)	242
5. Regio tympanica	243
a. Porus acusticus externus	243
b. Spina suprameatum	245
c. Os tympanicum (hyperostosis)	245
d. Os tympanicum (perforation)	248
e. Exostoses auriculares	249
f. Tuberculum articulare	253
g. Processus postglenoidalis	253

		Page
6. Fossa temporalis		255
a. Sulcus sphenoparietalis		255
b. Sutura sphenoparietalis (stenocrotaphy)		257
c. Os epiptericum		259
7. Fossa infratemporalis		262
a. Crista infratemporalis		262
b. Tuberculum spinosum		262
c. Crista infraorbitalis		264
8. Regio zygomatica		266
a. Arcus zygomaticus		266
b. Processus marginalis		270
c. Angulus zygomaticotemporalis		271
d. Sutura transversozygomatica		273
Norma frontalis		275
1. Regio frontalis		275
a. Tubera frontalia		275
b. Sutura frontalis s. metopica		275
c. Torus sagittalis ossis frontalis (Bartels)		276
d. Pars nasalis ossis frontis		279
2. Regio supraorbitalis		281
a. Glabellar development		281
b. Supraorbital prominences		282
3. Regio orbitalis		283
a. Shape of orbit		283
b. Incisura (foramen) frontalis		285
c. Incisura (foramen) supraorbitalis		285
d. Fovea and spina trochlearis		287
e. Cribra orbitalia		287
f. Canalis nasolacrimalis		290
4. Regio nasalis		290
a. Ossa nasalia		290
α. Shape		290
β. Nasal bridge		294
b. Foramina nasalia		295
c. Sutura internasalis		296
d. Sutura nasofrontalis		299
e. Nasion		301
f. Spina nasalis anterior		301
g. Incisura nasalis inferior		303
h. Margo piriformis inferior		304
5. Regio maxillaris		307
a. Fossa canina		307
b. Crista infrazygomatica		309
c. Sutura (foramen) infraorbitalis		311
Norma occipitalis		315
1. Occipital contour		315
2. Relief of squama		317
a. General remarks		317
b. Protuberantia occipitalis externa		318
c. Torus occipitalis (Ecker)		318
d. Fossa supratoralis (Klaatsch)		320
e. Os incae		323
f. Os apicis		325

CONTENTS.

	Page
3. Regio mastoidea	328
a. Foramen mastoideum	328
b. Asterion	330
Mandible	331
1. Corpus	331
a. General remarks	331
b. General appearance of lower jaw	331
c. Incisura praemuscularis (Klaatsch) s. praeangularis (Frizzi); "Schaukelunterkiefer" (Stahr)	332
d. Chin	333
e. Incisura submentalis / Spina interdigastrica (Klaatsch)	335
f. Foramen mentale	336
g. Spina mentalis interna	337
2. Ramus	338
a. General proportions	338
b. Incisura subcoronoidea / Incisura subcondyloidea (Klaatsch)	339
c. Processus condyloideus / Processus coronoideus / Incisura mandibularis (condylocoronoidea)	341
d. Trigonum postcoronoideum	343
e. Fossa praecoronoidea / Trigonum postmolare (Klaatsch)	343
f. Medial relief in general	344
Sutures and Wormian bones	346
Teeth	350
Summary to Part II: Cranioscopy	354
1. Facts and limitations	354
2. Norma verticalis	355
3. Norma basilaris	356
4. Norma lateralis	359
5. Norma frontalis	365
6. Norma occipitalis	368
7. Mandible	369
8. Sutures and Wormian bones	370
9. Teeth	371
Conclusions	372
1. General appearance	372
2. Specific appearance	372
a. Racial characteristics	372
b. Deformatory effects	374
α. Direct changes	374
β. Indirect changes	374
3. General morphologic evaluation	375
a. Inferior traits	375
b. Advanced traits	375
4. Extraneous characteristics	375
Final summary	375
Bibliography	377
Index	379
Tables of measurements	

LIST OF ILLUSTRATIONS.

SUMMARIES.

1—103, in Part I: Craniometry
104—177, „   „ II: Cranioscopy

ILLUSTRATIONS.

a. Metrical diagrams
I. Undeformed-deformed average deviations (p. 131).
II. Average tribal deviations of the Undeformed (p. 136).
III. Mongolo-mongoloid average deviations (p. 142).
IV. Lillooet affinities (p. 145).
V. Mongolo-mongoloideo-caucasid average deviations (p. 146).

b. Plates
I. Superposed median-sagittal tracings of deformed skulls.
II. Median-sagittal and horizontal tracings, males and females superposed, of the undeformed. varieties.
The five cranial normae of each:
III. Male Lillooet (2618).
IV. Female Kamloops (1410).
V. Male Spences Bridge (99).
VI. „   Haida (3751).
VII. „   Eskimo from Indian Point, Siberia (3776).
VIII. „ Salish, North Saanich (2644 A).
IX. „   Chinook (2676).
X.   „   Nimkish (1671).
XI. „   Koskimo (3642).

c. Text-figures

					Page
1. Median-sagittal perigram of a female Chinook (4473)					19
2. „ „ „ „ male Koskimo (3242)					20
3. „ „ „ „ Salish (2644 A)					21
4. „ „ „ „ „ Salish from a shell heap, Lower Fraser R. (1544) .					22
5. Scheme of angular relation between the ear-eye and glabella-lambda planes					27
6. Scheme of angular relation between the basion-bregma line and glabella lambda plane ("Zentralwinkel" K l a a t s c h)					28
7. Scheme of angular relations between the cranial height line and ear-eye and glabella-lambda planes					30
8. Median-sagittal frontal tracings superposed to show differences of index and declination.					56
9. Scheme of averages of frontal angle					58
10a. Superposition of median-sagittal parietal tracings coinciding with divisional averages . .					61
10b. Same superposition as in a, uniformly oriented according to the Undeformed angle . .					61
10c. Same superposition as in b, the parietal chords reduced to equal lengths					61
11. Scheme of averages of the parietal angle . . . . , ...					63

[VII]

VIII LIST OF ILLUSTRATIONS.

	Page
12. Scheme of averages of the occipital angle	67
13. Occipital angles paired	68
14. Superposition of occipital outlines at their individual angles in opisthion orientation	69
15. Same superposition as in fig. 14, in inion orientation	69
16. Interoccipital angles paired	71
17a. Scheme of angular possibilities between the foramen magnum and ear-eye planes	78
17b. Averages of angular relation between the foramen magnum and ear-eye planes	78
18. Comparative scheme of the cranio-basal, foramen magnum and basio-foramen magnum angles in ear-eye orientation	80
19. Superposition of facial triangles in ear-eye orientation	86
20. Scheme of average conditions of the ramus angle of the lower jaw	124
21. Superposition of ramus outlines in alveolar and coronoid vertical orientation	125
22. Illustrating the angular possibilities between the condylo-coronoid tangent and the alveolar plane	128
23. Os bregmaticum	166
24. Ossification of ligamentum apicis dentis epistrophei in a skull from Eburne near Vancouver	172
25. Condylus tertius	176
26. Precondylar tuberclus	176
27. Ankylosis atlantis (male Kwakiutl 4256)	179
28. Thorn-like projections in the foramen condyloideum (male Haida 3738)	185
29. Processus paracondyloideus (female Haida 1611)	191
30. Double-sided processus paracondyloideus (male Nootka 4568)	191
31. Fossa pharyngea and anomalies in pars basilaris (infantile Chukchee 3845)	198
32. Fossa pharyngea (male Bellacoola 4627)	198
33. Processus pterygoideus with muscular ridges and spina Civinini (male Bellacoola 4625)	201
34. Foramen pterygospinosum (Civinini) in a female Chukchee (3844)	202
35. Lamina externa of processus pterygoideus with reinforced margo maxillaris and a perforation (male Haida 3743)	202
36. Thorn-like formation in foramen ovale (male Chinook 4518)	203
37. Thorn and spicula formations in foramen ovale (male Haida 3735)	203
38. Foramen pterygospinosum (*Civinini*) incomplete (male Bellacoola 4627)	203
39. Foramen pterygospinosum (*Civinini*) almost complete (male Tsimshian 4586)	203
40. Foramen pterygospinosum (*Civinini*) verum (male Tsimshian 4647)	203
41. Various forms of sutura palatina transversa	211
42. Various forms of sutura incisiva	213
43. Various forms of foramen incisivum	213
44. Two different forms of the "keel" termination of the torus palatinus	217
45. Occipital outlines to show protrusion of upper squama	222
46. Squama temporalis: most frequently occurring forms	225
47. Irregular suturae squamosae	226
48. Various forms of incisura parietalis	229
49. Incisurae parietales with Wormian bones	230
50. Crista supramastoidea forming triangular projection upon parietal bone (male Bellacoola 4626)	232
51. Crista supramastoidea extending over sutura squamosa (male Haida 3738)	232
52. Sutura sphenosquamosa with sharp forward turn (female Salish 1784)	234
53. Variations in the bilateral occurrence of the processus frontalis	237
54. Sutura mastoideosquamosa (male Eskimo 3771)	239
55. Sutura mastoideosquamosa with pit-like depression (male Kwakiutl 4248)	239
56. Tympanic hyperostosis in Eskimo skulls	246
57. Bilateral exostoses auriculares (male San Miguel Island 312)	249
58. Exostoses auriculares (male Chinook 4470, 4513)	252
59. Perforated processus postglenoidalis (inf. II Salish 2735)	255
60. Sutura sphenoparietalis encroaching upon ala magna (female Haida 3742)	259

LIST OF ILLUSTRATIONS.

		Page
61.	Epiptericum varieties	260
62.	Crista infratemporalis (female Koskimo 3841)	266
63.	Various forms of arcus zygomaticus	267
64.	Superposition of human and anthropoid forms of arcus zygomaticus	268
65.	Angulus zygomaticotemporalis	270
66.	Various forms of sutura transversozygomatica	273
67.	Various stages of glabellar development	282
68.	Median-sagittal tracings of nasal roof	295
69.	Abnormal courses of sutura internasalis	296
70.	Abnormal excursions of sutura nasofrontalis	299
71.	Variation in the development of the spina nasalis anterior	303
72.	Three fundamental types of crista infrazygomatica	309
73.	Mutual relation between "Jugalwulst" (Klaatsch) and the roots of the first upper molar	311
74.	Variations in the foramen and sutura infraorbitalis	312
75.	Tuberculum linearum inferius (male Haida 3755)	317
76.	Variation of tuberculum linearum inferius	317
77.	Protuberantia occipitalis externa: narrow tongue-shape	318
78.	Protuberantia occipitalis externa: broad tongue-shape	318
79—81: Different shapes of fossa supratoralis		321
82.	Ossification scheme of occipital squama (modified after Ranke)	323
83.	Os incae verum s. proprium (inf. II Kwakiutl 4246)	325
84.	Os incae tripartitum	325
85.	Lambdoid portions of lambdoid sutures suggesting fontanel bones	326
86, a—d. Ossa lambdoidea partly complicated by Wormian bones		327
87, a—c. Ossa apicis, simple, transversely and sagittaly divided		328
88.	Corpus mandibulae with strong masseteric ridges and a clasp-like appendage in the incisura praeangularis (male Haida 3740)	332
89.	Basal outlines of lower jaws	332
90.	Fossa mentalis (inf. II Chukchee 3847)	333
91.	Mandibular outlines to show Klaatsch's three stages of chin development	334
92.	Horizontal curve systems of chin variation: median, lateral, rounded	335
93.	Mm. genioglossus and geniohyoideus origins, $\frac{2}{1}$, in a male Haida (3741)	338
94.	Mm. genioglossus and geniohyoideus origins, $\frac{1}{2}$, in a male Yakima (4334)	328
95.	Mm. genioglossus and geniohyoideus origins, $\frac{groove}{1}$ in an inf. II Yakima (4326)	338
96, a—b. Superposition of ramus outlines in alveolar and postmolar orientation representing height-breadth proportions indicated by highest and lowest index		339
97, a—d. Outlines of anthropoid mandibles in lateral projection and alveolar orientation		340
98.	Proc. coronoideus in a closed and open mandible of a carnivore. After W. Wright	342
99.	Superposition of mandibular rami to show mutual behavior of condyloid and coronoid processes	342
100.	Lingula mandibulae of unusual size (male Salish 2644 A)	345
101.	Sulcus mylohyoideus bridged (female Haida 3742)	345
102, a—c. Single and multiple Wormian bones in the coronal suture		349
103, a—b. Multiple Wormian bones in the partes complicatae of coronal sutures		349
104.	Wormian bone in the sutura internasalis (inf. II Lillooet 2629)	349
105.	Shovel-shape incisor with labial compensatory bulging (male Haida 1606)	350
106.	Crowded out left upper premolar (male Kamloops 1284)	352
107.	Third right upper molar of extraordinary size (male Bellacoola 4546)	352

INTRODUCTION

The skeletal material collected by the various members of the Jesup Expedition was entrusted in the autumn of 1913 by Professor Boas, to the present author for systematic investigation. The greater part of the work was carried on in the American Musum of Natural History where the collections of the Jesup Expedition are housed. Although the facilities of that institution were at the author's disposal the progress of the work was at times interrupted due to the exigencies of the war. Moreover, because of the complicated nature of the material which required a rather exacting methodical treatment, continued progress was still further hampered. It was the author's good fortune, however, to have handled the material in the condition it was brought in from the field, and in which unprepared state it had been stored in the Museum for future examination.

This report concerns itself with the craniology of the Pacific Northwest, the specific field of the Jesup Expedition, although much of the material, besides the skulls, consists of skeletons, more or less complete, and numerous single bones.

Owing to the artificial deformations to which about three fourths of the skulls had been subjected, a definite plan of craniological investigation immediately suggested itself. First of all, the undeformed and deformed crania had to be studied separately in order to prove the tribal differences and to show the effects of deformation. The practical approach to the problem, therefore, lay by way of craniometric as well as cranioscopic procedure especially adapted to the case. It was advisable, consequently, to arrange the skulls in serial units according to the three principal methods of deformation: the Cowichan, Chinook and Koskimo methods. With regard to the undeformed material, however, this arrangement appeared to be rather precarious, since Eskimo from Bering Strait and Siberia, and Chukchee were included. But as the description of this series as a whole seemed to be the most promising means of arriving at a general quantitative characterization, scruples over such a disparity in treatment were finally set aside in consideration of the fact that in the course of the proposed studies each tribal group in the undeformed series was also to be treated individually. Many of the tribal groups, however, were represented by so few specimens that their metrical evaluation remained rather uncertain.

The entire material, then, was arranged into four series: (1) Undeformed, (2) Cowichan deformation, (3) Chinook deformation and (4) Koskimo deformation. While the Undeformed are always referred to as such in the following investigations, the deformed series are spoken of as Cowichan, Chinook and Koskimo, or as Cowichan deformation, etc. These four series are designated as "divisons" and their averages as "divisional averages", in contradistinction to group means both derived in the customary way from the divisions and the tribal subdivisions. The metrical findings are individually listed in the tables of measurements appended at the end of the report, where also the ranges and means of the groups constituting the divisions, together with the ranges and averages of the divisions, are attached. Condensed summaries are given in the text together with the discussion of each of the metrical observations. These summaries contain the number of individuals classified according to males, females, juveniles and infantiles; the divisional averages; the standard deviations and physiological ranges. The cranioscopic summaries on the other hand, give the actual and percental frequencies of the morphologic features discussed in the different normae.

The tribal grouping within each division is arranged according to geographical location and, when necessary, the groups are named according to their geographical provenience, proceeding from north to south. The exact number and class of specimens contained in each group and division have been listed in summaries 1–5, and on p. 7. The numbers of the specimens wherever they occur in the text, legends and measuring tables, correspond to those of Catalogue 99 of the American Museum of Natural History.

Owing to the heterogeneity of our material and the insufficient number of undeformed specimens, the metrical and morphological disparities in the groups should be confirmed by studies upon more extensive material. The craniological results embodied in the following chapters therefore aim rather to represent a basis for future investigation than to establish a definite and conclusive interpretation of the racial conditions pertaining to the North Pacific regions. The more or less monographic treatment of the underlying subject matter suggested itself as the most promising.

The craniological report represented in this volume was divided for practical purpose into a craniometric and a cranioscopic division, followed by résumés and a conclusive chapter. The bibliography at the close of the work comprises only such titles as have direct reference to the regions and tribes studied, quotations being indicated in the text by parenthesized year and page numbers. The numerous papers referring to morphologic, anatomic or other specific features are listed in footnotes at the bottom of their respective pages. In cases of repeated reference to the same paper, the footnote reads as follows: *l. c.*, *p.* .. (...), where *p.* .. indicates the page of the present work, and the parenthesized plain number that of the paper referred to.

The illustrations of the text and the photographic tables reproduced in this report were ably executed by Messrs. Rudolf Weber and William Baake.

New York.   Bruno Oetteking.

THE MATERIAL

The entire skull material was grouped into four principal divisions: (1) the Undeformed, (2) the Cowichan deformation, (3) the Chinook deformation and (4) the Koskimo deformation. The specimens contained in each of the four divisions are listed in the following summaries according to their state of preservation. The latter is classified as follows: (1) cranium, the complete skull with lower jaw; (2) calvarium, the skull without lower jaw; (3) calvaria, the skull without face and lower jaw, and (4) calva, the skull-cap or calotte. Additional rubrics are reserved for (5) portions of the skull not classifiable according to the above definitions and for (6) single jaws. Further subdivision is made into males, females, juveniles and infantiles, the state of maturity or immaturity depending upon the closure of the synchondrosis spheno-occipitalis. The matures are represented by the adult, mature and senile stages, the immatures by the juveniles and the infantiles I and II stages, referred to in the tables of measurements and otherwise as: ad., mat., sen., juv., inf. I and II.

For their identification European standards[1] were used because they could unhesitatingly be employed, since only the different stages of life and not the individual ages were to be distinguished. It must, however, be emphasized that the determination of sex is not to be considered as final. Although error in regard to sex identification of a number of mature but conspicuously small skulls, almost child-like in appearance, was quite improbable, such identification in others was rendered extremely difficult. The disproportion in numbers of male and female skulls, the latter being greatly in the minority, is demonstrated in the summaries and appended tables of measurements. The characteristic smallness of the female Indian skull has frequently been pointed out by Virchow and later by Hrdlička, and can be fully substantiated by the present writer.

1. The *Undeformed*. For a more generalizing metrical evaluation of the undeformed craniological material, varying in type, of the North Pacific coast, all of the available undeformed crania are comprised in this division. They are grouped as follows: Athapascan (Alaska); Haida (Queen Charlotte Islands); Salish tribes of the Interior: Lillooet, Nicola Lake, Spences Bridge, Lytton, Kamloops; Eskimo from St. Lawrence Island (Bering Strait) and from Indian Point (Siberia), and Chukchee from Mariinsky Post (Anadyr, Siberia).

---

[1] Martin, Rudolf, 1914. Lehrbuch der Anthropologie, pp. 476–477.

The classification of the Undeformed and their frequency is recorded in *summary 1*. The relatively largest groups are those of the Haida and Eskimo,

Summary. 1.

The Undeformed: Classification and frequency of specimens

Tribe	Cranium				Calvarium				Calvaria				Calva				Portions of crania		Mandibula (single)				Total
	♂	♀	juv.	inf.	♂	♀	juv.	inf.	♂	♀	juv.	inf.	♂	♀	juv.	inf.	mat.	immat.	♂	♀	juv.	inf.	
Athapascan	4	1	—	1	2	—	—	—	—	—	—	—	—	—	—	—	—	—	—	—	—	—	8
Haida	8	6	—	3	8	2	1	2	2	—	—	—	—	—	—	—	—	—	6	—	—	—	38
Lillooet (Salish Interior)	2	2	—	3	—	—	—	2	—	—	—	—	—	—	—	—	—	—	—	—	—	1	10
Nicola Lake	3	1	—	—	1	—	—	—	—	—	—	—	—	—	—	—	1	1	—	—	—	—	7
Spences Bridge	1	1	—	—	1	—	—	—	—	—	—	—	—	—	—	—	—	—	—	—	—	—	3
Lytton	3	1	—	1	1	2	—	—	2	1	—	—	—	—	—	—	—	1	3	—	1	1	17
Kamloops	2	1	—	—	3	1	—	—	—	—	—	—	—	—	—	—	—	1	1	2	—	2	13
Eskimo	1	—	—	—	32	12	—	—	—	—	—	—	—	—	—	—	—	—	—	—	—	—	45
Chukchee	2	1	—	1	2	—	—	—	—	1	—	—	—	—	—	—	—	—	—	—	—	—	7
Total	26	14	—	9	48	19	1	5	4	1	—	—	—	—	—	1	—	4	8	4	—	4	148

while the others are but meagerly represented. The entire number of Undeformed skulls, with or without lower jaws, is 122, of which 74 are males, 33 females, 1 juvenile and 14 infantiles. In addition there are 16 single lower jaws, 5 calvariae, 1 calva und 4 portions of crania, bringing the entire number of specimens to 148. As shown in the total column on the extreme right, 45 of these are Eskimo and 38 Haida. Among the smaller groups the Lytton is the largest, numbering 17, the Kamloops 13 and the Lillooet 10. The frequencies of the remaining groups range below 10.

2. The *Cowichan* deformation. The specimens of this division come from the coast of the British Columbia mainland, the neighboring islands, especially Vancouver Island, and the coast districts of the State of Washington. In *summary 2* tribal names are listed together with the names of the localities in which the skull material was collected. Attention should be called to the fact that although the Tsimshian and Yakima did not as a rule practice head deformation, yet in those instances where it did occur they had to be incorporated in the Cowichan division. Both these series of tribal specimens were taken from their familiar habitats, the Tsimshian from Skeena River and the Yakima from Tampico, Ellensburg and Priest Rapids, Wash.

The specimens enumerated in *summary 2* comprise 121 skulls, of which 86 are male, 28 female, 2 juvenile and 5 infantile. The number of crania amounts to 50, calvaria 71, calvariae 4, portions of crania 5 and single lower jaws 29. The entire number of specimens as summed up on the extreme

Summary 2.

The Cowichan deformation: Classification and frequency of specimens

Tribe	Cranium				Calvarium				Calvaria				Calva				Portions of crania		Mandibula (single)				Total.
	♂	♀	juv.	inf.	♂	♀	juv.	inf.	♂	♀	juv.	inf.	♂	♀	juv.	inf.	mat.	immat.	♂	♀	juv.	inf.	
Tsimshian (British Columbia)	1	—	—	—	6	1	—	—	—	—	—	—	—	—	—	—	—	—	1	—	—	—	9
Yakima	5	2	2	1	1	—	—	—	—	—	—	—	—	—	—	—	1	—	—	—	—	2	14
Bellabella	—	—	—	—	9	1	—	—	—	—	—	—	—	—	—	—	—	—	—	—	—	—	10
Bellacoola	1	—	—	—	15	2	—	1	—	—	—	—	—	—	—	—	1	—	—	—	—	—	20
about Vancouver (Salis Coast)	7	4	—	—	12	5	—	—	3	—	—	—	—	—	—	—	2	—	14	2	—	3	52
North Saanich	9	—	—	—	3	—	—	—	—	—	—	—	—	—	—	—	1	—	1	—	—	—	14
Comox	—	1	—	—	—	—	—	—	—	—	—	—	—	—	—	—	—	—	—	—	—	—	1
Nanaimo	4	2	—	1	2	2	—	—	—	1	—	—	—	—	—	—	—	—	—	—	—	1	13
Point Roberts (State of Washington, U.S.)	—	—	—	—	1	—	—	—	—	—	—	—	—	—	—	—	—	—	—	1	—	—	2
Stanwood	1	2	—	—	1	—	—	—	—	—	—	—	—	—	—	—	—	—	—	—	—	—	4
San Juan de Fuca	2	1	—	—	—	—	—	—	—	—	—	—	—	—	—	—	—	—	1	—	—	—	4
Port Williams	—	—	—	—	1	—	—	—	—	—	—	—	—	—	—	—	—	—	—	—	—	—	1
Dungeness	2	1	—	1	2	4	—	1	—	—	—	—	—	—	—	—	—	—	2	—	—	1	14
Markham	—	—	—	—	1	—	—	—	—	—	—	—	—	—	—	—	—	—	—	—	—	—	1
Total	32	13	2	3	54	15	—	2	3	1	—	—	—	—	—	—	5	—	19	3	—	7	159

right of the summary aggregates 159, of which the largest series, namely 52, come from around Vancouver, while the remaing groups have frequencies in diminishing order down to one specimen for Comox and Markham.

3. The *Chinook* deformation. There are according to *summary 3*

Summary 3.

The Chinook deformation: Classification and frequency of specimens

Tribe	Cranium				Calvarium				Calvaria				Calva				Portions of crania		Mandibula (single)				Total
	♂	♀	juv.	inf.	♂	♀	juv.	inf.	♂	♀	juv.	inf.	♂	♀	juv.	inf.	mat.	immat.	♂	♀	juv.	inf.	
Chinook	3	—	—	—	54	25	4	6	—	—	—	—	—	—	—	—	—	—	1	—	—	—	93
Coupeville	1	—	—	—	—	—	—	—	—	—	—	—	—	—	—	—	—	—	—	—	—	—	1
Total	4	—	—	—	54	25	4	6	—	—	—	—	—	—	—	—	—	—	1	—	—	—	94

altogether 94 specimens. Most of them come from Memalose Island, in the lower course of Columbia River, a famous burial ground of the Chinook. A single male skull from Coupeville, Washington, is embodied with the others in the Chinook table because of its similar deformation. The number of

Chinook skulls aggregates 93, 4 of them being male crania, the rest calvaria, of which 54 are male, 25 female, 6 juvenile and 4 infantile. There is an additional single lower jaw.

4. The *Koskimo* deformation. The provenience of the specimens deformed in the Koskimo fashion is restricted to Vancouver Island, particularly to its northern, northeastern, northwestern and western coast districts. Most of the Kwakiutl skulls come from around Fort Rupert and the islands in its vicinity, the Nimkish from the Nimkish River district and Alert Bay. The Koskimo skulls come from Quatsino Sound and the Nootka and Clayoquot from the west coast of Vancouver Island. In *summary 4* the number of skulls in the

Summary 4.

The Koskimo deformation: Classification and frequency of specimens

Tribe	Cranium				Calvarium				Calvaria				Calva				Portions of crania		Mandibula (single)				Total
	♂	♀	juv.	inf.	♂	♀	juv.	inf.	♂	♀	juv.	inf.	♂	♀	juv.	inf.	mat.	immat.	♂	♀	juv.	inf.	
Kwakiutl	8	5	—	—	46	16	1	3	—	—	—	—	—	—	—	—	—	—	2	—	—	—	81
Nimkish	14	3	—	1	11	5	—	2	1	—	—	—	1	—	—	—	—	—	3	—	—	—	41
Koskimo	2	3	—	—	7	1	—	1	—	—	—	—	—	—	—	—	—	—	—	—	—	—	14
Nootka	—	—	—	—	10	3	—	—	—	1	—	—	—	—	—	—	1	—	—	—	—	—	15
Clayoquot	—	1	—	—	4	1	1	1	—	—	—	—	—	—	—	—	—	—	—	—	—	—	8
Total	24	12	—	1	78	26	2	7	1	1	—	—	1	—	—	—	1	—	5	—	—	—	159

Koskimo division aggregates 159. The male skulls number 102, 24 of them being crania and 78 calvaria, the females being represented by 12 and 26 specimens respectively of these classes. Besides these there are 1 infantile cranium, 2 juvenile and 7 infantile calvaria. Two calvariae, 1 calva, 1 cranial part and 5 single mandibles complete the total number of 159 specimens. Of these 81, as shown in the column of totals, belong to the Kwakiutl and 41 to the Nimkish. The other tribes are represented by considerably fewer numbers.

The entire collection comprises 560 specimens which are tabulated in *summary 5*. The number of male skulls is 320, 86 crania and 234 calvaria, as against 124 female skulls of which 39 are crania and 85 calvaria. The immatures total 9 juveniles with 2 crania and 7 calvaria, and 33 infantiles with 13 cranià and 20 calvaria. There are 11 calvariae, 8 male and 3 female, 2 calvae, 1 male and 1 female, 10 portions of skulls and 51 single lower jaws, of which 33 are male, 7 female, and 11 infantile. In the total compilation of the deformed, the Cowichan and Koskimo aggregate 159 each, while the Chinook have only 94. The Undeformed comprise 148 specimens.

Summary 5.

Total frequency in the four divisions

Series	Craninm				Calvarium				Calvaria				Calva				Portions of crania		Mandibula (single)				Total
	♂	♀	juv.	inf.	♂	♀	juv.	inf.	♂	♀	juv.	inf.	♂	♀	juv.	inf.	mat.	immat.	♂	♀	juv.	inf.	
Undeformed	26	14	—	9	48	19	1	5	4	1	—	—	—	—	1	—	4	—	8	4	—	4	148
Cowichan (deformation)	32	13	2	3	54	15	—	2	3	1	—	—	—	—	—	—	5	—	19	3	—	7	159
Chinook (deformation)	4	—	—	—	54	25	4	6	—	—	—	—	—	—	—	—	—	—	1	—	—	—	94
Koskimo (deformation)	24	12	—	1	78	26	2	7	1	1	—	—	1	—	—	—	1	—	5	—	—	—	159
Total	86	39	2	13	234	85	7	20	8	3	—	—	1	—	1	—	10	—	43	7	7	—	560

The majority of the specimens was in a fair state of preservation; quite a number, in fact, were in splendid condition, even down to the smaller bones of the face and the teeth. Of the incomplete skulls the best specimens were selected and their measurements added to those of the complete ones. It is to be regretted, however, that so many of the skulls are without lower jaws and complete dentures, which is not so much the fault of the collectors as that of the primitive burials from which in the course of disintegration the bones became separated either by animals or by geologic and climatic actions.

TECHNIQUE.

The *instruments* used in the craniometrical study of this report were the sliding and spreading calipers, the cubus craniophore and the diagraph, the steel tape and the camera lucida. The first four of these were devised by R. Martin, and are manufactured by P. Hermann in Zurich, Switzerland.

The *methods of measurement* employed in the study of the material are those set forth by Rudolf Martin in his "Lehrbuch der Anthropologie" (1914).

The *cranial capacity* was taken with millet and measured in the graduated cylinder. For classification that of the cousins Sarasin was adopted, who distinguished the grouping as follows:

	♂	♀
oligencephalic . . .	x–1300	x–1150
euencephalic	1301–1450	1151–1300
aristencephalic . . .	1451–x	1301–x

The *ear-eye horizontal* is the plane of orientation used for investigating the angular proportions of the skulls. The profilation (prognathism) is thus expressed in terms with reference to that plane. Flower's gnathic or alveolar index was not considered in the following studies.

The *orbital width* was taken from the maxillofrontale as the medial measuring point, its location being identical with the point of intersection of the prolongation of the crista lacrimalis anterior with the sutura maxillo-frontalis. The maxillo-frontale-ektokonchion width measurement affords a truer conception of the orbital width than the lacrimale-ektokonchion measurement. Since, however, the lacrimale has been extensively used in previous works, the present writer, for comparative purposes, has followed his routine of also accounting for and including the lacrimale measurement.

A dioptograph for making *orthogonal tracings* not being available, the camera lucida was used in its place, particularly in drawing the lateral projections of all the lower jaws. Into these projections the *alveolar plane line* was then drawn in order to facilitate their comparative study. There is, however, a great deal of uncertainty about the definition, application and evaluation of this line of orientation. Klaatsch,[2] who introduced it, does not accurately describe his method. There is according to him ". . . . . nur *ein*

---

[2] Klaatsch, Hermann, 1909. Kraniomorphologie und Kraniotrigonometrie. Arch. Anthrop., n. s., v. VIII, pp. 101–123.

Horizont .... gegeben durch eine Ebene, welche die Randpartien der Alveolen umfasst" (p. 102); and a little further on: "Ich nehme daher den Alveolarrand im Bereiche der Incisiven und *des*[3] letzten Molaren. Diese miteinander verbunden geben die Horizontale ...." (pp. 102–103). R. Martin's (Lehrbuch, 1914, 484) definition of the alveolar plane is considerably clearer. He says, "Dieselbe wird bestimmt durch die tiefsten Punkte der Alveolarränder der mittleren Incisiven und *der*[4] letzten Molaren ...." It is quite essential to indicate the lowest points on the margins of the incisival alveoli as the anterior points through which the alveolar plane line should pass,[5] since the marginal outline of those alveoli is usually concave rather than straight. But as this concavity is quite variable, the present writer has had recourse to another point, namely, that given by the greatest protrusion of the slight, but nevertheless distinct, horizontal ridge formed by the thickened edges of the alveoli, which protrusion is fairly constant and continuous all around the alveolar processes of both the upper and lower jaws. This touches upon the exact location of the prosthion inferius (infradentale) which, like the prosthion superius of the upper jaw, may differ according to the purpose involved. For computing the facial height measurement, anthropologists are agreed to use the lowermost point of the alveolar border located on the septum interalveolare between the two upper middle incisors. On the other hand, measurements for facial length and prognathism involve the most projecting point of the alveolar border. Similar procedures for the lower jaw likewise suggest the most projecting point for establishing the alveolar plane line.

This problem has received further attention in the conscientious efforts of Hans Virchow[6] who rejects Klaatsch's proposition for the reason that his line of orientation is not derived directly from the morphological conformation of the jaw, but is merely laid upon the projection drawing (1916, 138). H. Virchow recommends and employs in his studies an alveolar line of orientation representing a plane that is based on the infradental points, i. e., the summit points of the septa interalveolaria between the two middle incisors, and the m_2 and m_3 of each side. For the first of these points that author suggests the name "katoprosthion" in contradistinction to the "anoprosthion"

---

[3] Italics mine. Klaatsch speaks expressly of the last molar, not molars, having doubtless observed that the buccal margins of the alveoli of the three molars only rarely coincide with a horizontal plane line.

[4] Italics mine. In the sense of the preceding footnote the plural form does not seem to be justified here and is apparently a misprint, unless not meant to apply collectively to the last molars but individually either to the third, or in its absence, to the second, as the case may be.

[5] One of these points, preferably the left, is, of course, sufficient for establishing the alveolar plane. For the sake of greater exactness, however, both points might be horizontally connected and thus the projection on the median sagittal plane determined and marked on the specimen.

[6] Virchow, Hans, 1916. Über das Verhältnis der Alveolarebene des Oberkiefers zur Horizontalebene. Zschr. Ethnol., v. XLVIII, pp. 136–142.

——— 1920. Die menschlichen Skeletreste aus dem *Kämpfe*'schen Bruch im Travertin von Ehringsdorf bei Weimar. Jena. 141 pp.

of the upper jaw. The present writer, for two reasons, has not accepted H. Virchow's method, although he realizes its morphological exactness. First of all, as H. Virchow himself admits (1916, 138), specimens with one of these septa interalveolaria injured, cannot be considered for examination, and secondly, the septa, particularly the interincisival, were found so variable in height as compared to the greater stability of the most projecting anterior point of the alveolar border just defined, that the preference lay with the latter point and the corresponding lateral one. In the present report, however, only angular measurements were referred to the alveolar plane line, while for the absolute dimensions the object itself was utilized.

The method of preparing a lower jaw for diagraphical reproduction by means of the camera lucida was as follows. An ordinary rubber band was fastened around the alveolar process and the rami and made to coincide with the alveolar plane line in accordance with the principles proposed here. The length of the object was then ascertained by measuring the distance between the prosthion inferius and the bisecting point on the ramus-to-ramus extension of the rubber band, while the points of intersection of the latter with the anterior and posterior borders of the left ramus were indicated by pencil marks, as was the prosthion inferius. The rubber band was then removed and the length of the jaw and the breadth of its left ascending ramus, as indicated by the pencil marks, reproduced on the drawing paper. The object was then placed in position on a level with the camera lucida, but in such a way that the median-sagittal bisecting line of the jaw was made to coincide with the plane of projection. After moving the object so that the points indicated thereon coincided with the pencil marks on the drawing paper, the tracing was made. It will be noticed that in the described orientation, the camera being focused on the postmolar point, the farther right ramus is covered in perspective by the nearer left one and, furthermore, that the projection of the lower jaw is in the physiological position, since not the corpus mandibulae and the adjoining basal portion of the ascending ramus were made to coincide with the plane of projection, but the median-sagittal halving line of the mandible. After marking the points on the diagram through which the alveolar plane line is to pass and indicating the latter, the drawing is ready for examination. The measurements derived therefrom are discussed in the chapter on the mandibula.

DEFORMATION OF THE HEAD.

1. Nature of deformation and general distribution.

From prehistoric times down to the present day the custom of deforming the head has been in vogue. This practice, varying more or less in intensity, has been widely distributed over all parts of the world.[7] Disregarding the deformations that are caused by pathological processes, such as scaphocephaly, plagiocephaly and some other forms produced in most cases by premature synostosis of cranial sutures, a distinction has been made between unintentional and intentional deformation. There is, according to *Hrdlička*,[8] only one form of *unintentional* deformation which is widely distributed, namely, that which results from "prolonged contact of the occiput of the infant with a resistant head support in the cradleboard." The effect of this is that part of the occipital region, and in extreme cases the entire occiput, becomes flattened. *Intentional* deformation may be reduced to two distinctly different types. One mode is characterized by a depression of the forehead which is produced by the application of a board or resistant pads, while from behind the force of pressure from the cradleboard, supplemented in certain cases by special pads in the lambda region, causes the head to be compressed as in a vise, with the result that both the frontal and occipital regions become flattened, while the unobstructed parietals expand in a sideward direction.[9] The other type of deformation is caused by winding bandages, or pads and bandages, over the frontal region and under the occiput and completely encircling the braincase, from which even pressure all about, the head acquires a rounded contour where the bandages are applied, but the region about the vertex and posterior of it extrudes upward and backward.

Unintentional and intentional deformation can be effected only at the

---

[7] See *Virchow, R*, 1901. Über Schädelform und Schädeldeformation. Corr.-Bl. Ges. Anthrop., v. XXXII, pp. 135–139 (138). A general account of the geographical distribution of head deformation may also be found in: *Bräss, Martin*, 1887. Beiträge zur Kenntnis der künstlichen Schädelverbildungen. Mitt. Ver. Erdk. Leipzig, pp. 131–180 (174–180).

[8] *Hrdlička, Aleš*, 1912. Artificial head deformation, in: Handbook of American Indians north of Mexico v. I, pp. 96–97.

[9] *J. Imbelloni* (Sur un appareil de déformation du crâne des anciens Humahuacas. Proc. XXI. Internat. Congr. Am. Göteborg, 1924, pp. 607–618) has described an apparatus for anteroposterior head deformation used by the ancient Humahuacas of Argentina, consisting of two board arrangements between which the infant's head was compressed to produce either the "déformation fronto-occipital oblique ou élévée," according to whether the occipital board was applied to the upper occipital squama or to the entire squama.

tenderest age while the membrane bones of the neonate's head are still in the process of formation and can, for some time after birth, be moulded like wax by continuous effort. The softness of the growing membrane bones as well as the mobility of their sutures, while the fontanelles are not yet closed, is of importance for the definite shaping of the infant's head under the deforming influences. The membrane bones are mutually pliable in the sagittal direction so that, under pressure, either the parietals with their anterior and posterior borders overlap the frontal and occipital bones, or these latter the parietal bones.

A great variety of cradles and numerous methods of bandaging are employed to bring about a desired head form.[10] Bandages for such purposes are made of deer skin, kelp or bladder-wrack (Fucus vesiculosus), or cedar bark, and bound around the forehead and under the occiput. In some cases a transverse groove-like, postbregmatic depression occurs in this deformation. The same sort of groove is not infrequently found in fronto-occipital deformation, produced by the pressure on the forehead and the yielding of the margo frontalis region of the parietals. In the case of the Koskimo, however, it may be due to the pressure of another bandage which is wound over the postbregmatic region and under the lower jaw at right angles to the first one. This practice seems also to have been in vogue among the ancient Peruvians, whose deformatory practices are in principle identical with those described above. In North America the art of bandaging appears to have been prevalent only in certain regions of the northwest. In South America *Posnansky* relates that the Peruvian Highlanders use the "circular" deformation caused by bandaging the infant's head,[11] and bandaging seems also to be the custom among certain tribes in Africa.[12]

Strain and pressure, intentionally or unintentionally applied to the body, invariably cause not only an obstruction to growth, but involve processes of compensation in addition to direct changes. Such deformations come within the category of arrested and accelerated growth, and they result sometimes in pathological conditions. Thus, if the osseous growth of the head is impeded

---

[10] See: *Mason, Otis, T.*, 1887. Cradles of the American aborigines. Rep. Nat. Mus. Washington, v. XI, pp. 161–212.

[11] *Posnansky, Arthur*, 1914. Eine prähistorische Grabstätte in Südamerika, Berlin. The author speaking here of a "zirkulare Verunstaltung" unquestionably means a cylindrical or conical one.

[12] Mr. *Herbert Lang*, of the American Museum of Natural History, who spent five years on an expedition in the Congo State, tells me that the Mangbatu mothers use plaited bandages made of bast from Raphia vinifera *P. B.* and Raphia monbuttorum *Drude*, two domestic varieties of palms. The plaited bands are from one fourth to one half inch in width, and are bound around the head to produce the occipital elongation.

The bandages are worn almost constantly up to the closing of the fontanelles and taken off only for a day when the infant seems to suffer excessive pain. They are worn even later, probably partly in the belief that they will help to retain the acquired deformity better, and partly for ornament. The women, who naturally spend more time and care on their hair than the men, are also more conservative in wearing the bandages, thus succeeding in the better preservation of the distorted head form which in men often appears to become less pronounced.

in one direction, compensation in another is the rule. But as the skull represents a complex of many different bones, the size and shape of the parts bordering those under direct strain, are also affected. The investigations by *Dillenius*[13] of the influence of fronto-occipital deformation on the parietals of Calchaqui crania are quite illuminating. She writes: "Der starke, hauptsächlich auf den Mittelkopf konzentrierte Druck hat den oberen Abschnitt in vielen Fällen an seiner gesetzmässigen Entwickelung gehindert, während der untere Scheitelbeinabschnitt sich mehr ausdehnen konnte." She is of the opinion, for instance, that in the deformed skulls which she studied, the peculiar sharp forward turn of the coronal suture in the region of the linea temporalis is due to the influence of deformation, and is comparable to similar conditions in the orang-utan and other anthropoid apes. Such observations show how a systematic inquiry into the interdependence of parts of the skull under strain and pressure may reveal interesting cranio-morphological findings.

The direct mechanical changes brought about by deformation are most evident in the membrane bones of the brain-case in which, therefore, a flattening of the vaulted portions of the frontal and occipital bones occurs. On the other hand, a marked increase in sideward and backward vaulting in the parietals is sometimes shown.[14]

In the Jesup material there are instances of a deformation which differs quite distinctly from those described above. This method consists of a bilateral flattening which involves more or less either the whole brain-case or its anterior portion with a strong depression of the occiput from inion to obelion. *H. J. Smith* (1900–1908, v. II, pp. 139, 354) calls attention to the fact that such deformed skulls occur also in cairns and shell heap burials around the lower part of the Gulf of Georgia and on upper Puget Sound.[15] As these burials suggest, and in all probability represent, an older ethnic layer, his findings may have a bearing on the ethnogenetic problem of the Northwest and are referred to later (see chapter "Conclusions," of part two). Bilateral deformation of a more frontal character was also observed by *Hrdlička*[16] in the Lenape Indians, in skulls from Arkansas and Louisiana, and also in those from certain coast districts of Peru. Among very old individuals, senile atrophy is sometimes noticed as the cause of bilateral deformation. Exclusive occipital flattening caused by

---

[13] *Dillenius, A. J.*, 1912. Das Scheitelbein unter dem Einfluss der fronto-occipitalen Schädeldeformation. Arch. Anthrop., n. s., v. II, pp. 113–139 (137).

[14] Plagiocephaly is quite frequently connected with antero-posterior deformation. *Boas, Franz*, 1889, in: Deformation of heads in British Columbia. Science, v. XIII, p. 365, offers the following explanation: "It is a noteworthy fact that in the majority of cases the left side of the head is more prominent than the right side. Presumably this is due to the fact that the child mostly lies on his right side when in his cradle."

[15] See here also *Boas'* measurements of bilaterally deformed skulls, 1900–1908, v. II, pp. 188–190, and Zschr. Ethnol., 1890a, v. XXII, pp. 29–31 (31).

[16] *Hrdlička, Aleš*, 1916. Physical anthropology of the Lenape or Delawares and of the eastern Indians in general. Bur. Amer. Ethnol. Bull. LXII, p. 16. — See also: 1909. Report on an additional collection of skeletal remains from Arkansas and Louisiana. Journ. Ac. Nat. Sci. Philadelphia, v. XIV, pp. 174–240 (184).

mechanical manipulation as an hitherto unknown type of cranial deformation has been described of late in skulls from ruins (Mochicas) in Peru.[17]

Cranial deformation, although effecting conspicuous changes in outward appearance, does not seem in any way to impair the growth or function of the brain nor the general health of the individual.[18] Deleterious effects upon the optical nerve have been described as resulting from premature obliteration of cranial sutures (Enslin). But as a pathological condition is involved here, it might be conjectured that in this case a steadily increasing strain induces complications and that the organic disturbance has much deeper effects than mechanical pressure applied from the outside. That the latter, however, may also produce harmful effects, for the time being, is claimed by *Woldt-Jacobsen* (1884, 62) in the following statement: "Die Indianer von Nooette, Koskimo und Quatsino pressen die Köpfe ihrer kleinen Kinder, besonders der Mädchen, durch eine eigentümliche Art von Binde so fest zusammen, dass die Schädel allmählich die Form von Zuckerhüten annehmen. Der Druck der Kopfpresse wird oft so sehr verstärkt, dass den armen Säuglingen das Blut aus der Nase tritt."[19] From this statement we gain the impression that preferably girls were subjected to the custom of head deformation, which is also *Boas*' view, l. c., p. 14 (365); *Eaton* (see reference in this paragraph) expresses himself in a similar way,[20] but contrary to *Hrdlička's* assertion l. c., p. 12 (358) who found it on the whole more pronounced and common in males than in females.

The observations upon the material under investigation did not reveal any sex preference. Individual instances of excessively deformed skulls were noticed in the Chinook and Koskimo groups with an apparently equal frequency among the two sexes. The more or less pronounced deformations of individuals may be ascribed rather to the variations in the size of the head and the conditions of its growth, or the size of the neck and its muscles and ligaments, both of which would exercise their influence on the position of the head in the cradle. They may also be due to modifications in the form and use of deforming devices, such as cradles or bandages which in themselves

---

[17] See *Posnansky, Arthur*, 1925. Die erotischen Keramiken der Mochicas und deren Beziehungen zu occipital deformierten Schädeln. Festschrift Band II, Frankfurter Ges. Anthrop. Ethnol. Urgesch., pp. 67–74 (72).

[18] This is also the view of *George F. Eaton*, 1916. The collection of osteological material from Machu Picchu. Mem. Connecticut Ac. Arts. Sci., v. V, pp. 1–96 (83): "Probably no part of the human skeleton can be artificially deformed with less harmful results than the skull." — See also *Hrdlička, Aleš*, l. c., p. 12 (97). However, *Rüdinger, N.*, 1887. Ueber künstlich deformierte Schädel und Gehirne von Südseeinsulanern. Abh. K. Bayer. Ak. Wiss. II. Cl. München, v. XVI, Abth. II, describes the degeneration of certain cerebral parts due to deformatory strain.

[19] *Imbelloni*, l. c., p. 12 (612), speaks of "taches obscures que les liquides physiologiques ont laissées bien visibles à la surface du bois, et qui indiquent la zone de contact direct avec le crâne."

[20] In addition, with regard to *Jacobsen's* plan to engage natives from Fort Rupert, Vancouver Island, for exhibition in Europe, *Woldt* also states (1884, 130): "Am meisten lag mir daran, Frauen zu engagieren, da sich hauptsächlich unter ihnen die ausgeprägtesten Langköpfe befinden." — *MacCurdy* also states that "intentional deformation... was more in vogue with the female sex than with the male;" see *MacCurdy, George Grant*, 1923. Human skeletal remains from the highlands of Peru. Am. Journ. Phys. Anthrop., v. VI, no. 3, pp. 218–329 (229).

might seem to be quite unimportant. The influence of the length of time that head deforming devices are applied, and their continuous or intermittent application, must also not be underrated. The most intensive growth of the head takes place during the first year and this is the time that deformation is most effective. The general character of deformity established during this period remains unchanged in later life. As special investigations have shown, however, that the growth of the head continues up to the age of twenty, and probably later, and that physiological processes, such as puberty, exercise a stimulating influence,[21] it may not be erroneous to assume that established deformations are liable later to undergo certain limited modifications due to the various causes enumerated, without, however, altering the general type. The varieties thus created have only individual significance.[22]

2. Tribal methods of deformation and metrical interpretation.

Not all the tribes of the Northwest practiced head deformation. Neither the Salish of the interior of British Columbia, nor the Haida of Queen Charlotte Islands, nor the Athapascan and Eskimo followed this peculiar custom. *Teit* (1900–1908, v. II, 262; 586) relates of the Lillooet and Shuswap that the custom of compressing and deforming children's heads was held by them in contempt, while *Hrdlička* (1905, 360–361) reports of the Klamath, South Columbia River, that "they regard a long head, i. e., a non-deformed head, with derision. They say it is slave-llke, that their slaves had such, and that a man with such a head is not fit to be a great man in the tribe. Deformed heads are called 'good heads'." It is thus apparent that social distinctions, prompting disdain or esteem, were in a way established by the practice or non-practice of bandaging. It appears, however, that since primitive times head deformation became associated with a preferred social position.

With regard to the deformation of the head observed in the area under investigation, three principal types or modes were distinguishable, thus con-

---

[21] See *R. Martin*, Lehrbuch, 1914, 641. In the following pages references to the "Lehrbuch" will be indicated as follows: (*R. Martin*, 1914, 800). The latter number stands for the page.

[22] *Boas*' (1921, 666 et seq.) account of the practice of deformation in the Kwakiutl, based on authentic notes and data collected by *George Hunt*, is highly illuminating as regards the causes of modifications which occur in the head form of one and the same type of deformation. From these notes it appears that the principal device used for bringing about the desired head deformation is the kelp band which is applied in specific ways and for a certain period of time, distinction being made whether boys, girls or twins are concerned. Thus, girls were subjected to the treatment most intensively, the kelp band being kept on for twelve days at a time when it was removed in order to oil the bands and the child's head, and when the infant was ten months old, the treatment was permanently discontinued. It was somewhat less intensively applied to the heads of boys, namely, for a period of ten days and taken off after eight months, while in twins it was changed every four days over a period of four months. The most interesting observation in these statements is the fact that lasting deformities may be produced from the relatively short time, four to ten months, within which the bandages are applied. That artificial head deformation was more frequently and pronouncedly practiced upon females than upon males, is further corroborated in the observations made by travellers and investigators.

firming *Boas'* (1890*b*, 808, 812; 1891, 647–655) statement, who designated them as Chinook, Cowichan and Koskimo. The centers of radiation from which these tribal methods of deformation emanated, are fairly well established. The two distinctive, and one might say pure, forms, namely, the antero-posterior compression, and the conical shape produced by bandaging, are found in the extreme south and in the extreme north of that area respectively. The former prevails among the Chinook tribes, while the other, i. e. the Koskimo mode, was in vogue among the majority of the Kwakiutl and Nootka tribes on Vancouver Island. It is also found on the opposite mainland, north of Bute Inlet. The Koskimo method is applied most intensively in the north, particularly around Quatsino Sound, on the northwest coast of Vancouver Island. The northernmost division of the Kwakiutl-Nootka group, the Bellabella about Milbank Sound and on the adjoining mainland, practiced the Cowichan method, however. This latter method is distinguished from the two preceding ones by the employment of specific mechanical devices and the effect produced thereby, which is essentially an antero-posterior flattening. Side cushions which they use together with bandages somewhat mitigate the effects characteristic of the Chinook method, i. e. the excessive sagittal compression of the parietals which involves the flattening of the frontal and occipital bones and the compensatory expansion of the parietals. The Cowichan may thus be classified as an intermediate type between the Chinook and Koskimo, tending gradually toward the latter. *Boas* points out the Çatloltq (Comox) especially as conforming to this type, while its center of radiation seems to lie among the Cowichan near the southeast end of Vancouver Island. It is used by most of the coast Salish tribes of Vancouver Island and the adjoining mainland, and is referred to in these studies as the Cowichan method of deformation. A fourth method, the bilateral compression, should be mentioned, which is described in the preceding section (see p. 14) and which occurs only sporadically in archaeological remains of the Fraser Delta.

The occurrence of these distinct types of deformation within a limited section of a large continent is remarkable. Identical conditions have been recorded on the South American continent for different sections of Peru. They are related to similar forms of specialization in the realm of material culture. It may be mentioned in this connection that a number of authors have pointed out the fallacy of identifying tribes by deformatory fashions. Thus Gosse [23] criticises Tschudi's attempt to that end. Joseph Barnard Davis [24] must also be cited, saying, "This collection of American crania shows that there have been various modes of distortion of the skull among the aboriginal races, which were evidently not confined to particular tribes. Certain tribes within

---

[23] *Gosse*, L. A., Dissertation sur les races qui composaient l'ancienne population du Pérou. Mém. Soc. Anthrop. Paris, v. I, p. 148.

[24] Catalogue of the skulls of the various races of man. London, 1867, p. 249.

themselves have distorted the head in different ways; and distinct tribes have adopted the same mode of distortion, even when that mode was most artificial and required a very complex apparatus."

In addition to the photographic reproductions of the five normae (see pls. III–XI), the median-sagittal perigram has been employed to demonstrate the differences between the various forms of head deformation. Lateral changes, such as expansions or depressions measurable at right angles to the median-sagittal plane, cannot be recorded on the median-sagittal perigram. Such breadth records, however, are of minor importance, as compared to the more conspicuous changes which involve the distortion and shift of extensive parts of the skull occurring in the cranial length and height dimensions and which are directly and exactly traceable in the median-sagittal perigram. In order to demonstrate the specific nature of each method of deformation and to bring out their relation to one another, a special method was employed (see figs. 1–4). The perigram was oriented according to the ear-eye plane (E–E'), after which a line, x–y, was constructed to indicate the specific trend of each mode, i. e. the approximate direction in which the skull bones had given way most markedly under pressure of the deforming mechanisms. This line, x–y,[26] is obtained by connecting the vertex, v, i. e., the point of highest elevation above the parietal chord, b–l, with the mid-point, r, on a cranial base line between the nasion and opisthion, n–o. This latter line was adopted in preference to the nasion-basion line, n–ba, which does not take in the lower portion of the occiput and hence does not account for it anatomically. The nasion-opisthion line, however, affords support to the entire base of the neurocranium, including the occipital region. Furthermore, the vertex point, v, connected with the nasion, n, and opisthion, o, completes the cranial triangle n–v–o, which again is divided into two triangles, v–n–r and v–r–o by the x–y line. The sides of the triangle n–v–o form angles with each other and with the x–y line which in themselves are devoid of decisive value. Their relation, however, to the ear-eye plane affords a valuable means of comparison. The three angles of characteristic value in this respect are: 1. $\angle v$–n–e', formed by the nasion-vertex line and a parallel to the ear-eye plane e–e', indicating the declination of the anterior portion of the brain-case. 2. $\angle v$–t–E', formed by the vertex-opisthion line and the ear-eye plane proper E–E', indicating the declination of the posterior portion of the brain-case. 3. $\angle v$–s–p, formed by the x–y line and the ear-eye plane, which illustrates the general deformatory deviation. Letter s here signifies the intersection between the horizontal E–E' and the line x–y.

The different deformations are each illustrated by a typical perigram. Fig. 1 represents the skull of an adult female, showing the typical Chinook

---

[25] "Axe général" according to *Topinard, P.*, 1885. Anthropologie générale. Paris, pp. 742–746.

deformation. The forehead and occiput are excessively flattened, the latter to such an extent that the curved line between the lambda and opisthion is only very slightly convex, the normal protrusion of the inion region being repressed. The parietals project into the acute angle which is formed by the cradle and the board that compresses the forehead. Their contour reveals a marked sagittal compression whereby the chord is shortened and the vertex raised into a narrowly vaulted culmination. The vertex tends in a backward

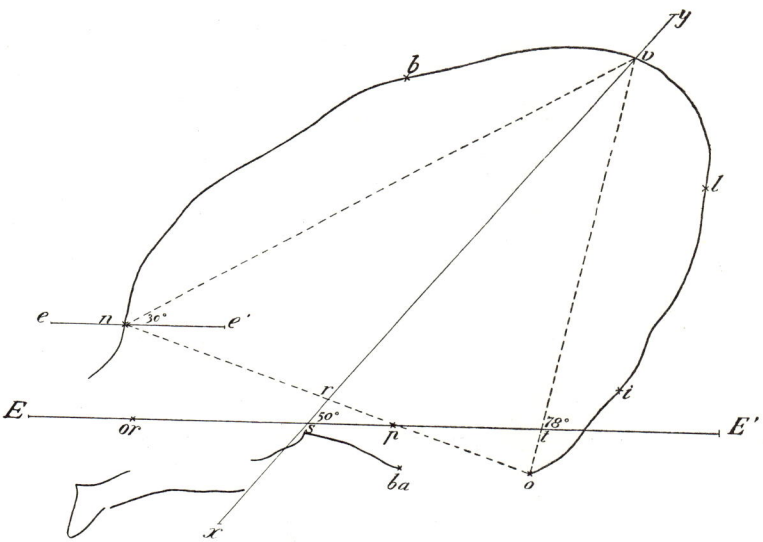

Fig. 1. Median-sagittal cranial perigram of an adult female Chinook (4473). 2/3.
$E-E'$, ear-eye plane; $e-e'$, parallel to ear-eye plane laid through nasion; $x-y$, line indicating general deformatory deviation; v, vertex, highest elevation above bregma-lambda chord; r, midpoint of nasion-opisthion line, intersected by $x-y$; s, point of intersection between $x-y$ line and ear-eye plane. Other letters represent craniological measuring points. Cranial triangle: $v-n-o$. Angles: $\angle$ $v-n-e'$, angle of anterior (frontal) declination; $\angle$ $v-t-E'$, angle of posterior (occipital) declination; $\angle$ $v-s-p$, angles of general deformatory deviation.

and upward direction and fairly coincides with the highest elevation of the post-bregmatic region. The angle of anterior declination amounts to 30°, that of the posterior to 78°, and that of general deviation to 50°.

Fig. 2 is the median-sagittal perigram of an adult Koskimo male. The enormous elongation of the skull is an illustration of the remarkable degree to which the infantile head can be made to yield to deforming influences. The Koskimo, as was mentioned before, practice the conical or cylindrical type of deformation to an excessive degree, while their kin, the Kwakiutl and Nootka tribes, employ milder forms of the same mode. The Koskimo perigram shows the vertex displaced still farther backward. The flattening of the forehead extends beyond the bregma whereby is produced a uniformly depressed area that begins at a short distance above the glabella and embraces about a third of the parietal contour. The latter, although artificially elongated, is not so narrowly arched as is the case in the Chinook. On the other hand, the occipital line is drawn out considerably farther and in a pronouncedly slanting direction. The impressions made by the bandages are recognizable at different places of the perigram. The three angles under

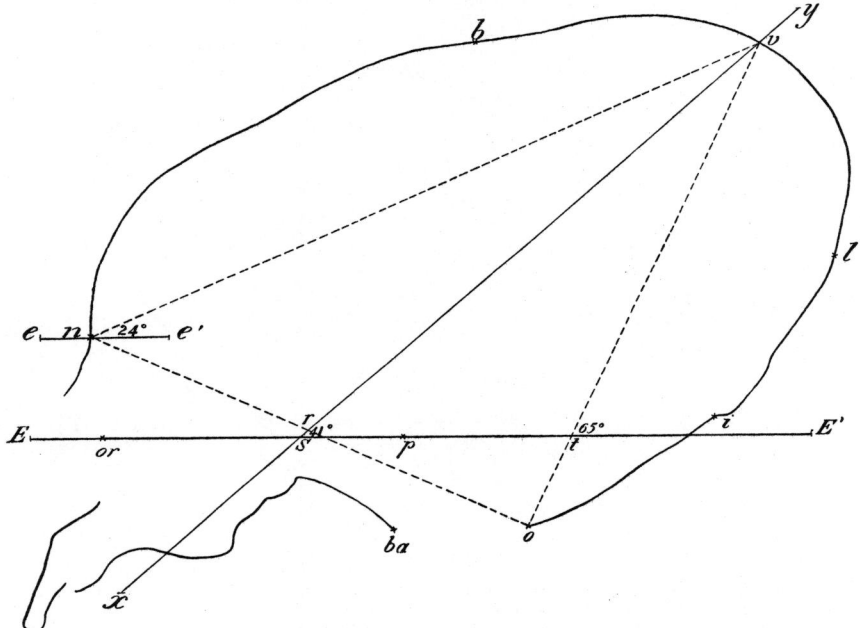

Fig. 2. Median-sagittal cranial perigram of an adult male Koskimo (3242). Lettering as in fig. 1. $^2/_3$.

consideration are smaller here than those of the Chinook skull. While the angle of anterior declination has only 24°, that of posterior declination is 65°. The general deviation shows 41°.

The Cowichan type of deformation is depicted in fig. 3. It represents the median-sagittal perigram of an adult male skull from North Saanich which is situated in the southeastern part of Vancouver Island. The effects of fronto-occipital compression appear here in a milder form. The frontal region is only slightly flattened, but in the occipital it is somewhat more pronounced, especially near the lambda, while the inion region appears unimpaired. The parietal curve is also only slightly changed, the vertex pointing more in an upward direction. The Cowichan type of deformation, being related in its specific trend more nearly to the Chinook than the Koskimo, is also characterized by larger angles, amounting to 32° for the anterior and 88° for the posterior declination, while the general deformatory deviation is 56°.

The fourth mode, that of bilateral deformation, is illustrated in fig. 4, which represents an adult male skull from a shell heap on the lower Fraser River. The perigram does not show the lateral flattening. While the frontal and, indeed, the whole anterior region of the brain-case seems to be sagittally unimpaired, the occipital region between the obelion and inion is quite depressed,

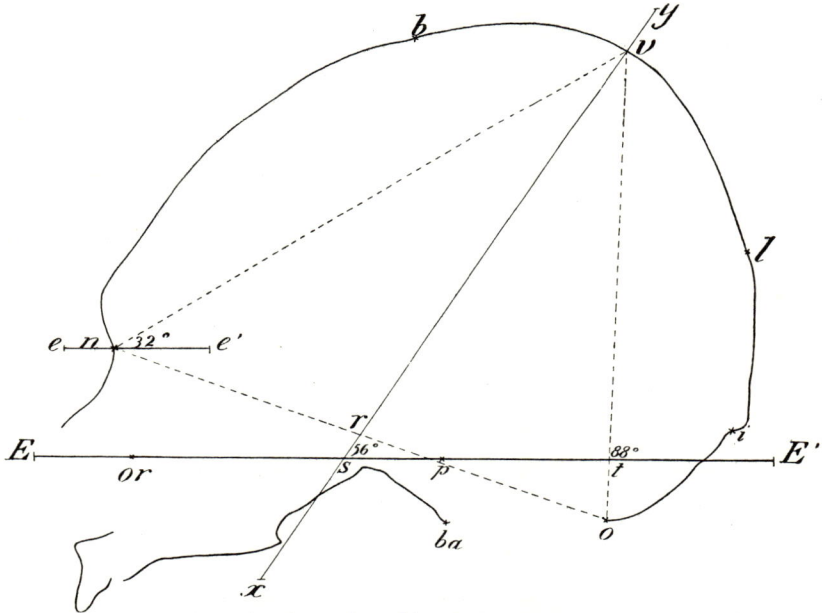

Fig. 3. Median-sagittal cranial perigram of an adult male from N. Saanich, Vancouver Is. (2644A). Lettering as in fig. 1. 2/3.

so much so, in fact, that an almost straight line is formed between those two points of the perigram. It seems probable that bilateral compression, especially in the anterior, as the part narrower *per se*, of the skull, may expand the medial periphery of the skull and thus produce a well curved frontal outline and an extended basion-bregma height. The postbregmatic elevation might have been increased by both factors, the bilateral and occipital depression, which condition *Boas* (1890, 31) refers to as "pyramidal." The frontal declination amounts to 37°, thus representing the highest angularity of the four types of deformation. The occipital declination of 88° corresponds to that of the Cowichan mode, while the general deviation angle of 61° also exceeds those of the other cases.

For a general comparative review, the metrical findings discussed in the preceding paragraphs have been listed in the following table, where $\angle\ v\text{-}s\text{-}p$,

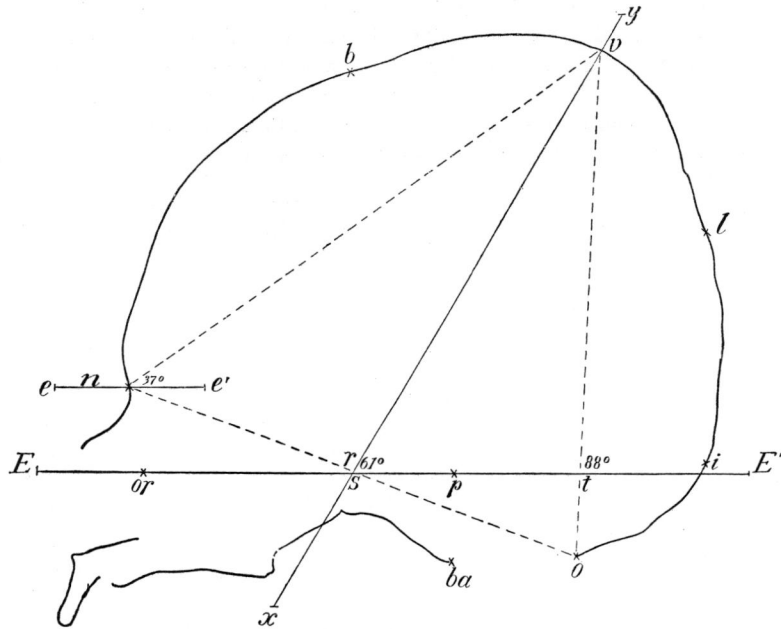

Fig. 4. Median-sagittal cranial perigram of an adult male from a shell heap of the Lower Fraser R. (1544). Lettering as in fig. 1. ²/₃.

as stated above, indicates the general deformatory deviation, $\angle\ v\text{-}t\text{-}E'$ the posterior, and $\angle\ v\text{-}n\text{-}e'$ the anterior declination.

Mode of deformation	ANGLES OF DEFORMATION			
	number, sex, age	$\angle\ v\text{-}s\text{-}p$	$\angle\ v\text{-}t\text{-}E'$	$\angle\ v\text{-}n\text{-}e'$
Bilateral	1544 ♂, ad.	61°	88°	37°
Cowichan	2644A ♂, mat.	56°	88°	32°
Chinook	4473 ♀, ad.	50°	78°	30°
Koskimo	3642 ♂, mat.	41°	65°	24°
Haida (undeformed)	1610 ♂, ad.-mat.	51°	82°	27°

For further comparison with the angles of an undeformed skull, those of a Haida male were added. It will be noticed that a steady increase in the sizes of all the angles occurs in the following order: Koskimo, Chinook, Cowichan and bilateral deformations. This is in keeping with the changing position of the vertex point, and the subsequent changes of the anterior and posterior declinations as well as the general deformatory deviation. The measurements of the undeformed skull are quite instructive here. Its general deviation angle, $\angle v\text{--}s\text{--}p$, of 51° falls between the excessive Chinook and Koskimo modes and the Cowichan and bilateral ones, the vertex points of which two latter are directed more upward and forward. This is also the condition with regard to the posterior declination, $\angle v\text{--}t\text{--}E'$, whose angle of 82° falls between the Chinook and Cowichan deformations. The Haida angle of anterior declination of 27°, $\angle v\text{--}n\text{--}e'$, ranges between the Koskimo and Chinook deformations, illustrating the latter's more upwardly displaced vertex point, which is still further expressive of the Cowichan and bilateral modes of deformation.

ORIENTATION.

1. General remarks.

The proper orientation of an object is essential in comparative study. The skull should be horizontally placed so that it is as nearly as possible in its natural, physiological position. This position, for the purposes of craniometry, must be accurately defined so that angular relations to the horizontal plane may be recognized.

Different planes of orientation which are used by the various schools and authors are not conducive toward the unification of comparative results. Such planes and lines, for instance, are: the ear-eye plane; the glabella-inion and the nasion-inion planes; the glabella-lambda plane; the alveolo-condylar plane. The cranial base plane (nasion-basion line) has also been used in the orientation of the skull, while the inclination of the plane of the foramen magnum has been considered only on account of its morphological significance. Keith [26] proceeded on more purely anatomical lines. His base line corresponds roughly with the lower margin of the cerebrum, and is indicated on the surface of the cranium anteriorly by the fronto-zygomatic suture and posteriorly by the lower angle of the parietal, the craniological point of the 'asterion'.

Bolk [27] made use of a base line that passes through points in the skull cavity, and which can be determined only after the skull has been halved in the median-sagittal plane. [28] The anterior point is the 'fronton,' where the interior surface of the frontal bone turns sharply to participate in the formation of the nasal cavity. In man this coincide fairly well with the anterior border of the foramen coecum. The posterior point is the 'occipiton,' the point of the interior occipital region that is farthest removed from the 'fronton.' This base line was used by Bolk in a special investigation into the changes of position of the foramen magnum.

Pointing out the inefficiency of most of the modes of orientation, including

---

[26] *Keith, Arthur*, 1925. The antiquity of man. London. 2. ed., v. II, chapter 31.

[27] *Bolk, Louis*, 1915. Über Lagerung, Verschiebung und Neigung des Foramen magnum am Schädel der Primaten. Ztschr. Morph. Anthrop., v. XVII, pp. 611–692 (614 et seq.).

[28] Reference is made to an instrument by which intracranial measurements can be taken without injuring the skull, by *Weinert, Hans*, 1922. Neue Untersuchungen über die Calotte des Pithecanthropus erectus. Zschr. Ethnol., v. LIV, pp. 199–207 (201).

the ear-eye plane, Pycraft[29] suggested the "meatonasion line, passing from the nasion backward through the center of the auditory meatus."

These are the more important of the numerous planes proposed by various authors. However, it is not the object of these studies to pass upon them critically.

The material under investigation was oriented according to the 'ear-eye' plane, which is indicated by the two 'poria' and the left 'orbitale'.

Angular relations of the ear-eye plane with other bases of orientation vary more or less. In late years the glabella-lambda plane[30] has gained greater interest and for that reason a systematic investigation into its angular differences with the ear-eye plane was carried out.

2. The angular relation between the ear-eye and glabella-lambda planes.

The angle formed by these two plane lines opens posteriorly in most cases, while occasionally parallelism between the two is encountered.

Summary 6.[30a]

Averages of the angular relation between the ear-eye and glabella-lambda planes.

	Undeformed			Deformation according to the three modes											
					Cowichan				Chinook				Koskimo		
Sex, Age	Cases	Range	Average	σ	Cases	Range	Average	σ	Cases	Range	Average	σ	Cases	Range	Average	σ
♂	76	0–16	6.7	± 3.47	76	2–19	10.1	± 3.44	57	7–18	12.4	± 2.53	104	0–16	7.1	± 3.12
♀	30	4–10	7.5	± 2.09	23	7–17	10.9	± 2.84	25	8–19	12.0	± 2.47	35	1–16	8.2	± 3.39
juv.	1	—	10.0	—	2	10; 11	10.5	—	4	10–17	14.0	—	2	6; 7	6.5	—
inf.	8	5–13	8.1	—	4	8–18	13.0	—	6	6–23	14.5	—	6	5–18	11.2	—

In the Undeformed division, as shown in *Summary 6*, the variation of this angle ranges from 0° to 16° in the males, and from 4° to 10° in the females. They oscillate around 7° in both sexes. The juvenile and infantile values also fall well within the general range. Of the groups constituting the Undeformed division, it is only the Haida and Eskimo whose numbers are large

---

[29] *Pycraft, W. P.*, 1916. Report on the human crania collected by the British Ornithologists' Union Expedition and the Wollaston Expedition in Dutch New Guinea. British Museum. 42 pp. (1; 24 et seq.).

1925. On the recognition of several species of post-Mousterian man: and the necessity for superseding the Frankfort base-line. Man, no. 105.

[30] This line of orientation was first introduced by *E. T. Hamy*, and later utilized in a novel and ingenious way by *Klaatsch* in his craniological works. He was able to point out what appear to be natural correlations in the architecture of the skull, to which reference will be made repeatedly in the present report (see pp. 26–28).

[30a] Metrical designations like *cc.*, cubic centimeter; *cm.*, centimeter; *mm.*, millimeter; %, per cent.; °, degree have been omitted in the summaries and tables of measurements and may be easily inferred from the nature of the measurements.

enough to justify the use of their means in comparative study.[31] The Haida means with 7.5° in both sexes are seen to fall in line with the general averages of the Undeformed division, while those of the Eskimo with 5.4° in the males and 6.7° in the females range below them.

The deviations in the deformed divisions depend largely on the mode of deformation to which the skulls have been subjected. Realizing the changeable position of the lambda point even under normal conditions, it is self-evident that its forcible displacement will bring about considerable variation. The least deviation as regards the angular relation of the two planes under discussion, is effected by the Koskimo deformation as practiced by the Kwakiutl and Nootka. Their range and average correspond fairly well to those of the Undeformed skulls. The average is grouped around 8° with a tendency toward a lower value in the males. This is also true of the Bellabella, a tribe related to the Kwakiutl and living in the region of Milbank Sound, who apply the Cowichan mode of deformation. In the latter the position of the lambda is shifted upward in various degrees according to the intensity with which the deforming devices were applied. The upper limit rises to 19°, the male and female averages being around 10°, with an apparent inclination of the females to produce higher means.

A single individual from Coupeville, Wash., enumerated with the Cowichan division, is deformed in the Chinook manner and, therefore, added to their number. Its high individual value coincides with the high figures found among the Chinook skulls, in which the lambda has suffered a considerable displacement. The effect of this shows quite plainly in the infantiles and juveniles with means of 14.5° and 14.0°, the upper limit of the infantile type even rising to 23°, while the lower limits are respectively 6° and 10°. Later development of the head, brought about by the growth of the brain and membrane bones, probably modify such extreme conditions. Yet the Chinook averages of 12.4° in the males and 12.0° in the females are the highest of our four divisions, conditions also reflected by their higher individual values as expressed in the ranges of variation. In the other deformed groups, changes brought about by artificial deformation are also more pronounced in the immature than in the mature age. It may be observed, however, that the undeformed infantile skulls also exceed the values of the undeformed adults, so that the conditions in the deformed skulls again appear as an exaggeration.

Summary treatment of each division shows also that the undeformed female skulls have higher averages than the males. It will be noticed in summary 6 that the same conditions obtain more or less in the deformed divisions with the exception of the Chinook skulls, where the males have an average that slightly exceeds that of the females: 12.4° by 12.0°. The infantiles have still higher values, both in the undeformed and deformed groups. The Chinook juveniles hold a high average, which corresponds to that of the infantiles, while the juveniles of the other groups fit in with the adults.

The variability throughout is nearly the same. There is hardly any difference to speak of between the figures of the standard deviation in the Undeformed and those in the deformed skulls.

A graphic representation of the conditions here discussed is shown in fig. 5, where, within the total range of all four divisions their respective total averages are indicated by differentiated lines.

3. Klaatsch's central angle ("Zentralwinkel").

The reinstitution by Klaatsch of the glabella-lambda plane as a line of orientation for the median-sagittal perigram of the skull revealed a phenomenon unknown up to that time. Klaatsch[32] was able to demonstrate a rectangular

---

[31] The number of individuals contained in each group and division; the means referring to the former and the averages to the latter; and the ranges of variation, are recorded in the appended tables of measurements. The summaries in the text contain the total frequencies, averages and the standard deviation; the last-named was computed for the mature specimens only, separately, however, for males and females.

[32] l. c., p. 9 (120).

relation of the cranial height line (basion-bregma) to the glabella-lambda horizontal. Under normal conditions the point of intersection of the two lines is more or less centrally located in the cranium. For this reason Klaatsch

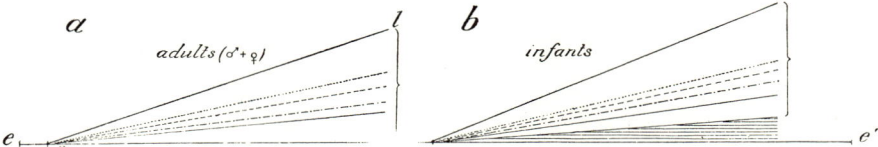

Fig. 5. Scheme of the angular relation between the ear-eye and glabella-lambda planes in (a) the adults, males and females combined and (b) the immatures. $e-e'$, parallel to ear-eye plane; $gl.$ glabella; $l.$ lambda.

——— Undeformed:	∠ l-gl-e'	6.9°, immatures	8.1°
- - - - Cowichan :	„ „	10.3°, „	13.0°
. . . . Chinook :	„ „	12.3°, „	14.5°
— · — · Koskimo :	„ „	7.4°, „	11.2°
Total range:	„ „	0° to 19°, „	5° to 23°

chose the term "Zentralwinkel", i. e. central angle. The latter is formed by the two chords, bregma-center and glabella-center, and opens frontally.

Although special investigations for testing Klaatsch's assertion are not numerous, they have, nevertheless, proved the correctness of that author's statement. Still, there exists in any series of normal, i. e. undeformed skulls, an oscillation around 90° in the relation of the two diameters in question. This was also realized by Klaatsch and mentioned in his writings.

Summary 7.

Averages of the angular relation between the basion-bregma and the glabella-lambda lines ("Zentralwinkel", Klaatsch).

Sex, Age	Undeformed				Deformation according to the three modes											
					Cowichan				Chinook				Koskimo			
	Cases	Range	Average	σ	Cases	Range	Average	σ	Cases	Range	Average	σ	Cases	Range	Average	σ
♂	74	86–100	91.6	± 2.44	75	86–100	93.9	± 3.23	57	93–105	99.9	± 3.66	134	89–105	96.6	± 3.66
♀	30	86–96	90.9	± 2.17	23	89–103	95.6	± 3.16	24	93–107	99.2	± 3.57	35	91–110	96.5	± 3.48
juv.	1	—	92.0	—	2	95; 97	96.0	—	4	97–100	98.5	—	2	93; 94	93.5	—
inf.	7	90–96	91.8	—	4	95–101	97.5	—	5	94–108	101.0	—	6	90–100	95.5	—

Even in the Undeformed, as will be observed in *Summary 7*, the oscillation around 90° is very considerable, covering a total range from 86° to 100°. The highest female value, however, is only 96°, and the less extended female range gives rise to a slightly lower average of 90.9° as against a male one of 91.6°.

The ranges and averages of the three deformed divisions considerably exceed those of the

Undeformed, and this occurs in even proportion to their degree of distortion. It is apparent that the displacement of the lambda was most pronounced in the Chinook as was also shown for the preceding measurement, and that the displacement of the lambda occurred less strenuously upward than backward in the Koskimo deformation. The least distortion is noticed in the Cowichan mode of deformation although its averages also remarkably exceed those of the Undeformed.

That a rectangular relation of the two lines under discussion, is preserved in deformed skulls, was shown by Falkenburger[33] in his study upon Peruvian skulls. This is readily understood when one considers that the relative position of the bregma and lambda points to one another, and that of both in relation to the glabella, was not disturbed by the deformation.

The observations on the infantile skulls corroborate our previous statement (see p. 12) that the deforming influences are strongest at an early age. Excepting the Koskimo type, the angle in the infantiles exceeds in size that found among the adults. The averages of the juveniles again are more in keeping with the latter. This difference between immature and mature ages proves true also for the undeformed skulls. Their infantiles have an average of 91.8°, which is a trifle higher than the adult male average. The only undeformed juvenile has an angle of 92.0°.

The standard deviation is seen to be lowest in the Undeformed; it ranges here below ± 3. while in the deformed divisions it rises above ± 3, and is relatively highest in the Chinook.

Here, again, a graphic scheme of the conditions just expounded was resorted to (fig. 6). Attention may be called to the fact that in the diagram

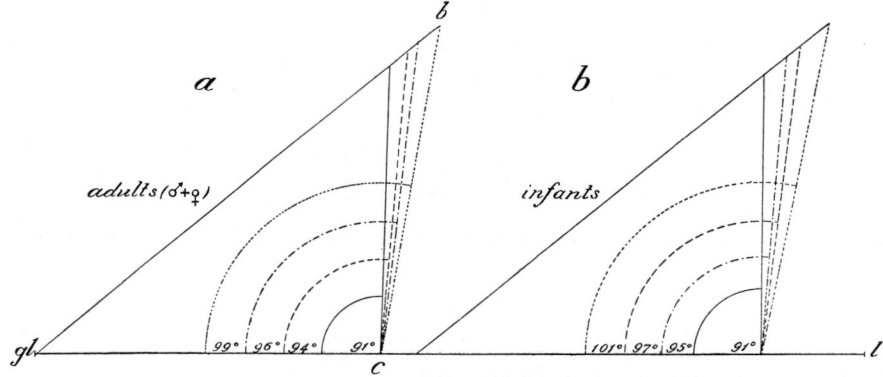

Fig. 6. Scheme of the angular relation between the basion-bregma (*c–b*) line and the glabella-lambda (*gl–l*) plane in the adults, males and females combined, and in the immatures, *c*, center of skull (intersecting point of the two lines named), ∠ *b–c–gl*. central angle („Zentralwinkel" Klaatsch).
——— Undeformed; - - - - Cowichan, ... Chinook, – · – · – · Koskimo deformations.

the order of lines representing the infantiles of the Salish (Cowichan) and Koskimo divisions is reversed as compared with the Salish and Koskimo adults, while the infantiles in general represent higher values than the adults.

[33] *Falkenburger, Fritz*, 1913. Diagraphische Untersuchungen an normalen und deformierten Rassenschädeln. Arch. Anthrop., N. F., v. XII, p. 81–85.

4. The angle formed by the basion-bregma height line with the ear-eye plane.

This angle is closely related to the angles discussed above. Its deviations in the different deformations are somewhat analogous to those of the central angle ("Zentralwinkel"). The difference between the two depends on the differences of the angular relation between the ear-eye and glabella-lambda planes. These latter, as was shown, form an angle whose vertex lies in the glabella point, i. e. the angle opens backward. Sometimes this angle is zero, as was stated above.

Summary 8.

Averages of the angular relation between the basion-bregma line and the ear-eye plane.

		Undeformed			Deformation according to the three modes											
					Cowichan				Chinook				Koskimo			
Sex, Age	Cases	Range	Average	σ	Cases	Range	Average	σ	Cases	Range	Average	σ	Cases	Range	Average	σ
♂	74	77–96	84.8	± 3.58	73	78–90	83.9	± 2.94	58	78–92	87.6	± 3.63	104	81–99	88.5	± 3.09
♀	30	79–96	83.4	± 3.14	22	79–90	85.1	± 3.24	24	79–93	87.2	± 3.82	35	83–98	88.3	± 3.39
juv.	1	—	82.0	—	2	85; 86	85,5	—	4	80–90	84.5	—	2	86; 88	87.0	—
inf.	7	80–86	83.7	—	4	82–87	84.2	—	5	83–89	86.0	—	6	77–90	84.3	—

For the angle indicated in the heading of this section ∠ b–c–e of fig. 7, the individual values in the Undeformed series, as specified in *Summary 8*, run as high as 96° in both sexes, while their lowest values with 77° in the males and 79° in the females remain considerably below those registered for the central angle, and reach only in the females up to the highest individual values. The ranges do not reach upward as high in the Cowichan and Chinook divisions, but exceed the Undeformed range in the Koskimo. It is in this division also that the highest averages occur, due to the extent of backward shifting of the bregma which is slightly less noticeable in the Chinook and still less so in the Cowichan. The male average of the last named ranges even below that of the Undeformed. The immature values agree more or less with those found among the adults.

The variability corresponds almost entirely to that of the central angle. It will be noticed that the Cowichan exceed the Undeformed in the values of the central angle. This must doubtlessly be laid to the greater stability of the ear-eye horizontal as being less involved in the distorting influences of deformation. Through the mobility of the lambda point, on the other hand, the glabella-lambda plane is directly affected by the gradually increasing strains of the different modes of deformation. This, in turn, influences the gradually increasing sizes of the angle under discussion.

In order to demonstrate graphically the angular relations of the basion-bregma height line to the ear-eye and glabella-lambda planes, the following scheme was constructed (fig. 7, a–d): the basion (ba) is shifted upward to the level of the ear-eye horizontal e–e', laid through c, the point of intersection of the cranial height line and the glabella-lambda plane. The cranial height line itself extends from this point c ($= ba$) to point b, the bregma. Through

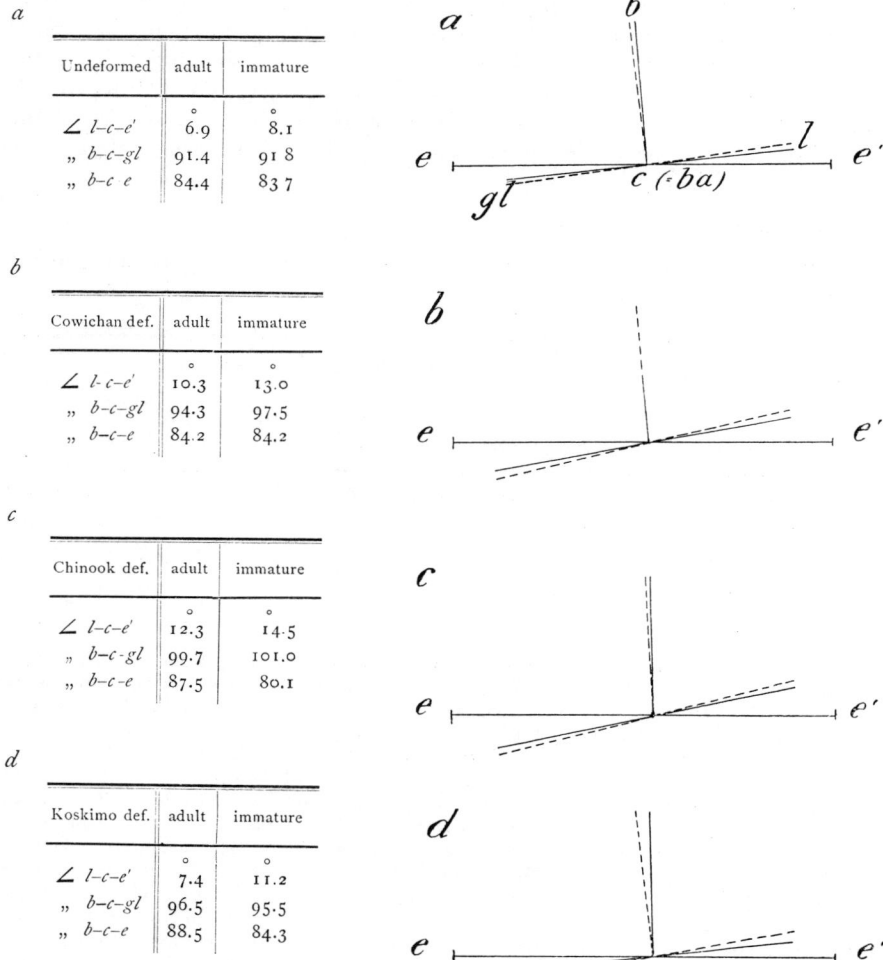

	Undeformed	adult	immature
a	∠ l-c-e'	6.9°	8.1°
	„ b-c-gl	91.4	91.8
	„ b-c-e	84.4	83.7

	Cowichan def.	adult	immature
b	∠ l-c-e'	10.3°	13.0°
	„ b-c-gl	94.3	97.5
	„ b-c-e	84.2	84.2

	Chinook def.	adult	immature
c	∠ l-c-e'	12.3°	14.5°
	„ b-c-gl	99.7	101.0
	„ b-c-e	87.5	80.1

	Koskimo def.	adult	immature
d	∠ l-c-e'	7.4°	11.2°
	„ b-c-gl	96.5	95.5
	„ b-c-e	88.5	84.3

Fig. 7. a–d, illustrating the angular relations of the cranial height line (ba–b) to the ear-eye (e–e') and glabella-lambda (gl–l) planes, in (a) the Undeformed; (b) the Cowichan, (c) Chinook, and (d) Koskimo deformation. c, center of skull (intersecting points of height line and the two planes). ———— adults, males and females combined, - - - infantiles. The basion is shifted upward and coincides with point c, through which a parallel of the ear-eye plane is laid.

point c were also laid the glabella-lambda planes of both the adults and infants, and their lines carried to points gl forward of c, and point l backward of c, the glabella and lambda points.

The diagrams thus show a combination of angular conditions; (1), of the glabella-lambda plane to the ear-eye plane: $\angle l$-c-e'; (2), of the cranial height line to the glabella-lambda plane: $\angle b$-c-gl, and (3), of the cranial height line to the ear-eye plane: $\angle b$-c-e.

The immatures are seen, practically in every instance, to fall short of the adults, excepting the two lines of orientation. It is only in the Undeformed skulls that they yield equal central angles ($\angle b$-c-gl), and in the Cowichan deformation, that they obtain uniform b-c-e angles. This latter angle, in every case, falls below 90°. In none of the instances represented here do the differences between the adults and immatures exceed four degrees.

In order to facilitate the interpretation of fig. 7, summaries containing the averages of the adults, males and females, and of the immatures have been added to diagrams a-d.

CRANIAL CAPACITY.

The general observation that artificial deformation of the head does not impair the intellectual qualities of the individual is correlated to the apparently justified assumption that the size of the brain also does not suffer any detriment therefrom. Quantitative differences were found, however, in the cranial capacities of the deformed series, with a gradual increase in the order of the Cowichan, Chinook and Koskimo deformations, the Cowichan in their turn exceeding the Undeformed. We might be tempted, therefore, to ascribe the increase to the deforming influences. But since we are unable to reconstruct the normal proportions of the skulls, and since we do not know the exact extent of compensatory expansion, further speculation is futile. Unless we assume that the mechanical strains act as organic stimuli for cranial enlargement, differences of cranial capacity, although measurable and comparable, must be considered a feature not directly traceable to deforming influences.

The high degree of variability of cranial capacity is a peculiar feature noticed in most large series of human skulls. It is not surprising, then, that the individual capacities in the skulls under investigation should cover a range which extends from 980 ccm. to 1640 ccm., including adult males and females. Under the classification as indicated before (see chapter on technique p. 9) it will be found that the variation of all four divisions comprises oligencephalic, euencephalic and aristencephalic elements in different proportions which are treated of later on. None of the male group means for the Undeformed series rises above the euencephalic upper limit of 1450 ccm.

Summary 9.

Averages of cranial capacity.

Sex, Age	Undeformed				Deformation according to the three modes											
					Cowichan				Chinook				Koskimo			
	Cases	Range	Average	σ	Cases	Range	Average	σ	Cases	Range	Average	σ	Cases	Range	Average	σ
♂	73	1100–1640	1349.5	± 127.75	69	1120–1590	1365.3	± 97.05	57	1150–1630	1388.8	± 112.50	96	1170–1635	1396.3	± 100.55
♀	32	1100–1620	1243.8	± 95.15	25	980–1350	1209.6	± 96.25	25	1020–1390	1251.6	± 100.50	36	1100–1410	1264.2	± 101.75
juv.	1	—	1350.0	—	2	1160;1250	1205.0	—	4	1070–1460	1227.5	—	2	1320;1350	1340.0	—
inf.	11	1020–1540	1268.2	—	4	1085–1400	1242.5	—	6	1200–1400	1301.7	—	4	1270–1400	1010.0	—

Summary 9 contains the averages of the four divisions. Males and females of all divisions have euencephalic averages. The males are seen to exceed the females in every instance by over 100 ccm., thus repeating the general observation among the human races and, in particular, among the American Indians. The sex differences amount to 105.7 ccm. in the Undeformed; and to 150.1 ccm. in the Cowichan, 137.2 ccm. in the Chinook, and 132.1 ccm. in the Koskimo deformations. The gradual increase in the averages, male and female, in the order, Undeformed, Cowichan, Chinook and Koskimo deformations, was pointed out at the beginning of this chapter. The only exception to this order occurs between the females of the Undeformed and the Cowichan deformation, with an average of 1243.8 ccm. for the former and 1209.6 ccm. for the latter. The immatures in each case range below the matures.

The variability ranges around ± 100, and is higher in the males than in the females, except in the Koskimo where both series are fairly equal.

Summary 10.

Cranial capacity of the combined four tribal divisions: sex averages and percental frequencies.

Total	Cranial capacity				
	total average	difference	Percental frequency		
			oligencephaly	euencephaly	aristencephaly
♂	1379.7 (1100–1640)	134.8	20.6	49.7	29.7
♀	1244.9 (980–1620)		11.2	62.4	26.4

The combination of all the males and females of the four divisions, of their ranges, averages and percental classification has been attempted in *Summary 10*. The total averages there amount to 1379.7 ccm. for the males and 1244.9 ccm. for the females, with a difference between the two of 134.8 ccm. These figures do not in any way change the individual status of the two sexes within the four divisions. In the percental distribution, the highest percentages are seen to belong to euencephaly with 49.7°/₀ in the males and 62.4°/₀ in the females. Considerably lower percentages are listed for the oligencephalic and aristencephalic classes, the latter noticeably exceeding the former.

PRINCIPAL DIAMETERS AND INDICES OF THE SKULL.

1. Maximum length of the skull.

Summary 11.
Averages of the maximum cranial length.

Sex, Age	Undeformed				Deformation according to the three modes											
					Cowichan				Chinook				Koskimo			
	Cases	Range	Average	σ	Cases	Range	Average	σ	Cases	Range	Average	σ	Cases	Range	Average	σ
♂	79	164–196	175.6	± 8.11	81	145–197	169.8	± 7.64	57	155–182	166.6	± 5.66	104	163–207	183.0	± 6.36
♀	34	162–183	170.3	± 5.03	27	144–180	161.8	± 7.71	25	148–166	160.7	± 5.77	39	165–190	175.5	± 6.28
juv.	1	—	170.0	—	2	151;162	156.5	—	4	144–169	152.8	—	2	166;169	167.5	—
inf.	13	145–178	160.9	—	4	153–171	155.0	—	6	151–166	157.2	—	8	153–179	167.5	—

The great variability of this measure, as shown in *summary 11*, is demonstrated by the ranges pertaining to the Undeformed series, and which extend from 164–196 mm. in the males, and from 162–183 mm. in the females. The differences between the shortest and the greatest length thus amount to 32 mm. in the former, and 21 mm. in the latter. The averages of 175.6 mm. for the males and 170 3 mm for the females fall in line with the smallest averages for this measurement as given by *R. Martin* (Lehrbuch, 1914, 661), and also indicate a sex difference of 5.3 mm., which corresponds well with the proportions obtaining, in general, in the human groups. The Haida males with 184.4 mm., and the Eskimo males with 181.9 mm. show the highest figures among the group means of the Undeformed division, the females yielding correspondingly high figures of 172.0 mm. and 173.2 mm. In striking contrast to these figures are seen the rather small values of the Lillooet males and females with averages of 164.5 mm. and 166.0 mm., the Lillooet immatures yielding an average of only 153.0 mm.

The Koskimo, on account of the excessive lengthening of their heads, naturally produce higher averages than the Undeformed. This is already suggested by the ranges which extend as high as 207 mm. in the males, and 190 mm. in the females, thus exceeding the two sexes in the Undeformed ranges by 11 mm. and 7 mm. The averages in the Koskimo deformation are 183.0 mm. for the males and 175.5 mm. for the females, resulting in a sex difference of 7.5 mm. Even the infantile average attains as high a figure as 167.5 mm., i.e., 6.6 mm. in excess of the average of the Undeformed infantiles. Among the tribal groups of the Koskimo division, it is the Koskimo themselves who claim the highest individual values as well as the highest male and female means as against the Kwakiutl, Nimkish, Nootka and Clayoquot of the same division. The averages of the Koskimo immatures fairly correspond in proportion to those of the Undeformed immatures.

The two remaining divisions of deformed skulls, the Cowichan and Chinook, range both below the Undeformed and Koskimo. Representing the effects of more strenuous antero-posterior compression, the Chinook naturally have the smaller averages of 166.6 mm. in the males and 160.7 mm. in the females as against 169.8 mm. and 161.8 mm. in the Cowichan deformation. This proportion does not repeat itself in the infantiles, the Chinook mean of 157.2 mm. exceeding the Cowichan by 2.2 mm. The few juveniles, however, conform with the adults. The sex differences in both adult groups amount to 8.0 mm. in the deformed Salish skulls, and 5.9 mm. in the Chinook. They thus repeat the conditions met with in normal series.

It may here be pointed out, which also holds true for quite a number of measurements discussed in this work, that the modifications or variations of the Cowichan and Koskimo deformations give rise to a very pronounced variability, more so in fact than is the case with the Chinook mode, which latter is conducive to more unified results on account of the more uniform changes produced by their specific way of deforming the head.

The standard deviation expresses these conditions in rather high figures, the highest one of which is that for the Undeformed males at ± 8.11, due to the strong local variations combined in this division. Relatively low are the nearly uniform figures in the Chinook, both in the males and females.

2. Maximum breadth of the skull.

Differences resulting from the peculiarities of specific deformation are obvious also in the breadth of the skull which may be seen in *summary 12*.

Summary 12.

Averages of the maximum cranial breadth.

Sex, Age	Undeformed				Deformation according to the three modes											
					Cowichan				Chinook				Koskimo			
	Cases	Range	Average	σ	Cases	Range	Average	σ	Cases	Range	Average	σ	Cases	Range	Average	σ
♂	79	129–152	140.8	± 5.65	80	131–174	151.2	± 8.58	57	143–170	156.3	± 6.33	103	127–158	138.7	± 5.69
♀	34	130–150	136.5	± 4.79	27	132–161	144.4	± 7.38	25	138–161	149.8	± 6.23	39	124–145	134.0	± 4.14
juv.	1	—	142.0	—	1	—	149.0	—	4	142–154	148.3	—	2	131;141	136.0	—
inf.	13	130–157	139.5	—	4	134–150	141.0	—	6	145–161	153.2	—	8	122–144	135.1	—

Higher averages are attained by the Cowichan and Chinook deformations, the latter surpassing the former, as might have been expected, but both exceeding the Undeformed specimens, which latter present about medium conditions of the skull breadth. The skulls deformed in the Koskimo fashion have the lowest averages, and thus range below the other three divisions. The differences between the averages of the Undeformed and Koskimo, however, are very small when compared with those of the Cowichan and Chinook deformations. Thus, while the Cowichan averages exceed those of the Undeformed by 10.4 mm. in the males and 7.9 mm. in the females, they are in turn exceeded by the Chinook by 5.1 mm. and by 5.4 mm. in the two sexes.

A review of the group means among the Undeformed skulls shows comparatively higher, means for the Haida, Lillooet and Nicola, if comparative value be allowed for the small numbers of individuals in the last two tribes. Slight differences prevail also in the other divisions.

The variability ranges highest in the Cowichan and Chinook deformations, namely around ± 8 in the former and ± 6 in the latter. The Undeformed and Koskimo are slightly less variable.

3. Basion-bregma height of the skull.

Summary 13.

Averages of the basion-bregma height.

	Undeformed				Deformation according to the three modes											
					Cowichan				Chinook				Koskimo			
Sex, Age	Cases	Range	Average	σ	Cases	Range	Average	σ	Cases	Range	Average	σ	Cases	Range	Average	σ
♂	75	110–148	134.2	± 5.87	74	117–147	131.6	± 6.47	57	115–145	127.8	± 6.16	102	122–147	131.9	± 4.74
♀	33	115–141	130.2	± 5.72	25	115–135	126.4	± 5.41	24	102–134	121.4	± 6.86	37	116–138	127.3	± 5.09
juv.	1	—	133.0	—	2	121;123	122.0	—	4	109–127	118.5	—	2	124;132	128.0	—
inf.	8	112–128	121.0	—	4	110–128	116.3	—	5	110–124	119.4	—	4	124–128	126.0	—

The height of the skull appears not to have been changed by deformation to such an extent as the cranial breadth. Assuming that the Undeformed heights, with averages of 134.2 mm. and 130.2 mm. for the adults of both sexes, as shown in *summary 13*, represent about medium and, therefore, normal conditions obtaining in Indians of the North Pacific area, the averages of the other divisions will be found to range below them. There is an obvious similarity between the averages of the Cowichan and Koskimo divisions, while the Chinook averages with 127.8 mm. for the males and 121.4 mm. for the females are the lowest. This latter may be laid entirely to the effects of excessive deformation. The sex differences within the four divisions are fairly stable, they amount to about 4 mm. in the Undeformed and Koskimo, to 5 mm. in the Cowichan and to 6 mm. in the Chinook deformations.

The infantile averages range in every case below those of the adults.

The group means within the divisions vary less with regard to the cranial height than the means obtained for the length and breadth measurements. It will be noticed, however, that of the larger groups the Haida means exceed the Undeformed averages in both sexes, while the Eskimo means rather conform with them. Similar instances might be pointed out with regard to the group means of the deformed series, but they are altogether too small to be of analytical importance.

The variability amounts to ± 4.74 in the Koskimo males, and lies between ± 5 and ± 6 in the Cowichan and Koskimo females, and in both sexes of the Undeformed. It falls above ± 6 in the Chinook, both males and females.

4. Comparative aspect of the three principal diameters of the skull.

The mutual relations between the length, breadth and height diameters of the skull will best be recognized from the two comparative *summaries 14 and 15*, where the absolute measurements and the differences between them are recorded. The latter is especially instructive. The different methods of deformation show quite plainly the changes in the mutual proportion. The

Summary 14.

Averages of the three principal cranial diameters in the four divisions.

Sex and Age	The three principal cranial diameters									
	Undeformed			Cowichan			Chinook			Koskimo		
	length	breadth	height	length	breadth	height	length	breadth	height	length	breadth	height
♂	175.6	140.8	134.2	169.8	151.2	131.6	166.6	156.3	127.8	183.0	138.7	131.9
♀	170.3	136.5	130.2	161.8	144.4	126.4	160.7	149.8	121.4	175.5	134.0	127.3
juv.	170.0*	142.0*	133.0*	156.5	149.0	122.0	152.8	148.3	118.5	167.5	136.0	128.0
inf.	160.9	139.5	121.0	155.0	141.1	116.3	157.2	153.2	119.4	167.5	135.1	126.0

* Only one individual could be recorded here.

Summary 15.

Differences between the three principal cranial diameters.

Sex and Age	Differences between the three principal cranial diameters									
	Undeformed			Cowichan			Chinook			Koskimo		
	l–b*	l–h	b–h	l–b	l–h	b–h	l–b	l–h	b–h	l–b	l–h	b–h
♂	34.8	41.4	6.6	18.6	38.1	19.6	10.3	38.8	28.5	44.3	51.1	6.8
♀	33.8	40.1	6.3	17.4	35.4	18.0	10.9	39.3	28.4	41.5	48.2	6.7
juv.	28.0	37.0	9.0	7.5	34.5	27.0	4.5	34.3	29.8	31.5	39.5	8.0
inf.	21.4	39.9	18.5	13.9	38.7	14.8	4.0	37.8	23.8	32.4	41.5	9.1

* l, length; b, breadth; h, height

shortened length diameters in the Cowichan and Chinook deformations gradually lower the differences between the cranial length and breadth in the males to 18.6 mm. and 10.3 mm. These figures are considerably lower than the difference of 34.8 mm. between the same diameters of the Undeformed which, in turn, is appreciably exceeded by the Koskimo difference of 44.3 mm., owing to the artificially lengthened head of the Koskimo deformation. Almost the same conditions which are met in the males obtain for the females, and are expressed by only slight differences in the figures representing the two sexes. The comparison clearly demonstrates that the impairment of the length and the compensatory bilateral expansion in the Cowichan and Chinook deformations both bear upon the differences between the length and breadth in the same direction, i.e. that of diminution. A more radical change of size even falls to the breadth, as a comparison of the lengths and breadths in *summary 14* readily shows. There the differences between the Undeformed males on the one hand, and those of the Cowichan and Chinook deformations on the other, would range for the length in the following order: 5.8 mm. and 9.0 mm. in favor of the Undeformed, and for the breadth exceeding the Undeformed: 10.4 mm. and 15.5 mm., i.e. when the length of the Cowichan skulls loses 5.8 mm., their breadth gains 10.4 mm., and when the length of the Chinook skulls loses 9.0 mm., their breadth gains 15.5 mm.

The basion-bregma height decreases steadily but slowly from the Undeformed to the Cowichan, to the Chinook deformations, but increases again in the Koskimo, whose height averages correspond with those of the Cowichan division. The ratio of the decrease and subsequent increase in figures is about 3 mm. each, showing the height of the skull to be the least variable quantity. The differences between the length and height, and the breadth and height diameters, then, are influenced more by the greater variability of the cranial length and breadth than by the more stable height. The difference between the Undeformed male length and height, amounting to 41.4 mm., is exceeded by 10 mm. in the Koskimo deformation, but not attained by that of the Cowichan and Chinook, both of which register 38.1 mm. and 38.8 mm. The reason for this latter condition must be sought in the even decrease in values of the length and height diameters in both deformations. Slight modifications in the female measurements somewhat change the proportional aspect of the female differences. The length diameters of the female Cowichan and Chinook divisions differ by only 1.1 mm. as against 3.2 mm., in the males, their heights by 5.0 mm. as against 3.8 mm. The female length-height difference is therefore a little greater in the Chinook as compared with the Cowichan, and does not conform with the male figures of even proportion. The excessive length of the Koskimo skulls raises their female length-height difference to the high figure of 48.2 mm.

The greater variability of the breadth shows its influence quite distinctly in the breadth-height proportion. Rising to only a fraction above 6 mm. in the Undeformed and Koskimo, the difference between the male breadth and height diameters yields 19.6 mm. in the Cowichan and 28.5 mm. in the Chinook deformations. The figures for the females here are about equal to those for the males in the four divisions.

Although the infantile diameters fall short of those of the adults, it is particularly the more extensive infantile breadth diameter than the shortened length diameter which bears on the differential results.

5. Length-breadth index.

Summary 16.

Averages of the cranial length-breadth index.

Sex, Age	Undeformed				Deformation according to the three modes											
					Cowichan				Chinook				Koskimo			
	Cases	Range	Average	σ	Cases	Range	Average	σ	Cases	Range	Average	σ	Cases	Range	Average	σ
♂	79	70.8–92.7	78.0	± 3.94	81	76.4–110.3	89.4	± 6.62	58	81.6–108.4	92.1	± 5.92	103	64.2–89.1	76.3	± 4.42
♀	34	71.6–88.5	80.0	± 3.75	27	73.3–110.3	90.9	± 7.94	25	83.1–102.3	93.2	± 4.36	39	66.8–85.4	76.9	± 3.93
juv.	1	—	83.5	—	2	92.0; 92.0	92.0	—	4	89.9–103.4	96.5	—	2	66.8–84.9	81.2	—
inf.	13	79.2–97.5	85.0	—	4	87.6–103.9	94.6	—	6	93.4–103.3	97.5	—	8	68.2–90.0	81.0	—

The data concerning this index are listed in *summaries 16 and 17*.

Regarding the shape of the human skull, the general observation that the female tends to be shorter than the male is confirmed by the cranial length-breadth index also for our Undeformed series. The index average of the Undeformed males is mesocranial at 78.0, of the females brachycranial at 80.0, although indicating only the border line between mesocrany and brachycrany. These male and female averages are outranged by those of the Cowichan and Chinook deformations, the latter of which still exceeds the former by 2.7 in the males and 2.3 in the females. We find hyper-brachycranial averages of 90.0 and higher in both these deformations. The averages in the Koskimo deformation with 76.3 in the males and 76.9 in the females are mesocranial; they range, however, below those for the Undeformed skulls.

A comparison of the ranges of the two latter divisions, the Koskimo and the Undeformed, demonstrates, however, the occurrence in the Koskimo groups of considerably lower individual values, 64 in the males and 66 in the females, while the Undeformed ranges begin with individual values of 70 and 71 in the two sexes. There is, therefore, a preponderance of dolichocrany in the Koskimo groups. The frequency in the divisions of the length-breadth index as well as the percental participations therein may be seen in *summary 17*. The phenomenon that first impresses

Summary 17.

Cranial length-breadth index: actual and percental frequency.

Range	Undeformed			Deformation according to the three modes								
				Cowichan			Chinook			Koskimo		
	Cases		%	Cases		%	Cases		%	Cases		%
	♂	♀	♂+♀	♂	♀	♂	♂	♀	♂+♀	♂	♀	♂+♀
64.2	—	—	—	—	—	—	—	—	—	1	—	0.7
65.0–69.9	—	—	—	—	—	—	—	—	—	3	1	2.8
70.0–74.9	14	2	14.3	—	1	1.0	—	—	—	39	10	34.8
75.0–74.9	46	15	54.5	3	1	3.6	—	—	—	43	21	45.4
80.0–84.9	14	14	25.0	21	6	24.8	4	1	6.0	15	4	13.5
85.0–89.9	2	3	4.5	26	8	31.2	11	5	19.3	3	1	2.8
90.0–110.3	2	—	1.7	32	11	39.4	43	19	74.7	—	—	—

one in comparing the deformed series with the Undeformed is the crowding of the index in the Koskimo deformation into the lower divisions. The contrary occurs in the Cowichan and Chinook deformations. The percentage of extreme brachycrany rises in the latter to 75°/₀, as against 39°/₀ in the former. An adjustment of some sort takes place here in so far as a higher percentage of frequency manifests itself in the lower grades of brachycrany in the Cowichan division (25°/₀), while the Chinook start with a lower percentage (6°/₀). It must be noticed, furthermore, that the Chinook deformation represents only brachycranial values while in the Cowichan deformation small mesocranial and even dolichocranial percentages occur.

The Koskimo deformation, as already pointed out, demonstrates the other extreme, most of its individuals being represented in the mesocranial and dolichocranial divisions of the index. Although some frequency in the brachycranial region is to be noticed, it will be readily discerned that the main characteristic of the Koskimo deformation is the tendency toward extreme long-headedness. The subdolichocranial and ultradolichocranial individuals are furnished by the Koskimo themselves, as was to be expected.

The Undeformed finally maintain something like a medium position as compared with the deformed series. Their greatest frequency of 55°/₀ occurs in the mesocranial division, leaving 25°/₀ to brachycrany and 14°/₀ to dolichocrany, while hyperbrachycrany and ultrabrachycrany are represented by only 4°/₀ and 2°/₀ respectively.

The groups composing the Undeformed division, and representing a variety of tribal elements, will merit a special discussion, which is justified in view of the importance held by the cranial length-breadth index as an ethno-analytical means. The Undeformed group means are mostly mesocranial to brachycranial. The pronounced roundheadedness of the Lillooet is rather remarkable with a male mean of 91.5 and a female one of 87.0. Contrary to the general condition among the sexes, it appears that the females are less shortheaded than the males. Represented by only two individuals of each sex, their comparative consideration here, in spite of their small number, may be justified for the reason that they seem to represent a distinct type of skull. The Haida, somewhat apart, with an index about the middle of the mesocranial division, list their males with an index mean of 76.3, approximating the Eskimo mean of 77.0. Four Chukchee males yield a mean of 77.9. Just as the female exceed the male means in nearly every case, so also the status of the infantiles is generally found *per se* to be considerably more shortheaded than the adults. The single Haida juvenile with an index of 83.5 fairly conforms with the infantile of the same tribe.

The Cowichan deformation affords quite an array of group means. The variability there is an expression of the great variety of modifications of head-form produced by one and the same deforming device. There are, for instance, cases like the Nanaimo, where the effects of deformation approach quite near the extreme state of fronto-occipital compression as represented by the Chinook. The Nanaimo register a male group mean of 99.7, but a female one of only 85.7. An explanation for the high male mean may be seen in the probability that a head tending toward brachycephaly under normal conditions may have gained in shortheadedness under the intense strain of deforming devices. This might have been less strenuous in the females who yield a lower index. Males and females are represented here, however, by only small numbers. Such is the case with almost all the other deformed Salish groups. The most numerous one, that from "about Vancouver", lists an index mean of 87.1 from twenty males, and one of 90.8 from nine females. The generally observed condition of shorter headed females in contrast with males which in their case applies to deformed skulls also, is here restored. The latter does not hold true, however, among the Chinook, who yield equal means of 93.8 and of 93.2 in the two sexes. Slightly varying conditions are also in evidence in the groups deformed according to the Koskimo fashion. The prolongation of the length diameter of the skull brought about in this deformation, does not, however, suffice to render all the specimens dolichocranial. A transition to such an effect is noticeable only in the Koskimo themselves, who represent index means of 72.9 for the males and 72.3 for the females. The Clayoquot males number only four individuals, from whom an index mean of 74.4 is derived. All the other group means in the Koskimo division are mesocranial, the highest index means of 77, and above, belonging to the Kwakiutl of both sexes, and the Nimkish and Nootka females, while the Nootka and Nimkish males yield an index of 75.7 each.

The statement of greater shortheadedness in the infantiles of the Undeformed can also be upheld for the deformed ones. On the whole, uniform results were obtained within groups or tribes which have been subjected to the same mode of deformation. Certain proportional differences between the indices of Undeformed adults and infantiles, are almost identically repeated in the deformed divisions. Modifications of type or other characteristics, as are often met in larger series of adult skulls are, on the other hand, liable to be blurred under the influence of deforming devices. An index taking in the principal diameters only, does not further any specific analytical purpose, whether in normal or artificially deformed skulls, serving, as has been stated, only to point out general proportions. But what has been said of the infantiles, applies also to the juveniles: they are more shortheaded than the adults, but as a rule less so than the infantiles.

It has been shown in section 4 of this chapter that of the principal diameters of the skull which are involved in the length-breadth index of the Cowichan and Chinook deformations, the breadth diameter is mostly responsible for the pronounced change in index and average values. The shortening of the length diameter does not seem to be so effective here. The lower index of the Koskimo skull, however, must be laid to the excessive elongation of the head as a result of the Koskimo mode of deformation, while the breadth is hardly impaired showing, when compared with the Undeformed, a difference of only 2.1 mm. in favor of the latter.

The variability manifests its highest phase in the Cowichan deformation where it rises to $\pm$ 6.62 in the males and to $\pm$ 7.94 in the females. In the other deformations and in the Undeformed it oscillates around $\pm$ 4.

6. Length-height index.

In the four main divisions of the series under investigation, the basion-bregma height diameter was recognized to be less variable than that of the length, so that the averages of the length-height index appear to be more directly influenced by the length than by the height measurements. The average of 74.3 for the Undeformed males is exceeded by the Cowichan male average of 77.7, which in turn equals the Chinook, where a uniform diminution of both diameters is involved. The lower Koskimo male average of 72.0 is due to their greater cranial length, notwithstanding the greater height which equals that of the Cowichan males. The female averages at 76.5 and 78.1 range a little higher in the Undeformed and in the Cowichan deformation respectively. The Chinook females, on the contrary, range below the males with 75.6 against 77.3, which must be attributed to the greater decrease in height as compared with the less shortened length diameter in the female skull.

Summary 18.

Averages of the cranial length-height index.

Sex, Age	Undeformed				Deformation according to the three modes											
					Cowichan				Chinook				Koskimo			
	Cases	Range	Average	σ	Cases	Range	Average	σ	Cases	Range	Average	σ	Cases	Range	Average	σ
♂	75	65.1–82.9	74.3	± 3.44	73	68.0–88.3	77.7	± 4.22	57	69.8–87.3	77.3	± 4.49	102	63.8–79.0	72.0	± 3.59
♀	33	69.3–82.5	76.5	± 3.38	24	69.4–93.1	78.1	± 4.95	24	62.2–84.8	75.6	± 5.38	37	66.7–83.1	72.5	± 3.22
juv.	1	—	78.2	—	2	75.9–80.1	78.0	—	4	72.2–85.2	76.9	—	2	73.4–79.5	76.5	—
inf.	8	71.3–77.1	74.2	—	4	69.0–81.9	75.2	—	5	66.7–82.1	75.7	—	4	69.8–83.0	75.7	—

Applying, then, the classification of the length-height index, *summary 18*, it is seen that the Undeformed males show an orthocranial average only a fraction below the lower limit of the hypsicranial, in which division also the Undeformed females are found. The Cowichan and Chinook deformations have also hypsicranial averages in both sexes, while the Koskimo male and female averages are encountered in the orthocranial division. The infantiles appear in general to range just a little below the adults. The Koskimo infantiles, however, range decidedly higher. This probably holds true also for the juveniles, who, still fewer in number, render futile any definite conclusions.

Summary 19.

Cranial length-height index: actual and percental frequency.

Range	Undeformed			Deformation according to the three modes								
				Cowichan			Chinook			Koskimo		
	Cases		%	Cases		%	Cases		%	Cases		%
	♂	♀	♂+♀	♂	♀	♂+♀	♂	♀	♂+♀	♂	♀	♂+♀
62.2–69.9	5	1	5.5	3	1	4.1	1	4	6.2	31	8	28.0
70.0–74.9	37	8	41.7	13	3	16.5	16	5	25.9	49	22	51.1
75.0–93.1	33	24	52.8	57	20	79.4	40	15	67.9	22	7	20.9

The percental distribution of the four divisions within the total range of variation for the length-height index is shown in *summary 19*. Hypsicrany furnishes the greatest percentage in the Undeformed, and in the Cowichan and Chinook deformations, amounting to $53°/_0$, $79°/_0$ and $68°/_0$. The Koskimo deformation assembles most of its specimens, i.e. $51°/_0$, in the orthocranial index, only $21°/_0$ being hypsicranial. Orthocrany is represented by smaller percentages in the other three divisions. Of the Undeformed, $42°/_0$ are orthocranial and $53°/_0$ hypsicranial; and of the Cowichan deformation only $17°/_0$ are orthocranial and $79°/_0$ hypsicranial, while in the Chinook deformation $26°/_0$ belong to the former and $68°/_0$ to the latter. Thus, the greatest divergence between the percentages of hypsicrany and orthocrany is found in the Cowichan deformation. Chamaecrany occurs but very slightly in the last named three divisions, causing the most pronounced divergence in the Undeformed, where $5°/_0$ are chamaecranial and $42°/_0$ orthocranial. The other two divisions comprise $4°/_0$ in the chamaecranial class as against $17°/_0$ in the orthocranial for the Cowichan deformation, and $6°/_0$ in the former as against $26°/_0$ in the latter for the Chinook deformation. An altogether different proportion obtains in the Koskimo deformation where $51°/_0$ are orthocranial, while in the two extreme classes, hypsicrany comprises $21°/_0$ and chamaecrany $28°/_0$. In summing up, it may be restated that the Koskimo deformation manifests the most even distribution of its individuals over the three divisions, or classes, of the index. A decided preponderance of hypsicrany is to be observed in the Cowichan and Chinook deformations, which must be attributed to their impaired length. The Undeformed show more normal proportions, their hypsicranial quota developing from a substantial orthocranial basis. The small percentage of chamaecrany here appears therefore somewhat out of proportion, while the skulls of the Cowichan and Chinook deformations seem to be divided between chamaecrany and orthocrany on the one hand and hypsicrany on the other.

The group means in each of the four main divisions do not present any differences to speak of. The lowest individual index value of 65.1 belongs to the Eskimo who, however, carry a mean in conformity with the total average of the Undeformed. The next highest individual index of 67.6 lies with the Nicola, who also represent the lowest group mean of 69.7. But as they number only three males and two females, any importance that might be attached to that group mean could not be considered typical. Similar conditions prevail in the groups of different deformation.

The variability centers around ± 4, which is somewhat smaller in the Undeformed and in the Koskimo deformation, and slightly higher in the Cowichan and Chinook deformations.

7. Breadth-height index.

The discussion of comparative *summaries 14 and 15*, in which the principal diameters of the skull and their differences are enumerated, has disclosed the greater variability of the breadth over the height. The index computed from these two factors is more influenced, therefore, by the variable breadth than by the more constant height. The Cowichan and Chinook deformations with their enlarged breadths, compensating the impaired lengths, and slightly reduced heights, express these particular proportions in their indices.

As shown in *summary 20*, there is no difference to speak of in the sexes in each of the four divisions. The averages, around 95, of the Undeformed and Koskimo deformation are of striking similarity, being metriocranial in both sexes. The high averages are due to the fact that in the two divisions under discussion, the difference between the two diameters involved in the index amounts to only 6 mm. The males and females of the Cowichan deformation are tapeinocranial with average indices of 87.3 and 87.9, and so are the Chinook with naturally smaller index averages of 82.6 and 81.2. The infantile averages, also tapeinocranial, range below the adults. In spite of their small number, it may be instructive to point out the greater variability of the height diameter in the infantiles, contrary to the conditions prevailing in the adults.

Tribal differences as suggested by their means do not seem to prevail among the Undeformed

Summary 20.
Averages of the cranial breadth-height index.

Sex, Age	Undeformed				Deformation according to the three modes											
					Cowichan				Chinook				Koskimo			
	Cases	Range	Average	σ	Cases	Range	Average	σ	Cases	Range	Average	σ	Cases	Range	Average	σ
♂	75	77.8–106.1	95.5	±4.92	74	71.3–106.9	87.3	±6.81	57	69.9–92.7	82.6	±5.12	101	84.1–105.3	95.0	±4.16
♀	33	83.3–106.3	95.6	±5.22	24	74.2–97.1	87.9	±6.42	24	65.4–92.7	81.2	±6.08	37	83.4–103.9	94.7	±4.52
jnv.	1	—	93.7	—	2	82.5–87.0	84.6	—	4	74.5–82.5	79.6	—	2	93.6–94.7	94.2	—
inf.	6	83.8–93.4	89.8	—	4	73.0–88.1	79.9	—	5	68.3–82.4	77.2	—	4	86.8–91.8	90.0	—

groups. The male mean of the Athapascans is acrocranial at 98.8, just above the metriocranial upper line of demarcation, and so is that of the Lytton at 98.2, while the females of the latter group show only 96.5. This is also the mean of the Eskimo males and females, while the Haida. Kamloops and four Chukchee males present gradually diminishing means, all of which, excepting the Athapascan and Lytton males, are metriocranial. Of the remaining two divisions, the group means of the Koskimo tribes are more uniform than those of the Cowichan deformation, which tends to demonstrate the greater variability of the latter.

Summary 21.
Cranial breadth-height index: actual and percental frequency.

Range	Undeformed			Deformation according to the three modes								
				Cowichan			Chinook			Koskimo		
	Cases		%	Cases		%	Cases		%	Cases		%
	♂	♀	♂+♀	♂	♀	♂+♀	♂	♀	♂+♀	♂	♀	♂+♀
65.4–91.1	14	8	20.4	55	18	74.5	56	23	97.5	25	10	25.3
92.0–97.9	37	16	49.0	16	6	22.4	1	1	2.5	60	18	56.6
98.0–106.9	24	9	30.6	3	—	3.1	—	—	—	16	9	18.1

As shown in *summary 21*, the percental distribution of the breadth-height index proves again the conformity of metriocranial averages in the Undeformed and Koskimo deformation. Metriocrany is represented with 49% in the Undeformed and with 57% in the Koskimo, males and females combined. The frequencies in the tapeinocranial and acrocranial classes of the index are reversed in the same two divisions, however. Tapeinocrany lists 20% in the Undeformed as against 25% in the Koskimo deformation, while the frequency in acrocrany is 31% and 18%. In the Cowichan and Chinook deformations, on the other hand, tapeinocrany shows the predominating frequencies of percentages as high as 75% and 97% respectively. The remaining 3% in the Chinook belong to metriocrany, while the Salish of Cowichan deformation claim 22%, the remainder of 3% being acrocranial. As in the preceding index, it is thus seen that the relatively stationary cranial height manifests its marked influence also in the breadth-height index. This is especially shown in the Cowichan and Chinook deformations, owing to the artificially increased breadths which are responsible for their high percentages of tapeinocrany. The probable but slightly impaired cranial breadth of the Koskimo deformation fairly conforms with the normal conditions encountered in the Undeformed.

The variability in the Undeformed, the Koskimo, and the Chinook males, centers around ±5, while in both sexes of the Cowichan deformation, and the Chinook females the variability exceeds ±6,

MEDIAN-SAGITTAL ARC

1. Median-sagittal arc.

The nasion-opisthion, i.e., the median-sagittal, arc is definitely correlated with the size and shape of the skull, since both a large cranial capacity and particularly longheadedness represent a greater extension of the arc. If this observation holds true for the normal skull, it must be still more effective in the case of specifically deformed skulls. The enforced elongation of the head in the Koskimo deformation, for instance, involves a greater extension of the median-sagittal arc. The impairment of the sagittal diameter by fronto-occipital compression and consequent lateral expansion tends, on the other hand, to modify the extension of the arc.

Summary 22.

Averages of the median-sagittal arc.

Sex, Age	Undeformed				Deformation according to the three modes											
					Cowichan				Chinook				Koskimo			
	Cases	Range	Average	σ	Cases	Range	Average	σ	Cases	Range	Average	σ	Cases	Range	Average	σ
♂	77	317–395	363.6	± 14.56	76	319–383	347.2	± 14.07	56	306–372	339.8	± 12.65	103	341–410	368.0	± 12.33
♀	32	325–380	350.1	± 12.14	25	308–359	331.6	± 14.84	25	305–365	324.2	± 12.32	37	336 383	353.7	± 12.26
juv.	1	—	344.0	—	2	320; 329	324.5	—	4	299–337	318.5	—	2	351; 352	351.5	—
inf.	13	308–366	339.9	—	5	313–348	326.0	—	6	318–334	325.7	—	7	333–368	357.1	—

The figures recorded in *summary 22* verify these suppositions, as will be seen later on. The study of the ranges shows, first of all, a sex difference, as all the highest female fall below the male values, while this is the case only in part with the lowest values of the ranges. But the female ranges are in every instance less extended than those of the male. The Undeformed male and female averages of 363.6 mm. and 350.1 mm. are outranged by the Koskimo with averages of 368.0 mm. and 353.7 mm. for both sexes. The Cowichan and Chinook figures, on the other hand, illustrate the conditions brought about by their particular modes of deformation. The averages of both keep below those of the Undeformed and Koskimo divisions, while among themselves the Chinook show the lower averages of 339.8 mm. and 324.2 mm. in the sexes as against the distinctly higher Cowichan averages of 347.2 mm. and 331.6 mm. All the infantile and juvenile skulls range below the adults. Attention might be called to the fact, however, that the infantile values range higher than the juvenile in almost all cases, due to the accidental smallness of the few juveniles. Moreover, both groups are not divided according to sex.

Group means in the adults vary considerably, as might be inferred from their cranial capacities. Among the Undeformed skulls, the Haida present the relatively high male and female mean of 371.2 mm. and 355.2 mm. respectively. The Salish of the interior Undeformed, have rather small means which are exceeded by the Athapascan and Eskimo, which in turn do not come up to those of the Haida. In the groups deformed in the Koskimo fashion, it is naturally the Koskimo themselves who hold the highest means, 379.0 mm. for the males and 365.0 mm. for the females. Their range rises to 410 mm., while the ranges of the Cowichan and Chinook deformations reach only 383 mm. (about Vancouver), and 372 mm. (Chinook) as their highest values.

A variability of $\pm$ 12 and slightly above is of fairly uniform occurrence in all the divisions, rising to $\pm$ 14, however, in the Cowichan deformation and the Undeformed males.

2. Divisions of median-sagittal arc.

The frontal, parietal and occipital divisions of the median-sagittal arc may be considered from two angles: that of their absolute extension and relative participation in the length of the entire median-sagittal arc. A third point of interest concerns the mutual relation between the frontal and parietal arcs, both of which undergo important phylogenetic changes.

Summary 23.

Averages of the median-sagittal frontal arc.

	Undeformed				Deformation according to the three modes							
					Cowichan				Chinook			
											Koskimo	
Sex, Age	Cases	Range	Average	σ	Cases	Range	Average	σ	Cases	Range	Average	σ	Cases	Range	Average	σ
♂	80	109–145	127.2	± 7.03	88	108–135	121.1	± 6.16	58	109–133	117.2	± 5.23	104	117–145	127.8	± 5.80
♀	34	113–135	122.3	± 5.40	30	100–128	117.0	± 5.85	26	109–128	115.0	± 5.59	39	113–136	122.7	± 5.37
juv.	1	—	122.0	—	1	—	115.0	—	6	103–113	109.5	—	2	120; 128	124.0	—
inf.	14	111–139	119.2	—	7	100–117	110.9	—	4	107–118	112.7	—	8	112–126	117.6	—

In the *frontal* arc, summary 23, averages of 127.2 mm. and 122.3 mm. in the two sexes of the Undeformed skulls occur. Averages of nearly the same value obtain in the skulls of the Koskimo deformation. Judging from these averages, it appears that the Koskimo deformation does not seem in any way to have affected the length of the frontal arc. Showing a more or less pronounced depression only in its upper or bregma section, the Koskimo frontal arc differs somewhat in appearance from those of the Cowichan and Chinook divisions. The latter two, particularly the Chinook deformation, produce an almost total depression of the arc, which begins at the glabella point and ends a short distance in front of the bregma, thus causing the depressed arc line to run almost parallel to the nasion-bregma chord of the frontal perigram.[34] The Cowichan and Chinook averages of 121.1 mm. and 117.0 mm. for both sexes in the former, and of 117.2 mm. and 115.0 mm. in the latter, show a decided depression in the Chinook figures, falling short of

---

[34] These conditions will be found more thoroughly discussed in the section on the os frontale (see p. 55).

the Cowichan, due very probably to the intensive frontal depression in the Chinook, as well as a sex difference that is little less emphasized in these two divisions as compared with the Undeformed and Koskimo skulls.

The group means and ranges of the frontal arc reveal several conspicuous facts. It is, for instance, the Haida and Eskimo males whose ranges extend as high as 145 mm., both yielding means of 129.3 mm., i. e., the highest in the Undeformed skulls. The Athapascan and Chukchee males follow with 126.3 mm. each, while the Salish of the interior keep below these figures. The results in the deformed groups are fairly uniform. In the Koskimo deformation, the Koskimo themselves, as was to be expected, carry the highest means in both sexes.

The means of the immatures in general fall below those of the adults.

The variability in most cases is a little above ± 5; rising, however, to ± 7.03 and ± 6.16 in the Undeformed and the Cowichan males.

Summary 24.

Averages of the median-sagittal parietal arc.

Sex, Age	Undeformed				Deformation according to the three modes											
					Cowichan				Chinook				Koskimo			
	Cases	Range	Average	σ	Cases	Range	Average	σ	Cases	Range	Average	σ	Cases	Range	Average	σ
♂	78	88–139	119.0	± 8.93	84	89–132	112.2	± 8.40	58	89–130	105.0	± 8.20	104	98–149	119.2	± 8.56
♀	34	102–131	115.9	± 6.10	28	87–124	103.4	± 9.88	26	89–112	100.8	± 7.19	39	93–135	111.2	± 9.85
juv.	1	—	110.0	—	2	101; 104	102.5	—	4	92–119	103.8	—	2	122; 123	122.5	—
inf.	13	104–125	112.2	—	5	90–118	102.8	—	6	90–109	100.2	—	8	98–135	113.5	—

Sex differences naturally obtain also in the length of the *parietal* arcs. The measurements are listed in *summary 24*. Sex differences are most pronounced in the Cowichan and Koskimo divisions, namely 8.8 mm. and 8.0 mm. respectively, while in the Undeformed skulls and those of the Chinook deformation they amount to only 3.1 mm. and 4.2 mm. As with the frontal, the parietal arcs also are longest in the Undeformed and Koskimo males, whose averages of 119.0 mm. and 119.2 mm. are listed in *summary 24*. The length of the Koskimo parietal arc, with values as high as 149 mm. in the males and 135 mm. in the females, although less noticeable in the average, is quite extreme in individual cases. On the other hand, there is to be noticed a decided diminution in the length of the arc in the Cowichan and Chinook deformations, with male averages of 112.2 mm. and 105.0 mm., and female averages of 103.4 mm. and 100.8 mm. The Chinook averages range lowest.

The group means, like those for the frontal arc, among the Undeformed are highest in the Haida, Athapascan and Eskimo of both sexes, which also holds true for the Koskimo group in the Koskimo division.

The infantiles and juveniles in general range below the adults, excepting the Koskimo juveniles with high individual values of 122 mm. and 123 mm., of which the latter slightly exceeds the Kosklmo male group mean of 122.4 mm.

The variability oscillates around ± 8, dropping, however, to ± 6.10 in the Undeformed females, and rising to ± 9.85 in the Koskimo females, and ± 9.88 in the Cowichan of the same sex.

The general aspect as regards the length of the *occipital* arc in the four main divisions of this series, corresponds to the conditions as described for the frontal and parietal arcs. The effects of deformation here are fairly similar in the different modes, consisting mainly in a general flattening of the occipital vaulting with modifications, however, where the deforming means had been less intensively applied or the cradle-board pressure less strenuously effective.

Summary 25.

Averages of the median-sagittal occipital arc.

	Undeformed				Deformation according to the three modes											
					Cowichan				Chinook				Koskimo			
Sex, Age	Cases	Range	Average	σ	Cases	Range	Average	σ	Cases	Range	Average	σ	Cases	Range	Average	σ
♂	78	103–140	117.6	± 7.79	77	97–136	115.5	± 9.23	57	95–125	111.8	± 6.84	103	101–148	120.3	± 10.07
♀	33	98–123	112.0	± 5.32	25	98–125	113.3	± 7.95	25	99–131	108.6	± 8.37	37	105–141	116.6	± 8.55
juv.	1	—	112.0	—	2	101; 104	102.5	—	4	94–119	105.3	—	2	102; 109	105.5	—
inf.	13	95–125	108.5	—	5	97–121	110.2	—	6	98–128	112.8	—	7	100–134	118.7	—

Sex differences between the averages, according to *summary 25*, amount to 5.6 mm. in the Undeformed and 2.2 mm. in the deformed Cowichan, the Chinook and Koskimo falling in between those extremes with 3.2 mm. and 3.7 mm. respectively. The greatest length of the occipital arc is reached by the Undeformed and Koskimo, the former with 117.6 mm. and 112.0 mm., the latter with 120.3 mm. and 116.6 mm. for the sexes. The Chinook here also range below the Cowichan.

The highest individual values of the Koskimo division are not found this time in the Koskimo group, whose range extends to 133 mm., but in the Kwakiutl where it runs up to 148 mm. The Haida and Eskimo males attain 140 mm. and 137 mm., with group means of 122.0 mm. in the former and 116.2 mm. in the latter, which is not excessively high as compared with the means of some of the Undeformed groups. Male group means as high as 116 mm. and 119 mm. fall even to the Bellabella of the Cowichan deformation, to the skulls from Vancouver, the Nanaimo and the Bellacoola. The female mean of the Nanaimo rises even to 118.4 mm.

Of the infantiles, the high average of 112.8 mm. of the Chinook stands out plainly, exceeding even the adult figures. The Koskimo infantiles have an average of 118.7 mm., which stands between their male and female averages, while the infantile average in the Cowichan division ranges below the adult. Peculiarly enough, the deformed juveniles yield smaller averages than the undeformed infantiles. It must be borne in mind, however, that the immature groups comprise only a few individuals.

Here the variability also centers around ± 8. The females are somewhat less variable in the Undeformed, Cowichan and Koskimo groups, but exceed the males of the Chinook deformation.

3. Participation of the frontal, parietal and occipital divisions in the median-sagittal arc.

The mutual relation of the three portions composing the median-sagittal arc, is somewhat variable in the material under investigation. The almost typical proportion throughout all the Primates including the Hominidae, is indicated by the order: occipital-parietal-frontal arc, where the occipital arc is the shortest, and the frontal the longest. Modifications of this order occur in two ways, between the occipital and parietal, and between the frontal and parietal arcs.[35] The first modification, of the occipital arc exceeding the parietal, is only encountered in some of the apes (Cynocephalus; Hylobates syndactylus; Orang-utan; Gorilla), while an equal length of the two arcs is evident in others (Hylobates agilis and Anthropopithecus). The second modification, of a larger parietal arc exceeding the frontal, occurs only in man and is signified by *Schwalbe* as a particularly anthropine occurrence (Alamans; Merowingians; Chinese; Japanese; Senoi).

Summary 26.

Comparative table of the frontal, parietal and occipital sections of the median-sagittal arc in the four tribal divisions.

Sex and Age	Sections of the median-sagittal arc[1]											
	Undeformed			Cowichan			Chinook			Koskimo		
	frontal	parietal	occipital	frontal	parietal	occipital	frontal	parietal	occipital	frontal	parietal	occipital
♂	127.2	119.0	117.6	121.1	112.2	115.5	117.4	105.0	111.8	127.8	119.2	120.3
♀	122.3	115.9	112.0	116.9	103.4	113.3	115.0	100.8	108.6	122.7	111.2	116.6
juv.	122.0[2]	110.0[2]	112.0[2]	115.0[2]	102.5	102.5	109.5	103.8	105.2	124.0	122.5	105.5
inf.	119.6	112.0	108.5	110.9	102.8	110.2	112.7	100.2	112.8	117.6	113.5	118.7

1) The other dimensions of the frontal, parietal and occipital bones are discussed in their respective chapters.
2) Only one specimen in this group.

The conditions obtaining in the North Pacific skulls may be found specified in *summary 26.* It will be seen that the Undeformed skulls repeat the conditions typical of the Primates in general, while in the three deformed divisions the occipital arcs exceed the parietal, although very slightly in the Koskimo division. From the observations recorded in the preceding pages, it may be inferred that the normal development of the parietal arc was impaired the most, and it is thus self-evident that in the deformed skulls also the frontal arc should exceed the parietal and repeat the conditions prevailing in the Undeformed.

Interpreting the mutual proportions by means of symbols, the letters F, P and O, indicating the three segments of the median-sagittal arc, the latter's proportions are:

$$\text{Undeformed: } F > P > O$$
$$\text{Deformed: } F > P < O$$

---

[35] *Martin, R.*, 1914, Lehrbuch, pp. 659—661.

The deviations in the deformed skulls from the assumed normal conditions in the Undeformed are furthermore expressed by accounting for the differences of the three averages in the following tabulation:

$$\begin{array}{rrcc}
 & & F - P & - O \\
 & & \text{mm.} & \text{mm.} \\
\text{Undeformed:} & \male & 8.2 > & > 1.4 \\
 & \female & 6.4 > & > 3.9 \\
\text{Cowichan def.:} & \male & 8.9 > & < 3.3 \\
 & \female & 13.5 > & < 9.9 \\
\text{Chinook def.:} & \male & 12.4 > & < 6.8 \\
 & \female & 14.2 > & < 7.8 \\
\text{Koskimo def.:} & \male & 8.6 > & < 1.1 \\
 & \female & 11.5 > & < 5.4 \\
\end{array}$$

The length differences between the divisions of the median-sagittal arc are here in every case greater in the deformed skulls, where again the female in every instance exceed the male values. It will be noticed furthermore that the differences between the frontal and parietal arcs markedly exceed those recorded between the parietal and occipital. The greatest differences are found among the Chinook, and it is only in the parieto-occipital proportion that they are outranged by the Cowichan females, the differences being 7.8 mm. to 9.9 mm. The reason for the pronounced excess in the Chinook values must doubtless be laid to the effects of excessive deformation which hampers or diverts the normal development of the parietal bones.

The infantiles follow the adults in every detail of the above statements. The immatures have been recorded in summary 26 only for the sake of completeness. Because of their small number, definite evaluation should not be attached to their averages.

4. Percental ratio between frontal and parietal arcs.

The investigation of the percental ratio between the frontal and parietal divisions of the median-sagittal arc is of interest because of the changes of proportion between the two, which in the *Hominidae* are apparently in process of development. The comparison of the two arcs gives rise to the following possible proportions in human series: (1) where the frontal arc exceeds the parietal; (2) where both are of equal length and, (3) where the parietal exceeds the frontal.

Summary 27.

Percental ratio between the frontal and parietal arcs in the four tribal divisions.

Sex and Age	Percental ratio between the frontal and parietal arcs									
	Undeformed			Cowichan			Chinook			Koskimo		
	F>P	F=P	F<P	F>P	F=P	F<P	F>P	F=P	F<P	F>P	F=P	F<P
♂	82.1	3.8	14.1	82.1	1.2	16.7	96.6	—	3.4	74.3	5.7	20.0
♀	82.3	5.9	11.8	89.3	3.6	7.1	100.0	—	—	74.4	—	25.6
Juv.	100.0	—	—	100.0	—	—	75.0	—	25.0	50.0	—	50.0
inf.	69.2	—	30.8	100.0	—	—	83.3	—	16.7	37.5	—	62.0

7 — JESUP NORTH PACIFIC EXPED., VOL. XI.

A consultation of *summary 27* shows that 14.1% of the Undeformed male skulls have a longer parietal arc, that in 3.8%, the frontal and parietal arcs are of equal length, leaving 82.1% to the proportion $F > P$. About the same conditions prevail in the females.

The infantile values reveal the interesting fact that the percentage of $F < P$ rises here to 30.8%, leaving 69.2% to the proportion $F > P$, with no occurrence of $F = P$. The infantile conditions thus show, by their regional differences, the direct correlation between the growth of the brain and that of the osseous brain-case. Among the deformed skulls, the Chinook have preserved the status of $F > P$ the best, with 96.6% in the males and 100.0% in the females. The Chinook infantiles join with 83.4% in this proportion, while the other 16.7% are represented by the $F < P$ proportion. The Cowichan deformation approaches nearest the Undeformed skulls, while the Koskimo deformation represents an increased status of $F > P$, with 20% in the males and 25.6% in the females, with a radical turn towards this proportion in the infantiles, namely, 62.5%. The status of the Undeformed infantiles is thus repeated in the deformed divisions.

OS FRONTALE.

1. Minimum frontal breadth.

The absolute breadth measurements of the forehead are naturally somewhat smaller in females than in males. According to *summary 28*, the minimum frontal breadth of the Undeformed males

Summary 28.

Averages of the minimum frontal breadth.

Sex, Age	Undeformed				Deformation according to the three modes										
					Cowichan				Chinook				Koskimo		
	Cases	Range	Average	σ	Cases	Range	Average	σ	Cases	Range	Average	σ	Cases	Range	Average	σ
♂	78	83–106	94.1	± 4.80	84	83–106	95.5	± 5.39	58	89–109	98.6	± 4.92	103	83–105	94.1	± 4.62
♀	34	82–104	91.4	± 5.38	28	78–100	91.1	± 5.01	25	86–102	93.9	± 3.96	39	82–101	91.3	± 4.36
juv.	1	—	97.0	—	2	87; 89	88.0	—	4	87–98	92.8	—	2	96; 98	97.0	—
inf.	12	83–95	88.5	—	7	84–98	91.9	—	6	87–97	94.0	—	7	81–101	92.1	—

averages 94.1 mm., which coincides with that of the Koskimo males. The male average of the Cowichan deformation amounts to 95.5 mm., which is exceeded by the Chinook males at 98.6 mm. The same order of increase obtains in the females except that the Undeformed, Koskimo and Cowichan females share a minimum frontal breadth of 91 mm. plus, while the Chinook females rise to 93.9 mm. The sex differences comprise only a few units, all in favor of the males, amounting to 2.7 mm. in the Undeformed, 2.8 mm. in the Koskimo, 4.4 mm. in the Cowichan and 4.7 mm. in the Chinook. The ranges cover more than twenty units in most cases, except in the Chinook and Koskimo females where they fall below. The ranges are smaller, of course, in the immatures, where the individuals appear to be less variable. They repeat, to a certain extent, the numerical order of averages pertaining in the adults. The few juveniles hold rather high individual values within the total range of variation.

There are no conspicuous differences among the group means. The Kamloops males among the Undeformed might be mentioned, however, with a relatively low mean of 89.6 mm., derived from five individuals with a range from 83—95 mm.

The variability is grouped around ± 5, dropping to ± 3.96 in the Chinook females.

2. Maximum frontal breadth.

Approximately the same conditions as observed in the minimum frontal breadth obtain for the maximum frontal breadth. The Undeformed and Koskimo male averages enumerated in *summary 29*, with 115.5 mm. and 115.9 mm., coincide, while a gradual increase is noticed in the

Summary 29.

Averages of the maximum frontal breadth.

Sex, Age	Undeformed				Deformation according to the three modes											
					Cowichan				Chinook				Koskimo			
	Cases	Range	Average	σ	Cases	Range	Average	σ	Cases	Range	Average	σ	Cases	Range	Average	σ
♂	76	105–127	115.5	± 4.75	80	103–141	120.4	± 6.35	58	112–133	123.1	± 5.04	100	102–125	115.9	± 4.65
♀	33	102–125	112.5	± 4.45	25	106–123	114.4	± 4.80	25	109–126	118.4	± 4.01	38	101–118	109.1	± 4.28
juv.	1	—	115.0	—	2	115; 117	116.0	—	4	112–120	116.0	—	2	112; 117	114.5	—
inf.	13	106–122	111.0	—	7	103–127	113.1	—	6	110–122	117.8	—	8	100–116	108.9	—

Cowichan and Chinook deformations, where the male averages are 120.4 mm. and 123.1 mm. The Koskimo female average of 109.1 mm., however, falls below that of the Undeformed females at 112.5 mm. The gradual increase in the male averages of the Cowichan and Chinook divisions recurs in the female with 114.4 mm. in the former and 118.4 mm. in the latter. Both males and females of the Cowichan and Chinook divisions exceed those of the Undeformed and Koskimo divisions in their averages, thus repeating the findings for the minimum frontal breadth. The sex differences are somewhat more pronounced. They amount to 6.0 mm. and 6.8 mm. in the Cowichan and Koskimo deformations, and to 4.7 mm. and 3.0 mm. in the Chinook deformation and the Undeformed. All the averages of the immatures range below those of the adults, including the females, thus exhibiting a different behavior from that recorded for the minimum breadth. Their ranges are also somewhat more extended as are also those of the adults, where the maximum extension from 103—141 mm. occurred in the Cowichan males.

Among the group means those of the Lillooet are remarkable for their high figures of 119.5 mm. in the males, and 118.0 mm. in the females. The Haida means also exceed the total average with 117.8 mm. and 114.5 mm. for the sexes.

The variability at ± 6.35 is highest in the Cowichan males and registers ± 5.04 in the Chinook males, amounting to ± 4 in all the other instances.

Deforming causes are responsible for the broadening of the frontal bone in the Cowichan and Chinook divisions, with an emphasis in the latter as expressed by the absolute measurements, their means and averages. The Koskimo division seems to be less affected, due to their special practice of deforming the head, which either leaves the frontal breadth measurements unaltered or, in extreme cases, serves even to diminish them.

3. Transverse frontal index.

The proportional relation of the minimum and maximum breadths of the forehead finds its expression in the transverse frontal index. A higher transverse index is more frequently met in females than in males, giving rise to the distinction of "frontal" and "parietal" skull types (*Manouvrier*, *Pittard*), the former applying to the female, the latter to the male skull.

The Undeformed, however, do not bear out that statement. Their averages are fairly equal in the sexes, as shown in *summary 30*. The Cowichan and Chinook divisions likewise have fairly

Summary 30.

Average of the transverse frontal index.

Sex, Age	Undeformed				Deformation according to the three modes											
					Cowichan				Chinook				Koskimo			
	Cases	Range	Average	σ	Cases	Range	Average	σ	Cases	Range	Average	σ	Cases	Range	Average	σ
♂	76	75.2–88.3	81.6	± 3.36	78	62.9 (72.2)–83.9	79.5	± 4.22	58	72.9–86.5	78.7	± 2.59	99	72.8–90.5	81.9	± 3.50
♀	33	73.0–88.3	80.9	± 3.61	25	70.9–86.4	79.9	± 4.28	25	73.7–84.1	79.3	± 2.63	38	71.8–90.3	83.7	± 3.81
juv.	1	—	84.3	—	2	76; 85	80.9	—	4	77.7–82.3	79.5	—	2	83.8; 85.7	84.8	—
inf.	14	73.8–84.0	87.7	—	7	76.7–86.4	81.4	—	6	77.5–83.6	79.7	—	7	80.2–90.2	83.3	—

equal averages for the sexes, although slightly smaller than those of the Undeformed, so that the averages decrease in the order, Undeformed, Cowichan, Chinook, with male values of 81.6, 79.5 and 78.7, and female ones of 80.9, 79.9 and 79.3. The dissimilar Koskimo mode causes the index to ascend again. Here the male average with 81.9 and the female with 83.7 exceed all others. There is, moreover, a female surplus of 1.8 units of the index in the Koskimo division. The averages of the Undeformed immatures exceed those of the adults by about six units (infantiles), while they agree fairly well in the other divisions, where an affinity with the female averages might be stated providing an adult sex difference in the Cowichan and Chinook divisions is taken at all into account. The entire ranges cover about eighteen units in the males, and twenty in the females. The highest individual values at 90.5 male and 90.3 female are encountered in the Koskimo division, the lowest at 72.2 male and 70.9 female in the Cowichan deformation. Here the extremely low index of 62.9 belongs to a Nanaimo male.

Tribal differences are represented by the Athapascan and Chukchee male means which range above the total average, while the Eskimo and Haida means conform with it. The Lillooet and Nicola means fall decidedly below the total average, while an intermediate position is held by the Kamloops. There is an indication of the so-called female "frontal" type in only a few groups, including the Haida, but not the Eskimo. The Koskimo group means are fairly uniform in the males, somewhat less so in the females. The latter quite uphold the "frontal" type theory of the female skull, of which the total average gave another proof.

The obvious heterogeneousness of the Cowichan division is responsible for a greater variability at ± 4.22 in the males, and ± 4.28 in the females. The lowest figures are attained by the Chinook with a male variability of ± 2.59 and a female one of ± 2.63. The Undeformed and Koskimo divisions range around ± 3.

4. Transverse fronto-parietal index.

The index of the minimum frontal and the maximum cranial breadths affords a useful means for comparative estimation of the transverse dimensions of the brain-case which shows best in the norma verticalis.

The transverse fronto-parietal index, as indicated in *summary 31*, yields decreasing averages in the order, Undeformed, Cowichan and Chinook deformations, but rises again and exceeds the

Summary 31.

Averages of the transverse fronto-parietal index.

Sex, Age	Undeformed				Deformation according to the three modes											
					Cowichan				Chinook				Koskimo			
	Cases	Range	Average	σ	Cases	Range	Average	σ	Cases	Range	Average	σ	Cases	Range	Average	σ
♂	78	59.3–73.9	66.8	± 3.41	78	47.7–73.6	63.4	± 4.20	58	56.0–67.8	62.1	± 3.57	101	52.9–76.6	67.4	± 3.70
♀	33	60.7–73.7	66.6	± 3.67	25	56.8–68.1	63.1	± 3.88	25	57.4–67.4	62.7	± 4.28	39	60.1–75.8	68.3	± 3.38
juv.	1	—	68.3	—	2	59.7; 62.6	61.2	—	4	61.0–64.5	63.3	—	2	69.5; 73.3	71.4	—
inf.	13	57.3–69.3	63.5	—	4	62.4–65.3	63.8	—	6	59.0–66.9	62.6	—	7	64.7–82.8	68.5	—

three other divisions in the Koskimo deformation. There is no sex difference to speak of between the male and female averages. The immatures of the deformed divisions are fairly in accord with the adults, but there is a more marked difference in the Undeformed where the infantiles range about three units below the Undeformed adults.

The group means do not present results that might be explained as differences of type.

The less variable quantity of the dimensions contained in this index is the minimum frontal breadth. The maximum cranial breadth undergoes direct and effective changes under the deforming pressure in the Cowichan and Chinook deformations. The Koskimo mode served to reduce the cranial breadth, which together with a slightly impaired frontal breadth produced the highest total averages. It seems plausible, therefore, that the Cowichan and Chinook averages range below, and the Koskimo above the Undeformed.

According to the classification of the index, the latter two divisions turn out metriometopic averages, while both the Cowichan and Chinook averages are stenometopic. Eurymetopic averages do not occur, although there is a slight eurymetopic frequency, especially in the Undeformed and Koskimo divisions, but none in the Chinook. The lowest or stenometopic individual indices occur in the Cowichan deformation.

The variability lies between ± 3 and ± 4.

5. Median-sagittal frontal arc.

This measurement has been treated of in connection with the median-sagittal arc, of which it forms the frontal segment (see p. 45).

6. Median-sagittal frontal chord.

The conspicuous feature about this measurement is its predominant length in the Koskimo skulls over those of the other three divisions. *Summary 32* shows the Koskimo to yield averages of 114.2 mm. and 110.7 mm. in the sexes. The other male averages are 112.6 mm. in the Undeformed and the Chinook, and 111.1 mm. in the Cowichan deformation, while the female averages are uniform at 107 mm in these three divisions. The sex differences amount to 4–5 mm. in general. The immature averages naturally range below the adult, and drop as low as 100.5 mm. in the Cowichan deformation and 102.0 mm. in the Undeformed. This is also shown by the lesser extension of their ranges which naturally keep below those of the adults.

The Undeformed Haida and Eskimo are characterized by the a high male means of 113.8 mm.

Summary 32.

Averages of the median-sagittal frontal chord.

Sex, Age	Undeformed				Deformation according to the three modes											
					Cowichan				Chinook				Koskimo			
	Cases	Range	Average	σ	Cases	Range	Average	σ	Cases	Range	Average	σ	Cases	Range	Average	σ
♂	80	101–130	112.6	± 4.92	88	101–122	111.1	± 4.78	58	103–121	112.6	± 4.52	104	106–132	114.2	± 4.72
♀	34	100–117	107.9	± 3.95	29	91–119	107.0	± 5.51	26	102–116	107.0	± 4.30	39	102–127	110.7	± 5.05
juv.	1	—	104.0	—	1	—	104.0	—	4	96–105	101.8	—	2	107; 113	110.0	—
inf.	14	87–115	102.0	—	6	92–107	100.5	—	6	101–109	104.3	—	9	100–111	108.4	—

and 109.0 mm. and 110.2 mm. for the female means. The Lillooet males and females attain only to 103.5 mm. in both sexes. The high averages of the Koskimo division have already been referred to, the group means of the Koskimo themselves rising to 117 mm. in the sexes.

The frontal chords of the Cowichan and Chinook appear to be of equal length with those in the Undeformed, but deforming influences must be ascribed to the Koskimo mode of deformation, the production of which apparently is responsible for the lengthened median-sagittal frontal chord there.

The variability lies around ± 4, but rises to ± 5.05 and ± 5.51 in the Koskimo and Cowichan females.

7. Sagittal frontal index.

The sagittal vaulting of the forehead preserves natural proportions in the Undeformed skulls. The higher the vaulting of the forehead, then, the lower the sagittal frontal index and vice versa.

Summary 33.

Averages of the sagittal frontal index.

Sex, Age	Undeformed				Deformation according to the three modes											
					Cowichan				Chinook				Koskimo			
	Cases	Range	Average	σ	Cases	Range	Average	σ	Cases	Range	Average	σ	Cases	Range	Average	σ
♂	80	84.9–99.2	88.7	± 2.76	88	86.8–97.3	90.5	± 2.26	58	89.0–96.6	93.2	± 1.77	105	85.6–99.2	90.2	± 2.34
♀	34	84.8–91.1	88.3	± 1.70	29	88.5–94.9	91.6	± 2.08	26	88.9–95.4	93.0	± 2.17	38	87.1–93.4	90.3	± 1.97
juv.	1	—	85.2	—	2	90.4; 90.4	90.4	—	4	92.7–93.7	93.2	—	2	88.3; 89.2	88.8	—
inf.	14	82.7–93.4	86.6	—	7	87.7–93.6	90.4	—	6	90.6–94.4	92.7	—	8	86.3–90.8	86.7	—

In the Undeformed, as shown in *summary 33*, it produces a male average of 88.7 and a female one of 88.3, while in the Chinook with their intensely flattened foreheads, the index averages rise to 93.2 and 93.0 in the sexes. More moderate changes, caused by the Cowichan and Koskimo modes of deformation, find expression in averages around 90 plus, while the Cowichan females rise to 91.6. Sex differences, however, are almost entirely absent. The Koskimo immatures of deformed skulls appear to have preserved a more normal vaulting, yielding, like the Undeformed immatures, an average of 86. The immatures of the Cowichan and Chinook deformations hold averages on a level with their adults.

Among the Undeformed the group means of the Lillooet and Nicola, with 91.3 and 95.1 in the males, 88.1 and 90.0 in the females, outrange the total averages of that division. The other means here occur slightly above it, and the Athapascan males with 87.9 a little below. A number of deviating means are demonstrable in the Cowichan division, while the Koskimo groups exhibit more stable conditions.

The variability here is manifestly low. It oscillates around ± 2 with a frequent drop below that amount.

Figure 8 a illustrates the conditions prevalent in the sagittal vaulting of the forehead in the four divisions. As recorded in the legend, they are

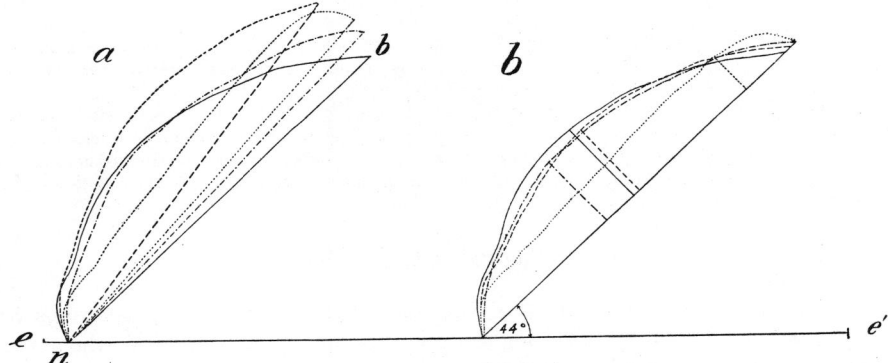

Fig. 8. The sagittal frontal index. *a.* Superposition of median-sagittal frontal tracings representing individual indices coinciding with divisional averages, the chords in their individual angularity. *e–e'*, parallel to ear-eye plane passing through *n*, nasion, the nasia coinciding; *b*, bregma.

——— Undeformed (Haida ♂, 3703): index 88.4; elevation 25 mm.; ∠ *b–n–e'* 44°
- - - - Cowichan (Bellabella ♂, 4638):   „   90.0;   „   23 „ ;   „   „   54°
· · · · Chinook (Chinook ♂, 4459):   „   92.9;   „   12 „ ;   „   „   49°
– · – · Koskimo (Koskimo ♂, 3648):   „   90.8;   „   23 „ ;   „   „   47°

b. superposed tracings same as in *a* oriented on the frontal chord of the Undeformed (Haida) at the latter's individual angle of 44°. The elevation above the frontal chord is indicated by vertical lines. ²/₃.

represented by four individual cases from the series with indices coinciding with their divisional averages. The four tracings are superposed in such a way that their nasion points (*n*) are made to coincide on a parallel of the ear-eye plane (*e–e'*) passing through those points.

The Undeformed arc manifests a fairly even vaulting that corresponds with an almost perfect segment of a circle. Its highest elevation at 25 mm. is found above the midpoint of the frontal chord. The other extreme is represented by a Chinook frontal arc whose general flattening causes its curve to run almost parallel with the nasion-bregma line. Its highest elevation occurs near the bregma, where it reaches 12 mm. Between these two extremes pass the Bellabella and Koskimo curves with equal indices. They differ, however, in so far as the highest elevation of the former occurs in the upper half of the segment, that of the latter in the lower half, while in both the highest elevation amounts to 23 mm. The frontal chords ($n-b$) of the four tracings form angles with the parallel of the ear-eye plane, which are likewise specified in the legend. In order to afford a direct comparison between the four arcs under discussion a uniform orientation was given them by making their chords coincide. This is seen in figure 8b, where the chords of the deformed specimens coincide with those of the Undeformed at 44°. The comparison is facilitated by the fact that the frontal segment, i. e., their chords, are almost of equal size. The two extremes as represented by the Undeformed and Chinook curves are easily recognized. The Bellabella and Koskimo curves passing between them, intersect each other a little below the middle between nasion and bregma, while the Koskimo curve overlaps the Bellabella curve in the lower region, and the latter curve overtakes the former in the upper. Another intersection of the two outlines near the bregma is caused by the slight difference in sizes. A flattening influence of the Cowichan mode of deformation in the lower region of the frontal bone is not very conspicuous, while an exaggeration of it is demonstrated in the Chinook skull; the Koskimo suffers an applanation in the region near the bregma.

8. Frontal angle.

The angle of the frontal bone as formed by the nasion-bregma chord and a parallel to the ear-eye plane line laid through the nasion is recorded in *summary 34*. The average amounts to

Summary 34.

Averages of the frontal angle.

	Undeformed				Deformation according to the three modes											
					Cowichan				Chinook				Koskimo			
Sex, Age	Cases	Range	Average	σ	Cases	Range	Average	σ	Cases	Range	Average	σ	Cases	Range	Average	σ
♂	75	40–54	46.0	± 3.16	77	41–57	48.9	± 3.44	58	40–55	46.2	± 3.29	104	37–52	44.5	± 3.17
♀	30	43–54	48.1	± 2.59	24	42–55	48.3	± 4.04	26	38–53	45.6	± 3.79	35	37–51	44.5	± 3.05
juv.	1	—	52.0	—	2	42; 55	49.0	—	4	45–55	48.8	—	2	47; 49	48.0	—
inf.	10	—	52.1	—	4	48–55	50.3	—	6	48–55	51.2	—	6	47–58	52.5	—

46.0° in the Undeformed males, while the Undeformed females with their somewhat more erect foreheads average 48.1. Owing to the equalizing effects of the deforming strains, sex differences either disappear almost entirely in the deformed divisions, or are reduced to fractions of a degree. A certain similarity to the Undeformed is shown by the Chinook averages. Their males also yield 46.2°, their females, however, 45.6°, leaving the latter 2.5° short of the Undeformed females. The Cowichan mode of deformation with a male average of 48.9°, and a female one of 48.3°, shows the former slightly in excess to the frontal angle in the Undeformed males, the females equalling the Undeformed of the same sex. The greatest disparity is seen in the Koskimo division, where the averages of both male and female drop to 44.5°. Interestingly enough, all the immatures possess higher averages than the adults. The infantile skulls present average angles from 50.3° to 52.5°, while the juveniles hold an intermediate position with averages from 49.0° to 40.0°. The single Undeformed juvenile has an angle of 52°, which, on the whole, comes within the immature range. Among the group means the Haida males stand out with an average of 43.6°, the Haida females yielding 50.4°. There seems to be a tendency toward higher figures in the Lillooet and Lytton, their respective male averages registering 49.5° and 50.0°. The females of these groups range still higher with means a little above 50°, even reaching 53.0° in the Lillooet. The latter, however, are represented by only a small number. The Cowichan group means are fairly uniform. It appears from these statements that the longer headed groups tend toward smaller frontal angles, which is confirmed in a way by the artificially elongated heads, especially those of the Koskimo division. The Koskimo group itself has the lowest means of 41.3° in the males and 40.3° in the females, which does not seem astonishing in consideration of the extreme distortion.

The variability is grouped around ± 3, rising to ± 4.04 in the Cowichan females and dropping to ± 2.59 in the Undeformed females.

The average conditions of the frontal angle in the four divisions are illustrated in figure 9.

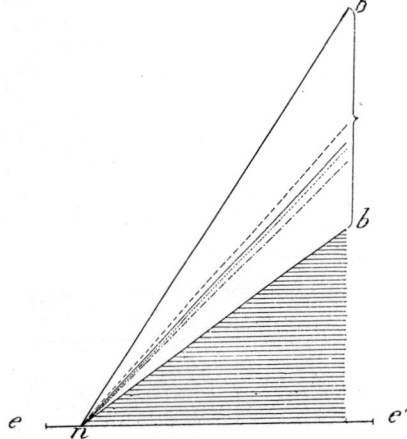

Fig. 9. Scheme of averages of the frontal angle in the four divisions, males and females combined, $e-e'$, parallel to ear-eye plane passing through n, nasion, the nasia coinciding: b, bregma.

——— Undeformed	: ∠ $b-n-e'$	46.6°	$b-b$,
- - - - Cowichan	: „ „	48.7°	total range:
. . . . Chinook	: „ „	46.8°	37° to 58°.
—·—· Koskimo	: „ „	44.5°	

(Cowichan, Chinook, Koskimo braced as "deformation")

The free sides of the angle, the vertex of which rests on the parallel to the ear-eye plane ($e-e'$) in the nasion point (n) represent the total range of variation, covering 21° (37–58°). The varied lines between them give the divisional averages of the four divisions, males and females combined. They are recorded in the legend to figure 9.

OS PARIETALE.

1. Median-sagittal parietal arc.

This measurement has been treated of in connection with the median-sagittal arc of the skull of which it forms the central segment (p. 46).

2. Median-sagittal parietal chord.

Like its arc, the median-sagittal parietal chord shows in a similar way the changes mechanically brought about on the head. The measurements are specified in *summary 35*. The Unde-

Summary 35.
Averages of the median-sagittal parietal chord.

Sex, Age	Undeformed				Deformation according to the three modes											
					Cowichan				Chinook				Koskimo			
	Cases	Range	Average	σ	Cases	Range	Average	σ	Cases	Range	Average	σ	Cases	Range	Average	σ
♂	78	82–120	106.7	± 7.06	84	82–112	96.7	± 7.60	58	80–111	91.0	± 6.53	104	89–119	105.2	± 5.85
♀	34	93–115	103.0	± 5.68	28	76–112	90.5	± 9.22	26	78–97	87.4	± 4.82	39	87–113	99.8	± 6.69
juv.	1	—	101.0	--	2	90; 93	91.5	—	4	80–91	86.8	—	2	104; 105	104.5	—
inf.	13	80–109	98.8	—	5	84–105	91.4	—	6	81–90	86.5	—	8	88–116	98.9	—

formed and Koskimo males have about equal averages of 106.7 mm. and 105.2 mm. The female figures also resemble those for the arc, in which the smaller Koskimo averages caused a greater sex difference with the Undeformed, their chord averages amounting to 103.0 mm. in the Undeformed and 99.8 mm. in the Koskimo. The Chinook averages, 91.0 mm. and 87.4 mm. in the sexes, again range below those of the Cowichan division with 96.7 mm. and 90.5 mm., both falling noticeably below the Undeformed and Koskimo averages. Fronto-occipital pressure under compensatory lateral expansion is thus shown greatly to modify the sagittal dimensions of the parietal bone, absolutely as well as relatively. On the other hand, the same dimensions in the Koskimo mode of deformation seem to be free of any pronounced alteration, as comparison with those of the Undeformed suggests. Changes occur there rather in the occipital and frontal regions, as might be anticipated.

The averages of the immatures fall mostly below those of the adults. Occasional high individual values like those of the Undeformed and Koskimo juveniles (101.0 mm.; 104.5 mm.) are indications of a rather wide range of variation.

Wide ranges of variation are also responsible for the obvious differences in group means. This not only applies to the Undeformed, but to the deformed divisions as well.

The variability is rather irregular. It is highest in the Cowichan division at ± 7.60 and ± 9.22, males and females, and at ± 7.06 in the Undeformed males. In the other classes it centers around ± 6, with the exception of the Chinook females with only ± 4.82.

3. Sagittal-parietal index.

The insignificant difference between the Undeformed male and female indices of 89.7 and 88.9, as shown in *summary 36*, is to be attributed to the slight preponderance of the female arc

Summary 36.

Averages of the sagittal parietal index.

Sex, Age	Undeformed				Deformation according to the three modes											
					Cowichan				Chinook				Koskimo			
	Cases	Range	Average	σ	Cases	Range	Average	σ	Cases	Range	Average	σ	Cases	Range	Average	σ
♂	78	81.3–93.2	89.7	± 2.34	84	79.6–92.9	87.1	± 3.19	58	77.1–91.1	85.5	± 3.94	104	76.5–95.6	87.6	± 3.11
♀	34	85.1–91.2	88.9	± 1.73	28	81.1–91.8	86.9	± 2.82	26	79.8–91.5	86.9	± 3.32	39	81.5–93.5	87.4	± 3.26
juv.	1	—	91.8	—	2	84.5; 86.5	85.5	—	4	76.5–88.6	84.0	—	2	84.5; 86.1	85.8	—
inf.	13	76.9–92.5	88.2	—	5	84.0–93.3	87.1	—	6	78.0–92.4	86.6	—	8	77.6–93.9	85.5	—

over the male. Similar proportions prevail also in the Koskimo division with male and female index averages of 87.6 and 87.4. The reverse, however, takes place in the Cowichan and Chinook divisions, the male averages ranging a little below those of the females, amounting to 87.1 and 87.9 in the former, and to 85.5 and 86.9 in the latter. The immature averages are about on the same level with those of the adults. In the Koskimo they show a tendency to range lower. The averages are altogether an expression of the changes brought about by the different modes of deformation. The Chinook averages, the lowest in summary 36, are indicative of the most pronounced artificial parietal bulging.

The ranges, naturally, are more concentrated than are those for the segments of the index. It is only in the Koskimo males that the range acquires an extension of nineteen units, the next lowest being fourteen units in the Chinook males, with twelve in the Koskimo females, while the least extended range is with the Undeformed females, where it comprises only six units.

There are no disparities to speak of in the group means of the Undeformed. This is also true of the other divisions. In the Koskimo deformation, means lower than the divisional average are held by the Koskimo proper. They amount to 86.2 and 86.8 in the sexes, and correspond with the Nootka male mean of 86.3, while the Nootka female mean is 88.6.

The variability lies around ± 3, but drops to ± 2.34 and ± 1.73 in the Undeformed males and females.

An illustration of these conditions is given in figure 10, *a–c*. The four individual tracings of figure 10*a* represent the average conditions of the sagittal parietal index of the four divisions. They are oriented on a parallel of the ear-eye plane (*e–e′*) laid through the lambda (*l*). Obvious differences are manifested in the degree of declination of the parietal chord (*b–l*) toward the line of orientation. This point will be discussed more thoroughly in the next section of this chapter. It must be mentioned, however, that the four cases here depicted do not give the average angularity of the four divisions, although their order of gradation conforms in this respect with the actual status. The elevation of the four arcs above their chords, amounting to 24 mm. in the Undeformed, Chinook and Koskimo, and to 25 mm. in the Cowichan deformation is fairly equal in the four instances, while the individual indices at 85.3 for the Chinook, 87.3 for the Koskimo, 87.5 for the Bellabella (Cowichan deformation) and 89.8 for the Undeformed correspond with the index averages. The vertical lines upon the parietal chords, denoting the extent of the elevation in each case, are seen almost to halve the parietal segment in the Undeformed and the Bellabella. In the Chinook and Koskimo they are shifted backwards, i. e., beyond the bisecting point on the parietal chords. This is still better observed in figure 10b, where the chords and lines of elevation of the same tracings are made to coincide. The individual angularity of the deformed specimens is dispensed with here in favor of a uniform orientation on the parietal chord which is that of the Undeformed average at 28.5°. A definite conception of the conditions under discussion cannot be obtained, however, without introducing another modification, namely, the reduction of the four segments to equal proportions. For that rea-

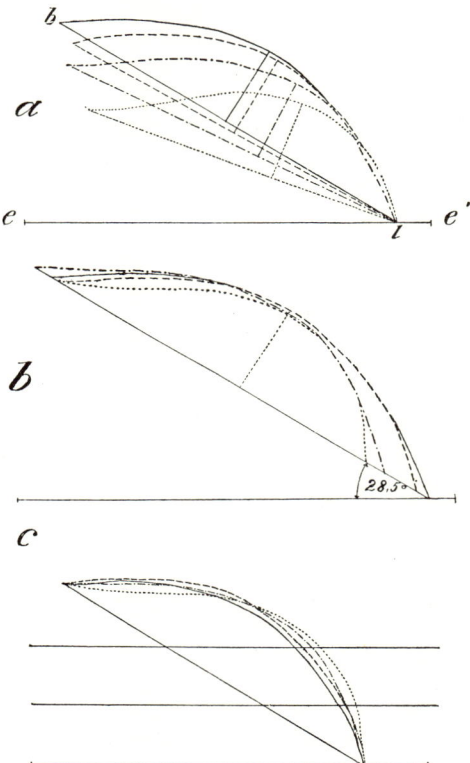

Fig. 10a. Superposition of median-sagittal parietal tracings representing individual indices coinciding with the divisional averages. The highest elevation above the parietal chords is indicated by vertical lines, the chords in their individual angularity. e–e', parallel of the ear-eye plane passing through the lambda (l), the lambdas coinciding; b, bregma. Reduced.

Fig. 10b. The same superposed tracings as in a oriented on the parietal chord of the Undeformed at the latter's divisional angle of 28.5°. The vertical lines, indicating the individual elevation of the arcs, also coincide. Lettering as in a. Reduced.

Fig. 10c. Superposition of the same tracings and orientation as in b. The tracings are reduced to the size of the shortest bregma-lambda chord (Chinook). The additional horizontals trisect the space between the bregma and the lambda parallel of the ear-eye plane. Lettering as in a. Reduced.

——— Undeformed (Haida ♂, 1610): index 89.8; elevation 24 mm. ∠ c–l–b 31°.
- - - - Cowichan (Bellabella ♂, 4643): index 87.5; elevation 25 mm. ∠ c–l–b 30°.
. . . . Chinook (Chinook ♂, 4445): index 85.3; elevation 24 mm. ∠ c–l–b 20°.
–·–·– Koskimo (Koskimo ♂, 3837): index 87.3; elevation 24 mm. ∠ c–l–b 26°.

son their cords have been made to conform with the length of the smallest, which in this case is that of the Chinook. This is realized in figure 10c. What has been said before with regard to the different elevations is recapitulated here. The Haida and Bellabella tracings, of which the latter exceeds the former, represent almost perfect segments of the circle. The shifting of the points of highest elevation in the Chinook and Koskimo toward the lambda region, indicating the effects of their specific practices of head deformation, is shown here quite clearly. At the same time, a postbregmatic depression is to be observed, which is rather pronounced in the Chinook. The two auxiliary parallels drawn in equal thirds between the ear-eye parallel and the bregma level show, after a uniform start of the four curves, in the lower and middle thirds the trespassing of the Koskimo and Chinook curves across those of the Haida and Bellabella, while in the upper third they again drop below them.

The figures, it may be repeated, illustrate only average conditions represented by individual cases corresponding with them. In individual cases at the extreme ends of the ranges of variation the average conditions are considerably exaggerated.

4. Parietal angle.

The declination of the parietal bones expressed by the angle of its median-sagittal chord with a parallel to the ear-eye plane passing through the lambda, is practically uniform in the Undeformed males and females, as shown in *summary 37*. The averages here amount to 28.7° and 28.2° in the sexes.

Summary 37.
Averages of the parietal angle.

Sex, Age	Undeformed				Deformation according to the three modes											
					Cowichan				Chinook				Koskimo			
	Cases	Range	Average	σ	Cases	Range	Average	σ	Cases	Range	Average	σ	Cases	Range	Average	σ
♂	75	18–38	28.7	± 4.62	75	18–37	27.7	± 4.40	57	13–33	23.6	± 4.56	104	13–39	26.9	± 4.47
♀	31	19–34	28.2	± 3.42	24	17–33	25.2	± 4.84	25	10–29	22.6	± 4.30	35	16–36	25.1	± 4.56
juv.	1	—	24.0	—	2	24; 29	26.5	—	4	12–25	19.0	—	2	30; 33	31.5	—
inf.	10	24–31	27.3	—	4	16–26	22.3	—	6	12–27	21.3	—	6	17–30	25.2	—

All the deformed averages fall below these in the order: Cowichan, Koskimo, Chinook deformations with male averages of 27.7°, 26.9° and 23.6°, and female, of 25.2°, 25.1° and 22.6°. Although small sex differences exist here in favor of the males, they probably do not differentiate tribal characters. The immatures do not reach the adult figures, although their individual values occasionally reach high places in the range of variation. Such is the case, for instance, with the two Koskimo juveniles at 30° and 33°; but in no case do the highest immature figures equal the highest adult ones.

Some significance might be attached to the higher group means in the Eskimo, 30.2° for the males and 29.5° for the females, since in this group they coincide with greater cranial heights. This would also hold true for the Lytton males, but not for the Haida, Athapascan or Chukchee, whose parietal angles rather conform with average conditions.

The variability, fairly uniform in the divisions and sexes, centers around ± 4.

The accompanying figure 11 illustrates the angular relation of the parietal chords (b–l) to the lambda parallel of the ear-eye plane (e–e'). The total range of variation from 10° to 39° is indicated by heavy solid lines. Between

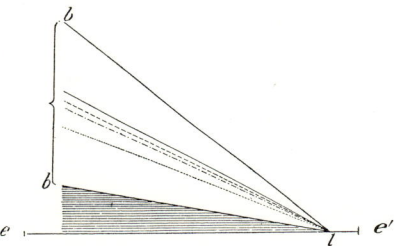

Fig. 11. Scheme of averages of the parietal angle in the four divisions, males and females combined. e–e', parallel to the ear-eye plane passing through the lambda, the lambdas coinciding; b, bregma.

```
———— Undeformed :  ∠ b–l–e  28.5°  ⎫
- - - - Cowichan  :    „   „    27.1°  ⎪  b to b,
. . . . Chinook   :    „   „    23.3°  ⎬  total range:
—·—· Koskimo   :    „   „    26.4°  ⎭  10° to 39°.
```

them are seen the divisional averages, males and females combined, in the order: Undeformed, Cowichan, Koskimo, Chinook. The most interesting observation here is the gradual depression of the bregma region in the deformed divisions, due to the specific deformatory influences which appear to have been most effective in the Chinook. Here more so than in the Cowichan deformation has the intense frontal compression brought forth a proportionally strong counter-effect at the occiput, so that the lambda region appears to have been pressed upward, thus still further diminishing the size of the angle.

OS OCCIPITALE.

1. Median-sagittal occipital arc.

The discussion of the occipital segment of the median-sagittal arc is embodied in the chapter treating of the latter (p. 46).

2. Median-sagittal occipital chord.

Summary 38 shows averages of the median-sagittal occipital chord in the Undeformed males and in those of the Cowichan deformation of nearly equal length at 96.2 mm. and 96.9 mm. They are

Summary 38.
Averages of the median-sagittal occipital chord.

Sex, Age	Undeformed				Deformation according to the three modes											
					Cowichan				Chinook				Koskimo			
	Cases	Range	Average	σ	Cases	Range	Average	σ	Cases	Range	Average	σ	Cases	Range	Average	σ
♂	78	83–113	96.2	± 5.70	77	81–111	96.9	± 7.04	57	86–109	97.4	± 5.26	103	86–125	102.1	± 7.21
♀	33	81–113	93.6	± 5.68	25	87–110	95.8	± 5.78	25	87–115	96.4	± 6.23	37	89–120	100.0	± 6.80
juv.	1	—	94.0	—	1	—	87.0	—	4	88–105	95.8	—	2	88; 93	90.5	—
inf.	14	80–97	91.0	—	6	81–94	93.5	—	6	87–111	100.5	—	7	88–110	100.9	—

exceeded by the Chinook and Koskimo male averages at 97.4 mm. and 102.1 mm., the difference between the latter two amounting to 4.7 mm. All the female range below the male averages. The sex differences at 2.6 mm. in the Undeformed and at 2.1 mm. in the Koskimo, 1.1 mm. in the Cowichan and 1.0 mm. in the Chinook deformations are rather inconspicuous. The infantile averages range below those of the adults in the Undeformed and the Cowichan, but exceed them in the Chinook and approach with an average of 100.9 mm. the adult averages in the Koskimo deformation. The few juveniles occupy rather low places in the divisional ranges, the total extensions of the latter covering values from 87–105 mm. As expected, the highest individual values are found in the Koskimo deformation.

The group means repeat in general the status of the divisional averages in regard to sex differences. There is, however, in the Undeformed a gap of 6.3 mm. between the Haida males and females, due to the high male mean of 100.2 mm., which arises from a high range of 92–113 mm. A rather high mean of 96.8 mm. is that of the Eskimo females, while the means of the smaller groups are more or less in keeping with the total average. The highest means in the Koskimo deformation are those of the Koskimo themselves, the males with 107.1 mm. and 105.4 mm. in the sexes. It is obvious that the longer occipital chords of the Chinook and Koskimo deformations are the result of deforming influences. Deformation, as pointed out, is also responsible for the excessive length of the occipital arc in the Koskimo division in spite of the strong flattening, simultaneously, of the occipital bone.

The variability is not so high here as for the arc. It lies around ± 6, but rises above ± 7 in the Cowichan and Koskimo males.

3. Sagittal occipital index.

As listed in *summary 39*, there is a gradual increase to be noted in the averages of this index in the order: Undeformed, and Cowichan, Koskimo and Chinook deformations, ranging

Summary 39.

Averages of the sagittal occipital index.

Sex, Age	Undeformed				Deformation according to the three modes											
					Cowichan				Chinook				Koskimo			
	Cases	Range	Average	σ	Cases	Range	Average	σ	Cases	Range	Average	σ	Cases	Range	Average	σ
♂	78	75.2–91.2	82.3	±3.08	77	76.7–95.1	83.5	±3.92	57	80.4–93.9	88.6	±3.17	103	73.6–95.7	85.7	±4.38
♀	33	77.6–88.7	83.8	±3.04	25	73.0–91.1	84.6	±4.52	25	80.9–96.0	88.9	±3.63	37	79.4–91.9	86.1	±3.31
juv.	1	—	83.9	—	2	88.1; 88.5	88.3	—	4	88.2–93.6	90.9	—	2	85.3; 87.1	86.2	—
inf.	13	77.6–87.1	83.6	—	5	81.0–89.7	84.9	—	6	85.9–91.1	88.9	—	7	80.6–96.5	84.9	—

in the males from 82.3–88.6, and in the females from 83.8–88.9. The sex differences, amounting to only 1.5 in the Undeformed, dwindle to fractions of an index unit in the other divisions, illustrating the uniform effects of the different modes of deformation. The higher index, expressing the greater applanation of the occipital bone, here shows that the Chinook deformation had the most intense influence in such a direction.

Among the immatures the findings for the adults are repeated quite faithfully.

The ranges of the index in both the matures and immatures are naturally more concentrated than those listed for its components, i. e., the occipital arc and chord. They are shortest in the Undeformed and in the Chinook deformation. The Cowichan and Koskimo deformations do not quite attain the Chinook degree of uniformity, and represent, for that reason, a greater individual variability manifested by wide ranges.

The group means of the Undeformed resemble the status of the divisional average with regard to the somewhat flatter occipitale in the females, as expressed by the higher figures for the latter. The males here have lower means than the total average, with the exception of the six Lytton skulls and the Eskimo whose means range somewhat higher. The contrary may be noticed in the females. In the Koskimo deformation the fact stands out that the Koskimo proper with their exaggeratedly protruding occipita coincide with the Koskimo average. The Koskimo female mean runs up to 88.6, thus exceeding the average. Four Clayoquot males have a mean only of 82.3, four Nootka females of only 84.7.

The variability rises only in the Cowichan females and the Koskimo males to a fraction above ± 4. It lies between ± 3 and ± 4 in all the other categories.

4. Occipital angle.

This angle, formed by the occipital chord (opisthion-lambda) and a parallel to the ear-eye plane laid through the opisthion, opens forward, i. e., toward the cavity of the skull. It shows the sagittal declination of the occipital bone in ear-eye orientation.

Summary 40.

Averages of the occipital angle.

Sex, Age	Undeformed				Deformation according to the three modes											
					Cowichan				Chinook				Koskimo			
	Cases	Range	Average	σ	Cases	Range	Average	σ	Cases	Range	Average	σ	Cases	Range	Average	σ
♂	75	101–134	117.4	± 5.79	73	103–126	112.7	± 4.81	57	105–130	114.2	± 4.67	104	112–138	123.3	± 4.78
♀	31	110–126	117.3	± 3.66	24	100–123	112.2	± 6.12	24	102–123	115.2	± 4.65	35	112–234	122.1	± 5.11
juv.	1	—	114.0	—	2	112; 121	116.5	—	5	110–118	113.5	—	2	121; 125	123.0	—
inf.	9	113–125	118.8	—	4	110–117	113.3	—	6	107–133	117.0	—	5	108–123	116.2	—

There are significant differences between the four divisions revealed by *summary 40*. The Undeformed averages of this angle at 117° plus in the sexes are greater by 5° than those of the Cowichan deformation at 112° plus. The Chinook averages of 114.2° and 115.2° respectively, fall between the former two, while all three divisions are considerably outranged by the Koskimo averages, 123.3° in the males and 122.1° in the females. Sex differences in the adults are so small that they may be disregarded. The averages of the infantiles only slightly exceed those of the adults in the Undeformed, and in the Cowichan and Chinook deformations. It seems, however, that the effects of deformation, showing so unequivocally in the adults, are not yet fully established in the immatures. This is still more plainly demonstrated in the Koskimo infantiles, whose average of 116.2° falls short about 6° of the adult averages of the same division.

The effects of deformation are clearly shown by these figures, most obviously in the Koskimo division, where the entire occiput, including the lambda point and region, undergo the most effective applanation. The Cowichan and Chinook deformations, resulting in a flattening of the occipital vaulting mostly by the mechanical counteraction of the cradle board against the frontal pressure and in an automatic rising of the lambda region, result in smaller angles of the former. The more intense pressure upon the forehead in the Chinook deformation, on the other hand, not only causes the lambda to rise, but, at the same time, to retreat, with the result that their occipital angle exceeds that of the Cowichan deformation. The large Koskimo angles are an expression of the strong protrusion of the occiput brought about by the Koskimo mode of deformation. While the divisional ranges in general are of fairly equal extension, it is shown that the lowest and highest individual values outrange in height the corresponding ones in the other divisions. They also include the ranges of the immatures.

The group means run unusually high in the Eskimo, Chukchee and Athapascan where they amount to 120.7°, 122.0° and 119.0° in males, and 118.6° in twelve Eskimo females. The Haida mean coincides with the divisional average of the Undeformed, as does the Nicola, while the Lillooet male mean attains only 107.0°. Regarding the normal, i. e., undeformed skull, it may be safe to conclude that longheadedness produces greater occipital angles than shortheadedness. This condition is artificially and exaggeratedly brought about in the Koskimo division, in which the Koskimo group attains means as high as 125.2° and 126.5° in the sexes.

The variability is somewhat irregular. It amounts to ± 3.66, or a fraction below ± 4 in the Undeformed females, and lies between ± 4 and ± 5 in the Cowichan males, the Chinook of both sexes and the Koskimo males but rises above ± 5 in the Undeformed males and the Koskimo females and above ± 6 in the Cowichan females.

An illustration of the average conditions of the occipital angle is given in figure 12, where the divisional averages, males and females combined, are represented by varied lines indicating the opisthion-lambda chords ($o-l$). The total range of variation ($l-l$) in the angular relation between the occipital chord and the parallel to the ear-eye plane through the opisthion ($e-e'$) comprises occipital angles ($\angle e-o-l$) of 100° to 138°. The two extremes are afforded by the Cowichan and Koskimo divisions, whose averages amount to 112.6° and 123.2°. The Chinook with 114.4° only slightly exceed the Cowichan, while the Undeformed with 117.3° maintain an intermediate position between the Chinook and Koskimo divisions. This intermediate status is quite significant in view of the deforming influences which force the occipital region more or less forward in the Cowichan and Chinook, thus diminishing the degree of declination there. The forced elongation of the head in the Koskimo, on the other hand, produces also the higher degree of occipital declination which quite appreciably exceeds the other three divisions.

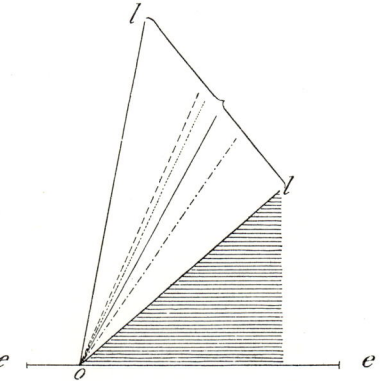

Fig. 12. Scheme of averages of the occipital angle in the four divisions, males and females combined. $e-e'$, parallel to the ear-eye plane passing through, o, opisthion, the opisthia coinciding; l, lambda.

———— Undeformed: $\angle e-o-l$ 117.3°
- - - - Cowichan : „ „ 112.6°
· · · · Chinook : „ „ 114.4°
—·—· Koskimo : „ „ 123.2°

l to l, total range: 100° to 138°.

In order to demonstrate these conditions by actual cases from the series, and simultaneously show the variation within a given group as represented here by each of the deformed divisions, the following scheme was employed: two occipital tracings are superposed at their individual angles and made to coincide in the opisthia through which passes a parallel to the ear-eye plane.

The deviation from normal conditions, shown by an interrupted line which stands for the average occipital angle of the Undeformed division at 117.3°, is added to each scheme by means of paired tracings. This is illustrated in figure 13, *a–c*. On the whole, conditions are similar to those of figure 12.

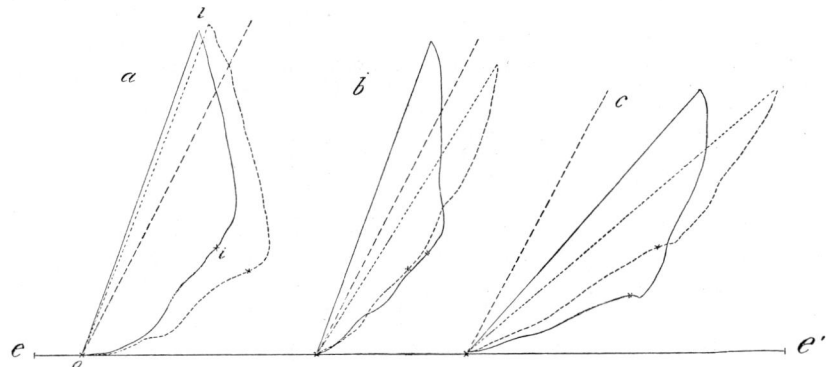

Fig. 13. Occipital angles paired to show different findings within the same deformed division of (*a*) Cowichan, (*b*) Chinook, (*c*) Koskimo, oriented on a parallel to the ear-eye plane (*e–e'*) passing through the opisthion (*o*), the opisthia coinciding. *l*, lambda; *i*, inion. Reduced.

Cowichan		Bellacoola ♂, 4546:	∠ *e–o–l* 109°;	84.2	
„		„ ♂, 4633:	„ „ 110°;	76.7	occipital
Chinook	deformation	Chinook ♀, 4459:	„ „ 109°;	88.9	sagittal
„		„ ♂, 4473:	„ „ 120°;	96.0	index
Koskimo		Kwakiutl ♂, 1725:	„ „ 130°;	85.0	
„		Koskimo ♂, 3642:	„ „ 138°;	95.7	

The broken straight line (- - - -) signifies the Undeformed average of the occipital angle to show the deviations in the deformed specimens.

The two Cowichan cases (*a*) with angles of 109° and 110° fall short of the Undeformed, while in the other extreme, represented by the Koskimo (*c*), the occipital angles at 130° and 138° exceed the Undeformed average. It is only in the Chinook that the two cases depicted under *b* differ from the average conditions of figure 12, in so far as one Chinook angle at 109° falls short of, and the other one at 120° exceeds, the Undeformed average. Similar variable conditions may also be noticed in the vaultings of the occipital arcs above their individual chords. In each pair of tracings there is one which appears less affected by their particular mode of deformation. This is especially noticeable in the excessive Chinook and Koskimo modes where the less distorted individuals have also the smaller occipital angles, while the strongly depressed ones yielded to the greater strain and, consequently, produced larger angles.

The sagittal occipital indices, interpreting the vaulting of the occipital squama, amount to 88.9 and 96.0 for the two Chinook, and to 85.0 and 95.7 for the two Koskimo, thus showing a more pronounced applanation of the occipital region in the Chinook deformation. While the applanation in these two divisions affects, as a rule, both the upper and lower occipital squamae, sometimes to a marked degree — the index maximum in the Chinook amounts to 96.0, in the Koskimo to 95.7 — it is the upper squama that is relatively most affected in the Cowichan deformation. The inion region here appears less impaired as shown in figure 13*a*, where the two sagittal occipital indices remain with only 84.2 and 76.7 below the status of the other two divisions. These conditions are furthermore corroborated by the divisional averages of the sagittal occipital index.

A combination of a typical tracing from each of the three deformed divisions with an identical outline of an Undeformed is given in figures 14, *a–c*, and 15, *a–c*. The Undeformed outline is that of a Haida (3707 ♂), the

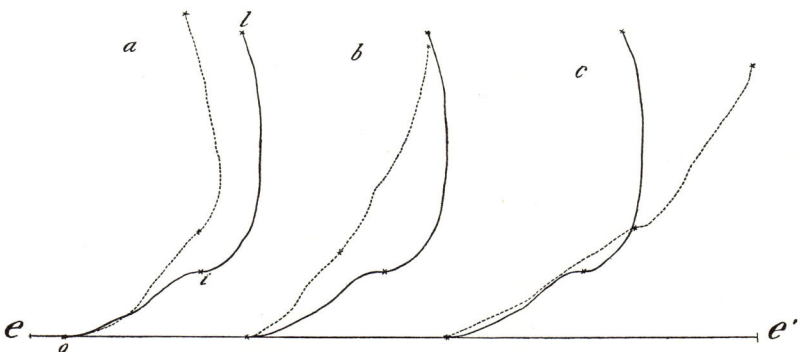

Fig. 14. Superposition of occipital outlines at their individual occipital angles, combining an Undeformed (Haida ♂, 3707) with a representative of (*a*) the Cowichan (Bellacoola ♂, 4546), (*b*) Chinook (♀, 4473), and (*c*) Koskimo (♂, 3642) deformations, oriented on a parallel to the ear-eye plane (*e–e'*) laid through the opisthion (*o*), the opisthia coinciding. *l*, lambda; *i*, inion. Reduced.

deformed divisions being represented by a Bellacoola (4546 ♂), and by typical cases from the Chinook and Koskimo series 4473 ♀, and 3642 ♂). The orientation is on the opisthion parallel to the ear-eye plane (*e–e'*) in figure 14,

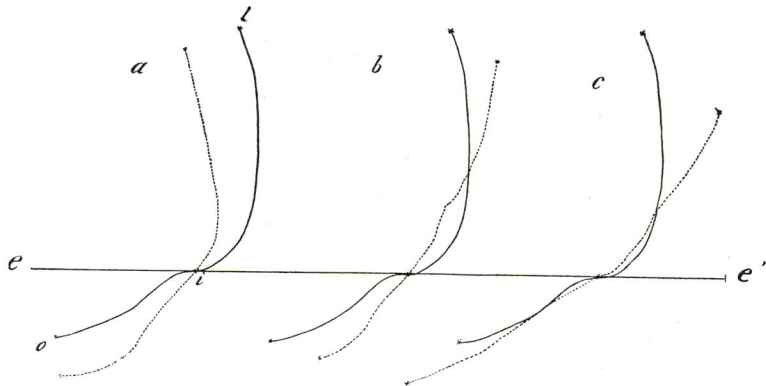

Fig. 15. Superposition of the same outlines as in fig. 14, the parallel to the ear-eye plane (*e–e'*) laid through the inion (*i*), the inia coinciding. *o*, opisthion; *l*, lambda. Reduced.

and on the inion parallel of the same plane line in figure 15, opisthia and inia coinciding in the respective cases. All the tracings are shown in their individual angular relations to the plane lines named. Both sets of tracings exhibit the characteristics of their series, namely, the gradual increase in posterior declination of the occipital squamae in the order: Cowichan, Chinook and Koskimo deformations. This behavior has been pointed out in each case as the result of specific deformation.

5. Interoccipital angle.

The median-sagittal chords of the upper and lower occipital squamae form an angle between themselves, the vertex of which is identical with the inion point and which opens toward the cranial cavity.

Summary 41.

Averages of the interoccipital angle.

Sex, Age	Undeformed				Deformation according to the three modes											
					Cowichan				Chinook				Koskimo			
	Cases	Range	Average	σ	Cases	Range	Average	σ	Cases	Range	Average	σ	Cases	Range	Average	σ
♂	76	108–136	124.3	± 6.41	73	110–140	123.5	± 7.10	57	123–149	135.4	± 6.39	104	111–144	127.9	± 7.32
♀	31	96–140	126.2	± 8.09	23	112–143	128.6	± 7.19	24	120–157	137.1	∓ 7.21	35	117–145	129.8	± 6.87
juv.	1	—	126.0	—	2	137; 141	139.0	—	4	140–153	146.8	—	2	128; 134	131.0	—
inf.	9	110–130	124.3	—	4	120–236	127.8	—	6	135–174	144.3	—	6	121–133	125.2	—

As specified in *summary 41*, the Undeformed males have an average angle of 124.3°, and the females one of 126.2°. There is only a small difference between these averages and those of the Cowichan deformation with 123.5° and 128.6° in the sexes. The Koskimo averages turn out somewhat higher with 127.9° for the males and 129.8° for the females. The Chinook figures range considerably higher, presenting 135.4° for the males and 137.1° for the females. Even higher figures are those of the Chinook immatures at 144.3° in the infantiles and 146.8° in the juveniles, thus considerably outranging the adult averages. The immature averages in the other divisions are more or less in keeping with the adult figures. The Koskimo infantiles with an average of 125.2° range below the adults of the same division, while the Cowichan infantiles with 127.8° slightly exceed them and the Undeformed ones with 124.3° equal the averages of the Undeformed males. The ranges show rather wide extensions, due to the great variability in the lengths of the two parts involved, viz. the inion-lambda and the inion-opisthion chords. The widest range is that of the Undeformed females, with an extension from 96° to 140°, or forty-five units. The highest individual value is that of a Chinook infant at 174°.

Among the group means of the Undeformed are those of the Eskimo which are rather high at 127.9° and 129.2° in the males and females. The other large groups conform with the total average, or range a little below it. The groups which constitute the Koskimo division give means mostly in keeping with the total average, excepting the Koskimo themselves, whose means rise to 135.6° in the males and 135.8° in the females. The effects of deformation then appear more pronounced in the most strongly deformed skulls, i. e., the Koskimo. Their highest means, therefore, coincide with the Chinook averages which are the product of another deforming device of great tension.

The variability centers around ± 7. It is only in the Undeformed females that a figure above ± 8 is attained. Here the widest range of variation was also found.

In order to show the variable conditions of the interoccipital angle in one and the same deformed division, two of their individual occipital outlines are superposed in figure 16, *a–c*. They are oriented in their natural positions on a parallel to the ear-eye plane (*e–e'*) laid through the inion (*i*), the vertex point of the angle ($\angle$ *o–i–l*); the inia coincide. Of particular interest is the

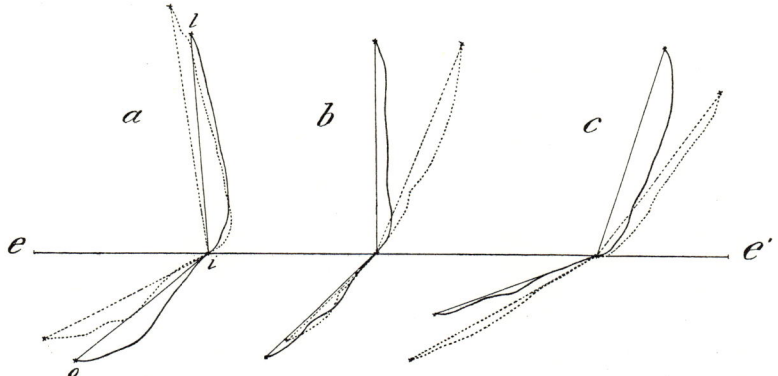

Fig. 16. Interoccipital angles paired to show different findings within the same deformed division of (*a*) the Cowichan, (*b*) Chinook, and (*c*) Koskimo, oriented on a parellel to the ear-eye plane (*e–e'*) laid through the inion (*i*), the inia coinciding. Same tracings as in fig. 13. Reduced.

Cowichan		——— Bellacoola	♂, 4546:	$\angle$ *l–i–o*	120°
„		·········· „	♂, 4633:	„ „	110°
Chinook	deformation	——— Chinook	♂, 4459:	„ „	135°
„		·········· „	♀, 4473:	„ „	157°
Koskimo		——— Kwakiutl	♂, 1725:	„ „	128°
„		·········· Koskimo	♂, 3642:	„ „	156°

behavior of the occipital squama above the inion (squama occipitalis superior). Repeating, in substance, also in the inion orientation the general status of the occipital squama in the three deformed divisions, it will be noticed, furthermore, that in each of the three combinations the stronger declination of the upper squama occurs simultaneously with an equal condition in the lower one. This correlation, of course, stands for the more intense depression of the occipital squama as a whole, and, at the same time, for larger occipital angles, amounting in the extreme cases to 120°, 157° and 156° in the Cowichan, Chinook and Koskimo deformations. The less depressed occipita have interoccipital angles of 110°, 135° and 128° respectively.

CRANIAL BASE.

1. Length of cranial base (nasion-basion).

The length of the cranial base depends largely on the degree of flexure of the skull in the phylogenetic course of development. The investigations of Schwerz [36] have shown that while during the process of growth the "Schädelbasislänge im Laufe der Entwicklung bei Menschen und Affen schneller wächst als die Länge der Deckknochen", in man it seems to be correlated with the size of the skull rather than with the craniological type. Racial and sex differences must be viewed principally from this angle. The following investigations may also shed some light on the question whether artificial deformation influences the mutual relation between the cranio-basal length and the size of the skull.

Summary 42.

Averages of the cranial base length.

Sex, Age	Undeformed				Deformation according to the three modes											
					Cowichan				Chinook				Koskimo			
	Cases	Range	Average	σ	Cases	Range	Average	σ	Cases	Range	Average	σ	Cases	Range	Average	σ
♂	76	94–113	102.7	± 4.38	73	87–111	99.6	± 5.12	57	87–107	98.6	± 4.14	102	91–110	100.5	± 3.68
♀	33	90–105	97.9	± 3.66	25	88–100	94.1	± 3.51	24	80–103	89.5	± 5.75	37	88–105	96.1	± 3.36
juv.	1	—	98.0	—	2	89; 91	90.0	—	4	85–97	89.5	—	2	89; 94	91.5	—
inf.	8	—	86.1	—	4	82–86	83.8	—	5	80–88	84.8	—	4	81–89	85.0	—

The male averages as dependent on the physical size of the skull range are, in every case, higher than the female ones. They are enumerated in *summary 42*, the differences amounting to several millimeters, as much as 9.1 mm in the Chinook. The Undeformed are recorded with the highest male average of 102.7 mm. and are followed by the Koskimo, Cowichan and Chinook deformations with 100.5 mm, 99.6 mm. and 98.6 mm. The females maintain the same order. Although all the deformed averages fall below the normal, i. e. undeformed average, it is impossible to prove whether head deformation in individual cases influences the growth of the basion-nasion diameter. The immature averages naturally fall considerably below those of the adults, although

---

[36] *Schwerz, Franz,* 1910. Untersuchungen über das Verhältnis von Frontal-, Parietal- und Occipitalsehne zur Schädelbasislänge. Arch. Anthrop., N. F., v. IX, pp. 50–52 (52).

individual values occur as high as the lowest values of the adult ranges. The juveniles hold rather an intermediate position between the infantiles and the adults.

Although from the craniological point of view the cranio-basal axis shows a priori a certain metrical stability in the cranial complex, this may be best expressed by comparison with other more variable measurements of the skull. The ranges are, nevertheless, rather wide and cover 20 mm., 16 mm. and 13 mm. in the Undeformed males, females and infantiles. They are partly exceeded in the Cowichan and Chinook deformations.

The relations obtaining in the four divisions between the averages and ranges are repeated with more or less constancy in the groups which compose the divisions.

Cameron's [37] interesting statement of a comparatively great length of the cranial base in the eastern Eskimo exceeding that in the Negroes and Whites could not be upheld for the western Eskimo of our series whose averages attained 102.6 mm. and 98.1 mm. in the sexes as over against 106.7 mm. and 98.8 mm. in *Cameron's* material from the Canadian Arctic Expedition (see bibliography). His statement is corroborated by *Hrdlička's* data,[38] but not by those of the present author [39] upon Greenland and Labrador skulls with cranial base lengths 100.9 mm. in the sexes.

The variability lies around ± 4, but rises above ± 5 in the Cowichan males and the Chinook females.

2. Angular relation between cranial base and ear-eye plane.

The cranio-basal angle formed by the nasion-basion line of the skull and a parallel to the ear-eye plane laid through the basion, varies very slightly in different races. *R. Martin* (Lehrbuch, 1914, 485) gives racial averages from 25.3° to 30.5°.

Summary 43.

Averages of the cranio-basal angle.

Sex, Age	Undeformed				Deformation according to the three modes											
					Cowichan				Chinook				Koskimo			
	Cases	Range	Average	σ	Cases	Range	Average	σ	Cases	Range	Average	σ	Cases	Range	Average	σ
♂	74	23–37	30.2	± 2.89	73	23–36	28.6	± 2.62	57	23–35	28.2	± 2.39	103	24–36	31.3	± 2.35
♀	30	25–35	29.9	± 2.65	22	25–35	29.4	± 2.75	24	25–35	29.2	± 2.59	35	25–36	30.4	± 2.54
juv.	1	—	31.0	—	2	23; 31	27.0	—	4	24–31	28.3	—	2	30; 32	31.0	—
inf.	7	23–30	27.4	—	4	25–30	27.8	—	5	27–31	29.2	—	4	28–30	29.3	—

[37] *Cameron, John*, 1926. Shortening of the nasion-basion length in the white races. Am. Jour. Phys. Anthrop., v. IX, no. 3, pp. 329–333.
[38] *Hrdlička, Aleš*, 1910. Contribution to the anthropology of Central and Smith Sound Eskimo. Anthrop. Pap. Am. Mus. Nat. Hist., v. V, no. 2, pp. 177–280.
[39] *Oetteking, Bruno*, 1908. Ein Beitrag zur Kraniologie der Eskimo. Abh. Ber. Kgl. Zool. Anthrop. Ethnogr. Mus. Dresden, v. XII, no. 3, 54 pp.

With a male and female average of 30.2° and 29.9°, our Undeformed, as shown in *summary 43*, conform to the highest averages. The sex difference amounts only to a fraction of a unit in favor of the males. The Cowichan and Chinook deformations are uniform with male averages of 28.6° and 28.2°, and range below the Undeformed males by 1.6° and 2.0°. Uniformity of average is found in the females in these three divisions, but the sex difference at 0.8° and 1.0° in the Cowichan as well as in the Chinook are in favor of the females. The averages of the Koskimo division at 31.3° in the males and 30.4° in the females are the highest of all. They differ from the Undeformed by 1.1° and 0.5°, both in favor of the Koskimo males and females whose sex difference amounts to 0.9°, also in favor of the males. The infantile averages differ in only a mild degree from the adult, the Cowichan and Koskimo divisions falling short of these only slightly. It is only in the Chinook that the infantile rises to the female average, which in turn exceeds the male average.

Deformatory effects, if any, upon the cranio-basal angle are not easily perceived.[40] In this kind of measurement, however, one can scarcely speak of direct distortion of the parts involved, but rather of a sort of correlative change, the amount of distortion for that reason being comparatively slight. The small deviations that do occur may, nevertheless, be taken into account. The averages of the Cowichan and Chinook, the two divisions deformed in more or less identical fashion, range below the Undeformed averages, while those of the Koskimo exceed them. The averages for the males are more significant than those for the females, which show a remarkable constancy in the Undeformed, Cowichan and Chinook, while the Koskimo females, like the rest of the Koskimo division, exceed the average of the Undeformed. It is, of course, impossible to determine to what extent tribal characters may be responsible for such disparities in the deformed series, all the more so since an examination of the group means reveals the fact that the Eskimo register the highest means of 31.6° and 31.0° in the sexes.

The variability lies around ± 2.5 in all the divisions.

The average conditions of the angular relation between the cranial base line and the ear-eye horizontal are illustrated in figure 18, in connection with the angular relations of the foramen magnum plane (see p. 80).

3. Length of cranial base in relation to other metrical quantities of the skull.

The specific nature of the crania under investigation does not encourage experiment for ascertaining the correlation of certain definite and more or less stable metrical conditions of the skull with its principal diameters, since these latter have undergone decided changes under the strain of artificial deformation. Nevertheless, a comparison has been attempted between the nasion-basion or cranial base line and metrical quantities of a more neutral character which do not seem to be directly influenced by deformation.[41] The cranial capacity and the angle formed by the cranial base line and a parallel to the ear-eye plane passing through the basion have been selected for that purpose. The averages derived from the combined males and females, besides the individual averages of the sexes are listed in *summary 44*.

---

[40] See however: *Oetteking, Bruno*, 1924. Declination of the pars basilaris in normal and in artificially deformed skulls. Ind. Notes Monogr., No. 27, pp. 1–25 (24).

[41] Racial differences in the relation of the nasion-basion length to other cranial measurements have been pointed out by: *Schultz, Adolph H.*, 1917. Anthropologische Untersuchungen an der Schädelbasis. Arch. Anthrop. N. F., v. XVI, pp. 1–103 (5–18).

Summary 44.

Relation between the length of the cranial base, the cranial capacity and the cranial base angle.

Series		Comparative averages							
		Length of cranial base			Cranial capacity			Angle of cranial base $\angle$ n–ba/e–e' *)		
		♂	♀	♂+♀	♂	♀	♂+♀	♂	♀	♂+♀
Undeformed		102.7	97.9	101.2	1349.5	1243.8	1317.2	30.2	29.9	30.1
Cowichan	deformation	99.6	94.1	98.1	1360.3	1209.6	1320.2	28.6	29.4	28.7
Chinook		98.6	89.5	95.9	1388.8	1251.6	1347.0	28.2	29.2	28.5
Koskimo		100.5	96.1	99.3	1396.3	1264.2	1360.7	31.3	30.4	31.0

The gradual changes disclosed by the sex averages appear to be reiterated and intensified in the combined averages. The decrease in the cranio-basal length and angle occurs, in the order: Undeformed, Cowichan and Chinook deformations, and an increase again in the Koskimo deformation, whose angle even exceeds the Undeformed value. In the cranial capacity, however, a gradual increase is noticed in the four main divisions and in the order of their enumeration just cited.

Taking the cranial capacity as a comparative model, it is shown that with a steady increase in the order: Undeformed, Cowichan, Chinook and Koskimo deformations, both the length of the cranial base and the angle formed by it with the ear-eye horizontal decline, with the exception, however, of the Koskimo deformation which shows a decided increase in all the three factors under discussion.

One is tempted, then, to assume that the length of the cranial base and especially its angle undergo certain modifications due to deformation. The fundamental uniformity of the Cowichan and Chinook devices which center their greatest strain over the forehead somewhat vertically, may indirectly exercise a certain amount of pressure upon the cranial base, thus impeding the latter's erection. This, in proportion with the increasing strains in the Cowichan-Chinook deformations, may show in the gradual decrease in the size of the nasion-basion length and the cranio-basal angle. The peculiarity, on the other hand, of the Koskimo deformation, resulting in the removal or transition of the deforming strain to the posterior part of the skull, may suggest a freer development of the cranial base, and even afford an opportunity for its rise. This may be recognized by the increase of both the cranio-basal length and the angle over the Cowichan and Chinook stages and, in the case of the angle, also over the Undeformed, while the lengths fall slightly short of the Undeformed length. One is also tempted to assume that the cranial capacity profits by deformation, the latter perhaps affording certain stimuli for enforced expansion in the directions of greatest stress (see p. 32). Speculation of this sort, however, must remain rather vague, since experiment is out of the question.

*) See fig. 18.

FORAMEN MAGNUM.

1. Length of foramen magnum.

Summary 45.
Averages of the length of the foramen magnum.

Sex, Age	Undeformed				Deformation according to the three modes											
					Cowichan				Chinook				Koskimo			
	Cases	Range	Average	σ	Cases	Range	Average	σ	Cases	Range	Average	σ	Cases	Range	Average	σ
♂	74	31–44	36.2	± 2.25	72	29–43	33.4	± 2.50	57	28–41	34.3	± 2.35	103	30–41	34.5	± 2.15
♀	32	31–40	34.4	± 1.83	24	30–38	33.5	± 2.12	25	30–36	32.7	± 1.23	36	29–36	32.7	± 2.12
juv.	1	—	37.0	—	2	31; 36	33.5	—	4	30–35	33.0	—	2	33; 34	33.5	—
inf.	9	32–41	35.9	—	6	29–37	33.2	—	5	30–37	33.4	—	4	34–38	35.5	—

Summary 45 reveals only slight differences in the lengths of the foramen magnum. The Undeformed have the highest averages with 36.2 mm. for the males and 34.4 mm. for the females. They are followed in decreasing order by the Koskimo, Chinook and Cowichan deformations, in which latter the averages at 33.4 mm. and 33.5 mm. are quite uniform in the sexes. The lowest averages, however, are those of the Chinook and Koskimo females at 32.7 mm. Sex differences in this measurement, which is naturally a short one, are very slight and even nil in the Cowichan deformation. The immature averages as well as the ranges are similar to the adult ones. None of the immature values lies below the starting point of the adult ranges, their highest values even exceeding the highest female ones in three of the four divisions. The female ranges throughout are less extended than the male ranges. The highest individual value is at 44 mm. in the Undeformed males.

Slight differences are likewise manifested by some of the Undeformed group means, the highest being that of the Eskimo males at 37.1 mm., the Haida males following with 35.7 mm. The group means of the deformed skulls show even more uniform results.

The standard deviation is around ± 2 in all the divisions.

2. Width of foramen magnum.

The differences in the width of the foramen magnum are still less significant than those for its length. The highest averages, as specified in *summary 46* are held by the Chinook and Koskimo males at 30.4 mm. each. Both the Undeformed males and those deformed in the Cowichan fashion have averages of 29.6 mm. The female averages fall a trifle lower. The greatest sex difference is 2.4 mm. in the Koskimo deformation, 1.3 mm. in the Chinook deformation, 1 mm. and even

Summary 46.
Averages of the foramen magnum width.

Sex, Age	Undeformed				Deformation according to the three modes											
					Cowichan				Chinook				Koskimo			
	Cases	Range	Average	σ	Cases	Range	Average	σ	Cases	Range	Average	σ	Cases	Range	Average	σ
♂	73	26–38	29.6	± 2.04	72	24–35	29.6	± 2.25	57	27–35	30.4	± 1.91	103	25–35	30.4	± 2.50
♀	32	26–32	28.6	± 1.76	24	23–33	28.8	± 2.09	25	26–32	29.1	± 1.86	36	24–32	28.0	± 1.91
juv.	1	—	25.0	—	2	26; 31	28.5	—	4	27–31	28.5	—	2	29; 30	29.5	—
inf.	9	28–30	29.0	—	6	26–30	27.7	—	5	27–29	28.0	—	4	27–27	27.0	—

less in the Undeformed skulls and the Cowichan deformation. These differences as well as those between the matures and immatures are to be judged from the view point of physical size only.

The group means show such close similarity that their discussion is unnecessary.

This holds also true for the ranges, with the exception, possibly, of the Chinook deformation, in which the range extends from 27 mm. to 35 mm., or nine units, in the males, and from 26 mm. to 32 mm., or seven units, in the females, while all the other ranges are somewhat more extended.

These conditions are further illustrated by almost uniform variabilities around ± 2.

3. Foramen magnum index.

Contrary to what might have been expected from the relative uniformity of the length and width averages of the occipital foramen, the averages of the foramen magnum index vary somewhat in the four divisions. The width, particularly, is almost uniform in the four divisions. The slight variations in the width and the more obvious differences in the length are revealed in the index. The Undeformed adults whose average length was the greatest, have an index of 82 plus in both sexes.

Summary 47.
Averages of the foramen magnum index.

Sex, Age	Undeformed				Deformation according to the three modes											
					Cowichan				Chinook				Koskimo			
	Cases	Range	Average	σ	Cases	Range	Average	σ	Cases	Range	Average	σ	Cases	Range	Average	σ
♂	73	62.8–106.3	82.0	± 6.98	71	71.4–106.3	86.9	± 7.09	57	73.7–100.0	89.1	± 5.85	103	71.4–106.4	86.1	± 6.21
♀	32	70.3–96.9	82.9	± 6.41	24	76.7–96.7	86.0	± 4.50	25	83.9–100.0	88.7	± 3.88	36	74.3–100.0	86.7	± 6.58
juv.	1	—	67.6	—	2	83.9; 86.1	85.0	—	4	82.4–90.0	86.5	—	2	85.5–90.9	88.1	—
inf.	9	70.7–93.8	83.2	—	6	77.1–89.7	83.6	—	5	75.7–93.3	84.2	—	4	71.0–79.4	76.2	—

They are followed in *summary 47* by the Cowichan and Koskimo deformations with averages of 86 plus in the sexes, while the highest index averages are those of the Chinook who possess the relatively greatest width. The male index here is 89.1 and the female 88.7. In other words, the Chinook have a more rounded occipital foramen. It is less wide in the Cowichan and Koskimo divisions, and least in the Undeformed. It is also in the latter division that as low an individual index as 62.8 is found which, in fact, is the lowest of the entire series.

The index of the Undeformed infantiles is greater at 83.2 than that of the adults, and coincides with the index of the Cowichan infantiles at 83.6. The Chinook infantiles range only a little higher with an average of 84.2. The remaining four Koskimo infantiles present a pronounced decline. Their average is 76.2, the lowest in the entire series, indicating a relatively narrow and, at the same time, long foramen magnum.

Among the group means of the Undeformed, those of the Eskimo and the Chukchee are noticeably low. Their males register 78.7 and 78.8, their females 80.4, and the single Chukchee female 75.0. The Haida and Athapascan form the other extreme with male means of 84.1 and 85.7, while the Haida females register 85.8. In a few cases the Cowichan division deviates greatly from the total average. There are, for instance, the Nanaimo at 93.0, the Nanaimo females rising only to 88.2. The group means of the Koskimo deformation do not manifest any unusual deviations. They are grouped in a restricted range around their total average and in no wise duplicate or corroborate the low infantile average of 76.2.

The variability centers in most of the cases around ± 6. It rises to ± 7.09 in the Cowichan males, while in the females it drops to ± 4.50, and in the Chinook females to ± 3.88.

4. Angular relation between the foraman magnum and ear-eye planes.

The angle formed by the foramen magnum plane with a parallel to the ear-eye horizontal passing through the basion is a positive one when the opisthion lies above the parallel; it is negative when it falls below, and neutral when the two lines coincide. These possibilities are schematically shown in

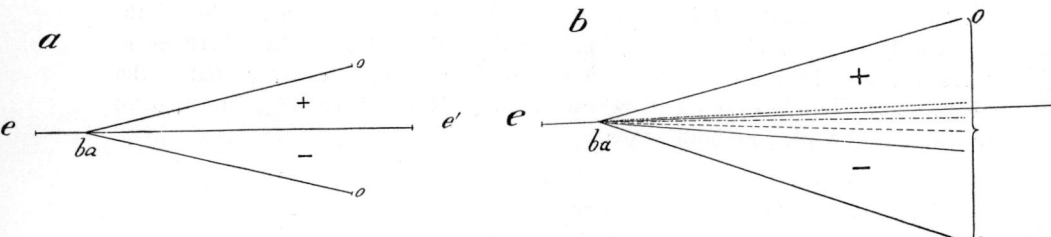

Fig. 17a. Scheme of possible deviations of the foramen magnum plane: +, deviation above, —, deviation below e–e', parallel to the ear-eye plane passing through ba, basion, o, opisthion.

Fig. 17b. Scheme of deviations of the foramen magnum plane from a parallel to the ear-eye plane laid through the basion, males and females combined. Lettering as in fig. 17a.

——— Undeformed:	∠ o–ba–e'	— 6.6°	total range:	
- - - - Cowichan :	„ „	— 3.3°	o–o,	
. . . . Chinook :	„ „	+ 0.3°	— 20° to 14°.	
—·—· Koskimo :	„ „	— 1.8°		

figure 17. All three stages occur among Hominidae, a negative angle signifying a progressive stage in the phylogenetic sense.

Differences in the angular relations between the two plane lines in question are quite apparent in the series under discussion and are treated in *summary 48*.

Summary 48.
Averages of the foramen magnum angle.

Sex, Age	Undeformed				Deformation according to the three modes											
					Cowichan				Chinook				Koskimo			
	Cases	Range	Average	σ	Cases	Range	Average	σ	Cases	Range	Average	σ	Cases	Range	Average	σ
♂	74	+6 to −19	−6.7	±8.43	72	+10 to −15	−3.6	±6.57	57	+14 to −15	+0.6	±6.01	103	+12 to −16	−1.1	±5.60
♀	29	+11 to −20	−6.5	±8.88	20	+3 to −11	−2.7	±4.64	24	+7 to −10	−0.5	±4.51	35	+5 to −15	−3.7	±6.27
juv.	1	—	+3.0	—	2	+10; −8	+1.0	—	4	+8 to 0	+3.0	—	2	−1 to −6	−3.5	—
inf.	7	−6 to −15	−10.7	—	4	−2 to −13	−7.5	—	5	+7 to +4	+5.2	—	5	−2 to −9	−5.6	—

The Undeformed crania have negative angles which amount to — 6.7° and — 6.5° in the sexes. The same condition, although less pronounced, prevails in the Cowichan and Koskimo deformations, where the male angles are — 3.6° and — 1.1° respectively, the female — 2.7° and — 3.7°. In the Chinook, both planes nearly coincide in the sexes, with averages of + 0.6° in the males and — 0.5° in the females. Sex differences are so slight in the divisions that in the Undeformed and in the Cowichan deformation the males exceed the females only by a fraction of a unit toward a more advanced state, while the Chinook and Koskimo divisions signify the reverse, the sex difference in the latter being as high as — 2.6° in favor of the females.

The ranges show fairly similar extensions. The greatest minus values are with the Undeformed, while the extreme plus values in the Chinook exceed those of the other divisions. The infantiles and juveniles of this same division differ considerably from those of the others. They emphasize the plus side of the measurement throughout the individual values, thus anticipating the final status of the adults. All the other immatures represent minus values with the exception of a single Cowichan juvenile and a single Undeformed juvenile.

The total adult range of variation comprising all the divisions and the divisional averages are shown in figure 17b, where male and female values are combined. The deviations of the foramen magnum plane above and below (+, —) a parallel to the ear-eye horizontal (e–e') passing through the basion (ba) is denoted by the two lines (ba–o) which comprise a range of variation from — 20° to + 14°. The divisional averages, males and females combined in each instance, are represented by lines radiating from ba to o in such a way that the Undeformed, the Cowichan and Koskimo deformations fall below, or to the minus side of, the ear-eye parallel and the Chinook above it. The averages, in the same order, amount to — 6.6°, — 3.3°, — 1.8°, and + 0.3°.

The group means show little diversity in comparison to the total average. Of the larger groups, the Eskimo and Chukchee with male means of — 7.1° and — 9.3° exceed the average, the Eskimo females outranging the female average and yielding a mean of — 9.8°. The latter also possess the highest individual value of all the groups, namely — 20°. The group means of the Haida and Athapascan, both male and female, range below the total average. High minus values are likewise conspicuous in the Lillooet and Nicola, with — 12.0° and — 8.0° in the males, and — 10.5° and — 8.5° in the females. In the Cowichan division it is the Nanaimo males with — 7.8°, the Yakima males with — 5.8°, and the male crania from "about Vancouver" with — 5.1°, which hold the highest minus values, while the female means conform fairly well with the female total average. In the Koskimo division, the high group means of the Nootka male angle of — 6.6°, and a female one of — 7.3° are rather surprising, while the Clayoquot means are — 5.3° and — 5.0° in the sexes, and in the Kwakiutl females — 5.0°. The remaining means are fairly uniform with the total average of the Koskimo deformation.

No doubt, deformation, particularly the extreme Chinook and Koskimo modes, has influenced the behavior of the foramen magnum angle. First of all, while the direct deformatory strain may be held responsible for any deviations from the normal, later on, the physical necessity of adjusting and correcting the changed conditions of the cephalic equilibrium may have a bearing on the cranial base and particularly on the declination of the foramen magnum. Racial differences can hardly be assumed here.

The variability is, peculiarly enough, smaller in the deformed divisions, where it amounts to a fraction over ± 6 in the Cowichan and Chinook males, and to a fraction over ± 4 in the females of the same divisions. The Koskimo division reverses this ratio, attaining ± 5.60 in the males and ± 6.27 in the females. All these figures are surpassed by the Undeformed, where both sexes show a variability of a fraction above ± 8. It is probable that the uniformity of distortion as brought about by uniform modes of deformation may also account for uniform physiological changes as demonstrated by a lesser variability in such a series.

5. Angular relation between cranial base and foramen magnum plane.

The angular relation of the cranial base (nasion-basion line) and the foramen magnum horizontal (basion-opisthion line) is best observed when oriented on the ear-eye plane, or rather its parallel passing through the basion. Correlative deviations are known to occur in this respect during the different age periods in the individual human being as well as phylogenetically.[41] If certain changes of angular relation of either of the two implicated lines were due to the effects of deformation, as has been assumed, it must now be shown whether a correlation can be stated between the same two lines in the different modes of deformation. The cranial base and the foramen magnum plane, representing the average conditions in the four divisions, males and females combined, are oriented on the ear-eye plane in figure 18.

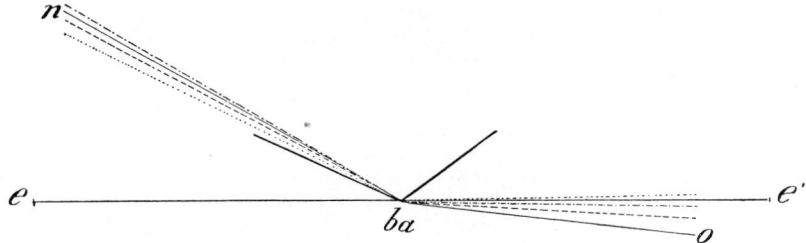

Fig. 18. Comparative scheme of divisional averages, males and females combined, of the cranio-basal ($\angle$ n–ba–e), foramen magnum ($\angle$ o–ba–e'), and basio-foramen magnum ($\angle$ n–ba–o) angles. e–e', parallel to ear-eye plane passing through ba, basion; n, nasion; o, opisthion.
——— Undeformed, - - - - Cowichan, ... Chinook, —·—· Koskimo deformations. — Orang-utan.

For phylogenetic considerations, an adult male Orang-utan (No. 124, American Museum of Natural History) was introduced into the figure. Its cranial base angle ($\angle$ n–ba–e) at 25° is smaller than any of those of the human divisions with which it is collated. The most remarkable discrepancy, however, lies

---

[41] *Birkner, F.*, 1913. Die Rassen und Völker der Menschheit. Berlin, 548 pp. (74).

in the position of the foramen magnum plane. With an angle ($\angle$ o–ba–e′) of $+37°$ it exceeds by far any human status.

Taking the Undeformed of the present series as a comparative model, their cranial base and foramen magnum angles amount to 30.1° and — 6.6°, the Cowichan deformation yields 28.6° and — 3.3°, and still smaller angles are produced by the Chinook at 28.2° and $+$ 0.3°. The Koskimo deformation upsets this apparent graded regularity, exceeding with 31.0° the averages of the angle of the cranial base as yielded by the other divisions, and falling with their foramen magnum angle of — 1.8° between the Cowichan and Chinook averages.

Summary 49.

Averages of the cranial base angles, males and females combined. Compare fig. 18.

Series	Angles of cranial base		
	cranio-basal $\angle$ n–ba–e	foramen magnum $\angle$ o–ba–e′	basio-foramen magnum $\angle$ n–ba–o*
Undeformed	30.1	— 6.6	156.5
Cowichan (deformation)	28.6	— 3.3	155.0
Chinook (deformation)	28.2	$+$ 0.3	151.5
Koskimo (deformation)	31.0	— 1.8	150.8
Orang-utan	25	$+$ 37	118.0

The tabular statement of *summary 49* aids in the identification of these conditions. A correlation is quite apparent here: when the angle of the cranial base decreases, as in the Cowichan and Chinook deformations, a corresponding decrease in the absolute value of the angle takes place in the declination of the foramen magnum plane. An increase, on the other hand, of the cranial base angle in the Koskimo division, even in excess of all the other divisions, is met with a slight increase also in the direction of the occipital foramen, its angle falling between the Chinook and Cowichan, as has been shown. The basio-foramen magnum angle, *Broca's* "angle basilaire", $\angle$ n–ba–o in *summary 49*, combines the results described, gradually declining, in the order: Undeformed, Cowichan, Chinook and Koskimo, with angles of 156.5°, 155.0°, 151.5° and 150.8°. It will be noticed, furthermore, that the slight deviation in the Koskimo from the order of decrease in the size of the foramen magnum angle, does not change the order of decrease in the size of the basio-foramen magnum angle, which places the Koskimo at the end of the divisional averages. The angle of the Orang-utan here amounts only to 118.0°.

* *Broca's* "angle basilaire."

FACE.

1. Upper facial height.

The predominance of the male over the female measurement is apparent in all the divisions and groups. According to *summary 50*, the Undeformed averages are 75.0 mm. and 70.2 mm. in

Summary 50.
Averages of the upper facial height.

Sex, Age	Undeformed				Deformation according to the three modes											
					Cowichan				Chinook				Koskimo			
	Cases	Range	Average	σ	Cases	Range	Average	σ	Cases	Range	Average	σ	Cases	Range	Average	σ
♂	76	65–85	75.0	± 4.38	81	62–86	72.8	± 4.75	56	68–83	73.6	± 3.34	102	64–89	76.0	± 4.74
♀	33	63–79	70.2	± 4.70	26	62–78	68.7	± 4.35	25	62–78	69.2	± 3.82	34	64–80	73.1	± 3.95
juv.	1	—	64.0	—	2	62;64	63.0	—	4	60–69	63.3	—	2	66;68	67.0	—
inf.	14	46–64	56.9	—	7	52–63	57.4	—	6	55–67	60.0	—	6	55–67	60.0	—

the sexes. The Cowichan and Chinook deformations, with averages of 72.8 mm. and 68.7 mm. in the former, and 73.6 mm. and 69.2 mm. in the latter, range below the Undeformed. The highest upper faces belong to the Koskimo deformation with 76.0 mm. in the males and 73.1 mm. in the females. The infantile averages, on the whole, range considerably below the adult, while the few juveniles hold an intermediate position between the immatures and the adults. The ranges are rather wide and cover values from 15 mm. to 26 mm. in the males of the different divisions, the smallest range belonging to the Chinook, the highest to the Koskimo, while the female ranges uniformly comprise seventeen units in each division.

In the Undeformed division, it is the Eskimo and the Haida who exceed the total averages with their means, all the other means ranging below. Distinct differences are also noticed in the Koskimo division, where the Koskimo proper lead with means of 80.2 mm. and 76.5 mm. in the sexes. They are followed by the Kwakiutl and Nimkish who conform rather with the divisional averages, while the Nootka and Clayoquot range below them.

Consulting *R. Martin's* (Lehrbuch, 1914, 790) table of averages, it will be noticed that all the averages and means of our series occupy rather high positions. *Martin's* highest averages are those for the Eskimo at 77.0 mm. and 72.0 mm. in the sexes, figures exceeded by our Koskimo group.

The variability is concentrated around ± 4, exceeding this figure in both sexes of the Undeformed and the Cowichan deformation and in the Koskimo males, while the females of this and the Chinook division vary at a figure below ± 4 in the sexes.

2. Bizygomatic breadth.

Summary 51.

Averages of the bizygomatic breadth.

Sex, Age	Undeformed				Deformation according to the three modes											
					Cowichan				Chinook				Koskimo			
	Cases	Range	Average	σ	Cases	Range	Average	σ	Cases	Range	Average	σ	Cases	Range	Average	σ
♂	70	125–156	138.5	± 6.78	65	125–163	142.7	± 8.34	57	133–151	141.8	± 5.07	99	128–153	138.4	± 6.10
♀	34	117–140	129.6	± 5.25	17	125–146	134.0	± 5.67	24	123–140	132.6	± 4.69	37	115–142	129.7	± 5.48
juv.	1	—	132	—	2	120; 128	124.0	—	4	112–126	120.0	—	2	124; 125	124.5	—
inf.	14	104–120	110.9	—	2	106; 120	113.0	—	6	108–120	116.8	—	6	110–117	111.3	—

Summary 51 shows the divisional averages of both the Undeformed and the Koskimo deformation to be identical in the sexes. The two remaining divisions of the Cowichan and Chinook deformations have higher averages, while throughout the series the sexes differ by about 9 mm. The infantile averages fall decidedly lower, which in the Cowichan and Chinook deformations conform proportionately with the higher adult averages of these divisions. The few juveniles fall between the averages of the adults and the infantiles. The divisional ranges show a rather wide extension, that of the Cowichan males being the greatest.

Since the bizygomatic breadth is an important factor in racial diagnosis, a certain significance must be attached to the group means. With slight modifications, all the group means are in accordance with the divisional averages which maintain similarly high places in *R. Martin's* (Lehrbuch, 1914, 790/91) list of bizygomatic averages. This also holds true for the slightly smaller averages of the Undeformed and Koskimo deformation.

Taking the Undeformed as a comparative model, the broadening of the bizygomatic breadth by means of their special deformatory practices, might be suspected in the coast Salish (Cowichan) and Chinook deformations. It is to be observed, however, that the more intensive application of the deforming devices in the Chinook has not brought about a proportionately greater bizygomatic average breadth, which is slightly lower than that of the Cowichan. It will be remembered that the minimum and maximum breadths of the frontal bone in those two divisions had also undergone broadening changes (see *summaries* 28 and 29), but that the Chinook as the more strenuously affected by antero-posterior compression had also produced the higher averages. This observation, i. e., the more pronounced frontal in correlation with a lesser bizygomatic broadening in the Chinook deformation, and the reverse in the Cowichan deformation, will at least let the direct deformatory effect on the broadening of the face appear somewhat doubtful. The Koskimo method apparently has neither changed the feature here discussed nor the frontal breadth, both of which conform with those of the Undeformed.

The variability is rather irregular. It is grouped around ± 5 in all the females and in the Chinook males; it rises above ± 6 in the Undeformed and Koskimo males, and even above ± 8 in the Cowichan males. In these the widest range was also found.

3. Upper facial index.

The differences in the two principal diameters of the upper face, demonstrated by the divisional averages and group means discussed above, produce indices which particularly emphasize the influence of the varying bizygomatic or facial breadth on them. They are specified in *summary 52*.

Summary 52.

Averages of the upper facial index.

Sex, Age	Undeformed				Deformation according to the three modes											
					Cowichan				Chinook				Koskimo			
	Cases	Range	Average	σ	Cases	Range	Average	σ	Cases	Range	Average	σ	Cases	Range	Average	σ
♂	69	41.4–61.8	54.1	± 3.80	64	44.4–60.2	51.4	± 3.46	56	46.8–57.6	52.0	± 2.16	97	48.1–65.4	55.4	± 3.42
♀	32	49.6–61.0	54.2	± 3.49	16	46.3–58.5	52.6	± 3.81	24	47.7–56.8	52.2	± 2.25	33	47.2–61.1	56.1	± 3.81
juv.	1	—	48.0	—	2	49.6; 51.7	50.7	—	4	49.2–54.3	52.5	—	2	53.2; 54.4	53.8	—
inf.	14	41.8–58.7	51.0	—	2	49.1; 52.5	50.8	—	6	47.5–56.8	51.4	—	5	49.6–61.5	54.2	—

The greater facial breadth in the Cowichan and Chinook divisions produce lower indices, with averages of about 52 for the sexes. The small excess of facial breadth in the Cowichan thus appears to be compensated in the index by the somewhat greater height of the Chinook faces. The Undeformed and the Koskimo deformation, on the other hand, have index averages which indicate the somewhat higher Koskimo faces, while the breadths coincide in both divisions. The Koskimo averages with 55.4 in the males and 56.1 in the females, therefore, slightly exceed those of the Undeformed at 54.1 and 54.2. All the infantile averages, indicating relatively broader faces, range below those of the adults. They yield about 51 in the Undeformed and in the Cowichan and Chinook deformations, while the Koskimo infantile average of 54.2 denotes a higher face, which is already noticeable in early age. The few juveniles scarcely submit to comparative deductions.

Of the ranges, that of the Undeformed males shows the greatest extension with twenty-one units, all the others being considerably shorter.

The averages of the Undeformed, the Cowichan and Chinook divisions thus are seen to be mesēnic with a tendency toward leptēny in the Undeformed, and toward euryēny in the Cowichan and Chinook. The Koskimo averages, on the contrary, are leptēnic, just across the line of demarcation between mesēny and leptēny. The averages of all the immatures are mesēnic in the infantiles with a tendency toward euryēny also in the Undeformed, the Koskimo immatures manifesting an inclination toward leptēny, following the Koskimo adults. The juveniles fall in line with the infantiles.

The group means of the immatures exhibit conditions which in the larger groups might be taken as tribal characteristics. The Eskimo, for instance, with a male mean of 55.7 and a female one of 55.5 prove to be higher and less broad-faced than the Haida with index means of 52.5 and 54.0. The Athapascan male mean of 56.8 — the single Athapascan female has an index of 54.7 — ranges with the Eskimo mean. There is to be noticed, then, a propensity toward leptēny in the Athapascan and Eskimo, both, in fact, possessing leptēnic means, while the Haida and Chukchee means occupy positions in the lower mesēnic domains. The varying means of the smaller groups present rather individual conditions, although the Lillooet male mean of 49.3 and the index of the single Spences Bridge male at 41.4 are significantly low. The Cowichan means indicate conditions between euryēny and mesēny. This is also the case with the Chinook, as mentioned before. The leptēnic Koskimo group means of the Kwakiutl and Nimkish with 55.8 and 55.3 in the sexes of the former, and 55.5 and 58.0 in the latter, are exceeded by a still greater degree of leptēny in the Koskimo themselves, their means amounting to 57.7 in the males and 56.4 in the females. The Nootka and Clayoquot turn out low mesēnic means save for the two Clayoquot females who have a leptēnic mean of 57.4.

The variability in all the classes oscillates around ± 3.

4. Facial length.[42]

Summary 53.

Averages of the facial length.

Sex, Age	Undeformed				Deformation according to the three modes											
					Cowichan				Chinook				Koskimo			
	Cases	Range	Average	σ	Cases	Range	Average	σ	Cases	Range	Average	σ	Cases	Range	Average	σ
♂	71	88–111	101.6	± 4.67	68	90–117	101.6	± 5.24	56	88–112	101.7	± 5.58	99	88–108	100.7	± 4.67
♀	31	88–105	97.6	± 4.06	21	85–107	97.1	± 6.01	24	88–108	97.2	± 4.82	34	90–103	97.8	± 4.22
juv.	1	—	94.0	—	2	89; 89	89.0	—	4	85–95	91.3	—	2	88; 94	91.0	—
inf.	8	79–87	82.3	—	4	80–89	82.5	—	5	81–90	86.2	—	3	75–83	78.7	—

The length of the face, as revealed in *summary 53*, appears to be a measurement of unusual constancy in all the four divisions. The male averages amount to 101 mm. plus in the Undeformed and the Cowichan and Chinook deformations, and to 100.7 mm. in the Koskimo deformation. All the female averages at 97 mm. plus thus give rise to uniform sex differences of about 4 mm. The infantile averages at 82 mm. plus in the Undeformed and the Cowichan deformation, naturally, fall distinctly short of the adult ones. Diverging from these, the Chinook infantiles are registered with 86.2 mm. and the Koskimo only at 78.7 mm., due very probably to their limited numbers. The few juveniles range between the adult and infantile ages.

The group means, in general, repeat the conditions of the divisional averages. The Haida means, however, at 104.5 mm. in the males, and 99.8 mm. in the females, might be pointed out as exceeding the rest of the groups. The means of the latter conform fairly well with the divisional averages, although it must be borne in mind that means of only a limited number of individuals seem at times to distort the average proportions. Such a consideration is also in order for the Cowichan deformation. The very slight inclination toward smaller means in the Koskimo division as indicated by its slightly lower male average, is offset by the group means of the Koskimo proper, where both the males and females exceed the related tribes with means of 102.2 mm. and 100.0 mm. in the sexes.

The variability lies a little above ± 4 in the Undeformed and Koskimo of both sexes, and in the Chinook females. It rises above ± 5 in the males of the Cowichan and Chinook deformations and above ± 6 in the Cowichan females.

---

[42] The basion-prosthion, or facial length diameter is discussed here because it forms one of the sides of the facial triangle (see part 5 of this chapter), in whose construction the facial length averages are employed. The averages for the total facial height and the lower facial length, involving the lower jaw for one of the measuring points (gnathion), have not been treated here on account of the relative paucity of complete crania. The individual measurements those of two diameters, however, will be found recorded with the other measurements in the appended tables.

5. Facial triangle.

The facial triangles of the four divisions composed of the average diameters, males and females combined, of the cranial base (nasion-basion), the upper facial height (nasion-prosthion) and the facial length (prosthion-basion) are seen superposed in figure 19, and oriented on a parallel to the ear-eye plane (e–e') passing through the basion. After constructing the cranial

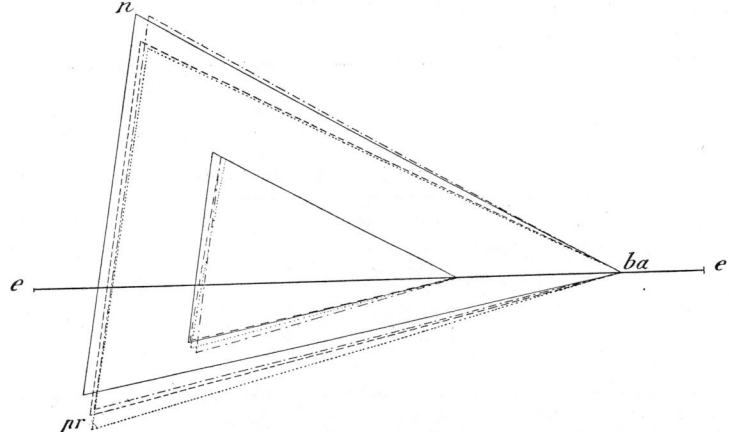

Fig. 19. Superposition of facial triangles oriented on a parallel to the ear-eye plane (e–e') passing through ba, basion, the basia coinciding; n, nasion; pr, prosthion; males and females combined. ———— Undeformed; - - - - Cowichan; . . . . Chinook; – · – · Koskimo deformations. Reduced.
Inner triangles the same triangles with coinciding cranial base lines (n–ba). $^1/_2$ of outer triangles.

base lines of the four divisions at their average angularities on the e–e' horizontal, the basia coinciding, the facial length diameter was indicated in each case by means of the compass, the upper facial height diameter being similarly drawn to intersect the arc indicating the facial length, the intersecting points of the two arcs being the prosthia. The facial triangle of the Undeformed being taken as a comparative model, an examination of the other triangles shows the cranial bases and the facial length diameters at variance to a greater extent than the facial height diameters. It will be noted that the cranial bases of the Cowichan and Chinook, in this order of enumeration, pass in close proximity below the Undeformed cranial base as well as below the Undeformed facial length line. The Koskimo cranial base, on the other hand, exceeds the Undeformed one, as well as the Undeformed facial length line. It does not, however, pass below the two facial length lines of the Cowichan and Chinook divisions, but moves between these and the facial length of the Undeformed. This latter fact is not astonishing because the facial height of the Koskimo division exceeds that of the other three. The more significant features, however, in the comparative view of the facial triangles are, first, the apparent depression of the facial triangles of the Cowichan and Chinook and, secondly, the obvious elevation of the Koskimo triangle. Both conditions are quite probably the effects of the two distinctly different modes of deformation. Even the effect of the more strenuous pressure applied to the Chinook forehead, which influences the entire facial region there, may be recognized in contradistinction to the effects of the less intensive pressure as practiced by the Cowichan. The Koskimo deformation, on the other hand, may have only a secondary effect on the facial region. The influence of its pressure being exerted backward rather than downward as in the Cowichan and Chinook modes, tempts one to assume that the slight elevation of the Koskimo triangle is due to their special mode of deformation. The facial height lines of the three deformed divisions forming the anterior sides of the facial triangle and depending, of course, on the average extensions of the cranial base and facial length diameters, are seen to fall short of the Undeformed. It may be rather deluding, however, to attribute this particular feature to the deformatory influences, all the more so since their divisional angularities hardly differ from the status of the Undeformed. The inserted scheme of triangles with the coinciding cranial base lines (n–ba) brings out still better the differences discussed in the preceding paragraphs.

6. Profilation.

a. Profile angle of the upper face.

The angular relation between the nasion-prosthion line and a parallel to the ear-eye plane passing through the prosthion shows the greatest angles in the Undeformed, as seen in *summary 54*, where an average of 82.3° is attained by both males and females.

Summary 54.
Average of the profile angle of the upper face.

Sex, Age	Undeformed				Deformation according to the three modes											
					Cowichan				Chinook				Koskimo			
	Cases	Range	Average	σ	Cases	Range	Average	σ	Cases	Range	Average	σ	Cases	Range	Average	σ
♂	69	72–92	82.3	± 3.96	72	72–89	81.3	± 3.31	55	73–87	80.7	± 3.67	102	74–88	81.1	± 3.22
♀	31	77–88	82.3	± 2.67	23	74–88	80.7	± 3.83	25	71–86	79.5	± 3.91	33	76–86	81.2	± 3.32
juv.	1	—	82.0	—	2	81; 82	81.5	—	4	73–83	79.5	—	2	76; 86	81.0	—
inf.	10	73–90	85.8	—	4	84–86	85.3	—	5	77–83	79.8	—	5	80–88	85.4	—

The Cowichan and Koskimo deformations fall only slightly lower with male and female averages of 81.3° and 80.7° in the former, and 81.5° and 81.2° in the latter. The lowest averages of 80.7° and 79.5° in the sexes are furnished by the Chinook. The sex differences are only nominal, amounting to fractions of a unit in the Cowichan and Koskimo divisions, while in the Chinook the sex difference rises to 1.2°, the averages of the Undeformed having been shown to be alike in both. The averages of all the divisions are thus to be characterized as mesognathous, except the Chinook females who at 79.5° are prognathous, although closely approximating mesognathy. The mesognathous averages, on the other hand, manifest an inclination toward prognathy. Only the Undeformed with their average of 83.2° in the sexes, appear to be a little more advanced in mesognathy, occupying nearly an intermediate position between mesognathy and orthognathy. The infantile averages with 85° plus in the Undeformed and in the Cowichan and Koskimo deformations, just enter the orthognathous domain the lower boundary of which lies at 85°. The few juveniles in these divisions conform with the adult status. An interesting exception, however, is afforded by the Chinook infantiles with 79.8°, who give rise to a prognathous average, in which they are joined by the juveniles with an average of 79.5°, both conforming with the status of the Chinook females, who also give a prognathous average, as just pointed out.

The group means, in general, in the Undeformed as well as in the Cowichan and Koskimo deformations, corroborate the mesognathous condition of their averages. The examination of the ranges, however, reveals the fact that in all the divisions including the Undeformed, prognathy as well as orthognathy are represented, although in various degrees as shown in *summary 55* of

Summary 55.

Profile angle of the upper face: actual and percental frequency.

	Undeformed			Deformation according to the three modes								
				Cowichan			Chinook			Koskimo		
Range	Cases		%	Cases		%	Cases		%	Cases		%
	♂	♀	♂+♀	♂	♀	♂+♀	♂	♀	♂+♀	♂	♀	♂+♀
71–79	12	4	16.0	16	8	25.3	17	12	35.8	31	13	32.6
80–84	42	21	63.0	42	12	56.8	30	11	50.6	57	17	54.8
85–92	15	6	21.0	14	3	17.9	9	2	13.6	14	3	12.6

actual and percental distribution. The greatest number of cases is assembled in the mesognathous domain of each of the four divisions, amounting to 63% in the Undeformed, and diminishing over 56% in the Cowichan deformation to 51% in the Chinook, but rising again to 54% in the Koskimo division. A similar gradation may be observed in the orthognathous domain where, however, both the Chinook and Koskimo deformations attain the smallest frequency of 13% each. Much more decided is the increase of prognathism, rising from 16% in the Undeformed to 25% in the Cowichan division, and even to 36% in the Chinook, while the Koskimo deformation with 33% ranges only slightly below the Chinook.

It is not entirely improbable that deformatory influences are the cause to an appreciable degree of increase in prognathy in the order: Undeformed, Cowichan, Chinook. The conditions in the Koskimo are nearly uniform with those of the Chinook, signifying the similarity of effects of extreme deformation which result, if only to a slight degree, in the retraction of the upper region of the face and of the forehead.

The variability lies between ± 3 and ± 4 in all the classes except the Undeformed females who attain ± 2.67.

b. Profile angle of the middle face.

This angle formed by the nasion-nasospinale line and a parallel to the ear-eye horizontal passing through the nasospinale, differs from the former by several degrees in favor of an inclination toward orthognathy, which is the condition generally observed in the human cranium.

Summary 56.

Averages of the profile angle of the middle face.

Sex, Age	Undeformed				Deformation according to the three modes											
					Cowichan				Chinook				Koskimo			
	Cases	Range	Average	σ	Cases	Range	Average	σ	Cases	Range	Average	σ	Cases	Range	Average	σ
♂	68	72–93	84.6	± 4.44	71	74–92	84.1	± 3.89	54	74–89	83.8	± 4.36	96	76–93	83.0	± 3.42
♀	31	78–91	84.6	± 3.01	22	76–91	83.5	± 3.81	25	73–88	81.8	± 4.13	32	77–89	82.7	± 3.68
juv.	—	—	—	—	2	83;84	83.5	—	4	74–84	80.8	—	2	79;92	84.0	—
inf.	10	73–94	86.6	—	3	85–87	86.0	—	5	79–84	81.4	—	5	79–92	86.6	—

Summary 56 shows all the divisions to have mesognathous averages in the sexes. Sex differences are limited to fractions of a unit in the Cowichan and Koskimo deformations, rising, however, to 2° in the Chinook deformation, all in favor of the males, while the Undeformed present equal averages of 84.6° in the sexes. As in the profile angle of the upper face, the angles of middle face profilation are exceeded by those of the infantiles, which are orthognathous at 86.6° in the Undeformed and Koskimo divisions, and 86.0° in the Cowichan deformation. The Chinook infantiles are mesognathous and so are the juveniles of the same division at 80.8°. The Cowichan and Koskimo juveniles are also mesognathous with 83.5° and 84.0°, the latter rising above the Koskimo adults.

Summary 57.

Profile angle of the middle face: actual and percental frequency.

Range	Undeformed			Deformation according to the three modes								
				Cowichan			Chinook			Koskimo		
	Cases		%	Cases		%	Cases		%	Cases		%
	♂	♀	♂+♀	♂	♀	♂+♀	♂	♀	♂+♀	♂	♀	♂+♀
72–79	6	1	7.0	6	2	8.6	13	6	24.1	12	6	14.1
80–84	27	14	41.5	31	11	45.2	29	12	51.8	56	14	54.7
85–92	33	16	49.5	34	9	46.2	12	7	24.1	27	12	30.4
93	2	—	2.0	—	—	—	—	—	—	1	—	0.8

Consulting *summary 57* of percental distribution, it is readily seen that the percentage of prognathism is considerably reduced here as compared with the same figures of the upper face in *summary 55*. The middle face angle shows a prognathous frequency of 7°/₀ in the Undeformed, and of 9°/₀ in the Cowichan deformation. Much higher, but nevertheless considerably lower than the percentage of prognathism of the upper face, is that of the middle face in the Chinook and Koskimo divisions, with 24°/₀ in the former and 14°/₀ in the latter. Orthognathy, on the other hand, gains markedly, yielding 51°/₀ in the Undeformed, 46°/₀ in the Cowichan, 24°/₀ in the Chinook and 31°/₀ in the Koskimo divisions. Included in these latter figures is hyperorthognathy at 2°/₀ in the Undeformed and at 1°/₀ in the Koskimo. The remaining percentages in the four divisions belong to mesognathy. It is thus shown that with a lessening degree of prognathy the highest frequency is shifted to orthognathy in the Undeformed and Cowichan deformation, while the amount of mesognathy remains constant in the Chinook and Koskimo deformations, although orthognathy increases considerably here at the expense of prognathism.

The variability turns out a trifle higher here than that observed for the profile angle of the upper face. It falls above ± 4 in the Undeformed males, and in the Chinook of both sexes. All the other classes vary between ± 3 and ± 4.

c. Profile angle of the pars alveolaris.

Corresponding with the nature of this angle prognathy is much more evident in the pars alveolaris than the other facial regions concerned.

Summary 58.

Averages of the profile angle of the pars alveolaris.

Sex, Age	Undeformed				Deformation according to the three modes											
					Cowichan				Chinook				Koskimo			
	Cases	Range	Average	σ	Cases	Range	Average	σ	Cases	Range	Average	σ	Cases	Range	Average	σ
♂	69	61–68	75.9	± 5.96	72	58–85	72.9	± 6.35	55	61–88	75.9	± 6.63	103	62–90	75.2	± 5.77
♀	31	61–83	72.9	± 5.20	22	61–83	72.6	± 5.73	26	56–83	71.2	± 6.26	32	56–79	72.8	± 4.71
juv.	—	—	—	—	2	74; 75	74.5	—	3	66–80	72.3	—	2	68; 79	73.5	—
inf.	10	63–90	81.0	—	4	83–86	84.5	—	5	67–77	72.4	—	3	78–88	82.0	—

Rather low averages are recorded in *summary 58* for all the classes. The Undeformed, Chinook and Koskimo have male averages of 75° plus, while the males of the Cowichan deformation amount only to 72.9°, and conform thus with the female status in the Undeformed and in the Cowichan and Koskimo deformations. The Chinook females yield an average only of 71.2°. The infantile averages range almost uniformly far above the adults in illustration of the development of the alveolar region only just begun in the immature skull. The Undeformed infantiles show an average of 81.0°, four Cowichan of 84.5° and three Koskimo of 82.0°. The five Chinook infantiles, peculiarly enough, anticipating the adult status, produce an average only of 72.4°, which rises slightly above the Chinook female average of 71.2°. The few juveniles conform rather with the adults. The individual status of alveolar prognathy is quite variable within an ethnic group, and since the ranges of variation are, as a rule greatly extended, as they also are in this particular case, the distribution of the individual values within the ranges seems to be of greater interest than the behavior of the group means. From *summary 59* it will readily be recognized that the

Summary 59.

Profile angle of the pars alveolaris: actual and percental frequency.

Range	Undeformed			Deformation according to the three modes.								
				Cowichan			Chinook			Koskimo		
	Cases		%	Cases		%	Cases		%	Cases		%
	♂	♀	♂+♀	♂	♀	♂+♀	♂	♀	♂+♀	♂	♀	♂+♀
56–59	—	—	—	1	—	1.1	—	2	2.5	—	1	0.7
60–69	10	9	19.0	21	7	29.8	11	5	20.0	17	5	16.3
70–79	37	18	55.0	38	12	53.2	25	15	50.0	64	26	66.7
80–84	19	4	23.0	9	3	12.7	15	3	22.5	21	—	15.6
85–90	3	—	3.0	3	—	3.2	4	—	5.0	1	—	0.7

greatest number of individuals are found assembled in the prognathous group of the ranges in all four divisions. The frequencies of prognathy are, therefore, very high with 55% in the Undeformed, and 53%, 50% and 67% in the Cowichan, Chinook and Koskimo divisions, males and females combined. These figures are increased by additional percentages of hyperprognathy and ultraprognathy, which increase the entire amount of prognathy to 74% in the Undeformed, and 84% in the Cowichan, 73% in the Chinook and 83.7% in the Koskimo deformations. The remainder belongs to mesognathy, and even orthognathy is represented to a small degree in each division, the lowest at 0.7% in that of the Koskimo.

As usual, the variability here is rather high. It centers around ± 6, while the Koskimo females attain only ± 4.71.

CRANIO-FACIAL PROPORTIONS.

1. Transverse cranio-facial index.

The two factors involved in the transverse cranio-facial index are quite variable in the human races. The bizygomatic breadth, however, being the more stable measurement in the series under investigation, disparities among the divisional averages of the transverse cranial-facial index must rather be sought in connection with the more variable maximum breadth of the skull.

Summary 60.

Averages of the transverse cranio-facial index.

Sex, Age	Undeformed				Deformation according to the three modes											
					Cowichan				Chinook				Koskimo			
	Cases	Range	Average	σ	Cases	Range	Average	σ	Cases	Range	Average	σ	Cases	Range	Average	σ
♂	70	90.7–108.5	98.5	± 4.09	64	81.8–104.9	94.1	± 5.13	57	81.3–99.3	90.8	± 3.61	98	87.3–111.7	99.1	± 4.08
♀	34	87.0–103.8	95.3	± 3.47	17	84.5–99.3	92.0	± 3.80	24	82.3–99.3	88.6	± 3.78	37	86.2–104.0	96.6	± 3.93
juv.	1	—	93.0	—	2	86.3; 86.6	86.5	—	4	79.2–84.5	80.9	—	2	84.4; 94.6	89.5	—
inf.	13	69.4–85.4	79.6	—	2	75.5; 79.1	77.3	—	6	73.9–81.1	76.7	—	6	79.1–89.3	82.9	—

In *summary 60* the Undeformed are listed with averages of 98.5 and 95.3 in the sexes. The insignificantly higher Koskimo averages of 99.1 and 96.6 are due to a narrower cranial breadth, the differences in this measurement between the Undeformed and Koskimo averages, however, amounting only to 2.1 mm. in the males and 2.5 mm. in the females. The considerably broader skulls of the Cowichan and Chinook deformations are determined only to a slight extent by correlatively and proportionately broader faces. The facial breadth of the two last named divisions exceeds, on an average, the breadth of the Undeformed faces by 3.9 mm. and 4.4 mm. in the Cowichan males and females, while the Chinook figures exceed the Undeformed only by 3.3 mm. and 3.0 mm. But it is here, as has been mentioned before, that the index average is distinctly altered by the maximum breadth of the skull brought about by deformation, which exceeds the Undeformed by 10.4 mm. and 7.9 mm. in the two sexes of the Cowichan deformation, and by 15.5 mm. and 13.3 mm. in the Chinook deformation. These decrease, therefore, to 94.1 and 90.8 in the Cowichan and Chinook males and to 92.0 and 88.6 in the females of the same divisions. The sex differences are thus shown to amount to two or three units in each case in favor of the males, which is in accord with the general behavior of the sex averages of this index. The infantile averages fall far below those of the adults, indicating the undeveloped facial breadth of the immatures.

They are 79.6 for the Undeformed, and rise from 76.3 in the Chinook to 77.3 in the Cowichan and to 82.9 in the Koskimo. The juveniles with more matured, i. e., broader faces, also produce higher indices without, however, reaching the adults.

The means of the larger groups in the Undeformed division scarcely vary. Low values in the Lillooet and Kamloops males at 95.4 and 95.2, respectively, the females yielding 91.7 and 90.1, are probably of some significance, indicating a broader head in the one and a narrower face in the other group. The Eskimo and Haida hold uniform male means of 98 plus, while means of 97 plus are attained by the Athapascan and Chukchee. Similar disparities are noticed in the Cowichan division, where seven Tsimshian males, for instance, produce an average of 99.0, while six Nanaimo males have only 91.3. The Koskimo groups, on the other hand, are fairly alike in their means.

The variability is assembled around ± 4 and below this figure in all the classes, but rises to ± 5.13 in the Cowichan males.

2. Jugo-frontal index.

The shape of the face, particularly with regard to its lateral outlines, depends greatly on the proportional behavior, superiorly, between the bizygomatic and minimum frontal breadths, and inferiorly between the bizygomatic breadth and the bigonial width of the lower jaw. The two indices computed from these quantities and to be discussed in the following paragraphs are: (1) the jugo-frontal and (2) the jugo-mandibular index.

Summary 61.

Averages of the jugo-frontal index

Sex, Age	Undeformed				Deformation according to the three modes									
					Cowichan				Chinook				Koskimo			
	Cases	Range	Average	σ	Cases	Range	Average	σ	Cases	Range	Average	σ	Cases	Range	Average	σ
♂	70	59.7–77.2	68.1	± 3.48	63	54.2–75.0	66.7	± 4.38	57	63.9–75.5	68.4	± 2.88	99	60.6–74.8	68.0	± 3.32
♀	34	64.0–84.5	70.6	± 4.29	18	63.9–77.2	68.9	± 3.77	24	65.4–76.9	71.0	± 3.08	37	62.4–77.4	70.7	± 4.07
juv.	1	—	73.5	—	2	69.0;72.5	70.8	—	4	72.5–80.4	76.8	—	2	77.4;78.4	77.9	—
inf.	14	74.8–83.3	80.7	—	2	79.2;81.7	80.5	—	6	78.8–81.5	80.5	—	5	79.5–92.7	83.2	—

The jugo-frontal index, as specified in *summary 61*, yields averages of noteworthy similarity in the sexes of the Undeformed and the Chinook and Koskimo deformations, the male averages amounting to 68.1, 68.4 and 68.0 in the divisions enumerated, and the female to 70.6, 71.0 and 70.7. An examination of the two factors involved in the index shows the exact equality of their average values in the Undeformed and Koskimo deformation, the minimum frontal breadth yielding 94.1 mm. and 91.3 mm. in the sexes of the two divisions, the bizygomatic breadth 138.4 mm. and 129.7 mm. The Chinook figures here are at 141.8 mm. and 132.6 mm. But as the increase occurs at an even rate in both factors, they give rise to an index similar to that of the Undeformed and Koskimo. The Cowichan are the only indices that do not conform with the others, their averages being 66.7 in the males and 68.9 in the females. This is entirely due to a greater facial breadth of 142.7 mm. in the males and 132.0 mm. in the females, thus exceeding even the Chinook values, while the minimum frontal breadths at 95.5 mm. and 91.1 mm. correspond with those of the Undeformed and Koskimo. The female averages everywhere are seen to range about two units higher than the male, thus signifying a somewhat narrower female face. The infantile averages occur considerably higher than the adult ones. They yield 80 plus in the Undeformed and in the Cowichan and Chinook divisions, and 83.2 in the Koskimo. As was the case in the cranio-facial index, the relatively high infantile figures result from the undeveloped bizygomatic breadth. The juveniles have indices which range between those of the infantiles and the adults, indicating somewhat more mature faces.

The group means of the Undeformed vary somewhat in the case of the Athapascan who furnish the highest figures in the division, namely, 72.8 in the males and 73.5 in the females. The rather low male means of the Lillooet and Nicola groups are indicative of broader faces. This, however, may be purely accidental as only two individuals are concerned in each group. The Cowichan group means are fairly alike, although the exceptionally low mean of 63.0, derived from six Nanaimo males and due to their unusually broad faces, cannot escape notice. Great similarity of group means also prevails in the Koskimo division, and here it is only the Koskimo females at 73.2 who exceed the total average by more than two units.

The variability oscillates around ± 4, but drops to ± 2.88 in the Chinook males.

3. Jugo-mandibular index.

The jugo-mandibular index, the second one enumerated in the introductory paragraph to part 2 of this chapter expresses the ratio between the bizygomatic breadth and the bigonial width of the lower jaw. The indications here are that the lower the index the broader the face or, which is equivalent, the narrower, in proportion, the bigonial width of the lower jaw. The number of complete skulls, i. e., with mandibles, is somewhat limited, although sufficient for average treatment, with the exception perhaps of the Chinook who, as noted in *summary 62*, are represented by only four males and one female.

Summary 62.

Averages of the jugo-mandibular index.

Sex, Age	Undeformed				Deformation according to the three modes											
					Cowichan				Chinook				Koskimo			
	Cases	Range	Average	σ	Cases	Range	Average	σ	Cases	Range	Average	σ	Cases	Range	Average	σ
♂	23	67.8–85.1	76.9	± 4.77	22	63.1–78.1	72.4	± 3.69	4	68.7–74.8	71.9	—	24	62.3–84.8	74.0	± 5.36
♀	14	69.9–85.8	75.9	± 4.42	8	67.7–82.1	74.1	± 4.65	1	—	74.8	—	10	72.2–88.8	77.9	± 4.00
jnv.	—	—	—	—	1	—	76.7	—	—	—	—	—	—	—	—	—
inf.	9	67.5–85.1	75.6	—	2	76.7;86.3	72.4	—	—	—	—	—	—	—	—	—

The averages of the deformed divisions range by various amounts below those of the Undeformed, except in the Koskimo females who exceed the Undeformed females by two units. Within the divisions the Undeformed males exceed the females, while in the other divisions the higher indices belong to the females. This is to be attributed not so much to the greater bigonial width of the females as rather to the greater bizygomatic breadth of the males, the sex difference in the latter measurement exceeding that in the former. The few infantiles in the Undeformed and Cowichan divisions conform with the adults, both their measurements, as involved in the index, being proportionally smaller in comparison with those of the adults.

The group means derived from individuals, too few in number to be of comparative value, need not be considered.

The variability centers around ± 4.

A comparative review of the principal cranio-facial proportions is presented in *summary 63*.

Summary 63.

Comparative averages of cranio-facial proportions, males and females combined.

Series	Comparative averages			
	cranio-facial index	bizygomatic breadth	jugo-frontal index	jugo-mandibular index
Undeformed	97.4	135.6	68.9	76.5
Cowichan (deformation)	93.7	140.9	67.2	72.8
Chinook (deformation)	90.1	139.1	69.2	72.5
Koskimo (deformation)	98.4	136.0	68.7	75.2

With the bizygomatic breadth are collated the cranio-facial, the jugo-frontal and the jugo-mandibular indices. Of particular interest is the comparison of the latter two indices which signify the characteristic differences with reference to the facial contour. The jugo-mandibular index will be found in each division to exceed the jugo-frontal index, a condition which indicates a greater bigonial width of the lower jaw, meaning in this relation a lateral facial contour that broadens out downward. The differences in the average conditions of the bizygomatic breadth are seen reflected more by the jugo-mandibular index than by the jugo-frontal index, in which latter a greater uniformity is attained through the proportionally greater minimum frontal breadth, the other factor involved in this index. The status of the cranio-facial index is to its greatest extent dependent on the markedly broadening cranial breadth in the Cowichan and Chinook deformations, and which, in spite of the higher bizygomatic breadth, produce their lower index averages as compared with the conspicuously higher index averages of the Undeformed and Koskimo deformations where they fall high in spite of their lower bizygomatic breadths.

4. Cranio-facial angle.

Among the metrical correlations between the parts of the cranium there is one of particular interest because it involves the two cranial complexes of the brain-case and the face: the angular relation between the nasion-basion, or the cranial base line, and the prosthion-bregma line which produces angles around 90° at their point of intersection. *Falkenburger*[47] termed this the cranio-facial angle, and has studied it also in deformed skulls.

---

[47] l. c., p. 28.

Summary 64.
Averages of the cranio-facial angle.

Sex, Age	Undeformed				Deformation according to the three modes											
					Cowichan				Chinook				Koskimo			
	Cases	Range	Average	σ	Cases	Range	Average	σ	Cases	Range	Average	σ	Cases	Range	Average	σ
♂	67	83–96	89.3	± 2.41	69	84–97	90.3	± 2.89	56	83–97	91.8	± 3.02	103	85–96	90.4	± 2.32
♀	30	84–93	89.2	± 2.36	21	84–95	89.9	± 2.83	25	87–99	92.3	± 3.02	32	86–96	91.4	± 2.51
juv.	1	—	88.0	—	2	89;91	90.0	—	2	90;93	91.5	—	2	86;90	88.0	—
inf.	7	85–89	88.3	—	4	87–92	89.8	—	4	88–93	90.0	—	3	80–91	85.3	—

The cranio-facial angle as specified in *summary 64*, shows only slight deviations in the averages of the four divisions. It will be noticed that on the whole the Undeformed and Cowichan female averages fall a little below and the Koskimo averages a little above 90°. The Chinook with 91.8° and 92.3° in the sexes are seen to produce the highest, and the Undeformed with 89.3° and 89.2° the lowest averages. The individual values even drop to 83° in the Undeformed and Chinook males, while values of 97° occur in the Cowichan and Chinook males, and one as high as 99° in a Chinook female. It was here that the highest divisional average of 92.3° was attained; the male one at 91.8° also exceeding the upper limit of rectangularity, which may be ascribed to the deformatory effects so excessively pronounced in this division. This may also hold true for the Koskimo, and in a lesser degree for the Cowichan deformation. Deformatory effects, on the whole, are thus seen to be only slight, although the minute deviations may be considered as rather significant.

The infantile averages somewhat corroborate the adult status. The low average of only 85.3° in the Koskimo infantiles is rather disturbing. In accordance with their mode of deformation a higher value might have been expected. This discrepancy, however, is to be attributed to their paucity, all the more since the lowest infantile value is only 80°, which is the lowest of the entire series.

The larger Undeformed groups produce a mean of 89.0° in the Haida males and 88.1° in Haida females, both the Eskimo and Athapascan having means of 88 plus. The Chukchee males, on the other hand, amount to 90.5° and all the (undeformed) Salish groups of the Interior also fall above 90°, or slightly below. Among the Koskimo groups, the Koskimo themselves have the highest means at 91.2° in the males and 93.3° in the females, thus emphasizing the significance of excessive deformatory effects in this group.

The variability is rather low and lies in all the classes between ± 2 and ± 3, except in the Chinook where both males and females list a variability of ± 3.02.

UPPER JAW

1. Maxillo-alveolar length.

Summary 65.
Averages of the maxillo-alveolar length.

Sex, Age	Undeformed				Deformation according to the three modes											
					Cowichan				Chinook				Koskimo			
	Cases	Range	Average	σ	Cases	Range	Average	σ	Cases	Range	Average	σ	Cases	Range	Average	σ
♂	62	47–60	53.7	± 2.79	79	47–61	54.2	± 3.04	52	49–60	54.2	± 2.73	100	46–61	53.5	± 3.59
♀	31	45–57	51.3	± 2.81	26	43–57	51.7	± 3.35	25	46–58	50.6	± 2.79	34	43–58	51.8	± 3.22
juv.	—	—	—	—	2	46;46	46.0	—	4	43–48	44.8	—	2	39;45	42.0	—
inf.	13	32–44	37.1	—	6	35–44	39.7	—	6	38–46	41.3	—	5	36–43	38.6	—

There is according to *summary 65* only a very slight difference in the maxillo-alveolar lengths. The divisional averages are grouped around 54 mm. in the males and 51 mm. in the females. Sex differences reach their highest figure of 3.6 mm. in the Chinook, 2.5 mm. and 2.4 mm. in the Cowichan deformation and the Undeformed, and 1.7 mm. in the Koskimo. The extension of the divisional ranges varies in the adults between fifteen units in the Chinook and nineteen units in the Cowichan and Koskimo deformations, while the Undeformed also cover only sixteen units. The lowest individual values of 43 mm. as well as the highest of 61 mm. are contained in the Cowichan and Koskimo divisions, the former being females, the latter males. The infantile averages at 37.1 mm. in the Undeformed and 41.3 mm. in the Chinook naturally range considerably below those of the adults. The juveniles range between these and the adults.

The Haida stand conspicuously high among the Undeformed group means, rising to 56.0 mm. in the males and 53.5 mm. in the females. At the same time, both sexes contain the highest individual values in the divisional ranges. A corresponding position is held by the Koskimo group in the Koskimo division. Both sexes exceed their divisional averages, the males with 57.0 mm. by 3.5 mm., the females with 54.3 mm. by 2.5 mm. The other group means fairly conform with the divisional average.

The variability is concentrated quite steadily around ± 3, and a little below in the Undeformed and Chinook males and females, and in the Koskimo males, while in both sexes of the Cowichan and in the Koskimo males it rises slightly above.

2. Maxillo-alveolar breadth.

This measurement is somewhat more variable in its averages than the preceding one. *Summary 66* shows the male average of the Undeformed to be 65.4 mm. and the female 61.9 mm.

Summary 66.

Averages of the maxillo-alveolar breadth.

Sex, Age	Undeformed				Deformation according to the three modes											
					Cowichan				Chinook				Koskimo			
	Cases	Range	Average	σ	Cases	Range	Average	σ	Cases	Range	Average	σ	Cases	Range	Average	σ
♂	61	55–71	65.4	± 4.43	79	56–73	63.9	± 3.72	51	61–73	66.5	± 3.16	103	56–76	66.2	± 4.29
♀	30	53–69	61.9	± 3.51	27	56–67	60.4	± 3.05	23	58–68	62.9	± 2.43	33	55–69	62.0	± 3.15
juv.	—	—	—	—	2	59;59	59.0	—	4	58–66	61.5	—	2	64;64	64.0	—
inf.	13	50–59	55.7	—	6	52–60	56.5	—	6	59–60	59.2	—	5	55–59	56.8	—

These figures are slightly exceeded in the Chinook and Koskimo divisions where they amount to 66 mm. plus in the males and 62 mm. plus in the females. An exceptional position is held by the Cowichan deformation with averages of 63.9 mm. and 60.4 mm. in the sexes, both being the lowest averages recorded. The sex differences in all divisions are between 3 mm. to 4 mm., rising, however, to 4.2 mm. in the Koskimo. The Chinook division provides the highest infantile average of 59.2 mm. which thus foreshadows the slight tendency toward a greater maxillo-alveolar breadth in the adult Chinook. The remaining infantile averages are at 56 mm. plus in the Cowichan and Koskimo deformations, and at 55.7 mm. in the Undeformed. The juveniles fall, as usual, between the infantiles and adults.

As in the maxillo-alveolar length the Haida produce rather high group means of maxillo-alveolar breadth at 66.5 mm. and 64.5 mm. in the sexes. Their ranges also contain the highest individual values among the Undeformed of either sex. The high male mean of 68.0 mm. from three individuals from Nicola Lake, the particularly low one of 62.0 mm. from four Kamloops, and 61.0 mm. from three Chukchee males, may be purely accidental and due to the smallness of the series. Among the larger Cowichan groups the males from "about Vancouver" are listed with a rather low mean of 61.7 mm., the females with 59.6 mm. Comparatively high group means in excess of the average are produced by the Koskimo proper with 70.3 mm. and 65.7 mm. in the sexes. The Kwakiutl male mean of 67.5 mm. is also rather high, while the Nimkish and Nootka males and females with lengths of 64.4 mm. and 63.5 mm. fall short of the divisional average.

The variability also appears to be a little more unstable than that found for the maxillo-alveolar length. It oscillates around ± 3. The Koskimo males, however, have a variability as high as ± 4.29, the Chinook females as low as ± 2.43.

3. Maxillo-alveolar index.

The index averages reflect the oscillations of the maxillo-alveolar breadth in proportion to the more constant maxillo-alveolar length. The slight inclination toward a greater breadth in the Chinook deformation finds its expression in a higher index, the averages of which are enumerated in *summary 67* with 126.4 and 124.7 in the sexes. Next to them are the Undeformed, with averages of 122.4 and 120.8. The latter figure is also uniformly found in both sexes of the Koskimo, while the Cowichan with their relatively smallest maxillo-alveolar breadth, have also the relatively lowest indices, their averages amounting to 118.2 in the males and 117.2 in the females. The females, in consequence of slightly narrower upper jaws, are seen in three divisions to range below the males, in one, viz. the Koskimo, both sexes have equal averages.

Summary 67.

Averages of the maxillo-alveolar index.

Sex, Age	Undeformed				Deformation according to the three modes											
					Cowichan				Chinook				Koskimo			
	Cases	Range	Average	σ	Cases	Range	Average	σ	Cases	Range	Average	σ	Cases	Range	Average	σ
♂	61	108.8–138.8	122.4	± 6.25	79	91.8–137.2	118.2	± 8.62	51	105.2–138.5	126.4	± 8.20	98	103.5–139.1	120.8	± 6.47
♀	30	109.4–130.6	120.8	± 5.46	26	105.7–132.5	117.2	± 6.12	23	110.9–141.7	124.7	± 8.12	33	110.3–137.8	120.8	± 7.04
inf.	—	—	—	—	2	128.3;128.3	128.3	—	4	125.0–153.5	137.2	—	2	130.6;142.2	136.4	—
juv.	13	131.8–160.7	150.6	—	6	136.6–151.4	142.8	—	6	128.3–155.3	143.7	—	5	132.5–155.3	147.4	—

According to the classification of the index, all the adults have brachyuranic averages in a certain gradation, not too far removed, however, from the mesuranic domain. Possessing upper jaws which are more broad than long, they represent a condition encountered in most of the human groups, in contradistinction to the simian condition of longer upper jaws as indicated by indices below 100.

Considerably higher even than the adult averages are those of the infantiles, whose averages with 150.6 in the Undeformed and 142.8, 143.7 and 147.4 in the Cowichan, Chinook and Koskimo deformations exceed even the highest individual adult values. The juveniles again maintain an intermediate position between the infantiles and the adults.

Somewhat contrasting group means, falling above and below the average, are found in the Undeformed by the larger groups of the Haida and Eskimo males, the former yielding 120.3, the latter 123.5. The smaller groups of the Lillooet and Nicola have comparatively high means in both sexes, amounting to 130.4 and 128.5 in the males, and to 118.3 and 124.2 in the females. High means are also seen in the Yakima and Bellabella groups of the Cowichan deformation, with 122.4 and 123.0 in the males, the other groups conforming mostly with the divisional average. The figures for the Nimkish and Koskimo males are somewhat higher with means above 123, while both the Nootka and Clayoquot males with means of 117.7 and 118.2 fall below the total average. The female means throughout the Koskimo division are more in keeping with the average.

The variability is rather high, thus revealing a pronounced variation in the maxillo-alveolar proportions. Amounting to ± 5.46 in the Undeformed females, it rises to ± 6 in the Undeformed and Koskimo males and in the Cowichan females, to ± 7 in the Koskimo females and above ± 8 in the Cowichan males and both sexes of the Chinook.

The actual and percental distribution of all the cases among the index classes is shown in *summary 68*. It demonstrates the extraordinary predominance of brachyurany in the four divisions of which there are 85% in the Undeformed and 89% in the Chinook. Lower percentages of 79% and 64% obtain in the Koskimo and Cowichan divisions. In the latter the percentage of mesurany rises to 22%, while 18% are found in the Koskimo, 13% in the Undeformed and 8% in the Chinook. Only small percentages of dolichurany, namely, 2% in the Undeformed and 3% in both the Chinook and Koskimo divisions, are represented, the Cowichan, however, producing as much as 14%. The latter division thus shows a proportionately graded distribution of individual values over the entire range of the index, with a decided predominance, however, to brachyurany.

Summary 68.

Maxillo-alveolar index, males and females combined: actual and percental frequency.

Range	Undeformed			Deformation according to the three modes								
				Cowichan			Chinook			Koskimo		
	Cases		%	Cases		%	Cases		%	Cases		%
	♂	♀	♂+♀	♂	♀	♂+♀	♂	♀	♂+♀	♂	♀	♂+♀
91.8–109.9	1	1	2.2	11	4	14.3	2	—	2.7	4	—	3.0
110.0–114.9	8	4	13.2	19	4	21.9	4	2	8.1	14	9	17.6
115.0–141.7	52	25	84.6	49	18	63.8	45	21	89.2	80	24	79.4

The other three divisions, on the other hand, although containing a certain percentage of mesurany, have by far the greatest number of individuals assembled in the brachyuranic section, leaving only minimum percentages to dolichurany.

4. Palatal length.

The maxillo-alveolar and palatal lengths are quite similar. They differ in favor of the former around 7 mm. on an average in the four divisions. Differences around 2 mm., as may be gained

Summary 69.

Length of palate.

Sex, Age	Undeformed				Deformation according to the three modes											
					Cowichan				Chinook				Koskimo			
	Cases	Range	Average	σ	Cases	Range	Average	σ	Cases	Range	Average	σ	Cases	Range	Average	σ
♂	59	39–52	46.7	± 2.60	79	43–56	47.8	± 3.09	50	42–51	47.1	± 2.47	99	41–53	47.0	± 2.64
♀	29	39–50	44.6	± 2.53	23	39–52	46.6	± 2.90	23	40–52	44.3	± 2.86	34	39–51	45.1	± 2.42
juv.	—	—	—	—	2	39; 41	40.0	—	4	40–42	40.8	—	2	40; 45	42.5	—
inf.	14	29–39	34.3	—	6	32–37	36.5	—	6	35–43	37.8	—	5	32–39	36.2	—

from *summary 69*, occur likewise between the male and female averages of the palatal length, while the immatures range markedly below the matures.

The variability lies around ± 3, also corresponding to that of the maxillo-alveolar length.

5. Palatal width.

The maxillo-alveolar breadth and the palatal width show proportionally greater average differences than the length averages due to the anatomical conditions of the upper jaw. The averages of the two measurements just mentioned differ around 24 mm. in the males and from 20 mm. to 23 mm. in the females. The sex differences between the averages of the palatal length, listed in *summary 70*, amount to 2 mm. plus in the Undeformed, and the Koskimo and Chinook deformations, and drops to 1.4 mm. in the Cowichan. The immatures range appreciably below the matures.

Summary 70.

Width of palate.

	Undeformed				Deformation according to the three modes											
					Cowichan				Chinook				Koskimo			
Sex, Age	Cases	Range	Average	σ	Cases	Range	Average	σ	Cases	Range	Average	σ	Cases	Range	Average	σ
♂	57	34–49	42.0	± 2.72	78	33–47	40.5	± 2.74	50	32–48	42.5	± 2.84	94	34–47	41.4	± 2.52
♀	29	36–45	39.6	± 2.54	23	34–44	39.1	± 3.03	23	35–45	40.1	± 2.42	32	32–44	38.8	± 2.68
juv.	—	—	—	—	2	34; 39	36.5	—	4	34–38	36.0	—	2	37; 40	38.5	—
inf.	14	27–36	32.4	—	6	29–37	32.5	—	6	32–38	34.5	—	5	30–34	32.0	—

The variability, like that of the preceding measurement, is rather modest, amounting to ± 3 minus in all the classes except the Cowichan females who deviate at ± 3.03.

6. Palatal index.

Summary 71.

Palatal index.

	Undeformed				Deformation according to the three modes											
					Cowichan				Chinook				Koskimo			
Sex. Age	Cases	Range	Average	σ	Cases	Range	Average	σ	Cases	Range	Average	σ	Cases	Range	Average	σ
♂	57	73.9–115.4	90.1	± 8.20	75	62.3–102.2	80.5	± 7.97	50	76.2–104.4	90.4	± 6.27	95	68.2–104.9	87.9	± 6.24
♀	29	80.3–100.0	89.1	± 5.81	24	76.9–95.8	82.5	± 5.42	23	72.5–102.4	90.6	± 7.06	33	66.7–102.5	85.9	± 7.78
juv.	—	—	—	—	2	87.2; 95.1	91.2	—	4	80.9–95.0	88.4	—	2	82.2; 100.0	91.1	—
inf.	14	77.1–112.5	94.1	—	6	82.5–92.5	89.1	—	5	79.1–105.6	92.1	—	5	81.1–106.2	90.1	—

The averages of the palatal index, as specified in *summary 71*, are brachystaphyline with the exception of those of the Cowichan males and females who are mesostaphyline at 80.5 and 82.5 respectively. There is some inconsistency obtaining in the sex averages of the four divisions. Thus, while there is a uniformity of averages of 90 plus to be noticed in the Chinook sexes, those of the Undeformed and the Koskimo differ in favor of the males by one unit in the former and two in the latter, and, contrary to these, the Cowichan by two units in favor of the females. All the immatures, including the Cowichan, have brachystaphyline averages, and comprise in their ranges the highest individual values of the four divisions, exceeded only in the Undeformed by an Eskimo male at 115.4.

The variability is rather irregular, reaching its highest figure with ± 8.20 in the Undeformed males and its lowest at ± 5 plus in the Undeformed and Cowichan females.

Summary 72.

Palatal index: actual and percental frequency.

Palatal index	Undeformed			Deformation according to the three modes								
				Cowichan			Chinook			Koskimo		
	Cases		%	Cases		%	Cases		%	Cases		%
	♂	♀	♂+♀	♂	♀	♂+♀	♂	♀	♂+♀	♂	♀	♂+♀
62.3–79.9	6	—	7.0	17	7	26.3	2	1	4.1	12	7	14.9
80.0–84.9	8	9	19.8	17	9	28.6	6	2	11.0	17	8	19.5
85.0–115.4	43	20	23.2	33	8	45.1	42	20	84.9	66	18	65.6

The actual and percental distribution of the individual values into the classes of the palatal index is shown in *summary 72*. In all the divisions the decided tendency toward brachystaphyliny will be noticed, so much so that in the Undeformed and in the Chinook and Koskimo deformations the brachystaphyline exceed the combined leptostaphyline and mesostaphyline frequencies. This is, strange enough, not the case in the Cowichan deformation where leptostaphyliny and mesostaphyliny are present in appreciable frequencies, and in their combination distinctly outrival brachystaphyliny.

7. Maxillo-cranial correlations.

The quantitative position of the maxillo-palatal complex in the facial configuration is relatively easily estimated even without comparative metrical procedures. It seemed, on the other hand, interesting to investigate the correlations, if any, between the maxillo-alveolar and palatal and the cranial diameters as well as their proportional conditions. For that reason the several length and breadth measurements as well as the length-breadth indices were studied, and are listed in *summary 73*. It is self-evident that investigations like these should be made only upon the normal, i. e., the undeformed skull.

Using the cranial length and breadth as bases, their ranges were suitably divided into three regions and for each of these regions the rellated individual maxillo-alveolar and palatal length and breadth values as well as their arithmethic means ascertained. It will first be noticed that in this tripartition the greatest number of individuals is assembled in the middle group of the basic range which is rather in accord with the natural behavior of any range of variation, but which is of significance here for the reason that the greatest assemblage takes place in the two correlated factors. The two regions of the basic range adjoining the central ones above and below contain either an equal number of individuals as in the palatal length of the males, or contrasting numbers, i. e., either the higher of the lower regions exceed one another in the number of individuals. Where, however, a more limited female range admits only of a bipartition as in the two maxillary length measurements, a distortion in proportion takes place in such a way

Summary 73.

Maxillo-cranial correlations: actual and percental frequency.

Cranial length	Maxillo-alveolar length					
	male			female		
	cases	range	average	cases	range	average
162—174	8	47—55	51.0	25	45— 57	51.1
175—189	46	49—59	53.8	4	49—55	52.0
190—196	5	51—60	56.0	—	—	—
do	Palatal length					
162—174	6	45—48	46.3	24	39—50	43.6
175—189	44	39—52	46.7	4	42—46	44.3
190—196	6	45—52	47.8	—	—	—
Cranial breadth	Maxillo-alveolar breadth					
126—134	8	59—70	63.9	12	53—66	60.3
135—144	36	55—73	65.6	14	56—67	62.9
145—152	14	63—71	66.6	3	60—69	64.0
do	Palatal width					
126—134	9	37—43	39.9	12	34—42	39.8
135—144	32	34—49	42.2	13	36—45	40.2
145—152	13	40—47	43.2	3	37—43	40.3
Cranial length-breadth index	Maxillo-alveolar index					
70—74	12	108—138	120.7	1	126	126.0
75—79	33	114—131	121.9	12	109—130	120.3
80—92	13	111—136	125.7	16	113—125	120.4
do	Palatal index					
70—74	12	75—115	87.5	1	93	93.0
75—79	30	79—108	90.0	13	79—95	87.4
80—92	12	73—104	88.0	15	80—100	88.9

that by far the greater frequency occurs in the lowest region of the basic range, while only a small frequency goes to the central range of the region.

The indices were disposed of in a similar way, only that with regard to the basic cranial length-breadth index, the three divisional regions were afforded by the index classification into dolicho-, meso- and brachycrany. As to the individual distribution of the maxillo-alveolar and palatal indices, it will be noticed that in the females an increasing number of individuals are assembled successively in the three cranial index classes.

The final results of this experiment in correlation are revealed by the average figures which invariably increase in the basic tripartition, i. e., with the increase of the cranial length and breadth, a proportional increase takes place in the maxillary measurements, while with the increase of the cranial length-breadth index an increase of maxillo-alveolar and palatal indices is more or less distinctly correlated. In other words: longer skulls have longer and narrower dental arches and palates, and shorter skulls have shorter and broader or wider ones.

NOSE.

1. Nasal height.

The nasal height averages of our series range in part with the highest in *R. Martin's* (Lehrbuch, 1914, 833) table of racial averages.

Summary 74.

Averages of the nasal height.

Sex, Age	Undeformed				Deformation according to the three modes											
					Cowichan				Chinook				Koskimo			
	Cases	Range	Average	σ	Cases	Range	Average	σ	Cases	Range	Average	σ	Cases	Range	Average	σ
♂	76	47–63	53.1	± 3.32	83	43–62	51.8	± 4.12	57	48–60	52.5	± 2.68	103	47–61	53.8	± 3.12
♀	33	45–56	51.4	± 4.40	27	44–54	48.9	± 2.50	25	44–57	49.6	± 3.25	37	46–57	50.4	± 2.86
juv.	1	—	46.0	—	2	42; 49	45.5	—	4	44–48	45.5	—	2	45; 49	47.0	—
inf.	14	15–45	37.7	—	7	35–45	41.0	—	6	42–44	43.7	—	5	41–47	51.4	—

They are, as specified in *summary 74*, fairly alike at 53 plus in the Undeformed and in the Koskimo males. The Chinook and the Cowichan males with 52.5 mm. and 51.8 mm. fall somewhat lower. The nasal height of the females decreases gradually from 51.4 mm. in the Undeformed to 50.4 mm. in the Koskimo, 49.6 mm. in the Chinook and 48.9 mm. in the Cowichan deformations. Sex differences, as will be shown in part 2 of this chapter, are naturally somewhat more pronounced in the nasal height as compared with the nasal width. Amounting only to 1.7 mm. in the Undeformed, the sex differences are 2.9 mm. in both the Cowichan and Chinook divisions, and 3.4 mm. in the Koskimo division. The ranges are rather wide in the males and cover twenty units in the Cowichan deformation, while the highest individual value of 63 mm. falls to the Undeformed males. The female ranges on the whole are somewhat narrower excepting that of the Chinook with one unit in excess of the male range. The infantiles yield averages considerably below those of the adults. An interesting exception, however, is that of the Koskimo infantiles whose average of 51.4 mm. falls between the male and female averages of the same division. The few juveniles occur between the adults and infantiles in the Undeformed and in the Cowichan and Chinook deformations, while in the Koskimo they fall with 47.0 mm. below the adult and infantile averages.

Among the Undeformed the Eskimo exceed the divisional average with means of 54.9 mm. and 52.3 mm. in the sexes. Three Nicola males even yield 55.3 mm. with all their individual values above the Undeformed average. All the other Undeformed group means fall below the average. The Yakima among the deformed Inland tribes fall peculiarly low with group means of 49.4 mm. in the males and 46.5 mm. in the females. The larger groups here, like the Tsimshian,

Bellacoola and Nanaimo range somewhat above the averages in both sexes. Relatively high group means are also attained in the Koskimo division by the Kwakiutl males with 57.5 mm. and the Koskimo themselves with 56.2 mm., while the others conform more with the divisional average.

The variability is centered mostly about ± 3, exceeding ± 4 in the Undeformed females and Cowichan males.

2. Nasal width.

Summary 75.

Averages of the nasal width.

Sex, Age	Undeformed				Deformation according to the three modes											
					Cowichan				Chinook				Koskimo			
	Cases	Range	Average	σ	Cases	Range	Average	σ	Cases	Range	Average	σ	Cases	Range	Average	σ
♂	74	19–29	24.7	± 2.15	83	20–29	23.7	± 1.96	57	20–29	24.2	± 1.76	102	20–29	23.8	± 1.68
♀	33	21–28	24.0	± 2.00	26	21–27	23.6	± 1.66	25	20–26	22.7	± 1.74	36	20–26	23.1	± 1.68
juv.	1	—	21.0	—	2	21; 22	21.5	—	4	21–23	22.3	—	2	23; 23	23.0	—
inf.	14	18–22	20.2	—	4	19–24	20.3	—	6	19–21	19.8	—	6	19–21	20.2	—

Disregarding very slight differences, the nasal width is fairly alike in the four divisions. It is seen from *summary 75* that all the averages are grouped around 24 mm. and thus range with the lowest averages of *R. Martin's* (Lehrbuch, 1914, 833) racial table. Only the Chinook females yield as low an average as 22.7 mm. There are no sex differences to speak of; they amount to fractions of 1 mm. in the Undeformed, and the Cowichan and Koskimo divisions, and to 1.5 mm. in the Chinook. The infantile figures fall short of the adult to the extent of about 4 mm. The few juveniles range slightly higher than the infantiles and maintain an intermediate position between the latter and the adults. The range of the females comprises seven units in each of the three deformations as against ten units in the males. The Undeformed ranges exceed the deformed by 1 mm. in each sex, bringing the male range up to 11 mm. and the female to 8 mm.

Among the Undeformed groups the Haida are conspicuous for their comparatively great nasal width with 26.0 mm. in the males and even 27.0 mm. in the females. Similarly high are the means of the Lillooet and Nicola males. In the Cowichan deformation the divisional average is exceeded by the N. Saanich and Nanaimo males with group means of 25.2 mm. and 25.3 mm. The few females of the same groups conform with the female average of the division. There are no digressions worth mentioning in the group means of the Koskimo division.

The variability amounts to ± 2 in the Undeformed females, and to ± 2.15 in the Undeformed males, falling between ± 1 and ± 2 in all the other classes.

3. Nasal index.

All the female averages as will be seen from *summary 76*, range above the male. There is in addition a complete uniformity to be observed in the averages of the Undeformed and the Cowichan deformation, both male and female. The discussion of the factors involved in this index showed both the Cowichan measurements to be somewhat shorter in equal proportion which then causes the uniform index averages. The Chinook and Koskimo averages, both male and female, follow in a slightly decreasing order as a result rather of a somewhat greater nasal height

Summary 76.

Averages of the nasal index.

Sex, Age	Undeformed				Deformation according to the three modes											
					Cowichan				Chinook				Koskimo			
	Cases	Range	Average	σ	Cases	Range	Average	σ	Cases	Range	Average	σ	Cases	Range	Average	σ
♂	74	36.5–57.1	46.5	± 5.19	84	40.0–56.2	46.7	± 4.31	57	36.2–58.0	45.5	± 4.63	102	36.8–54.7	44.7	± 4.14
♀	33	37.5–57.1	48.4	± 5.16	26	46.0–56.8	48.8	± 4.12	25	38.5–56.8	45.9	± 4.44	36	38.5–54.3	45.8	± 4.00
juv.	1	—	45.6	—	2	42.9; 52.4	47.7	—	4	47.7–51.1	48.9	—	2	46.9; 51.1	49.0	—
inf.	14	46.5–60.6	51.2	—	6	45.6–57.1	51.8	—	6	40.0–48.8	45.6	—	6	34.5–50.0	45.4	—

than width. Their sex difference amounts only to 0.4, increasing to 1.1 in the Koskimo, 1.9 in the Undeformed and 2.1 in the Cowichan, all in favor of the females, as already mentioned. The infantile averages at 51.2 in the Undeformed and at 51.8 in the Cowichan division are separated from the adults of the same divisions by several units, while the Chinook and Koskimo infantile averages, on the contrary, with 45.6 and 45.4 conform with them. The juvenile figures fall within the divisional ranges, although the fact is interesting that five Chinook juveniles yield an average of 48.9, which is about three units in excess of the Chinook adults and infantiles, accounting for lower noses in the juveniles, while the nasal width equals that of the adults.

Regarding the classification of the nasal index, all the male averages are shown to be leptorrhinic, although closely approximating the mesorrhinic border in the Undeformed and Cowichan. Somewhat more pronounced is the leptorrhinic status of the Chinook and Koskimo males. Mesorrhinic averages about intermediate between mesorrhiny and chamaerrhiny are held by the Undeformed and Cowichan females, while the Chinook and Koskimo females have leptorrhinic averages in conformity with the male averages of the same divisions. Mesorrhiny with a tendency toward leptorrhiny is the general state in the American Indian. Exquisite types of leptorrhiny are known in the Eastern Eskimo. The Western Eskimo of our series at 44.2 and 46.0 in the sexes are likewise leptorrhinic. The Haida males, on the other hand, at 51.5 are just within the chamaerrhinic class, while the Haida females at 50.9 are on the verge between mesorrhiny and chamaerrhiny. Chamaerrhinic averages are also found in the Undeformed and Cowichan infantiles as against leptorrhinic averages in the Chinook and Koskimo infantiles. The few juveniles appear on the average to be mesorrhinic.

That the divisional ranges extend fairly well into the chamaerrhinic domain of the index, is demonstrated by *summary 77* of actual and percental frequencies. It reveals the interesting fact, already anticipated by the divisional averages, that leptorrhiny increases constantly from 47% in the Undeformed to 58% in the Cowichan, to 67% in the Chinook and to 70% in the Koskimo. Chamaerrhiny decreases somewhat differently in the four divisions. While there is 24% of it in the Undeformed and in the Cowichan deformation, the percentage suddenly drops to 9% in the

Summary 77.

Nasal index, males and females combined: actual and percental frequency.

Range	Undeformed			Deformation according to the three modes								
				Cowichan			Chinook			Koskimo		
	Cases		%	Cases		%	Cases		%	Cases		%
	♂	♀	♂+♀	♂	♀	♂+♀	♂	♀	♂+♀	♂	♀	♂+♀
36.2–46.9	36	14	46.7	50	14	57.7	38	17	67.1	74	22	69.6
47.0–50.9	22	9	29.1	16	4	18.0	14	5	23.2	22	11	23.9
51.0–57.9	16	10	24.2	18	9	24.3	4	3	8.5	6	3	6.5
58.0	—	—	—	—	—	—	1	—	1.2	—	—	—

Chinook and 7% in the Koskimo, with an additional 1% of hyperchamaerrhiny in the Chinook. Mesorrhiny is fairly evenly distributed with 29% in the Undeformed, 23% and 24% in the Chinook and Koskimo, but only 18% in the Cowichan. The tendency toward narrower noses is thus manifest in the Chinook and Koskimo, who also produce the lowest leptorrhinic individual figures, although, on the other hand, there was a hyperchamaerrhinic nose to be noticed in the Chinook in addition to the small percentage of chamaerrhiny as compared with the Undeformed and Cowichan divisions. The conditions within the divisions as reflected by the group means rather reiterate the divisional status.

The variability in the nasal index lies around ± 5, the Koskimo females dropping to ± 4.0.

ORBIT.

1. Orbital height.

Summary 78.

Averages of the orbital height.

Sex. Age	Undeformed				Deformation according to the three modes											
					Cowichan				Chinook				Koskimo			
	Cases	Range	Average	σ	Cases	Range	Average	σ	Cases	Range	Average	σ	Cases	Range	Average	σ
♂	78	32–42	35.9	± 1.93	84	30–41	36.1	± 2.03	57	33–40	36.3	± 1.50	101	34–42	37.1	± 1.60
♀	33	32–41	34.9	± 2.02	27	33–39	36.3	± 1.64	25	32–40	36.3	± 1.87	37	33–42	36.7	± 1.93
juv.	1	—	32.0	—	2	32; 34	33.0	—	4	31–37	33.3	—	2	34; 35	34.5	—
inf.	13	31–37	33.0	—	7	31–34	31.6	—	6	31–36	33.8	—	9	31–41	27.0	—

Summary 78 shows for the orbital height a slow rise in the male averages of the four divisions in the order of the Undeformed with 35.9 mm., the Cowichan with 36.1 mm., the Chinook with 36.3 mm. and the Koskimo with 37.1 mm. The female averages are still more concentrated with 34.9 mm. in the Undeformed, 36.3 mm. in both the Cowichan and Chinook deformations and 36.7 in the Koskimo deformation. All the male and female averages, except that of the Undeformed females, thus exceed *R. Martin's* (Lehrbuch, 1914, 857) list of racial averages. A sex difference occurs only in the Undeformed, where it amounts to 1 mm. in favor of the males. In the other three divisions differences of less than a unit occur, in the Cowichan in favor of the females, in the Koskimo of the males, while the Chinook have uniform averages for both sexes. The ranges vary between twelve and seven units in the Cowichan males and females. The ranges of the other classes fall within these extremes.

The lowest infantile average of 27.0 mm., strangely enough, belongs to the Koskimo who otherwise possess the highest adult averages and which may be assumed as having been brought about by deformation, i. e., the retraction of the forehead by means of bandaging the head. The average of the Cowichan infantiles is 31.6 mm., while the Undeformed and Chinook infantiles have 33.0 mm. and 33.8 mm. The group means in all the divisions are more or less in keeping with the divisional averages. A stronger digression, however, is to be observed in the Koskimo division where the Koskimo themselves are distinguished by the high means of 39.2 mm. and 38.7 mm. in the sexes. Only insignificant deviations are noticeable in the other groups of this division.

The variability lies around ± 2, expressing only slight deviations in this measurement and in the different divisions.

2. Orbital width.

Of the three medial measuring points of the orbital width used by different schools and authors, namely, the lacrimale, dacryon and maxillofrontale, the latter is receiving increasing recognition. Situated at the intersection point of a line prolonging the crista lacrimalis anterior upward and the maxillofrontal suture, it presents a point directly upon the medial rim of the orbit which is better for ascertaining a truer orbital width than the two other points which are found rather inside the orbital cavity. Since, however, the lacrimale width had been widely employed in the metrical treatment of the orbit prior to the introduction of the maxillofrontale width, the lacrimale measurement has also been considered in the following investigations in order to facilitate the comparison with racial figures derived in such a way. This applies not only to the orbital width as such but also to the orbital index in which it is involved.

Summary 79.

Averages of the orbital width (maxillofrontale).

Sex, Age	Undeformed				Deformation according to the three modes											
					Cowichan				Chinook				Koskimo			
	Cases	Range	Average	σ	Cases	Range	Average	σ	Cases	Range	Average	σ	Cases	Range	Average	σ
♂	78	40–50	44.2	± 2.12	84	39–48	43.5	± 2.02	57	40–49	43.8	± 1.73	102	39–49	44.2	± 2.13
♀	34	38–44	41.6	± 1.49	27	39–45	41.9	± 1.65	25	38–47	42.0	± 2.05	37	39–47	42.4	± 2.0
juv.	1	—	42.0	—	2	36; 40	38.0	—	4	37–42	39.3	—	2	40; 41	40.5	—
inf.	14	34–41	37.3	—	7	35–39	37.9	—	6	36–39	38.2	—	8	35–41	38.0	—

The orbital width with the maxillofrontale as its medial measuring point varies but slightly in the four divisions. *Summary 79* accounts for uniform male averages of 44.2 mm. in the Undeformed and in the Koskimo deformation, while the Cowichan and Chinook deformations yield 43.5 mm. and 43.8 mm. Still less variation is exhibited by the females with averages of 41.6 mm. and 41.9 mm. in the Undeformed and in the Cowichan deformation, and 42.0 mm. and 42.4 mm. in the Chinook and Koskimo deformations. The sex difference is greatest in the Undeformed at 2.6 mm., but fairly uniform in the deformed divisions with 1 mm. plus. The ranges are almost alike in the males, comprising ten units on an average which in itself, however, is rather a high figure for measurements of a smaller range. The females are listed with ranges of seven units in the Undeformed and Cowichan deformation, their ranges comprising, however, 10 mm. in the Chinook and 9 mm. in the Koskimo females.

The infantile averages of the orbital width naturally range below the adult figures. They amount to 37 mm. plus in the Undeformed and in the Cowichan deformation, and to 38 mm. plus in the Chinook and Koskimo deformations. The juveniles, in not a single instance rising to the adult status, fall somewhat higher.

In the Undeformed the Haida with 45.3 mm. and 42.1 mm. in the sexes possess conspicuously high group means. The highest male value is here 50 mm., which is likewise encountered in the Eskimo. The means of the latter, however, like most of the others of the Undeformed division, conform with the divisional averages. Similar conditions as found in the Undeformed occur in the Cowichan. There the lowest male mean of 41.7 mm. is held by seven Yakima. Four Dungeness males yield 42.3 mm., and sixteen from Vancouver 42.9 mm., all of them falling short of the total average. Above the latter range six Nanaimo males with a mean of 45.2 mm., nine Bellabella males with 44.1 mm., and a number of individual values from other localities. In the Koskimo division the Nootka and Clayoquot males are seen to range below the average with means of 42.8 mm. and 42.5 mm. The Koskimo proper exceed this somewhat with 45.1 mm., a condition which also obtained in the orbital height; while the Kwakiutl and Nimkish conform with the average. As regards the orbital width, in both the Cowichan and Koskimo deformations the females in general are seen to fall short of the males.

The variability lies fairly uniform around ± 2.

Summary 80.

Averages of the orbital width (lacrimale).

	Undeformed				Deformation according to the three modes											
					Cowichan				Chinook				Koskimo			
Sex, Age	Cases	Range	Average	σ	Cases	Range	Average	σ	Cases	Range	Average	σ	Cases	Range	Average	σ
♂	77	37–46	40.1	± 1.91	82	36–43	39.5	± 1.70	57	37–45	39.7	± 1.58	101	36–44	40.1	± 1.75
♀	32	35–40	37.9	± 1.59	25	36–41	38.2	± 1.35	25	35–43	38.3	± 1.89	35	35–42	38.4	± 1.59
juv.	1	—	40.0	—	2	33; 36	34.5	—	4	33–38	35.3	—	2	37; 37	37.0	—
inf.	13	32–36	34.1	—	7	31–36	34.6	—	6	32–36	34.8	—	7	31–38	34.4	—

The lacrimale width shows similar proportions among the divisional averages and group means as encountered in the maxillofrontale width. This is specified in *summary 80*, while in the comparative *summary 81* the averages of both widths are listed side by side, demonstrating there a uniform difference of 4 mm. between the two measurements in every division, in favor, naturally, of the maxillofrontale width.

Summary 81.

Averages of the orbital widths: (1) maxillofrontale-ectokonchion, (2) lacrimale-ectokonchion, males and females combined.

Series	Orbital width		
	maxillo-frontale	lacrimale	difference
Undeformed	43.5	39.5	4.0
Cowichan ⎫	43.1	39.2	3.9
Chinook ⎬ deformation	43.2	39.2	4.0
Koskimo ⎭	43.7	39.7	4.0

The variability for the lacrimale width in all divisions and classes lies between ± 1 and ± 2, thus ranging in every case below the variability of the maxillofrontale width.

3. Orbital index.

Summary 82.

Averages of the orbital index (maxillofrontale).

Sex, Age	Undeformed				Deformation according to the three modes											
					Cowichan				Chinook				Koskimo			
	Cases	Range	Average	σ	Cases	Range	Average	σ	Cases	Range	Average	σ	Cases	Range	Average	σ
♂	78	70.0–92.9	81.7	± 5.08	86	70.8–95.1	83.1	± 4.77	57	73.3–92.9	83.8	± 4.62	102	73.9–97.4	84.9	± 5.02
♀	33	74.4–97.6	83.8	± 4.79	27	77.8–97.5	86.1	± 4.51	25	74.4–92.3	86.4	± 4.53	37	76.7–93.0	86.6	± 4.82
juv.	1	—	76.2	—	2	85.0; 88.9	87.0	—	4	73.8–92.5	84.9	—	2	85.0; 85.1	85.5	—
inf.	14	86.1–94.9	88.8	—	7	82.0–88.6	85.2	—	6	86.1–92.3	88.6	—	8	85.4–100.0	90.4	—

The orbital index for the maxillofrontale width, as specified in *summary 82*, shows the same slow but constant increase as the orbital height in the order: Undeformed, and the Cowichan, Chinook and Koskimo deformations. This measurement, as compared with the orbital width, was shown to be more variable. The male averages of the index amount to 81.7 in the Undeformed, rising to 83.1 in the Cowichan, 83.8 in the Chinook and 84.9 in the Koskimo divisions. All the female averages with 83.8 in the Undeformed and 86 plus in the three deformed divisions exceed the male, and this is due to the greater variability of the female orbital width, while, at the same time, the orbital height exhibits pronouncedly uniform divisional averages in both sexes. All the male averages are mesokonchic width a tendency toward hypsikonchy, which places the highest, the Koskimo, average of 84.9 exactly on the dividing line between those two index classes. The females are hypsikonchic, with the exception of the Undeformed who, with an average of 83.8 list a high mesokonchic average. The females thus repeat the sex proportions, which in regard to the orbital index obtain as a rule in the human varieties. High hypsikonchic averages are also found in the infantiles, where that of the Koskimo stands out conspicuously with 90.4. The averages of both the Undeformed and Chinook infantiles amount to 88 plus, while the Cowichan infantiles fall lowest in hypsikonchy with an average only of 85.2. The juveniles represent all the three index classes in their divisional ranges. These latter are rather extended in the cases of the adults where they also comprise a certain amount of chamaekonchy as specified in *summary 83*.

Summary 83.

Orbital index (maxillofrontale), males and females combined: actual and percental frequency.

Range	Undeformed			Deformation according to the three modes								
				Cowichan			Chinook			Koskimo		
	Cases		%	Cases		%	Cases		%	Cases		%
	♂	♀	♂+♀	♂	♀	♂+♀	♂	♀	♂+♀	♂	♀	♂+♀
70.0–75.9	8	1	8.1	6	—	5.3	2	1	3.6	5	—	3.6
76.0–84.9	50	22	64.9	52	9	54.0	42	8	61.0	50	16	47.5
85.0–97.6	20	10	27.0	28	18	40.7	13	16	35.4	47	21	48.9

Among the male group means of the Undeformed the Athapascan and Haida are seen to range below the average, which also holds true for the smaller groups of the Lillooet and Chukchee. The Eskimo males exceed the divisional average and the same holds true in a similar proportion for the female Eskimo. Varying group means are also noticed in the deformed divisions. Most conspicuous among the Koskimo group means are those of the Koskimo themselves with 85.9 and 89.6 in the sexes, both figures, especially the latter, in excess of the divisional average and typifying hypsikonchy to a pronounced degree.

The variability of the maxillofrontale orbital index centers around ± 5.

The actual and percental distribution over the range of variation, as listed in *summary 83*, males and females combined, shows the greatest percentage belonging to mesokonchy in the Undeformed, and the Cowichan and Chinook divisions, where it amounts to 65%, 54% and 61% respectively. An exception to this statement occurs in the Koskimo division, where the greatest percentage is hypsikonchial, namely 49% as against 48% mesokonchial. Hypsikonchy is also of marked occurrence in the other divisions where it represents 27% in the Undeformed, 41% in Cowichan and 35% in the Chinook. The Cowichan deformation thus is seen to range next to the Koskimo as regards the percental frequency of hypsikonchy, while the Undeformed rank lowest and the Chinook between the Undeformed and the Cowichan. The percentage of chamaekonchy is quite insignificant in each division as compared with the high percentages of mesokonchy and hypsikonchy. There is, however, 8% of it in the Undeformed, but only 5% in the Cowichan and 4% in both the Chinook and Koskimo deformations.

The proportions in general between the orbital height and width as revealed in the maxillofrontale index are repeated in the index with the lacrimale width, except that the tendency toward hypsikonchy is very much more pronounced here. This is shown in *summaries 84 and 85*, where

Summary *84.*

Averages of the orbital index (lacrimale).

	Undeformed				Deformation according to the three modes											
					Cowichan				Chinook				Koskimo			
Sex, Age	Cases	Range	Average	σ	Cases	Range	Average	σ	Cases	Range	Average	σ	Cases	Range	Average	σ
♂	77	76.7–102.6	90.0	± 5.56	84	80.9–105.4	91.5	± 5.59	57	82.2–102.6	91.7	± 4.75	101	80.9–105.6	94.0	± 5.52
♀	31	82.0–100.0	91.7	± 5.02	25	85.4–102.6	93.5	± 4.27	25	82.0–102.9	95.0	± 4.88	35	84.6–105.3	95.2	± 4.90
juv.	1	—	80.0	—	2	94.4; 97.0	95.7	—	4	81.6–102.8	94.6	—	2	91.9; 94.6	93.5	—
inf.	13	93.9–103.1	97.3	—	7	91.2–100.0	95.0	—	6	94.3–100.0	97.1	—	7	86.1–111.1	99.3	—

in the latter the percental distribution of hypsikonchy amounts to 90% in the Undeformed and the Cowichan deformation, to 96% in the Chinook and to 94%, in the Koskimo deformation, males and females combined. Small percentages thus are left to mesokonchy, namely, 4% in the Chinook, 6% in the Undeformed and the Koskimo deformation, and 10% in the Cowichan deformation. In addition there is a percentage of 4% of chamaekonchy in the Undeformed. Comparing with the orbital index of the maxillofrontale width, and the percental distribution of individual values of these, it is seen that the classification of that index affords a more reliable expression of the metrical proportions of the orbit. Both indices, however, show that the morphological character of the orbit in the tribes of the North Pacific regions is mesokonchic with a tendency toward hypsikonchy. That the latter might be due to artificial head deformation in the Koskimo tribe has been mentioned in connection with the discussion of the orbital height.

The variability of the lacrimale index as that of the maxillofrontale centers around ± 5 in the four divisions.

Summary 85.

Orbital index (lacrimale), males and females combined: actual and percental frequency.

Range	Undeformed			Deformation according to the three modes								
				Cowichan			Chinook			Koskimo		
	Cases		%	Cases		%	Cases		%	Cases		%
	♂	♀	♂+♀	♂	♀	♂+♀	♂	♀	♂+♀	♂	♀	♂+♀
76.7–80.0	4	—	3.7	—	—	—	—	—	—	—	—	—
80.1–85.0	5	2	6.5	11	—	10.1	2	1	3.7	7	1	5.9
85.1–103.1	68	29	89.8	73	25	89.9	55	24	96.3	94	34	94.1

4. Anterior interorbital breadth.

The anterior interorbital breadth as measured between the two maxillofrontalia is equivalent to the breadth development of the nasal process of the frontal bone, or the interorbital septum, a characteristic of racial significance. The greater interorbit breadth apparently is an advanced morphological condition. The average results in our four divisions are extraordinarily uniform, lying around 17 mm., and therewith signifying a decidedly low position in R. Martin's (Lehrbuch, 1914, 865) comparative table of averages.

Summary 86.

Averages of the anterior, interorbital breadth (maxillofrontale).

Sex, Age	Undeformed				Deformation according to the three modes											
					Cowichan				Chinook				Koskimo			
	Cases	Range	Average	σ	Cases	Range	Average	σ	Cases	Range	Average	σ	Cases	Range	Average	σ
♂	78	13–23	17.7	±1.97	82	14–24	17.9	±2.06	58	15–24	18.7	±2.00	102	14–22	17.8	±1.76
♀	34	13–22	16.9	±2.03	29	14–24	17.2	±2.57	25	14–20	17.7	±1.43	37	15–20	17.4	±1.70
juv.	1	—	18.0	—	2	18; 19	18.5	—	4	15–20	17.8	—	2	16; 17	16.5	—
inf.	14	14–18	16.0	—	7	15–18	16.3	—	6	15–17	16.7	—	7	13–18	15.9	—

The Chinook males, however, as specified in *summary 86*, rise to 18.7 mm. and with 17.7 mm. of the Chinook females represent the relatively highest sex averages of the four divisions. The Undeformed females, on the other hand, attain an average only of 16.9 mm. The sex differences, in every case in favor of the males amount only to 0.4 mm. in the Koskimo, 0.7 mm. in the Cowichan and 1.0 mm. in the Chinook deformations, while the difference in the Undeformed amounts to 0.8 mm. The two extreme averages of 16.9 mm. in the Undeformed females and 18.7 mm. in the Chinook males are thus seen to yield a difference of 1.8 mm. The individual differences range from 5 mm. to 10 mm., the latter occurring in the Undeformed and in the Cowichan males and females, indicating here a considerable variety of interorbital breadth. The infantile averages range below the adult from 1 mm. to 2 mm., while the juvenile values fit well into the adult ranges without, however, reaching their highest figures.

Among the Undeformed group means, the Eskimo and the Haida represent extremes, the former with 16.5 mm. in the males and 15.3 mm. in the females, the latter with 19.2 mm. and 18.6 mm. in the sexes. A mean of 19.3 mm. is also attained by three Nicola males, the two females of the same tribe yielding 18.5 mm. The larger Cowichan groups produce means deviating only slightly from the divisional average, and the same may likewise be said of the Koskimo groups. The variability centers around ± 2.

5. Sagittal declination of the orbit.

The angle of sagittal declination is formed by the vertical midorbital height line and the ear-eye plane, and is measured toward the orbital cavity. Neither in the Undeformed nor the deformed divisions do the angles reach 90° on an average, and are smaller in the females in a varying degree, as shown in *summary 87*.

Summary 87.

Averages of the angle of sagittal orbital declination.

Sex, Age	Undeformed				Deformation according to the three modes											
					Cowichan				Chinook				Koskimo			
	Cases	Range	Average	σ	Cases	Range	Average	σ	Cases	Range	Average	σ	Cases	Range	Average	σ
♂	73	82–98	89.6	± 4.42	75	81–100	89.2	± 3.88	57	78–100	88.1	± 4.25	98	79–104	88.5	± 3.92
♀	31	79–94	89.0	± 3.77	23	82–97	88.5	± 3.72	25	79–97	86.8	± 3.90	34	77–93	86.3	± 3.84
juv.	1	—	90.0	—	2	87; 90	88.5	—	4	77–88	84.8	—	2	87; 95	91.0	—
inf.	10	90–98	93.1	—	4	88–94	91.0	—	6	82–92	88.0	—	6	85–95	89.5	—

The highest male averages of 89° plus are yielded by the Undeformed and the Cowichan deformation. The females of these two divisions have averages of 89.0° and 88.5°, giving rise to sex differences of 0.6° and 0.7°. The Chinook and Koskimo divisions produce somewhat lower averages, male ones of 88° plus and female ones of 86° plus. The sex differences amount to 1.3° and 2.2° in these two divisions. Although the divisional averages are rather uniform, there is nevertheless a slight diminution to be noticed in the order: Undeformed, and the Cowichan, Chinook and Koskimo deformations. These are all the more important, however, from the view point of deformatory effects as regards metrical conditions where even minute deviations may come to be of diagnostic significance. If the divisional disparities, then, are assumed to be due to the influences of deformation, it is not surprising that the divisional ranges show only slightly such effects. As regards individual values, the Koskimo division not only contains the lowest and highest individual angles at 77° and 104°, but higher individual values occur even in the Cowichan and Chinook divisions when compared with those of the Undeformed. Deforming influences, however, quite probably tell already on the infantile orbits with averages of 93.1° in the Undeformed and 91.0° in the Cowichan, 88.0° in the Chinook and 89.5° in the Koskimo divisions.

The measurements show, that with increasing fronto-occipital compression (Cowichan-Chinook) the sagittal declination of the orbit also increases, i. e., forms smaller angles, and that, always considering the averages, the Koskimo mode of deformation produces similar effects in this respect. On the whole, and particularly in regard to the Undeformed skull, it seems that the morphologically advanced condition is signified by greater angles of sagittal orbital declination, but that the Mongoloids rather tend to produce right angles or such below 90°.

Among the group means of the Undeformed, the Eskimo fall rather low with 87.0° in the males and 85.9° in the females. Conspicuously high, on the other hand, are the Lillooet males and females with averages of 95.0° and 92.0° respectively. The Kamloops males have 95.5°. In fact all the Salish means from the Interior exceed the 90° degree mark, while the Haida attain a mean of 90.0° in the sexes, and the Athapascan males only 88.8°. The group means within the Cowichan deformation show scarcely any aberration from the divisional average. Contrasts are exhibited, however, by the Tsimshian with a male mean of 91.1° and the Yakima with one of 87.8°. The Koskimo means are almost uniform.

The variability is comparatively high considering the minute proportions of this measurement. It oscillates around ± 4, with fractions above in the Undeformed and Chinook males, and below in all the other classes.

MANDIBLE. [48]

With the exception of the absolute dimensions of the lower jaw, regarding the measurements of which there can scarcely be any doubt, the investigation of the angular conditions of its parts has been executed after the method advised by *Klaatsch* (1909) [49], but slightly modified by me (see chapter on technique). I have preferred to relate the angular deviations in the parts of the lower jaws of our series to the line of orientation described there, and have used the calipers for the absolute measurements. The alveolar plane has been used in this chapter under section 8, *a–d*.

1. Bicondylar breadth.

Summary 88.

Averages of the bicondylar breadth of the lower jaw.

Sex, Age	Undeformed				Deformation according to the three modes											
					Cowichan				Chinook				Koskimo			
	Cases	Range	Average	σ	Cases	Range	Average	σ	Cases	Range	Average	σ	Cases	Range	Average	σ
♂	30	97–136	123.9	± 8.46	44	110–142	124.6	± 8.76	4	118–135	126.5	—	31	109–128	119.1	± 5.39
♀	17	103–127	115.7	± 7.79	12	105–135	118.5	± 8.02	1	—	118.0	—	10	105–126	112.7	± 4.25
juv.	—	—	—	—	1	—	113.0	—	—	—	—	—	—	—	—	—
inf.	12	80–109	95.0	—	9	85–108	95.9	—	—	—	—	—	1	—	85.0	—

In this measurement a distinct gradation appears in the divisional averages, as shown in *summary 88*, in the order: Undeformed, Cowichan and Chinook deformations. The Koskimo range below the Undeformed. The sex difference is greatest at 8.2 mm. in the Undeformed, the Cowichan and Koskimo deformations yielding 6.1 mm. and 6.4 mm. The sex difference of 8.5 mm. in the Chinook conforms with the Undeformed, but lacks comparative value because of the presence of only a single female jaw. The infantiles, remaining considerably below the adult figures, yield uniform averages of 95.0 mm. and 95.9 mm. in the Undeformed and Cowichan deformation, the only Koskimo mandible at 85 mm. accidentally maintaining the order observed in the adults where the Koskimo averages were found to fall below those of the other divisions. The ranges are considerably extended in the Undeformed, where they cover forty units in the

---

[48] The number of lower jaws, either separate or belonging to crania, is rather limited in the present series. There are, however, a sufficient number of mandibles to justify their special treatment.

[49] l. c. p. 9 (102).

males and twenty-five in the females. Even the infantiles here vary thirty units. The ranges in the other divisions are somewhat less extended.

A discussion of the group means is hardly justifiable on account of the paucity of lower jaws.

Regarding the gradation as noticed in the divisional averages, the interesting fact presents itself that with intensified antero-posterior compression as instanced by the Cowichan-Chinook modes of deformation, the bicondylar breadth also increases. This is perceivable, however, in the adult state only where the full effects of deformation are evident, the infantiles, at least in the Undeformed and Cowichan deformation, maintaining uniform averages. For the sake of comparison it is rather unfortunate that infantile mandibles of the Chinook were not available. The Koskimo adult averages, on the other hand, apparently show the effects of their specific mode of deformation in averages falling below those of the Undeformed.

The variability is rather irregular, quite high in the Undeformed and Cowichan deformation where it centers around ± 8 in the sexes. In the Koskimo, on the other hand, the males register ± 5.39, the females ± 4.25.

2. Bigonial breadth.

Summary 89.

Averages of the bigonial breadth of the lower jaw.

Sex, Age	Undeformed				Deformation according to the three modes											
					Cowichan				Chinook				Koskimo			
	Cases	Range	Average	σ	Cases	Range	Average	σ	Cases	Range	Average	σ	Cases	Range	Average	σ
♂	30	85–117	106.0	± 7.51	43	82–120	103.3	± 8.61	4	101–108	104.0	—	30	88–119	103.4	± 8.89
♀	17	86–110	98.0	± 6.10	13	82–102	97.1	± 7.41	1	—	104.0	—	11	91–111	100.5	± 5.69
juv.	—	—	—	—	1	—	92.0	—	—	—	—	—	—	—	—	—
inf.	8	72–97	80.4	—	9	79–86	80.3	—	—	—	—	—	1	—	75.0	—

The comparison of *summary 89* with the preceding one shows that a gradation between the averages as noticed in the bicondylar breadth is not observed in the bigonial breadth. The relative uniformity of average figures is, therefore, not suggestive of deformatory effects which one was tempted to assume for the bicondylar breadth.

The ranges, however, show everywhere considerable extension similar to the conditions met in the preceding measurement.

The group means again are derived from too few numbers to be of comparative value. It may be worth mentioning, however, that the few Lillooet exhibit the high means of 116.0 mm. and 105.5 mm. in the sexes, which might be attributed to their marked shortheadedness.

The variability is unusually high at ± 8 plus in the Cowichan and Koskimo males and at ± 7 in the Undeformed males and the Cowichan females. The Undeformed females yield ± 6.10 and the Koskimo females ± 5.69.

3. Breadth index.

The observation of an increasing bicondylar breadth in the order: Undeformed, and the Cowichan and Chinook deformations, the latter apparently representative of deformatory effects, and a foreshortening of the same breadth in the Koskimo as a probable result of their mode of deformation, is clearly reflected by the breadth index of the lower jaw, all the more so since its other factor, the bigonial breadth, proves to be the more stable of the two.

Summary 90.

Averages of the breadth index of the lower jaw.

Sex, Age	Undeformed				Deformation according to the three modes											
					Cowichan				Chinook				Koskimo			
	Cases	Range	Average	σ	Cases	Range	Average	σ	Cases	Range	Average	σ	Cases	Range	Average	σ
♂	30	76.9–94.4	85.9	± 4.01	44	71.3–94.6	83.3	± 4.15	4	77.7–82.1	79.1	—	30	71.7–98.6	86.1	± 6.54
♀	17	67.5–94.0	84.6	± 6.11	12	74.6 96.2	82.2	± 6.52	1	—	88.1	—	11	81.4–93.2	88.0	± 3.15
juv.	—	—	—	—	—	—	—	—	—	—	—	—	—	—	—	—
inf.	12	74.3–102.1	85.8	—	9	75.9–96.5	84.1	—	—	—	—	—	—	—	88.0	—

As specified in *summary 90*, the male averages in the above named order amount to 85.9 in the Undeformed, 83.3 in the Cowichan and 79.1 in the Chinook, while the Koskimo males with 86.1 even slightly exceed the Undeformed males. The female averages in the Undeformed and Cowichan deformation with index averages slightly below the males maintain the same order. The single Chinook female at 88.1 lacks comparative value, but the Koskimo female average at 88.0, like the male one, ranges also highest, exceeding the Undeformed female average by 3.4 units. A slight diminution is also noticeable between the Undeformed and Cowichan infantiles, with averages of 85.8 and 84.1, the one Koskimo infantile preserving, accidentally, also here the order repeatedly mentioned, while on the whole they conform to the adult averages.

The group means are more or less in keeping with the averages. The divisional ranges, however, are everywhere quite extended, amounting at their highest to 26.9 in the Koskimo males.

The variability falls above ± 6 in the Undeformed and Cowichan females and in the Koskimo males; above ± 4 in the Undeformed and Cowichan males and above ± 3 in the Koskimo females.

4. Height of ramus.

The height of the ascending ramus of the lower jaw, as stated before, was taken on the object itself between the condylion and gonion. The latter is not always easily determined, but difficulties will readily be overcome by following *R. Martin's* (Lehrbuch, 1914, 517) instruction.

The ramus height, as shown in *summary 91*, is fairly uniform in the male mandibles where it yields averages of 61.9 mm. in the Undeformed and 62.3 mm., 60.8 mm. and 62.6 mm. in the

Summary 91.

Averages of the ramus height of the lower jaw.

Sex, Age	Undeformed				Deformation according to the three modes											
					Cowichan				Chinook				Koskimo			
	Cases	Range	Average	σ	Cases	Range	Average	σ	Cases	Range	Average	σ	Cases	Range	Average	σ
♂	33	48–78	61.9	± 5.51	52	50–74	62.3	± 5.93	4	56–61	60.8	—	31	57–74	62.6	± 4.10
♀	18	46–66	56.4	± 4.59	16	47–62	53.9	± 4.18	1	—	52.0	—	11	50–65	58.2	± 3.51
juv.	—	—	—	—	2	44; 51	47.5	—	—	—	—	—	—	—	—	—
inf.	13	30–49	41.8	—	10	36–49	40.2	—	—	—	—	—	1	—	43.0	—

Cowichan, Chinook and Koskimo deformations. The female averages, indicating the smaller size of the female mandible, are somewhat less uniform at 56.4 mm. in the Undeformed, 53.9 mm. in the Cowichan, 52.0 mm. in the Chinook and 58.2 mm. in the Koskimo divisions. The Chinook value, however, being an individual one and leaving, therefore, out of consideration its sex difference, the greatest sex difference, then, is seen to occur in the Cowichan division of 8.4 mm. which is followed by the Undeformed with 5.5 mm. and the Koskimo with only 4.4 mm.

The infantile averages naturally keep far below the adult status with 41.8 mm. and 40.2 mm. in the Undeformed and Cowichan, the single Koskimo infantile accidentally following the adults which were seen to yield the highest male and female averages. The two juveniles of the Cowichan division with an average of 47.5 mm. keep about midway between the infantiles and females of that division.

The ranges here also show a considerable extension which covers as many as thirty-one units in the Undeformed males, and even twenty units in the infantiles of the same division. The physiological range of the ramus height, as given by R. *Martin* (Lehrbuch, 1914, 882) for the human varieties, i. e., 50–77 mm., is, with reference to the North Pacific Coast Indians, slightly to be expanded to 46–78 mm.

The group means are derived from altogether too few individuals to be of definite comparative value. The Haida male mean, however, derived from fourteen specimens yields as high an average as 65.4 mm. thus exceeding the Undeformed average by 3.5 mm., while the female mean of the same group exceeds the divisional average by 2.1 mm. This condition seems to be of some significance because the Haida ranges commence at a comparatively high figure, and also contain the highest individual values of the division. In the Cowichan division the jaws from Vancouver show a rather low mean of 59.3 mm. in the males, who thus fall short of the divisional average by 3.0 mm., while the female mean of the same group slightly exceeds the divisional average. Slight oscillations also occur in the Koskimo means.

The variability in the Undeformed and Cowichan males lies above ± 5; between ± 4 and ± 5 in the Undeformed and Cowichan females and in the Koskimo males, and drops with ± 3.51 below ± 4 in the Koskimo females.

5. Breadth of ramus.

As in the ramus height, the average of the ramus breadth at 38.7 mm. slightly exceeds in the Koskimo males the averages of the other divisions which register 37.7 mm in the Undeformed and 36.6 mm. and 36.0 mm. in the Cowichan and Chinook deformations (see *summary 92*). At the same time these latter three decrease very little. The female averages in all the divisions and

Summary 92.

Averages of the ramus breadth of the lower jaw.

Sex, Age	Undeformed				Deformation according to the three modes											
					Cowichan				Chinook				Koskimo			
	Cases	Range	Average	σ	Cases	Range	Average	σ	Cases	Range	Average	σ	Cases	Range	Average	σ
♂	33	29–44	37.7	± 3.13	53	31–46	36.6	± 2.95	4	34–38	36.0	—	31	34–43	38.7	± 2.54
♀	18	29–40	34.2	± 2.73	16	29–39	34.4	± 2.52	1	—	27.0	—	11	31–41	34.6	± 3.14
juv.	—	—	—	—	2	32; 34	33.0	—	—	—	—	—	—	—	—	—
inf.	13	22–31	26.8	—	10	22–32	26.7	—	—	—	—	—	1	—	23.0	—

34 mm. plus. The single Chinook jaw at 27 mm. cannot be compared with the average figures. The sex differences at 4.1 mm. are highest in the Koskimo and somewhat less in the Undeformed at 3.5 mm. and in the Cowichan at 2.2 mm., all of them, however, in favor of the males. The infantile averages and the two Cowichan juveniles naturally range below the adults. The ranges, considering the particular nature of the measurement, are somewhat more concentrated than those of the preceding measurement.

Among the Undeformed group means, the Haida, both male and female, range the highest, repeating thus the condition observed in connection with the preceding measurement, while the Athapascan, on the other hand, fall below the divisional average. However insignificant such differences may appear, their importance grows when it is considered that the variability of minute measurements may be an expression of group characteristics. Slight differences of group means are also noticeable in the Cowichan and Koskimo divisions.

The variability centers around ± 3.

6. Ramus index.

Summary 93.

Averages of the ramus index of the lower jaw.

Sex, Age	Undeformed				Deformation according to the three modes											
					Cowichan				Chinook				Koskimo			
	Cases	Range	Average	σ	Cases	Range	Average	σ	Cases	Range	Average	σ	Cases	Range	Average	σ
♂	33	48.7–72.7	61.3	± 5.06	52	48.6–82.7	62.2	± 6.43	4	58.1–62.7	61.0	—	31	52.3–74.1	61.7	± 5.14
♀	18	50.9–68.5	60.8	± 4.63	16	53.2–74.9	64.6	± 5.27	1	—	71.2	—	11	49.2–69.6	60.8	± 7.11
juv.	—	—	—	—	2	62.7; 77.3	70.0	—	—	—	—	—	—	—	—	—
inf.	13	58.7–77.5	65.1	—	10	57.1–74.4	66.4	—	—	—	—	—	1	—	53.5	—

The male averages of this index as listed in *summary 93* are almost uniform in the four divisions at 61 plus. The exact uniformity of the female averages of 60.8 in the Undeformed and

Koskimo is met by a somewhat higher average of 64.6 in the Cowichan females, due apparently to the relatively lesser ramus height of the latter. There is a sex difference of 2.4 in their favor, while in the other divisions the females fall slightly below the males. The two infantile averages, the Undeformed and Cowichan at 65.1 and 66.6, exceed the adult ones of the same divisions by several units, thus expressing the character of the infantile ramus with its undeveloped height extension. The two Cowichan juveniles at 70.0 represent two values occurring in the extreme upper end of the total range of variation.

The divisional ranges as such are of considerable extension, amounting at their highest to thirty-five units in the Cowichan males, the others being somewhat less extended but still comprising in the Undeformed females nineteen units at the lowest. Our findings corroborate R. Martin's (Lehrbuch, 1914, 882) statement of an index range from 40.3–74.6. In his table of averages (p. 882) he lists the Mongols with 60.1, to which the North Pacific averages fairly conform.

The Haida group means of 61.0 in the sexes, derived from measurements slightly in excess of the average conditions in the Undeformed, as was shown in the two preceding sections, correspond here with the divisional average. Exceeding the Cowichan average are the Vancouver group means of 64.0 and 66.9 in the sexes, resulting evidently from a slightly reduced ramus height as well as a somewhat enlarged breadth diameter of the ramus as expressed by their averages. The Koskimo means are grouped closely around their divisional average.

The variability at ± 7.11 is rather high in the Koskimo females. The males of the Cowichan have ± 6.43, while those of the Koskimo and Undeformed divisions and the Cowichan females vary around ± 5, and the Undeformed females at ± 4.63.

7. Height of chin.

Summary 94.

Averages of the height of the chin.

Sex, Age	Undeformed				Deformation according to the three modes											
					Cowichan				Chinook				Koskimo			
	Cases	Range	Average	σ	Cases	Range	Average	σ	Cases	Range	Average	σ	Cases	Range	Average	σ
♂	32	28–41	35.7	± 3.39	52	31–40	34.8	± 2.34	4	32–36	34.3	—	33	30–42	35.2	± 3.06
♀	18	26–37	32.7	± 3.04	16	26–39	32.6	± 3.06	1	—	32.0	—	10	31–38	34.3	± 2.26
juv.	—	—	—	—	2	27; 28	27.5	—	—	—	—	—	—	—	—	—
inf.	13	19–28	24.5	—	10	22–28	25.0	—	—	—	—	—	1	—	24.0	—

This measurement is treated of here as one of the factors involved in the "antero-basal" angle (see under 8c, this chapter).

Few disparities are noted in the averages of the chin height. The male averages, according to *summary 94*, are grouped around 35 mm., the female at 32 mm. plus, rising to 34.3 mm. in the Koskimo females. Sex differences amount to 3.0 mm. in the Undeformed and 2.2 mm. in the Cowichan, but only to 0.9 mm. in the Koskimo. The infantile averages are similarly uniform, although noticeably lower.

The ranges are rather extended in spite of the minuteness of the measurement and the close similarity of the adult averages. They run highest in the Undeformed males and the Cowichan females, namely, from 28 mm. to 41 mm., and from 26 mm. to 39 mm., and lowest from 31 mm. to 38 mm. in the Koskimo females, thus covering fourteen units in the Cowichan and nine units in the latter.

The variability centers quite uniformly around ± 3, dropping to ± 2 plus in the Cowichan males and the Koskimo females.

8. Angular relations.

a. Angular relations between alveolar plane and ramus tangent ("ramus angle").

The angular relation between the ramus tangent and the alveolar plane, which might be designated the "ramus angle" of the lower jaw, and which naturally differs from the ramus angle (angulus mandibularis) between the ramus tangent and the base of the mandible, exhibits a certain gradation in the divisional averages as well as a distinct sex difference.

Summary 95.

Averages of the "ramus angle" of the lower jaw.

Sex, Age	Undeformed				Deformation according to the three modes											
					Cowichan				Chinook				Koskimo			
	Cases	Range	Average	σ	Cases	Range	Average	σ	Cases	Range	Average	σ	Cases	Range	Average	σ
♂	34	55–79	69.0	± 5.71	52	59–85	71.9	± 5.56	4	64–73	68.5	—	32	60–87	75.9	± 4.87
♀	18	57–70	64.2	± 3.34	16	65–74	65.1	± 5.38	1	—	77.0	—	10	68–78	72.6	± 4.25
juv.	—	—	—	—	2	65; 66	65.5	—	—	—	—	—	—	—	—	—
inf.	12	46–63	55.9	—	10	49–62	55.2	—	—	—	—	—	1	—	55.0	—

The Undeformed male average of 69.0°, as shown in *summary 95*, is exceeded by that of the Cowichan and Koskimo males with 71.9° and 75.9° respectively. The Chinook average of 68.5° falls below that of the Undeformed males, but its comparative value as derived from only four individuals is somewhat uncertain. The female averages increase in the same order as the male, yielding 64.2° in the Undeformed and 65.1° and 72.6° in the Cowichan and Koskimo deformations. While the increase between the Undeformed and the Cowichan deformations is not exceedingly strong, a peculiar upward trend takes place between the averages of the Cowichan and Koskimo deformations, the differences in the first instance amounting to 2.9° in the males and to 0.9° in the females, and in the second to 4.0° and 7.5° respectively. The sex difference within the divisions is highest at 6.8° in the Cowichan deformation, amounting to 4.8° in the Undeformed and 3.3° in the Koskimo deformation. The infantile averages of the Undeformed and Cowichan uniformly yield 55° and fractions, a figure which the single Koskimo infantile jaw also attains.

The variability oscillates around ± 4, but rises above ± 5 in the Undeformed males, and in both sexes of the Cowichan deformation.

A problem of peculiar interest arises here with regard to the gradually progressing erectness of the ascending ramus of the lower jaw as indicated by the "ramus angle" in the order: Undeformed-Cowichan-Koskimo, and dependent apparently on the mode and degree of deformation in the different divisions. The causation of this phenomenon is a matter not easily ascertained and is probably implicated with functional action and counteraction under deformatory strains.

Figure 20 illustrates the angular relation under discussion. In *a* the divisional deviation is schematically illustrated, males and females combined,

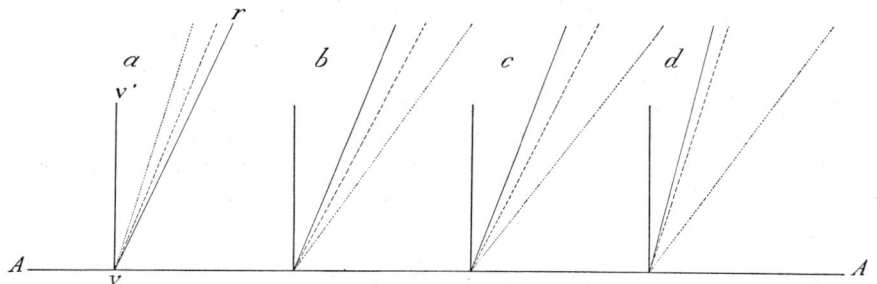

Fig. 20. Scheme of average conditions of the ramus angle of the lower jaw ($\angle r\text{-}v\text{-}A'$). $A\text{-}A'$, alveolar plane; $v\text{-}v'$; orienting perdendicular.
a, divisional averages, males and females combined: ——— Undeformed; - - - - Cowichan, ... Koskimo deformations, the same varied lines signifying males, females and immatures in *b*, *c* and *d*, the letters representing the Undeformed, Cowichan and Koskimo divisions.

by varied lines representing the average declination of the ramus tangent on the alveolar plane line in the Undeformed and the Cowichan and Koskimo deformations. In the following schemes the same three lines signify the male, female and infantile angularity, in (*b*) the Undeformed, (*c*) the Cowichan and (*d*) the Koskimo deformations. An orienting perpendicular is attached to each diagram.

The combined males and females of *a* produce angle averages of 67.3° in the Undeformed, 70.3° in the Cowichan 75.1° in the Koskimo deformations. In *b*, *c* and *d* the male angles in each case, indicating a more pronounced erectness of the ramus at 69.0° in the Undeformed, 71.9° in the Cowichan and 75.9° in the Koskimo, exceed the female. The latter, in the same divisional order, yield angles of 64.2°, 65.1° and 72.6°, and the infantiles fall short of the females at 55.9°, 55.2° and 55.0°.

The striking feature about the posterior border of the ascending ramus, as was pointed out before, is its gradually increasing erectness with intensified deformation. Fig. 20 plainly demonstrates this feature. In fig. 21 three cases from the Haida series are superposed, a male (no. 3741), a female (no. 1608) and an infantile (no. 3752). They are oriented on the alveolar plane line ($A\text{-}A'$) and made to coincide on their coronoid verticals ($c\text{-}v$). The posterior outlines of the rami are thus separated for better comparison and their tangents drawn in conformity with the varied lines distinguishing the three outlines. The ramus angles here repeat the average angularities as shown in fig. 20, pointing out at the same time what appear to be typical differences of ramus declination in the male, female and infantile mandibles, amounting to 69°, 63° and 46°.

b. Angular relations between the ramus and basal tangents ("postero-basal" angle).

The angle formed by the ramus and basal tangents, which may properly be termed "postero-basal", is closely dependent on the behavior of the ramus tangent in the four divisions. It is fairly identical with the ramus angle (angulus mandibularis) secured with the gnathometer. The "postero-basal" angle treated of in this section, it may be repeated, was taken from the mandibulogram.

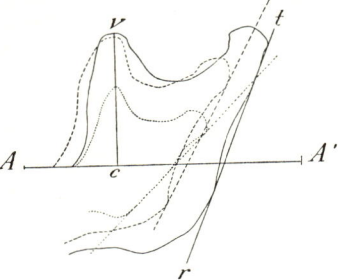

Fig. 21. Superposition of ramus outlines of lower jaws oriented on the alveolar plane ($A-A'$) and coronoid vertical ($c-v$), to show the typical deviation of the ramus tangent ($r-t$) in the male (——— Haida, 3741, at 69°), female (- - - Haida, 1608, at 63°), and infantile (.... Haida, 3752, at 46°). Reduced.

Summary 96.
Averages of the "postero-basal" angle of the lower jaw.

Sex, Age	Undeformed				Deformation according to the three modes									
					Cowichan				Chinook				Koskimo			
	Cases	Range	Average	σ	Cases	Range	Average	σ	Cases	Range	Average	σ	Cases	Range	Average	σ
♂	34	100–137	118.4	± 6.75	52	99–131	114.4	± 6.80	4	115–125	118.8	—	32	101–130	112.5	± 5.51
♀	18	116–131	124.2	± 4.90	15	113–133	122.1	± 5.52	1	—	115.0	—	10	110–124	118.4	± 4.50
juv.	—	—	—	—	2	120; 125	122.5	—	—	—	—	—	—	—	—	—
nf.	13	122–140	129.3	—	10	122–137	130.2	—	—	—	—	—	1	—	130.0	—

From *summary 96* it will be seen that in both sexes average angles decrease in the order: Undeformed, Cowichan and Koskimo deformations, and do so in direct correlation with the varying averages of the ramus angle (see *summary 95*).

The female averages conforming to the order of the males, exceed the males, which is likewise coincident with the smaller female ramus angle. The four male Chinook with a "postero-basal" angle of 118.8° disrupt the progressing order of averages. Since, however only, a very limited number of lower jaws are involved here, the definite evaluation of the Chinook average is rather uncertain. The sex difference at 7.7° is highest in the Cowichan division, while the Undeformed and Koskimo divisions differ equally at 5.8° and 5.9°. The infantile averages exhibit the same constancy as found in the preceding measurement. They exceed the adults in about the same proportion as was realized between the male and female averages. The ranges are rather wide in the males, and somewhat less extended in the fewer females. The widest male range is found in the Undeformed where it comprises thirty-eight units, the widest female with twenty-one units belonging in the Cowichan deformation. But even the still fewer infantiles show ranges from 122° to 140° in the Undeformed, and from 122° to 137° in the Cowichan.

The variability is only slightly higher than in the preceding measurement. It rises above ± 6 in the Undeformed and Cowichan males, above ± 5 in the Cowichan females and Koskimo males, and lies between ± 4 and ± 5 in the Undeformed and Koskimo females.

The size of the "postero-basal" angle, as stated before, depends on the extent of declination of the ramus tangent, and only in a minor degree on that of the basal tangent. The greater constancy of the latter may be judged from the following tabular statement, in which the angular relations of the ramus and basal tangents to the alveolar plane line are listed side by side.

Series	Angles of tangents with alveolar plane	
	ramus	basal
Undeformed, ♂ + ♀	67.3°	7°
„ males	69.6°	7°
„ females	64.2°	6°
„ infantiles	55.9°	4°
Cowichan, ♂ + ♀	70.3°	5°
„ males	71.9°	4°
„ females	65.1°	7°
„ infantiles	55.2°	4°
Koskimo, ♂ + ♀	75.1°	8°
„ males	75.9°	8°
„ females	72.6°	10°
„ infantiles	55.0°	4°

The divisional averages of these two angles, males and females combined, amount to 67.3° and 7° in the Undeformed, and to 70.3° and 5° in the Cowichan, giving rise to differences of 3° and 2° between the corresponding angles. The Koskimo averages of 75.1° and 8° compared with those of the Undeformed, increase the difference between the ramus tangents to 7.8°, while that between the basal tangents amounts only to 1°. Similar and more pronounced conditions are met between the sexes and the immatures in each division.

Regarding the angularity of the basal tangent on the gonion parallel to the alveolar plane, it must be borne in mind that there are two quantities involved; the height of the chin and that of the corpus mandibulae, both of them bearing on the angularity. The corpus height, almost without exception, remains below that of the chin in all the specimens. There are, however, a few cases in which the chin height remains slightly below that of the corpus, thus producing angularities between the alveolar plane and the basal tangent of −1°, i.e., forming an angle which opens backward. The greatest deviation, on the other hand, does not exceed $+13°$ in favor of a higher chin. Corresponding, on the whole, to the morphological conditions most generally encountered in the Mongoloid mandible, the corpus and chin heights of the Indian mandible also differ very little, and thus produce only slight basal deviations.

c. Angular relations between chin vertical and basal tangent ("antero-basal" angle).

The "antero-basal" angle of the lower jaw as formed by the chin vertical and the basal tangent is primarily dependent on the height of the chin, and consequently on the angular relation of the basal tangent with the alveolar plane. Both factors present only slight sex differences, and repeat that condition in the "antero-basal" angle.

Summary 97.
Averages of the "antero-basal" angle of the lower jaw.

Sex, Age	Undeformed				Deformation according to the three modes										
					Cowichan				Chinook				Koskimo		
	Cases	Range	Average	σ	Cases	Range	Average	σ	Cases	Range	Average	σ	Cases	Range	Average	σ
♂	34	69–89	81.8	± 4.52	52	76–91	83.2	± 3.57	4	77–82	79.8	—	32	72–86	80.0	± 3.04
♀	18	72–86	80.5	± 4.47	15	75–87	81.7	± 3.72	1	—	77.0	—	10	67–83	77.8	± 4.21
juv.	—	—	—	—	2	79; 84	81.5	—	—	—	—	—	—	—	—	—
inf.	13	72–86	83.1	—	10	79–86	82.9	—	—	—	—	—	1	—	83.0	—

The averages, as specified in *summary 97*, lie around 80°. Compared with the Undeformed of both sexes, there is a slight rise of averages to be noted in the Cowichan deformation and a slight relapse in the Koskimo. These results are entirely prompted by corresponding conditions in the chin height, causing the greater height to produce smaller angles, and vice versa. The condition of mutual equipoise of the two factors involved is likewise present in the infantiles. Their chin heights, especially, as well as their alveolar plane-basal tangent angles remain considerably below the mature state. The average of 83.1° in the Undeformed infantiles is slightly in excess of the Undeformed adults, and the average of 82.9° in the Cowichan infantiles, which latter figure almost conforms with the average of the Cowichan males.

The ranges show considerable extension, varying from thirteen units in the Cowichan females to twenty-one units in the Undeformed males.

The variability turns out accordingly and centers around ± 4, but drops to ± 3.04 in the Koskimo males.

d. Angular relations between the alveolar plane and condylo-coronoid line ("condylo-coronoid" angle).

The "condylo-coronoid" angle formed by the condylo-coronoid tangent and a parallel to the alveolar plane passing through the coronion, the summit point of the coronoid process, may be neutral, negative or positive. In the first case the condylo-coronoid tangent and the alveolar plane coincide; the negative and positive angles open backward either above (−) or below (+) the coronion parallel of the alveolar plane line, in direct expression of the condition of the processus coronoideus which either exceeds or falls short of the processus condyloideus. These conditions are illustrated in fig. 22 by three representative cases in the superposition of the ramus outlines above the alveolar plane line. Oriented on the alveolar plane, the coronia coinciding, they represent a Haida female (———— 3742) at 0°; a Lillooet female (- - - 2624) at −8°; and a Haida infantile (.... 1615) at + 15°.

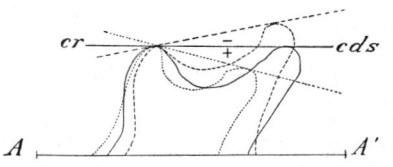

Fig. 22. Illustrating the angular possibilities between the condylo-coronoid tangent *cr* (coronion) − *cds* (condylion superius) and the alveolar plane (*A–A'*). ———— neutral (*O*); - - - - positive (−); ..... negative (+) angle. Reduced.

Summary 98.

Averages of the "condylo-coronoid" angle of the lower jaw.

Sex, Age	Undeformed				Deformation according to the three modes											
					Cowichan				Chinook				Koskimo			
	Cases	Range	Average	σ	Cases	Range	Average	σ	Cases	Range	Average	σ	Cases	Range	Average	σ
♂	34	−18 to +18	+0.4	±7.22	52	−18 to +20	−1.2	±8.22	4	−12 to −1	−7.0	—	32	−24 to +8	−5.2	±6.54
♀	18	−12 to +12	−1.4	±6.44	16	−17 to +11	−1.9	±7.79	1	—	−8	—	10	−16 to +9	−6.6	±6.19
juv.	—	—	—	—	2	−6; +5	−0.5	—	—	—	—	—	—	—	—	—
inf.	12	−8 to +28	+12.8	—	10	+4 to +20	+12.5	—	—	—	—	—	1	—	+26	—

Summary 98 reveals the surprising fact that the averages of the deformed series exceed the Undeformed averages in the increase of the negative state of the "condylo-coronoid" angle, i. e., when the coronoid height remains below the condyloid height. The averages of the Undeformed amount to + 0.4° in the males and — 1.4° in the females, those of the Cowichan deformation to — 1.2° and — 1.9° in the sexes. Although the increase is only slight here, it is quite pronounced in the Koskimo division with a male average of — 5.2° and a female one of — 6.6°, i.e., in excess even of the Cowichan averages to the amount of — 4° in the males and of — 4·7° in the females. Four Chinook males yield as high an average as — 7.0°.

One is tempted to lay this behavior to deformatory influences, although a convincing proof is exceedingly difficult. It is well known that the physiological task of mastication in conjunction with the successive eruption of the permanent denture and general osseous growth has a direct influence on the shaping and angular position of the ascending ramus, so that in the adult state the latter reaches not only its best adapted morphological form, but also its greatest degree of erectness. While the relative height of the processus coronoideus is quite probably a rather stationary moment in the morphology of the lower jaw, particularly in view of racial expression in the adult state, one would have to consider the possibility of greater erectness of the ramus in the case of increased physiological demands ("Beanspruchung") and, as a secondary result, the receding coronoid height as compared with the rising condyloid one. Such changes are, of course, very minute but recordable by metrical interpretation. A cause might be given in the shifting of muscular attachment as a result of artificial head deformation, but such speculations appear rather vague.

The peculiar trend of the averages of the "condylo-coronoid" angle is distinctly corroborated by the averages of the ramus angle which are listed beside the former in the following table where males and females are combined:

Series	Condylo-coronoid angle	Ramus angle
♂ + ♀		
Undeformed	$-0.2°$	$67.3°$
Cowichan ⎫ deformation	$-1.4°$	$70.3°$
Koskimo ⎭	$-4.7°$	$75.1°$

The correlation between these two series of figures is clearly demonstrated i. e., that with the increase in the size of the negative "condylo-coronoid" angle, the increase of the ramus angles goes hand in hand. From the mechanical point of view the argument may even be reserved in so far as the increase of the "condylo-coronoid" angle, i.e., its minus state, may be considered a result of the erection of the ascending ramus.

The physiological nature of the problem is furthermore emphasized by the behavior of the infantile jaws. They have naturally positive angles at averages of $+12.8°$ in the Undeformed and $+12.5°$ in the Cowichan, the single Koskimo infantile jaw even listing an individual value of $+26°$.

The divisional ranges are exceedingly wide, both sides, the minus and plus, participating in their extensions, and are equivalent in the Undeformed, where the male range runs from $+18°$ to $-18°$, the female one from $+12°$ to $-12°$. This proportion is distinctly changed in the Koskimo division with a male range from $+8°$ to $-24°$, and a female one from $+9°$ to $-16°$.

The variability is as high as ± 8.22 in the Cowichan males, and lies above ± 7 in the Undeformed males and Cowichan females, while the Undeformed females and both sexes of the Koskimo vary at figures above ± 6.

SUMMARY TO PART I: Craniometry.

1. Comparative aspect of the four series (divisions).

In consideration of the peculiar nature of the skull material collected by the Jesup Expedition, the division into four independently treated series suggested itself. A distinction was therefore made between undeformed and deformed crania, the latter resulting from the various methods of mechanical head deformation which have been described in a special chapter (see p. 12), and which may be reduced to two fundamental types: the antero-posterior and the conical compression. The skull material then comprises in addition to the Undeformed, the three series deformed in the Cowichan, Chinook and Koskimo fashions. The cranio-metrical treatment of the Cowichan and Chinook series representing the anteroposterior deformation in an increasing measure, and of the Koskimo series deformed by the conical method, has shown that from the quantitative point of view, the physiological ranges as such hardly differ from those of the normal, i. e., undeformed skulls. This proves not only the natural difference in physical size, but the extent of individual yielding to the deformatory strains and, still more important, the measure of individual retention of the effects of deformation. Although not directly provable, the range, i. e. the variation of such effects suggests, nevertheless, the probability, in individual cases, of a partial reversion toward the normal after the discontinuation of the deformatory practice. *Kunike, Hugo*, 1911, Beiträge zur Anthropologie der Calchaqui-Täler. Arch. Anthrop., N. F., v. X, pp. 203—237 (218), expresses himself similarly in saying "Wie es uns bei genauer vergleichender Betrachtung der Schädel namentlich jüngerer und älterer Individuen erscheinen will, verliert sich die Deformation mit zunehmenden Alter. Die Schädel haben offenbar also in sich die Tendenz, sich selbst zum Normaltypus zu restituieren." This probability doubtless accounts for the occasionally pronounced divagation of average conditions of groups (called means in our specific case) comprised in a deformed series or division, and which are recorded in the tables of measurements.

The quantitative treatment, applying the customary methods equally to the undeformed and deformed crania, was intended to assertan, first of all, the metrical data, which in average expressions were then used for serial comparison. The latter was carried on for a legitimate expression of deviation from the normal, not only between the deformed series, but between these and the Undeformed.[50] As already outlined in the introductory chapter, all the undeformed groups for this purpose were combined in order to gain generalized average expressions of normal cranial dimensions in contradistinction to such derived from the distorted ones. This appeared to be permissable under the reservation of individual treatment in this discussion, of the various tribal elements constituting the Undeformed division.

The effects of deformation upon the head may be recognized as direct or indirect results of deformatory strain. In the former class, for instance, fall the cranial length, breadth and height variations including the changes in cranial vaulting, the angular relations of cranial parts to a plane of orientation, in our case the ear-eye plane, and the angular intracranial relations such as the cranio-facial and "central" angles. Changes, on the other hand, in the angularity of the cranial base, the foramen magnum plane, orbital declination and prognathy, increase in bicondylar breadth, and a number of others very probably come about indirectly, i. e. through a combination of factors, complicated pressure effects and physiological adjustments. *Hrdlička*[51] likewise points out that "the deformation, if marked, affects the base, the orbits and the facial parts of the skull", where direct as well as indirect effects must be accounted for.

A comparative list of the more significant divisional averages is contained in *summary 99,* where the differences between the averages of the deformed series and those of the Undeformed are expressed in multiples of the latter's standard deviations according to the formula: $\frac{\text{difference}}{\sigma}$, and which represent the σ-quotients here and in the following summaries. This summary is supplemented by the metrical diagram I. The measurements in both the summary and chart have been arranged for practical reasons in the order: cranial capacity; length, breadth and height measurements of both the cerebral and facial cranium; indices and angles.

a. Cerebral cranium.

The study of the metrical diagram I immediately reveals the fact that the greatest deviations as judged by the Undeformed conditions, occur in the cranial dimensions which were under direct deformatory stress, and in the indices and angles in which they are involved. This means for the Cowichan and Chinook a foreshortening of the *cranial length* (2), a modified *height* (15),

---

[50] As early as 1890, *Boas* (1890, 812) in his report to the British Association for the Advancement of Science, on the Indians of British Columbia, conceived of a comparative craniometrical investigation of skulls deformed in various ways, saying that "It may be of interest to show the effect of these methods upon the length and width of the crania."

[51] *Hrdlička Aleš*, 1920. Anthropometry. Philadelphia, p. 48.

Summary 99. Metrical differentiation: the four main divisions. Basis: Undeformed. Males and females combined (see diagram 1).

Measurement	Undeformed Average	σ ±	Cowichan Average	Differ-ence	σ-quo-tient	Chinook Average	Differ-ence	σ-quo-tient	Koskimo Average	Differ-ence	σ-quo-tient
1. Capacity	1317.2 ♂ 1349.5 ♀ 1243.8	111.45	1320.2 ♂ 1360.3 ♀ 1209.6	+ 3.0	+ .03	1347.0 ♂ 1388.8 ♀ 1251.6	+29.8	+ .3	1360.7 ♂ 1396.3 ♀ 1264.2	+43.5	+ .4
Length											
2. cranial	174.0	6.57	167.8	— 8.2	— 1.2	164.8	— 9.2	— 1.3	180.9	+ 6.9	+ 1.0
3. cranial base	101.2	4.02	98.2	— 3.0	— .8	95.9	— 5.3	— 1.3	99.3	— 1.9	— .5
4. foramen magnum	35.7	2.04	33.4	— 2.3	— 1.1	33.8	— 1.9	— 1.0	34.1	— 1.6	— .8
5. facial	100.4	4.35	100.5	+ .1	+ .02	100.3	+ .1	+ .02	99.9	— .5	— .1
6. maxillo-alveolar	52.9	2.80	53.6	+ .7	+ .3	53.0	+ .1	— .03	53.2	+ .3	+ .1
Breadth											
7. cranial	139.5	5.22	149.4	+ 9.9	+ 1.9	154.3	+14.8	+ 2.8	137.3	— 2.2	— .4
8. minimum frontal	93.3	5.90	94.3	+ 1.0	+ .2	97.2	+ 3.9	+ .7	93.3	=	=
9. 1 izygomatic	135.7	6.01	140.8	+ 5.3	+ .9	139.1	+ 3.4	+ .5	136.0	+ .3	+ .1
10. maxillo-alveolar	64.9	3.47	63.0	— 1.9	— .5	65.4	+ .5	+ .1	65.3	+ .4	+ .1
11. orbital (mf)	43.4	1.80	43.1	— .3	— .2	43.2	— .2	— .1	43.7	+ .3	+ .2
12. anterior interorbital	17.4	2.0	17.7	+ .3	+ .2	18.4	+ 1.0	+ .5	17.6	+ .2	+ .1
13. nasal	24.5	2.75	23.7	— .8	— .3	23.7	— .8	— .3	26.6	+ 2.1	+ .8
14. bicondylar	120.8	8.12	123.2	+ 2.4	+ .3	123.6	+ 2.8	+ .3	117.4	— 3.4	— .4
Height											
15. cranial	133.1	5.79	130.3	— 2.8	— .5	126.6	— 6.5	— 1.1	134.7	+ 1.6	+ .3
16. upper facial	73.6	4.54	71.8	— 1.8	— .4	72.3	— 1.3	— .3	75.5	+ 1.9	+ .4
17. orbital	35.7	1.97	36.2	— .5	+ .3	36.3	+ .6	+ .3	37.0	+ 1.3	+ .7
18. nasal	52.6	3.86	51.1	— 1.5	— .4	51.6	— 1.0	— .3	52.9	+ .3	+ .1
Index											
19. cranial L—Br	78.6 ♂ 78.0 ♀ 80.0	3.94	89.7 ♂ 89.4 ♀ 90.9	+11.1	+ 2.8	92.4 ♂ 92.1 ♀ 93.2	+13.8	+ 3.5	76.4 ♂ 76.3 ♀ 76.9	— 2.2	— .6
20. „ L—H	75.0 ♂ 74.3 ♀ 76.5	3.41	77.8 ♂ 77.7 ♀ 78.1	+ 2.8	+ .8	76.8 ♂ 77.3 ♀ 75.6	+ 1.8	+ .5	72.1 ♂ 72.0 ♀ 72.5	— 2.9	— .9
21 „ Br—H	95.5 ♂ 95.5 ♀ 95.5	5.70	87.5 ♂ 87.3 ♀ 87.9	— 8.0	— 1.4	82.2 ♂ 82.6 ♀ 81.2	—13.3	— 2.3	94.6 ♂ 95.0 ♀ 94.7	— .9	— .2
22. upper facial	54.1 ♂ 54.1 ♀ 54.2	3.64	51.7 ♂ 51.4 ♀ 52.6	— 2.4	— .7	52.0 ♂ 52.0 ♀ 52.0	— 2.1	— .6	55.5 ♂ 55.4 ♀ 56.1	+ 1.4	+ .4
23. transverse fronto-parietal . .	66.7 ♂ 66.8 ♀ 66.6	3.54	63.3 ♂ 63.4 ♀ 63.1	— 3.4	— 1.0	62.3 ♂ 62.1 ♀ 62.7	— 4.4	— 1.3	67.7 ♂ 67.4 ♀ 68.3	+ 1.1	+ .3
24. transverse cranio-facial . . .	97.3 ♂ 98.5 ♀ 95.3	3.73	93.7 ♂ 94.1 ♀ 92.0	— 3.6	— 1.0	90.1 ♂ 90.8 ♀ 88.6	— 7.2	— 2.0	98.4 ♂ 99.1 ♀ 96.6	+ 1.1	+ .3
25. orbital (mf)	82.3 ♂ 81.7 ♀ 83.8	4.93	83.8 ♂ 83.1 ♀ 86.1	+ 1.5	+ .3	85.6 ♂ 83.8 ♀ 86.4	+ 3.3	+ .7	85.3 ♂ 84.9 ♀ 86.6	+ 3.0	— .6
26. nasal	47.1 ♂ 46.5 ♀ 48.4	5.17	47.2 ♂ 46.7 ♀ 48.8	+ .1	+ .01	45.6 ♂ 45.5 ♀ 45.9	— 1.5	— .3	45.0 ♂ 44.7 ♀ 45.8	— 2.1	— .4
27. maxillo-alveolar	121.9 ♂ 122.4 ♀ 120.8	5.85	118.0 ♂ 118.2 ♀ 117.2	— 3.9	— .7	125.9 ♂ 126.4 ♀ 124.7	+ 4.0	+ .7	120.8 ♂ 120.8 ♀ 120.8	— 1.1	— .2
Angle											
28. frontal	46.6	2.87	48.7	+ 2.1	+ .7	46.0	— .6	— .2	44.5	— 2.1	— .7
29. parietal	28.5	4.02	27.1	— 1.4	— .4	23.3	— 5.2	— 1.3	26.4	— 2.1	— .5
30. occipital	117.3	4.72	112.6	— 4.7	— 1.0	114.4	— 2.9	— .6	123.2	+ 5.9	+ 1.3
31. interoccipital	124.8	7.25	124.6	— .2	— .02	135.9	+11.1	+ 1.5	128.3	+ 3.5	+ .5
32. cranial base	30.1	2.77	28.7	— 1.4	— .5	28.5	— 1.6	— .6	31.0	+ .9	+ .3
33. foramen magnum	— 6.6	8.65	— 3.0	+ 3.6	+ .4	+ .3	+ 6.9	+ .8	— 1.7	+ 4.9	+ .6
34. vertical orbital	89.4	4.09	89.0	— .4	— .1	87.7	— 1.7	— .4	88.0	— 1.4	— .3
35. facial	82.3 ♂ 82.3 ♀ 82.3	3.31	81.2 ♂ 81.3 ♀ 80.7	— 1.1	— .3	80.3 ♂ 80.7 ♀ 79.5	— 2.0	— .6	81.1 ♂ 81.1 ♀ 81.2	— 1.2	— .4
36. alveolar	74.9 ♂ 75.9 ♀ 72.9	5.58	72.8 ♂ 72.9 ♀ 72.6	— 2.1	— .4	74.2 ♂ 75.9 ♀ 71.2	— .7	— .1	74.6 ♂ 75.2 ♀ 72.8	— .3	— .1
37. ramus	67.3 ♂ 69.0 ♀ 64.2	4.52	70.3 ♂ 71.9 ♀ 65.1	+ 3.0	+ .7	70.0 ♂ 68.5 ♀ 77.0	+ 2.7	+ .6	75.1 ♂ 75.9 ♀ 72.6	+ 7.8	+ 1.7

[132]

and a marked increase in *cranial breadth* (7), while the reverse is true of the Koskimo. The *cranial indices* reflect these conditions particularly in the *length-breadth* (19) proportion, and only slightly less so in the *length-height* (20) and the *breadth-height* (21), and the *transverse fronto-parietal* (23) and *cranio-facial* (24) *indices*. The angles of *frontal* (28), *parietal* (29) and *occipital* (30) declination, and the *interoccipital* (31) angle show the Chinook and Koskimo to deviate below the Undeformed standard in the frontal and parietal declinations marking the different degress of artificial depression. In the parietal declination they are joined by the Cowichan whose angle of frontal declination, however, is greater than that of the Undeformed, showing that the milder form of Cowichan (antero-posterior) depression tends not only to preserve the natural frontal angularity, but also somewhat to diminish it, i.e. producing a greater angle. The occipital depression, as may be expected, is greatest in the Koskimo series, i. e. in excess of the Undeformed condition, while by means of strong occipital counteraction the extent of occipital depression is obviously modified in the Cowichan and Chinook. The interoccipital angle demonstrates in the most intensively deformed series the flattening of the occiput by the production of greater angles in the order Koskimo-Chinook. The same angle in the Cowichan is left rather unimpaired; it coincides with that of the Undeformed, first for the reason of less intensive deformatory strain and secondly because of the more localized occipital counterpressure somewhat above the inion region. There is also to be noted an increase of the *minimum frontal breadth* (8) in the Cowichan-Chinook deformations, correlative to their increasing cranial breadths. It places their before mentioned *transverse fronto-parietal indices* (23) in negative deviation below the Undeformed level, while the Koskimo are found above it. The comparative shortness in the three deformations, of the *cranial base* (3) and the *foramen magnum* (4), whatever significance there might be suggested by their order of decrease, will be difficult to prove as results of deformation. Whether deformation has anything to do with size and shape of the foramen magnum will be difficult to decide. *MacCurdy*[52], who noticed a smaller foramen in the deformed skulls from Peru, is of the opinion that "it would seem therefore that Aymara deformation when carried to excess tends to reduce the dimensions of the spinal canal at its uppermost portion." This observation may be corroborated by the foramen magnum length of our series, but not by the width. Such is the case, likewise, in regard to the *cranial capacity* (1) which, by their averages, suggests an increase over the Undeformed average in the order Cowichan-Chinook-Koskimo. Somewhat more plausible as indirect effects of deformation, however, appear the *depression of the cranial base and the foramen magnum plane* as illustrated by their respective angles (32, 33). In the former,

---

[52] l. c., p. 15 (230).

however, it is only the Cowichan and Chinook deformations that show such a depression, while the angle of the Koskimo is slightly in excess of that of the Undeformed. This is coincidental with the behavior of certain facial dimensions of the Koskimo, the significance of which will be commented on in the next section. The depression of the foramen magnum plane, on the other hand, reaching its most pronounced state in the Chinook, is marked by angles smaller than our Undeformed standard of comparison.

b. Facial cranium.

Of the principal facial dimensions, the *facial length* (5) is fairly uniform in the four series, in contrast to the more variable *upper facial height* (16) and the *bizygomatic breadth* (9). In the deformed divisions, the latter exceeds the Undeformed average in such a way that the strongest deviations are to be noticed in the Chinook-Cowichan order, while the Koskimo exceed the Undeformed only very slightly. Reflecting these conditions in the *upper facial index* (22), the Koskimo with their leptēnic average rise slightly above the Undeformed who with the gradually declining Chinook and Cowichan mark the increasing degrees of mesēny. The deviation of the Koskimo in the *transverse cranio-facial index* (24) is, likewise only slight, while the excessive broadening of the head in the Cowichan-Chinook series, frustrating their greater bizygomatic averages, gives rise to considerable deviations below the Undeformed standard. The pronounced Chinook-Cowichan deviation in the bizygomatic breadth, however, is coincident with their smaller *upper facial* and *nasal heights* (18), contrary to the conditions in the Koskimo division. It is thus seen that with the latter's greater facial and, coincidentally, nasal heights, the greater cranial base angle discussed in the preceding paragraph appears to be correlated (compare in this connection the facial triangles of fig. 19). One is indeed tempted to attribute the broadening and depression of the face, the foreshortening of the nasal height, and the obvious depression of the cranial base and foramen magnum planes in the Cowichan and Chinook skulls to the effects of antero-posterior deformation contrary to the conical deformation of the Koskimo with its probable stretching effects. The other alternative of identifying these deviations with tribal or typal characteristics might be investigated upon undeformed skull material of the groups here studied which, however, lay outside the present possibilities. Of particular interest from this angle of observation is the *orbital height* (17) which coincident with the greater upper facial and nasal heights of the Koskimo, exceeds here conspicuously the same measurement of the other three divisions. If head deformation were responsible for this feature, one might expect depressed orbits in the Cowichan and Chinook divisions which, however, is not the case since also their orbital heights exceed the Undeformed type. Assuming, therefore, that a comparatively great orbital height be a Mongolian characteristic, one may assume in addition to this recognition the effect of deformation in the Koskimo.

The maxillo-alveolar complex in the four divisions shows fairly identical *maxillo-alveolar length* (6) measurements. The *maxillo-alveolar breadth* (10), although likewise rather uniform, tends to be narrower in the Cowichan, a condition expressed by a lower *maxillo-alveolar index* (27), while the contrary holds true for the Chinook.

Facial prognathy (35) deviates toward the negative in the order Cowichan-Koskimo-Chinook, while in *alveolar prognathy* (36) the order is reversed to Chinook coinciding with Koskimo and Cowichan. It was shown in *summaries 55, 57* and *59*, that prognathy, facial and alveolar as well as that of the middle face (ear-eye orientation) increased in the deformed divisions as compared with the Undeformed, conditions which suggest also here the effects of deformation which, with perhaps still more justification, may be realized in the increasing *vertical orbital* (34) declination, both conditions expressed by comparatively smaller angles.

c. Intracranial correlations.

Among the intracranial relations not accounted for in either *summary 99* or diagram I, the angular relation between the ear-eye plane and glabella-lambda line (*Klaatsch's* "central angle"), and between the prosthion-bregma and basion-nasion lines (*Falkenburger's* "cranio-facial" angle) seems to be the most important. Consulting *summaries 7* and *64*, it is evident that the former suffered the greater distortions in the deformed series in the order Cowichan-Koskimo-Chinook, reaching in the latter an average of about 100°, males and females combined. The observation is quite interesting, as was already pointed out in the discussion to *summary 7*, that in the infants, at least in the Cowichan and Chinook, the angles are higher in consequence of the greater pliability of the infantile head, as yet untampered. Later on adjustments take place due almost entirely to cerebral growth. The more or less rectangular relation of the two lines involved in the "central angle" may be retained in antero-posterior and even conical deformation, if the anterior and posterior pressures compensate each other, so that the bregma points, although pushed upwards, preserve their relative positions in the cranial configuration.

The cranio-facial angles, also oscillating around 90°, appear much less affected by deformation. A glance at *summary 64* reveals the fact that plus deviations over the Undeformed state are very slight on the average. They increase in the order Cowichan-Koskimo-Chinook, thus accounting for the strongest deviations in the series of most intensive deformatory strain. The average angularity in the Chinook skulls, however, does not exceed 92.5°, males and females combined. It follows then that the displacement of the bregma, which was seen to be of greater effect in the vertical, i. e. height consideration, shows lesser effects in its oblique application, i. e. the relation of the slanting prosthion-bregma line to the cranial base line. It must be remembered, however, that in the cranio-facial angle also such quanta are involved as the length and declination of the cranial base line, the height of the face and the amount of prognathy, particularly the alveolar.

d. Lower jaw.

Of the mandibular measurements only the phylogenetically and functionally important *bicondylar breadth* (14) and the *ramus angle* (37) are accounted for in the chart. The increase former, of the due, from a general point of view, to the phylogenetic broadening of the cranial base appears to be still further emphasized in the antero-posteriorly compressed heads of the Cowichan and Chinook, while there is a minus deviation to be stated in the Koskimo corresponding to their moderate cranial breadth falling short of the Undeformed cranial breadth. It is indeed interesting enough that the conditions in the Koskimo coincide with their mode of deformation by which the head is elongated and narrowed. It is rather difficult to decide, however, whether they really result from it or whether we have to deal here with a type character. It is also rather puzzling that the *ramus angle* (37) with the alveolar plane conspicuously exceeds in the deformed series that of the Undeformed, and it is again in the Koskimo that the greatest deviation is reached. There is a possibility that the phylogenetic erection under functional influence of the mandibular ramus may likewise be influenced by the mechanical distortion of the head and the subsequent adjustment of the parts that cooperate in the masticatory function, which, however, is difficult to prove.

2. The non-deformed tribal elements.

Following the order of the preceding section, the skulls of the non-deformed tribal elements, i. e. our Undeformed series, has been treated comparatively in *summary 100* and diagram II. In the latter, the undeformed Salish (Lytton, Nicola Lake, Spences Bridge and Kamloops) afforded the basis ($\sigma \pm$), while the Lillooet, Haida and Eskimo were traced according to their group deviations in the manner explained above (p. 131). Males and females combined.

a. Cerebral cranium.

At a glance, the chart reveals the fact that in the absolute measurements both the Haida and the Eskimo move above the basic horizontal in more or less close association. The outstanding feature here is the behavior of the

Summary 100. Metrical differentiation: the principal tribal elements of the Undeformed. Basis: Salish (see diagram II). Males and females combined.

Measurement	Salish (Lytton, Nicola, Spences Bridge, Kamloops)		Lillooet			Haida			Eskimo		
	Average	σ ±	Average	Difference	σ-quotient	Average	Difference	σ-quotient	Average	Difference	σ-quotient
1. Capacity	1295.5 ♂1390.0 ♀1177.5	132.5	1202.5 ♂1190.0 ♀1215.0	−93.0	.7	1375.3 ♂1402.2 ♀1315.1	+79.8	+.6	1312.8 ♂1335.4 ♀1250.8	+17.3	+.1
Length											
2. cranial	173.7	7.46	165.2	−8.7	−1.2	180.6	+6.9	+.9	179.5	+5.8	+.8
3. cranial base	100.5	4.90	95.8	−4.7	−.9	102.8	+2.3	+.5	101.4	+.9	+.2
4. foramen magnum	34.7	2.19	33.3	−1.4	−.6	35.2	+.5	+.2	36.7	+2.0	+.9
5. facial	99.0	5.11	97.0	−2.0	−.4	102.9	+3.9	+.8	100.1	+1.1	+.2
6. maxillo-alveolar	51.0	2.91	51.0	—	—	55.1	+4.1	+1.4	52.6	+1.6	+.6
Breadth											
7. cranial	138.0	5.70	147.5	+9.5	+1.2	142.1	+4.1	+.7	138.8	+.8	+.1
8. minimum frontal	91.5	5.47	93.2	+1.7	+.3	94.4	+2.9	+.5	93.4	+1.9	+.3
9. bizygomatic	132.3	9.20	138.0	+5.7	+.6	138.4	+6.1	+.7	136.4	+4.1	+.4
10. maxillo-alveolar	62.4	1.41	63.2	+.8	+.6	65.8	+3.4	+2.4	64.7	+2.3	+1.6
11. orbital (mf)	41.7	2.14	44.0	+2.3	+1.1	44.2	+2.5	+1.2	43.8	+2.1	+1.0
12. anterior interorbital	17.8	1.60	18.0	+.2	+.1	19.1	+1.3	+.8	16.2	−1.6	+1.0
13. nasal	23.6	1.89	25.5	+1.9	+1.0	25.5	+1.9	+1.0	24.1	+.5	+.3
14. bicondylar	116.8	10.43	126.3	+9.5	+.9	124.8	+8.8	+.8	126.1	+9.3	+
Height											
15. cranial	129.5	5.90	122.2	−7.3	−1.2	136.2	+6.7	+1.1	133.9	+4.4	+.7
16. upper	69.6	4.85	69.5	−.1	—	74.3	+4.7	+1.0	75.9	+6.3	+1.3
17. orbital	34.5	1.89	35.3	+.8	+.4	35.5	+1.0	+.5	36.4	+1.9	+1.0
18. nasal	50.6	3.25	49.5	−1.1	−.3	50.7	+.1	—	55.4	+4.8	+1.5
Index											
19. cranial L—Br	79.8 ♂79.1 ♀80.7	3.03	89.2 ♂91.5 ♀87.0	+9.4	+3.1	78.8 ♂77.8 ♀83.0	−1.0	−.3	77.5 ♂77.0 ♀77.9	−2.3	−.8
20. „ L—H	74.9 ♂74.4 ♀75.6	3.39	74.7 ♂73.6 ♀76.2	−.2	−.1	75.4 ♂74.6 ♀77.6	+.5	+.1	74.7 ♂74.2 ♀76.6	−.2	+.1
21. „ Br—H	93.9 ♂94.1 ♀93.7	5.86	83.9 ♂80.4 ♀87.6	−10.0	−1.7	95.8 ♂95.9 ♀95.7	+1.9	+.3	96.5 ♂96.5 ♀96.7	+2.6	+.4
22. upper facial	52.0 ♂51.4 ♀52.8	3.88	50.4 ♂49.3 ♀51.7	−1.6	−.4	53.0 ♂52.5 ♀54.0	+1.0	+.2	55.7 ♂55.7 ♀55.5	+4.9	+.9
23. transverse fronto-parietal	65.5 ♂65.4 ♀65.7	3.94	63.2 ♂61.8 ♀64.7	−2.3	−.6	66.7 ♂66.5 ♀67.2	+1.2	+.3	67.0 ♂67.4 ♀66.4	+1.5	+.4
24. transverse cranio-facial	95.5 ♂98.8 ♀92.9	4.76	93.2 ♂95.4 ♀91.7	−2.3	−.5	97.0 ♂98.5 ♀96.0	+1.5	+.3	97.9 ♂98.9 ♀97.1	+2.4	+.5
25. orbital (mf)	82.6 ♂82.4 ♀83.0	4.42	80.1 ♂80.5 ♀79.9	−2.5	−.6	80.6 ♂78.9 ♀84.1	−2.0	−.5	84.0 ♂83.3 ♀85.1	+1.4	+.3
26. nasa	47.5 ♂46.2 ♀49.5	3.88	51.5 ♂53.1 ♀50.0	+4.0	+1.0	50.5 ♂51.5 ♀50.9	+3.0	+.8	44.6 ♂44.2 ♀46.0	−2.9	−.7
27. maxillo-alveolar	121.9 ♂124.4 ♀119.2	6.27	124.3 ♂130.4 ♀118.7	+2.4	+.4	120.4 ♂120.3 ♀120.6	−1.5	−.2	122.8 ♂123.5 ♀121.4	+.9	+.1
Angle											
28. frontal	47.9	3.78	51.3	+3.4	+.9	45.1	−2.8	−.7	46.1	−1.8	−.5
29. parietal	27.5	3.63	25.2	−2.3	−.6	27.5	—	—	30.0	+2.5	+.7
30. occipital	114.6	4.97	113.0	−1.6	−.3	117.7	+3.1	+.6	118.2	+3.6	+.7
31. interoccipital	120.8	4.71	125.5	+4.7	+1.0	123.0	+2.2	+.5	128.2	+7.4	+1.6
32. cranial base	28.7	2.60	26.3	−2.4	−.9	29.9	+1.2	+.5	31.4	+2.7	+1.0
33. foramen magnum	−6.2	4.20	−11.3	−5.1	−1.2	−5.0	+1.2	+.3	−7.9	−1.7	−.4
34. vertical orbital	93.1	3.60	93.5	+.4	+.1	90.7	−2.4	−.7	86.7	−6.4	−1.8
35. facial	83.0 ♂82.8 ♀83.4	4.31	84.2 ♂86.0 ♀82.5	+1.2	+.3	81.5 ♂81.7 ♀81.3	−1.5	−.3	82.0 ♂81.9 ♀82.3	−1.0	−.2
36. alveolar	75.2 ♂76.3 ♀73.4	6.46	71.0 ♂74.0 ♀68.0	−4.2	−.6	74.7 ♂75.5 ♀73.4	−.5	−.1	75.5 ♂76.5 ♀73.0	+.3	—
37. ramus	66.9 ♂68.6 ♀64.5	5.77	68.0 ♂70.3 ♀64.3	+1.1	+.2	68.5 ♂70.3 ♀64.3	+1.6	+.3	66.0 ♂66.0 ♀—	−.9	−.2

Lillooet who in the *cranial capacity* (1), *cranial length* (2) and *height* (15) fall short of all the other groups, while in *cranial breadth* (7) they exceed them. Their *cranial base* (3) and *foramen magnum length* (4) are in accord with the smallness of their cranial length. The Eskimo-Haida order of positive cranial length-deviations is reversed as regards the foramen magnum length, indicating, perhaps a characteristic feature of the types, the longer foramen magnum of the Eskimo against the shorter one of the Haida. These conditions are not correlated with their respective cranial or cranio-basal lengths as shown in the tracings of the diagram. The excessive cranial breadth of the Lillooet skulls is not conditioned by a similarly excessive *minimum frontal breadth* (8). Although deviating above the basic average, it falls short of the same measurement of the Haida, but coincides with that of the Eskimo. The obvious shortness and breadth of the Lillooet skull is characterized by the strong positive deviation of their *cranial length-breadth index* (19), while those of the Haida and Eskimo fall short of the basic horizontal, thus contrasting the excessive brachycrany of the Lillooet with the different mesocranial stages of the three other groups. The *cranial length-height index* (20) is fairly uniform in the four groups here compared owing to the more uniform deviations in each of the two factors involved in the index. The indices indicate ortho-hypsicranial conditions. In the *breadth-height* proportion (21), however, involving the cranial breadth and height factors which were seen to be excessive in the Lillooet in diametrically opposed directions, their index falls conspicuously below the average horizontal while the Haida and Eskimo of less diverging breadth and height diameters have more uniform indices above the basic average. In this index the distinctly tapeinocranial mean of the Lillooet stands out against the mesocranial means of the other groups, gradually increasing in the order Salish-Haida-Eskimo. The excessive cranial breadth of the Lillooet in proportion to only a moderately deviating minimum frontal breadth causes also a decided minus-deviation of their transverse *fronto-parietal index* (23) which denotes a somewhat stenometopic condition in the Lillooet skulls as against the metriometopic one of the other groups.

The angles of the cerebral cranium bear out what might be expected in the case of pronounced brachycrany of the Lillooet: there is a positive deviation noticed in *frontal declination* (28), while the *parietal* (29) and *occipital* (30) angles deviate negatively. The contrary is true of the Haida and Eskimo. The *interoccipital angle* (31) rises in the three groups above the basic horizontal in the order Haida-Lillooet-Eskimo in expression of the average conditions of inial flexion in the occiput. The *cranial base angle* (32) already pointed out in connection with the deformed conditions (p. 133) appears to bear definite correlations to the *upper facial height* (16) which is quite clear in the progressing Salish-Haida-Eskimo order, but not between the Salish and Lillooet who, possessed of identical upper facial heights, have a smaller cranial base angle in the latter. This diversion may justly be attributed to the relative length of the cranial base at equal upper facial heights, interdependent factors well meriting a special investigation. The *foramen magnum angle* (33) shows its most pronounced negative deviation in the Lillooet, identical in this case with a more progressive condition in the phylogenetic sense, less so in the Eskimo, Salish and Haida. All of them, however, mark progressive stages if judged by the minus-deviations of their foramen magnum planes from the plane of general cranial orientation, i.e. the ear-eye plane.

b. Facial cranium.

Among the principal dimensions of the face the *bizygomatic breadth* (9) appears to be the least deviating of the compared groups. All of these, however, deviate toward the plus-side in the order Eskimo-Lillooet-Haida. The same order obtains regarding the *facial length* (5), only that on account of the greater intervals the deviations seem to be more significant. The latter is likewise the case with regard to the *upper facial height* (16) which coincides in the Lillooet with that of the basic horizontal while conversely the Haida and Eskimo deviate markedly toward the positive side. Their excessive cranial breadth on the one hand and their comparatively small upper facial height on the other place the Lillooet with regard to their *transverse cranio-facial* (24) and *upper facial* (22) *indices*, conspicuously below the Salish basis and the other two groups with which they are compared. With their average upper facial index of 50.4, the Lilìooet show a strong tendency toward euryëny, while the Salish and Haida are mesēnic in a progressive order and the Eskimo even more distinctly leptēnic. The *orbital* (17) and *nasal* (18) *height* of the Eskimo appear to be in accordance with their upper facial height thus distinctly exceeding in deviation the other groups of the chart. Such a correlation is likewise true of the Lillooet and Haida who, however, exhibit a close relationship in these two dimensions, contrary to the Haida-Eskimo affinity of the upper facial height dimension. This shows that a correlation between the upper facial, orbital and nasal height measurements which was recognized in the Eskimo, does not prevail in the Haida, and in the Lillooet only with regard to the orbital height. More equally disposed appear the *orbital breadths* (11) of the three groups traced in the metrical diagram which are clustered together in pronounced positive deviation in the order Eskimo-Lillooet-Haida. The latter two coincide in a positive deviation of the *nasal breadth* (13) identical with that for the orbital breadth, while the Eskimo range conspicuously lower in close proximity to the basic Salish. The *orbital* (25) and *nasal* (26) *indices* reflect these proportions by the negative deviation of the former in the Haida and Lillooet, and by the positive deviation of the latter in the same order of intensity. The Eskimo deviate in a contrary way, indicating their stronger tendency toward hypsikonchy and leptorrhiny which is also that of the Salish, while the Lillooet show chamaekonchic and chamaerrhinic propensities wherein they conform to the Haida. The *anterior interorbital breadth* (12) deviates quite decisively and positively in the Haida and Eskimo as compared to the Lillooet who fairly coincide with the Salish basis. The greater interorbital breadth (between the two maxillofrontalia points) has been referred to as a progressive feature in another place of this work (p. 114). As a feature of configurative significance, however, it is naturally also dependent upon the general proportions of the specimen, as demonstrated, for instance, by a comparison of the absolute measurement in question with the bizygomatic and maxillo-alveolar breadths in *summary 100*, where the coincidence of greater and smaller measurements is quite plain in the Lillooet and Haida on one side and the Salish and Eskimo on the other.

The angle of *vertical orbital declination* (34), deviating positively, but slightly, in the Lillooet, and quite decisively in the Haida and Eskimo, appears to be correlated with the cranial length-breadth index where similar deviations were noticed. Further proof for such an assumption must be seen in the fact that in the Mongolids the average condition of the angle in question is that of a right one or even exceeding it, and that at the same time they show a strong tendency toward brachycrany. The marked negative deviation of the Eskimo is in line with their distinctly mesocranial average. *Prognathism of the face* (35) indicates mesognathous to orthognathous conditions, which is particularly noticeable in the Lillooet who deviate above the horizontal. Peculiarly enough, this condition is reversed with regard to the *alveolar prognathism* (36) wherein the Lillooet deviate negatively as against the Haida and Eskimo who fairly coincide with the basic average. All the Mongoloids including the American Indians, however, are possessed of stronger alveolar prognathy, i. e. relatively lower angles, than the true Mongols, a phenomenon which will be referred to again later on (p. 153).

c. Intracranial correlations.

Klaatsch's "central angle" and *Falkenburger's* craniofacial angle which have not been accounted for in *summary 100* and diagram II, are recorded in the following small summary where the males and females are combined:

Angle	Salish (undeformed)	Lillooet	Haida	Eskimo (West)
"Central angle" (*Klaatsch*)	91.1	89.5	91.3	91.9
Cranio-facial (*Falkenburger*)	91.2	92.0	88.7	88.6

It will be noticed immediately that with the exception of the Lillooet the averages of the "*central angle*" in the Salish, Haida and Eskimo exceed 90°, while the Lillooet range slightly below. Although these differences had to be noted, one must carry in mind, on the other hand, that a slight margin is to be allowed above and below the average of a physiological range. Applying this consideration to the rectangular relations resulting in the two angles in question, margins of 2° in either direction may be allowed for. It will then be seen that also the averages of the *cranio-facial angle* fall within the presumed range, although the Salish and Lillooet range above, the Haida and Eskimo below 90°. A correlation between the two angles appears to be quite interesting, namely that with a rising "central angle" a diminishing cranio-facial angle occurs, as in the Haida and Eskimo, while in the Lillooet the conditions are reversed. Peculiarly enough, these correlations are enhanced by increased or diminished cranial, facial, cranial base, foramen magnum and maxillo-alveolar lengths as well as by a number of angles, conditions which likewise merit a special investigation.

d. Lower jaw.

The *bicondylar breadth* (14) in the Lillooet is quite significant for the reason that it appears to be correlated with their excessive cranial breadth, a phenomenon in a way proved in the Cowichan and Chinook modes of deformation, and touched upon on p. 136. The three groups here compared coincide in rather marked positive deviations which from the view point of correlation is all the more interesting since also the Haida and Eskimo who are less broadheaded have nevertheless remarkable bicondylar breadths. This must be understood, of course, as an adaptation to a typically broad cranial base, which observation, however, does not hold true for the basic Salish, whose bicondylar breadth average ranges conspicuously below the averages of the other groups, as a glance at *summary 100* will reveal. A methodical and comparative study of the various cranial breadth extensions in undeformed skulls may disclose interesting correlations. The *ramus angle* (37) between the ramus tangent and the alveolar plane is seen to deviate only slightly in the groups. It deviates, however, positively in the hyperbrachycranial Lillooet, and negatively in the slightly mesocranial Eskimo. This apparent correlation is counteracted by the strongly mesocranial Haida, who even exceed the positive deviation of the Lillooet.

3. Mongolo-mongoloid differentiation.

The resolution of the Mongolids (*Baur–Fischer–Lenz*) into their constituent elements, the Mongols and Mongoloids has given rise to the following differential study. This racial problem, however, will be referred to again in the concluding chapter. Accepting, for the time being, the Chukchee, Athapascan and western Eskimo of our Undeformed series as mongoloid, these have been compared with the Mongols of *Hrdlička's* Catalogue (1924, pp. 40—47) who apparently represent a racial unit as true to type as may be desired. For the various measurements given there, the standard deviations as well as in addition the transverse cranio-facial index and its standard deviation were calculated by the writer, and the σ's made the basis of the comparative diagram III. The latter has furthermore been enlarged by the addition of the angles of facial and alveolar prognathy with the ear-eye plane, of *Reicher's* (1913, tables) combined Buriats, Kalmucks and Mongol-Torgouts. The various calculations, males and females combined, are contained in *summary 101*, to which, as in diagram III, eastern Eskimo of Greenland and Labrador (*Oetteking* 1908) have been added for further comparison.

a. Cerebral cranium.

It will be noticed that in many respects the four groups of diagram III, traced in varied lines are rather uniform in their behavior toward the Mongol basis, deviating from the latter either positively or negatively, but in a few instances coinciding with it fairly well. Regarding the size in general, as expressed by the *cranial capacity* (1) and *module* (2), the Mongoloid groups do not reach up to the Mongol level, although in the module the western Eskimo come very near it. Of the three principal cranial diameters, it is the *breadth* (4) and *height* (8) that show decisive deviations in the four groups, negative in the former measurement as against the broader head of the Mongol, and positive in the latter measurement as against his lower head. The Chukchee in each case, however, deviate slightly less. The *cranial length* (3) deviations, negative in the three western groups, resemble exactly those for the cranial module. The eastern Eskimo possessed of longer heads deviate positively. The two *cranial indices* (12, 13) deviating decidedly negatively, indicate the meso-dolichocranial and orthocranial mongoloid conditions as compared with the brachy-hypsicranial Mongols. The strong deviation of the eastern Eskimo illustrates their pronounced dolichocrany by which, as also by the two factors involved, they differ distinctly not only from their western relatives but also from the American Indians in general.

b. Facial cranium.

In both principal dimensions of the face, the *bizygomatic breadth* (5) and the *upper facial height* (9), the Mongolids, with the exception of the western Eskimo in the latter measurement, deviate negatively. The order of negative

Summary 101.

Metrical differentiation: mongolo-mongoloid. Basis: Mongols (*Hrdlička, A.*, 1924, 40-46 and *Reicher, M.*, 1913, tables). See diagrams III and IV. Males and females combined.

Measurement	Mongols		Chukchee			Athapascan			Eskimo (West)			Eskimo (East)			Salish (Lytton, Nicola, Spences Bridge, Kamloops)			Lillooet		
	Average	σ ±	Average	Difference	σ-quotient	Average	Difference	σ-quotient	Average	Difference	σ-quotient	Average	Difference	σ-quotient	Average	Difference	σ-quotient	Average	Difference	σ-quotient
1. Capacity	1506.6 ♂1753 ♀1406	133.55	1306.0 ♂1310.0 ♀1290.0	−200.6	−1.5	1258.6 ♂1280.0 ♀1130.0	−248.0	−1.8	1295.5 ♂1335.4 ♀1250.8	−211.1	−1.6	1351.8 ♂1351.8 ♀—	−144.8	−1.1	1295.5 ♂1390.0 ♀1177.5	−211.1	−1.6	1202.5 ♂1190.0 ♀1215.0	−304.1	−2.3
2. Module *	151.2 ♂155.1 ♀147.3	5.24	147.7 ♂148.2 ♀146.0	−3.5	−.7	149.6 ♂150.3 ♀145.3	−1.6	−.3	150.7 ♂152.4 ♀147.5	−.5	−.1	149.9 ♂149.9 ♀—	−1.3	−.3	149.5 ♂150.2 ♀148.8	−1.7	−.3	145.0 ♂144.3 ♀145.7	−6.2	−1.2
Length																				
3. cranial	180.1	7.74	174.8	−5.3	−.7	178.7	−1.4	−.2	179.5	−.6	−.1	182.3	+2.2	+.3	173.7	−6.4	−.8	165.2	−14.9	−1.9
Breadth																				
4. cranial	147.4	6.55	137.8	−9.6	−1.5	135.3	−12.1	−1.8	138.3	−8.6	−1.3	137.7	−14.7	−2.2	138.0	−9.4	−1.4	147.5	+.1	+.01
5. bizygomatic	137.9	7.15	135.4	−2.5	−.3	128.5	−9.4	−1.3	136.4	−1.5	−.2	134.2	−3.7	−.5	133.3	−5.6	−.8	138.0	+.1	+.01
6. orbital(la)	39.1	1.97	39.2	+.1	+.1	39.7	+.6	+.3	39.8	+.7	+.4	38.8	−.3	−.2	37.9	−1.2	−.6	38.8	−.3	−.2
7. nasal	26.8	2.05	24.8	−2.0	−1.0	23.6	−3.2	−1.5	24.1	−2.7	−1.3	22.8	−4.0	−1.9	23.6	−3.2	−1.6	25.5	−1.3	−.6
Height																				
8. cranial	128.6	5.49	130.6	+2.0	+.4	134.9	+6.3	+1.1	133.9	+5.3	+1.0	134.6	+6.0	+1.1	129.5	+.9	+.2	122.2	−6.4	−1.2
9. upper facial	74.7	5.81	72.6	−2.1	−.4	72.3	−2.4	−.4	75.9	+1.2	+.2	71.6	−3.1	−.5	69.6	−5.1	−.9	69.5	−5.2	−.9
10. orbital	35.5	2.10	34.0	−1.5	−.7	35.7	+.2	+.1	36.4	+.9	+.4	36.4	+.9	+.4	34.5	−1.0	−.5	35.3	−.2	−.1
11. nasal	54.8	4.40	51.4	−3.4	−.8	51.1	−3.7	−.8	55.4	+.6	+.1	51.4	−3.4	−.8	50.6	−4.2	−1.0	49.5	−5.3	−1.2
Index																				
12. cranial L.-Br.	81.9 ♂81.4 ♀82.4	3.74	78.0 ♂77.9 ♀78.1	−3.9	−1.1	75.6 ♂76.4 ♀71.6	−6.3	−1.7	77.5 ♂77.0 ♀79.0	−4.4	−1.2	72.8 ♂72.8 ♀—	−9.1	−2.6	79.8 ♂79.1 ♀80.7	−2.1	−.6	89.2 ♂91.5 ♀87.0	+7.3	+1.9
13. cranial L.-H.	78.9 ♂78.4 ♀79.1	3.11	74.0 ♂72.4 ♀80.5	−4.9	−1.6	75.5 ♂75.4 ♀76.1	−3.4	−1.1	74.7 ♂74.2 ♀76.2	−4.2	−1.4	73.7 ♂73.7 ♀—	−5.2	−1.2	74.9 ♂74.4 ♀75.6	−4.0	−1.3	74.7 ♂73.6 ♀76.2	−4.2	−1.4
14. transverse cranio facial	93.3 ♂95.1 ♀91.6	3.78	98.3 ♂97.7 ♀100.7	+5.0	+1.3	96.3 ♂97.0 ♀92.1	+3.0	+.8	98.4 ♂99.0 ♀97.1	+5.1	+1.3	100.8 ♂100.8 ♀—	+7.5	+2.0	95.9 ♂— ♀—	+2.6	+.7	93.2 ♂95.4 ♀91.7	−.1	−.02
15. upper facial	53.8 ♂54.5 ♀53.1	3.07	53.6 ♂53.2 ♀55.2	−.2	−.1	56.2 ♂56.5 ♀54.7	+2.4	+.8	55.7 ♂55.7 ♀55.5	+1.9	+.6	54.3 ♂54.3 ♀—	−.5	−.2	52.0 ♂51.4 ♀52.8	−1.8	−.6	50.4 ♂49.3 ♀51.7	−3.4	−1.1
16. orbital(la)	92.3 ♂90.2 ♀93.1	5.11	89.4 ♂88.0 ♀92.1	−2.9	−.6	88.5 ♂88.5 ♀—	−3.8	−.7	91.9 ♂91.8 ♀92.3	−.4	−.1	93.2 ♂93.2 ♀—	+.9	+.2	90.5 ♂89.8 ♀91.5	−1.8	−.4	90.8 ♂91.0 ♀90.5	−1.5	−.3
17. nasal	49.0 ♂48.8 ♀49.4	3.95	48.3 ♂49.4 ♀44.2	−.7	−.2	46.1 ♂45.5 ♀50.0	−2.9	−.7	44.6 ♂44.2 ♀46.0	−4.4	−1.1	44.3 ♂44.3 ♀—	−4.7	−1.2	47.5 ♂46.2 ♀49.5	−1.5	−.4	51.5 ♂53.1 ♀50.0	+2.5	+.6
Angle																				
18. facial	86.7 ♂86.7 ♀86.2	3.08	82.6 ♂82.8 ♀82.0	−4.1	−1.3	83.1 ♂83.2 ♀83.0	−3.6	−1.2	82.0 ♂81.9 ♀82.3	−4.7	−1.5	82.6 ♂82.6 ♀—	−4.1	−1.3	83.0 ♂82.8 ♀83.4	−3.7	−1.2	84.2 ♂86.0 ♀82.5	−2.5	−.8
19. alveolar	78.4 ♂78.4 ♀78.3	6.59	72.6 ♂72.3 ♀74.0	−3.8	−.6	75.1 ♂75.7 ♀72.0	−3.3	−.5	75.5 ♂76.5 ♀73.0	−2.9	−.4	76.0 ♂76.0 ♀—	−2.4	−.4	75.2 ♂76.3 ♀73.4	−11.5	−1.7	71.0 ♂74.0 ♀68.0	−7.4	−1.1

* Cranial length + breadth + height / 3

deviation in the bizygomatic breadth is seen to bring the western Eskimo and Chukchee closest to the Mongol basis; slightly below it deviate the eastern Eskimo, and conceivably so the Athapascan in expression of their gradually narrowing faces. Lower facial heights as compared with the Mongol basis distinguish the mongoloid groups in a more uniformly negative manner, except the western Eskimo who, as already noted, deviate to the plus-side. These statements are somewhat contradicted by the relative behavior of the two factors involved in the *upper facial index* (15), leaving the Chukchee below and the other three groups above the basic horizontal in the order eastern Eskimo-Athapascan-western Eskimo. However, the Chukchee and eastern Eskimo remain in close proximity to the Mongols in expression of their slightly less or more mesēnic conditions, while the Athapascan and western Eskimo rise to a leptēnic state, due in the former to a markedly smaller bizygomatic breadth and in the latter to a greater upper facial height. The *transverse cranio-facial index* (14) likewise involving the bizygomatic breadth, appears to be more radically influenced, however, by the cranial breadths, ranging in different degrees of intensity below the Mongol basis. The four mongoloid groups deviate distinctly above the underlying Mongols, thus indicating more the formers' narrower skulls than their correspondingly narrower faces. The greatest deviation, as in a number of other instances, is given by the eastern Eskimo who are possessed of the narrowest crania. The *orbital width* (6) between the lacrimale and ektokonchion points deviates only slightly in the four mongoloid groups of which may be recognized as the more significant one the minus deviation of the eastern Eskimo which is brought about by a distinct positive deviation of the *orbital height* (10). This is shared, however, by the western Eskimo. The Chukchee are seen to decline quite distinctly which keeps their *orbital index* (16) likewise on a low level where it fairly coincides with that of the Athapascan. The two Eskimo groups deviate only slightly, the eastern above, the western below the Mongol basis, indicating in the former, since all the compared groups have hypsikonchic averages, the relatively greatest amount of hypsikonchy. The *nasal width* (7) and *height* (11) show negative deviations in the former in the order Chukchee-western Eskimo-Athapascan-eastern Eskimo, while in the latter negative deviation is more uniform although less pronounced. In the latter measurement, however, the western Eskimo deviate positively, i. e. in excess of the basic Mongols which is coincidental with the other cranial and facial height measurements of the same group. The *nasal index* (17) of the Chukchee coincides with that of the Mongols, the other groups range distinctly below them illustrating the leptorrhinic condition particularly of the two Eskimo groups as against the slightly less pronounced leptorrhiny of the Athapascan and the mesorrhinic conditions in the Chukchee and Mongols. The angles of *facial* and *alveolar prognathy* (18, 19) render a fairly uniform picture of the more prognathous conditions in the Mongoloids with even relatively greater deviations in the facial angle. This corresponds to similar observations of a number of other authors.

c. Lillooet affinities.

The comparative study of mongolo-mongoloid affinities has been supplemented by diagram IV, tracings of which are based on the metrical calculations contained in the last two columns of *summary 101*. The horizontal line represents, as in the preceding chart, the Mongol data, upon which the deviating undeformed Salish and the Lillooet of diagram II are traced. It was particularly with regard to the latter whose exceptional type had been recognized in the discussion to *summary 100* and diagram II, that a special combination with a Mongol basis was essayed (diagram IV), and which was amplified by the addition of the undeformed Salish just mentioned. It will be noticed immediately that in a number of proportions the Lillooet and Mongols coincide or that the Lillooet even overlap the latter toward the side of greater intensity, or positive deviation, while the undeformed Salish remain in negative deviation with the exception of only the cranial height. Not attaching too much significance to the behavior of the absolute measurements with their direct reference to the size of the specimens, it is nevertheless to be realized that the markedly smaller Lillooet as compared with the Mongols show identical or nearly identical *cranial, bizygomatic* and *orbital breadth* (4, 5, 6), and *orbital height* (10) dimensions which produce similarly identical *transverse craniofacial* and *orbital indices* (14, 16). These were recognized in the preceding sections as illustrating the greater cranial breadth of the true Mongols in the former index, and of a hypsikonchic condition characteristic for both the Mongols and Mongoloids. The *cranial length-breadth index* (12), on the other hand, due to the markedly smaller cranial length of the Lillooet while their breadth coincides with that of the Mongols, rises considerably above the basic horizontal, designating their hyperbrachycranial state. The *length-height index* (13), however, of the Lillooet, ortho-to hypsicranial falls conspicuously short of the hypsicranial Mongols, and coincides with the Salish. The *nasal dimensions* (7, 11) of the Lillooet and undeformed Salish are seen to range below the Mongols. The *nasal index* (17) of the former, however, deviates positively and that of the Salish negatively, in illustration of the Lillooet's more chamaerrhinic, and the Salish's almost leptorrhinic condition. *Prognathism* (18, 19) as a typical feature, being more pronounced in the Mongoloids as against the true Mongols, is shown to deviate duly negative. But while the Lillooet are seen to deviate to a lesser degree in both angles of *facial* (18) and *alveolar* (19) *prognathism*, the fact stands out that in both groups alveolar exceeds the facial prognathism contrary to the conditions described and illustrated in the preceding summary and diagram.

4. Mongolo-mongoloideo-caucasid differentiation.

For the sake of wider comparison, a Caucasid element, namely the author's Ancient Egyptians [53], has been introduced in the following investigation and which is supported by *summary 102* and diagram V. In the latter the basic horizontal, representing the mongoloid element, is afforded by our Undeformed series of *summary 100* and diagram II, while the Mongol element of *summary 101* and diagram III is represented by the solid line and the Caucasid by the interrupted one.

a. Cerebral cranium.

Regarding the *cranial capacity* (1), the Mongols demonstrate a strong positive deviation due very probably to their greater lateral expansion as compared with Mongoloids and the Ancient Egyptians. Fairly uniform in their *modules* (2), rather pronounced positive deviation in close association is seen in regard to the *cranial length* (3) of the Mongols and Caucasids. A strong divergence, resulting in a marked positive deviation of the Mongols and a negative one of the Ancient Egyptians occurs in the *cranial breadth* (4) which may indeed be considered a distinctive feature. The *cranial height* (8) which in the Mongols and the Caucasids as well falls short of the Mongoloids behaves quite differently, but in such a way that the former overlaps the latter thus showing a less pronounced negative deviation. The *cranial length-breadth index* (12) influenced by the strongly opposing cranial breadth measurements just commented on, reflects these conditions in the positive deviation of the Mongols and the negative of the Ancient Egyptians, illustrating the brachycrany of the former and the mild mesocrany of the latter as against the decided mesocrany of the mongoloid Salish. The *length-height index* (13) repeats the relative positions of the two races here compared, slightly emphasized, however, with regard to the positive deviation of the Mongols who indicate hypsicrany, while the Ancient Egyptians do not reach up fully in orthocrany to that of the Salish. Very similar proportional differences between the *cranial* and *bizygomatic breadths* (5) place the two *transverse cranio-facial indices* (14) in close association below the basic horizontal of the undeformed Salish in illustration of the broader mongoloid and the somewhat narrower mongol and caucasid faces.

b. Facial cranium.

The *bizygomatic breadth* (5), however, as an absolute measurement predominates in the Mongols and Mongoloids which is well demonstrated in its combination with the *upper facial height* (9). The *upper facial index* (15), although mesēnic in the three compared groups reveals its tendency toward leptēny in the caucasoid Ancient Egyptians. Both the *orbital heights* (10)

---

[53] *Oetteking, Bruno* 1909. KraniologischeStudien an Altägyptern. Arch. Anthrop., N.F., vol. VIII. pp. 1–90.

Summary 102. Metrical differentiation: mongolo-mongoloideo-caucasid. Basis: Undeformed Salish; Mongols as in *summary 101*; Caucasids: Ancient Egyptians (*Oetteking, B.*, Arch. Anthrop., 1909, vol. VIII). Males and females combined. See diagram V.

Measurement	Undeformed		Mongols			Caucasids (Ancient Egyptians)		
	Average	r ±	Average	Difference	σ-quotient	Average	Difference	σ-quotient
1. Capacity	1317.2 ♂ 1349.5 ♀ 1243.8	111.45	1506.6 ♂ 1753 ♀ 1406	+ 189.4	+ 1.7	1336.4	+ 19.2	+ .2
2. Module	149.2 ♂ 150.5 ♀ 143.9	5.86	150.4 ♂ 152.4 ♀ 147.2	+ 1.2	+ .2	149.7	+ .5	+ .1
Length								
3. cranial	174.0	6.57	180.1	+ 6.1	+ .9	181.5	+ 5.7	+ 1.1
Breadth								
4. cranial	139.5	5.22	147.4	+ 7.9	+ 1.5	136.2	− 3.3	− .6
5. bizygomatic	135.7	6.01	137.9	+ 2.2	+ .4	126.9	− 8.8	− 1.5
6. orbital(la)	39.5	1.75	39.1	− .4	− .2	37.4	− 2.1	− 1.2
7. nasal	24.5	2.75	26.8	+ 2.3	+ .8	24.2	− .3	− .2
Height								
8. cranial	133.1	5.79	128.6	− 4.5	− .8	131.4	− 1.7	− .3
9. upper facial	73.6	4.54	74.7	+ 1.1	+ .2	69.3	− 4.3	− .8
10. orbital	35.7	1.97	35.5	− .2	− .1	33.4	− 2.3	− 1.2
11. nasal	52.6	3.86	54.8	+ 2.2	+ .6	49.7	− 2.9	− .7
Index								
12. cranial L—Br . . .	78.6 ♂ 78.0 ♀ 80.0	3.94	81.9 ♂ 81.4 ♀ 82.4	+ 3.7	+ .9	75.1	− 3.5	− .9
13. cranial L—H . . .	75.0 ♂ 74.3 ♀ 76.5	3.41	78.9 ♂ 78.4 ♀ 79.1	+ 3.9	+ 1.1	73.7	− 1.3	− .4
14. transverse cranio-facial . . .	97.3 ♂ 98.5 ♀ 95.3	3.73	93.3 ♂ 95.1 ♀ 91.6	− 4.0	− 1.1	93.1	− 4.2	− 1.1
15. upper facial . . .	54.1 ♂ 54.1 ♀ 54.2	3.64	53.8 ♂ 54.5 ♀ 53.1	− .3	− .01	54.5	+ .4	+ .1
16. orbital(la)	90.5 ♂ 90.0 ♀ 91.7	5.29	92.3 ♂ 90.2 ♀ 93.1	+ 1.8	+ .3	89.8	− .7	− .1
17. nasal	47.1 ♂ 46.5 ♀ 48.4	5.17	49.0 ♂ 48.8 ♀ 49.4	+ 1.9	+ .4	49.6	+ 2.5	+ .5
Angle								
18. facial	82.3 ♂ 82.3 ♀ 82.3	3.31	86.7 ♂ 86.7 ♀ 86.2	+ 4.4	+ 1.3	84.0	+ 1.7	+ .5
19. alveolar	74.9 ♂ 75.9 ♀ 72.9	5.58	78.4 ♂ 78.4 ♀ 78.3	+ 3.5	+ .6	78.3	+ 3.7	+ .7

and breadths (*la*, 6) are fairly alike in the Mongols and Salish, but slightly smaller in the Ancient Egyptians. The *orbital index* (16) is hypsikonchic, somewhat higher in the Mongols but fairly equal in the Mongolids and Caucasids as shown in the chart. The nasal dimensions differ quite interestingly with regard to the *nasal height* (11) which in the Ancient Egyptians remains markedly below the basic horizontal in negative deviation conforming with the general height proportions of the face, while the positively deviating nasal height of the Mongols is in accord with their other facial height dimensions. The *nasal breadth* (7) in a way corresponds to these deviations. In the *nasal index* (17) a tendency toward chamaerrhiny is shown by the mesorrhinic Mongols and Ancient Egyptians as compared to the leptorrhinic Mongoloids who on their side tend toward mesorrhiny. *Facial prognathy* (18) is notoriously less pronounced in the Mongols who are seen to deviate even more strongly above the mongoloid standard than the caucasid Ancient Egyptians, rendering the former orthognathous and the latter mesognathous as opposed to the less mesognathous Salish. These proportions are repeated among the three groups. Their angles of *alveolar prognathy* (19) fall in the prognathous class, but are less so in the Mongols and Ancient Egyptians who possess uniform angles in excess of the undeformed Salish.

5. Cranio-typological differentiation.

In *summary 103*, a final condensed table of metrical differentiation, the general typological behavior of our four series has been recorded. In addition to the cranial module and capacity, and the angles of facial and alveolar prognathy, the more important and differentiating indices of the two cranial complexes have been listed there according to their classificatory evaluation in percental occurrences, the arithmetic means, the standard deviations ($\sigma \pm$) and the coefficients of variation (v). Except where drastic distortions gave rise to markedly different proportional expressions (indices), the tabulated results are directly comparable.

Judged by European standards [54] of male and female average *cranial* capacities of 1450 cc. and 1300 cc., in a range of 1100—1700 cc., the averages of our four series fall rather low. If compared with the average of 1440 cc. for American Indians *(Welcker)*, they must be considered submedium. Such is the average condition in spite of certain high individual values of our range, 1640 cc. and 1620 cc. in the sexes, counterbalanced by the extremely low male value of 1100 cc. coinciding with the lowest value of the European range quoted above and our lowest female value of 980 cc. remaining conspicuously below it. The latter condition is due to the frequent astonishingly small crania of the adult female Indian, a characteristic occa-

---

[54] For these, the reader is referred to *Rud. Martin's* Lehrbuch der Anthropologie, 1914.

Summary 103. Metrical differentiation: cranio-typological. General metrical condensation. Males and females combined.

Measurement	Undeformed				DEFORMATION									
					Cowichan				Chinook				Koskimo			
	Percent	Average	σ ±	v	Percent	Average	σ ±	v	Percent	Average	σ ±	v	Percent	Average	σ ±	v
Capacity																
oligencephalic...	23.8	1317.2			18.1	1320.2			18.3	1347.0			9.9	1360.7		
euencephalic ...	55.2	♂1349.5	111.5	8.5	58.5	♂1360.3	96.7	7.3	48.8	♂1388.8	106.5	7.9	56.8	♂1396.3	101.4	7.5
aristencephalic...	21.0	♀1243.8			23.4	♀1209.6			23.9	♀1251.6			33.3	♀1264.2		
Module.........		149.3				149.6				148.6				149.8		
		♂150.5				♂151.4				♂150.4				♂151.3		
		♀143.9				♀144.4				♀144.3				♀145.7		
Length-breadth index																
dolichocranial...	14.3	78.6			1.0	89.7			—	92.4			38.3	76.4		
mesocranial....	54.5	♂78.0	3.9	4.9	3.6	♂89.4	7.3	8.3	—	♂92.1	5.2	5.5	45.4	♂76.3	4.2	5.5
brachycranial...	31.2	♀80.0			95.4	♀90.9			100.0	♀93.2			16.3	♀76.9		
Length-height index																
chamaecranial..	5.5	75.0			4.1	77.8			6.2	76.8			28.0	72.1		
orthocranial....	41.7	♂74.3	3.4	4.6	16.5	♂77.7	4.6	6.0	25.9	♂77.3	5.0	6.7	51.1	♂72.0	3.4	4.7
hypsicranial....	52.8	♀76.5			79.4	♀78.1			67.9	♀75.6			20.9	♀72.5		
Upper facial index																
euryēnic	4.9	54.1			33.8	51.7			15.0	52.0			3.8	55.5		
mesēnic	52.5	♂54.1	3.7	6.9	50.0	♂51.4	3.7	7.2	73.8	♂52.0	2.2	4.3	38.5	♂55.4	3.6	6.5
leptēnic	42.6	♀54.2			16.2	♀52.6			11.2	♀52.2			57.5	♀56.1		
Orbital index (mf)																
chamaekonchic..	8.1	82.3			5.3	83.8			3.6	85.6			3.6	85.3		
mesokonchic ...	64.9	♂81.7	5.0	6.1	54.0	♂83.1	4.7	5.7	61.0	♂83.8	4.6	5.5	47.5	♂84.9	4.9	5.6
hypsikonchic ...	27.0	♀83.8			40.7	♀86.1			35.4	♀86.4			48.9	♀86.6		
Nasal index																
leptorrhinic....	46.7	47.1			57.7	47.2			67.1	45.6			69.6	45.0		
mesorrhinic....	29.1	♂46.5	5.2	11.1	18.0	♂46.7	4.2	9.0	23.2	♂45.5	4.5	9.9	23.9	♂44.7	4.1	9.2
chamaerrhinic..	24.2	♀48.4			24.3	♀48.8			9.7	♀45.9			6.5	♀45.8		
Maxillo-alveolar index																
dolichuranic ...	2.2	121.9			14.3	118.0			2.7	125.9			3.0	120.8		
mesuranic.....	13.2	♂122.4	5.9	4.9	21.9	♂118.2	7.4	6.3	8.1	♂126.4	8.2	6.5	17.6	♂120.8	6.8	5.6
brachyuranic...	84.6	♀120.8			63.8	♀117.2			89.2	♀124.7			79.4	♀120.8		
Facial prognathy																
prognathous....	16.0	82.3			25.3	81.2			35.8	80.3			32.6	81.1		
mesognathous ..	63.0	♂82.3	3.4	4.1	56.8	♂81.3	3.6	4.4	50.6	♂80.7	3.9	4.9	54.8	♂81.5	3.3	4.1
orthognathous..	21.0	♀82.3			17.9	♀80.7			13.6	♀79.5			12.6	♀81.2		
Alveolar prognathy																
prognathous....	74.0	74.9			84.1	72.8			72.5	74.2			83.7	74.6		
mesognathous ..	23.0	♂75.9	3.7	4.9	12.7	♂72.9	3.9	5.4	22.5	♂75.9	4.3	5.9	15.6	♂75.2	3.6	4.8
orthognathous...	3.0	♀72.9			3.2	♀72.6			5.0	♀71.2			.7	♀72.8		

sionally referred to by *R. Virchow, Hrdlička, et al*. The highest percental occurrences among the three classes of the cranial capacity fall, in our four series, to euencephaly. Oligencephaly and aristencephaly occurring in fairly equal percentages in the Undeformed, change this proportion in favor of aristencephaly in the order Cowichan-Chinook-Koskimo. The capacities of the tribal groups composing the Undeformed series or division have been discussed in section 2 of this chapter. The relatively highest averages are those of the Eskimo and Haida; they are only euencephalic, however, except in the Haida females whose average is aristencephalic. A general conception of the cranial size may furthermore be obtained from the average *cranial module* which at 149 mm. plus or minus, males and females combined, is practically uniform not only in our four major divisions but likewise in the subdivisions of the Undeformed. Naturally the male module is higher at 150–151 mm. as against the female at 143–145 mm. Comparing our averages with those from eastern Indians given by *Hrdlička*[55] which range from 152.2–160.4 mm. in the males and from 146.4–150.0 mm. in the females, it will easily be recognized that the Indians of the North Pacific Coast do not reach up to the modular size of the eastern tribes[56]. They exceed, however, the San Miguel Islanders (Chumash) of Southern California (Museum of the American Indian, Heye Foundation) with averages of 148.9 mm. and 142.6 mm. in the sexes, or at a combined average of 145.7 mm., thus rendering them intermediate between those two extremes.

The distribution among the classes of the *length-breadth index* shows in the Undeformed the characteristic mongolid predominance of mesocrany tending toward brachycrany, while dolichocrany occurs at a relatively small percentage. In the latter the numeral participation of the following groups: Chukchee (1); Lytton (1); Haida (3); Athapascan (4); Eskimo (7), appears to be quite significant. The distortion of the cranial length and breadth in the deformed divisions produces artificial brachycrany in the Cowichan and Chinook, to the amount of 100°/₀ in the latter and as much as 95.4°/₀ in the former. On account of distortions in the opposite directions mesocrany with a strong tendency toward dolichocrany prevails in the Koskimo, contrary to the behavior of the index in the Undeformed. The extreme distortion of the Koskimo proper, frequently referred to in this report, gives rise to markedly dolichocranial averages of 72.9 and 72.4 in the sexes, with minimum values as low as 64.2 in the males and 66.8 in the females.

Here may be the place for a brief comment on the speculative restoration

---

[55] l. c., p. 14 (118).
[56] This holds likewise true for the southern Indians whose averages the same author records as 151.7–155.5 mm. (single individuals from S. Carolina and Mississippi are listed with 159.3 mm. and 161.3 mm. for the males and 145.3–149.8 mm. for the females in: *Hrdlička, Aleš*, 1922. The anthropology of Florida. The Florida State Hist. Soc. (Deland, Fla.), 140 pp. (111–112).

of deformed skulls to their norms. The readjustment of artificially changed skull proportions, although offering possibilities of speculative experimentation must be considered extremely tedious and unfruitful. One of the main difficulties is the uncertainty as to the extent to which organic reaction influences the purely mechanical deformatory strains in the production of artificially changed and fixed head form. The only true standards of estimation in the author's opinion are the undeformed heads and skulls of a tribe or group otherwise given to head deformation. However, from a general point of judgment it may be reasonable to assume that rounder heads yield more easily to anteroposterior compression than heads with a tendency toward longheadedness, but that the latter yield more readily to artificial elongation by means of circular bandagery. Lacking the other alternative, the last expressed opinion may furnish some slight clue in the diagnosis of cranial deformation. Regarding unintentional deformation *Hooton*[57] expresses himself in a somewhat similar way when he says, "The examination of the Tennessee series confirms our conclusion that accidental occipital deformation affects dolichocephalic crania very little, mesocephalic crania slightly, and brachycephalic crania most of all."

In the *cranial length-height index* the tendency toward hypsicrany is quite obvious in the undeformed series; it even exceeds the appreciable percentage of orthocrany, leaving only a negligible amount of chamaecrany. The index average duly reflects these conditions with a value of 75.0, i. e. upon the border between ortho- and hypsicrany. By their average of 76.5, the females exhibit a somewhat more pronounced tendency toward hypsicrany than the males whose average of 74.3 marks them orthocranial. The group means are more or less in accord with the divisional, i. e. serial averages. Anteroposterior compression proves to be very favorable in the production of hypsicrany as examplified by the Cowichan and Chinook averages and percental frequencies, while the conical elongation of the Koskimo tends to produce chamaecrany.

The *upper facial index* produces preeminently mesēnic averages tending strongly toward leptēny in the Undeformed and toward euryēny in the Cowichan, while the Chinook list almost three-fourths of their number as mesēnic, the remaining fourth going to euryēny and leptēny with a slight emphasis on the former. The Koskimo series shows the highest frequency of leptēny, and the mesēnic frequency is likewise considerable, thus leaving only $3.8°/_0$ to euryēny. Their average of 55.5, therefore, indicates leptēny, although marking the border line between mesēny and leptēny. The averages of the other divisions are mesēnic, the highest one of 54.1 being that of the Undeformed. Only the Eskimo and Athapascan are truly leptēnic among, the latter with averages of 55.7 and 56.2, and it is they who in the Undeformed influence

---

[57] *Hooton, Earnest A.*, 1920. Indian village site and cemetery near Madisonville, Ohio. Pap. Peabody Mus. Am. Arch. Ethnol. Harvard Univ., v. VIII, n⁰. I, pp. 83–137 (89).

positively the percental amounts of ortho- and hypsicrany. In the four series and the tribal groups of the Undeformed the sex difference, if any, is rather slight, the tendency toward female leptēny being, therefore, quite indistinct. The reason for this must be attributed to the fact that the positive difference between the upper facial height in the sexes is rendered ineffective in the index by the difference in zygomatic breadth which latter is proportionally greater in the males.

The *orbital index* with the maxillofrontale width exhibits the predominating mongolid mesokonchy with its strong leaning toward hypsikonchy in its averages and percental distribution among the index classes. The somewhat exaggerated trend in this direction, particularly in the Koskimo, was assumed to be influenced by artificial deformation (p. 134). The negligible percentages of chamaekonchy amounting in the Undeformed to 8.1% at its highest, concern almost entirely the male orbit, where chamaekonchic indices as low as 70.0 are witnessed. This occurs in the Haida who likewise yield the altogether lowest male group mean of 78.9, which however is mesokonchic. In close proximity are seen the Athapascan, Chukchee and Salish males, while the Eskimo with a male group mean approach rather the meso-hypsikonchic border. The low mesokonchic condition of the Lillooet is rendered somewhat uncertain in the sexes by their paucity, both mesokonchy and hypsikonchy being represented. It will be noticed that the Chinook and Koskimo total averages are hypsikonchic. If the sexes are separated this is true only of the female averages in which also the Salish females join, while the Undeformed female average is mesokonchic like that of the males.

As regards the skeletal nose, the marked tendency toward leptorrhiny is of interest in our four series. For the *nasal index* the highest percental frequencies occur in that index class in the order Undeformed-Cowichan-Chinook-Koskimo at figures of 46.7% in the first named series and 69.6% in the last. Chamaerrhiny occurs with only small percentages in the Chinook and Koskimo, but somewhat more numerous, i.e. about a fourth of the total, in the Undeformed and Salish. The remainder are mesorrhinic with 18% the lowest frequency in the Cowichan. The total averages of the combined sexes fall in the Chinook and Koskimo slightly below the lepto-mesorrhinic border line, i.e. they are leptorrhinic, while in the Undeformed and Cowichan they fairly coincide with it, i.e. they are just mesorrhinic. This condition is rendered still more interesting by the sex differences which in all the series yield the higher averages to the females, thus confirming the general racial proportions. These, however, are likewise leptorrhinic in the Chinook and Koskimo, but distinctly mesorrhinic in the Undeformed and Cowichan. All the male averages, on the other hand, are leptorrhinic in the order Koskimo-Chinook-Undeformed-Cowichan ranging between 44.7 and 46.7. Among the more numerous groups of the Undeformed, the Eskimo are leptorrhinic, not in the same degree, however, as their eastern kin, while the Haida show a decided trend toward chamaerrhiny. The Athapascan and Salish hold the middle between these extremes with lepto-mesorrhinic averages. On the whole it appears that the Mongols (see *summary 102*) are more pronouncedly mesorrhinic than the northwestern Indian tribes, except the Haida who fairly coincide with them, and that the tendency toward leptorrhiny, as stated above, is rather pronounced in natives of the North Pacific Coast.

Although in the *maxillo-alveolar index* the highest percental frequencies in the four divisions occur in the brachyuranic class, which renders their averages likewise brachyuranic, there are conspicuous differences to be noticed in the latter. As already indicated by the comparatively highest frequency of brachyurany at 89.2% in the Chinook, their divisional average of 125.9 represents the highest among the four averages, to be followed at some distance by the Undeformed and Koskimo averages of 121.9 and 120.8, and finally the Cowichan with the relatively low average of 118.0. It is in the latter division that mesurany and dolichurany are likewise well represented at 21.9% and 14.3% respectively as over against the minimal percentages particularly of dolichurany in the other divisions. The males are somewhat more dolichuranic than the females as shown by the average conditions. This, however, does not seem to represent the general racial conditions as proved by *Martin's* comparative table of maxillo-alveolar indices (p. 824), where it is furthermore shown that most of the human varieties are brachyuranic and the Mongols pronouncedly so.

The angle of *facial prognathy* referred to the ear-eye plane of general cranial orientation reveals average mesognathous conditions in the four divisions with a tendency toward prognathy in the deformed series which is less clear in the Undeformed. This is indicated in the former by the percental excess of prognathy over orthognathy and the reverse in the latter. The male and female averages fairly coincide showing those of the Chinook just above and below the border line between prognathy and orthognathy. The possibility was hinted at above (p. 135) of a deformatory influence upon prognathy in the tribes addicted to artificial head distortion, which, however, it will be difficult to prove, first of all, on account of the minuteness of the metrical disparity. Another point of observation, however, referred to above (p. 144, 145) seems to be of greater interest, namely, the closer or more distant racial affinity to the Mongol stock. It was shown there in reiteration and corroboration of the statements of various authors that the profile angles of the Mongol stock is less prognathous than in the mongoloid varieties. Applying this observation to some of our Undeformed groups, it would seem that, for instance, the Athapascan and Lillooet with their higher group means do not divagate, if any, from average mongolian conditions. These conditions should be proved upon a more numerous material.

The *alveolar profile angle* is overwhelmingly prognathous in its percental frequency as well as its averages where it appears that, excepting the Cowichan where the male and female averages are identical, the female angles are noticeably smaller than the male or, what is equivalent, more prognathous than the latter. The Cowichan at the same time exhibit the strongest degree of prognathy in the divisional average of 72.8°. What was said in the preceding paragraph about the mongolo-mongoloid divergence applies also and even more strongly to alveolar prognathy. However, the group means among the Undeformed fairly coincide and do not exhibit divergences which would place certain mongoloid groups closer to the Mongol stock. With *Martin's* (p. 810) ranges of averages for the angle of alveolar prognathy from 62° to 86°, and of individual angles from 49° to 100°, it appears that our series hold about a medium position. The same author points out that pronounced alveolar orthognathy is to be considered a rather individual condition.

The variability, already indicated by the *standard deviation* ($\sigma \pm$) in the summaries of the numerous measurements discussed in the craniometric part of this report, where the deviations were accounted for separately in the sexes, have been condensed in the present general *summary 103* to mark the serial or divisional deviations. In addition the *coefficient of variation* may be found in the last column pertaining to each of the four divisions. It will be noticed that the variability is stronger in the deformed divisions, particularly in such cranial dimensions which were influenced by direct deformatory strain, and the indices computed from them. Others like the *upper facial index* where the deformatory influence is less pronounced, vary in fairly equal degree in both the undeformed and deformed crania, with the exception of the Chinook whose σ and v fall conspicuously lower. A lesser variability in the deformed divisions as against the Undeformed is to be noticed in the *orbital* and *nasal indices*, while the reverse is true again with regard to the maxilloalveolar index where in excess of the Undeformed and the other deformed series, the Chinook show the greatest variability with a standard deviation of ± 8.2 and a coefficient of variation of 6.5. It was likewise the Chinook who exceeded all the other divisions with regard to their brachyuranic index of 125.9. The two *angles of prognathy* reveal a fairly similar variability in the four divisions, although, taking the Undeformed as a model, a slight increase might be stated in the Cowichan and Chinook. A slight relapse, similar in proportion, occurs in the Koskimo.

In conclusion, it may be stated, that there is no stable proportion in the cranial variability of the sexes as shown in the numerous craniometrical summaries of this part, and that, on the whole, the variability represents average conditions of series more or less mixed in character; it is, in other words, rather moderate than excessive.

SUMMARY.

The results of our craniometrical investigation upon the skull material collected by the Jesup Expedition, laid down in the different chapters and the discussion preceding this final statement may be summarized as follows:

Deformed skulls.

a. Voluntary, intentional or artificial head deformation is reducible to two fundamental types: anteroposterior and conical compression, both of which are variable with regard to their range of intensity.

b. A third type, that of bilateral compression is only sporadically met with, and then mostly in connection with anteroposterior, more seldom with conical deformation.

c. From the viewpoint of skull deformation, several well defined localities present themselves as centers of radiation: Vancouver Island for the milder form of anteroposterior compression (Cowichan) and for the conical method; anteroposterior compression in an extreme degree as practiced by the Chinook of lower Columbia River; bilateral compression as occurs in skulls from lower layers of shell heaps around Vancouver City [58].

d. Intentional head deformation produces articificial long- and shortheadedness.

e. The distortions in the skull due to direct deformatory strain are augmented by such as are acquired indirectly in physiological adjustment of the disturbed conditions of cerebral growth and expansion, and cranial equilibrium. Direct changes occur in connection with the cranial diameters (elongation, foreshortening, compensatory expansion) and the angular positions of the parts concerned with reference to the plane of orientation (ear-eye plane); indirect changes are brought about through the intermediary of parts or complexes working upon each other (orbital, foramen magnum, cranial base declination; central and craniofacial angles; orbital height diameter; facial breadth, height and prognathy; cranial capacity [?]; and a number of other conditions more difficult to be traced and therefore more uncertain).

---

[58] Bilateral deformation, however, was also reported in relatively recent skulls from the southern regions of the United States. It occurs likewise in the South American center of head deformation, Ancient Peru, where the deformatory practices were the same in principle as in our Northwest.

Undeformed skulls.

a. On the whole the skulls of the Undeformed, with the exception of the somewhat sturdier Haida, are of a rather delicate texture, non-robust in appearance and of moderate to sub-moderate size (euencephalic); manifest a tendency toward mesobrachy- and hypsiorthocrany; have medium high to high faces (mesēnic–leptēnic); are mesokonchic and mesorrhinic with leanings toward hypsikonchy and leptorrhiny; pronouncedly brachyuranic; mesognathous in facial and prognathous in alveolar prognathy, and have moderately developed chins.

b. The sex and age differences are those which obtain likewise in other human varieties.

c. When compared with the Mongol stock, tribal varieties of the Undeformed show a tendency toward greater longheadedness and lowheadedness, slighter facial breadth, narrower noses, higher orbits and a stronger facial and alveolar prognathy.

d. Among the tribal varieties comprised in the Undeformed series, the Lillooet have been recognized as a special type characterized by extreme shortheadedness, comparatively low cranial and facial heights and considerable facial breadth, somewhat low orbits and rather broad nasal apertures. Although in some characters conforming with the Mongol stock, the Lillooet are decidedly more prognathous.

e. There is a distinct difference between the Eskimo of the West and East, mostly with regard to the principal cranial diameters; the sagittal crest of the cranial vault, the extreme narrowness of the nasal aperture and the orbits approaching in orientation the frontal plane, being characteristic of the eastern Eskimo.

f. The tribal varieties of the Undeformed complex, in spite of slight craniometrical differences among themselves, show fundamental type affinities which in turn appear to be more or less closely related to the characteristics of the Mongol stock. Applying to them the term of Mongoloids to which variety the American Indians of the Northwest (undeformed as well as deformed) are herewith definitely allotted (see however the final chapter), marks them in the sense of *Baur–Fischer–Lenz* as belonging to the great racial domain of the Mongolids which comprise the true Mongol and the groups of mongolian affinities, i. e. the Mongoloids.

PART II. — CRANIOSCOPY.

General remarks.

Under the caption of cranioscopy, which comprises the descriptive branch of craniology, the form differences of the skull in its various aspects as well as the morphologic detail from the normal and abnormal points of view, will be treated. The latter represent either anomalous or pathological conditions. Quantitative methods, which form the basic purport in craniometry, need therefore not be considered in cranioscopy, and are only employed here as a means of ascertaining the frequency and occasionally the dimensions of certain traits.

The method generally employed in cranioscopy, i.e., the study of the skull in the five normae, is also pursued in this part. Emphasizing the fact that the form differences of the skull, particularly in the norma verticalis, cannot be expressed in terms of proportional relations, i.e., the cranial indices, the Italian School of *G. Sergi* and his followers have substituted a method by which the cranial contour is patterned upon a suitable geometrical figure and named accordingly, viz., ellipsoides, sphaeroides, etc. *Sergi* has gone even further in identifying the different contours as characteristic of specific races. But realizing that the skull is "a tridimensional body whose peculiar form it is impossible to determine by a planimetric outline of a single norma" (*R. Martin*, Lehrbuch, 1914, 587), *Sergi*[59], supplementing his system of horizontal outlines, had recourse also to those of the norma lateralis, i. e., the median-sagittal contours. This is the "tassonomic method" of the Italian School. The present writer has found it useful for descriptive purposes, without, however, following *Sergi* in the attempt to draw any conclusions from the viewpoint of racial diagnosis.

Besides the description of the cranial contours, an individual method of investigation has been established and adhered to in the following chapters. Since the anatomy of the skull forms the foundation for any and all morphologic observations, the present writer has systematically examined the anatomical details in each norma as to their frequency and individual development, and

---

[59] *Sergi*, G., 1893. Le varietà umane. Torino (English translation by *D. G. Brinton*, in: Miscell. Coll. Smiths. Inst., 1894, n⁰. 969)
—— 1905. Die Variationen des menschlichen Schädels und die Klassifikation der Rassen. Arch. Anthrop., v. XXXI (N. F., v. III), pp. 111—121.

has grouped them according to their regional occurrence. Many of these, like, for instance, the frontal process of the temporal squama, the torus palatinus, the fossa pharyngea, etc., have already been established as racial peculiarities. For less varying characters, having no anthropological record so far, figures are offered here for future comparison with results from other related and unrelated series.

The examination of the five normae is carried on in the following order: verticalis; basilaris; lateralis; frontalis, and occipitalis.

The morphologic features occurring in these normae were listed in cranioscopic observation sheets and graded individually according to their specific appearance (cranial contours, shape of the foramen magnum, course of the sutura nasofrontalis, etc.), or by the letters: *a*, *b*, and *c*, designated to indicate the intensity of development as slight, medium or pronounced. Special cases of pronounced aberration, either negative or positive, had to be pointed out as such by special marks. In the following paragraphs descriptive reference is made to the features enumerated, supplemented by comparative summaries and occasional illustrations [60]. The various skull types are visualized by the median-sagittal and horizontal tracings as well as by the photographic reproductions contained in Plates I–XI.

---

[60] *Sullivan, Louis R.*, in his "Anthropology of the Siouan tribes" (Anthrop. Pap. Amer. Mus. Nat. Hist., 1920, v. XXII, p. 91), is correct in stating, that: "The value of descriptive characters is not very great, due, not to any great extent to the fault of the observers, but to the use of unsatisfactory standards and the unavoidable range of personal estimation in evaluating minute differences in terms of relative magnitude". For some cranial features, such as the spina nasalis, the glabellar development, the shape of the nasal bones, etc., satisfactory standards facilitate description. There are other traits however, like the fossa canina, the crista marginalis of the palate bone, etc., for which it might be difficult to create a graded scale of development, unless figurative representation of the individual case, or metrical interpretation is resorted to. Altogether it might be said that a careful investigation carried out by the same observer will render a uniform interpretation, uniform at least from the viewpoint of personal observation.

NORMA VERTICALIS.

1. Cranial contour.

The principal types of cranial outlines, as described by *G. Sergi* and employed in his tassonomic method, are relatively easily discernible. They are, besides the ellipsoides and sphaeroides which represent the two fundamental cranial types, the rhomboides, depending upon strongly protruding parietal bosses and as such occurring most frequently in the immature ages, and the intermediary forms between the former two, such as the ovoides, pentagonoides, sphenoides and byrsoides, which are subject somewhat to personal estimation. But such is the fate, more or less, of many descriptive characters.

The classification in *summary 104* shows the numerical and percental distribution of the undeformed and the typically deformed skulls among the seven geometrical classes as marked in outlines at the head of that summary.[61] The groups composing the Undeformed division are furthermore individually listed.

The greatest number of individuals here is shown to belong to the ovoides cranial outline, namely, 39.1%, of which 45% are males and 38% females. Relatively high frequencies occur also in the byrsoides[62] and sphenoides, while smaller percentages are expressive of the pentagonoides and rhomboides. This latter contour is represented by two males, three females and six infantiles who contribute the larger number in accordance with the above statement of preferred occurrence. The Cowichan and Chinook skulls with their flattened and broadened occipita have the greater number of individuals with the sphenoides. This is particularly true in the Chinook, of whom there is only one deviating male classed as ovoides, thus bringing their percentages to 98.9% and 1.1%. The deformed Salish vary somewhat more, their frequency for the sphenoides amounting to 77.1%, while the ovoides, rhomboides, byrsoides and pentagonoides in diminishing percentages make up the balance. In the Koskimo deformation the ovoides at 45.3% comprise the bulk in which the males participate with 51% and the females with 33%. The unequal intensity of deformation in this division is also responsible for larger percentages in the byrsoides and sphenoides. Smaller percentages go to the ellipsoides and pentagonoides, the rhomboides here being represented by one male and two infants.

Disregarding the deformed skulls with their more decided prevalence of cranial contour due to their specific modes of deformation, the figures of this list demonstrate a rather pronounced variability in the Undeformed. The two

---

[61] On account of their paucity, the percental frequencies in the immatures have throughout not been accounted for.

[62] Byrsoides is taken from the Greek where βύρσα means, the skin stripped off, a wine-skin (see Liddell and Scott's Greek-English Dictionary). The shape had reference to that of a purse and the word is used in this sense.

Summary 104.

Cranial contours in norma verticalis: actual and percental frequency.

| SERIES | Cranial contour in norma verticalis |||||||||||||||||||||
| | 1 Ellipsoides ||| 2 Pentagonoides ||| 3 Rhomboides ||| 4 Ovoides ||| 5 Sphenoides ||| 6 Sphaeroides ||| 7 Byrsoides |||
	♂	♀	im-mat	♂	♀	im-mat	♂	♀	im-mat	♂	♀	im-mat	♂	♀	im-mat	♂	♀	im-mat	♂	♀	im-mat
Undeformed Salish (Int'r) Athapascan	—	—	—	1	—	1	1	—	—	2	—	—	1	—	—	—	—	—	1	1	—
Haida	—	—	—	2	—	1	—	1	2	8	2	1	3	4	1	—	—	—	5	2	—
Lillooet	—	—	—	—	1	2	—	—	1	—	—	—	2	1	1	—	—	—	—	1	—
Nicola	—	—	—	—	1	—	—	1	—	2	—	—	1	—	—	—	—	—	—	—	—
Lytton	—	—	—	—	—	1	—	—	1	5	3	—	—	1	—	—	—	—	1	—	—
Spences Bridge	—	—	—	—	1	—	—	—	—	1	—	—	—	—	—	—	—	—	—	1	—
Kamloops	—	—	—	—	—	—	1	—	—	3	2	—	1	—	—	—	—	—	—	—	—
Eskimo	—	—	—	4	—	—	—	1	—	11	6	—	7	2	—	—	—	—	10	4	—
Chukchee	—	—	—	—	—	—	—	—	2	3	1	—	—	—	—	—	—	—	1	—	—
cases	—	—	—	7	3	5	2	3	6	35	14	1	15	8	2	—	—	—	18	9	—
sex percentage	—	—	—	9.0	8.0	—	3.0	8.0	—	45.0	38.0	—	20.0	22.0	—	—	—	—	23.0	24.0	—
total	—			11.7%			8.6%			39.1%			19.5%			—			21.1%		
Cowichan	—	—	—	1	2	—	3	3	2	12	3	—	74	22	5	—	—	—	3	1	—
sex percentage	—	—	—	1.0	6.0	—	3.0	10.0	—	13.0	10.0	—	80.0	71.0	—	—	—	—	3.0	3.0	—
total	—			2.3%			6.1%			11.5%			77.1%			—			3.0%		
Chinook	—	—	—	—	—	—	—	—	—	1	—	—	56	25	10	—	—	—	—	—	—
sex percentage	—	—	—	—	—	—	—	—	—	1.8	—	—	98.2	100.0	—	—	—	—	—	—	—
total	—			—			—			1.1%			98.9%			—			—		
Koskimo	6	5	1	2	3	1	1	—	2	52	13	3	16	8	1	—	—	—	26	10	—
sex percentage	6.0	13.0	—	2.0	8.0	—	1.0	—	—	51.0	33.0	—	15.0	21.0	—	—	—	—	25.0	25.0	—
total	8.0%			4.0%			2.0%			45.3%			16.7%			—			24.0%		

fundamental forms, viz. ellipsoides and sphaeroides, are entirely absent, and the former, especially characteristic of certain Negro tribes, would hardly be looked for in this connection.

2. Pathological cranial forms.

The only pathological deformation of the skull recorded in these series is that of plagiocephaly,[63] due mostly to premature obliteration of the lambdoid

---

[63] There are several causes responsible for this cranial anomaly, which might be divided into mechanical and organic. *R. Virchow* (1892, 56), goes even so far as to trace it to intrauterine conditions when he states:

suture on one side of the occiput. From *summary 105* it appears that anteroposterior compression, as practiced by the Coast Salish (Cowichan deformation), and in more intensive fashion by the Chinook, is very apt to produce *artificial* plagiocephaly. It occurs less frequently in the Koskimo deformation.

In all the series, undeformed as well as deformed, left-sided plagiocephaly predominates; the male frequency in most cases exceeding the female. Left-sided plagiocephaly occurs, for instance, in the male Undeformed in ten individuals out of eighty, and in the females in two out of thirty-four. Right-sided plagiocephaly occurs only in one female, and in one infantile skull out of fourteen.

Summary 105.

Plagiocephaly: actual and percental frequency.

Sex and Age	Plagiocephaly											
	Undeformed				Cowichan				Chinook				Koskimo			
	Right		Left		Right		Left		Right		Left		Right		Left	
	no.	%	no.	%	no.	%	no.	%	no.	%	no.	%	no.	%	no.	%
♂	—	—	10	10.3	5	5.7	33	37.5	11	19.0	22	30.8	—	—	4	3.8
♀	1	2.9	2	5.1	7	24.1	5	17.2	5	19.2	8	30.8	1	2.6	3	7.7
juv.	—	—	—	—	—	—	2	—	—	—	2	—	—	—	—	—
inf.	1	—	—	—	2	—	2	—	1	—	3	—	—	—	—	—
Frequencies	2	1.6	12	9.8	14	11.6	42	34.7	17	18.3	35	37.6	1	0.7	7	4.7
Total	11.5 %				46.3 %				55.9 %				5.3 %			

The frequency is considerably higher in the Cowichan deformation and attains the highest figure in the males for its occurrence on the left cranical side. Right-sided plagiocephaly occurs in the same sex only in five individuals. This order is reversed in the females, where left-sided plagiocephaly was found in 17.2 % as against 37.5 % in the males, and right-sided plagiocephaly in 24.1 % as against 5.7 %. In the immatures, the two juveniles, and two infantiles out of five, show left-sided, two other infantiles right-sided plagiocephaly.

"Der Druck ist hervorgebracht durch den Widerstand der Beckenknochen oder anderer Teile des Fötus oder eines Zwillings im Mutterleibe. Diese, in der ersten Zeit nach der Geburt zuweilen recht auffällige angeborene Difformität gleicht sich durch natürliche Wachstumsverhältnisse ziemlich oft so sehr aus, dass man nach einigen Jahren wenig oder nichts davon bemerkt. Indess giebt es auch Fälle in denen eine bleibende Verunstaltung dadurch bewirkt wird."

Among the mechanical causes in extrauterine life producing a plagiocephalic condition, are to be mentioned the ways of holding the infant or carrying it about, (see footnote 14) and its position at rest in the cradle or bed. The latter, in fact, does not vary much from the cause of occipital depression as represented in a milder degree by some cases of the Cowichan deformation. The most frequent of the organic and, therefore, truly pathological causes is the premature one-sided obliteration of the lambdoid suture resulting in compensatory expansion on the other cranial side. The occurrence of plagiocephaly in the undeformed skulls of the present series is generally due to this cause. In no case could it be laid to osseous diseases.

The relatively highest frequency of simultaneous occurrence in the adult sexes is seen in the Chinook deformation. Left-sided plagiocephaly occurs here in twenty-two cases out of a total of fifty-eight males, or 30.8 %, the same percentage being had for eight females out of twenty-six. Right-sided plagiocephaly yields also equal percentages in the two sexes, namely, 19.0 % for eleven males and 19.2 % for five females. The number of immature plagiocephalic skulls in the Chinook equals that in the Cowichan deformation. The Chinook juveniles numbering four, present two left cases, the six infantiles three, while one infantile shows the right-sided deformation. These figures are relatively high considering the paucity of immatures in both series, the Cowichan and Chinook deformation, but they corroborate what has been pointed out in footnote 63 with reference to artificially formed plagiocephaly.

The Koskimo deformation does not evince artificial plagiocephaly to the same extent. Only four cases out of a total of one hundred-four males, and three out of thirty-nine females exhibit left-sided plagiocephaly, while one female shows it on the right side. The total absence of plagiocephaly in the immatures rather bears out what has been said concerning the different modes of deformation which produce artificial plagiocephaly.

The total percentages verify these detailed statements.

3. Postorbital constriction.

The morphological significance of postorbital constriction is commensurate with its relation to the development of the frontal and temporal lobes of the cerebrum. Its usefulness as a means of differentiation becomes manifest then, not only in comparison between the anthropoids and the Hominidae, but also between the latter and the different varieties of Homo sapiens.

The postorbital constriction as measured behind the zygomatic processes of the frontal bone, fairly coincides with the minimum frontal diameter, as pointed out by *R. Virchow* (1892, 34: "minimale Stirnbreite"), and *Schwalbe*.[64] The averages of this measurement, 94 mm. and 91 mm. (see p. 51) in the Undeformed and Koskimo respectively, were shown to be equal in the sexes, while those of the Cowichan and Chinook deformations exceeded the former in successive order at 95 mm. and 98 mm. in the males, and 91 mm. and 93 mm. in the females, the increase being due doubtless to deformatory influence.

As a comparative feature postorbital constriction is of diagnostic value only in the normal, i. e., the undeformed skull. A few data from the lists of *Schwalbe* and *Nehring*[65] may be of interest. The former gives a range of averages from 81—116 mm., the extreme values belonging to Veddah and Weissthurmthor skulls. Pithecanthropus has a postorbital constriction or

---

[64] *Schwalbe*, G., 1899. Studien über Pithecanthropus erectus Dubois. Zschr. Morph. Anthrop., v. I, pp. 16—240 (62—63).

[65] *Nehring*, A., 1905. Menschenreste aus einem Sambaqui von Santos in Brasilien. Zschr. Ethnol., v. XXVII, pp. 710—721; discussing the causation of postorbital constriction, is of the opinion that muscular traction and pressure, especially of the great masticators, is responsible for that trait in the anthropoids. This view he supports by comparing the immature and mature stages of cranial development in man and apes, their apparent similarity in early life and their pronounced divergence in the adult. Granted the effects of muscular action, aided by the strong dentitions of the apes, *Nehring* leaves out of consideration, however, the different modes of cerebral growth and expansion. These are continued in man during the entire period of physical growth, while in the apes changes are quite insignificant on account of the cessation of cerebral growth at a considerably earlier period of life. In view of this the two adult stages are not directly comparable.

minimum frontal width of 87 mm., Spy I, Spy II, and Neandertal each of 104 mm., 109 mm. and 112 mm. respectively.

The Undeformed averages of the present series namely, 94.1 mm. for the males and 91.1 mm. for the females would then fall between the values of Pithecanthropus and the other fossils. According to *Schwalbe*'s list this is where the greatest frequency occurs, including the values from 90—94 mm. *Nehring's* [66] Sambaqui skull at 90 mm., although below the averages of the present series, would also come under that group.

The range of variation includes individual values as low as 83 mm. in the males and 82 mm. in the females of the Undeformed. It is quite plausible, however, that in general the absolute size of a skull with an extremely low postorbital constriction must be taken into consideration, and that a true evaluation of the feature under discussion can be had only when brought into relation with other cranial dimensions. On the other hand, the arithmetic means of the groups comprising the lowest male value, viz. the Eskimo and the Kamloops, are 94.5 mm. and 89.6 mm., the former conforming to the average of the Undeformed division, the latter, however, falling distinctly below it. The low female value of 82 mm. is one of the two Nicola Lake specimens, the other measuring 90 mm. The lowest male mean is that of the Kamloops at 89.6 mm., the highest at 95.2 mm. that of the Athapascans. The Eskimo at 94.5 mm. and 90.3 mm. conform to the general average.

4. Foramina parietalia.

No cases of extremely large foramina parietalia, as described in anthropological literature by *W. Gruber, L. Plenk, A. Maciesza, Th. Simon*, et al., have been recorded for the present series. But a peculiarity of a different nature was not infrequently met in connection with the foramina. The obelion region, where they are situated, represented in a number of cases marked elevations with rugged, uneven surfaces, on top of which the foramina were to be seen. The simplest appearance of such elevation or bulging is that of a circular isolated knoll of narrower or wider circumference, showing at its summit the foramen parietale with smoothed-off or depressed edges. The typical occurrence of such elevations is twofold corresponding to the typical number of foramina. A further complication is that of a connecting ridge across the sagittal suture between the two isolated knolls. This ridge, directed transversely, is also seen, more or less broad, to widen in extreme cases so as to transform the entire obelion region into an extended uniform prominence of the typical appearance of a muscular tuberosity. The nature of this formation is not quite clear. It occurs in both the normal and deformed Indian

---

[66] *Nehring* registers 88—92 mm., of which the mean of 90 mm. was calculated above.

skulls. But as a cranial locality of retarded ossification is concerned here, a larger frequency of this formation apparently occurs in the deformed skulls so that its cause to some extent may be sought in deforming influences affecting the process of ossification in the obelion region.

The typical number of foramina parietalia is two, one on each side of the sagittal suture. The number, however, may be not only increased on one or both sides, but none at all may be found. In the case of total absence a number of small pores are sometimes observed in place of the foramina. Still another variety is the foramen parietale impar, i. e., the occurrence of a foramen parietale in the sagittal suture. The sizes also may vary in one and the same skull. However, large-sized ones, as stated above, were not encountered.

Anomalous conditions as to number and distribution of the foramen parietale occur in all the series, and are listed as to their actual and percental frequency in *summary 106*.

The plan pursued therein is the assemblage in the four series of all the individuals under special captions, showing either the normal number of the foramina parietalia, namely, two (t), and their equal size ($r = l$), or variations of both number and size. The first four columns following the sex and age rubric, and headed by the letters t, r, l and o, refer to the number. t means that the normal number of two foramina are present; r and l indicate that either the right or the left foramen only is in place, and o that both are absent. The next three columns refer to the size, and interpret the status of t directly, the two foramina being either of equal size ($r = l$), or the right one larger than the left ($r > l$); or the right one smaller than the left ($r < l$). The last column contains the anomalies. The number in front of the letter indicates the number of foramina, while the number in parentheses give the number of cases.

As regards their number, it is seen then that the normal, i. e., the presence of two foramina, as listed at the foot of each column t, predominates in each division. With the exception of the two equal percentages of 63.0 % in the Chinook deformation, it will also be observed that the male exceed the female percentages. The presence of only the right foramen (column r) shows the next highest figures in the four divisions, signifying at the same time the higher frequency of this condition as against the presence of only the left one (column l). Comparatively high percentages are reached for the total absence of the foramina parietalia in the Undeformed and Cowichan deformation. In the former, the females exceed the males, in the latter this condition is reversed. The percentage for the same condition is astonishingly low in the Chinook, where both sexes are each represented by one case only. As the greater occurrence of absence is thus shown to occur in Undeformed skulls, it may not be entirely improbable that excessive deformation as practiced by the Chinook serves as a sort of preventive against the obliteration of these typical cranial outlets (emissaria venosa). The status in the Koskimo deformation would partly corroborate such an assertion, although the frequency in the females amounts to six, or 15%, as against only two in the males, or 2 %.

Equality in size of the two foramina appears to be the normal condition in the undeformed as well as in the deformed skulls. It is represented by total percentages as high as 51.1 % in the Chinook, and by somewhat lesser ones in the other three divisions. Male and female percentages vary from a comparative angle. While the Undeformed and Koskimo males exceed the females, the reverse is true of the Cowichan and Chinook divisions.

Inequality in size in which the right foramen predominates shows a greater frequency than the contrary condition. Of this latter there are represented only two male specimens in all the Undeformed, while the Cowichan and Chinook males number three, and the Chinook and Koskimo females only one each. The Koskimo males, however, number ten specimens at 17%. The frequency of the greater right foramen lies considerably above the last discussed status. The highest

Summary 106.

Foramina parietalia: actual and percental frequency, and anomalies. t, presence of the two typical foramina, r, l, of right or left foramen only; o, absence.

Sex and age	Foramina parietalia													Anomalies	
	Undeformed														
	t		r		l		o		r=l		r>l		r<l		no.	%
	no.	%	no.	%	no.	%	no.	%	no.	%	no.	%	no.	%		
♂	39	51.0	15	20.0	8	11.0	10	13.0	24	62.0	13	33.0	2	5.0	3r (1);* r, 2l (1); r, 3l (1) 2t (1);	5.0
♀	11	30.0	11	30.0	3	8.0	9	24.0	5	45.0	6	55.0	—	—	r, 2l (1); 2l (1)	8.0
juv.	—	—	1	—	—	—	1	—	—	—	—	—	—	—	—	—
inf.	5	—	—	—	2	—	4	—	2	—	3	—	—	—	—	—
Total frequencies	55	44.0	27	21.6	13	10.4	24	19.2	31	24.0	22	17.6	2	1.6	6	4.8
Cowichan deformation																
♂	28	35.0	20	25.0	8	10.0	18	22.0	19	68.0	6	21.0	3	11.0	2t (2); r, 2l (2) 2r (2); 2l (1); 2r, l (1)	8.0
♀	7	26.0	8	30.0	1	3.0	3	11.0	7	100.0	—	—	—	—	2r (1); 2l (1) 3r (2); r, 2l (3)	30.0
juv.	2	—	—	—	—	—	—	—	2	—	—	—	—	—	—	—
inf.	2	—	—	—	1	—	1	—	2	—	—	—	—	—	2t (1)	—
Total frequencies	39	33.9	28	24.4	10	8.7	22	19.1	30	26.1	6	5.2	3	2.6	16	13.9
Chinook deformation																
♂	34	63.0	10	19.0	5	9.0	1	2.0	27	79.0	4	12.0	3	9.0	2t (1); 2r (2); 2l (1) 2t (1); 2r, 3l (1)	7.0
♀	17	63.0	3	11.0	2	7.0	1	4.0	14	82.0	2	12.0	1	6.0	2r, l (1); r, 2l (1)	15.0
juv.	3	—	1	—	—	—	—	—	2	—	1	—	—	—	—	—
inf.	3	—	1	—	1	—	—	—	3	—	—	—	—	—	—	—
Total frequencies	57	63.3	15	16.7	8	8.9	2	2.2	46	51.1	7	7.8	4	4.4	8	8.9
Koskimo deformation																
♂	58	55.0	15	14.0	14	14.0	2	2.0	36	62.0	12	21.0	10	17.0	2t (5); r, 2l (3) 2r (8); 4r, l (1) 2r (1); r, 3l (1)	15.0
♀	13	33.0	7	18.0	5	13.0	6	15.0	6	46.0	6	46.0	1	8.0	r, 2l (2); 2r, l (4) 2r, l (1);	21.0
juv.	—	—	1	—	1	—	—	—	—	—	1	—	—	—	—	—
inf.	4	—	—	—	1	—	—	—	3	—	1	—	—	—	—	—
Total frequencies	75	49.3	23	15.1	20	13.2	8	5.3	45	29.6	19	12.5	11	7.2	26	17.1

* Figures in parentheses indicate frequency.

percentage of 17.6 %, is reached in the Undeformed, which exceeds that of the Koskimo by 5.1 %, while the Cowichan and Chinook percentages fall considerably lower, although higher than in the rubric $r < l$.

The immatures reflect more or less the condition as stated for the matures.

The anomalies are concerned only with equal or unequal repetition of numbers above the normal two foramina. They also comprise the cases of unilateral absence of a foramen and multiplication on the opposite side. The percentages fall relatively low in the Undeformed. They yield higher figures in each of the deformed divisions, reaching 17.1 % in the Koskimo.

5. Os bregmaticum.

The os bregmaticum occurs so seldom that its evaluation as a racial characteristic is rather negative. Of particular interest, however, is its causation and shape. The os bregmaticum resembles in morphological significance the Wormian bones of the sutures, i. e., both are derived from accessory ossification centers and both are furthermore met with in close association. Pathological conditions such as hydrocephaly and premature obliteration of sutures may also cause the formation of our anomaly, but the number of investigations is too small as yet to admit of definite conclusions.

A typical fontanel bone, like the os epiptericum and os apicis (see normae lateralis and occipitalis), the os bregmaticum fills in more or less completely the primary osseous gap known as fonticulus frontalis. As a rule, its greatest extension is posteriorly directed, while frontal projections occur more seldom, and then generally in conjunction with metopism. Occasional multiplicity of osseous formations in the anterior fontanel has been mentioned by *Barclay-Smith* [67] who found at least thirteen ossicles there in a full-time fetus, and four in a young male of 21 years.

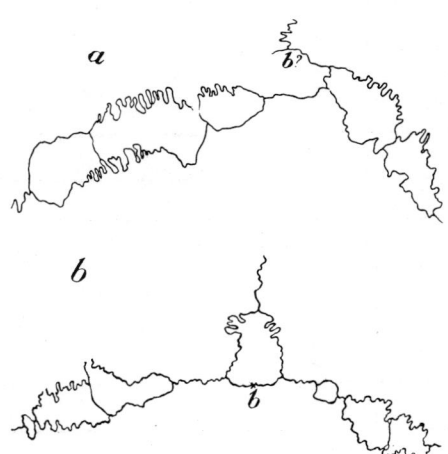

Fig. 23. *Os bregmaticum.*

In our specific case it seems that artificial deformation of the head favored the production of the feature under discussion, since both the recorded cases (Kwakiutl male 3893, and Chinook female 4484) belong to the deformed series and are further distinguished by simultaneous occurrence of numerous Wormian bones in the coronal suture (see fig. 23, *a* and *b*). The

---

[67] *Barclay Smith, E.*, 1908/9. A rare condition of Wormian ossification. Jour. Anat. Physiol., London, v. XLIII (3. ser., v. IV), pp. 277—278.

1909/10. Two cases of Wormian bone in the bregmatic-fontanelle. do, v. XLIV (3. ser., v. V), pp. 312—314.

first case represents an os bregmaticum incomplete in so far as its right side is fully merged with the parietal bone, similar cases being recorded by other authors. It is also marked by a continuous line of Wormian bones in the coronal suture closing in upon the os bregmaticum from both sides. The case is further complicated by the uncertainty of the bregma position, which may be identified either at its typical place at the point of intersection of the coronal and sagittal sutures, but more probably somewhat nearer to the center of the ossicle. In the original state its transverse diameter exceeded the longitudinal one. The second case represents a fine example of os bregmaticum of almost rectangular shape with a longitudinal diameter of 19 mm. and a transverse one of 10—15 mm.[68] Posteriorly and laterally its otherwise simple sutures appear quite enlivened. This case is likewise complicated by the occurrence of Wormian bones which, however, do not crowd in upon the bregma bone as in the preceding case.

The percental frequency in accordance with its rare occurrence is naturally very low. The Chinook and Koskimo series taken singly where the two recorded cases occur, the frequencies amount to 1.8% in the former, and 0.6% in the latter, while for our entire material from the Northwest as small a percentage as 0.39% would obtain. This is in close proximity to *Russell*'s[69] finding of 0.5% in American skulls and *Hrdlička*'s[70] of 1.0% in 20 Lenape Indians. Higher percentages like that for Eskimo at 1.9% or that given by *Koumaris*[71] at 1.08% are far too insignificant to be of diagnostic value. *Schultz*,[72] who has made a comprehensive study of the os bregmaticum, states that the very extensive statistics over 16,000 human skulls yielded a frequency only of 0.6%. Of interest, on the other hand, are the high percentages of occurrence found by him in various mammals, such as Erinaceus europaeus (68%); Castor canadensis (64%); Erethizon (51.0%), and Procyon crancrivorus (45.4%).

6. Vertical aspect of arcus zygomaticus.

The behavior of the arcus zygomaticus in norma verticalis is expressed by the terms: phaenozygy, orthozygy, and cryptozygy. The two contrasting conditions, phaenozygy and cryptozygy, signify either the visibility or non-visibility of the arcus zygomaticus in the vertical aspect, while orthozygy designates a state of coincidence of the zygomatic and cranial outlines in norma

---

[68] *Martin, R.,* (Lehrbuch, 1914, 757) gives a dimensional range from below 1 mm. to 4.7 mm. for the os bregmaticum.
[69] *Russell, Frank,* 1900. Studies in cranial variation. Amer. Natural., v. XXXIV, pp. 737—745.
[70] l. c., p. 14 (36).
[71] *Koumaris, Jean G.,* 1919. Sur quelques variations des os "des crânes grecs anciens." Anthrop., v. XXIX, pp. 29—36 (32).
[72] *Schultz, Adolph H.,* 1923. Bregmatic fontanelle bones in mammals. Jour. Mamm., v. IV, pp. 65—77.

verticalis. The three conditions of the zygomatic arch in the order as indicated above reflect a successive development from the comparative and phyletic viewpoints. Thus, in addition to its correlation to postorbital constriction, the extent of frontal and lateral extension of the zygomatic arch must particularly be considered; the latter, as is well known, is a Mongolian characteristic. Both factors, then, are involved here.

Phaenozygy predominates in all four divisions, as will be gathered from *summary 107*. The males at the same time show markedly higher percentages, a result due to the greater actual breadth of the female forehead as expressed by the difference of the minimum frontal diameters which, as mentioned at various times, is the equivalent of postorbital constriction. The highest total percental occurrence is shown by the Koskimo deformation, where phaenozygy amounts to 83.6%. The gradual and even decrease of phaenozygy in the following order is significant: Cowichan, Chinook and Undeformed with frequencies of 73.5%, 71.3% and 49.6%. Of special interest is the decrease of orthozygy in the reverse divisional order; the Undeformed yielding 27.6% of orthozygy, the frequency diminishes in the Cowichan to 16.8%, in the Chinook to 11.7% and in the Koskimo to 6.6%. It will be noticed that the sex order of percentage is also reversed in such a way that in orthozygy the females attain the higher percentages. The principal reason for this, as suggested above, is the different morphological development of the anterior frontal region in the sexes, and the different relative widths of the zygomatic arch, even from the viewpoint of racial characteristics. But the intensity of deformation likewise seems to be an influence. The Cowichan and Chinook modes, in spite of their broadening tendencies, apparently favor phaenozygy, while orthozygy suffers a diminution in a similar proportion. The Koskimo deformation, particularly with its lengthening and narrowing influences upon the skull seems to overreach the effects of the other two, increasing the amount of phaenozygy and decreasing that of orthozygy.

The cryptozygous condition is rather irregularly represented in the four divisions. In the males it amounts only to 9% in the Undeformed and to as low as 3% in the Koskimo. The higher female percentages, however, confirm in a general way the assertion regarding the morphological characteristic of the broader female skull It is also in accord with general morphological conditions that the immatures should be found classed with the cryptozygous skulls, a fact which causes the total percentages of the Chinook and Koskimo to exceed their orthozygous figures.

Summary 107.

Arcus zygomaticus: actual and percental frequency of behavior in vertical aspect.

Sex and Age	Arcus zygomaticus					
	Undeformed					
	Phaenozygous		Orthozygous		Cryptozygous	
	no.	%	no.	%	no.	%
♂	52	69.0	18	23.0	7	9.0
♀	11	30.0	17	46.0	9	24.0
juv.	—	—	—	—	2	—
inf.	—	—	—	—	11	—
Total frequencies	63	49.6	35	27.6	29	22.8
	Cowichan deformation					
♂	64	78.0	11	13.0	7	9.0
♀	19	68.0	7	25.0	2	7.0
juv.	—	—	—	—	2	—
inf.	—	—	1	—	—	—
Total frequencies	83	73.5	19	16.8	11	9.7
	Chinook deformation					
♂	48	84.0	7	12.0	2	4.0
♀	19	70.0	4	15.0	4	15.0
juv.	—	—	—	—	4	—
inf.	—	—	—	—	6	—
Total frequencies	67	71.3	11	11.7	16	17.0
	Koskimo deformation					
♂	96	92.0	5	5.0	3	3.0
♀	31	77.0	5	13.0	4	10.0
juv.	—	—	—	—	1	—
inf.	—	—	—	—	7	—
Total frequencies	127	83.6	10	6.6	15	9.8

NORMA BASILARIS.

1. Foramen magnum.

a. *Shape.*

From the cranioscopic viewpoint the shape of the foramen magnum is quite variable and admits of a number of subdivisions which illustrate the conditions prevailing in different series of crania. *Hooton*,[73] in the Madisonville crania, distinguishes between: irregular, round, diamond, half-diamond and hexagonal shapes, but for our series the shapes of the foramen magnum were designated as elliptic, oval with bases situated anteriorly or posteriorly, round and rhomboid. The oval shapes approximate more or less the elliptic or the round, for both of which there are good instances. Regarding its final appearance, however, the shape of the foramen magnum depends in a number of cases upon the behavior of the occipital condyles. By their degree of projection into the lumen they are apt to modify the shape of the foramen, particularly toward the production of angular conditions, to which some of the foramina owe their rhomboid character.

A decided prevalence of any one shape as peculiar of the four principal divisions is not apparent in *summary 108*, except that of the rounded one in the Chinook. The high occurrence here of $6\;.6°/_o$ is in harmony with their high foramen magnum index of 89.1 and 88.7 in the sexes. The rhomboid shape, on the other hand, throughout the series is of limited frequency. Occurring in the Chinook in only $1.1°/_o$, somewhat higher percentages are met in the other divisions, yielding their highest in the Cowichan deformation at $7.0°/_o$. It is also in the Chinook that the elliptic shape occurs at the low percentage of $3.3°/_o$, while in the Undeformed and Cowichan it ranges above $20°/_o$, and in the Koskimo even above $30°/_o$. The oval-shape foramen magnum, with its base situated forward, yields its highest frequencies of $31.0°/_o$ in the Undeformed and $16.1°/_o$ in the Koskimo division, while the Cowichan and Chinook figures remain quite low. The oval-shape foramen magnum with posteriorly situated base, on the other hand, has its highest frequency in the latter two divisions.

Thus it is seen, with the exception of the high frequency of round-shape foramina in the Chinook, that there is scarcely any other proportion sufficiently represented to proclaim it a racial trait. Yet the observations among the Undeformed groups shows that the majority of the Lillooet and Lytton possess the round-shape foramina, and the Eskimo and Haida the oval-shape with anteriorly directed bases. The Eskimo at the same time show a tendency toward the elliptic.

---

[73] l. c., p. 151 (112).

Summary *108*.

Foramen magnum: actual and percental frequency of shapes.

Sex and Age	Foramen magnum (shape) Undeformed									
	1 Elliptic		2 Oval (base anterior)		3 Oval (base posterior)		4 Round		5 Rhomboid	
	no.	%	no.	%	no.	%	no.	%	no.	%
♂	21	30.0	20	28.6	7	10.0	18	25.6	4	5.8
♀	6	18.8	9	28.1	9	28.1	7	21.9	1	3.1
juv.	1	—	1	—	—	—	—	—	—	—
inf.	—	—	5	—	1	—	2	—	1	—
Total frequencies	28	24.8	35	31.0	17	15.0	27	23.9	6	5.3
Cowichan deformation										
♂	16	22.6	5	7.0	15	21.1	29	40.8	6	8.5
♀	4	18.2	1	4.5	9	40.9	7	31.8	1	4.6
juv.	1	—	—	—	—	—	1	—	—	—
inf.	1	—	2	—	1	—	1	—	—	—
Total frequencies	22	22.0	8	8.0	25	25.0	38	38.0	7	7.0
Chinook deformation										
♂	1	1.8	1	1.8	13	23.2	40	71.4	1	1.8
♀	1	3.9	3	11.5	7	26.9	15	57.7	—	—
juv.	—	—	2	—	—	—	2	—	—	—
inf.	1	—	—	—	1	—	2	—	—	—
Total frequencies	3	3.3	6	6.7	21	23.3	59	65.6	1	1.1
Koskimo deformation										
♂	37	36.3	19	18.6	9	8.8	34	33.4	3	2.9
♀	9	25.0	4	11.1	8	22.2	15	41.7	—	—
juv.	—	—	—	—	—	—	1	—	—	—
inf.	2	—	—	—	—	—	—	—	2	—
Total frequencies	48	33.5	23	16.1	17	11.9	50	35.0	5	3.5

It appears from these slight indications that there might be some correlation between the shapes of the foramen magnum and of the skull. But specific investigations, although meagre as yet, do no bear out such a supposition. Quite a number of skulls both of the undeformed and deformed series have unusually small foramina magna which may be indicative of small stature, as frequently pointed out by *Hrdlička* and others. Although probably true, these two assumptions will require thorough investigation upon more numerous material.

b. *Anterior border.*

At the anterior border of the foramen magnum anomalous osseous formations are occasionally noticed which have received considerable attention in anthropological literature. According to their nature they may be classified as ossifications, formations of rudimentary and vestigial significance, and of functional origin. Osseous eminences at the anterior edge which project into the lumen of the foramen magnum are generally specified under the caption of "condylus tertius". [74] Its various forms are of different causation. [75] The simplest form is that of a medially situated conical or thorn-like excrescence, provided sometimes with a slight articular surface. In most cases this form is due to ossification of the ligamentum apicis dentis epistrophei and, in connection therewith, to that of the ligamentum cruciatum atlantis, or still more correctly, its crus superius. Such a case is that of a male (1762) from "about Vancouver" (Eburne). The osseous formation here rises directly from the anterior border of the foramen magnum and its cerebral surface. It is peglike, situated in the median line and projects about 3 mm. into the lumen of the foramen magnum. It is fairly cylindrical and about 2.5 mm. thick. Although not of extraordinary size,[76] there occurs a

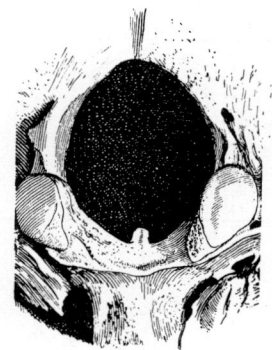

Fig. 24. Ossification of ligamentum apicis dentis epistrophei in a skull from Eburne near Vancouver, B. C. (n⁰. 1762).

---

[74] How vague the meaning of the term is may be seen from the many interpretations given it by *R. Havelock Charles*. Nevertheless, these are still valid. He says (Contributions to the craniology and craniometry of the Punjab tribes. Journ. Anat Physiol., 1893, v. XXVII [n. s., v. VII], pp. 5—20 [15]) "The 3rd condyle... may either be an articular depression, a single and medium tuberosity with an articular facet, a bilateral facetted tuberosity or, lastly, an unilateral or bilateral non-articular tubercle. It may articulate either with the anterior arch of the atlas, medially or laterally, or with the odontoid process. It may be developed in the suspensory ligament, or in the anterior lateral occipito-atloid ligament."

Koumaris, Jean G., l. c., p. 167 (30), on the other hand, distinguishes between "troisième condyle" and "éminences accessoires", for which latter he proposes the term "pseudocondyles". This distinction is quite important from the evolutionary viewpoint, since it takes notice of their different causation.

[75] See under section d of this chapter: "Manifestation of the occipital vertebra", p. 175.

[76] Among similar cases that described by *Schlaginhaufen* in a Battak-skull is of particular interest. The ossification attained the respective lengths of 10 mm. and 13 mm., the latter measurement representing the intra-

complication in connection with it which adds to the importance of the case. The entire region close to and in advance of the anterior border of the foramen magnum and between the condyles appears depressed, sloping somewhat posteriorly and above to anteriorly and below. This is plainly illustrated in fig. 24, where anteriorly the slope terminates in a transverse ridge in continuation of the anterior ends of the condyles. But the significant feature is a slight groove-like depression of articular origin.[77] Thus, while there cannot be any doubt regarding the odontoid articulation, the atlantal one by means of the anterior arcus is also evident. Unfortunately a fuller description of this condition cannot be given on account of absence of the adjoining cervical vertebrae.

The question whether artificial head deformation is in any way responsible for the production of these anomalies cannot easily be answered.

There may be noticed, in *summary 109*, a frequency of abnormal formations at the anterior border of the foramen magnum in the Undeformed, amounting even to 13.1%. But higher percentages of 16.0% and 16 5% occur in the Cowichan and Koskimo deformations, while the Chinook yield as much as 18.3%. It is rather interesting that ossifications of the described order occur only in the adult individuals of our series, and that the frequencies of the deformed series exceed the percentage attained by the Undeformed; and, furthermore, that among the former, the Chinook, the series of most strenuous deformation, possess the highest percentage of anomalies. Pronounced cases, however, are exceedingly rare, as will be seen in *summary 109*, the greatest frequencies belonging to occurrences marked "slight". It is the Chinook again who exceed the other divisions in the medium and pronounced cases.

c. *Posterior border*.

At the posterior border of the foramen magnum incisures more or less deep are occasionally met in the median plane area. Attention has been called to the casual artificial lengthening of the foramen through scraping the bone in mechanical maceration. In the pursuit of tribal rites[78] this was done by certain tribes after disinterring their deceased Such cases, however, are relatively easily discerned. A so-called incisura marginalis posterior (*Toldt*) s. occipitalis posterior (*Bolk*), on the other hand, is the result of the non-mergence of a small bone developing independently in the ontogenetic state or other ossificatory anomalies in the opisthion region: the Os Kerckringi s. manubrium squamae occipitalis (*Virchow*). The edges of such an incisure are at times seen to be curved or double-curved, showing straight medial surfaces

---

cranial length of the process. *Schlaginhaufen, Otto*, 1907. Ein Fall von Ossification des Ligamentum apicis dentis epistrophei beim Menschen und entsprechende Bildungen bei den Affen. Morph. Jahrb., v. XXXVII, pp. 120—128.

[77] A thickening and sloping of the anterior margin, an additional transverse ridge between the condyles and probably an articular surface, somewhat similar to our case, occurring in a Kindiga skull was described and illustrated by *Ried, H. A.*, 1915. Zur Anthropologie des abflusslosen Rumpfschollenlandes im nordöstlichen Deutsch-Ost-afrika. Abh. Hamburg. Kolonialinst., v. XXXI, pp. 1—295 (65/66).

[78] See: *Hrdlička, Aleš*, 1907. Skeletal remains suggesting or attributed to early man in North America. Bur. Am. Ethnol., Bull. 33 (p. 91).

Summary 109.

Foramen magnum: actual and percental frequency of ossifications at anterior border.

Sex and Age	Foramen magnum (ossifications at anterior border)						
	Undeformed						
	Slight		Medium		Pronounced		Grand total
	no.	%	no.	%	no.	%	
♂	10	12.5	—	—	1	1.3	
♀	4	11.8	1	2.9	—	—	13.1 %
juv.	—	—	—	—	—	—	
inf.	—	—	—	—	—	—	
Total frequencies	14	10.7	1	0.8	1	0.8	
	Cowichan deformation						
♂	13	14.8	—	—	2	2.3	
♀	5	17.2	—	—	—	—	16.5 %
juv.	—	—	—	—	—	—	
inf.	—	—	—	—	—	—	
Total frequencies	18	14.1	—	—	2	1.2	
	Chinook deformation						
♂	7	12.1	3	5.2	—	—	
♀	3	11.5	3	11.5	1	3.8	18.3 %
juv.	—	—	—	—	—	—	
inf.	—	—	—	—	—	—	
Total frequencies	10	10.8	6	6.5	1	1.07	
	Koskimo deformation						
♂	14	13.5	1	0.9	1	0.9	
♀	7	18.9	1	2.7	—	—	16.0 %
juv.	—	—	—	—	—	—	
inf.	—	—	—	—	—	—	
Total frequencies	21	14.0	2	1.3	1	0.6	

as if cut out. A good instance of failure to develop the Os Kerckringi, the so-called node of *Kerckring* is shown by *Mac-Curdy* in his Peruvian studies.[79]

With the exception of very slight indications, there were no incisurae marginales posteriores to be noticed in the present series. The position of the opisthion in each case, even in more pronounced ones, could approximately be reconstructed without difficulty.

d. "*Manifestation of the occipital vertebra*"

A number of irregular formations about the borders of the foramen magnum have led *Kollmann*[80] to speak of the "manifestation of the occipital vertebra." The latter is, according to *Froriep*,[81] the most caudal of the three or four metameres observed by him as rudimentary vertebrae in the embryonic basi-occipital of certain mammals. During the process of growth and until its definite mergence into the pars basilaris this particular metamere acquires somewhat more advanced forms. Residua, giving rise to the "manifestation of the occipital vertebra" in *Kollmann*'s sense, consist in such irregular formations as: condylus tertius; labia foraminis magni; enlarged massae laterales; bipartition of canalis hypoglossi, "and perhaps a few more features." As such he names in another place the canalis intrabasilaris (intraoccipitalis *Swjetschnikow*),[82] the incisura marginalis posterior, the processus basilares and paracondyloidei.

In accordance with ontogenetic facts such manifestations appear to be correctly traced and named. But it is with reference to the third condyle and precondylar tubercles that differing explanations have been advanced of late by *Bolk*.[83] This author assumes the condyles to migrate laterally and posteriorly, while their medial ends, under specific conditions, remain stationary. Their inherent thriving tendency ("positive Entwicklungspotenz") would result at the same time in their mergence and the formation of such anomalies as condylus tertius and tubercula basilaria. The present author has remarked elsewhere,[84] that if *Bolk*'s theory should prove correct, a plausible explanation

---

[79] l. c., p. 15 (plate XL).

[80] *Kollmann, J.*, 1905. Varianten am Os occipitale, besonders in der Umgebung des Foramen occipitale magnum. Anat. Anz., v. XXVII, Verh. Anat. Ges. (19. Vers. Genf), pp. 231—236 (235). See also: Anat Anz., 1907, v. XXX, nos. 22 and 23.

[81] *Froriep, August*, 1882. Ueber ein Ganglion des Hypoglossus und Wirbelanlagen in der Occipitalregion. Arch. Anat. Physiol , Anat. Abt., pp. 279—301.

— 1886. Zur Entwicklungsgeschichte der Wirbelsäule, insbesondere des Atlas und Epistropheus und der Occipitalregion. do. pp. 69—150.

[82] *Swjetschnikow, S.*, 1906. Über die Assimilation des Atlas und die Manifestation des Occipitalwirbels beim Menschen. Arch. Anat. Physiol., Anat. Abt., pp. 155—193 (181).

[83] *Bolk, L.*, 1921. Die verschiedenen Formen des Condylus tertius und ihre Entstehungsursache. Anat. Anz., v. LIV, pp. 335—347.

— 1922. Über unregelmässig assimilierte letzte Occipitalwirbel beim Menschen. *Ibid.*, v. LV, pp. 156—162.

[84] *Oetteking, Bruno*, 1923. On the morphological significance of certain cranio-vertebral variations. Anat. Rec., v. XXV, pp. 339—353 (345).

would have been found and the theory of ontogenetic residua of the occipital vertebra, at least in a number of cases, discredited. In this connection, however, it must be mentioned that *Weigner*,[85] following up *Froriep*'s investigations, has brought forward valuable embryological proofs in corroboration of that author's theories.

From our series two of several cases of particular interest merit detailed description, although they show no hitherto unknown features. The first one, fig. 25, Yakima male (4334), is that of a well developed true third condyle. Its situation is directly on the anterior border of the foramen magnum medially between the occipital condyles from which it is separated by narrow passages. Both the extracranial basilar and the intracranial clivus surfaces are continuous with the anterior and posterior sides of the accessory condyle, which is only anteriorly very slightly set off against the pars basilaris, above which it rises to about 4—6 mm. Its transverse diameter amounts to 14 mm. as against a longitudinal one of 12 mm. The articular surface is slightly concave and roughened. This feature is somewhat contrary to the general condition of articular surfaces. It is, furthermore, almost horizontally

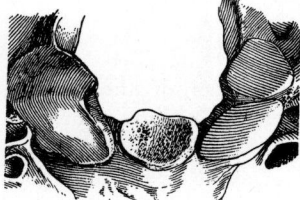

Fig. 25. Condylus tertius.

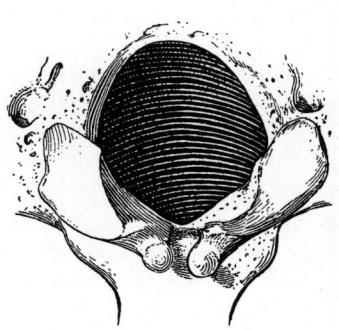

Fig. 26. Precondylar tubercles.

directed, rising only slightly from below and before to above and behind. Other indications of a manifestation of the occipital vertebra are the quite distinct posterior labia foraminis magni in continuation with the posterior halves of the condyles. They do not unite in the median line, however, but stop short about 1 cm. of the opisthion on either side. The condyles themselves are transversely flexed; the articular surfaces of the anterior and posterior halves, uniting in distinct transverse edges, form angles between themselves of about 115° on the left, and 128° on the right side. The massae laterales show a fair, but by no means extraordinary, development. The canalis hypoglossi is medium-sized and undivided.

The second case, fig. 26, Haida male (1606), shows precondylar tubercles in connection with the mesially lengthening and thinning occipital condyles. The tubercles, or labia foraminis magni anteriora according to *Kollmann*, are club-like, slightly pea-shape at their ends, and almost meet in the median line. Rising about 6 mm. above the posterior portion of the pars basilaris of the

---

[85] *Weigner*, *K.*, 1911. Über die Assimilation des Atlas und über die Variationen am Os occipitale beim Menschen. Anat. Hefte, v. XLV, no. 135.

occipital bone, the ends run clear of their basis. It is only between them that the border of the foramen magnum acquires its normal appearance. The elongated occipital condyles show, on their main masses, medially downward and outward sloping surfaces. There is, in connection with well developed lateral masses, an indication of a processus paracondyloideus on the right side; the labia foraminis magni posteriora are represented by rough ridges otherwise well merged with the bone, but not connecting mesially as in the preceding case; the canales hypoglossi are not bipartite but have the quite considerable width of 5 mm. This specific case is similar to *Bolk*'s drawing of a specimen in the Amsterdam anatomical collection used by *Kollmann* (1907, p. 556; see footnote p. 175).

Here also the question arises as to the influence of artificial head deformation upon the manifestation of the occipital vertebra. Regarding ontogenetic conditions, it might easily be dismissed, since the *anlage* of occipital vertebrae is noticeable only in the embryonic stage. During early infantile age, when the deforming practices are applied, the pars basilaris begins to take on its final typical appearance, while rudimentary or vestigial remnants of the last caudal occipital vertebra occur as anomalies long before the effects of deformation are traceable. The problem, however, represents itself in a different light. if *Bolk*'s theory of irregular differentiation is considered. It then would seem not at all improbable that mechanical pressure exercises a certain influence in this region favorable to the formation of the anomalies under discussion. Recognizing these different viewpoints it may be of interest to show the actual and percental frequency of the manifestation of the occipical vertebra in our four series. In *summary 110* the occurrences are qualified as slight, apparent and pronounced.

The last are lacking entirely in the Cowichan and Koskimo deformations, while there is one case recorded in the Chinook and three in the Undeformed, amounting to 1.1 % and 2.2 % respectively. With the exception of the single Chinook case, the manifestations occur only as indications marked slight in the three deformed series, while there three are in the column of apparent cases in the Undeformed. The highest total percentage is attained by the Koskimo with 28.0 %, the smallest by the Chinook with 4.3 %, between which extremes the Undeformed and Cowichan fall with 14.8 % and 13.3 %.

e. *Assimilation of atlas.*

Although not represented in our series, this anomaly should be mentioned for the sake of completeness. As compared with the preceding hyperplastic anomaly, the assimilation of the atlas is a hypoplastic formation, for which *Swjetschnikow*[86] offers three reasons: (1) acquired through pathological causes; (2) acquired in utero through pressure in consequence of abnormal construction of the pelvis; (3) congenital as a result of the anomalous mergence of the

---

[86] l. c., p. 175 (172).

Summary 110.

"Manifestation of the occipital vertebra": actual and percental frequency.

Sex and Age	Manifestation of occipital vertebra						
	Undeformed						Grand total
	Slight		Apparent		Pronounced		
	no.	%	no.	%	no.	%	
♂	10	12.5	3	3.8	3	3.8	
♀	2	5.9	—	—	—	—	14.8%
juv.	—	—	—	—	—	—	
inf.	—	—	—	—	—	—	
Total frequencies	12	9.2	3	2.2	3	2.2	
	Cowichan deformation						
♂	13	14.8	—	—	—	—	
♀	4	13.8	—	—	—	—	13.3%
juv.	—	—	—	—	—	—	
inf.	—	—	—	—	—	—	
Total frequencies	17	13.3	—	—	—	—	
	Chinook deformation						
♂	2	3.4	—	—	—	—	
♀	1	3.8	—	—	1	3.8	4.3%
juv.	—	—	—	—	—	—	
inf.	—	—	—	—	—	—	
Total frequencies	3	3.2	—	—	1	1.1	
	Koskimo deformation						
♂	31	29.8	—	—	—	—	
♀	11	25.6	—	—	—	—	28.0%
juv.	—	—	—	—	—	—	
inf.	—	—	—	—	—	—	
Total frequencies	42	26.1	—	—	—	—	

atlas-sclerotome with the sclerotomes of the precervical vertebrae. The extent of assimilation as recorded in anthropological literature is quite variable. But the significant feature about all of them is the replacement of the occipital condyles by the inferior articular surfaces of the atlas.

A few cases showing simultaneous atlas assimilation and the manifestation of the occipital vertebra, according to *Kollmann*, are recorded in the quite extensive special anthropological literature, where that described by *Dwight*[87] is of particular interest. He points out, in support of *G. Elliot Smith*, that isolated cases of assimilation are of rare occurrence and generally associated with other anomalies in the same region. It is to be regretted, therefore, that the parts involved, i. e., the adjoining vertebrae, or still better, the entire vertebral column, are seldom extant for thorough investigation.

f. *Ankylosis atlantis.*

The causes mentioned in the preceding section for the assimilation of the atlas apply more or less also to the form of articulation between the atlas and the occipitale, known as ankylosis. As such, however, it lacks evolutionary significance. *Hrdlička*,[88] enumerates six causes for the anomalous articulation and the different stages of fusion between the two parts. It is apparently to the first cause, resulting from some inflammatory process, that our own case, Kwakiutl male (4256), is due. Its atlas as well as the occipital parts concerned are entirely unimpaired as may be seen from fig. 27. The occipital condyles and articular foveae of the atlas are fully united except at the posterior left side. The coalesced parts have rough edges, more so posteriorly than anteriorly, suggesting some ostitic process as being responsible for the anomalous articulation. An elliptically shaped and horizontally oriented passage to the normal extension between the articular parts, the so-called spatium atlanto-occipitale anterius, is left between the upper margin of the anterior atlantal arch and the pars basilaris. But there is no resorption of material evident in the coalesced areas.

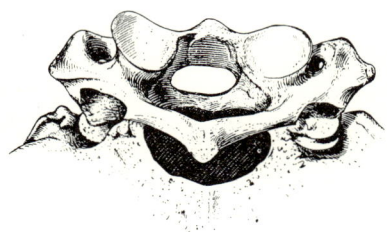

Fig. 27. Ankylosis atlantis (male Kwakiutl 4256).

The processus jugulares of our case are well developed, but not extraordinarily so. There is a slight indication on the right side of a processus paracondyloideus, but an articulation here or between the posterior arch of the

---

[87] *Dwight, Thomas*, 1909. I. Concomitant assimilation of the atlas and occiput with manifestation of an occipital vertebra. II. Notes on a hypochordal brace. Anat. Rec., v. III, pp. 321—333.

[88] *Hrdlička, Aleš*, 1904. Anomalous articulation and fusion of the atlas with the occipital bone. Washington Med. Journ., v. III, n⁰. 1, pp. 34—35.

atlas and the occipital does not exist. However, regarding the position of the atlas in relation to the foramen magnum, it appears to be shifted somewhat to the fore, which brought the tuberculum anterius more forward and underneath the pars basilaris, and the tuberculum posterius fairly within the lumen of the foramen magnum.

The percental frequency of this single case of ankylosis amounts to 0.7% in the Koskimo series, while a frequency of 0.2% is derived if applied to the entire number of crania.

2. Regio occipitalis lateralis.

a. *Condyli occipitales.*

Throughout the entire series, shape and size of the occipital condyles conform with *Strecker*'s [89] instance 3, being intermediate between instances 1 and 2, which are described by him as low and broad, and high and long. Number 1 of these conditions is declared to be characteristic of Negroes and Ainus, number 2 of Malays, while the intermediate one distinguishes the Europeans, Mongols and Indians.

The percental frequency of moderately high, long and broad condyles amounts then to 100% in the four divisions, except the Undeformed where two Eskimo, one male and one female, were recorded with high and long condyles. They represent for this trait a frequency of 1.9%, leaving 98.1% to the prevailing condition described as 3.

There are two features, however, which merit special mention. From general observation it would appear that the height of the condyles increases with the increasing inclination of the foramen magnum plane toward the minus-orientation, i. e., the rising of the basion or, what is equivalent, the increased dropping of the opisthion point below a coordinate of the ear-eye plane laid through the basion. A morphological adjustment like this appears quite plausible since it means the adaptation of the articular parts concerned in the occipito-vertebral articulation. Such a condition was seen in the skull of an Eskimo female (3710). [90]

The other feature referred to was seen in a Kwakiutl male (3879). The condyles here appear deeply set and fairly overlapped by the surrounding bone, particularly in the posterior portions. As this condition is not rare in the deformed skulls, it does not seem improbable that cranial deformation is responsible for it.

There are also a few cases recorded of transversely divided condyles

---

[89] *Strecker*, C., 1887. Über die Condylen des Hinterhaupts. Arch. Anat. Physiol., Anat. Abt., pp. 301—338.
[90] A reduction in height of the condyles is seen to occur sometimes on the right side, a peculiarity which has been correlated with right-handedness.

showing double-facetted articular surfaces in remininscence of the two parts involved in their formation.

b. *Fossa and canalis condyloideus*.

The fossa condyloidea is quite variable in depth and circumference, which appear to be proportionally correlated. Excessive conditions are very rare, a fundibuliform fossa occurring in an Eskimo male (3773).

The classification of shallow, moderately deep, and deep fossae, as carried out in *summary III*, shows quite a preponderance of medium conditions, representing in each division about half the cases, with a slight increase in the deformed in proportionate order, Cowichan, Chinook, Koskimo. The frequency among the latter, at 54.1°/₀ coincides with that of the Undeformed at 54.7°/₀. Shallow and deep fossae occur about equally in the Undeformed and Chinook, while the shallow exceed the deep by 10°/₀ in the Cowichan deformation, and by as much as 39°/₀ in the Koskimo, leaving in the latter only 3.5°/₀ to the deep fossae.

Whether deformation is in any way responsible for this condition must remain doubtful. It can be imagined, however, that the changed static conditions of the head, brought about by the Koskimo deformation might, by increased muscular action, have counterbalanced the posterior increase in weight. In this way occipito-atlantal articular pressure might have been somewhat relieved posteriorly and thus had a bearing on the size and depth of the fossa which, besides vascular pressure, doubtless are to some extent related to it.

The canalis condyloideus (s. foramen condyloideum) is, as *Hrdlička*[91] expresses it, "of interest only because of more or less frequent absence from one or both sides in different racial groups." Under normal conditions it transmits the emissarium condyloideum, a veinous connection between the sinus sigmoideus and the plexus vertebralis cervicalis. *Summary 112* accounts for six different modifications of width and frequency.

The moderately wide size predominates in all the divisions at percentages slightly above 50°/₀ in the Undeformed and Chinook deformation, but considerably above that amount in the Cowichan and Koskimo divisions, reaching even 75.4°/₀ in the former. The two extremes, narrow and wide, occur in equal percentages of 14.6°/₀ in the Undeformed. The occurrence is still less in the other divisions, the wide canales exceeding the narrow in the Cowichan, and the narrow the wide in the Chinook and Koskimo. The Chinook have the smallest number, 5.5°/₀, of wide canales condyloidei, which is exceeded by the narrow at 13.2°/₀, representing thus a greater discrepancy than the other divisions. The frequencies of absence and one-sided occurrence are quite variable. Total absence reaches its highest frequency in the Undeformed and Chinook with 5.7°/₀ in the former and 7.7°/₀ in the latter. Very small percentages are yielded by the Cowichan and Koskimo at 1.9°/₀ and 2.7°/₀ respectively. Similar conditions are specified only for one-sided occurrences. Right and left absence occurs at equal percentages of 5.7°/₀ in the Undeformed. Right absence is exceeded by left in the Cowichan and Chinook, the reverse being true of the Koskimo. The highest figures here are reached by the Chinook where right absence occurs in 12.0°/₀ and left in 7.7°/₀.

Hrdlička[91] finds the feature under discussion "exceptionally normal" in the Munsee, with no anomalies in the females but left absence in one male

---

[91] l. c., p. 14 (47).

Summary III.

Fossa condyloidea: actual and percental frequency.

Sex and Age	Fossa condyloidea					
	Undeformed					
	Shallow		Moderately deep		Deep	
	no.	%	no.	%	no.	%
♂	11	15.9	35	50.7	23	33.3
♀	6	18.2	23	69.7	4	12.1
juv.	1	—	1	—	—	—
inf.	8	—	5	—	—	—
Total frequencies	26	22.2	64	54.7	27	23.1
	Cowichan deformation					
♂	31	40.2	32	41.6	14	18.2
♀	3	9.4	18	56.2	11	34.4
juv.	—	—	2	—	—	—
inf.	2	—	2	—	—	—
Total frequencies	36	31.3	54	47.0	25	21.7
	Chinook deformation					
♂	16	27.6	26	44.8	16	27.6
♀	4	16.0	16	64.0	5	20.0
juv.	—	—	2	—	1	—
inf.	1	—	3	—	1	—
Total frequencies	21	23.1	47	51.6	23	25.3
	Koskimo deformation					
♂	42	40.4	57	54.8	5	4.8
♀	13	41.9	18	58.1	—	—
juv.	2	—	—	—	—	—
inf.	4	—	3	—	—	—
Total frequencies	61	42.4	78	54.1	5	3.5

Summary 112.

Canalis condyloideus: actual and percental frequency.

Sex and Age	Canalis condyloideus									
	Undeformed									
	0		Narrow		Moderately wide		Wide		Left only		Right only	
	no.	%	no.	%	no.	%	no.	%	no.	%	no.	%
♂	6	7.6	9	11.4	40	50.6	16	20.3	3	3.8	5	6.3
♀	1	3.5	2	6.9	19	65.5	2	6.9	3	10.3	2	6.9
juv.	—	—	—	—	2	—	—	—	—	—	—	—
inf.	—	—	7	—	5	—	—	—	1	—	—	—
Total frequencies	7	5.7	18	14.6	66	53.7	18	14.6	7	5.7	7	5.7
	Cowichan deformation									
♂	2	2.7	7	9.3	53	70.6	8	10.7	3	4.0	2	2.7
♀	—	—	—	—	22	88.0	1	4.0	2	8.0	—	—
juv.	—	—	—	—	1	—	—	—	1	—	—	—
inf.	—	—	—	—	4	—	—	—	—	—	—	—
Total frequencies	2	1.9	7	6.6	80	75.4	9	8.5	6	5.7	2	1.9
	Chinook deformation									
♂	4	7.3	7	12.7	28	50.9	5	9.1	8	14.5	3	5.5
♀	2	7.7	2	7.7	16	61.6	—	—	3	11.5	3	11.5
juv.	1	—	1	—	2	—	—	—	—	—	—	—
inf.	—	—	2	—	3	—	—	—	—	—	1	—
Total frequencies	7	7.7	12	13.2	49	53.9	5	5.5	11	12.0	7	7.7
	Koskimo deformation									
♂	4	3.8	8	7.7	73	69.5	10	9.5	3	2.8	7	6.7
♀	—	—	7	20.6	24	70.6	2	5.9	—	—	1	2.9
juv.	—	—	—	—	2	—	—	—	—	—	—	—
inf.	—	—	1	—	4	—	—	—	—	—	1	—
Total frequencies	4	2.7	16	10.9	103	70.1	12	8.2	3	2.1	9	6.1

skull out of five, equalling 20%, while another 20% have diminutive right canales, 60% being normal. The total occurrence of anomalies in the present series, which is considerably more numerous, amounts to 17.1% in the Undeformed, 9.5% in the Cowichan, 27.4% in the Chinook and 10.9% in

Summary 113.
Canalis condyloideus: frequency of anomalous occurrence.

Sex and Age	Canalis condyloideus					
	Undeformed					
	r>l	r<l	r/2 l*	r 2/l	r 2/l 2	l 2/r o
♂	1	1	1	1	—	—
♀	1	—	1	—	1	—
Total	2	1	2	1	1	—
	Cowichan deformation					
♂	4	1	—	—	—	—
♀	2	—	—	—	—	1
Total	6	1	—	—	—	1
	Chinook deformation					
♂	1	—	—	—	—	—
♀	1	—	—	—	—	—
Total	2	—	—	—	—	—
	Koskimo deformation					
♂	6	3	—	—	—	—
♀	—	—	—	—	—	—
Total	6	3	—	—	—	—

* Symbols refer on right (r) and left (l) sides to differences in size and number.

the Koskimo. A few additional anomalies not incorporated in *summary 112* which concern differences in size and occurrence, are enumerated in *summary 113*. However, racial conclusions drawn from these cursory observations would prove illusory.

Regarding the absence of the canales condyloidei, which is the rule in the anthropoids, or the presence of particularly small jugular foramina, a compensatory correlation between the two has been assumed by several authors. Thus, while *Ried*[92] observed an extraordinarily large fossa jugularis, and the absence of a foramen condyloideum, *Charles*[93] found that "when the jugular foramen was smaller than usual on one side, the post-condyloid foramen on the same side was larger". These observations can be corroborated more or less fully in the present series, although the great variability of both characters rather defeats a definite comparison.

Another feature, however, must not remain unmentioned, i. e., the bridging of the fossa condyloidea by thorn-like osseous processes arising from opposite sides of the fossa. This peculiarity occurs in a small number of cases and is illustrated in fig. 28, Haida male (3738). Although the cause of this variation seems to be unknown, it may safely be assumed that the emissarium passing through the canalis and fossa condyloidea was divided into two branches by means of the described bridging.

Fig. 28. Thorn-like projections in the foramen condyloideum (male Haida 3738).

c. *Canalis hypoglossi.*

The canalis for the transmission of the n. hypoglossus is of specific morphological interest on account of its position in the cranio-vertebral border region. This and the fact of its first appearance in the amniota have shown that the n. hypoglossus as an independent formation is not only a late acquisition in the phylogenetic sense, but also of complex origin from the ramifications of n. vagus and nn. cervicales. The ontogenetic proof of a number of occipital vertebrae more or less undifferentiated, the most caudal one being *Froriep*'s "vertebra occipitalis", has served to confirm that morphological finding.[94] Certain anomalous conditions in the cranio-vertebral border region, among which a bipartite canalis hypoglossi is also enumerated, have been attributed to the "manifestation of the occipital vertebra" (*Kollmann*), as previously discussed (see p. 175).

First taking into consideration the typical occurrence of two equal-sized canales, the width of the canalis hypoglossi has been classified in *summary 114* as narrow, medium and wide.

It will there be seen that the greatest frequency occurs in the medium class at percentages above 50 % in the deformed divisions, and slightly below in the Undeformed. Wide canales are

---

[92] l. c., p. 173 (12).
[93] *Charles, R. Havelock*, 1892. Notes on the craniometry of some of the outcaste tribes of the Panjab. Journ. Anat. Phys. London, v. XXVI (n. s., v. VI), pp. 1—25 (6—7).
[94] l. c., p. 175.

considerably more numerous than narrow ones, the highest percentage of 28.7% being yielded by the Undeformed, and 21.4% by the Cowichan as against percentages below 20% in the Chinook and Koskimo. Narrow canales are represented by very small percentages. In each of these classifications, equality of size for both right and left canalis is the rule. Only one case, that of a Salish of Cowichan deformation, was recorded with a larger right canalis.

Irregularities occur in four ways as specified in the last four categories of *summary 114*. A bipartite left canalis in combination with an absent right one was seen only in one Undeformed and one Cowichan male. The occurrences are more numerous of one right and two left canales, and two right combined with one left. A right and left bipartite canalis in the same individual is not so frequent as might have been expected from a superficial examination. The frequency here reaches its highest figure of 6.1% in the Koskimo and its lowest of 1.9% in the Cowichan deformation, while in between fall the Undeformed and Chinook with advantage to the latter.

It is inconceivable that irregularities in connection with the canalis hypoglossi should be caused by artificial head deformation. They are much more likely rooted in ontogenetic conditions referred to previously. The serial percentages of regular and irregular conditions, as shown in *summary 114* at the foot of each division, is quite interesting. The frequency of the former is there seen to decrease in the order, Undeformed, Cowichan, Chinook, Koskimo, while at the same time and in the same order the increase of irregularities will be noticed.

d. *Foramen jugulare*

The foramen jugulare is quite variable in size to that three principal conditions had to be accounted for, (1) where the foramina on both sides were of equal size, (2) the right foramen was larger, or, (3) smaller than the left one. Of particular interest among the irregularities here, but of almost typical occurrence in the human skull, is the division of the foramen into two unequal parts, a large lateral and a small medial one, brought about by the junction of the processus intrajugulares of the occipital and temporal bones. The foramen jugulare is generally of medium size and no cases of extreme largeness or smallness were observed; nor is the present author in a position to corroborate, beyond a general statement, the compensatory dependence of size between the foramina condyloideum and jugulare (see p. 185). He is also somewhat skeptical of *Hrdlička*'s (1906, 62) assumption: "The jugular foramina were generally smaller in whites. Perhaps that also coincides with small stature", although he admits that problems of correlation and interdependence of parts merit a thorough investigation.

Regarding the comparative sizes of the foramina, the earlier observation of a larger right one is confirmed in our series.

Summary 115 shows this particular condition $(r > l)$ in more than 50% in each of the four divisions. The next greatest frequency is seen in the equality of size of both foramina in the Cowichan and Chinook. In the proportion $r < l$, the Undeformed and Koskimo have frequencies equal to those for the $r = l$ status, while the Cowichan exceed that frequency by 1%. In the Chinook that order is reversed in favor of the $r = l$ proportion by fully 8%.

Summary 114.
Canalis hypoglossi: actual and percental frequency.

Sex and Age	Canalis hypoglossi																
	Undeformed																
	Narrow		Medium		Wide		r>l		r 0/l 2 *		r/l 2		r 2/l		r 2/l 2	
	no.	%	no.	%	no.	%	no.	%	no.	%	no.	%	no.	%	no.	%
♂	—	—	33	44.6	24	32.4	—	—	1	1.4	7	9.5	6	8.1	3	4.0
♀	1	3.0	17	51.5	9	27.3	—	—	—	—	5	15.2	—	—	1	3.0
juv.	—	—	1	—	1	—	—	—	—	—	2	—	—	—	—	—
inf.	3	—	7	—	1	—	—	—	—	—	—	—	—	—	—	—
Total frequencies	4	3.3	58	47.5	35	28.7	—	—	1	0.8	14	11.5	6	4.9	4	3.3
	79.5%						20.5%									
	Cowichan deformation																
♂	1	1.3	43	56.6	16	21.1	—	—	1	1.3	6	7.9	7	9.2	2	2.6
♀	—	—	11	44.0	6	24.0	1	4.0	—	—	2	8.0	5	20.0	—	—
juv.	—	—	1	—	—	—	—	—	—	—	—	—	1	—	—	—
inf.	—	—	4	—	1	—	—	—	—	—	—	—	—	—	—	—
Total frequencies	1	0.9	59	54.6	23	21.4	1	0.9	1	0.9	8	7.4	13	12.0	2	1.9
	76.9%						23.1%									
	Chinook deformation																
♂	—	—	30	53.6	8	14,3	—	—	—	—	11	19.6	4	7.1	3	5.4
♀	2	8.0	17	68.0	2	8.0	—	—	—	—	1	4.0	2	8.0	1	4.0
juv.	—	—	2	—	1	—	—	—	—	—	1	—	—	—	—	—
inf.	—	—	3	—	2	—	—	—	—	—	—	—	1	—	—	—
Total frequencies	2	2.2	52	57.1	13	14.3	—	—	—	—	13	14.3	7	7.7	4	4.4
	73.6%						26.4%									
	Koskimo deformation																
♂	1	1.0	47	44.7	20	19.1	—	—	—	—	16	15.2	15	14.3	6	5.7
♀	1	3.0	22	64.7	2	5.9	—	—	—	—	5	14.7	1	2.9	3	8.8
juv.	—	—	2	—	—	—	—	—	—	—	—	—	—	—	—	—
inf.	—	—	4	—	2	—	—	—	—	—	—	—	—	—	—	—
Total frequencies	2	1.4	75	51.0	24	16.3	—	—	—	—	21	14.3	16	10.9	9	6.1
	68.7%						31.3%									

* Symbols refer on right (r) and left (l) sides to differences in size and number.

Summary 115.

Foramen jugulare: actual and percental frequency.

Sex and Age	Foramen jugulare									
	Undeformed									
	r = l		r > l		r < l		r 2/l *		r/l 2		r 2/l 2	
	no.	%	no.	%	no.	%	no.	%	no.	%	no.	%

Sex	no.	%	no.	%	no.	%	no.	%	no.	%	no.	%
♂	10	14.5	49	71.0	10	14.5	6	—	3	—	(1)**	—
♀	5	15.6	21	65.6	6	18.8	—	—	1(1)	—	1	—
juv.	—	—	—	—	1	—	—	—	—	—	—	—
inf.	4	—	5	—	2	—	1	—	—	—	—	—
Total frequencies	19	16.8	75	66.4	19	16.8	7	5.5	5	3.9	2	1.6
Cowichan deformation											
♂	12	16.9	44	62.0	15	21.1	4(1)	—	2(1)	—	1	—
♀	6	27.3	12	54.5	4	18.2	(2)	—	(1)	—	—	—
juv.	1	—	—	—	1	—	—	—	—	—	—	—
inf.	1	—	2	—	1	—	1	—	—	—	—	—
Total frequencies	20	20.2	58	58.6	21	21.2	8	7.1	4	3.6	1	0.9
Chinook deformation											
♂	13	22.8	35	61.4	9	15.8	2	—	—	—	1	—
♀	8	33.3	13	54.2	3	12.5	1	—	—	—	—	—
juv.	1	—	1	—	2	—	—	—	—	—	—	—
inf.	1	—	3	—	1	—	2	—	—	—	—	—
Total frequencies	23	25.5	52	57.8	15	16.7	5	5.2	—	—	1	1.0
Koskimo deformation											
♂	10	14.5	49	71.0	10	14.5	7	—	2	—	5(1)	—
♀	5	15.6	21	65.6	6	18.8	2	—	2	—	—	—
juv.	—	—	—	—	1	—	—	—	—	—	—	—
inf.	4	—	5	—	2	—	—	—	—	—	—	—
Total frequencies	19	16.8	75	66.4	19	16.8	9	5.7	4	2.5	6	3.8

* Symbols refer on right (r) and left (l) sides to differences in size and number.
** Numbers in parentheses stand for incomplete bipartition.

Divided foramina, including the imperfectly divided ones, show without exception their greatest frequency on the right side, thus coinciding with the high percental occurrence of foramina of largest size. Smaller frequencies were encountered on the left side, the Chinook being devoid of any such condition. Still smaller frequencies around 1 % were specified for equal occurrence of divided foramina on both sides of the skull, the Koskimo, however, yielding 3.8 %, i. e., in excess of the frequency of left side occurrence of divided foramina.

e. *Processus paracondyloideus (s. paramastoideus).*

The attempt to remedy the confusion which exists in regard to these terms has been tried by *Uhde*[95] as early as 1867, and by *Corner*[96] in 1896. While both agree that the name "paramastoideus" should be restricted to a downward projection in the mastoid region of the temporal bone, *Uhde* wants a similar projection from the lateral portion of the occipital bone named "paracondyloideus", and *Corner* "paroccipitalis". *Corner* (p. 387) gives an exact description of four forms of processus paramastoideus, which in a general way correspond with different developmental stages of the inner lip of the digastric fossa or incisura mastoidea. But it is the processus paracondyloideus solely which will be discussed here. Situated toward the distal end of the jugular process, it is sometimes found of excessive size, more frequently, however, of medium growth, or as a mere indication. The process is supposed to be homologous with the paramastoid process of certain mammals (Canidae, Suidae, etc.), but it is also taken for an excessively developed transverse process of the embryonic occipital vertebra, and as such it would be one of the manifestations of the occipital vertebra, in the sense of *Kollmann* (see footnote p. 175). Corresponding, under normal conditions, with the place of insertion for m. rectus capitis lateralis, the abnormally large process may directly articulate with the transverse process of the atlas or even coalesce with it, thus affording only limited lateral movement of the head, or none at all. While the indicated and medium instances occur quite regularly on both sides, the excessive forms of the process seem to exist most frequently on one side only.

In the present series, as enumerated in *summary 116*, the excessive forms total three, and occur on the right side only in the Undeformed female, and on the left sides in a Cowichan male and a Chinook infant, giving rise to frequencies of 0.8 % in the former two divisions, and 1.1 % in the latter. A unilateral occurrence of a right medium-sized process was found in the Undeformed and Koskimo divisions resulting there in frequencies of 0.8 % in the former and 0.7 % in the latter. These percentages fairly coincide with those given by *Russell*,[97] namely, 0.7 % for American Indians, and 0.9 % for Peruvians. The summary furthermore shows quite a frequent occurrence of indications of a process in all four divisions, and a limited one of medium-sized processes. The males exceed the females considerably in both, while their combined percentages run quite high, particularly in the Cowichan and Chinook, amounting to 25.6 % and 36.6 %.

[95] *Uhde, C. F. W.*, 1867. Schiefstellung des Kopfes durch einen Processus paracondyloideus bedingt. Arch. Klin. Chir., v. VIII, pp, 34—37.

[96] *Corner, Edred M.*, 1896. The processes of the occipital and mastoid regions of the skull. Journ. Anat. Physiol. London, v. XXX (n. s., v. X), pp. 386—389.

[97] l. c., p. 167.

Summary 116.

Processus paracondyloideus: actual and percental frequency.

Sex and Age	Processus paracondyloideus							
	Undeformed							
	Slight		Medium		Large		Grand total	Right only	Left only
	no.	%	no.	%	no.	%	%	no. and %	no. and %
♂	13	17.6	3	4.1	—	—		1 slight 1 medium	—
♀	1	3.0	3	1.0	—	—	19.5	1 large	1 slight
juv.	—	—	—	—	—	—		—	—
inf.	4	—	—	—	—	—		—	—
Total frequencies	18	14.6	6	4.9	—	—	—	slight 0.8 medium 0.8 large 0.8	0.8
Cowichan deformation									
♂	24	28.2	—	—	—	—		—	1 large
♀	4	13.8	1	3.4	—	—	25.6	—	—
juv.	1	—	—	—	—	—		—	—
inf.	2	—	—	—	—	—		—	—
Total frequencies	31	24.8	1	0.8	—	—	—	—	0.8
Chinook deformation									
♂	17	29.3	2	34.5	—	—		—	—
♀	7	28.0	1	4.0	—	—	36.6	—	—
juv.	3	—	1	—	—	—		—	—
inf.	2	—	1	—	—	—		—	1 large
Total frequencies	29	31.2	5	5.4	—	—	—	—	1.1
Koskimo deformation									
♂	17	16.5	4	3.9	—	—		1 medium	—
♀	3	8.1	2	5.4	—	—	19.9	—	—
juv.	1	—	—	—	—	—		—	—
inf.	3	—	—	—	—	—		—	—
Total frequencies	24	15.9	6	4.0	—	—	—	0.7	—

Too great importance should not be attached to these figures, since the variability of the feature under discussion is quite wide, and only excessive cases are directly discernible as anomalous formations. It is significant for this reason that no two-sided occurrence of large processes have been accounted for in *summary 116*. For the same reason it is scarcely worth while to consider deformatory influences, although the deformed divisions show considerably higher "grand total" percentages than the Undeformed, except the Koskimo, who coincide with the latter in lower percentages of 19.9 % and 19.5 %.

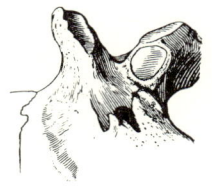

Fig. 29.
Processus paracondyloideus
(female Haida 1611).

In figs. 29 and 30, two cases are illustrated of a processus paracondyloideus of extraordinary size and unilateral occurrence, and of medium-sized processes occurring on both sides. The former is that of a Haida female (1611). The process is cone- or peg-shape, 19 mm. long laterally and 12 mm. medially, and is 15 mm. thick from fore to aft, and 12 mm. from side to side. On its extreme end and extending backward is a groove for the articulation with the atlas. In size it exceeds considerably that mentioned by *Klaatsch*[98] in an Australian skull from Northwest Queensland, the height and thickness of which amount to 10—12 mm. and 5—8 mm. respectively. Our own specimen shows a number of other anomalies: a double-faceted right condyle, pre-

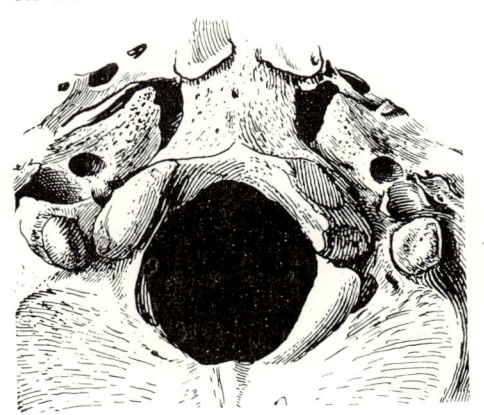

Fig. 30. Double-sided processus paracondyloideus
(male Nootka 4568).

condylar tubercles, and fossa condyloidea from the posterior border of which thorn-like projections arise that partly cover a wide foramen condyloideum.

The other case is that of a Nootka male (4568). In Fig. 30 are shown the medium-sized processes extending from the lateral extremities of the processus jugulares. They are plug- or stopple-shape and have no articular surfaces. In this case also a double-faceted left condyle may be noticed; a right foramen condyloideum is absent.

---

[98] *Klaatsch, Hermann*, 1908. The skull of the Australian aboriginal. Rep. Pathol. Lab. Lunacy Dep. Sidney, v. I, pt. III, pp. 44—167 (127).

Summary 117.
Incisura mastoidea: actual and percental frequency.

Sex and Age		Incisura mastoidea							
		Undeformed							
		Shallow			Moderately deep			Deep		
		Narrow	Medium wide	Wide	Narrow	Medium wide	Wide	Narrow	Medium wide	Wide
♂	no.	11	7	—	4	21	2	—	20	8
	%		24.7			37.0			38.3	
♀	no.	8	5	—	1	14	2	1	3	—
	%		38.3			50.0			11.7	
juv.		1	—	—	—	1	—	—	—	—
inf.		2	5	—	—	7	—	—	—	—
Total frequencies		22	17	—	5	43	4	1	23	8
			31.7%			42.3%			26.0%	
Cowichan deformation										
♂	no.	2	9	1	2	30	11	—	12	4
	%		16.9			60.6			22.5	
♀	no.	3	3	—	—	19	1	1	1	1
	%		20.7			69.0			10.3	
juv.		—	—	—	—	1	—	—	1	—
inf.		1	—	—	2	1	—	—	1	—
Total frequencies		6	12	1	4	51	12	1	15	5
			17.8%			62.6%			19.6%	
Chinook deformation										
♂	no.	—	5	—	1	26	7	—	9	4
	%		9.6			65.4			25.0	
♀	no.	3	—	—	4	13	—	—	5	—
	%		12.0			68.0			20.0	
juv.		2	—	—	—	1	—	—	—	—
inf.		3	2	—	—	1	—	—	—	—
Total frequencies		8	7	—	5	41	7	—	14	4
			17.5%			61.6%			20.9%	
Koskimo deformation										
♂	no.	4	16	2	2	41	31	—	2	5
	%		21.4			71.8			6.8	
♀	no.	2	6	—	2	20	2	—	—	2
	%		23.5			70.6			5.9	
juv.		—	—	—	—	1	—	—	—	—
inf.		1	1	—	1	3	—	—	—	—
Total frequencies		7	23	2	5	65	33	—	—	7
			22.2%			71.5%			6.3%	

f. *Incisura mastoidea.*

In *summary 117* the depth and width of the incisura mastoidea are specified for each division. Divided into shallow, moderately deep and deep incisures, these are subdivided further into narrow, medium-wide and wide. But while for these only the actual occurrence, i. e., the number of individuals is given, the depth on the whole is accounted for by percentals. It will readily be noticed that medium conditions prevail for both, although in graded order so that the Undeformed with 42.3% stand lowest, and the Koskimo with 71.5% highest. Between the two, inclining, however, toward the higher percentage of the Koskimo, fall the Chinook with 61.6% and the Cowichan with 62.6%. In the class of shallow incisurae, wide ones are represented by only a single instance in the Cowichan, and by two males in the Koskimo, while the Undeformed and Chinook are entirely devoid of this combination. Deviating from the general occurrence, the cases of narrow and shallow incisurae predominate over those of medium width in the Undeformed and the Chinook, but only slightly so in the latter. The shallow incisurae reach a relatively high frequency at 31.7% in the Undeformed. They are followed by the Koskimo with 22.2%, and with still lower percentages of 17.5% and 17.8% in the Chinook and Cowichan deformations. The remaining percentages go to the deep incisurae, where the Undeformed again lead with a percentage of 26.0%, thus falling short of the shallow ones of the same division by 5.7%. The low percentage of 6.3% of deep incisurae in the Koskimo is astonishing in proportion, however, to their exceedingly high frequency in the moderately deep incisurae and also of the relatively high percentage of shallow ones. The Cowichan and Chinook percentages for the deep incisurae slightly exceed those of the shallow and thus do not exhibit any extreme proportions. It may be pointed out that in the deep incisurae the combination of deep-wide predominates considerably over deep-narrow, and that the male percentages exceed the female in this category, while the conditions in the shallow and moderately deep classes are reversed.

A correlation between the conditions of the incisura mastoidea and the size of the processus mastoideus, see *summary 134*, does not seem to exist. Thus, for instance, the remarkably high percentage of 61.7% of large processus in the Chinook is not related to a similar percentage of deep incisurae. Nor does the incisura appear to be affected by deformatory influences.

g. *Fossa mandibularis (glenoidalis).*

Recent observations upon the fossa mandibularis (glenoidalis) have shown that its appearance is largely due to function and as such can hardly be considered a racial character. It was, however, so held by *Knowles*[99], who regarded a shallow fossa as an Eskimoid character, not, however, without having pointed out the influence of function, particularly the lateral grinding movements as caused by the use of crude food prepared in a primitive way. His view has of late been upheld by *Cameron* (1923, 40 c), while *Ritchie*[100] considers a shallow fossa as a result of edge to edge bite and occlusion. *Sullivan*[101] and others, however, have shown that shallow and flat fossae occur in very appreciable percentages in all the tribes of this continent and South

---

[99] *Knowles, F. H. S.*, 1915. The glenoid fossa in the skull of the Eskimo. Mus. Bull. no. 9. Anthrop. Ser. 4 (Geol. Surv. Ottawa), 24 pp.

[100] *Ritchie, Stephen G.*, The dentition of the Western and Central Eskimo. Rep. Canadian Arctic Exped. 1913—18, v. XII, pt. C, pp. c 59—66 c (64 c).

[101] *Sullivan, Louis R.*, 1917. Variations in the glenoid fossae. Am. Anthrop., n. s., v. XIX, pp. 19—23.

America, and in fact in other parts of the world. *Sullivan* (p. 21) proves the functional hypothesis by the interesting observation that asymmetry of the fossae was in a number of cases connected with unequal wear of the teeth in such a way that the teeth on the side of the more shallow fossae were worn more than those on the opposite side. In some cases differences in the form of the condylar process of the mandible were also observed. *Sullivan*'s characterization of the glenoid fossae as: deep and short; medium and short; shallow and elongated, and flat and elongated, were also applicable in the present series. Further observations on the morphology of our material revealed the fact that the depth of the fossa glenoidalis was almost exactly correlated to the height of the tuberculum articulare, and that the frequencies listed there (see *summary 40*) also apply in a way to the status of the fossa. Deep fossae were correlated furthermore with the more vertical position of the anterior wall of the tympanic bone.

3. Regio occipitalis posterior.

a. *Processus retromastoideus (Waldeyer)*.

This tubercular projection has quite frequently been observed in Papuan skulls and those of other South Sea groups. According to *Waldeyer*[102], who first described it, the process occurs where the upper lateral branch of the linea nuchae inferior meets upon the linea nuchae superior. It forms the point of insertion for the m. obliquus capitis superior. Although not a single case of this process was found in our series, its mention in connection with this report seemed to be justified for the sake of future cranioscopic observations upon Indian skulls, and in view of its isolation as a racial character.

b. *Fossula vermiana (Albrecht)*.

Situated endocranially and medially backward of the posterior circumference of the foramen magnum, the fossula vermania is a groove occasionally formed there by the division of the crista occipitalis interna into two branches. It is supposed to lodge the vermis inferior cerebelli, and its causation is attributed either to hypertrophic conditions of the vermis and circulatory system, or irregular ossification, in which the ossiculum Kerckringi (see p. 175) is concerned. *Le Double*[103] has shown this anomaly to occur in most mammals, and is inclined to pronounce it an atavism in man.

This is also *Black*'s [104] opinion, who states its occurrence as normal among the anthropoids in Hylobates only, where it lodges a definite part of the vermis.

---

[102] *Waldeyer, W.* 1908. Der Processus retromastoideus. Abh. Kgl. Preuss. Ak. Wiss., pp. 1—32 (10—16).
[103] *Le Double, A. F.*, 1903. Traité des variations des os du crâne de l'homme. Paris. p. 49.
[104] *Black, Davidson*, 1915/16. Endocranial markings of the human occipital bone and their relations to the so-called "vermiform fossa". Anat. Rec., v. X, pp. 182—185.

In the other anthropoid forms and in man, the formation of a deep cistern has "caused the postero-median lobe of the cerebellum to become completely separated.... from the endocranial surface of the occipital bone." Instead, the phylogenetically recent falx cerebelli is inserted into the osseous ridge, known as crista occipitalis interna.

The separation of the crista occipitalis interna into two branches corresponding with a similar condition in the falx cerebelli may in most cases be responsible for the triangular formation endocranially in the opisthion region. But it is indeed necessary to distinguish here between true grooves and triangular depressions. Formations of the latter kind obtain only in the skulls under discussion. Indications of a fossula occur quite frequently in the Undeformed and Chinook divisions, and in a considerably smaller percentage in the Cowichan and Koskimo, as shown in *summary 118*.

Far smaller frequencies are enumerated in the evident and distinct columns of the same summary, a well developed fossula being entirely absent in the Undeformed and Chinook. The total divisional frequencies yield as much as 24.6% and 28.0% in the Undeformed and Chinook, and only 10.7% and 6.7% in the Cowichan and Koskimo. If, however, only the evident and distinct cases were taken into consideration, the result would be fairly identical with *Russell*'s 4.8% for American Indians in general.

R. Martin (Lehrbuch, 1914, 737) quotes a frequency of 19% in Egyptians, 22% in Australians, and as much as 40% in Peruvians of the Aymará type. But whether racial prevalences really obtain, seems doubtful with regard to the uncertainty as to what form of the fossula was considered. And if, on the other hand, *Le Double*'s and *Black*'s conceptions of the atavistic nature of the fossula be true, the question of deformatory influences in its causation would also be discredited, since a relatively high percentage of indicated occurrences was also specified for the Undeformed. And again, pathological conditions producing the anomaly must rather be sought during ontogenetic stages.

4. Regio occipitalis anterior (basilaris).

a. *Tuberculum pharyngeum.*

The tubercular shape of this elevation for the insertion of lig. longitudinale anterius and m. constrictor pharyngis superior, is at times changed into a sagittally directed ridge. However, there is little variation and the former is the typical formation, rarely absent, as shown in *summary 119*.

Of the indicated, evident and distinct cases, the latter are not represented, and the cases of medium development are in all divisions considerably exceeded by those of slight development, except in the Chinook, where both show about the same frequency. The total divisional frequencies including all the cases of graded development, amount to slightly less than 100%, showing this feature in our series to be the anatomical condition in general. Of greater interest therefore is the trequency of total absence of the tuberculum, which is lowest in the Koskimo where it amounts fo 1.4%, and highest in the Chinook at 6.6%, the Undeformed and Cowichan falling between these extremes.

Summary 118.

Fossula vermiana (*Albrecht*): actual and percental frequency.

Sex and Age	Fossula vermiana							
	Undeformed							
	Indicated		Evident		Distinct		Grand total	
	no.	%	no.	%	no.	%	no.	%
(74) ♂	14	18.9	3	4.1	—	—	17	23.0
(33) ♀	6	18.2	—	—	—	—	6	18.2
(1) juv.	1	—	—	—	—	—	1	—
(14) inf.	5	—	1	—	—	—	6	—
Total frequencies	26	21.3	4	3.3	—	—	30	24.6
Cowichan deformation								
(85) ♂	5	5.9	2	2.4	1	1.2	8	9.4
(29) ♀	2	6.9	1	3.4	2	6.9	5	3.4
(5) juv.	—	—	—	—	—	—	—	—
(2) inf.	—	—	—	—	—	—	—	—
Total frequencies	7	5.8	3	2.5	3	2.5	13	10.7
Chinook deformation								
(58) ♂	14	24.1	2	3.4	—	—	16	27.6
(25) ♀	8	32.0	—	—	—	—	8	32.0
(4) juv.	1	—	—	—	—	—	1	—
(6) inf.	1	—	—	—	—	—	1	—
Total frequencies	24	26.0	2	2.2	—	—	26	28.0
Koskimo deformation								
(103) ♂	5	4.9	4	3.9	1	0.9	10	9.7
(47) ♀	—	—	—	—	—	—	—	—
juv.	—	—	—	—	—	—	—	—
inf.	—	—	—	—	—	—	—	—
Total frequencies	5	3.3	4	2.7	1	0.7	10	6.7

Summary 119.

Tuberculum pharyngeum: actual and percental frequency.

Sex and Age	Tuberculum pharyngeum Undeformed								Grand total, presence
	Absence		Indicated		Evident		Distinct		
	no.	%	no.	%	no.	%	no.	%	%
♂	3	4.1	39	53.4	31	42.5	—	—	
♀	1	3.2	16	51.6	14	45.2	—	—	94.8
juv.	—	—	1	—	1	—	—	—	
inf.	2	—	7	—	—	—	—	—	
Total frequencies	6	5.2	63	54.8	46	40.0	—	—	
	Cowichan deformation								
♂	5	6.4	44	56.4	29	37.2	—	—	
♀	—	—	13	59.1	9	40.9	—	—	95.3
juv.	—	—	2	—	—	—	—	—	
inf.	—	—	4	—	—	—	—	—	
Total frequencies	5	4.7	63	59.4	38	35.8	—	—	
	Chinook deformation								
♂	2	3.6	23	41.8	30	54.6	—	—	
♀	4	15.4	15	57.7	7	26.9	—	—	93.3
juv.	—	—	2	—	2	—	—	—	
inf.	—	—	3	—	2	—	—	—	
Total frequencies	6	6.6	43	47.8	41	45.6	—	—	
	Koskimo deformation								
♂	—	—	79	77.5	23	22.5	—	—	
♀	2	5.9	25	73.5	7	20.6	—	—	98.6
juv.	—	—	2	—	—	—	—	—	
inf.	—	—	2	—	2	—	—	—	
Total frequencies	2	1.4	108	76.1	32	22.5	—	· —	

b. *Fossa pharyngea*.

In place of a tuberculum pharyngeum and sometimes associated with it, a fossa pharyngea of variable size is occasionally encountered. There were a number of indications to be noticed, and a relatively low frequency of medium-sized fossae, while large ones did not occur except in the single case of an Undeformed infantile skull, as may be seen from *summary 120*.

The total occurrence of a fossa pharyngea, with the inclusion of slight indications of it, amounts to as high as 55.7% in the Koskimo. The lowest percentage of 16.1% occurs in the Undeformed, while the Cowichan and Chinook show frequencies of about 30% each.

The fossa pharyngea as a diagnostic factor was pointed out in the observations upon American skulls by *Sullivan*[105]. He observed high frequencies of 16.4% and 18.5% in tribes of the Uto-Aztecan linguistic stock of southwestern United States and Mexico, with the exception, however, of the Pueblo peoples of New Mexico and Colorado. The rather high percentages resulting from our own investigations which were completed prior to the appearance of *Sullivan*'s paper, supplement those found by him, and from a geographical standpoint, add the Northwest to the areas of greatest frequencies. It is necessary, however, to call attention to the rather low percentages of medium-sized fossae in *summary 120*, which were raised to the high total percentages only by the addition of indicated, i. e., small or shallow fossae. The cases marked evident and indicating a medium development of the trait in question present frequencies of only 2.7% in the Undeformed, and 1.1% in the Chinook. The Cowichan and Koskimo divisions have higher frequencies of 3.8% and 10.0% respectively. These figures conform rather with the frequency of 3.5% which *Sullivan* (p. 241) gives as a total for American skulls. In any case it is quite possible that the present results may undergo modifications by the application of still more exact methods of evaluation and classification.

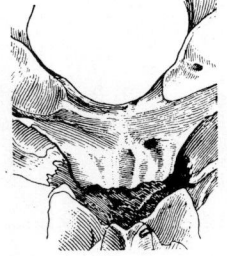

Fig. 31. Fossa pharyngea and anomalies in pars basilaris (infantile Chukchee 3845). Natural size.

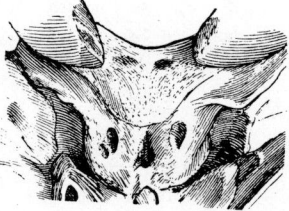

Fig. 32. Fossa pharyngea (male Bellacoola 4627). Natural size.

Two anomalous cases may be seen illustrated in figs. 31 and 32, the former being that of a Chukchee inf. I—II (3845) and the latter of a Bellacoola

---

[105] *Sullivan, Louis R.*, 1920. The fossa pharyngea in American Indian crania. Am. Anthrop., n. s., v. XXII. pp. 237—243.

———. 1922. The frequency and distribution of some anatomical variations in American crania. Anthrop. Pap. Am. Mus. Nat. Hist., v. XXIII, pt. V, pp. 207—258 (224—228).

Summary 120.

Fossa pharyngea: actual and percental frequency.

Sex and Age	Fossa pharyngea. Undeformed								Grand total, presence
	Absence		Indicated		Evident		Distinct		
	no.	%	no.	%	no.	%	no.	%	%
♂	61	84.7	9	12.5	2	2.8	—	—	16.1
♀	25	83.3	4	13.3	1	3.4	—	—	
juv.	2	—	—	—	—	—	—	—	
inf.	6	—	1	—	—	—	1	—	
Total frequencies	94	83.9	14	12.5	3	2.7	1	0.9	
	Cowichan deformation								
♂	55	72.3	18	23.7	3	3.9	—	—	30.2
♀	15	62.6	8	33.3	1	4.1	—	—	
juv.	1	—	1	—	—	—	—	—	
inf.	3	—	1	—	—	—	—	—	
Total frequencies	74	69.8	28	26.4	4	3.8	—	—	
	Chinook deformation								
♂	40	74.1	13	24.1	1	1.9	—	—	29.5
♀	15	60.0	10	40.0	—	—	—	—	
juv.	2	—	2	—	—	—	—	—	
inf.	5	—	—	—	—	—	—	—	
Total frequencies	62	70.5	25	28.4	1	1.1	—	—	
	Koskimo deformation								
♂	37	37.4	50	50.5	12	12.1	—	—	55.7
♀	20	57.2	13	37.1	2	5.7	—	—	
juv.	2	—	—	—	—	—	—	—	
inf.	1	—	3	—	—	—	—	—	
Total frequencies	60	42.9	66	47.1	14	10.0	—	—	

Summary 121.

Processus pterygoideus: actual and percental frequency.

Sex and Age	Processus pterygoideus			
	Undeformed			
	l = m *		l > m	
	no.	%	no.	%
♂	6	11.1	48	88.9
♀	5	25.0	15	75.0
juv.	—	—	1	—
inf.	3	—	10	—
Total frequencies	14	15.9	74	84.1
	Cowichan deformation			
♂	5	8.6	53	91.4
♀	5	22.7	17	77.3
juv.	—	—	2	—
inf.	—	—	5	—
Total frequencies	10	11.5	77	88.5
	Chinook deformation			
♂	4	7.6	49	92.4
♀	1	5.3	18	94.7
juv.	—	—	2	—
inf.	1	—	5	—
Total frequencies	6	7.5	74	92.5
	Koskimo deformation			
♂	7	7.8	83	92.2
♀	3	11.5	23	88.5
juv.	—	—	2	—
inf.	—	—	7	—
Total frequencies	10	8.0	115	92.0

* *l*, *m*, laminae lateralis and medialis.

male (4627). Both show irregular ossification, so much so that in the first case a complete canal is formed, with an outlet on the right side of the fossa. It represents quite probably a venous perforation and not a homologon of the craniopharyngeal canal. Another irregularity will be noticed in the pitted groove on the articular side between the first and second third of the right condyle, due probably to an anomaly of ossification between the two primary portions of the occipital bone participating in the formation of the occipital condyle. In fig. 32 additional grooves are shown on each side of the fossa pharyngea.

5. Regio pterygoidea.

a. *Processus pterygoideus.*

Waldeyer's [106] distinction of the processus pterygoideus into three forms is not fully applicable in the present series. The general status here is the prevalence of the lamina lateralis over the lamina medialis. At the same time, both show medium grades of development which insure a medium development also of the fossae pterygoidea and scaphoidea. This condition corresponds to *Waldeyer*'s form *B*, and is specified in *summary 121*, under l > m, where the percental frequencies are seen to be considerable. Only small percentages thus remain for a condition representing equal development of both laminae below medium size, which consequently in- volves a slighter development of the fossae produced by them. The percentages here, at least for the Undeformed, Cowichan and Chinook divisions, range in the opposite order from those of the preceding condition. While the equal development of the laminae conforms with *Waldeyer*'s form *A*, indicated in the summary as l = m, his form *C*, where all the details are but very slightly developed, was not met in the present series.

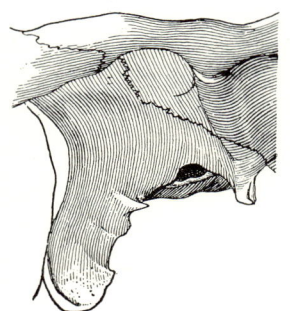

Fig. 33. Processus pterygoideus with muscular ridges and spina Civinini (male Bellacoola 4625). Natural size.

Referring particularly to *Waldeyer*'s form *A* and *C*, our own specified findings of a general preponderance of the size of the lamina lateralis must be upheld. A small number of cases, on the other hand, show abnormal conditions as to size and formation of the lamina. Three exceptional cases may be seen illustrated in figs. 33, 34 and 35. In addition to its greater size, the lamina externa in fig. 33, (Bellacoola male, 4625), shows on its external surface three transverse ridges, the upper and lower terminating in thorns which project beyond the posterior border of the lamina. These ridges

---

[106] *Waldeyer, W.*, 1893. Über Form- und Rassenverschiedenheiten der Flügelfortsätze des Keilbeins. Sitz. Ber. K. Preuss. Ak. Wiss., pp. 999—1002.

mark the origin of the pterygoideus externus muscle, and in a way may be taken as an expression of muscular demand upon the bone. Such may also be the case of more or less deep, groove-like depressions on the external surface of the lamina externa. The lamina, of quite extraordinary size in fig. 34 illustrating the condition as found in a Chukchee female skull (3844), fills in

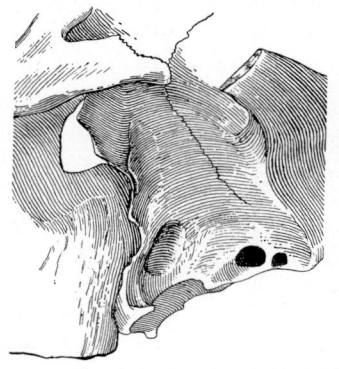

Fig. 34. Foramen pterygospinosum (Civinini) in a female Chukchee (3844). Natural size.

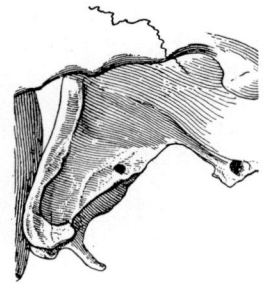

Fig. 35.
Lamina externa of processus pterygoideus with reinforced margo maxillaris and a perforation (male Haida 3743). Natural size.

the space toward the spina angularis, forming at the same time the foramen pterygospinosum (*Civinini*) treated at length in section *b* of this chapter. In addition to a deep and spacious groove on the outside of the lamina, there is another anomaly regarding the margo maxillaris of the external lamina which shows a very irregular course besides being reinforced and slightly turned outward. This is still more so the case in fig. 35, Haida male (3743), where the margo maxillaris appears to be fairly doubled up.

The abnormal size of the external pterygoid laminae and thorny prolongations at their posterior margin in Eskimo skulls was pointed out by several authors, and again of late by *Cameron* (1923, 39). Altogether, the better development of the processus pterygoideus in the Caucasoids and the prevalence of its external plate in the Mongoloids are characteristics, of which the latter particularly is a corroboration of *Waldeyer*'s racial findings in this respect, while primitive development marks the Negro.

b. *Foramen pterygospinosum (Civinini)*.

Much literature has accumulated since *Civinini* (1837) first called attention to the anomaly named after him, and authors generally also point out the variable conditions of the underlying details. Several of these details, backward of the pterygoid process, participate in the formation of what is known as the foramen pterygospinosum or Civinini, namely, (1) the lamina lateralis of that process, (2) the spina angularis of the sphenoid bone, (3) the ligamentum pterygospinosum, and indirectly (4) the foramina ovale and spinosum. In our series the foramen ovale was seen to be either long and narrow, or long and wide in different degrees, or circular. In certain cases, like that of a male Eskimo (3721), extraordinary dimensions of 10 mm. by 6 mm. on the left side, and 8 mm. by 5 mm. on the right, were noticed. Among irregularities regarding the foramen ovale incomplete ossification, particularly of its medial border, and merging with the foramen spinosum, whose size appears also to be quite variable, must be mentioned. In some cases the foramen ovale was also found completely

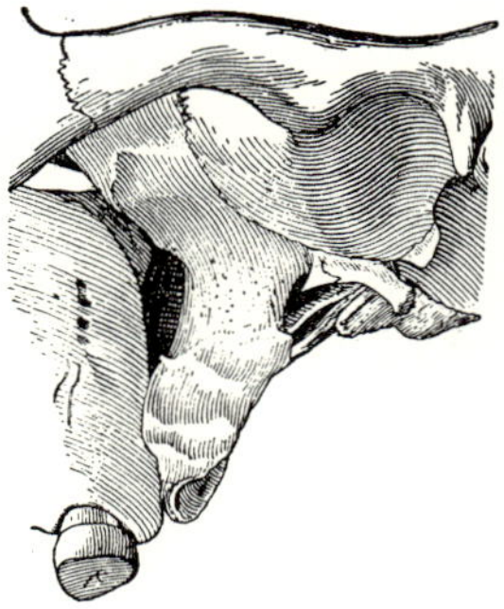

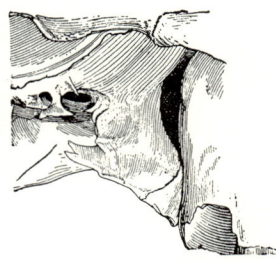

Fig. 36. Thorn-like formation in foramen ovale (male Chinook 4518). Natural size.

Fig. 37. Thorn and spicula formations in foramen ovale (male Haida 3735). Natural size.

or incompletely bridged by osseous projections issuing from one side or from opposite borders, apart from the real cause of the formation of the foramen Civinini, presently to be described. A thorn-like projection from the posterior border of the left foramen ovale and projecting into about half of its lumen, is shown in fig. 36, representing that condition in a

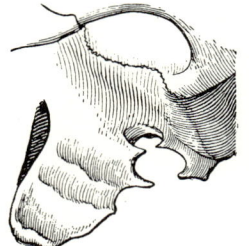

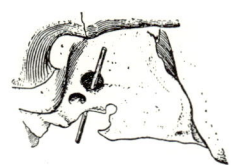

Fig. 38. Foramen pterygospinosum (*Civinini*) incomplete (male Bellacoola 4627). Natural size.

Fig. 39. Foramen pterygospinosum (*Civinini*) almost complete (male Tsimshian 4586). Natural size.

Fig. 40. Foramen pterygospinosum (*Civinini*) verum (male Tsimshian 4647). Natural size.

Chinook male skull (4518). Thorn-like projections and a real spicula around the foramen ovale and partly bridging it are shown in a male Haida (3735), fig. 37.

The spina angularis which acquires unusual sizes in Spy and the anthropoids, shows medium development in our series. Between the spina angularis and the spina Civinini of the external pterygoid plate, the higher one of its posterior projections mentioned in the preceding section, the ligamentum pterygospinosum, extends in the living. It is to the successive stages of ossification that the variations of the foramen Civinini are due. The incomplete formation [107] in the male Bellacoola (4627) of fig. 38 is complicated by an accessory pair of projections within the circumference of what by further differentiation would have become a true foramen Civinini. Such accessory projections were fittingly called spinae pterygospinosae spuriae by *Grosse* [108]. The almost complete union of the true spina Civinini and processus angularis is demonstrated in the male Tsimshian (4586) in fig. 39, while the male Tsimshian (4647) of fig. 40 represents a true foramen through which a probe is led. The posterior border of the lamina lateralis of this case shows below the foramen a florid notch suggesting other foramina which remained incomplete.

With regard to their percental frequencies the various forms of the foramen pterygospinosum or Civinini are listed in *summary 122*.

They are grouped according to absence, one-sided and two-sided occurrence, the latter again classified as a, b and c, signifying rudimentary, incomplete and complete conditions of the foramen. All the anomalous forms show, naturally, only small frequencies, as seen in the summary. The true foramen being of greatest interest has its percental frequencies enumerated in the last column, where both possibilities, one- and two-sided occurrences are summed up. The differences between the figures of the last two columns mark the one-sided occurrence of the true foramen. It is thus seen that out of a total frequency of $5.9\,°/_0$ of true foramina in the Undeformed, $1.7\,°/_0$ are two-sided and $4.2\,°/_0$ one-sided. For the other divisions and conditions the following percental proportions in an increasing order hold true: Cowichan, $4.4\,°/_0 = 3.5\,°/_0 + 0.9\,°/_c$; Chinook, $6.6\,°/_0 = 2.2\,°/_0 + 4.4\,°/_0$; Koskimo, $7.7\,°/_0 = 1.4\,°/_0 + 6.3\,°/_0$. These frequencies do not exactly correspond to *Hrdlička*'s statement that the foramen pterygospinosum is "rather common in Indians" (1906, 62). It is more to the point, however, if referred to the general tendency toward the formation of the foramen.

It is difficult to decide whether the gradual increase in the frequencies of the four divisions is of any functional significance. One may be tempted to assume such a cause in consideration of *R. Martin*'s (Lehrbuch, 1914, 788) figures of frequency who gives a European percentage of $4.8\,°/_0$ for the complete, and $18.3\,°/_0$ for the incomplete foramen, while extra-European races present frequencies of $15\,°/_0$ to $33\,°/_0$. But since the feature under discussion is a regular occurrence in the monkeys and anthropoid apes it may be safer to follow *von Brunn* [109] who conceives it to be of theremorphic significance.

6. Regio maxillaris.

a. *Dental arch.*

In its phylogenetic development the dental arch has obviously gone through changes of form which, according to *Bauer* [110], may best be described

---

[107] Rather for anatomical reasons in the recent state, *Faesebeck*, as early as 1840, had applied the term "foramen interruptum" for the anomaly under discussion. See *Faesebeck, J.*, 1840. Die Nerven des menschlichen Kopfes; nach einigen Untersuchungen geschrieben und durch Abbildungen erläutert. Braunschweig.

[108] *Grosse, Ulrich*, 1893. Über das Foramen pterygospinosum *Civinini* und das Foramen crotaphiticobuccinatorium *Hyrtl*. Anat. Anz., v. VIII, p. 321—348.

[109] *Brunn, A. von*, 1891. Das Foramen pterygospinosum (*Civinini*) und der Porus crotophiticobuccinatorius (*Hyrtl*). Anat. Anz., v. VI, pp. 96—104 [104].

[110] *Bauer, Moritz*, 1904. Beiträge zur Anthropologie des harten Gaumens. Zürich.

Summary 122.

Foramen pterygospinosum (Civinini): actual and percental frequency.

Sex and Age	Foramen pterygospinosum (Civinini)																					
	Undeformed																					
	Double-sided										One-sided						Totals of perfect foramina		
	Equal size						Unequal size														
	o Absent		a Indicated		b Imperfect		c Perfect		ra/lb*		rb/lc		rc/lb		ro/lc		lo/rb		lo/rc		One-sided	Two-sided	Grand Total
	no.	%	no.	%	no.	%	no.	%	no.	%	no.	%	no.	%	no.	%	no.	%	no.	%			
♂	53	73.6	8	11.1	2	2.8	2	2.8	—	—	2	2.8	—	—	2	2.8	2	2.8	1	1.3	4.2%	1.7%	5.9%
♀	25	80.6	2	6.4	3	9.7	—	—	1	3.3	—	—	—	—	—	—	—	—	—	—			
juv.	1	—	—	—	—	—	—	—	—	—	—	—	—	—	—	—	—	—	—	—			
inf.	9	—	4	—	—	—	1	—	—	—	—	—	—	—	—	—	—	—	—	—			
Total frequencies	88	74.6	14	11.9	6	5.1	2	1.7	1	0.8	2	1.7	—	—	2	1.7	2	1.7	1	0.8			
	Cowichan deformation																					
♂	46	56.1	25	30.5	5	6.1	3	3.7	2	2.4	—	—	1	1.2	—	—	—	—	—	—	3.5%	0.9%	4.4%
♀	18	69.2	5	19.2	2	7.7	1	3.9	—	—	—	—	—	—	—	—	—	—	—	—			
juv.	1	—	—	—	—	—	—	—	—	—	—	—	—	—	—	—	—	—	—	—			
inf.	2	—	2	—	—	—	—	—	1	—	—	—	—	—	—	—	—	—	—	—			
Total frequencies	67	58.8	32	28.1	7	6.1	4	3.5	3	2.6	—	—	1	0.9	—	—	—	—	—	—			
	Chinook deformation																					
♂	40	70.1	12	21.0	—	—	1	1.8	—	—	1	1.8	—	—	1	1.8	1	1.8	1	1.8	4.4%	2.2%	6.6%
♀	17	70.8	5	20.8	—	—	1	4.2	—	—	—	—	—	—	1	4.2	—	—	—	—			
juv.	3	—	1	—	—	—	—	—	—	—	—	—	—	—	—	—	—	—	—	—			
inf.	5	—	1	—	—	—	—	—	—	—	—	—	—	—	—	—	—	—	—	—			
Total frequencies	65	71.4	19	20.9	—	—	2	2.2	—	—	1	1.1	—	—	2	2.2	1	1.1	1	1.1			
	Koskimo deformation																					
♂	44	43.5	39	38.6	9	8.9	1	1.0	—	—	3	3.0	3	3.0	1	1.0	—	—	1	1.0	6.3%	1.4%	7.7%
♀	19	55.9	13	38.3	1	2.9	—	—	—	—	—	—	—	—	—	—	—	—	1	2.9			
juv.	1	—	1	—	—	—	—	—	—	—	—	—	—	—	—	—	—	—	—	—			
inf.	3	—	2	—	—	—	1	—	1	—	—	—	—	—	—	—	—	—	—	—			
Total frequencies	67	46.5	55	38.2	11	7.6	2	1.4	—	—	3	2.1	3	2.1	1	0.7	—	—	2	1.4			

* Symbols refer on right (r) and left (l) sides to differences in occurrence and state of completeness.

as U-shape (upsiloid), ellipsoid and paraboloid. Of these forms the last one appears to be the most advanced, and quite characteristic of all the Hominidae, while the upsiloid form is typical in the anthropoids and the ellipsoid in the monkeys. As a rule the form of the dental arch is rather variable and the three distinctions have been employed in our series, mindful of the fact that transitional forms between the three are not at all rare. Besides, there are certain states that can be linked directly to primitive conditions, like the transverse straightness of the anterior portion of the dental arch as characteristic of the chimpanzee. Here is concerned the os incisivum s. intermaxillare, of phylogenetic significance, which in the cases under discussion is more or less angularly set off against the sides of the dental arch which latter also frequently tend toward straightness, generally, however, posteriorly, in a minor degree of divergence. That this is truly a character of primitive morphology may be inferred from its greater frequency in primitive races as compared with the whites. It is to be seen in the Krapina F lower jaw, and *Fr. Sarasin* [111] states it for the New Caledonians and Loyalty-Islanders.

As has already been stated, the typical human form of the dental arch of the maxillary bone is paraboloid. In our series it also greatly exceeds the other forms, as shown in *summary 123*, yielding as high a frequency as 88.6% in the Undeformed, while the other divisions yield lesser ones, the Koskimo only 66.4%. For the other two forms the frequencies remain comparatively low in the Undeformed, the upsiloid form having its highest occurrence at only 6.0% in the Chinook as against 2.1% in the Undeformed, the ellipsoid at 29.5% in the Koskimo as against 9.3% in the Undeformed [112].

Whether there is a correlation between the form of the dental arch and the shape of the skull seems rather doubtful when only morphological considerations are concerned. Quantitatively conceived, however, it appears that broad and short arches are frequently found in brachycranial, and narrow and long ones in dolichocranial skulls. But this is not so without exception, and *Sullivan* [113] has shown that "the principle of dolichocephaly and brachycephaly, in itself, is not sufficient to explain the form of the alveolar arch." His comparative lists show that opposite conditions in the two factors are frequently met, the Eskimo representing a remarkable instance of long-headedness and width of palate. The association of these two characters in the Eskimo is ascribed by *Gregory* [114] to "a secondary narrowing of the braincase .... which may have been derived from mongoloids with a wide palate and short skull". In

---

[111] *Sarasin, Fritz*, 1916—1922. Anthropologie der Neu-Caledonier und Loyalty-Insulaner. Berlin, 651 pp. (285).

[112] *Hrdlička* in the Lenape, l. c., p. 14 (43), distinguishes between: ovoid, elliptic and paraboloid, while no approaches toward the U-shape (upsiloid) arches are mentioned. If by ovoid a form is meant with sides, distinctly diverging and slightly turned-in ends, such forms were, in the present series, united with the paraboloid, since their principal feature is strongly expressive of that form.

[113] *Sullivan, Louis R.*, 1918. The bearing of physical anthropology on the problems of orthodontia. Dental Cosmos, pp. 1—11 (10).

[114] *Gregory, William K.*, 1921. The origin and evolution of the human dentition, Part V, Later stages in the evolution of the human dentition. Journ. Dent. Research, v. III, pp. 87—228 (171).

Summary 123.
Dental arch: actual and percental frequency.

Sex and Age	Dental arch Undeformed					
	1 Upsiloid		2 Ellipsoid		3 Paraboloid	
	no.	%	no.	%	no.	%
♂	2	3.3	7	11.5	52	85.2
♀	—	—	2	7.4	25	92.6
juv.	—	—	—	—	—	—
inf.	—	—	—	—	—	—
Total frequencies	2	2.1	9	9.3	86	88.6
Cowichan deformation						
♂	2	2.9	21	30.4	46	66.7
♀	2	9.1	6	27.3	14	63.6
juv.	—	—	1	—	1	—
inf.	—	—	—	—	4	—
Total frequencies	4	4.1	28	28.9	65	67.0
Chinook deformation						
♂	2	3.9	14	26.9	36	69.2
♀	—	—	3	13.6	19	86.4
juv.	—	—	—	—	4	—
inf.	3	—	—	—	2	—
Total frequencies	5	6.0	17	20.5	61	73.5
Koskimo deformation						
♂	4	4.7	27	31.4	55	63.9
♀	—	—	8	26.7	22	73.3
juv.	1	—	1	—	—	—
inf.	—	—	—	—	4	—
Total frequencies	5	4.1	36	29.5	81	66.4

his summary, however, *Gregory* (p. 218) has questioned that finding. *Sullivan* (p. 9), on the other hand, has shown that there is a more constant relationship between the width of the face and that of the palate, a statement by which the prevailing conditions in the Mongoloids would be satisfactorily explained. Again, *Gregory's* (p. 170) assumption appears rather plausible that a widening of the skull base, causing an increase in the width of the intercondylar diameter, together with the increased size of the tongue, i. e., the moulding of the palatal arch and the lower jaw, around the greatly enlarged tongue, might be held responsible for the width of the palate. It remains doubtful if this sagacious bit of morphological insight could also be applied to skull bases secondarily broadened by strong deformation, like that practiced by the Chinook, or whether they have, per se, as tribal characteristics, the greatest maxillo-alveolar breadth and the highest maxillo-alveolar indices (see *summaries 66 and 67*).

b. *Sutura palatina mediana.*

There is so little variation in the course and general condition of this suture that a distinction into different descriptive types can be dispensed with. Its course, as it extends between the posterior border of the foramen incisivum and the termination of the spina nasalis posterior, is straight as a rule. Deviations sometimes occur in the anterior portion, which widens up into the foramen incisivum. Obliteration of the suture is very rare, except in the posterior portion, dividing the horizontal processes of the palatine bone. Here it is frequently entirely obscured by the "keel" of the torus palatinus (see section *f* of this chapter). In case a longitudinal medial depression of the palate toward the nasal cavity occurs, the suture is fouud at the bottom of it, the depression being called "negative torus" by *Bauer* [115].

c. *Sutura palatina transversa.*

In spite of the great variability of the sutura palatina transversa, three fundamental types were recognized by *Stieda* [116], namely, the straight one, and those of a medial excursion forward or backward. As causal in the formation of these types, he assumes the merging of an ossification point in the region where the joining of the maxillary and palatine parts of the hard palate is to occur, either with the processus palatinus of the maxillary bone, or with the pars horizontalis of the palatine bone. The result in the former case

---

[115] l. c., p. 204 (23).

[116] *Stieda, L.,* 1891. Der Gaumenwulst (Torus palatinus). Ein Beitrag zur Anatomie des knöchernen Gaumens. Internat. Beitr. Wiss. Med., I, 146—176.

would be the backward, and in the latter the forward excursion of the suture. Their simplest forms are those of triangles projecting foreward or backward between the two halves of the horizontal parts of either of the bones constituting the palate. While it appears that the straight transverse suture is most frequently met in man, the forward excursion, particularly its triangular shape, is typical in all mammals including the anthropoids. On the other hand, a triangular projection backward is considered by *Bartels*[117] as stressing the condition in man, a condition called by him "übermenschlich" (ultrahuman). These being the three fundamental types, their great variability has induced other authors[118] to establish a number of additional types which, with more or less justification, might be termed transitional. There is only one particular condition which merits special mention, namely, the irregular joining of the two halves of the transverse suture in the median line. Occurring in connection with the three fundamental types, their cause seems to be due to unequal ossification. This condition has been made note of in the last column of *summary 124*. The three forms mentioned above are listed in columns 2—4, while total obliteration is accounted for in the first column. The last named is quite rare in our series and corresponds to *Frédéric's* listings for Indians (see his table 1). He counts the sutura palatina transversa among the facial sutures of early obliteration (p. 408), and the percentages of frequency run rather high in Europeans ($32°/_o$ to $42°/_o$), Cameroon Negroes ($19°/_o$), and Melanesians ($40°/_o$).

The straight suture is the most frequent in our series except in the Koskimo, where the anteriorly projecting and irregularly joining ones acquire slightly higher percentages. The last named is quite appreciable in all the divisions, and attains even to $32.2°/_o$ in the Koskimo. Comparatively low frequencies are listed for the backward excursion of the suture, the highest one being $9.9°/_o$ in the Cowichan, while there is no occurrence of it in the Koskimo. The distance between the meeting points at the median suture of the two sections of the transverse suture is at times as much as 3 mm. to 4 mm. Summarizing, it may be restated that ossification is quite rare and that the straight course of the transverse suture is the predominating one, while the forward excursion and the irregular joining occur in appreciable percentages. The last is mostly met in the forwardly curved suture. The backward excursion is only of moderate occurrence.

The more variable of these types is without doubt the medial anterior excursion. In fig. 41, *a–c*, three different stages are illustrated. They represent a pointed projection, Nanaimo male (1826); a curved one, Chinook female (4457), and a semicircular one curving medially in upon itself, Kwakiutl male (3896). A suture curving backward is to be noticed in fig. 41, *d–f*, slightly curved in a male Salish (1596), somewhat pointed in a male Bellacoola (4543), and widely separated medially in a male Kwakiutl (1723). Irregular joining in a lesser degree occurs also in the medial backward excursion of the suture as shown in *e* and *f*.

---

[117] *Bartels, G.*, 1892. In discussion, in: *W., Waldeyer*, Anomalien des harten Gaumens. Zschr. Ethnol., v. XXIV, pp. 427—430 (428).
[118] The more important papers are those of: *Le Double, A. F.*, 1906. Traité des variations des os de la face de l'homme. Paris, 98—111. — *Killermann, S.*, 1894. — Über die Sutura palatina transversa und eine Beteiligung des Vomer an der Bildung der Gaumenfläche beim Menschenschädel. Arch. Anthrop., v. XXII, pp. 393—424 (Taf. VII). — *Frédéric, Jakob*, 1909. Untersuchungen über die normale Obliteration der Schädelnähte. Zschr. Morph. Anthrop., v. XII, pp. 371—440 (426).

Summary 124.

Sutura palatina transversa: actual and percental frequencies.

Sex and Age	Sutura palatina transversa								
	Undeformed								Irregular medial union	
	Obliterated		Straight		Excursion				
					Forward		Backward			
	no.	%	no.	%	no.	%	no.	%	no.	%
♂	—	—	32	49.2	14	21.6	5	7.7	14	21.5
♀	1	3.7	12	44.5	7	25.9	—	—	7	25.9
juv.	—	—	—	—	—	—	—	—	1	—
inf.	—	—	11	—	3	—	1	—	—	—
Total frequencies	1	0.9	55	50.9	24	22.2	6	5.6	22	20.4
	Cowichan deformation								
♂	2	2.9	25	36.2	16	23.2	8	11.6	18	26.1
♀	—	—	10	41.7	7	29.2	2	8.3	5	20.8
juv.	—	—	—	—	1	—	—	—	1	—
inf.	—	—	1	—	2	—	—	—	3	—
Total frequencies	2	2.0	36	35.7	26	25.7	10	9.9	27	26.7
	Chinook deformation								
♂	—	—	19	38.0	20	40.0	1	2.0	10	20.0
♀	—	—	12	54.6	5	22.7	—	—	5	22.7
juv.	—	—	2	—	1	—	—	—	—	—
inf.	—	—	3	—	2	—	1	—	—	—
Total frequencies	—	—	36	44.4	28	34.6	2	2.5	15	18.5
	Koskimo deformation								
♂	1	1.0	30	30.6	34	34.7	—	—	33	33.7
♀	2	5.9	10	29.4	13	38.2	—	—	9	26.5
juv.	—	—	—	—	1	—	—	—	1	—
inf.	—	—	2	—	2	—	—	—	2	—
Total frequencies	3	2.1	42	30.0	50	35.7	—	—	45	32.2

d. *Sutura incisiva* (Goethei).

Open at times in the infant, and therefore easily recognized, this suture separates the os intermaxillare s. incisivum s. praemaxillare from the adjoining part of the horizontal processes of the maxillary bone. Though obliterating very early, traces of it may be observed in varying degrees up to mature age. Such traces generally issue from the posterior end of the foramen incisivum transversely to both sides, at a distance generally less than 1 cm.

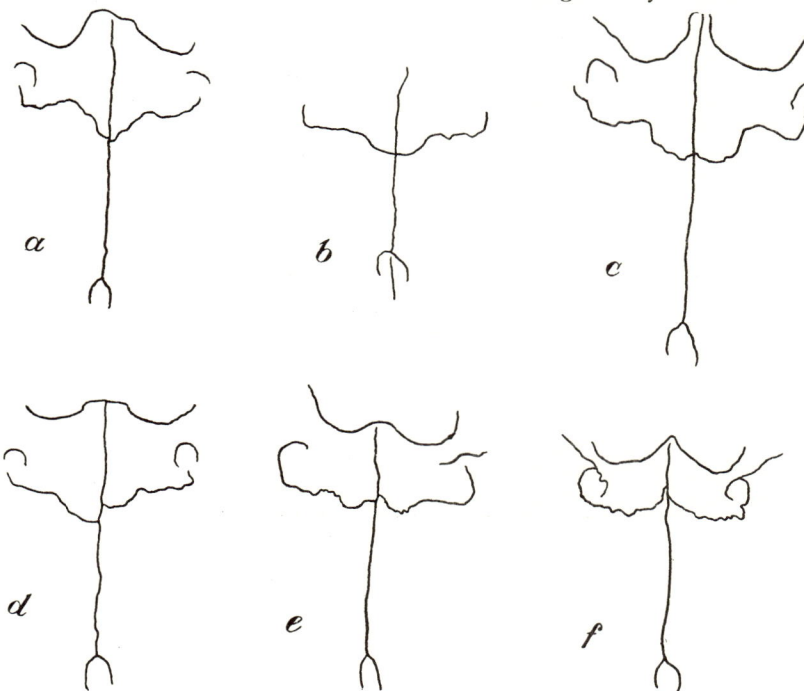

Fig. 41. Various forms of sutura palatina transversa. Natural size.

from the sutura palatina mediana, and take a forward turn toward the septum interalveolare between the lateral incisors and the canines.

From *summary 125* it will be observed that in the immatures not a single case of total obliteration occurred in our material. The frequencies of that condition, with more than 50 %, predominate in the matures of the Cowichan, Chinook and Koskimo divisions, while the immatures show the greatest frequency in the condition marked medium. Total persistence of the suture obtains in small percentages only, that of 4.5 % in the Undeformed being the highest, while there is no case recorded in the Koskimo. The condition of medium persistence is only moderately represented. The total frequencies, i. e., the combination of the different stages, yield percentages between 40 % to 50 % in the three deformed divisions, the Undeformed having as much as 64.0 %.

Summary 125.

Sutura incisiva (*Goethei*): actual and percental frequency.

Sex and Age	Sutura incisiva (Goethei)							
	Undeformed							
	Obliterated		Persistence					
			Slight		Medium		Total	
	no.	%	no.	%	no.	%	no.	%
♂	33	50.0	24	36.7	8	11.8	1	1.5
♀	7	23.3	20	66.7	3	10.0	—	—
juv.	—	—	1	—	—	—	—	—
inf.	—	—	4	—	6	—	4	—
Total frequencies	40	36.1	49	44.1	17	15.3	5	4.5
Cowichan deformation								
♂	39	66.1	18	30.4	2	3.4	—	—
♀	10	45.5	10	45.5	1	4.6	1	4.6
juv.	—	—	—	—	—	—	—	—
inf.	—	—	1	—	2	—	1	—
Total frequencies	49	57.5	29	34.0	5	5.9	2	2.4
Chinook deformation								
♂	32	62.8	15	29.4	4	7.8	—	—
♀	12	54.5	9	40.9	1	4.6	—	—
juv.	—	—	—	—	4	—	—	—
inf.	—	—	1	—	4	—	1	—
Total frequencies	44	53.0	25	30.1	13	15.7	1	1.2
Koskimo deformation								
♂	65	68.4	22	23.2	8	8.4	—	—
♀	17	45.9	16	43.3	4	10.8	—	—
juv.	—	—	1	—	2	—	—	—
inf.	—	—	1	—	5	—	—	—
Total frequencies	82	58.1	40	28.4	19	13.5	—	—

Consulting *Frédéric*'s [119] table, it is clear that a racial significance does not pertain to our findings, since high frequencies were also listed for other racial groups.

A few interesting cases are shown in fig. 42, where in *a—c* branches of the sutura incisiva take a course backward, apparently corresponding to the sutura longitudinalis lateralis, of which an instance is given by *Frédéric* (p. 417). Fig. 42, *d*, represents a condition in which the sutural remnants issue from the sides of a rather large foramen incisivum, a condition typical for many mammals. All these variations are from male Eskimo skulls (3775, 3767, 3782, 3715).

  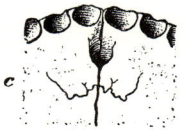 

Fig. 42. Various forms of sutura incisiva. Natural size.

e. *Foramen incisivum*.

The shape of the foramen incisivum is generally elliptic to roundish, the former frequently with pointed ends. A long and narrow foramen incisivum is seen in fig. 43, *a*, a more roundish one in *b*, and one of extraordinary size in *c*, as found in male Eskimo skulls 3714, 3715, and a male Bellacoola skull 4633. A few cases were observed in which from the posterior end a more or less distinct thorn- or peg-like projection issues, in which both horizontal processes of the maxillary bone participate. Such is the case in a female Eskimo skull (3710) and illustrated in fig. 43, *d*.

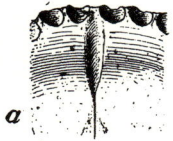 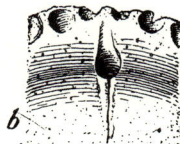 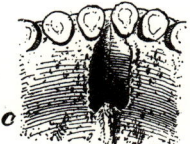 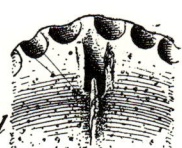

Fig. 43. Various forms of foramen incisivum. Natural size.

With regard to its size, the foramen incisivum was either small, medium or large. In *summary 126*, the highest frequencies around 80 °/₀ go to the medium-sized foramen in the deformed divisions, the Undeformed having only 61.8 °/₀. The latter, however, with 29.3 °/₀ of small-sized foramina greatly exceed the frequencies of the deformed divisions, while large foramina occur in only small numbers ranging below the frequencies of the small foramina, except in the Chinook, where the latter show a frequency of 4.4 °/₀ of small foramina as against 7.7 °/₀ of large ones.

f. *Torus palatinus*.

Bauer's [120] suggestion that any longitudinal elevation in the median line of the palate is a torus palatinus, was accepted for our own observations.

---

[119] l. c., p. 209 (413).
[120] l. c., p. 204 (25).

Summary 126.

Foramen incisivum: actual and percental frequency.

Sex and Age	Foramen incisivum					
	Undeformed					
	Small		Medium		Large	
	no.	%	no.	%	no.	%
♂	21	28.4	46	62.2	7	9.4
♀	7	20.6	23	67.6	4	11.8
juv.	1	—	—	—	—	—
inf.	7	—	7	—	—	—
Total frequencies	36	29.3	76	61.8	11	8.9
	Cowichan deformation					
♂	10	12.2	65	79.3	7	8.5
♀	3	11.5	21	80.8	2	7.7
juv.	—	—	2	—	—	—
inf.	2	—	5	—	—	—
Total frequencies	15	12.8	93	79.5	9	7.7
	Chinook deformation					
♂	2	3.6	49	87.5	5	8.9
♀	—	—	23	92.0	2	8.0
juv.	—	—	4	—	—	—
inf.	2	—	4	—	—	—
Total frequencies	4	4.4	80	87.9	7	7.7
	Koskimo deformation					
♂	12	11.5	90	86.6	2	1.9
♀	9	26.5	24	70.6	1	2.9
juv.	—	—	2	—	—	—
inf.	3	—	3	—	—	—
Total frequencies	24	16.4	119	81.5	3	2.1

Quite an abundant literature has accumulated on the torus since its discovery by *von Kupffer* (1879/80), and a number of classifications have been advanced in regard to its different forms. Following *Bauer*'s suggestion, however, and applying it to the series under discussion, the following distinctions were made, (1) non-occurrence or absence; (2) torus maxillaris, as restricted to the palatine processes of the maxillary bones; (3) pars palatina, restricted to the horizontal processes of the palatine bones, which is identical with *von Kupffer*'s "Kiel" (keel)[121]; (4) torus palatinus, extending over the entire length of the palate or the greater part of it, and including both horizontal parts of the two bones which constitute it. A distinction into broad and "spindle-shape" tori, as recognized by *Stieda*[122], was not significant enough to be carried out in our material.

It will be seen from *summary 127* that the torus palatinus in its perfect form occurs at nearly equal percentages around 80 % in all the four divisions, and even with a slight increase in the Chinook. The remaining frequencies go for the greatest part to the cases of non-occurrence, except in the Undeformed whose "keel"-shape formations upon the palatine bones exceed the cases of non-occurrence, The "keel" in its restricted form shows only very small frequencies in the other divisions, and is entirely absent in the Chinook.

The exceedingly high frequencies of a true torus palatinus in our material doubtless designates it as a racial feature[123]. But by other authors it was recognized as occurring in almost any racial group before its discoverer had pronounced it as a characteristic in Prussian-Lithuanian skulls. Its true nature, however, does not seem as yet to have been recognized, except that a pathological origin appears to be improbable. It is at least of interest that the torus does not occur in the anthropoids. This fact suggests to the present author the possibility that during the phylogenetic process of retraction of the alveolar process, which causes a certain limitation of development, a stimulus might be exercised upon the area of generation, i. e., upon the median sutural margins of the palatine processes of the maxillary bones, resulting in the hyperplasia of a torus. Regarding its racial frequency, the following data may be of interest as compared with an average of 80% in our series; they are quoted from *Martin* (Lehrbuch, 1914, 832) who lists 88% for Lapps, 72% for Australians, 60% for Eskimo, 56.3% for Peruvians, 52.0% for Italians, and as little as 13.8% for Bavarians.

Finally, it may be stated that the different degrees of development of the maxillary part of the torus do not always affect its palatine termination

---

[121] It does not seem superfluous to point out the fact that the "keel"-shape termination of the torus is the typical formation while the "keel", restricted to the horizontal processes of the palatine bones, is an exceptional occurrence.

[122] l. c., p. 208.

[123] *Russell* (1900), l. c., p. 167, lists only 14.4% of torus occurrence in American Indians, and *Hrdlička* on the Lenape Indians, l. c., p. 14 (43), says: "there is no torus worthy of notice." It is therefore quite probable that series other than those from the North Pacific Coast possess that character only to a limited degree, or, what is still more probable, that a diversity of method exists.

Summary 127.

Torus palatinus: actual and percental frequency.

Sex and Age	Torus palatinus							
	Undeformed							
	Absence		Torus maxillaris		Palatine "keel"		Torus palatinus	
	no.	%	no.	%	no.	%	no.	%
♂	6	8.3	2	2.8	11	15.3	53	73.6
♀	2	6.3	—	—	1	3.1	29	90.6
juv.	—	—	—	—	—	—	1	—
inf.	2	—	—	—	—	—	10	—
Total frequencies	10	8.5	2	1.7	12	10.3	93	79.5
	Cowichan deformation							
♂	16	19.8	1	1.2	—	—	64	79.0
♀	4	15.4	—	—	2	7.7	20	76.9
juv.	—	—	—	—	—	—	2	—
inf.	1	—	—	—	—	—	5	—
Total frequencies	21	18.3	1	0.9	2	1.7	91	79.1
	Chinook deformation							
♂	10	17.9	1	1.8	—	—	45	80.3
♀	2	8.3	—	—	—	—	22	91.7
juv.	—	—	—	—	—	—	4	—
inf.	2	—	—	—	—	—	4	—
Total frequencies	14	15.6	1	1.1	—	—	75	83.3
	Koskimo deformation							
♂	20	19.1	—	—	6	4.7	79	75.2
♀	3	9.4	—	—	1	3.1	28	87.5
juv.	1	—	—	—	—	—	1	—
inf.	—	—	—	—	—	—	7	—
Total frequencies	24	16.4	—	—	7	4.8	115	78.8

in the same way, that is to say, that the maxillary torus may be weakly developed while the palatine part is rather voluminous. The latter, again, may also differ in shape as broad and narrow, of which instances are shown in fig. 44, *a* and *b*, illustrating the respective conditions in two male Chinook

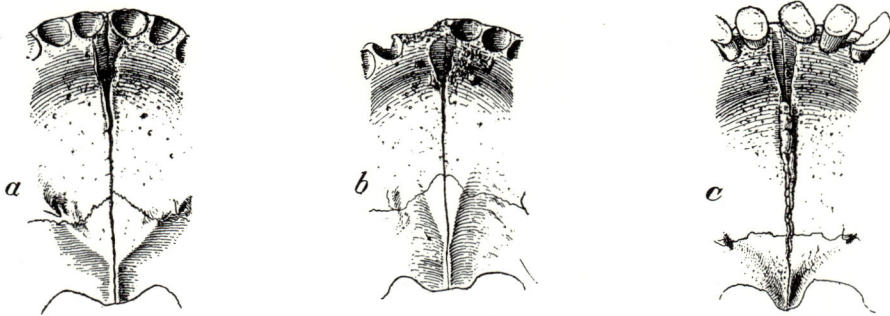

Fig. 44. Two different forms of the "keel" termination of the torus palatinus: *a* broad; *b* narrow; *c* "granulated" form of torus. Natural size.

skulls (4493, 4447). Another variation is more or less frequently found in granulations of different size in place of the torus, *Bauer*'s "diskontinuierliche Torusbildung" in a male Koskimo (3642), as illustrated in fig. 44, *c*.

g. *Spina nasalis posterior*.

Although the spina nasalis posterior, as formed by the two horizontal plates of the palatine bone, is sometimes found mentioned in literature and anomalous conditions in connection with it pointed out, a systematic investigation seems not to have been carried on with regard to the frequencies of certain forms in certain series. As an anomaly, the bipartite spina, also occurring in our series, appears first to have been described by *Waldeyer*[124], while *R. Martin* (Lehrbuch, 1914, 829) saw it in $30°/_0$ in the Battaks, *Bauer*[125] in $9.3°/_0$ in different races combined. In the present series the following forms of the spina were recognized: tapering, angular, rounded, trapezoid and bipartite. Of these the trapezoid is only another angular form broadly drawn out and of varying length (depth). It was so termed for the reason that if a line is drawn connecting the deepest points of the two notches as formed by the posterior borders of the palatine bones, the projecting parts (spina nasalis) form a more or less exact trapezoid. In *summary 128* these forms are seen exemplified at the top of their rubrics.

---

[124] *Waldeyer, W.*, 1892. Über den harten Gaumen. Corr. Bl. Deut. Anthrop. Ges., v. XXI, pp. 118—119.
[125] l. c., p. 205 (20, 25).

Summary *128.*

Spina nasalis posterior: actual and percental frequency.

Sex and Age	Spina nasalis posterior									
	Undeformed									
	1 Tapering		2 Angular		3 Rounded		4 Trapezoid		5 Bipartite	
	no.	%	no.	%	no.	%	no.	%	no.	%
♂	17	26.6	19	29.7	22	34.4	4	6.2	2	3.1
♀	10	35.7	8	28.6	6	21.5	2	7.1	2	7.1
juv.	1	—	—	—	—	—	—	—	—	—
inf.	5	—	3	—	1	—	2	—	3	—
Total frequencies	33	30.8	30	28.1	29	27.1	8	7.5	7	6.5
Cowichan deformation										
♂	24	32.4	25	33.8	12	16.2	6	8.1	7	9.5
♀	5	20.9	9	37.5	5	20.8	2	8.3	3	12.5
juv.	—	—	—	—	1	—	—	—	—	—
inf.	1	—	1	—	1	—	3	—	—	—
Total frequencies	30	28.6	35	33.3	19	18.1	11	10.5	10	9.5
Chinook deformation										
♂	12	26.1	20	43.5	6	13.0	5	18.9	3	6.5
♀	3	18.8	6	37.5	4	25.0	2	12.5	1	6.2
juv.	—	—	2	—	1	—	—	—	1	—
inf.	3	—	2	—	2	—	—	—	—	—
Total frequencies	18	24.6	30	41.1	13	17.8	7	9.7	5	6.8
Koskimo deformation										
♂	37	38.5	42	43.8	5	5.2	9	9.4	3	3.1
♀	8	24.2	16	48.5	2	6.1	6	18.2	1	3.0
juv.	2	—	—	—	—	—	—	—	—	—
inf.	1	—	3	—	—	—	1	—	1	—
Total frequencies	48	35.0	61	44.5	7	5.1	16	11.7	5	3.7

The angular form is the predominating one in the Cowichan, Chinook and Koskimo divisions, while the tapering one ranges as second in frequency. This proportion is reversed in the Undeformed, although the tapering form exceeds the angular one only slightly. Again, the rounded form here (27.1%) ranges only a little below the frequency of the angular one, the frequencies for the rounded form in the Cowichan and Chinook being somewhat farther removed from those of their tapering forms. The frequency of the Koskimo for the rounded form falls considerably lower than those for the three other divisions. Of the two remaining forms, the trapezoid is only moderately represented, which is still more true of the bipartite. Their occurrence with 6.5% and 6.8% is fairly alike in the Undeformed and the Chinook, while the Cowichan have 9.5%, and the Koskimo 3.7% of bipartite spinae. From *Bauer*'s list it must be assumed that the latter anomaly can hardly be considered a racial trait, but that as a morphological variation it occurs in almost any human race, as well as in the anthropoid apes.

h. *Foramina palatina majora and minora.*

Observations on the foramina are exceedingly rare in literature despite considerable variation in the number of lesser foramina, The larger ones vary little, only in size, which as a rule is quite conservative. A foramen majus of extraordinary size, 5 mm. long and 4 mm. wide, was seen in a male Kwakiutl (1729). In a female Kwakiutl skull (1911) the foramina majora and minora were merged because the crista marginalis which ordinarily separates the two was absent.

The usual number of lesser foramina situated on the processus pyramidalis of the palatine bone is generally two. However, careful observation here revealed such variable conditions in our material that twenty-one states of equal or unequal occurrence had to be accounted for.

Summary 129 shows that equal numbers up to four foramina occur on both sides. Then there are different combinations, from non-occurrence to four right foramina, with varying conditions on the left side, where as many as five foramina were counted in a single case. Bilateral absence was not observed. The highest frequencies in all four divisions are listed for bilateral occurrence of one and two foramina, the former exceeding the latter in every case. The percentages then gradually diminish as the combinations become more complicated.

It may be worth while to consider this trait in future investigations. A cursory examination of other series from other parts of the world (South America, Australia) did not reveal to the author similar variable conditions as found in the Northwest material.

Summary 129.

Foramina palatina minora: actual and percental frequency.

Sex and Age	Foramina palatina minora																				
	Undeformed																				
	r1/11*	r2/12	r3/13	r4/14	r0/11	r0/12	r0/13	r0/14	r1/12	r1/13	r2/10	r2/11	r2/13	r2/14	r2/10	r3/11	r3/12	r3/15	r4/11	r4/12	r4/13
♂	15	11	1	1	—	2	—	1	9	1	3	7	6	1	—	2	1	—	—	1	—
♀	9	2	—	—	—	1	1	—	2	1	—	3	2	—	1	2	2	—	—	—	—
juv.	—	—	—	—	—	1	—	—	—	—	—	—	—	—	—	—	—	—	—	—	—
inf.	4	2	—	—	—	—	—	—	2	2	—	—	—	—	—	—	—	—	—	—	—
Total frequencies (no.)	28	15	1	1	—	4	1	1	13	4	3	11	8	1	1	4	3	—	—	1	—
(%)	28.0	15.0	1.0	1.0	—	4.0	1.0	1.0	13.0	4.0	3.0	11.0	8.0	1.0	1.0	4.0	3.0	—	—	1.0	—
	Cowichan deformation																				
♂	20	14	2	—	1	2	—	—	8	3	—	7	6	2	—	3	3	—	—	1	—
♀	4	7	—	—	1	1	—	—	4	1	—	1	1	—	—	—	—	—	—	1	1
juv.	—	1	—	—	—	—	—	—	—	—	—	—	—	—	—	1	—	—	—	—	—
inf.	1	2	—	—	1	1	—	—	1	1	—	—	—	—	—	—	—	—	—	—	—
Total frequencies (no.)	25	24	2	—	3	4	—	—	13	5	—	8	7	2	—	4	3	—	—	2	1
(%)	24.3	23.3	1.9	—	2.9	3.9	—	—	12.6	4.9	—	7.8	6.8	1.9	—	3.9	2.9	—	—	1.9	1.0
	Chinook deformation																				
♂	16	8	1	1	—	—	—	—	8	4	—	4	—	—	—	4	5	—	1	—	1
♀	4	6	—	—	—	—	—	—	1	—	—	6	4	—	—	—	2	—	1	—	—
juv.	—	2	1	—	—	—	—	—	—	—	—	—	—	—	—	—	—	—	—	—	—
inf.	2	1	—	—	—	—	—	—	1	—	—	—	—	—	—	—	—	—	—	—	2
Total frequencies (no.)	22	17	2	1	—	—	—	—	10	4	—	10	4	—	—	4	7	—	2	—	3
(%)	25.6	19.7	2.3	1.2	—	—	—	—	11.6	4.7	—	11.6	4.7	—	—	4.7	8.1	—	2.3	—	3.5
	Koskimo deformation																				
♂	21	18	4	2	—	—	—	—	13	4	3	6	4	2	—	2	8	1	—	1	1
♀	9	7	2	—	1	—	—	—	5	2	—	—	3	—	—	1	—	—	—	1	1
juv.	1	1	—	—	—	—	—	—	—	—	—	—	—	—	—	—	—	—	—	—	—
inf.	3	2	—	—	—	—	—	—	—	—	—	—	—	—	—	—	—	—	—	—	—
Total frequencies (no.)	34	28	6	2	1	—	—	—	18	6	3	6	7	2	—	3	8	1	—	2	2
(%)	26.4	21.7	4.7	1.6	0.8	—	—	—	14.0	4.7	2.3	4.7	5.4	1.2	—	2.3	6.2	0.8	—	1.6	1.6

* Symbols refer on the right (r) and left (l) sides to the number of foramina.

NORMA LATERALIS.

1. Cranial contour.

The classification of the cranial outlines in the norma lateralis, according to *G. Sergi*'s tassonomic system, is not so easily effected as in the norma verticalis. The lateral contours are, first of all, less readily discernible, and, secondly, much more rarely true to type in the majority of cases in the different series. Nevertheless a classification was attempted for the reason that from a purely descriptive viewpoint a few definite types might facilitate a more or less adequate morphologic interpretation. What has been said with regard to the norma verticalis may be repeated here, namely, that with the employment of the tassonomic method, a racial diagnosis has not been attempted in the following paragraphs.

As the undeformed skulls in the present series, with a few brachycranial exceptions, belong to the mesocranial variety, *G. Sergi*'s subvarieties in lateral aspect of the ellipsoides of the norma verticalis are important here. They are, (1) the ellipsoides sphyroides (σφῦρον, heel), distinguished by a peculiar sharp flexion of the cranial outline at the inion; (2) the ellipsoides cuneatus with evenly and somewhat pointedly projecting occiput, and (3) the ellipsoides rotundus. Of these the sphyroid and rounded subvarieties have the inferior occipital outline from the inion to the opisthion directed almost horizontally, while it slopes more steeply in the cuneate subvariety. It seems unnecessary, with regard to the underlying material, to enter upon *G. Sergi*'s other subvarieties, all the more so since the variability is very slight and fully covered by the three subvarieties quoted above. The sphyroides which according to the Italian author retains the shape of the fetal occiput, occurs in the Haida and Eskimo only in a very faint indication. The male skull in general shows the characteristics of the ellipsoides cuneatus, recognizable even in the brachycranial Lillooet. The female skulls, on the other hand, shorter *per se* and more rounded than the male, conform with the ellipsoides rotundus. which is still more in evidence in the brachycranial Lillooet females. The infantile skull, whose characteristics in more than one respect are preserved by the female skull, exhibits also a rounded occipital contour. The frontal outline of the infantile skull throughout the Undeformed series maintains its steep ascendance, so characteristic of the immature skull and which is retained with little modification by the female.

The almost typical occurrence of a more or less pronounced depression at the lambda is of special interest in the cranial outline of the Eskimo, being, apparently, the result of the decided protrusion which the upper occipital squama undergoes. This feature was recently commented on also by *Cameron* who found that "the upper portions of the occipital bones exhibited a pronounced backward bulging" [126].

Quite marked likewise is the occipital protrusion in a female skull from Tenerife as depicted by *Hooton* [127], which appears to be more pronounced than the frequently occurring occipital protrusion as described by the present writer in the ancient Egyptians [128]. One assuredly cannot go amiss in attributing these conditions to intracranial pressure in reminiscence of early departures from a more generalized condition.

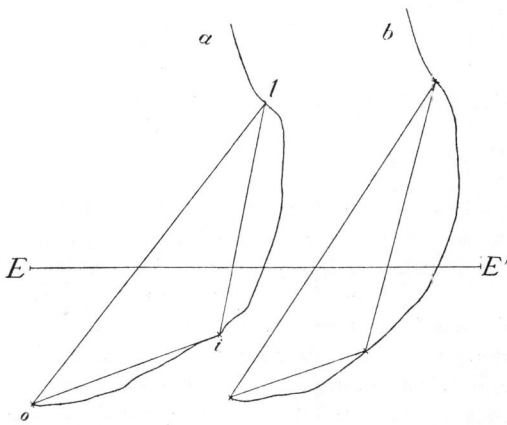

Fig. 45. Occipital outlines to show protrusion of upper squama. Two-thirds.

Two cases of the present series, Eskimo 3772 and 3782, males, are found illustrated in occipital outline in fig. 45. The first of the two diagrams depicts the peculiarity remarked on in conjunction with a more flattened upper squama, while in the second one the outline appears to be more rounded. There is not a single instance of this distinctly localized peculiarity found in any of the other groups to the degree exhibited by the Eskimo.

2. Lineae temporales.

The linea temporalis inferior shows a more marked development only in the pars temporalis, indentical there with the crista supramastoidea. The pars frontalis represents the typical appearance of the temporal line in this region, forming rather a crista temporalis of the frontal bone. Skulls of coarser habitus usually develop coarser ridges which are less pronounced in the female and in immature age.

The development of the crista temporalis of the frontal bone may in the

---

[126] l. c., p. 193 (40).
[127] *Hooton, Earnest, A.*, 1925. The ancient inhabitants of the Canary Islands. Harvard African Studies, v. VII, pl. 30.
[128] l. c., p. 146 (23—24).

present series be described as medium. Neither does its course manifest any abnormal conditions in the Undeformed groups. In the deformed skull, especially in the Chinook, the crista temporalis shows interesting behavior in that the strongly flattened forehead, sometimes set off almost at right angles from the facies temporalis of the frontal bone, causes the illusion of the high course of the crista. Viewing the configuration here more discriminatingly, one cannot fail to recognize that the general depression of the frontal region has also affected the course of the crista temporalis, i. e., it is rather low and in a number of cases excessively so. Similar results are produced in the Koskimo deformation, while in the Cowichan they are of a relatively milder degree.

A downward incurvation with somewhat typical recurrence takes place where the linea temporalis crosses the coronal suture. Passing upon the parietal bone the temporal line rises again, following first the course of the coronal suture and then proceeding on its more horizontal curve. The configuration at the coronal suture is sometimes quite complicated, caused by the latter's attitude in the stephanion region. It is here, where the pars complicata continues into the plainer pars temporalis, that the coronal suture may take an abrupt backward turn to form a pars horizontalis, resuming again the vertical course toward the bregma. This behavior is typical in the apes where, in connection with such occurrence, the behavior of the linea temporalis is quite as variable as it is in human skulls of similar conformation. It follows closely the horizontal turn of the suture either above, below or coincidingly, shaping its further course along the direction of the coronal suture, i. e., forming an upward curve around the posterior end of the pars horizontalis, or reaching the parietal bone in a straight course some distance above or below the horizontal part. Such cases have been described by *Ranke*[129], *Aigner*[130], *Dillenius*[131], et al., while the curve upward of the linea temporalis posterior of the sutura coronalis was explained by *Dalla Rosa*[132] as a result of the resistence offered by that suture against the gradual progression upward and forward of the line of origin of the temporal muscle, i. e. the linea temporalis inferior, in the course of growth.

Indications of all such conditions were observed in our series, but scarcely, with few exceptions, to such a degree as to present adequate illustrations. It may be stated, however, that in addition to the typical slight incurvation mentioned, the rather straight course of the crista temporalis into the linea temporalis inferior of the parietal bone, formed the rule in the Undeformed.

---

[129] *Ranke, J.*, 1900. Die überzähligen Hautknochen des menschlichen Schädeldaches. Abh. K. Bayr. Ak. Wiss. München, Math.-Physic. Kl., v. XX, Abt. 3 (Denkschrift).

[130] *Aigner, D.*, 1900. Über die Ossa parietalia des Menschen. Phil. Diss., Munich.

[131] *Dillenius, J. A.*, 1910. El hueso parietal baja la influencia de la deformación fronto-occipital. Publ. Seccion Anthrop. no. 7, Univ. Nacional, Buenos Aires.

[132] *Dalla Rosa L.*, 1886. Das postembryonale Wachstum des menschlichen Schläfenmuskels. Stuttgart.

The marked upward turn of the linea temporalis on the parietal side of the sutura coronalis is particularly well developed in a number of instances in the Chinook skulls. They may be taken as a sort of experimental proof of *Dalla Rosa*'s assertion referred to in the preceding paragraph.

The pars parietalis of the linea temporalis proper which here becomes the linea inferior, is as a rule weakly developed in all the skulls of the present series, and in a number of cases it is unidentifiable. This is also true to a more marked degree of the linea temporalis superior, although occasionally it is just this line which shows a ridge-like development [133]

The course of the two temporal lines upon the parietal bone, especially in their relation to the tuber parietale and sutura lambdoidea, is of greater interest than their development. Conditions here are in fact quite variable. *Aigner* (cited by *Dillenius*, see footnotes p. 224) pointed out five different conditions, (1) the tuber parietale is situated above the superior temporal line; (2) is traversed by it; (3) lies between the two temporal lines; (4) is traversed by the inferior temporal line; or (5) remains below it. Since the development also of the tuber parietale is frequently very slight, the identification of both elements, i. e., the lineae temporales and the tuber parietale, is sometimes rendered exceedingly difficult. It seems, however, that in the majority of the Undeformed cases, the superior temporal line traverses the tuber while the inferior one extends below it, reaching the crista supramastoidea soon thereafter in a sweeping curve. The superior temporal line strikes out considerably farther, taking its course along and anteriorly of the lambdoid suture. In the deformed skulls it is sometimes found to form strong ridges on the occipital side of the suture, continued over the sutura occipitomastoidea and into the more or less pronounced tuberosity of the m. splenius capitis insertion (crista mastoidea *Klaatsch*) upon the mastoid process. This causes the sulcus mastoideus (*Waldeyer*) not only to become quite deep, but also to extend more posteriorly between the two ridges produced by the cristae supramastoidea and mastoidea. Another interesting observation upon excessively deformed skulls (Chinook, Koskimo), where the parietal bones suffer pronounced distortion, is the fact that the tuber parietale remains within the "circummuscular zone" (*Dalla Rosa*) which extends between the two temporal lines. The temporal lines and the tubera yield simultaneously to the deformatory influences, causing them to retain their relative positions toward each other even in extreme extortion.

The discussion of the temporal part of the linea temporalis inferior will be found under crista supramastoidea in the following section of this chapter.

---

[133] The statement invariably found in text books of anatomy that the linea temporalis superior represents the line of attachment of the fascia temporalis, is questioned by *H. Virchow*, 1910. Muskelmarken am Schädel. Zschr. Ethnol., v. XLII, pp. 638—654 (641), when he says: "Die Angabe, dass an der Linea temporalis superior die Fascia temporalis befestigt sei, muss ich bestreiten und *Hyrtl* darin beistimmen, dass an ihr Periost und Galea nicht fester anheften als an anderen Stellen".

3. Squama temporalis.

a. Form and size.

The cranioscopic view of the squama temporalis discloses a number of forms which recur somewhat regularly in the Undeformed skulls. They are illustrated in fig. 46, *a–c*, of which the upper one, almost circular in its even roundness, is the typical infantile form, frequently met with also in the female skull. It belongs to a Haida inf. II (3752). The remaining two represent a short and a long form, the former as a rule combining shortness with a superior height, while the latter's length is generally prompted by relative and absolute lowness. These two conditions are evident in a male Athapascan (4339) and a male Haida (3741). Disregarding a metrical interpretation of the height and length extensions of the squama temporalis, it may be stated that its general shape maintains a certain affinity to the lateral outline of the skull. This is also true of the size, although within the latter's ranges, the three forms of fig. 46 have been seen to occur without preference. Among the Undeformed, the Eskimo are possessed of rather large squamae, long as well as high, which, somewhat in keeping with the dimensions of the Eskimo skull, might be taken as a racial peculiarity.

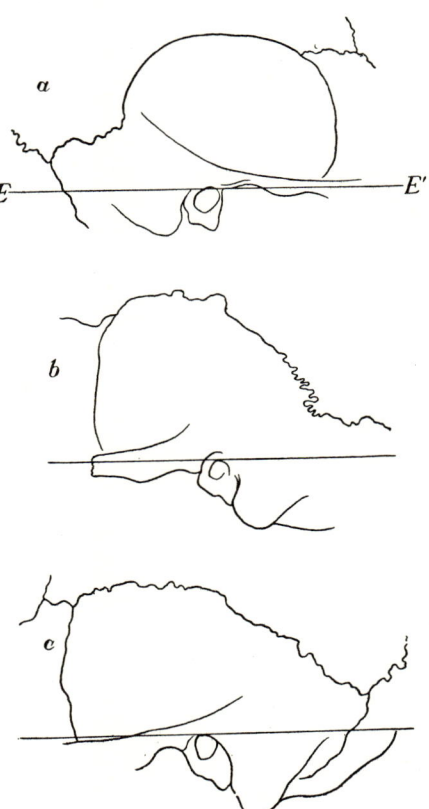

Fig. 46. Squama temporalis: most frequently occurring forms. About natural size.

Still more variable is the form of the temporal squama in the deformed skulls which frequently does not conform with the types of fig. 46. The form here at times assumes an irregular aspect, due to the altogether horizontal direction of the superior margin of the squama and its angular continuation into the posterior margin. In a number of cases the characteristic anthropoidal form was observed, representing a rather low squama with an upper margin evenly sloping towards the incisura parietalis. The variability of form might, to a certain degree, be attributed to the deforming influences which work secondarily upon the cranial regions that are not directly under the deforming strains. Thus the dimensions of the squama temporalis, while rather submedium in the Koskimo deformation, seem conspicuously large in the Chinook, and moderately so in the Cowichan deformation.

b. Sutura squamosa.

Form and size of the squama temporalis depend largely upon the direction of the sutura squamosa. Its course, on the other hand, may be quite irregular and thus serve at times to enliven the outline to a high degree of variability. In the immature ages, the suturae squamosae show, as a rule, a very regular, i. e., plain and even, course of almost circular outline, as was pointed out in the preceding section (see also fig. 46, a). Such a course is sometimes retained in the adult female skull, although during the process of growth, form and size of the squama change considerably, yielding, as an individual bone, to the trend of growth in phyletic kyphosis as well as to the laws governing the interdepence of the cranial parts. In consideration of this it appears that the sutura squamosa of the Undeformed male skull is subject to great variability. In the deformed skulls this is without doubt increased by the deforming pressure, so effective during the first stages of extra-uterine life. Not only are the suturae squamosae of the deformed skulls per se more irregular than those of the Undeformed, but in many instances attain a high degree of irregularity, particularly in the Chinook. Examples of this are seen in fig. 47, a and b. The first of the two male Chinook skulls (4456) preserves more of a meandering course, while the latter (4469) combines this with exceedingly strong serration.

Fig. 47. Irregular suturae squamosae. About natural size.

c. Processus parietalis.

This projection of the squama temporalis upon the os parietale was first described at length by *Adachi* [134], who saw it in about 50°/₀ of Japanese crania. It is situated at about the middle of the sutura squamosa, anterior of the sulcus arteriae temporalis mediae and frequently shields a blood vessel, an offshoot of the arteria meningea media, which, being transmitted through the sutura squamosa, emerges from under the end of the process in several small branches. Since indications of the process are met in lower forms of vertebrate animals, one is justified in attaching to it a certain phylogenetic importance [135].

Mere indications of the process were not considered in the present series and only the unequivocal cases recorded.

These, as shown in *summary 130* in the Undeformed males, amount to 7.5°/₀, in the females to 2.6°/₀, yielding a total in the Undeformed series of 6.1°/₀. In the infantile skulls only a few slight indications of the process were observed. Altogether the greatest frequency is found on the left side, while bilateral occurrence is quite rare. The Cowichan deformation presents a male frequency of 8.0°/₀, and a female one of 6.2°/₀. with a total for the series of 7.7°/₀. Successively higher percentages are reached in the Chinook and Koskimo deformations. The former attain 8.6°/₀ in the males, 3.8°/₀ in the females and a total of 7.4°/₀, and the latter 14.4°/₀ in the males, the females and infantiles being devoid of a processus parietalis. The total for the series rises here to 9.7°/₀.

What was stated with regard to the frequency in the Undeformed holds true also for the other divisions, namely that among the cases recorded, the greatest frequency was seen to occur on the left side of the skull, the right side being less favored, and bilateral occurrence restricted only to a few cases.

d. Incisura parietalis.

Loth [136] has called attention to the gradual appearance, phylogenetically, of the incisura parietalis. On the whole, it is absent in the lower apes, but in the orang he finds the first true incisura, comparable to similar conditions in the so-called lower races of man. Not until the squama temporalis gains in height, suggesting at the same time its arrest in width, does it attain the formation of an incisura parietalis.

This is, doubtless, correctly observed. It is obvious, from the purely cranioscopic viewpoint, however, that the great variation in form of the incisura parietalis other than phylogenetic, depends upon the individual behavior of the parts involved in its formation. These are primarily the suturae squamosa and parietomastoidea, and the junction of the margines squamosus and mastoideus of the parietal bone, more exactly, the latter's angulus mastoideus. All these elements may vary considerably in size and form and thus cause the high degree of variation of the incisura which might best be classified with reference to the angular deviation of the two sutures involved, taking the right angle

---

[134] *Adachi, B.*, 1907. Processus parietalis squamae temporalis. Zschr. Morph. Anthrop., v. X, pp. 485—488.

[135] In this sense the processus parietalis has been explained as an upgrowth into the lower portion of a vertical parietal suture of rare persistence.

[136] *Loth, E.*, 1911. Beiträge zur Kraniologie der Polen. Zschr. Morph. Anthrop., v. XIX, pp. 305—338 (320).

Summary 130.

Processus parietalis (squamae temporalis): actual and percental frequency.

Sex and Age	Processus parietalis (squamae temporalis)								Grand total
	Undeformed								
	Bilateral		Right		Left		Total		
	no.	%	no.	%	no.	%	no.	%	%
♂	2	2.5	—	—	4	5.0	6	7.5	} 6.1%
♀	—	—	1	2.6	—	—	1	2.6	
juv.	—	—	—	—	—	—	—	—	
inf.	—	—	—	—	—	—	—	—	
Total frequencies	2	1.6	1	0.8	4	3.1	—	—	
	Cowichan deformation								
♂	2	2.3	3	3.9	2	2.3	7	8.0	} 7.7%
♀	—	—	—	—	2	6.2	2	6.2	
juv.	—	—	—	—	—	—	—	—	
inf.	—	—	—	—	—	—	—	—	
Total frequencies	2	1.6	3	2.4	4	3.2	—	—	
	Chinook deformation								
♂	1	1.7	—	—	4	6.9	5	8.6	} 7.4%
♀	1	3.8	—	—	—	—	1	3.8	
juv.	—	—	—	—	—	—	—	—	
inf.	—	—	—	—	—	—	—	—	
Total frequencies	2	2.1	—	—	4	4.3	—	—	
	Koskimo deformation								
♂	1	1.0	5	4.8	9	8.7	15	14.4	} 9.7%
♀	—	—	—	—	—	—	—	—	
juv.	—	—	—	—	—	—	—	—	
inf.	—	—	—	—	—	—	—	—	
Total frequencies	1	0.6	5	3.2	9	5.8	—	—	

as a standard of comparison. Grouped around the right angle toward the minor side, are found obtuse angularity and either an entire absence of the incisura or only a slight indication of it, while the opposite side is represented by acute angularity at different degrees. Finally, asymmetries had to be recorded,

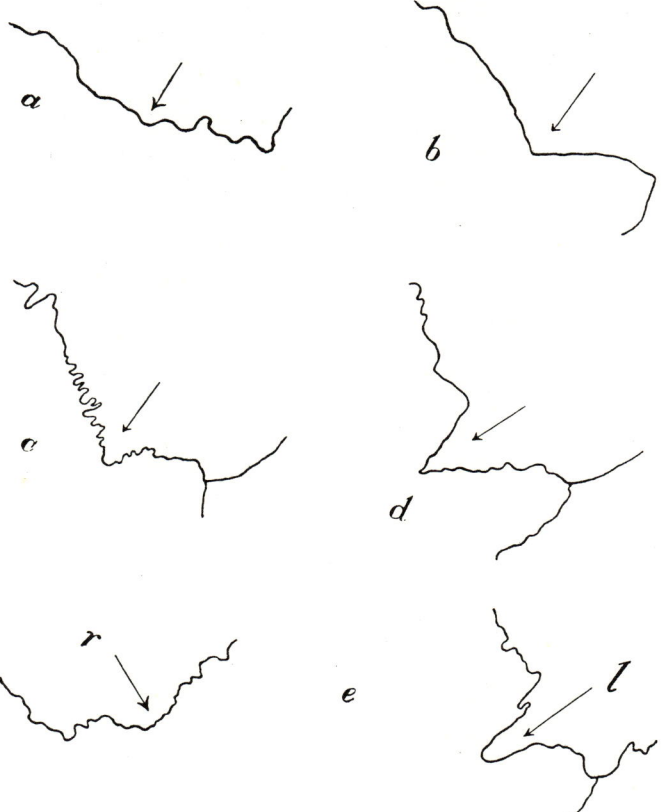

Fig. 48. Various forms of incisura parietalis. Natural size.

i. e., the cases of dissimilar behavior of the incisura parietalis upon the two sides of the skull, comprising almost all the possible combinations.

Attention may first be called to fig. 48, where the different forms are illustrated. Absence of an incisura or its slight indication, as depicted in *a* is particularly found in connection with a low temporal squama, the elevation of which produces such angular conditions as seen in *b*, *c* and *d*. These four conditions were seen in skulls of a female Chinook (4496); a Haida inf. II (1605); a Chukchee male (3849) and an Eskimo male (3776). Dissimilar behavior of the two sides of the skull gives rise to the formation of incisurae of acute and obtuse angularity, as seen in *e*, which conditions are represented in a male Athapascan (4337). In a number of cases Wormian bones were observed to fill up the entire triangle, such as seen in fig. 49, *a–c*. Their forms varied also, mostly in correlation with form and size of the incisurae parietales. Narrow bones in the form of chips, more long than wide, were found in connection with narrow incisurae, mostly in a diagonal position with their lower ends directed forward, of which an instance is given under *a*, of a male Haida skull (3747). Broader incisurae, in a number of cases devoid of any angular shape, but forming instead notches of irregular size, were sometimes seen to comprise also irregularly shaped Wormian bones either single as under *b*, in

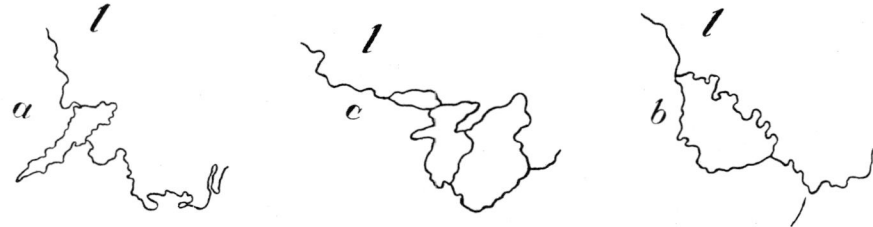

Fig. 49. Incisurae parietales with Wormian bones. Natural size.

a Chinook inf. I–II, (3845), or multiply divided as under *c*, in a Chinook male (4512).

The occurrence of Wormian bones in this particular place is less common than in the asterion region where such features are more frequently met. The Wormian bones of the incisura parietalis might better be explained then as ossa suturarum, since they occur in the course of a suture removed from any fonticulus, and not as fontanel bones like, for instance, the epiptericum. It must be borne in mind, however, that otherwise the locality of the incisura during growth gives rise to a number of complications which might favor the formation of Wormian bones in the individual skull in addition to the strains of deformation. In fact, in the deformed skulls of this series a greater frequency of the anomaly in question is seen.

The percental frequency of the incisura parietalis as listed in *summary 131* reveals quite interesting conditions. Rectangularity attains 16.9% in the Undeformed, exceeded by the Chinook and Koskimo deformations with 22.4% in the former and 29.6% in the latter. The Cowichan frequency at 13.2% ranges below the Undeformed. Obtuse angularity, indicated by $<$ R in our summary is listed with high percentages of 57.0% and 59.2% in the Cowichan and Koskimo deformations. Compared with these high frequencies, the Undeformed yield 29.9%, while the Chinook list only 4.1%. The Chinook, however, with 45.9% reveal a high frequency of shallow incisurae or none at all; the Cowichan deformation and the Undeformed have frequencies of 6.1% and 12.1%, while in the Koskimo deformation no shallow incisurae were noticed. Acute angularity, i. e., an incisura smaller than 90° ($<$ R), is only moderately represented. Appreciable percentages,

Summary 13f.

Incisura parietalis: actual and percental frequency.

Sex and Age	Incisura parietalis									
	Undeformed									
	Absent or slightly indicated		>R		=R		<R		Bilaterally dissimilar	
	no.	%	no.	%	no.	%	no.	%	no.	%
♂	8	10.0	16	20.3	15	19.9	16	20.3	24	30.4
♀	5	16.1	14	45.2	4	13.0	3	9.7	5	16.1
juv.	1	—	—	—	1	—	—	—	—	—
inf.	1	—	7	—	1	—	—	—	3	—
Total frequencies	15	12.1	37	29.9	21	16.9	19	15.3	32	25.8
	Cowichan deformation									
♂	2	2.5	46	58.2	11	13.9	12	15.2	8	10.1
♀	2	6.8	17	58.6	4	13.8	2	6.8	4	13.8
juv.	2	—	—	—	—	—	—	—	—	—
inf.	1	—	2	—	—	—	1	—	—	—
Total frequencies	7	6.1	65	57.0	15	13.2	15	13.2	12	10.5
	Chinook deformation									
♂	28	44.4	2	3.2	15	23.8	7	11.1	11	17.5
♀	12	48.0	1	4.0	6	24.0	1	4.0	5	20.0
juv.	1	—	1	—	—	—	—	—	2	—
inf.	4	—	—	—	1	—	—	—	1	—
Total frequencies	45	45.9	4	4.1	22	22.4	8	8.2	19	19.4
	Koskimo deformation									
♂	—	—	60	58.3	34	33.0	4	3.9	5	4.8
♀	—	—	26	66.7	9	23.0	1	2.6	3	7.7
juv.	—	—	1	—	—	—	1	—	—	—
inf.	—	—	3	—	2	—	—	—	3	—
Total frequencies	—	—	90	59.2	45	29.6	6	4.0	11	7.2

however, go to the bilateral dissimilarities, the Undeformed leading with 25.8%, the Koskimo listing only 7.2%, while the Chinook with 19.4% and the Cowichan with 10 5% are intermediate.

The most marked feature as revealed in *summary 131* is the preponderance of angular conditions larger than 90° in the deformed skulls. A certain tendency toward acute angularity might be noticed in the Undeformed. It will be rather difficult to decide whether deforming influences can be held responsible for percental discrepancies. The high percentage of non-occurrence of angles in the Chinook deformation and the lack of absence of incisures in the Koskimo, however, may suggest such influences.

e. Crista supramastoidea.

The temporal portion of the linea temporalis inferior, known as the crista supramastoidea, shows an unusual development, particularly in the male skulls of the present series, both undeformed and deformed. Continuing backward of the proces- sus zygomaticus of the temporal squama, it rises from the typical depression above the external auditory opening to form marked ridges upon bases of variable widths. The greatest height is generally attained toward the

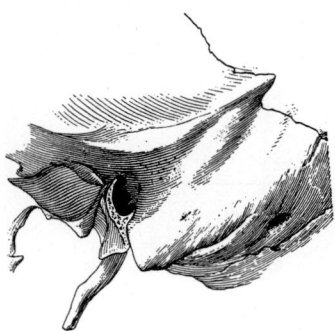

Fig. 50. Crista supramastoidea forming triangular projection upon parietal bone (male Bellacoola 4626). Natural size.

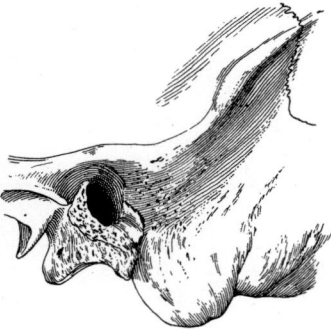

Fig. 51. Crista supramastoidea extending over sutura squamosa (male Haida 3738). Natural size.

end of its course, diminishing again in a tapering or pointed manner before it reaches the sutura squamosa. Quite frequently it may be seen to continue as a tooth or thorn-like projection of the temporal squama upon the parietal bone as found in a male Bellacoola (4626), and illustrated in fig. 50. At times again the ridge is carried on over the sutura squamosa upon the parietal bone and continued more or less directly into the parietal portion of the linea temporalis inferior. Such is the case in a male Haida (3738), as illustrated in fig. 51. Here the basis of the ridge is seen to widen and form a convexity upward before it traverses the sutura squamosa. The continuation of the ridge upon the parietal bone was invariably marked by a strong diminution of bulk, while its extension, rather limited as a rule, reached 41 mm. in the exceptional case of a Kwakiutl male (1912).

In the female skull the crista supramastoidea does not reach the same degree of development as found in the male. The percental frequency of marked development ranges there considerably lower, as will be seen farther on. The immature ages show scarcely any indication of a crista, and it is absent altogether in the infantiles.

Without exception the course of the crest posteriorly takes an upward turn. It appears, however, that a course less curved is often found correlated with a lower squama temporalis.

An estimate of the degree of development of the crista supramastoidea can be ventured only with regard to its general appearance in the different series.

The percental frequency of a more strongly developed crista supramastoidea as listed in *summary 132* was found highest in the Undeformed with a total adult frequency of 39.5%. Next come the Chinook with 35.7% for both sexes. The Cowichan deformation also ranges relatively high, yielding a total of 32.5%. The smallest percentage is that of the Koskimo with 20.2%.[137]

Summary 132.

Crista supramastoidea: actual and percental frequency.

Sex and Age	Crista supramastoidea		
	Undeformed		
	Actual frequency	Percental frequency	Total percental frequency
♂	40	50.0%	39.5%
♀	5	14.7%	
	Cowichan deformation		
♂	34	38.6%	32.5%
♀	4	13.8%	
	Chinook deformation		
♂	28	48.3%	35.7%
♀	1	3.8%	
	Koskimo deformation		
♂	27	25.0%	20.2%
♀	2	5.1%	

---

[137] R. *Martin*, (Lehrbuch, 1914/781) cites the following percental frequencies: Australians 72.5% (*Krause*); Oceanians 40.8% (*Volz*) and 31.1% (*Fridolin*); Americans 30.0% (*Rabl, Rückhard*); Asiatics 24.5°/° (*Broesike*); Europeans 10.0% (*Broesike*). The two contrasting figures, those of the Australians and Europeans reveal quite

The high percentage of the Undeformed seems to bear some significance first as a matter per se and then in comparison with the results derived from the deformed skulls. Deformation thus does not suggest an increase in the way of frequency, but rather of decrease. But upon closer examination one might be tempted, nevertheless, to attribute a certain influence to the deforming action since the feature under consideration contains many cases of pronounced development of the crista supramastoidea. This is essentially true in the Cowichan and Chinook deformations, while cristae of excessive dimensions seemed to be rather infrequent in the Koskimo deformation. On the other hand, it should be remembered that it is not solely function which is to be held responsible for deviations of size and form.

f. Tuberculum supramastoideum anterius (*Waldeyer*).

This term was applied by *Waldeyer* [138] to a more or less circular protuberance at the posterior end of the crista supramastoidea, anterior of the sutura squamosa but not passing beyond it. It is sometimes met by a deep depression on the parietal side of the suture. The tuberculum was seen in a number of Papuan skulls by *Broesike* and *Waldeyer*.

No cases of a tuberculum supramastoideum anterius have been recorded for the present series, although indications were suggested in certain individuals by the proportions of the crista supramastoidea.

g. Sutura sphenosquamosa.

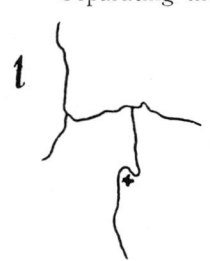

Fig. 52. Sutura sphenosquamosa with sharp forward turn (female Salish 1784). Add no size indication.

Separating the squama temporalis from the ala magna of the sphenoid bone, the sutura sphenosquamosa is most frequently slightly curved with a forward convexity, but in a number of cases rather straight. There are several instances recorded in our series where the suture takes a short angular forward turn while in others it produces a sort of loop-like bend. Such a case was seen in a female skull (1784) from Eburne (near Vancouver), and is illustrated in fig. 52. Since deviations like the one described occur generally in the pterion region, they may justly be associated with irregular ossification about the fonticulus sphenoidalis.

The two bones involved in the formation of the sutura sphenosquamosa join quite rarely on a level; much more frequently are their margins seen to rise against each other, either to form

---

interesting stages of morphologic development. The general status of our series would approximate those of the Americans and Asiatics of *R. Martin*'s citations, although the Undeformed at 39.5% exceed both, while the Koskimo at 20.2% range below them.

[138] l. c., p. 194 (18—19).

a sharp ridge or a bulging of varied magnitude. These conditions are often rendered still more pronounced through the longitudinal depression of the ala magna, the so-called sulcus sphenoparietalis (see under 6 of this chapter: Fossa temporalis). Ridge as well as bulging occur in both the undeformed and deformed skulls with an apparent increased frequency in the latter. It is particularly in the Chinook that both conditions seem to be emphasized due to their strenuous mode of deformation. The skulls deformed in the Cowichan and Koskimo fashions, on the other hand, do not show them in the same degree of frequency nor development. The Haida and Eskimo, however, seem to have the greatest frequency among the Undeformed.

h. Processus frontalis (squamae temporalis). [139]

The actual frequency of the processus frontalis is somewhat similar in the Undeformed, the Cowichan and Koskimo deformations. The two sexes are proportionately alike, four males to three females in the former, two to two and three to three in the latter two divisions. The Chinook number six males, but only one female. The immatures are represented by only one in the Undeformed, the Cowichan and Chinook divisions, but two in the Koskimo. No preference of occurrence obtains with regard to right or left. In all the males combined the processus was found five times on the right side, four times on the left, and six times where it occurred simultaneously on both sides. The female figures are two, two and five for the same conditions, the immature being one, one and three. The figures of simultaneous occurrence are thus seen to prevail over those of unilateral occurrence.

Summary 133 contains the actual and percental frequencies of the processus frontalis as described in this section. The total percental frequencies, including the immatures, amount to 6.2%, 3.2%, 8.5% and 5.2% in the four series, as listed in the summary.

Considering the phylogenetic significance of this morphological feature (see footnote 139), it will be quite difficult to decide whether its frequency can be attributed to the influences of deformation, although the higher percentage of strongest distortion in the Chinook division might justify such an assumption.

Summary 133 does not comprise the cases of incomplete development, as illustrated in fig. 53, *a–d*. The two sides of the skull, right and left, are seen placed in juxtaposition to one another. Under *a*, female Chinook (4498), they show an indication of a processus frontalis, on the right side one of

---

[139] The term processus frontalis was apparently introduced into anatomy by *R. Virchow*, 1875. Ueber einige Merkmale niederer Menschenrassen am Schädel. Abh. Kgl. Ak. Wiss. Berlin.(1876), Phys. Kl., 2 Abt., p. 49, when he says: "Es ist das die Verbindung der Schuppe des Schläfenbeins mit dem Stirnbein durch einen besonderen Fortsatz. Ich werde ihn Stirnfortsatz (Processus frontalis) nennen." He explains furthermore, that the processus as well as other anomalous formations of the pterion region originate: "wenn die vorhandene Bindesubstanz der Fontanelle nicht rechtzeitig und regelmässig zur Vergrösserung der benachbarten Knochen verwandt wird." Whether a pathological origin can legitimately be ascribed to the processus frontalis remains doubtful, since it occurs with great regularity in certain catarrhine forms (cercopithecus, 74%; cynocephalus, 80%; macacus, 90%), and with typical recurrence in the gorilla (100%) and the chimpanzee (77%). This speaks more for phylogenetic transmission. The formation of the processus is, according to *R. Virchow* facilitated by the way in which the ala magna of the sphenoid connects with the adjoining bones. While the ala magna overlaps the frontal and parietal bones with its margins, it is itself overlapped by the temporal squama in the sutura sphenosquamosa.

triangular form, the left of a narrow rectangle. Under *b*, Chinook inf. II (4468), the processes are still incomplete but markedly widened. The female Koskimo (3841), shown under *c*, has a complete process on the left side, while the right squama sends out a much narrower one which remains incomplete. Only *d*, male Kwakiutl (3878), possesses two fully developed processes meeting the frontalia with broad margins.

Summary 133.

Processus frontalis (squamae temporalis).

Series	Processus frontalis (squamae temporalis)												Total percental frequency		
	Actual frequency				Local occurrence										
	♂	♀	juv.	inf.	r	l	r+l	r	l	r+l	r	l	r+l	♂	♀	immat.
					♂			♀			immat.			%		
Undeformed	4	3	—	1	1	2	1	1	1	1	1	—	—	6.2		
Cowichan } deformation	2	2	—	1	1	—	1	1	—	1	—	—	1	3.2		
Chinook } deformation	6	1	—	1	2	2	2	—	1	—	—	—	1	8.5		
Koskimo } deformation	3	3	1	1	1	—	2	—	—	3	—	1	1	5.2		

4. Regio mastoidea.

a. Processus mastoideus.

The size of the mastoid process is as a rule conspicuously smaller in females and still more so in the immatures as compared with the males. But as its development occurs during the periods of general physical growth, it is more than likely that the effects of cranial deformation should also have a bearing on its definite appearance by means of the muscular traction needed in the correction and adjustment of the changed cephalic equilibrium. That the processus mastoideus as a relatively late acquisition in the phylogenetic sense is subject to individual adaptation, has already been pointed out by *Klaatsch*.[140] And this is particularly noticeable in the transitional stages from the half-upright to the upright gait.

The probability of deformatory effects is quite clearly indicated in the Chinook deformation where, according to *summary 134* the large male processes are listed with 91.1%, the medium-sized with 8.9%, while no small processes have been recorded. The females have as many as 25.0% falling to the large-sized group, and 75.0% to the group containing the medium-sized processes, while the small-sized group is here also not represented. The Chinook infantiles do not

---

[140] *Klaatsch, H.*, 1902. Occipitalia und Temporalia der Schädel von Spy verglichen mit denen von Krapina. Zschr. Ethnol., v. XXXIV, pp. 392—409 (403).

form an exception to the general infantile status of mastoid processes in the beginning stages. The other division of extreme deformation, the Koskimo, lists a small male percentage and a larger female one of small processes. Their greatest percentages are found in the medium group where the males amount to 63.8% and the females to 80.6%. This leaves for the large processes a male percentage of 34.3% and a female one of only 5.6%. The conspicuous feature then in the Koskimo division is the pronounced preponderance of medium processes in both sexes and the relatively small occurrence of large ones, somewhat in contrast with the behavior of the less strenuously deformed Cowichan and even of the Undeformed. In the case of the Koskimo deformation it must be pointed out, however, that the Koskimo themselves are among those with strongly developed processes. The Koskimo females follow somewhat the general tendency by yielding a fair percentage of small processes, while the bulk goes to the medium, leaving only a minor share to the large-sized. The Koskimo immatures repeat the status of the Chinook immatures.

The remaining two divisions, the Undeformed and the Cowichan deformation present fairly similar conditions. The high percentage of large processes in the Undeformed males is of interest, which with 45.9% exceed even the Cowichan with 42.9%. The medium-sized processes of the Cowichan males yield 50.0%, representing the majority there, while 45.9% of the Undeformed males conform with their percentage of large processes. Small mastoids are of rather infrequent occurrence in both divisions, where the immatures also repeat here the status as described above.

The total percentages of all the cases, including the immatures, mark the predominance of medium-sized mastoids in the Undeformed, Cowichan and Koskimo series with 41.9%, 47.5% and 65.8%. Large processes in the same serial order are second in the order of frequency and small-sized are third. The Koskimo frequency of only 8.7%, is conspicuously low. The Chinook division reverses the order somewhat, yielding as much as 61.7% for the large mastoids and 33.0% for the medium-sized, leaving only 5.3% for the small the latter in analogy to the Koskimo conditions.

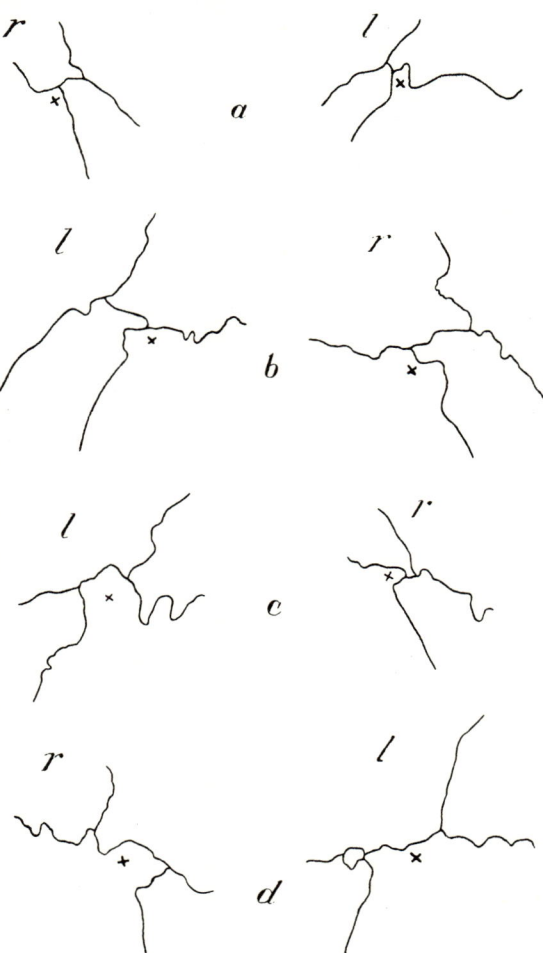

Fig. 53. Variations in the bilateral occurrence of the processus frontalis. Natural size.

Summary 134.

Processus mastoideus: actual and percental frequency.

Sex and Age	Processus mastoideus					
	Undeformed					
	Small		Medium		Large	
	no.	%	no.	%	no.	%
♂	6	8.2	34	45.9	34	45.9
♀	15	41.7	17	47.2	4	11.1
juv.	1	—	1	—	—	—
inf.	12	—	—	—	—	—
Total frequencies	34	27.4	52	41.9	38	30.7
	Cowichan deformation					
♂	6	7.1	42	50.0	36	42.9
♀	14	51.9	11	40.7	2	7.4
juv.	—	—	3	—	—	—
inf.	4	—	—	—	—	—
Total frequencies	24	20.3	56	47.5	38	32.2
	Chinook deformation					
♂	—	—	5	8.9	51	91.1
♀	—	—	21	75.0	7	25.0
juv.	2	—	2	—	—	—
inf.	3	—	3	—	—	—
Total frequencies	5	5.3	31	33.0	58	61.7
	Koskimo deformation					
♂	2	1.9	67	63.8	36	34.3
♀	5	13.8	29	80.6	2	5.6
juv.	—	—	2	—	—	—
inf.	6	—	—	—	—	—
Total frequencies	13	8.7	98	65.8	38	25.5

In addition to its size which, from the occasionally marked percental deviations, one may be justified to consider as being influences by deforming strains, it is the direction of the processus mastoideus that deserves attention. The cranioscopic graduation into steep, slightly and strongly slanting processes has not revealed any findings of importance. The records almost invariably show a medium tendency, with a slight indication, however, towards steepness in the Chinook. The cranioscopic method of description does not prove efficient in this special case. But it is quite possible that exact metrical procedures may yield more differentiated results.

b. Sutura mastoideosquamosa.

The independent origin of the squamous and petrous parts of the temporal bone finds expression through the sutura mastoideosquamosa which is obliterated at the end of the second year. The persistence of the suture in the adult human skull is exceedingly rare. Residues of it, however, are more frequently met, although not to any great extent.

Vestiges of the suture were seen in both the undeformed and deformed skulls of the present series, sometimes quite distinct, sometimes blurred by the

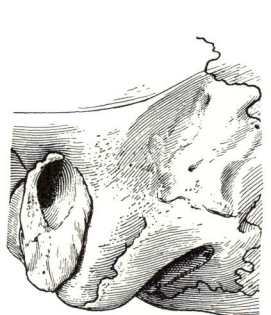

Fig. 54. Sutura mastoideosquamosa (male Eskimo 3771). Natural size.

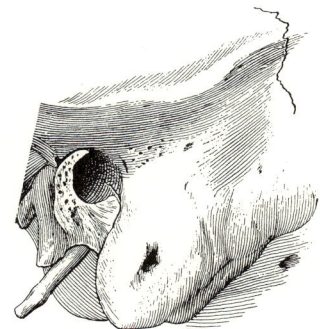

Fig. 55. Sutura mastoideosquamosa with pit-like depression (male Kwakiutl 4248). Natural size.

tuberosities of the mm. sternocleidomastoideus and splenius insertions which *Klaatsch*[141] called crista mastoidea. In such a case the residual suture appears on top of the ridges of muscular attachment. Its course is invariably from backward and above, to forward and below, generally in the direction of the processus mastoideus. Illustrative of this is the case of an Eskimo male (3771), fig. 54, whose processus mastoideus appears to be fairly bisected by a rather markedly persistent suture. It is the Eskimo, prevalently, who present this

---

[141] l. c., p. 236 (403).

trait at a relatively greater frequency than the other groups of the series *MacCurdy* [142] records a frequency of 10.0°/₀ in Peruvian Highland skulls.

A case of somewhat incomplete ossification between the two parts of the temporal bone under discussion, in the course, however, of the sutura mastoideo-squamosa, is illustrated in fig. 55 of a Kwakiutl male (4248). A gap or pit is seen there on the lateral surface of the processus mastoideus, somewhat deep, but not connected with the mastoid cellulae. Specific disturbances of growth in connection with the primary division and subsequent coalescence of the parts involved, have been observed by several authors. *Le Double* [143], for instances, writes: "La suture pétro-squameuse externe des adultes est parfois remplacée par un sillon ou interrompue dans une partie de son trajet." The ridge referred to, but not specified by *Le Double*, is doubtless the muscular tuberosity mentioned above as crista mastoidea *Klaatsch*, while the interruptions may show a number of different conditions.

c. Sulcus supramastoideus (*Waldeyer*).

The sulcus-like depression below and along the crista supramastoidea, and between the latter and the ridge-forming tuberosity of muscular attachment on the lateral side of the processus mastoideus (crista mastoidea *Klaatsch*), has been named and described by *Waldeyer*. [144] It is present, more or less marked, in the adult skull and only slightly, if at all, in the immature as shown in *summary 135*. Hereby is already predicted that the sulcus is most markedly shown in skulls with strongly developed cristae supramastoideae and mastoidal tuberosities. Since these occur to an appreciable extent in the Undeformed, the more pronounced stage of the sulcus is also found here, attaining a frequency of 12.2°/₀. It is met, however, also in the other divisions. Divisible into three different grades: shallow, medium deep and deep, the general condition of the sulcus is medium deep, while in a great number of cases it is quite shallow and even scarcely perceptible.

d. Tuberculum supramastoideum posterius (*Waldeyer*).

In contradistinction to the tuberculum supramastoideum anterius discussed above (see p. 234), *Waldeyer* [145] has also described a tuberculum supramastoideum posterius. This protuberance is situated at the angulus mastoideus of the parietal bone, anteriorly of the asterion point and occupying at times the entire length of the mastoideoparietal suture. Its form is more or less circular and in its perfect state probably more smooth than rugged. Both adjoining bones, the parietal with its angulus mastoideus and the temporal with its pars

---

[142] l. c. p. 15 (269). [143] l. c., p. 194 (295).
[144] l. c. p. 194 (20). [145] l. c., p. 194 (17—18).

Summary 135.

Sulcus supramastoideus (*Waldeyer*): actual and percental frequency.

Sex and Age	Sulcus supramastoideus					
	Undeformed					
	Shallow		Medium		Deep	
	no.	%	no.	%	no.	%
♂	22	27.8	42	53.2	15	19.0
♀	12	31.6	25	65.8	1	2.6
juv.	2	—	—	—	—	—
inf.	12	—	—	—	—	—
Total frequencies	48	36.6	67	51.2	16	12-2
	Cowichan deformation					
♂	24	27.3	55	62.5	9	10.2
♀	9	32.1	16	57.1	3	10.8
juv.	1	—	—	—	—	—
inf.	5	—	1	—	—	—
Total frequencies	39	31.7	72	58.5	12	9.8
	Chinook deformation					
♂	19	32.7	36	62.1	3	5.2
♀	12	46.2	14	53.8	—	—
juv.	3	—	1	—	—	—
inf.	6	—	—	—	—	—
Total frequencies	40	42.5	51	54.3	3	3.2
	Koskimo deformation					
♂	23	22.6	76	74.5	3	2.9
♀	11	32.4	23	67.6	—	—
juv.	—	—	2	—	—	—
inf.	3	—	—	—	—	—
Total frequencies	37	26.3	101	71 6	3	3.1

mastoidea, participate in the formation of the tuberculum in such a way that the sutura mastoideoparietalis passes through it.

The formation under discussion is significant from both the osteogenetic and figurative points of view. Situated in the area of the fonticulus mastoideus, it may be possible that irregularities of ossification, not exactly of a pathological character, together with the action of periosteum, galea and muscular attachment, is responsible for the formation of the tuberculum supramastoideum posterius. Thus far observations as to the nature and character of the tuberculum are not numerous and its value as a racial trait is, therefore, doubtful as yet. *Waldeyer* saw the tuberculum in skulls of Alfures, Tamara and Timor Laut.

The definite occurrence in our series of a tuberculum supramastoideum posterius is not easily determined. Rugged tuberosities in different degrees of development are discernible in a number of cases. Considering the better developed cases only with regard to some semblance of a tubercular elevation, it appears as if the frequency, although small on the whole, is greater in the deformed skulls. The Eskimo among the Undeformed, however, reveal a frequency of ten cases among the thirty-three males, and five among the twelve females. These cases have been recorded as medium-large. The almost total absence in the other Undeformed groups is significant. The greatest frequency in the deformed skulls is shown by the Chinook with fourteen male and three female cases among a total number of fifty-eight and twenty-six respectively. The Cowichan deformation is listed with nine and three cases among eighty-eight and twenty-nine, and the Koskimo deformation with seven and two cases among one hundred and four males and thirty-nine females.

The tuberculum supramastoideum posterius being established by *Waldeyer* as an independent morphological character, its closer examination from the generic and statistic angles with a view toward racial distribution is a desideratum. A more detailed treatment here was therefore left out of consideration, since also none of the cases mentioned came up to the degree of development as described by that author.

e. Processus asteriacus (*Haferland*).

A protuberance similar to the preceding one, but restricted to the angulus mastoideus of the parietal bone, was observed and described by *Haferland*[146] in Melanesian skulls. In that author's opinion it is related to a homologous formation in the chimpanzee skull. Disregarding a few very slight and indistinct indications, the present series is completely devoid of it.

---

[146] *Haferland, R.*, 1905. Ein Schädel mit einem Processus asteriacus. Zschr. Ethnol., v. XXXVII, pp. 207–208.

5. Regio tympanica.

a. Porus acusticus externus.

The two fundamental and predominating types, occurring also in our series, are the circular and elliptic ones. They result from the different ways through the merging of os tympanicum with pars petrosa; the round one is the typical occurrence in eastern apes and the elliptic one in man. In the latter, differences in the inclination of the longitudinal axis were to be noticed. Further peculiar modifications of this shape of the porus acusticus externus deserve special attention. The simplest modification is that of a narrow fissure-like, almost vertically directed opening, which in cases may be seen to be bilaterally constricted, and producing an opening in the shape of a dumb-bell. In a number of these the main axis of the porus slants from above and before to below and behind.

The actual and percental frequencies of the different shapes of the porus acusticus externus are listed in the five columns of *summary 136*. They represent, (1) the circular; (2) the vertical ellipse; (3) the diagonal ellipse; (4) the vertical and (5) the diagonally compressed or constricted shape. The circular shape, perhaps the primary one, yields altogether the highest percentages in the Undeformed and in the Cowichan deformation. Furthermore, it includes in the latter all the immatures of the Cowichan deformation, while only limited numbers of the immatures in the other divisions have circular pori. Considerably smaller percentages obtain for the same shape in the Chinook and Koskimo adults. As to sex proportions, it will be noticed that in the Undeformed the males exceed the females, the latter, however, presenting higher percentages in the three deformed divisions.

The vertical ellipse is represented by relatively small frequencies, of which those of the Undeformed and Koskimo deformation again range relatively high.

The diagonally oriented ellipse, on the other hand, repeats the high occurrence of the circular shape only in a reversed order. The Chinook and Koskimo divisions are seen to exceed the Undeformed and Cowichan in their total percentages. The sex proportions are also slightly different since the female numbers exceed the male in the Undeformed and Chinook divisions. The majority of the immature skulls are also found assembled here.

The vertically directed narrow, fissure-like shape of the porus acusticus externus occurs in very small percentages only. They do not even reach $1°/_0$ in the Undeformed and the Koskimo divisions, and only a fraction above $1°/_0$ in the remaining two. The diagonally directed narrow shape, however, attains as high as $21.5°/_0$ in the Chinook, and $4.2°/_0$ in the Cowichan deformation. The Koskimo deformation obtains only $1.3°/_0$. It will be noticed that the latter shape occurs only in the deformed divisions. The greater frequency of the diagonally directed ellipse seem also to be highly characteristic in the two divisisions of excessive deformation, the Chinook and Koskimo. Although obtaining also to an appreciable degree in the Undeformed and deformed Salish, and being in fact considered by some authors as a characteristic of the American skull, it is quite probable that head deformation is responsible for greater percentages of this shape in those two divisions.

The size of the porus acusticus externus, on the whole, is to be classified as medium, corresponding thus to the size of the skull. It is an interesting fact, however, that conspicuously large pori prevail throughout the Koskimo division (Kwakiutl, Nimkish, Koskimo, Nootka), suggesting here a distinct tribal peculiarity.

Summary 136.

Porus acusticus externus (shape): actual and percental frequency.

Sex and Age	Porus acusticus externus (shape)									
	Undeformed									
	1 ◯		2 ⬭		3 ⬭		4 ⧗		5 ⧗	
	no.	%	no.	%	no.	%	no.	%	no.	%
♂	44	57.1	15	19.5	17	22.1	1	1.3	—	—
♀	16	48.5	3	9.1	14	42.4	—	—	—	—
juv.	—	—	—	—	2	—	—	—	—	—
inf.	6	—	—	—	6	—	—	—	—	—
Total frequencies	66	53.2	18	14.5	39	31.5	1	0.8	—	—
	Cowichan deformation									
♂	47	54.7	6	7.0	26	30.2	2	2.3	5	5.8
♀	19	67.9	3	10.7	6	21.4	—	—	—	—
juv.	1	—	—	—	—	—	—	—	—	—
inf.	5	—	—	—	—	—	—	—	—	—
Total frequencies	72	60.0	9	7.5	32	26.6	2	1.7	5	4.2
	Chinook deformation									
♂	13	22.8	3	5.3	23	40.4	—	—	18	31.6
♀	6	23.1	3	11.6	14	53.8	1	3.8	2	7.7
juv.	1	—	1	—	2	—	—	—	—	—
inf.	2	—	—	—	4	—	—	—	—	—
Total frequencies	22	23.6	7	7.5	43	46.3	1	1.1	20	21.5
	Koskimo deformation									
♂	26	24.1	21	19.5	59	54.6	1	0.9	1	0.9
♀	16	44.4	4	11.1	15	41.7	—	—	1	2.8
juv.	—	—	—	—	3	—	—	—	—	—
inf.	3	—	—	—	4	—	—	—	—	—
Total frequencies	45	29.2	25	16.2	81	52.6	1	0.7	2	1.3

There was scarcely any difference observed in the shape of the porus acusticus externus on the two sides of the skull. A few exceptions occur in the excessively deformed skulls, where one side may present an elliptic shape, while the other shows a fissure-like porus. This is the case, for instance, in a Chinook skull (4481), whose special feature is the narrow porus on the side of the less pronounced compression, the opposite side showing the elliptic shape. This example goes to demonstrate that the greatest deforming strain and the effect produced do not always disclose even proportions.

b. Spina suprameatum.

The form of the spina suprameatum is most frequently that of a more or less distinct ridge or lamina fitting into the circumference of the porus acusticus externus. It is invariably situated at the beginning of the sulcus supramastoideus, being, therefore, a formation of the pars mastoidea of the temporal bone and not of its pars tympanica. Adjoining the spina posteriorly there occurs a typical pit-like depression as a fossa mastoidea, or foveola suprameatum (*Pensa*).[147] Regarding the nature of these characters *Pensa* distinguishes between four different types, where (1) spina and foveola are wanting; (2) coexisting; (3) and (4) either spina or foveola absent. In no case in our material was there encountered a thorn-like spina projecting into the lumen of the porus as depicted by *Pensa* (his table I, fig. 3), or a spine-like one caused by the detachment of the lower end of the lamina representing the spina, as figured by *Schlaginhaufen*.[148] A more thorough investigation into the nature of the spina suprameatum which, however, was not attempted here, might have occasioned its classification into several forms similar to those of *Pensa*'s. Unusually shaped cases not being encountered, dissimilarities from a general point of view were nevertheless to be observed. In the immatures there is, as a rule, only a slight development of the spina, and at times it is not even indicated. The sex difference in the adults is clearly demonstrated by better marked spinae in the males who also show deeper and wider foveolae. As far as could be seen the size of the spina suprameatum in the deformed skulls exceeds that in the undeformed. Deformatory influences may thus also be responsible for larger spinae.

c. Os tympanicum (hyperostosis).

The thickening or hyperostosis of the os tympanicum around the porus acusticus externus is a characteristic of certain primitive races and has been

---

[147] *Pensa, Antonio*, 1907. Osservazioni sulla "spina supra meatum." Boll. Soc. Med. Chir. Pavia, pp. 1–15 (4).
[148] *Schlagenhaufen, Otto*, 1906. Über eine Schädelserie von den Marianen. Jahrb. Naturw. Ges. St. Gallen, pp. 454—509 (491).

described in connection with the Neandertaloids and the Eskimo. It is also a typical characteristic of the North Pacific Indians throughout the entire series under investigation.

Its grades are specified in *summary 137* as slight, medium and pronounced, the first and last columns containing the percentages of absence and total frequency. The latter, in their very high percentages, show a gradual increase in the four divisions from $91.3°/_o$ in the Undeformed to $98.3°/_o$ in the Cowichan, $98.9°/_o$ in the Chinook and $100.0°/_o$ in the Koskimo deformations. Absence of hyperostosis of the os tympanicum was recorded for the Undeformed males and females at equal percentages, $9.0°/_o$ and $8.8°/_o$, and for the Cowichan males at $2.4°/_o$, besides one infantile in each of the Undeformed and Chinook divisions. No cases of absence were recorded for the Koskimo. Slight thickening yield almost negligible percentages — there is none in the Chinook deformation — so that the highest percentages in every division go to the medium and pronounced grades. The high frequency of $53.9°/_o$ of the pronounced state in the Undeformed males is due to the uniformly strong thickening of the tympanic bone in the Eskimo series of that division. The Undeformed females have a higher percentage of medium development, which holds also true for the sexes of the Cowichan and Koskimo deformations and the Chinook females. The Chinook males, on the other hand, present the highest frequency of pronounced thickening with $63.2°/_o$.

It is a distinguishing fact that all the immatures except two show tympanic thickening to some, mostly medium and strong, degree, proving that this feature develops quite early, perhaps at a period before the annulus tympanicus has assumed its final appearance. Mechanical causes, such as wearing heavy ear pendants, or artificial deformation, have been mentioned as conducive to the production of tympanic hyperostosis. If, however, the incipient stages of this anomaly must be sought at an early, perhaps intrauterine period, mechanical influences in later life should be of little importance. The thickened edge, as such, is quite variable in shape. Three different states from as many male Eskimo skulls (3719, 3793, 3776) may be seen depicted in fig. 56, *a–c*, where they advance from a

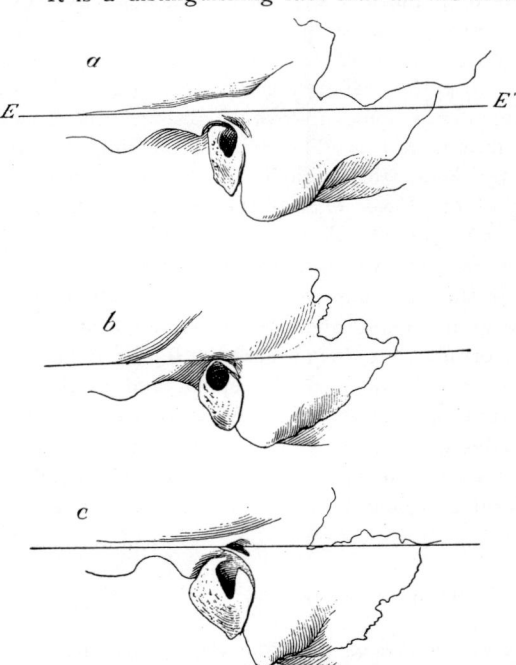

Fig. 56. Tympanic hyperostosis in Eskimo skulls. Natural size.

rather slender to a fairly rounded form of broad peripheral area. Although on the whole the thickening of the edges occurs rather typically in such a

Summary 137.

Os tympanicum (hyperostosis): actual and percental frequency.

Sex and Age	Os tympanicum (hyperostosis)							
	Undeformed							
	Absent		Slight		Medium		Pronounced	Grand total, present
	no.	%	no.	%	no.	%	no.	%	
♂	7	9.0	3	3.8	26	33.3	42	53.9	
♀	3	8.8	—	—	18	52.9	13	38.3	91.3 %
juv.	—	—	1	—	—	—	1	—	
inf.	1	—	3	—	5	—	4	—	
Total frequencies	11	8.6	7	5.5	49	38.6	60	47.3	
	Cowichan deformation							
♂	2	2.4	4	4.6	49	56.2	32	36.8	
♀	—	—	1	3.7	19	70.4	7	25.9	98.3 %
juv.	—	—	—	—	2	—	—	—	
inf.	—	—	—	—	5	—	—	—	
Total frequencies	2	1.7	5	4.1	75	62.0	39	32.2	
	Chinook deformation							
♂	—	—	—	—	21	36.8	36	63.2	
♀	—	—	—	—	15	57.7	11	42.3	98.9 %
juv.	—	—	—	—	1	—	4	—	
inf.	1	—	—	—	4	—	2	—	
Total frequencies	1	1.1	—	—	41	43.1	53	55.8	
	Koskimo deformation							
♂	—	—	1	1.0	67	64.4	36	34.6	
♀	—	—	—	—	22	59.5	15	40.5	100.0 %
juv.	—	—	—	—	1	—	1	—	
inf.	—	—	—	—	7	—	1	—	
Total frequencies	—	—	1	0.7	97	64.2	53	35.1	

way that the lower portion is frequently more drawn out than the sides, yet the anterior and posterior walls of the tympanicum may show irregular degrees of thickening by which either the former, the latter, or both are favored.

A few cases have been recorded with edges so excessively drawn out that these and the apices of the mastoid processes terminate upon one and the same level, the fissura tympanico-mastoidea being thus considerably lengthened.

d. Os tympanicum (perforation).

Perforations in the floor of the auditory meatus, or better, its anteriorly directed wall, are found in varying degrees of size and frequency in the immature as well as the mature skull. In the former they are due to incomplete ossification between the partes tympanica and petrosa which under normal conditions merge about the fifth year of infantile life. In the adult, however, an additional cause is given in the action of the mandibular joint in conjunction probably with atrophic processes. *Hyrtl*'s "spontaneous dehiscences"[149] seem to be of a quite different nature besides being restricted in their occurrence to the tegmen tympani.

Perforation of the anterior wall of the os tympanicum seems to be quite common in American skulls (*Hrdlička, Fuller*). The defects, generally roundish in shape in the present series, may also present quite irregular forms with longitudinal diameters up to 6 mm. The defective areae as a rule were found to be more or less depressed and, therefore, somewhat funnel-like with wrinkled margins. The perforations were invariably listed for both sides of the skull.

The statement by other authors of a higher female occurrence would be in accordance with the status of the present series (see *summary 138*), where the females in each division outrange the males by considerably higher figures in the Undeformed, and in the Cowichan and Koskimo deformations. In the Chinook this sex difference is quite inconspicuous, while at the same time the general total frequency amounts here only to 8.5% as against the much higher total percentages of 22.5% in the Undeformed, 22.2% in the Cowichan and 24.7% in the Koskimo deformations. Included in these figures are the immatures at frequencies proportional to those of the adults. The low percentage in the Chinook is of particular interest since it corresponds proportionately to the high percentages in this division of tympanic hyperostosis and exostoses. From this statement it may be inferred that osseous growth is more profuse in the Chinook which would also bear on the percental occurrence of osseous defects in such a way as appreciably to reduce them. The high percentages of tympanic perforation in the Koskimo, amounting to 33.3% in the females and 19.2% in the males conform with *Hooton*'s findings upon skulls from Madisonville, Ohio[150], which were for the greater part only slightly deformed by antero-posterior compression.

Although the general total percentage of tympanic perforations is fully as high in the Undeformed as in the Cowichan, but exceeded by the Koskimo,

---

[149] *Hyrtl, Joseph*, 1858. Über spontane Dehiscenz des Tegmen tympani und der Cellulae mastoideae. Sitz. Ber. K. Ak. Wiss. Wien, Math.-Naturw. Kl., v. XXX, pp. 275—282.

[150] l. c., p. 151 (113).

nevertheless, one may be induced to attribute effective influences upon the production of those osseous defects to artificial deformation, either in a prohibitive or stimulative way.

e. Exostoses auriculares.

Differing in character from the more diffuse growth of tympanic hyper ostosis, the exostoses auriculares are of a hard, ivory-like consistency. They occur as characteristically shaped outgrowths at the anterior and posterior ends of the os tympanicum. Their principal shapes are two: (1) pea-shape, and (2) crest-shape, which again may vary in form, size and frequency, and there may even be transitional forms between hyperostoses and exostoses, with reference to shape more than to texture. Thus *Kleiweg de Zwaan* [151] found in a series of Tanimbar skulls that: "De hyperostose van het os tympanicum herinnerde sterk aan de exostosen aan den uitwendigen gehoorgang der Peruanern». The pea-shape exostosis, restricted to the marginal area of the external auditory meatus is more or less pedunculated and may also occur

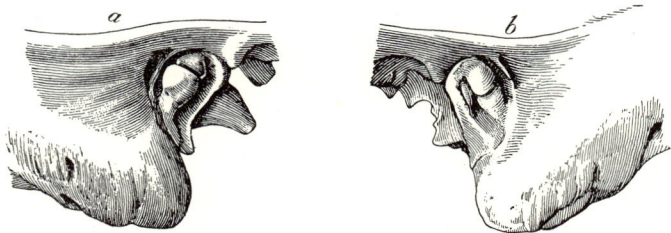

Fig. 57, *a* and *b*. Bilateral exostoses auriculares (male San Miguel Island 312). Natural size.

singly either upon the anterior or posterior wall of the meatus. In twofold occurrence they grow at times so large as almost to occlude the external meatus. Such cases may be seen illustrated in fig. 57, *a* and *b*, representing the two sides of an undeformed skull from San Miguel Is., California (312, Museum of the American Indian, Heye Foundation). The interesting feature here, besides the large growth of the exostoses, is the wandering upward and backward of the anterior one and the junction with the posterior one in front of the spina suprameatum. At the point of junction their vertices appear flattened, leaving only a very narrow cleft between them. The crest-shape form is elongated, frequently rolled in and extending from without inward. The crests also occur at the edges of the os tympanicum, but though they do not seem to reach the same height in the external auditory meatus as the

---

[151] *Kleiweg de Zwaan, J. P.*, 1917. Tanimbarschädels. In: Volkenkundige Opstellen I, Koloniaal Inst. Amsterdam, Mededeeling IX, Afdeeling Volkenkunde no. 3, pp. 1—90 (14).

Summary 138.
Os tympanicum (perforation): actual and percental frequency.

Sex and Age	Os tympanicum (perforation)							Total	Grand total
	Undeformed								
	Slight		Medium		Pronounced			
	no.	%	no.	%	no.	%		
♂ Both sides....	1	1.3	3	3.8	3	3.8		
Right only...	—	—	1	1.3	—	—	12.5%	
Left only....	—	—	2	2.5	—	—		
Total frequencies	1	1.3	6	7.5	3	3.8		22.5%
♀ Both sides....	2	5.9	1	2.9	3	8.8		
Right only...	1	2.9	—	—	—	—	29.4%	
Left only....	1	2.9	2	5.9	—	—		
Total frequencies	4	11.8	3	8.8	3	8.8		
juv.......	1 (1)	—	—	—	—	—	—	
inf.......	—	—	2	—	6	—	—	
	Cowichan deformation								
♂ Both sides....	2	2.3	5	5.7	7	8.0		
Right only...	1	1.1	1	1.1	1	1.1	20.4%	
Left only....	—	—	1	1.1	—	—		
Total frequencies	3	3.4	7	7.9	8	9.1		22.2%
♀ Both sides....	—	—	—	—	6	20.7		
Right only...	—	—	—	—	2	6.9	27.6%	
Left only....	—	—	—	—	—	—		
Total frequencies	—	—	—	—	8	27.6		
juv.......	—	—	—	—	—	—	—	
inf.......	—	—	1	—	1	—	—	
	Chinook deformation								
♂ Both sides....	—	—	1	1.7	2	3.4		
Right only...	—	—	—	—	—	—	6.9%	
Left only....	—	—	1	1.7	—	—		
Total frequencies	—	—	2	3.4	2	3.4		8.5%
♀ Both sides....	1	3.8	—	—	—	—		
Right only...	—	—	—	—	—	—	7.7%	
Left only....	—	—	—	—	1	3.8		
Total frequencies	1	3.8	—	—	1	3.8		
juv.......	—	—	—	—	—	—	—	
inf.......	—	—	1 (1)	—	1	—	—	
	Koskimo deformation								
♂ Both sides....	1	0.96	8	7.7	6	5.8		
Right only...	—	—	2	1.9	—	—	19.2%	
Left only....	1	0.96	1	0.96	1	0.96		
Total frequencies	2	1.9	11	10.6	7	6.7		24.7%
♀ Both sides....	1	2.6	1	2.6	7	17.9		
Right only...	1	2.6	1	2.6	—	—	33.3%	
Left only....	—	—	2	5.1	—	—		
Total frequencies	2	5.1	4	10.3	7	17.9		
juv.......	—	—	—	—	—	—	—	
inf.......	—	—	1 (r+1) 1 (1)	—	3	—	—	

Summary 139.
Exostoses auriculares: actual and percental frequency.

Sex and Age	Exostoses auriculares																						
	Undeformed							Deformed according to the three modes														
								Cowichan							Chinook							Koskimo	
	Crest-shape		Pea-shape		Total	Grand total		Crest-shape		Pea-shape		Total	Grand total		Crest-shape		Pea-shape		Total	Grand total		Crest-shape		Pea-shape		Total	Grand total
	no.	%	no.	%				no.	%	no.	%				no.	%	no.	%				no.	%	no.	%		
♂ Both sides	—	—	—	—	—			1	1.1	—	—				9	15.5	6	10.3				—	—	—	—		
Right only	—	—	—	—	—			—	—	—	—	2.3%			—	—	—	—	32.8%			1	0.96	—	—	1.9%	
Left only	—	—	—	—	—			1	1.1	—	—		1.6%		3	5.2	1	1.7		23.4%		1	0.96	—	—		1.9%
Total frequencies	—	—	—	—	—			2	2.3	—	—				12	20.7	7	12.1				2	1.9	—	—		
♀ Both sides	—	—	—	—	—			—	—	—	—				3	11.5	—	—				1	2.6	—	—		
Right only	—	—	—	—	—			—	—	—	—				—	—	—	—	15.4%			—	—	—	—	2.6%	
Left only	—	—	—	—	—			—	—	—	—				1	3.8	—	—				—	—	—	—		
Total frequencies	—	—	—	—	—			—	—	—	—				4	15.4	—	—				1	2.6	—	—		
juv.	—	—	—	—	—			—	—	—	—	—			—	—	—	—	—			—	—	—	—	—	
inf.	—	—	—	—	—			—	—	—	—	—			—	—	—	—	—			—	—	—	—	—	

pea-shape exostoses, their size is at times quite considerable. Fig. 58, *a* and *b*, depicts two male Chinook cases (4470, 4513) where the ridges arise on a rather

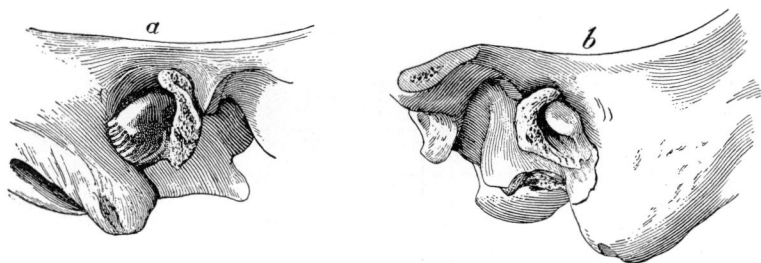

Fig. 58, *a* and *b*. Exostoses auriculares (male Chinook 4470, 4513). Natural size.

broad base from the posterior wall of the meatus, while anteriorly the tympanicum, thickened by hyperostosis, reaches up to the roof of the external meatus.

From *summary 139* it will be seen that no exostoses were recorded for the Undeformed. The general total percentage with 1.6°/₀ and 1.9°/₀ is rather insignificant in the Cowichan and Koskimo deformations, but rises to 23.4°/₀ in the Chinook. The summary furthermore shows the prevalence of crest-shape exostoses, not only as applied to the principal tribal divisions, but also to the sexes, i.e., in favor of the males. This statement is, however, not exactly true for the Koskimo, where the female percentage of crest-shape exostoses exceeds that of the males. Pea-shape exostoses were found only in the Chinook males. The immatures are entirely devoid of this anomaly.

The problem of the causation of auricular exostoses is by no means settled as yet. It is true that some sort of pathological process must be held responsible for the anomaly which again might be favored by mechanical motives such as head deformation and the wearing of heavy ear-pendants (see however, p. 246). It is generally accepted, though, that the extent of the influence of the latter is not at all confirmed since, as R. *Virchow*[152] puts it: "die stärksten Deformationen ohne Exostosen und die grössten Exostosen ohne Deformationen vorkommen". In corroboration, as it were, of this statement, the same author observes on strongly deformed Longheads from Vancouver Island (1892, 28): "Bei den Longheads von Vancouver-Island fand ich nur eigentümliche Verdickungen der Ossa tympanica, die nicht ganz denselben Charakter haben." This would be in harmony with the observations on the Koskimo of our series, whose strenuously deformed heads yielded only 1.9°/₀ of true auricular exostoses as stated above. However, the Chinook, who also practice excessive head deformation, show the anomaly in as high a percentage as 23.4°/₀, which is greatly in excess of the findings for the other series, and also for those of other authors on American material (*F. Russel*, *Hrdlička*, *Hooton*, *Fuller*, et al.). It thus appears that although artificial deformation

---

[152] *Virchow R.*, 1894. Schädel aus Süd-Amerika, insbesondere aus Argentinien und Bolivien. Zschr. Ethnol., v. XXVI, pp. 386—410 (406).

is not unequivocally responsible for auricular exostoses it may have a limited influence in their causation.

Although, according to Le Double [153], auricular exostoses occur in small percentages also in other races, and even in $1.03°/_o$ in Europeans, the highest frequency is met in American Indians, which that author determined at $8.3°/_o$ on an average (pp. 325—327).

f. Tuberculum articulare.

The size of the tuberculum articulare in man is an expression of growth and function. The accompanying *summary 140* shows most of the immatures assembled in the small class and only very few in the medium. In the adults there is also a fair percentage of small-sized tubercula, the greatest percentages going to the medium, while considerable percentages also belong to the large-sized class. All three indications bear also on the height of the tuberculum. There is an even percental occurrence, however, of the medium- and large-sized tubercula in the Undeformed at $41.2°/_o$ and $41.9°/_o$ respectively. Except in the Chinook where the male and female percentages in the medium class are alike at $48.2°/_o$, the preponderance of the female over the male percentages in the small and medium classes is quite significant. Still more so are the decidedly higher male percentages of large tubercula articularia in each of the four series, reaching the highest figure of $63.0°/_o$ in the Undeformed. The comparatively smallest male percentage here is that of the Koskimo at $40.8°/_o$, where also the females are listed lowest with only $10.3°/_o$.

Strenuous head deformation, particularly as practiced by the Chinook and Koskimo, is apparently of no consequence in the size development of the tuberculum articulare. While the total of the former at $36.9°/_o$ only slightly exceeds the Cowichan at $34.9°/_o$, the Koskimo total at $30.7°/_o$ ranges below the two, all three being peculiarly outranged by the Undeformed at $41.9°/_o$ of large tubercula. The figures do in fact suggest a negative effect of artificial head deformation upon the development of the tuberculum, and that again is in accord with the effects of increased demand upon the temporo-mandibular joint, discussed in connection with the fossa glenoidalis (see p. 194).

It may be mentioned in this connection that comparatively and racially the Neandertaloids and the Veddah of Ceylon have rather weakly developed tubercula articularia.

g. Processus postglenoidalis.

Posteriorly the glenoid fossa may be bounded by a more or less developed ridge arising from the root of the processus zygomaticus and joining with its posterior side the anterior wall of the tympanic bone in the fissura petrotympanica (*Glaseri*). In lateral aspect this ridge appears as a processus postglenoidalis (s. tuberculum articulare posterius s. tuberculum tympanicum). Where the tympanic plate assumes a more vertical position, it serves as the posterior boundary of the fossa mandibularis (s. glenoidalis) and is apt to preclude the formation of marked processus postglenoidales. This is the case in the recent skull with deep fossae where phylogenetically an anteroposterior compression has taken place, resulting in the narrowing of the subzygomatic and tympanic regions. For opposite reasons a well developed processus postglenoidalis is encountered in the anthropoid apes, the Hominidae, and among recent man

---

[153] l. c., p. 194 (325—327).

Summary 140.

Tuberculum articulare: actual and percental frequency.

Sex and Age.	Tuberculum articulare					
	Undeformed					
	Small		Medium		Large	
	no.	%	no.	%	no.	%
♂	5	6.9	22	30.1	46	63.0
♀	5	13.9	25	69.4	6	16.7
juv.	2	—	—	—	—	—
inf.	9	—	4	—	—	—
Total frequencies	21	16.9	51	41.2	52	41.9
	Cowichan deformation					
♂	7	9.6	32	43.8	34	46.6
♀	10	34.5	15	51.7	4	13.8
juv.	1	—	1	—	1	—
inf.	5	—	—	—	—	—
Total frequencies	23	21.1	48	44.0	38	34.9
	Chinook deformation					
♂	2	3.6	27	48.2	27	48.2
♀	7	25.9	13	48.2	7	25.9
juv.	2	—	1	—	—	—
inf.	6	—	—	—	—	—
Total frequencies	17	18.5	41	44.6	34	36.9
	Koskimo deformation					
♂	6	5.8	55	53.4	42	40.8
♀	7	17.9	28	71.8	4	10.3
juv.	1	—	1	—	—	—
inf.	6	—	—	—	—	—
Total frequencies	20	13.3	84	56.0	46	30.7

those possessing shallow or flat glenoid fossae, particularly the Eskimo and Eskimoid peoples. *Hooton* [154], however, points out that: "The so-called postglenoid process is dependent for its existence upon the position and form of the glenoid cavity. When the glenoid fossa is deep and situated well forward from the tympanic plate, the process is well marked; when the glenoid cavity is shallow or situated farther back and close to the tympanic plate the postglenoid process is absent or rudimentary". This clear definition explains satisfactorily the occurrence of the process in most modern races, in the statement of which *Hooton* follows *Angelotti*. [155]

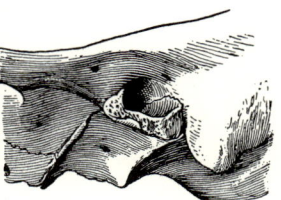

Fig. 59. Perforated processus postglenoidalis (inf. II Salish 2735). Natural size.

Processus postglenoidales of various sizes are not at all scarce in the present series, their occurrence being directly traceable to *Hooton*'s criteria. Cases of extraordinary development were not encountered. But an interesting feature was met in a number of cases in the presence of a vascular orifice upon the process. Their sizes are quite variable and at times quite large. In one case, inf. II Salish from Dungeness (2735), there was a direct communication noticed with the cranial cavity. This case is illustrated in fig. 59.

6. Fossa temporalis.

a. Sulcus sphenoparietalis.

The cleft between the frontal and temporal lobes of the cerebrum as given by the fissura cerebri lateralis (*Sylvii*) is marked externally by a longitudinal depression of the ala magna of the sphenoid and extending in cases upon the angulus sphenoidalis of the parietal bone. This depression known as fossa alaris or sulcus sphenoparietalis represents in its stronger development a progressive morphological character depending mostly on the increasing size and lateral expansion of the temporal lobe.

In the present studies the depressions referred to are treated collectively in *summary 141* as sulcus sphenoparietalis, which was furthermore defined as: shallow, medium and deep. The greatest number of cases are seen listed as medium in the Undeformed at 56.0°/₀, and the Cowichan and Chinook deformations at 53.1°/₀ and 48.9°/₀ respectively. The shallow and deep sulci are quite equally represented in the Undeformed, while there is a strong preponderance of the former in the Cowichan at 37.2°/₀ against their deep sulci at only 9.7°/₀, and in the Chinook at 30.4°/₀ as against 20.7°/₀. The findings in the Koskimo division differ considerably in as much as deep sulci do not occur here, while shallow ones reach the high frequency of 72.5°/₀, leaving only 27.5°/₀ to the medium class. The immatures of the Koskimo have only shallow sulci while in the other divisions they are almost equally divided between the shallow and medium.

---

[154] *Hooton, E. A.*, 1918. On certain Eskimoid characters in Icelandic skulls. Am. Journ. Phys. Anthrop. v. I, pp. 53—76 (64).

[155] *Angelotti, Guido*, 1909. Variazioni e lacune nella "pars tympanica" del temporale. Atti Soc. Rom. Antrop., v. XV, pp. 35—53.

Summary 141.

Sulcus sphenoparietalis: actual and percental frequency.

Sex and Age	Sulcus sphenoparietalis					
	Undeformed					
	Shallow		Medium		Deep	
	no.	%	no.	%	no.	%
♂	15	19.2	44	56.4	19	24.4
♀	3	9.4	18	56.3	11	34.3
juv.	1	—	1	—	—	—
inf.	6	—	7	—	—	—
Total frequencies	25	20.0	70	56.0	30	24.0
	Cowichan deformation					
♂	25	32.1	43	55.1	10	12.8
♀	15	51.7	13	44.8	1	3.5
juv.	—	—	1	—	—	—
inf.	2	—	3	—	—	—
Total frequencies	42	37.2	60	53.1	11	9.7
	Chinook deformation					
♂	17	29.3	29	50.0	12	20.7
♀	6	25.0	1	45.8	7	29.2
juv.	2	—	2	—	—	—
inf.	3	—	3	—	—	—
Total frequencies	28	30.4	35	48.9	19	20.7
	Koskimo deformation					
♂	71	68.9	32	31.1	—	—
♀	27	75.0	9	25.0	—	—
juv.	2	—	—	—	—	—
inf.	8	—	—	—	—	—
Total frequencies	108	72.5	41	27.5	—	—

The Koskimo findings immediately raise the question of deformatory influences. It seems quite probable that their mode of deformation causing the elongation of the brain and its lateral applanation would also bear on the outer relief of the skull in such a way as to hinder the formation of a sulcus sphenoparietalis. Astonishingly small, on the other hand, is the percentage of deep fossae in the Chinook and even that of 9.7% in the Cowichan as against 24.8% in the Undeformed. Anteroposterior compression, even if rigidly applied as in the Chinook, seems, therefore, also to have a prohibitive influence upon the development of a well marked sulcus when compared with the relatively high percentage of deep sulci in the Undeformed. The present writer is at a loss how to explain this phenomenon, all the more so since the visual examination of the Chinook conditions seemed to reveal a narrowing in the longitudinal sense of the fossa temporalis. In the Undeformed, on the other hand, there is to be noticed an unquestionable tendency toward a true sulcus in response to cerebral expansion. For it is a generally acknowledged fact that the expansive power of the brain is considerably more effectual in bringing about the external and, of course, the internal reliefs of the skull than muscular traction. And in the latter category mechanical influences such as deformation may in a certain sense also be counted.

b. Sutura sphenoparietalis and stenocrotaphy

The sutura sphenoparietalis in which, as a specific anthropine characteristic, the parietal bone and the ala magna of the sphenoid articulate, is as a rule well developed in the normal skull.

From *summary 142* it will be seen that its individual length may rise as high as 26 mm. in individual cases. Throughout the series the right and left sutures were found to differ. The averages reach their highest figures in the males of the Cowichan deformation with 12.9 mm. on the right, and 13.0 mm. on the left side, the females amounting to 10.6 mm. and 11.2 mm. Similar ratios, i. e., the males slightly exceeding the females, recur in the Chinook and Koskimo series. An exception from this order is noticed in the Undeformed where the female values exceed the male. A tendency toward shorter sutures may be seen in the Chinook and Koskimo deformations, a statement which to some extent will be affirmed later in the discussion of stenocrotaphy. The averages of the immatures, on account of their small numbers, are not exactly comparable to the status of the matures. It will be noticed, however, that the infantiles present rather high figures, which reach even 26 mm. in an individual case of the Undeformed.

The differences between the right and left averages are listed in column three of *summary 142*, indicated by plus and minus signs, which signify right or left predominance of measure. The positions vary somewhat. Thus, while in the Undeformed the right suture throughout exceeds the left in length, this order is reversed in the Cowichan deformation, only the infantiles being excepted. A similar condition prevails in the Koskimo whose minus order is interrupted by the female status of right equalling left. In the Chinook division right is seen to predominate in the females and infantiles, while left rules in the males and juveniles. Altogether the differences between the right and left averages are rather inconspicuous in the adults, although slightly greater in the immatures.

Special attention was devoted to the occurrence and frequency of stenocrotaphy in the present series. Designating a hypoplastic condition of the ala magna, stenocrotaphy is indicated

Summary 142.

Sutura sphenoparietalis: actual and percental frequency.

Sex and Age	Sutura sphenoparietalis							Stenocrotaphy 3—0 mm.		
	Undeformed									
	Right		Left		Difference of averages		Right	Left	Bilateral
	Average	Range	Average	Range	+	—			
	mm.									
♂	11.6	2—18	11.5	3—19	0.1	—	0.8%	1.6%	0.8%
♀	13.2	7—21	12.8	3—22	0.4	—			
juv.	13.5	9; 18	11.0	11	2.5	—			
inf.	17.2	6—26	14.7	6—22	2.5	—			
	Cowichan deformation									
♂	12.9	2—24	13.0	2—20	—	0.1	0.9%	2.8%	0.9%
♀	10.6	5—15	11.2	2—17	—	0.6			
juv.	11.0	5; 17	12.2	6—15	—	1.2			
inf.	13.0	13	10.7	9—12	2.3	—			
	Chinook deformation									
♂	11.9	2—25	12.2	3—24	—	0.3	1.6%	1.6%	—
♀	10.3	2—19	10.0	2—17	0.3	—			
juv.	8.6	6—13	10.0	6—12	—	1.4			
inf.	14.0	9—20	13.1	8—19	0.9	—			
	Koskimo deformation									
♂	10.7	2—22	10.8	2—21	—	0.1	5.2%	3.0%	1.5%
♀	10.4	2—15	10.4	3—15	—	—			
juv.	8.3	3—11	10.2	6—16	—	2.0			
inf.	10.2	7—13	13.3	8—20	—	3.1			

by a reduction of the sutura sphenoparietalis to the length of 3—0 mm.[156]. The last three columns of *summary 142* contain the percental records of stenocrotaphitic conditions occurring either separately on the right and left sides or simultaneously on both. The percentages rise slightly but somewhat irregularly in the order of the summary, the left side exceeding the right in the Undeformed and Cowichan deformation. The Chinook have equal percentages, but the right side predominates in the markedly higher ones of the Koskimo. This is made still clearer in the percentages of simultaneous occurrence which, however slight, progresses steadily from 0.8% in the Undeformed to 0.9% in the Cowichan, and 1.5% in the Koskimo. The Chinook are devoid of such occurrences.

[156] See *R. Virchow*, l. c., p. 235 (52).

A stenocrotaphitic tendency in normal, i. e., undeformed skulls, seems to be a racial trait in certain human varieties, such as *Kleiweg de Zwaan* [157] found in skulls from the island of Nias. It is quite probable on the other hand that artificial deformation bears upon the production of this feature, although the excessively deformed Chinook and Koskimo skulls might have been expected to show higher percentages of it, while *R. Martin* [158] states that in ancient Patagonian skulls deformation is not causal for the narrowing of the ala magna.

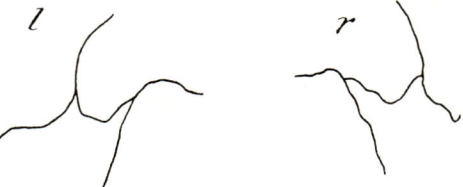

Fig. 60. Sutura sphenoparietalis encroaching upon the ala magna (female Haida 3742). Natural size.

In most cases the course of the suture is straight, but in a number of others it exhibits a marked downward concavity in the deformed skulls as well as the undeformed ones. Under such conditions the sphenoid angle of the parietal bone appears to project well into the upper end of the ala magna. The case illustrated in fig. 60 is that of a Haida female (3742).

c. Os epiptericum.

In *summary 143* only the true cases of epiptericum have been accounted for. In its true state the epiptericum is inserted between the four bones: frontal, parietal, squama temporalis and ala magna of the sphenoid, and joined to them by the suturae epipterico-frontalis, epipterico-parietalis, epipterico-squamosa, and epipterico-sphenoidalis. If incomplete, one or more of those connections are wanting. But even under such conditions the epiptericum betrays its derivation from a fontanelle bone that is destined to fill up the membranous interval of the infantile skull at the area of juncture of the four bones named above. But it may also be traced to an accessory membranous element that in man appears independently above the cartilaginous alisphenoid, and to which *Ranke* has called attention. True epipterica occurring in the male Nanaimo and Nootka skulls (1628, 4565) are instanced in fig. 61, *b* and *e*, all the other cases in that figure being spurious. The downward concave course of the sphenoparietal suture as referred to in the last paragraph of the preceding section and illustrated anew in fig. 61, *a* taken from a female Kwakiutl skull (4252), is probably a case of irregular ossification, influenced by deformation. From the genetic standpoint it does not seem improbable that the depressed sphenoparietal suture represents the epipterico-sphenoidal

---

[157] *Kleiweg de Zwaan, J. P.*, 1915. Die Insel Nias bei Sumatra: Kraniologische Untersuchungen niassischer Schädel. Haag. p. 37.

[158] *Martin, Rudolf*, 1896. Altpatagonische Schädel. Vierteljschr. Naturf. Ges. Zürich, v. XLI, pp. 496—539 (511).

Fig. 61. Various formations in the fonticulus sphenoidalis region, of which b and e are true epipterica in male Nanaimo and Nootka skulls (1628, 4565). a, c, d, f and g are spurious epipterica, in a female Kwakiutl (4252), an infantile Chinook (4485), a male Eskimo (3769), a male Nootka (4465) and an infantile Koskimo (3645). e and f, and g and h show bilaterally dissimilar formations, h presenting a true processus frontalis of the temporal squama. r, l, right, left. Natural size.

suture, and that the epipterico-parietal suture is fully obliterated through the coalescence of the parietal angulus sphenoidalis and the epipteric fontanelle bone. In the case under consideration this seems to be particularly confirmed by the sharp inturn of the coronal suture which helps to demarcate the upper boundary of what might have become a true epiptericum. In fig. 61, c and d, two incomplete epipterica of a similar kind are shown, a large one and a small one, both being devoid of connection with the squama temporalis. They were seen in an infantile Chinook (4485) and in a male Eskimo skull (3769). Differing conditions upon the two sides of the skull may be seen represented in fig. 61, e and f, and g and h, which are those of a male Nootka (4465) and an infantile Koskimo (3645). In e a true epiptericum exists on the right side, while on the left (f) a peculiar oval-shape and horizontally oriented sutural bone, with its strongly tapering end directed backward, presents itself. While from the standpoint of classification we have to deal here with a Wormian bone, the nature of fig. 61, g, is again doubtful and additionally complicated by a small processus frontalis which, as

Summary 143.
Os epiptericum: actual and percental frequency.

Sex and Age	Os epiptericum Undeformed						Total	Grand total
	Small		Medium		Large			
	no.	%	no.	%	no.	%		
♂ Both sides....	—	—	—	—	—	—	7.5%	6.2%
Right only ...	—	—	2	2.5	1	1.6		
Left only	—	—	1	1.6	2	2.5		
Total frequencies	—	—	3	3.8	3	3.8		
♀ Both sides....	—	—	—	—	1	2.9	5.9%	
Right only ...	—	—	1	2.9	—	—		
Left only	—	—	—	—	—	—		
Total frequencies	—	—	1	2.9	1	2.9		
juv.......	—	—	—	—	—	—		
inf.......	1	—	—	—	—	—		
Cowichan deformation								
♂ Both sides....	—	—	1	1.1	3	3.5	10.2%	9.5%
Right only ...	—	—	—	—	1	1.1		
Left only	1	1.1	1	1.1	2	2.3		
Total frequencies	1	1.1	2	2.3	6	6.8		
♀ Both sides....	1	3.4	—	—	1	3.4	10.3%	
Right only ...	—	—	—	—	—	—		
Left only	—	—	1	3.4	—	—		
Total frequencies	1	3.4	1	3.4	1	3.4		
juv.......	—	—	—	—	—	—		
inf.......	—	—	—	—	—	—		
Chinook deformation								
♂ Both sides....	—	—	2	3.4	1	1.7	10.3%	8.5%
Right only ...	—	—	—	—	1	1.7		
Left only	—	—	—	—	2	3.4		
Total frequencies	—	—	2	3.4	4	6.9		
♀ Both sides....	—	—	—	—	—	—	7.7%	
Right only ...	—	—	1	3.8	1	3.8		
Left only	—	—	—	—	—	—		
Total frequencies	—	—	1	3.8	1	3.8		
juv.......	—	—	—	—	1	—		
inf.......	—	—	2	—	—	—		
Koskimo deformation								
♂ Both sides....	1	0.96	—	—	—	—	6.7%	6.5%
Right only ...	2	1.96	1	0.96	2	1.96		
Left only	—	—	—	—	1	0.96		
Total frequencies	3	2.9	1	0,96	3	2.9		
♀ Both sides....	—	—	—	—	—	—	7.7%	
Right only ...	—	—	—	—	1	2.6		
Left only	—	—	1	2.6	1	2.6		
Total frequencies	—	—	1	2.6	2	5.1		
juv.......	—	—	—	—	—	—		
inf.......	—	—	1	—	1	—		

such, is of considerable size on the left side (h) of this Koskimo skull. From *summary 143* it will be seen that unilateral occurrence of the epiptericum is more frequent than bilateral. There is also a predominance of the larger-sized bones and of the male over the female frequencies. The total percentages are at 6.2% and 6.5% alike in the Undeformed and Koskimo. The Cowichan and Chinook deformations attain higher percentages of 9.5% and 8.5%, denoting hereby a preponderance of true cases in the skulls of anteroposterior deformation. Further reference on this condition will be made in the chapter on sutures and ossa suturarum.

7. Fossa infratemporalis.

a. Crista infratemporalis.

b. Tuberculum spinosum.

Different stages of development were noticed also in some of the details of the fossa infratemporalis. Dividing the latter from the fossa temporalis, the crista infratemporalis was observed either to be absent, or to show slight, medium or pronounced development as indicated in *summary 144*.

It is rather significant that absence of the crista obtains in 5.3% in the Undeformed against noticeably smaller percentages in the deformed divisions, dropping even to 0.9% in the Cowichan. Considering this, and taking the development of the crista as an expression of the muscular action of m. pterygoideus externus, it is interesting on the other hand to notice that the pronounced development of the crista infratemporalis yields the highest percentage of 23.0% in the Undeformed, and the lowest at 6.0% in the Koskimo deformation. The high percentage of pronounced occurrence in the Cowichan and Chinook seems to be due to their special mode of deformation. It is in the Chinook also that the highest percentage of medium development is found with 50.5% as against 43.1% in the Cowichan. But the Koskimo at 49.7% are on an equal basis with the Chinook, while the Undeformed at 42.5% conform with the Cowichan. Cristae of slight development are encountered at about equal percentages of 42.2% and 41.6% in the Cowichan and Koskimo divisions. Lesser percentages at 26.9% and 29.2% are those of the Chinook and Undeformed. Altogether it appears that the cristae of medium development predominate in the four divisions, and that the oscillations in the pronounced and absent stages show certain graded affinities to the different modes of deformation. A high percentage of strongly developed cristae, however, could be stated for the Undeformed. Female percentages from a general angle exceed the male in the absent and slight stages, while the reverse order holds true for the medium and pronounced stages. But it should be observed that absences were not registered in the Cowichan and Koskimo males, nor are they accounted for in the Chinook males and females. The immatures show to the greater extent a slight-to-medium development of the crista infratemporalis.

In appearance the crista very rarely represents a continuous horizontal ridge. Much more frequently a number of more or less sharply projecting tubercles are met with, or a number of vertically directed smaller ridges. Tubercular projections of a more distinct order are usually seen adjoining the sutura sphenosquamosa and at the anterior end of the crista, at and in

Summary 144.

Crista infratemporalis: actual and percental frequency.

Sex and Age	Crista infratemporalis							
	Undeformed							
	Absent		Slight		Medium		Pronounced	
	no.	%	no.	%	no.	%	no.	%
♂	3	4.2	13	18.3	32	45.1	23	32.4
♀	1	3.6	11	39.3	13	46.4	3	10.7
juv.	—	—	1	—	1	—	—	—
inf.	2	—	8	—	2	—	—	—
Total frequencies	6	5.3	33	29.2	48	42.5	26	23.0
	Cowichan deformation							
♂	—	—	31	36.9	38	45.2	15	17.9
♀	1	4.2	13	54.2	10	41.7	—	—
juv.	—	—	—	—	1	—	1	—
inf.	—	—	5	—	1	—	—	—
Total frequencies	1	0.9	49	42.2	50	43.1	16	13.8
	Chinook deformation							
♂	—	—	9	15.8	31	54.4	17	29.8
♀	—	—	11	42.3	13	50.0	2	7.7
juv.	—	—	2	—	2	—	—	—
inf.	2	—	3	—	1	—	—	—
Total frequencies	2	2.2	25	26.9	47	50.5	19	20.4
	Koskimo deformation							
♂	—	—	36	35.0	58	56.3	9	8.7
♀	3	8.4	18	50.0	15	41.6	—	—
juv.	—	—	1	—	1	—	—	—
inf.	1	—	7	—	—	—	—	—
Total frequencies	4	2.7	62	41.6	74	49.7	9	6.0

continuation of the crista sphenomaxillaris. This latter projection is known as the tuberculum spinosum which, as a place of muscular origin, appears to be still more variable than the crista infratemporalis.

The tuberculum spinosum reveals in its state of pronounced development certain analogies with the development of the crista infratemporalis.

Its highest and lowest frequencies, as may be gained from *summary 145*, are also met with in the same divisions, namely, $51.3°/_0$ in the Undeformed, and $33.8°/_0$ in the Koskimo. Of the two remaining divisions, the Chinook attain $48.3°/_0$, thus approximating the Undeformed, and the Cowichan $40.7°/_0$, which places them about halfway between the Koskimo and Chinook. The other extreme of slight development — absence does not occur in any of the divisions — is least represented in the Cowichan at $5.3°/_0$, and at fairly equal percentages of $7.7°/_0$ and $8.8°/_0$, and $8.9°/_0$ in the Chinook, Koskimo and Undeformed.

The medium-sized tuberculum is the predominating one as stated similarly for the crista infratemporalis, although the tubercula of pronounced development are rather an outstanding condition in the Undeformed, and predominate slightly also in the Chinook. It is quite significant that with regard to sex differences the female percentages exceed the male in the classes of slight and medium development, but range below them in the pronounced stage. It must be pointed out, however, that no cases of slight development were listed in the Undeformed and Chinook females. The immatures exhibit somewhat variable conditions of either equal distribution among the slight and medium stages as in the Undeformed; or, of higher frequency of medium-sized tubercula as in the Cowichan and Koskimo deformations; or, of higher frequency in those of slight development as in the Chinook. But there are also several immatures listed with pronounced tubercula.

The tuberculum spinosum is appropriately so termed on account of its spine-like appearance. Individual cases of extraordinary sizes are naturally encountered in the divisions that yield the greatest percental frequencies. Thus the Chinook were found to be possessed of rather large-sized tubercula. An exceedingly large tubercle of about 8—10 mm. in height was seen in a Nanaimo male (1628).

Notwithstanding the fact, however, that the Undeformed yielded the highest percentage of tubercula of pronounced size, visual observation proved that in most cases excessive sizes were met in the deformed skulls, particularly those of the Cowichan and Chinook.

c. Crista infraorbitalis.

In connection with the preceding features another might be discussed here which belongs rather to the norma frontalis, were it not for its bearing on the region under discussion. The crista infraorbitalis, which forms the lower margin of the orbital surface of the sphenoid bone, is as a rule smooth,

Summary *145*.

Tuberculum spinosum: actual and percental frequency.

Sex and Age	Tuberculum spinosum					
	Undeformed					
	Slight		Medium		Pronounced	
	no.	%	no.	%	no.	%
♂	3	4.1	25	34.3	45	61.6
♀	—	—	13	50.0	13	50.5
juv.	1	—	1	—	—	—
inf.	6	—	6	—	—	—
Total frequencies	10	8.9	45	39.8	58	51.3
	Cowichan deformation					
♂	3	3.9	36	46.1	39	50.0
♀	2	6.9	20	69.0	7	24.1
juv.	—	—	1	—	—	—
inf.	1	—	4	—	—	—
Total frequencies	6	5.3	61	54.0	46	40.7
	Chinook deformation					
♂	2	3.6	22	40.0	31	56.4
♀	—	—	15	57.7	11	42.3
juv.	2	—	1	—	1	—
inf.	3	—	2	—	1	—
Total frequencies	7	7.7	40	44.0	44	48.3
	Koskimo deformation					
♂	5	5.1	54	55.1	39	39.8
♀	4	10.0	25	62.5	11	27.5
juv.	—	—	2	—	—	—
inf.	4	—	4	—	—	—
Total frequencies	13	8.8	85	57.4	50	33.8

setting off that surface against the sphenomaxillary one of the same bone which is parallel to the former but removed slightly backwards. As a crest it forms the upper boundary of the fissura orbitalis inferior. Although a systematic investigation of this formation was not undertaken, an interesting deviation from the normal was nevertheless noticed in the Koskimo division, and principally in the Koskimo themselves. The crista infraorbitalis acquires here at times the appearance of a true lamina of considerable size, doubtless the result of deformation. Thus while the gap of the inferior orbital fissure is widened by the strain of artificial deformation, a stimulus was afforded at the same time for the crista infraorbitalis to moderate that gap by increasing growth. An illustration of the feature, quite marked in the Koskimo division, as already mentioned, and especially in the Koskimo themselves, may be seen in fig. 62 of a female Koskimo (3841),

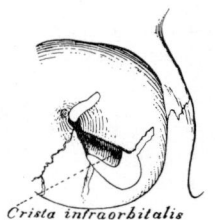

Fig. 62. Crista infraorbitalis in a female Koskimo (3841). Natural size.

8. Regio zygomatica.

a. Arcus zygomaticus.

Four distinct forms of the arcus zygomaticus were seen to occur in our series with a certain constancy. They are illustrated in fig 63, *a–d* and represent cases from the series under investigation. The distinguishing feature here is the upper edge of the zygomatic bridge, which in fig. 63, *a*, male Bellacoola (4542), is marked by a total though slight concavity; in *b*, male Nimkish (1671), a rather straight outline is represented which appears modified in *c*, male Spences Bridge (Upper Thompson) (99), in such a way that above the tuberculum articulare the upper edge slopes downward to form a short curve, rising again simultaneously with the lower outline. In lateral projection the zygomatic arch has thus the appearance of a band whose straight course is slightly changed by a downward turn after which it rises again going above the original level.[159] The fourth form, as illustrated in fig. 63, *d*, male Kwakiutl (3885), is in a way the most interesting since it resembles conditions found in certain apes, particularly the gorilla. The greater part of the upper outline of the arch is curved into a more or less regular convexity which begins its gradual ascent from the point of issue of the processus frontosphenoidalis and temporalis of the zygomatic bone, to become continuous with the upper outline

---

[159] A modification of *c* rather than an independent type in our series lies in the insignificant rising of the anterior portion of the zygomatic arch in connection with the posterior downward turn. It occurs as a distinct type, according to *Fr. Sarasin*, l. c., p. 207 (228), in the New Caledonians, where 45% of the upper margin represents a „Wellenform, mit einer hinteren, nach unten und einer vorderen, nach oben gerichteten Konvexität".

of the processus zygomaticus of the temporal squama. The starting point just mentioned corresponds to the vertex of an angle which may be appropriately termed angulus zygomaticotemporalis, *Lebzelter*[160] simply referring to it as "Beugestelle" of the two processes mentioned.

The form of the arcus zygomaticus just described has been likened by the cousins *Sarasin* to a bent handle and, therefore, called "Henkelform" It is, according to them, predominant in the Veddah, while *Klaatsch* claims

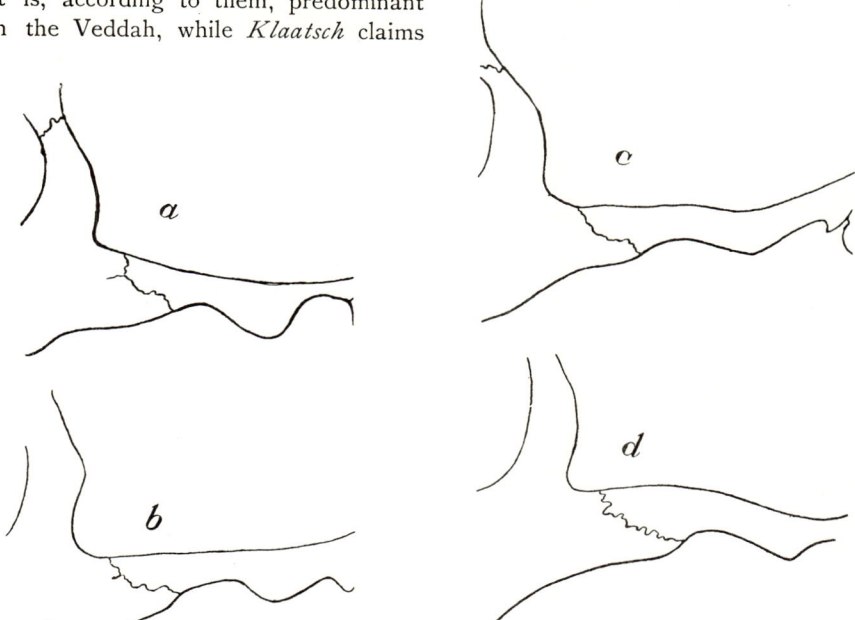

Fig. 63. Showing four typical forms of the arcus zygomaticus; *a*, upper border concave, in a male Bellacoola (4542); *b*, straight, in a male Nimkish (1671); *c*, sloping posteriorly, in a male skull from Spences Bridge, Upper Thompson (99); *d*, "Henkelform", in a male Kwakiutl (3885)? About natural size.

it to be a characteristic feature of the Neandertaloids and Australians. But it has also been found in several other races, according to *R. Martin* (Lehrbuch, 1914, 732) in the Senoi, Ainu, Negroes, Egyptians and New Caledonians. It is unlike simian forms, however, in so far as the vertex point of the convex upper edge is situated somewhat more foreward in the human skull, i. e., about in line with the lower end of the zygomaticotemporal suture, while in the simian skull it is in line either with the deepest point of the underside concavity, or may even fall into the area of the tuberculum articulare.

---

[160] *Lebzelter, Viktor*, 1913. Morphologische Untersuchungen über die Jochbogengegend und deren Beziehungen zur Frankfurter Horizontalebene. Mitt. Anthrop. Ges. Wien, v. XLIII (3. ser., v. XIII), pp. 325—342 (334).

These condition are illustrated in fig. 64, where the outline of fig. 63, d, reduced in size to conform with that of a Gorilla gina (*Lebzelter*, p. 335), appears in superposition, oriented according to the ear-eye plane, the anguli zygomaticotemporales being adjusted to a vertical. Disregarding the different degrees of vertical or sagittal orbital declination, it will be noticed that the simian angulus falls below the line of orientation, which is rather typical in the apes and which will be referred to again under section b of this chapter. Since the human angle lies above the plane line, and both outlines rise from the vertices of their respective angles, it is apparent that the simian curve reaches a greater height than the human. The vertex points of their concave outlines are indicated by verticals which at the same time mark the points at the lower outlines through which they pass.

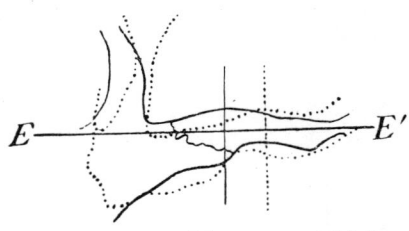

Fig. 64. Superposition of the arcus zygomatici of a male Kwakiutl (3885) of fig. 63, and a Gorilla gina, their sizes adjusted, to show the differences of the "Henkelform". —male Kwatiutl; ...... Gorilla gina (*Lebzelter, Viktor*, l. c., p. 267 (335)).

The straight form of the arcus zygomaticus appears also in *Klaatsch*'s [161] comparative figure and is assigned there to the Negro of West Africa, while the modification of the straight form, fig. 63, c, is designated by him as Japanese.

Turning now to the frequency of the different forms in *summary 146*, it will be noticed that the concave form (*a*) yields the highest percentages in the deformed divisions. The Chinook at 64.8% considerably exceed the Cowichan at 44.6%. One is tempted to attribute this condition to the effects of intensive deformation, all the more so since it is already apparent in the immatures of the Chinook, all of which are assembled here, as are the greater number of the Cowichan. The concave arch is likewise found in the Koskimo deformation, whose percental frequency of 39.4% falls below that of the other divisions, but nevertheless is the highest in their own. The straight arcus (*b*) attains here a frequency of 37.8%, and thus almost equals the percentage of the Koskimo for the concave form. The rather small Cowichan and Chinook figures of 31.3% and 12.5% for the straight arcus as over against their high frequencies of concaveness is significant, thus corroborating what has just been said about the effects of their specific modes of deformation. The modification of the straight arcus as represented by type *c*, has its lowest frequency in the deformed series which, on the other hand, were shown to have their highest occurrence with the concave arches. This is particularly true of the Chinook whose very high percentage of concave arcus exceeds not only the other figures of that series but of all the others too. The Undeformed percentages can serve in a limited way only as a key to the conditions as met in the deformed divisions. The concave arcus occurs there also at an appreciable percentage of 20.2% which, although considerably less than those for the deformed divisions, slightly mitigates their importance, but serves to show that an *a priori* existing peculiarity may be greatly enforced by mechanical influences. Higher and fairly equal percentages are attained by the forms *b* and *c* at 33.9% and 34.9%. The latter as the relatively highest Undeformed percentage in a way emphasizes the Mongoloid form of *Klaatsch*'s table mentioned above. It is this form which in the deformed skulls has quite probably added to the number of concave arcus, which themselves have suffered an exaggeration there.

---

[161] l. c., p. 236 (405).

Summary 146.

Arcus zygomaticus: actual and percental frequency.

Sex and Age	Arcus zygomaticus							
	Undeformed							
	a		b		c		d	
	Upper edge straight		Upper edge concave		Upper edge slightly convex		Upper edge pronouncedly convex	
	no.	%	no.	%	no.	%	no.	%
♂	17	25.8	13	19.7	27	40.9	9	13.6
♀	12	37.5	9	28.1	8	25.0	3	9.4
juv.	1	—	1	—	—	—	—	—
inf.	1	—	3	—	—	—	—	—
Total frequencies	31	33.9	26	20.2	35	34.9	12	11.0
	Cowichan deformation							
♂	21	31.3	27	40.3	17	25.4	2	3.0
♀	6	31.6	10	52.6	3	15.8	—	—
juv.	1	—	1	—	—	—	—	—
inf.	1	—	3	—	—	—	—	—
Total frequencies	29	31.5	41	44.6	20	21.7	2	2.2
	Chinook deformation							
♂	9	15.8	32	56.2	15	26.3	1	1.7
♀	2	9.1	16	72.7	4	18.2	—	—
juv.	—	—	3	—	—	—	—	—
inf.	—	—	6	—	—	—	—	—
Total frequencies	11	12.5	57	64.8	19	21.6	1	1.1
	Koskimo deformation							
♂	35	38.5	38	41.7	18	19.8	—	—
♀	10	33.3	11	36.7	9	30.0	—	—
juv.	2	—	—	—	—	—	—	—
inf.	1	—	1	—	2	—	—	—
Total frequencies	48	37.8	50	39.4	29	22.8	—	—

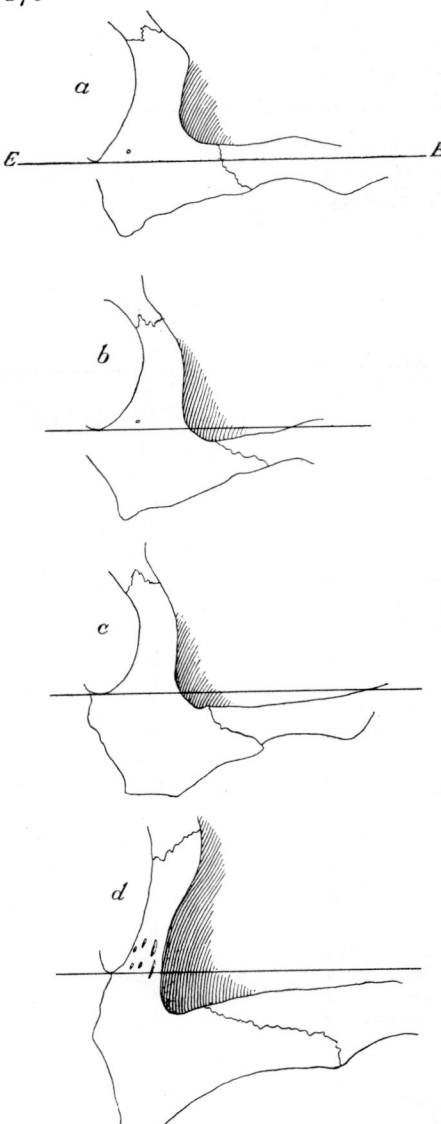

The simian or "Henkelform" (*d*) is represented by as many as 11.0% in the Undeformed and, compared with this, by the astonishingly small percentages of 2.2% in the Cowichan and 1.1% in the Chinook, while the Koskimo are entirely devoid of it. Whether such scarcities can justifiably be attributed to the more or less direct work of mechanical influences, is quite difficult to decide.

b. Angulus zygomaticotemporalis.

The angulus zygomaticotemporalis, so named above (see p. 267), is formed by the processus frontosphenoidalis and temporalis of the zygomatic bone. Its relative position to the ear-eye plane is of interest, since at times it falls below that line of orientation in reminiscence of phylogenetically inferior stages. The depressed position of the angulus involves also the entire arcus zygomaticus or part of it, or it may be restricted to the latter, as shown by *Lebzelter* [162] for the Bushmen. It is a characteristic of the apes, hence, about the relative position of the arcus to the line of orientation, *Lebzelter* (p. 335) could write: ".... er divergiert von ihr um so mehr, je tiefer der Affe im System steht". From the descriptive morphologic point of view *Gorjanović-Kramberger* [163] holds that similar conditions in the Krapina fossils are caused by the low position of the nasofrontal suture and the size of the frontosphenoid process. While now the ontogenic and phylogenetic nature of this feature is quite clear, its value as a racial character is rather limited.

Fig. 65. Showing the angulus zygomaticotemporalis above the ear-eye plane as in *a*, of a male Eskimo (3715), or below it as in *b–d*, of a male Eskimo (3711), a male Chinook (4447) and an Orang-utan (124). $E–E'$, ear-eye plane. Two-thirds.

---

[162] l. c., p. 267 (337).
[163] *Gorjanović-Kramberger, Karl*, 1906. Der diluviale Mensch von Krapina in Kroatien. Wiesbaden, pp. 113–104.

Of the few cases recorded in our material those of a male Eskimo (3711) and a male Chinook (4447) are depicted in fig. 65, *b* and *c*. They are inserted between *a*, male Eskimo (3715), with the line of orientation passing through the middle of the arcus, and *b*, an Orang-utan (124), where it passes considerably above the entire arcus. The two cases *b* and *c* are illustrative of the conditions described here as anomalous and approaching those in the Orang-utan. Applying in these two cases *Gorjanović-Kramberger*'s diagnostic criterea, — the relative positions of the orbitale and porion points, and the cephalo-orbital volumen indices (*Mantegazza*) as followed up by *Lebzelter*, — it might be stated: that a lower position of the nasofrontal suture as measured from the nasion to a median point on a line connecting the two upper orbital margins is not evident here. The measurements amounting to 7 mm. in the Chinook and 9 mm. in the Eskimo represent about medium conditions in the respective series. His second criterion, that of uncommon size of the frontosphenoidal process of the zygomatic bone, might be modified in so far as it is rather the posterior border of the process the length of which exceeds that of the anterior border, thus bringing about the depressed position of the angulus. The anterior border and also the orbital height seem ontogenetically of small importance.

It will be difficult to decide whether artificial head deformation exerts any influence in the development of this character. Judging by its occurrence also in the normal skull, it may be safe to say that its development was favored by deformation.

c. Processus marginalis.

In *summary 147* the percental frequency of large-sized processes beginning with those or about 6 mm. in height, is of particular interest. Extreme sizes not being present, the frequency of large processes is rather high at 31.4% in the Undeformed, and 36.9% in the Chinook. On a markedly lower level are seen those of the Cowichan and Koskimo with 19.1% and 21.4% respectively. A certain conformity, in the reverse order, however, in the two last named divisions, will also be noticed in the percentages of medium-sized processes. This category contains in fact the greatest frequencies as compared with the categories of small- and large-sized processes. It is not astonishing, however, that, from a general viewpoint, for the small and partly the medium ones the female percentages predominate, while for the large the opposite order obtains. The fact here is quite significant that the high percentage of 36.9% for the large-sized processes in the Chinook is prompted by the occurrence of three immatures in that category, while as a rule these latter possess mostly small and medium processes.

It seems not improbable that in the individual the development of the processus marginalis is influenced by artificial head deformation, particularly in the Chinook, where the strongly distorted area of origin of the temporal fascia exercises greater functional demands anteriorly. But, although the graded percentages here exhibit an obvious increase in the order of the summary, as compared, for instance, with the Undeformed status, the other division of excessive deformation, the Koskimo, shows quite a reverse order. The high

Summary *147*.

Processus marginalis: actual and percental frequency.

Sex and Age	Processus marginalis					
	Undeformed					
	Small		Medium		Large	
	no.	%	no.	%	no.	%
♂	11	14.9	34	45.9	29	39.2
♀	13	39.4	12	36.4	8	24.2
juv.	1	—	—	—	—	—
inf.	9	—	3	—	1	—
Total frequencies	34	28.1	49	40.5	38	31.4
	Cowichan deformation					
♂	18	22.2	43	53.1	20	24.7
♀	11	47.8	11	47.8	1	4.5
juv.	1	—	1	—	—	—
inf.	1	—	3	—	—	—
Total frequencies	31	28.2	58	52.7	21	19.1
	Chinook deformation					
♂	58	14.8	23	42.6	23	42.6
♀	25	17.8	15	53.6	8	28.6
juv.	3	—	—	—	1	—
inf.	2	—	2	—	2	—
Total frequencies	18	19.6	40	43.5	34	36.9
	Koskimo deformation					
♂	24	24.5	52	53.1	22	22.4
♀	12	34.2	15	42.9	8	22.9
juv.	1	—	2	—	—	—
inf.	2	—	2	—	—	—
Total frequencies	39	27.9	71	50.7	30	21.4

frequency of large-sized processes in the Undeformed is likewise liable to discredit the theory of deformatory effects.

d. Sutura transversozygomatica.

This suture, illustrative of a bipartite os zygomaticum is, in the present series, extant only in a residual form. While in its complete and typical appearance it divides the corpus of the zygomatic bone horizontally from the middle of the sutura zygomaticomaxillaris to the middle of the sutura zygomaticotemporalis, traces of it, invariably in connection with the latter, were found as simple indications or residual sutures of varying lengths. The former are marked as acutely angular indentations of the sutura zygomaticotemporalis as illustrated in fig. 66, *a*, male Nicola Lake (2611). Such indentations are also the rule where residual sutures occur as depicted in fig. 66, *b* and *c*, juv. Yakima (4319) and male Nanaimo (1624). In the latter, the lengths of the residual sutures amount to 5 mm. and 7 mm. upon the right and left sides of the skull.

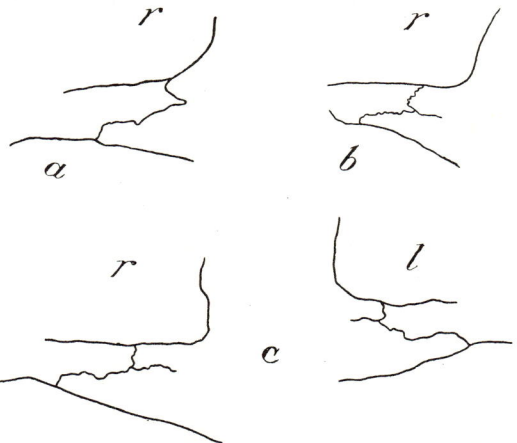

Fig. 66. Showing different stages of the sutura transversozygomatica, in a male skull from Nicola Lake (2611); a juvenile Yakima (4319) and a male Nanaimo (1624). *r, l*, right left. Natural size.

Simultaneous occurrence, however, is not invariably the rule, as may be seen from the adjoining *summary 148*, although the greater number of cases occur as such.

The total percentages, combining the unilateral and bilateral occurrences, are predominant with 13.2% and 12.7% in the Undeformed and Cowichan. Distinctly higher percentages of 18.2% and 20.8% are attained by the Koskimo and Chinook deformations. But it remains doubtful whether their modes of deformation can be held responsible for this altogether incomplete feature, since the ossification of the os zygomaticum is generally completed before the deformatory strain can be of any effect.

Summary 148.

Sutura transversozygomatica: actual and percental frequency.

Sex and Age	Sutura transversozygomatica									
	Undeformed								Grand total
	Both sides		Right only		Left only		Total		
	no.	%	no.	%	no.	%	no.	%	%
♂	6	7.5	2	2.5	—	—	8	10.0	⎫
♀	5	14.7	—	—	3	8.8	8	23.5	⎬ 13.2
juv.	—	—	—	—	—	—	1	—	⎪
inf.	—	—	—	—	—	—	—	—	⎭
Total frequencies	11	9.3	2	1.6	3	2.3	17	—	
Cowichan deformation										
♂	11	12.5	—	—	1	1.1	12	13.6	⎫
♀	2	6.9	—	—	—	—	2	6.9	⎬ 12.7
juv.	—	—	1	—	—	—	1	—	⎪
inf.	1	—	—	—	—	—	1	—	⎭
Total frequencies	14	11.1	1	0.8	1	0.8	16	—	
Chinook deformation										
♂	11	9.0	—	—	—	—	11	19.0	⎫
♀	4	15.4	—	—	2	7.7	6	23.1	⎬ 20.8
juv.	—	—	—	—	—	—	—	—	⎪
inf.	3	—	—	—	—	—	3	—	⎭
Total frequencies	18	18.8	—	—	2	2.1	20	—	
Koskimo deformation										
♂	13	12.3	3	2.9	5	4.8	21	20.2	⎫
♀	5	12.8	—	—	1	2.6	6	15.4	⎬ 18.2
juv.	—	—	—	—	—	—	—	—	⎪
inf.	1	—	—	—	—	—	1	—	⎭
Total frequencies	19	12.3	3	1.9	6	3.9	28	—	

NORMA FRONTALIS.

1. Regio frontalis.
a. Tubera frontalia.

The tubera frontalia are uniformly of medium size tending toward smallness, so that a percental calculation seemed to be uncalled for. This is still more emphasized due to the rather unpronounced vaulting of the frontal region of the Indian skull in general, and not even the female forehead, which as a sex character is somewhat better developed also in the American Indian, lessens this impression. In the more longheaded tribal groups, like the Athapascan, Haida and Eskimo, the forehead in frontal aspect is therefore rather flat and slopes gently backward, while in the more roundheaded groups like Lillooet and Lytton, and in the more roundheaded specimens of the other groups, this condition appears to be modified toward frontal bulkiness. In the immatures the tubera frontalia show to better advantage, as is the rule in general.

The flattening of the forehead as found in the Cowichan and Chinook series, and particularly the latter, causes the tubera frontalia to appear to still lesser advantage, on the whole quite considerably broadening the entire forehead region which becomes still more conspicuous against the dilated parietal region.

b. Sutura frontalis s. metopica.

The persistence of the fetal frontal suture which under normal conditions ossifies between the first and second years does not appear to be of phylogenetic derivation. Its almost total absence in the anthropoids and only rare occurrence in the morphologically more primitive human varieties as against an increasing frequency in the peoples of ancient and modern culture justify its assumption as a newly acquired, i. e., progressive, character commensurate with the development and expansive power of the frontal brain. The greater frequency therefore lies with short and broadheaded varieties, and it appears like a test experiment of nature when the hydrocephali possess the sutura metopica.

The true or complete sutura metopica being only of limited occurrence, its incomplete form occurs quite frequently and is represented by a number of vestiges. Particular features have been specified in *summary 149* as nasal triangle, pars nasalis and pars supraglabellaris, of which, according to *Mair* [164], only the second one can claim to be a part of the suture in question, while the two others are produced by peculiar processes in the ossification of the supranasal region [165].

In the majority of specimens no traces of a frontal suture were seen, so that absence of this feature attains 74.6°/₀ in the Koskimo division and somewhat smaller percentages in the other divisions. A true trigonum was observed in a Lillooet infantile as a solitary occurrence. Supranasal traces, however, stand second in frequency and run as high as 42.6°/₀ in the Undeformed, while the deformed series show lesser frequencies. A pars glabellaris was also noticed in a Koskimo male.

With regard to the final specification of the sutura metopica as complete and incomplete, the former, evaluating traces other than those already mentioned, accounts for two single cases, one in the Undeformed and the other in the Koskimo division, both male. The true, i. e. complete, suture occurs three times in the Undeformed, which is 2.5°/₀. The relatively highest frequency was found in the Cowichan deformation, namely, six at 5°/₀. If this had any relation to deformation, it is astonishing that the Chinook with their stressed antero-posterior distortion present only one case of a complete suture. The three occurrences in the Koskimo division produce a frequency there of 2.4°/₀, which is equal to that of the Undeformed.

Metopism then is only of infrequent occurrence in the North Pacific area, somewhat in excess, however, of the frequency of 1.1°/₀ which *Russell* [166] derived from American Indians of over one thousand specimens. Inferior frequencies of 1.0°/₀, according to *R. Martin*'s (Lehrbuch, 1914, 755) list, obtain also in the Negroes (Congo) and the Australians, while Europeans in general have 8.7°/₀, Frisians 11.4°/₀ and Germans 12.3°/₀ (*Welcker*).

c. Torus sagittalis ossis frontis (*Bartels*).

A torus-like sagittal elevation of the frontal bone which *Bartels* [167] has named torus sagittalis ossis frontalis, but which was also seen by others (*Schwalbe, Mingazzini, Le Double*), is quite probably a product of premature ossification of the frontal suture. It is perhaps this causation which attaches to it only a relative evaluation as a diagnostic feature. This same causation, however, seemed sufficiently interesting for the basis of investigation in our series. The various developmental stages of the torus are specified in *summary 150* as slight, medium and pronounced.

Absence is accounted for in the first column, attaining very high percentages in the deformed divisions, while in the Undeformed a frequency of only 38.2°/₀ obtains. It is in this division also that the pronounced form of the torus has by far its greatest frequency at 23.6°/₀ as against such

---

[164] *Mair, Rudolf*, 1923. Zur Kenntnis der Fontanella metopica und der Stirnnaht. Anat. Anz., v. LVII, pp. 149—157.

[165] The supranasal trigonum comes about through accessory osseous lamellae progressing mesially on the basis of the already ossified supranasal region. The non-union of these lamellae produce an apparent gap of triangular shape.

Mair claims a similar origin for the pars glabellaris in the formation of the glabellar eminence contrary to *Schwalbe* et al.

[166] l. c., p. 167 (138).

[167] *Bartels, Paul*, 1905. Über Rassenunterschiede am Schädel. Intern. Mschr. Anat. Physiol., v. XXI, pp. 137—194.

Summary 149.
Sutura frontalis s. metopica: actual and percental frequency.

Sex and Age	Sutura frontalis s. metopica									
	Undeformed									
	Absent		Nasal triangle		Pars nasalis		Pars glabellaris		Sutura frontalis	
									Incomplete		Complete	
	no.	%	no.	%	no.	%	no.	%	no.	%	no.	%
♂	38	50.0	—	—	36	47.4	—	—	1	1.3	1	1.3
♀	22	73.4	—	—	7	23.3	—	—	—	—	1	3.3
juv.	2	—	—	—	—	—	—	—	—	—	—	—
inf.	3	—	1	—	9	—	—	—	—	—	1	—
Total frequencies	65	53.3	1	0.8	52	42.6	—	—	1	0.8	3	2.5
	Cowichan deformation									
♂	51	60.7	—	—	28	33.3	—	—	—	—	5	6.0
♀	18	72.0	—	—	6	24.0	—	—	—	—	1	4.0
juv.	2	—	—	—	—	—	—	—	—	—	—	—
inf.	4	—	—	—	3	—	—	—	—	—	—	—
Total frequencies	75	63.6	—	—	37	31.4	—	—	—	—	6	5.0
	Chinook deformation									
♂	34	63.0	—	—	20	37.0	—	—	—	—	—	—
♀	15	68.2	—	—	6	27.3	—	—	—	—	1	4.5
juv.	3	—	—	—	1	—	—	—	—	—	—	—
inf.	3	—	—	—	3	—	—	—	—	—	—	—
Total frequencies	55	64.0	—	—	30	34.9	—	—	—	—	1	1.1
	Koskimo deformation									
♂	68	75.6	—	—	18	20.0	1	1.1	1	1.1	2	2.2
♀	25	86.2	—	—	4	13.8	—	—	—	—	—	—
juv.	—	—	—	—	1	—	—	—	—	—	—	—
inf.	1	—	—	—	4	—	—	—	—	—	1	—
Total frequencies	94	74.6	—	—	27	21.4	1	0.8	1	0.8	3	2.4

Summary 150.

Torus sagittalis ossis frontis (*Bartels*): actual and percental frequency.

Sex and Age	Torus sagittalis ossis frontis (*Bartels*)									
	Undeformed									
	Absent		Slight		Medium		Pronounced		Grand total	
	no.	%	no.	%	no.	%	no.	%	no.	%
♂	21	28.4	20	27.0	7	9.5	26	35.1	53	71.6
♀	19	57.5	10	30.3	2	6.1	2	6.1	14	42.4
juv.	1	—	—	—	—	—	—	—	—	—
inf.	6	—	6	—	2	—	1	—	9	—
Total frequencies	47	38.2	36	29.2	11	9.0	29	23.6	76	61.8
	Cowichan deformation									
♂	59	69.4	19	22.4	7	8.2	—	—	26	30.6
♀	18	62.1	10	34.5	—	—	1	3.4	11	37.9
juv.	2	—	—	—	—	—	—	—	—	—
inf.	4	—	3	—	2	—	—	—	5	—
Total frequencies	83	66.4	32	25.6	9	7.2	1	0.8	42	33.6
	Chinook deformation									
♂	34	58.6	15	25.9	2	3.4	7	12.1	24	41.4
♀	16	64.0	8	32.0	—	—	1	4.0	9	36.0
juv.	3	—	2	—	—	—	1	—	3	—
inf.	3	—	—	—	1	—	—	—	1	—
Total frequencies	56	60.2	25	26.9	3	3.2	9	9.7	37	39.8
	Koskimo deformation									
♂	77	74.7	25	24.3	—	—	1	0.9	26	25.2
♀	30	81.1	6	16.2	1	2.7	—	—	7	18.9
juv.	3	—	—	—	—	—	—	—	—	—
inf.	7	—	1	—	—	—	—	—	1	—
Total frequencies	117	77.5	32	21.1	1	0.7	1	0.7	34	22.5

insignificant ones of 0.8% in the Cowichan, 0.7% in the Koskimo and 9.7% in the Chinook deformations. The slight development is fairly equally represented at appreciable percentages of 20% plus, while the medium-sized torus shows enumeratively diminishing frequencies of 9.0% to 0.7% in the order of the four divisions. It will be gathered from the last column of *summary 150* that the total amount of torus formation at 61.8% in the Undeformed greatly exceeds those in the deformed divisions, which suggests the assumption that the development of the frontal region, undisturbed by deformatory strains as in the Undeformed, rather favors the production of the feature under discussion. This is naturally still better demonstrated by the frequencies of the pronounced state. If premature ossification of the sutura frontalis is to be accepted as its cause, the only slight occurrence of pronounced tori in the deformed series may be sufficiently explained. The higher percentage of complete sutura metopica in the Cowichan deformation might corroborate such a statement which, however, is only conditionally true for the other deformed divisions.

R. Martin, (Lehrbuch, 1914, 758), quotes a torus frequency of 44.2% in Australians and 56% in the crania of ancient Wends and Esths.

d. Pars nasalis ossis frontis.

The distinctiveness of the pars nasalis in the facial configuration lies rather with its quantitative than with its specific form. The metrical estimation therefore concerns itself with length or height and the breadth of the part under discussion. The breadth as extending between the two maxillofrontalia has been treated in the chapter on the orbit (see *summary 86*), where it was shown that the divisional averages around 17 mm. were markedly uniform. There the Chinook with their relatively highest averages of 18.7 mm. and 17.7 mm. in the sexes conform with the average of 18.5 mm. for Chinese in *R. Martin*'s list (Lehrbuch, 1914, 865), stationed at its lowest extremity as over against the Swiss with 21.7 mm. or the Egyptians with 20.6 mm.

The length of the nasal process shows a similar uniformity centering around 9 mm., as may be gathered from *summary 151* [168] The female averages slightly exceed the male in the Undeformed and the Cowichan and Koskimo deformations, while in the Chinook the reverse is true. The immatures are seen to come fully up to the adults which, observed also in other racial groups, caused *H. Virchow* [169] to recognize here the early appearance of a variable character. The ranges are quite extensive, comprising eleven units in the Undeformed (4–14 mm.) and the Koskimo (5–15 mm.) twelve in the Cowichan

---

[168] In his monograph on "The Santa Barbara skeletal remains. Part I: Craniology. Indian Notes Monogr., 1925, no. 39, p. 86, the present writer has stated his dissatisfaction with the measurement hitherto employed of the length of the pars nasalis between the supraorbitale and nasion points. The latter point being dependent on the encroachment of the nasal bones upon the frontal bone, the above named measurement varies according to the amount of encroachment. He therefore proposed his "infranasion", i. e., the midpoint of a line connecting the meeting points of the suturae nasomaxillaris, maxillofrontalis and nasofrontalis, and called by him "maxillo-nasofrontale" (*Oetteking, Bruno*, 1920. Morphological and metrical variation in skulls from San Miguel Island, California. I. The sutura nasofrontalis. Ind. Notes Monogr., v. VII, no. 2, pp. 51–85 [56]). The difference between the nasion and infranasion amounted to 3–5 mm. in the Santa Barbara crania and may run still higher in other series.

[169] *Virchow, H.*, 1915. Zur anthropologischen Untersuchung des Gesichtsskelettes. Zschr. Ethnol., v. XLVII, pp. 323—372.

Summary 151.
Pars nasalis ossis frontis: cases, averages, ranges.

Tribe	Pars nasalis ossis frontis (length)											
	Undeformed											
	Male			Female			Juvenile			Infantile		
	Cases	Average	Range	Cases	Average	Range	Cases	Average	Range	Cases	Average	Range
Athapascan ..	6	8.8	7—13	1	9.0	—	—	—	—	—	—	—
Haida	16	8.9	7—11	8	10.0	7—12	1	10.0	—	5	8.1	6—13
Lillooet	2	8.0	6 ; 10	2	7.5	7 ; 8	—	—	—	2	10.0	10 ; 10
Nicola Lake..	3	7.0	4—9	2	9.5	8 ; 11	—	—	—	—	—	—
Spences Bridge	1	10.0	—	2	8.5	8 ; 9	—	—	—	—	—	—
Lytton.....	4	8.0	4—12	2	6.5	5 ; 8	—	—	—	1	11.0	—
Eskimo	34	9.3	5—14	11	11.0	8—14	—	—	—	—	—	—
Chukchee ...	4	10.0	9—10	1	9.0	—	—	—	—	2	9.5	9 ; 10
Total	70	9.0	4—14	29	9.4	5—14	1	10.0	—	10	9.4	6—15
	Cowichan deformation											
Total	74	8.3	2—12	23	9.0	6—13	2	9.5	9 : 10	3	8.7	8—9
	Chinook deformation											
Total	55	9.7	6—16	25	8.8	4—13	4	10.0	9—11	6	9.5	6—12
	Koskimo deformation											
Kwakiutl ...	42	9.1	5—14	16	9.4	6—13	—	—	—	3	10.0	8—11
Nimkish.....	40	9.7	7—12	10	9.9	8—12	—	—	—	2	10.0	9 ; 11
Koskimo....	10	11.4	8—15	4	12.8	11—14	—	—	—	—	—	—
Nootka	10	8.9	6—12	3	10.3	8—14	—	—	—	—	—	—
Clayoquot ...	5	8.6	7—10	2	8.0	7 ; 9	—	—	—	1	6.0	—
Total	107	9.4	5—15	35	9.9	6—14	—	—	—	6	9.3	6—11

(2–13 mm.) and thirteen in the Chinook (4–16 mm.). There is also some variation in the group means of which the more conspicuous in the Undeformed are those of the Eskimo and Chukchee who exceed the divisional average, and of the Lillooet and Lytton who fall below it. Perhaps of greater importance are the high means, male and female, of the Koskimo in the Koskimo division which with 11.4 mm. and 12.8 mm. distinctly exceed the divisional average, suggesting thereby an effect of artificial deformation as brought about by the retraction of the forehead which likewise affected the height of the orbit.

From the viewpoint of racial and morphological comparison specific investigations have shown that a broad pars nasalis as estimated by the anterior interorbital breadth is a progressive characteristic. Its greater length, on the other hand, was recognized as primitive, pithecoid, etc. (*F.* and *P. Sarasin*, *Zuckerkandl*, *H. Virchow*). This characteristic then is shared by the tribes of the North Pacific Coast and quite probably by the American Indian in general, and proved by the former's averages around 9 mm. as against 6 mm. for European males mentioned by *F. Sarasin* [170].

2. Regio supraorbitalis.

a. Glabellar development.

The glabellar development must be considered both as a racial and sex characteristic. From the racial standpoint it is well known that a stronger protrusion of the glabella is encountered in primitive races like the Australians and the fossil Hominidae, while from the viewpoint of sex, the males in every racial group show a stronger glabellar development than the females. This is also true throughout our series. The glabellar protrusion, however, attains nowhere an extreme degree, and that seems to hold true for the Indian population in general; it is even quite weak in many of the male skulls. While this latter is the typical state in the females, it is frequently absent here and also in the immatures.

A detailed investigation [171] of the feature under discussion not having been attempted, the superposition of a number of individual cases characteristic as such or for the group or class, is shown in fig. 67, *a–d*. In *a* three different forms of the male state may be seen, of which the two solid lines represent equally strong protrusions but with narrower and wider curves. A fossa supraglabellaris so characteristic in the anthropoid apes and the Hominidae is only very faintly, if at all, indicated in the narrower glabellar curve here and in the other outlines of this figure. The interrupted line of *a*, on the other hand, is only slightly vaulted, and the supraglabellar portion of the curve ascends quite steeply into the cerebral outline as is typical of the female skull. This is still better shown by the female and infantile outlines of *b*, which illustrate not only the typically more or less pronounced non-occurrence of the glabellar protrusion, but also the steeper ascent of the frontal outline in the latter, and the better developed nasal bridge in the former. In *c* the sex difference of the glabellar outline is demonstrated in two cases from the Eskimo series,

---

[170] l. c., p. 207 (214).
[171] Individual methods of investigations have been proposed by: *Mollison*, *Theodor*, 1907. Beitrag zur Kraniologie und Osteologie der Maori. Zschr. Morph. Anthrop., v. XI, pp. 529–595 (575), and *Sarasin*, *Fritz*, l. c., p. 207 (211).

whose nasal bridge of rue Mongolid type will be referred to in the discussion of the regio nasalis of this section. The three male tracings of *d* are from specimens deformed in the three modes of deformation obtaining in our material, and it is readily seen that the Chinook skull, although possessing a glabellar protrusion, has suffered the most drastic depression change not only in this but

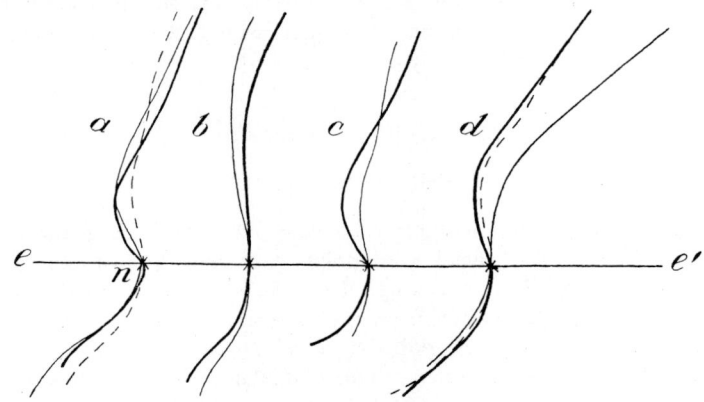

Fig. 67. Glabellar development in skulls of: *a*. three male Haida — 3751; — 1614; --- 3753), *b*. a female and inf. II Haida (— 1608; — 1615). *c*. a male and female Eskimo (— 3713; — 3718). *d*. males of the Cowichan, Chinook and Koskimo deformations (— North Saanich 2644 A; — Coupeville 2676; --- Koskimo 3644). Natural size. *e–e'*, parallel to ear-eye plane passing through *n*, nasion.

still more in the cerebral part of the frontal outline, while curiously enough its nasal outline exceeds the others in forward projection. Regarding the latter condition, however, projecting noses even in a marked degree seem to be a Chinookan characteristic, which also will be mentioned again further on The Cowichan and Koskimo modes of deformation seem to influence the glabellar outline to a much lesser degree.

b. Supraorbital prominences.

The resolution, after *Cunningham-Schwalbe* [172], of the over-eye prominences into several forms of an arcus superciliaris, afforded, in the present instance, the means of classification. The various forms are represented by (*a*) one of semilunar shape above the medial angle of each orbit, keeping clear of the supraorbital margin, and (*b*) its greater extension mesially as well as laterally, involving a more or less extended portion of the supraorbital margin and frequently the glabellar region, but not including the triangular anterior surface

---

[172] See *R. Martin*, Lehrbuch, 1914, 770.

of the zygomatic process of the frontal bone (trigonum supraorbitale). The merging of all these elements including the trigonum, gives rise to the formation of the torus supraorbitalis so familiar in the anthropoids and Hominidae, and frequently seen in the Australians.

Since none occurred in our collection, the torus has not been accounted for in *summary. 152*, while the two forms of the arcus are headed *a* and *b*. It will be noticed that throughout our series the milder form of the arcus is the prevailing one in the females, while the stronger form, excepting the Chinook, is found in the males, whereas in the immatures there is an irregular frequency of absence and the milder form. The total frequency of absence is as great as $12°/_0$ in the Undeformed and as small as $2.5°/_0$ in the Cowichan deformation. The two forms of the arcus are seen furthermore to occur at fairly similar total percentages in the Undeformed and Cowichan deformation. Decidedly higher percentages of the milder form are attained, however, in the Chinook deformation, while the opposite is true in the Koskimo deformation. It is not improbable that these conditions were brought about by deformation, which in the Chinook particularly impeded the normal development of supraorbital prominences.

3. Regio orbitalis.

a. Shape of orbit.

In the craniometrical part it was shown that, on an average, the size of the orbit in the North Pacific region tends rather toward largeness and furthermore that the width-height proportion shows a tendency toward hypsikonchy. The latter is still more pronounced in the females who thus repeat a sex difference generally met with in the human varieties. The shape of the orbit, however, depends on the behavior of its margins and the angles enclosed by them. The upper margin as a rule is somewhat straighter than the other sides of the aperture, and the supero-medial angle more acute, i. e., approaching a right angle much more than do the other angles. These are generally more smoothed off or rounded, particularly in the female skull and extremely so in the infantile. The general tendency toward a medio-lateral (horizontal) declination of the orbit, following *Cameron* [173], may well be attributed to the muscular traction of the temporal and masseter muscles. The most conspicuous result of this action is the downward traction of the infero-lateral angle which, however, seems to be more pronounced in the Caucasians than in the Mongolids where it is more rounded. The horizontal declination of the orbit therefore is less pronounced in the latter, for which (Japanese) *R. Martin* (Lehrbuch, 1914, 863)

---

[173] *Cameron, John*, 1920. Contour of orbital aperture in representatives of modern and fossil Hominidae. Am. Journ. Phys. Anthrop., v. III, pp. 476—488 (486).

Summary 152.

Supraorbital bulges: actual and percental frequency.

Sex and Age	Supraorbital bulges					
	Undeformed					
	Absence		Arcus superciliaris			
			a		b	
	no.	%	no.	%	no.	%
♂	3	3.8	23	29.5	52	66.7
♀	2	6.1	30	90.9	1	3.0
juv.	—	—	1	—	—	—
inf.	10	—	3	—	—	—
Total frequencies	15	12.0	57	45.6	53	66.7
Cowichan deformation							
♂	—	—	30	35.3	55	64.6
♀	1	3.5	23	79.3	5	17.2
juv.	—	—	2	—	—	—
inf.	2	—	3	—	—	—
Total frequencies	3	2.5	58	47.9	60	49.6
Chinook deformation							
♂	—	—	32	55.2	26	44.8
♀	—	—	23	95.8	1	4.2
juv.	—	—	3	—	—	—
inf.	3	—	3	—	—	—
Total frequencies	3	3.3	61	67.0	27	29.7
Koskimo deformation							
♂	1	1.0	27	26.4	74	72.6
♀	3	8.6	26	74.3	6	17.1
juv.	2	—	—	—	—	—
inf.	2	—	5	—	1	—
Total frequencies	8	5.4	58	39.5	81	55.1

gives male and female averages of 13.9° and 11.9°, as against 16.2° and 13.9° in the former. Although variable, it may be said that on the whole the orbits of the series under investigation are rather large with smoothly rounded angles and a moderate degree of horizontal declination. This holds true not only for those of average mutual width-height proportions, but also for the pronouncedly hypsikonchic Koskimo, and the Athapascan and Haida who range below their divisional (Undeformed) average.

b. Incisura (foramen) frontalis.

The statistical data about the incisure or foramen for the ramus frontalis of the supraorbital nerve and its accompanying blood vessels in the superomedial angle of the orbit are very scarce, but all of them confirm the limited frequency of the foramen. Our own data are in accord with such statements. They are listed in *summary 153*, where the incisura and the foramen have been recorded with regard to absence, bilateral, right or left, and mixed occurrence. Absence is represented at appreciable percentages in all the divisions, the highest being 31.0% in the Cowichan deformation, the lowest 18.5% in the Undeformed. The incisura frontalis in all the four divisions shows the highest frequencies, 60% in the Undeformed, and only nominally lower ones in the other divisions. It will also be seen that by far the greatest percentages go to the bilateral occurrence of the incisure, while the unilateral varies somewhat in the sexes as well as in the divisions. The considerably lower total frequency of the foramen frontale corresponds, however, in its constituency to that of the incisure, in so far as bilateral occurrence comprises the greatest number of cases. Unilateral occurrence was met only in individual cases. Mixed occurrence on opposite sides of incisure and foramen also attain appreciable percentages, partly equal, above, or slightly below those for the foramen, all of them, however, ranging below the figures denoting absence. By this latter condition it is indicated that both the incisura and foramen frontale on the whole do not occur with the same regularity as the slightly laterally situated notch or orifice for the supraorbital nerve and its accompanying blood vessels.

c. Incisura (foramen) supraorbitalis.

The incisura as well as the foramen supraorbitale form the passage for the n. supraorbitalis of n. frontalis and accompanying blood vessels coursing forward beneath the roof of the orbit. Although very variable in shape and ranging from wide and shallow to narrow and deep notches, from the incipient stages of closure to complete orifices, it seems that incisures designate the more primitive condition generally found in the fossil Hominidae and in the

Summary 153.
Incisura (foramen) frontalis: actual and percental frequency.

Sex and Age	Incisura (foramen) frontalis															
	Undeformed															
	Incisura								Foramen						r i/l f		r f/l i	
	o		Both sides		r*		l		Both sides		r		l					
	no.	%	no.	%	no.	%	no.	%	no.	%	no.	%	no.	%	no.	%	no.	%
♂	16	21.3	29	38.7	3	4.0	9	12.0	8	10.7	2	2.7	1	1.3	3	4.0	4	5.3
♀	3	8.6	16	45.7	3	8.6	5	14.3	2	5.7	1	2.8	—	—	5	14.3	—	—
juv.	1	—	—	—	—	—	—	—	—	—	—	—	—	—	1	—	—	—
inf.	4	—	11	—	—	—	2	—	—	—	—	—	—	—	—	—	1	—
Total frequencies	24	18.5	56	43.1	6	4.6	16	12.3	10	7.7	3	2.3	1	0.8	9	6.9	5	3.8
	60.0%								10.8%						10.7%			
	Cowichan deformation															
♂	29	33.0	33	37.5	8	9.1	2	2.3	4	4.5	1	1.1	1	1.1	7	8.0	3	3.4
♀	9	30.0	14	46.7	1	3.3	2	6.7	1	3.3	—	—	—	—	1	3.3	2	6.7
juv.	1	—	—	—	1	—	—	—	—	—	—	—	—	—	—	—	—	—
inf.	—	—	5	—	—	—	1	—	—	—	—	—	—	—	—	—	—	—
Total frequencies	39	31.0	52	41.2	10	7.9	5	4.0	5	4.0	1	0.8	1	0.8	8	6.3	5	4.0
	53.2%								5.5%						10.3%			
	Chinook deformation															
♂	17	29.3	24	41.3	3	5.2	2	3.5	5	8.6	1	1.8	1	1.8	2	3.4	3	5.2
♀	5	20.8	10	41.7	3	12.5	3	12.5	1	4.2	—	—	—	—	—	—	2	8.3
juv.	2	—	—	—	1	—	—	—	—	—	—	—	—	—	1	—	—	—
inf.	—	—	4	—	—	—	1	—	—	—	—	—	1	—	—	—	—	—
Total frequencies	24	26.1	38	41.3	7	7.6	6	6.5	6	6.5	1	1.1	2	2.2	3	3.3	5	5.4
	55.4%								9.8%						8.7%			
	Koskimo deformation															
♂	23	22.5	47	46.1	8	7.8	2	2.0	5	4.9	1	1.0	1	1.0	9	8.8	6	5.9
♀	11	32.4	17	50.0	1	2.9	—	—	—	—	—	—	—	—	2	5.9	3	8.8
juv.	—	—	2	—	—	—	—	—	—	—	—	—	—	—	—	—	—	—
inf.	2	—	2	—	—	—	—	—	1	—	—	—	—	—	—	—	—	—
Total frequencies	36	25.2	68	47.5	9	6.3	2	1.4	6	4.2	1	0.7	1	0.7	11	7.7	9	6.3
	55.2%								5.6%						14.0%			

* r, right; l, left; f, foramen; i, incisura.

primitive living. Absence, on the other hand, seems to be very rare and does not occur in our series.

The greatest frequencies are those of the foramen supraorbitale, attaining 61.4% in the Undeformed and 50% plus in each of the deformed divisions. The incisura occurs in percentages around 25% in the Undeformed and the Cowichan and Chinook divisions, but rises to 30.9% in the Koskimo. For both the incisura and the foramen the bilateral occurrence is usual. However, as may be gained from *summary 154,* there is a fair percentage of mixed occurrence to be noted which in the Cowichan deformation with 24.8% equals the frequency for the incisura.

The fact of a more numerous presence of the incisura in the immatures may suggest that it is a transitional stage toward the predominance of the foramen. This, however, is not carried out in every case, and besides, as mentioned above, the incisure is the prevailing condition in the more primitive Hominidae, not to speak of the anthropoids.

d. Fovea and spina trochlearis.

Fovea and spina trochlearis for the m. obliquus superior oculi do not frequently occur at the same time. The spina has not been sufficiently investigated to decide upon its diagnostic value. It represents, according to *Verga* [174], the ossified ligament which fastens the trochlea to the frontal bone, and not the ossified trochlea. The cases of bilateral occurrence of the spina, as listed in *summary 155,* are very few,

one in the Undeformed and two in the Koskimo equalling 0.9% and 1.4%, the cases of mixed occurrence of fovea and spina at the two sides of the skull are slightly more numerous, raising the total occurrence of the spina to 3.9% in the Cowichan deformation as the lowest, and to 6.8% in the Koskimo as the highest. The highest percentages listed in our summary go to the bilateral occurrence of the fovea trochlearis, which contains about two thirds of all the cases in the Undeformed and Cowichan, and even more in the Chinook and Koskimo divisions. In contrast to these figures are seen those indicating the absence of either fovea or spina, not in any way a negligible condition, attaining a frequency as high as 20.5% in the Cowichan division and 19.5% in the Undeformed. The lowest figure of absence is 12.2% as found in the Koskimo.

Le Double [175] points out a rather high percentage of spina trochlearis in whites, namely 15.9%, and adds "elle semblerait donc être infiniment plus commune dans la race jaune que dans la race caucasique". This statement, however, is not corroborated by his quotation from *Adachi* of 10.0% in Japanese and 8.8% in Ainus, nor by the still smaller percentages of *summary 155.*

e. Cribra orbitalia.

The sieve-like condition of the anterior portion of the orbital roof which latter is a part of the frontal bone, and called cribra orbitalia by *Welcker* [176],

---

[174] *Verga, A.,* 1889. Poche parole sulla spina trochleare dell' orbita umana. — Arch. Antrop., v. XIX, pp. 419—426.
[175] l. c., p. 194 (413).
[176] *Welcker, H.,* 1888. Cribra orbitalia, ein ethnologisch-diagnostisches Merkmal am Schädel mehrerer Menschenrassen. Arch. Anthrop., v. XVII, pp. 1—18.

Summary 154.
Incisura (foramen) supraorbitalis: actual and percental frequency.

Sex and Age	Incisura (foramen) supraorbitalis								
	Undeformed								
	Incisura (both sides)		Foramen (both sides)		ri/lf*		rf/li		Total of mixed occurrence	
	no.	%	no.	%	no.	%	no.	%	no.	%
♂	15	19.2	51	65.4	6	7.7	6	7.7	12	15.4
♀	9	27.3	21	63.6	1	3.0	2	6.1	3	9.1
juv.	1	—	1	—	—	—	2	—	2	—
inf.	7	—	5	—	—	—	—	—	—	—
Total frequencies	32	25.2	78	61.4	7	5.5	10	7.9	17	13.4
	Cowichan deformation								
♂	18	20.0	50	55.6	10	11.1	12	13.3	22	24.4
♀	10	33.3	13	43.3	5	16.7	2	6.7	7	23.4
juv.	2	—	—	—	—	—	—	—	—	—
inf.	2	—	2	—	1	—	2	—	3	—
Total frequencies	32	24.8	65	50.4	16	12.4	16	12.4	32	24.8
	Chinook deformation								
♂	15	26.8	28	50.0	8	14.3	5	8.9	13	23.2
♀	5	20.8	15	62.5	3	12.5	1	4.2	4	16.7
juv.	1	—	2	—	—	—	1	—	1	—
inf.	1	—	4	—	1	—	—	—	1	—
Total frequencies	22	24.4	49	54.5	12	13.3	7	7.8	19	21.1
	Koskimo deformation								
♂	28	27.2	55	53.4	8	7.8	12	11.6	20	18.4
♀	13	36.1	16	44.5	4	11.1	3	8.3	7	19.4
juv.	2	—	—	—	—	—	—	—	—	—
inf.	3	—	4	—	1	—	—	—	1	—
Total frequencies	46	30.9	75	50.3	13	8.7	15	10.1	28	18.8

* r, right; l, left; f, foramen; i, incisura.

Summary 155.

Fovea (spina) trochlearis: actual and percental frequency.

Sex and Age	Fovea (spina) trochlearis									
	Undeformed									
	Absence		Fovea both sides		Spina both sides		Mixed occurrence		Total frequency of spinae	
	no.	%	no.	%	no.	%	no.	%	no.	%
♂	15	21.7	53	76.8	—	—	1	1.5	1	1.5
♀	5	17.8	22	78.6	—	—	1	3.6	1	3.6
juv.	1	—	1	—	—	—	—	—	—	—
inf.	1	—	9	—	1	—	3	—	4	—
Total frequencies	22	19.5	85	75.2	1	0.9	5	4.4	6	5.3
	Cowichan deformation									
♂	19	21.6	65	73.9	—	—	4	4.5	4	4.5
♀	6	20.0	24	80.0	—	—	—	—	—	—
juv.	—	—	2	—	—	—	—	—	—	—
inf.	1	—	5	—	—	—	1	—	1	—
Total frequencies	26	20.5	96	75.6	—	—	5	3.9	5	3.9
	Chinook deformation									
♂	10	18.2	41	74.5	—	—	4	7.3	4	7.3
♀	4	16.7	20	83.3	—	—	—	—	—	—
juv.	—	—	4	—	—	—	—	—	—	—
inf.	—	—	6	—	—	—	—	—	—	—
Total frequencies	14	15.7	71	79.8	—	—	4	4.5	4	4.5
	Koskimo deformation									
♂	10	9.7	86	83.5	2	1.9	5	4.9	7	6.8
♀	7	20.0	26	74.3	—	—	2	5.7	2	5.7
juv.	—	—	2	—	—	—	—	—	—	—
inf.	1	—	6	—	—	—	1	—	1	—
Total frequencies	18	12.2	120	81.1	2	1.4	8	5.4	10	6.8

has been quite thoroughly investigated from the racial point of view. Due apparently to an osteophytic process which leaves the horizontal plates of the frontal bone in a spongeous condition, perforations of the parts concerned do not occur, at least not in the present series. *Summary 156* shows that almost without exception, the cribra are found simultaneously in both orbits at a frequency as high as 25.5°/₀ in the Undeformed. The noticeably lower frequencies in the other divisions, as low even as 13.6°/₀ in the Cowichan, make it clear that deformation does not seem to have any influence on the production of this anomalous condition. One-sided occurrence is exceedingly rare; it was found present in only two cases, one on the left side in an undeformed infant (Haida) and one on the right side in a male Kwakiutl.

R. Martin (Lehrbuch, 1914, 868) lists very high frequencies for Sokotos and Eastern Sudanese Negroes at 47.6°/₀ and 35.0°/₀, and Mongols and Mongolids from 8°/₀ to 19.7°/₀. Excepting our Undeformed frequency at 25.5°/₀, the frequencies of the deformed divisions fall well within that range. Altogether it appears that according to *R. Martin*'s listings for Europeans at 3.1°/₀ and 4.7°/₀ cribra orbitalia are much more frequently found in the yellow and black races.

f. Canalis nasolacrimalis.

Except for occasional remarks on the size of the canalis nasolacrimalis, specific data on this feature are rather rare. It seems on the whole that wide variation obtains in any racial group, and that cases of extreme width of the canalis are met with in Mongolids and Negroes. Our North Pacific groups, according to *summary 157*, show the highest frequencies for the wide canalis in the Chinook and Koskimo divisions at 8.3°/₀ and 7.9°/₀, the Undeformed attaining 5.8°/₀ and the Cowichan only 1.0°/₀. The greatest frequencies occur in the moderately and medium wide canales, the former having their highest percentages in the Undeformed and the Cowichan division, the latter in the Chinook and Koskimo divisions.

4. Regio nasalis.

a. Nasal bones.

α. Shape.

Following *R. Martin*'s (Lehrbuch, 1914, 839) classification of nasal bone outlines these were divided into a number of fundamental types and entered in *summary 158* as "narrow-constricted", "broad-constricted", "wing-shape" with rather narrow upper and spreading lower extremities, and "hylobatoid", broadish with somewhat parallel lateral outlines. The first two of these represent the

Summary 156.

Cribra orbitalia: actual and percental frequency.

Sex and Age	Cribra orbitalia							
	Undeformed							
	Absence		Both sides		r		l	
	no.	%	no.	%	no.	%	no.	%
♂	52	82.5	11	17.5	—	—	—	—
♀	19	65.5	10	34.5	—	—	—	—
juv.	1	—	1	—	—	—	—	—
inf.	6	—	5	—	—	—	1	—
Total frequencies	78	73.6	27	25.5	—	—	1	0.9
	Cowichan deformation							
♂	70	87.5	10	12.5	—	—	—	—
♀	25	86.2	4	13.8	—	—	—	—
juv.	1	—	1	—	—	—	—	—
inf.	6	—	1	—	—	—	—	—
Total frequencies	102	86.4	16	13.6	—	—	—	—
	Chinook deformation							
♂	47	87.0	7	13.0	—	—	—	—
♀	19	90.5	2	9.5	—	—	—	—
juv.	3	—	1	—	—	—	—	—
inf.	4	—	2	—	—	—	—	—
Total frequencies	73	85.9	12	14.1	—	—	—	—
	Koskimo deformation							
♂	89	86.4	13	12.6	1	1.0	—	—
♀	30	81.1	7	18.9	—	—	—	—
juv.	1	—	—	—	—	—	—	—
inf.	5	—	3	—	—	—	—	—
Total frequencies	126	83.9	23	15.4	1	0.7	—	—

Summary 157.

Canalis nasolacrimalis: actual and percental frequency.

Sex and Age	Canalis nasolacrimalis					
	Undeformed					
	Moderate		Medium		Wide	
	no.	%	no.	%	no.	%
♂	23	43.4	26	49.1	4	7.5
♀	11	47.8	11	47.8	1	4.4
juv.	1	—	—	—	—	—
inf.	9	—	—	—	—	—
Total frequencies	44	51.2	37	43.0	5	5.8
Cowichan deformation						
♂	37	52.9	32	45.7	1	1.4
♀	12	57.1	9	42.9	—	—
juv.	—	—	—	—	—	—
inf.	3	—	2	—	—	—
Total frequencies	52	54.2	43	44.8	1	1.0
Chinook deformation						
♂	12	22.6	35	66.1	6	11.3
♀	10	45.5	11	50.0	1	4.5
juv.	2	—	1	—	—	—
inf.	4	—	2	—	—	—
Total frequencies	28	33.3	49	58.3	7	8.3
Koskimo deformation						
♂	37	40.7	47	51.6	7	7.7
♀	13	43.3	14	46.7	3	10.0
juv.	1	—	1	—	—	—
inf.	4	—	—	—	—	—
Total frequencies	55	43.3	62	48.8	10	7.9

Summary *158*.

Ossa nasalia: actual and percental frequency.

Sex and Age	Ossa nasalia							
	Undeformed							
	Narrow-constricted		Broad-constricted		Wing-shape		Hylobatoid	
	no.	%	no.	%	no.	%	no.	%
♂	4	6.0	28	41.8	35	52.2	—	—
♀	1	4.6	16	72.7	5	22.7	—	—
juv.	—	—	1	—	—	—	—	—
inf.	1	—	2	—	7	—	—	—
Total frequencies	6	6.0	47	47.0	47	47.0	—	—
Cowichan deformation								
♂	5	7.9	40	63.5	18	28.6	—	—
♀	1	5.3	11	57.9	6	31.6	1	5.2
juv.	—	—	2	—	3	—	—	—
inf.	—	—	4	—	1	—	—	—
Total frequencies	6	6.5	57	62.0	28	30.4	1	1.1
Chinook deformation								
♂	4	10.0	25	62.5	11	27.5	—	—
♀	2	14.3	11	78.6	1	7.1	—	—
juv.	1	—	1	—	—	—	—	—
inf.	2	—	—	—	3	—	—	—
Total frequencies	9	14.8	37	60.6	15	24.6	—	—
Koskimo deformation								
♂	10	11.5	61	70.1	16	18.4	—	—
♀	3	9.1	17	51.5	11	33.3	2	6.1
juv.	—	—	1	—	1	—	—	—
inf.	—	—	5	—	—	—	4	—
Total frequencies	13	9.9	84	64.1	28	21.4	6	4.6

so-called "Sanduhrform" (hourglass shape), the narrow one being recognized by the cousins *Sarasin* as predominating in the Vedda of Ceylon.

It is the broader "Sanduhrform", however, which likewise predominates in our series with percentages noticeably above the half-hundred in the deformed divisions, slightly below at 47% in the Undeformed. The same frequency obtains in this division regarding the wing-shape nasalia, the percentages of which are considerably smaller in the deformations, the Koskimo attaining only 21.4% as over against their highest frequency of 64.1% of the broader constricted form. Compared to this latter, the narrower constriction was found in markedly lower percentages. The hylobatoid form, reminiscent of more primitive morphologic conditions and as such occurring sporadically, is not recorded in the Undeformed and Chinook divisions, but represented by one case or 1.1% in the Cowichan and six cases or 4.6% in the Koskimo deformations.

These figures are corroborated in a way by the transverse nasal bone index (see Table of measurements) which presents its lowest averages below 50.0 in the Undeformed males and females and the Koskimo males. It is in the Chukchee, Eskimo and Haida groups of the Undeformed division that the lowest averages are found with 41.0 and 27.3; 46.5 and 39.9; and 46.1 and 48.8 in the sexes. The lowest individual values below 40.0 and slightly above are those in the Koskimo and Undeformed juveniles.

Higher averages, representing straighter outlines of the nasal bones, are characteristic of the Europeans who, according to *R. Martin*'s (p. 840) list attain averages of 60.0 in Parisians and 62.7 in Auvergnats. Our own series shows rather high averages in the Chinook, namely 57.5 and 56.6 in the sexes, while the averages of the other divisions fit in with the Vedda = New Caledonian = Tamil group.

Anomalies like "catarrhiny" (*R. Virchow*) and "Os maxillo-naso-lacrimofrontale" (*Le Double*) or Proc. lateralis s. orbitalis (*Perna*) were not noticed in the series under investigation.

β. Nasal bridge.

The sagittal outline of the nasal roof best observed in lateral projection is of specific diagnostic interest. It is not only the more or less complete concavity of the nasal bridge that is recognized as a Mongolian trait, but also the upper part of the sagittal nasal curve receding behind a vertical dropped from the nasion. The latter particularly indicates the depressed condition of the nasal skeleton in its totality. However, there is a marked variability easily yielding to methodic investigation connected with these features. In fig. 68 several nasal outlines are seen oriented on a parallel to the ear-eye plane (e–e') passing through the nasion (n). From the latter point two auxiliary lines were drawn, one the nasion vertical (n–v) as mentioned above, and the other connecting in the median-sagittal plane the proximal and distal points of the nasal roof, i. e., the nasion and rhinion (n–r). The first two nasal outlines, *a* and *b*, show the typical concavity of the Mongolid nose in a Chinook male (4470) and a Kwakiutl female (1744), but in different orientation. Thus, while the former shows a markedly stronger projection as indicated by an angle of only 50° between the nasion-rhinion line and the ear-eye parallel, the latter's angle is 72°, due to the greater general depression of the nasal skeleton, emphasized by the recession of the nasal outline behind the nasion vertical hinted at above. In *c*, representing the nasal roof line of a Haida male (1614), the total curvature is given over in favor of a distal convexity. The tracing in its entirety represents thus a double curve not infrequently met in the Indian skull of the North Pacific region, and which in a way resembles the well projecting Caucasian nose. The point of difference, however, between these two forms lies in the generally unmistakable concavity right below the nasion in the nose of the Indian, while the nasal outline of the White shows

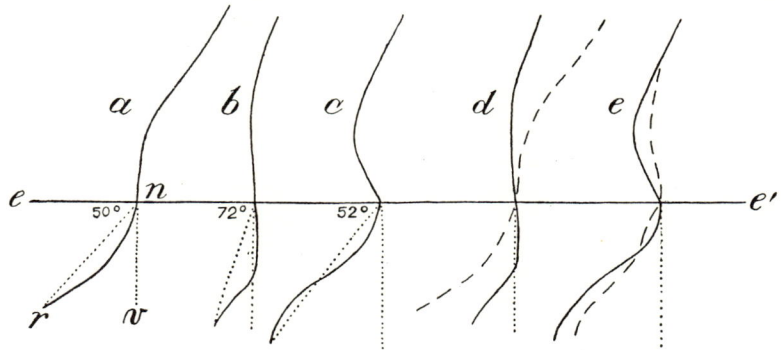

Fig. 68. Median-sagittal tracings of nasal roof in: *a*, male Chinook (4470); *b*, female Kwakiutl (1744); *c*, male Haida (1614); *d*, superposition of *a* and *b*; *e*, superposition of *c* and male Swabian (4554, - - - -). Natural size. *e–e'*, parallel to ear-eye plane through *n*, nasion; *n–v*, nasion vertical; *r*, rhinion; *n–r*, nasal roof line; ∠ *e–n–r*, angle of nasal roof projection.

in this portion a straighter and even projecting outline. These two conditions may be visualized in fig. 68, *e*, where the Kwakiutl outline of *c* and that of a Swabian male (4554) are superposed. Another superposition combines in *d* outlines *a* and *b*, in order to show by direct comparison the variable extent of projection of typical Mongolid noses. Incidentally, rather than due to deformation, the receding forehead of the Chinook is prompted by a stronger projecting nose as against the reverse conditions in the Kwakiutl outline. How great the variability of nasal roof projection might be, is demonstrated by *R. Martin's* (Lehrbuch, 1914, 814) figures which account for a Caucasian variation from 43° to 65°, and a Mongolid one (Kalmucks, Torgotes, Chinese) from 56° to 75°. Both ranges are seen to overlap.

b. Foramina nasalia.

These perforations of the nasal bones which transmit the ramus nasalis externus of the n. ethmoidalis anterior (n. ophthalmicus n. trigemini) vary in size, number and position. There is normally one foramen for each ramus situated in the middle of the bone, but they are sometimes seen farther upward, downward or at different levels. Large foramina were not observed, but a tendency toward smallness in size was rather apparent, as well as a certain multiple occurrence. In case of absence the ramus nasalis externus passes through a notch at the inferior end of the nasal bones and thus reaches the skin. The foramina nasalia have been accounted for in *summary 159* as either normal, i. e., two in number, absent, one-sided and as of multiple occurrence, either even or uneven. It will readily be discerned that in all four divisions the greatest frequency (71.0°/₀ to 77.0°/₀) falls to the normal occurrence, while the cases of uneven multiplicity (14.1°/₀ to 19.7°/₀) stand second in order. Total absence is very rare and represented by only one case in each the Undeformed, and the Cowichan and Chinook deformations. Slightly greater are the frequencies of one-sided occurrence and even multiplicity. There were no cases of the former noticed among the Koskimo.

c. Sutura internasalis.

The sutura internasalis as may be gathered from *summary 160* has a straight course in the median-sagittal plane only in a limited number of cases which seems to hold true for any human variety. The greater frequency lies with the curved and irregular courses at percentages of 32.3°/₀ and 19.2°/₀ in the Undeformed and somewhat lesser ones in the deformed divisions. Irregularity

Fig. 69. Abnormal sutura internasalis in: *a*, inf. II Nanaimo (1622); *b*, male "about Vancouver" (1567); *c*, male Nanaimo (1620); *d*, Krapina C specimen. Two-Thirds.

comprises undulating or serrate sutures as well as peculiar sudden deviations at the proximal extremities of the bones. Such curvatures may be either mild as in fig. 69, *a*, a Nanaimo inf. II (1622), or abrupt to the right or left as in *b* and *c*, a male skull from "about Vancouver" (1567), and a Nanaimo male (1620). Such anomalies, of course, are not restricted to our material and occur also in the human fossils, as for instance the Krapina C specimen [177] which is added as *d* to our fig. 69.

Another point of interest is the total or partial obliteration of the internasal suture. *R. Martin* mentions that it obliterates at an early age in the Simiidae, and that relatively early partial obliteration has been observed in

---

[177] l. c., p. 270 (pl. l, fig. 2).

Summary *159*.

Foramina nasalia: actual and percental frequency.

Sex and Age	Foramina nasalia							
	Undeformed							
	Normal		Absence		One-sided (right or left)		Multiplicity			
							Even || Uneven	
	no.	%	no.	%	no.	%	no.	%	no.	%
♂	34	73.9	1	2.1	2	4.4	2	4.4	7	15.2
♀	18	85.7	—	—	—	—	—	—	3	14.3
juv.	2	—	—	—	—	—	—	—	—	—
inf.	6	—	—	—	—	—	2	—	1	—
Total frequencies	60	76.9	1	1.3	2	2.6	4	5.1	11	14.1
Cowichan deformation										
♂	48	70.6	1	1.5	5	7.3	2	2.9	12	17.7
♀	15	75.0	—	—	1	5.0	—	—	4	20.0
juv.	1	—	—	—	—	—	—	—	—	—
inf.	2	—	—	—	—	—	1	—	1	—
Total frequencies	66	71.0	1	1.1	6	6.4	3	3.2	17	18.3
Chinook deformation										
♂	63	75.0	1	1.2	3	3.6	3	3.6	14	16.6
♀	20	80.0	—	—	2	8.0	—	—	3	12.0
juv.	1	—	—	—	—	—	—	—	—	—
inf.	5	—	—	—	—	—	—	—	1	—
Total frequencies	89	76.5	1	0.9	5	4.3	3	2.6	18	15.7
Koskimo deformation										
♂	32	76.2	—	—	—	—	1	2.4	9	21.4
♀	11	78.6	—	—	—	—	1	7.1	2	14.3
juv.	1	—	—	—	—	—	—	—	—	—
inf.	3	—	—	—	—	—	—	—	1	—
Total frequencies	47	77.0	—	—	—	—	2	3.3	12	19.7

Summary 160.

Sutura internasalis: actual and percental frequency.

Sex and Age	Sutura internasalis								
	Undeformed								
	Obliteration				Straight		Curved		Irregular	
	Part		Total						
	no.	%	no.	%	no.	%	no.	%	no.	%
♂	17	27.4	11	17.7	4	6.5	17	27.4	13	21.0
♀	5	20.8	—	—	4	16.7	10	41.7	5	20.8
juv.	—	—	—	—	—	—	1	—	1	—
inf.	1	—	1	—	5	—	4	—	—	—
Total frequencies	23	23.4	12	12.1	13	13.1	32	32.3	19	19.2
Cowichan deformation										
♂	25	36.8	11	16.2	4	5.9	12	17.6	16	23.5
♀	5	21.8	3	13.0	4	17.4	9	39.1	2	8.7
juv.	—	—	—	—	1	—	—	—	1	—
inf.	—	—	—	—	5	—	—	—	—	—
Total frequencies	30	30.6	14	14.3	14	14.3	21	21.4	19	19.4
Chinook deformation										
♂	15	31.9	4	8.5	7	14.9	16	34.1	5	10.6
♀	7	36.9	—	—	5	26.3	5	26.3	2	10.5
juv.	—	—	—	—	3	—	—	—	—	—
inf.	—	—	—	—	3	—	1	—	1	—
Total frequencies	22	29.7	4	5.4	18	24.3	22	29.7	8	10.9
Koskimo deformation										
♂	33	34.7	14	14.7	10	10.5	20	21.1	18	19.0
♀	5	16.7	4	13.3	6	20.0	11	36.7	4	13.3
juv.	—	—	—	—	2	—	—	—	—	—
inf.	—	—	—	—	3	—	3	—	—	—
Total frequencies	38	28.6	18	13.5	21	15.8	34	25.6	22	16.5

Hottentots, Bushmen, New Brittanians and Veddah. He also mentions that partial synostosis is quite frequent in deformed Americans. This statement is corroborated by our own observations showing that partial synostosis occurs in 23.4% to 30.6% and total synostosis from 5.4% to 14.3%. These ranges, however, include the Undeformed with 23.4% and 12.1% which demonstrates that the tendency toward synostosis of the sutura internasalis is not limited to the deformed groups.

d. Sutura nasofrontalis.

As in a previous paper [178], the writer has resolved the fundamental types of the sutura nasofrontalis into a number of subtypes, representing the straight and slightly curved, the upwardly convex or semicircular, the rectangular and trapezoid forms, while the angular form with steeply rising sides which join in the median-sagittal plane presents a type by itself.

As in the San Miguel skulls, the greatest frequency in our series, as shown in *summary 161*, lies with the semicircular form at a percentage as high as 43.1% in the Undeformed, while the lowest at 27.6% in the Koskimo is nevertheless the highest in the Koskimo series. Next in importance range the straight sutures, which are followed by the rectangular and curved ones still at appreciable frequencies. The low frequency of only 6% of straight sutures obtaining in the San Miguel series is greatly exceeded by the frequencies in the present series which run from 17.8% to 31.7%.

Although not representing the highest figures in each of our divisions, they nevertheless approach quite near to what *R. Martin* (Lehrbuch, 1914, 843) assumes to be a mongolid and negroid character. This assumption is confirmed to a degree by the negligible occurrence of angular sutures which the same author considers characteristic of Europeans, with 0.7% in the Koskimo, 0.8% in the Undeformed and Cowichan, but 4.4% in the Chinook. The status of the sutures in the immatures is rather indecisive so that a direct tendency toward a certain sutural form is not recognized there.

Two contrasting cases of sutural behavior are depicted in fig. 70, one of which *a*, a Koskimo male (3646), represents a straight course below the level of the maxillofrontal sutures, the other, *b*, a Koskimo inf. II (3645), an extremely high extension upon the nasal part of the frontal bone.

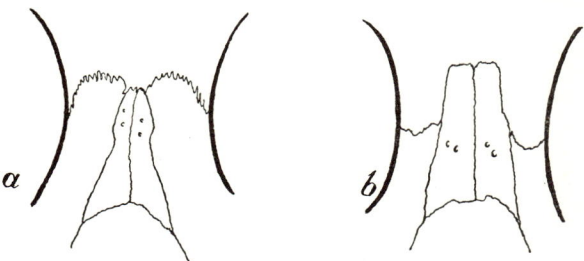

Fig. 70. Sutura nasofrontalis. Two extreme cases of sutural excursion in a male and immature Koskimo skull (*a*, 3646; *b*, 3645). Natural size.

---

[178] l. c., p. 279.

Summary 161.

Sutura nasofrontalis: actual and percental frequency.

Sex and Age	Sutura nasofrontalis Undeformed											
	Straight		Curved		Semicircular		Rectangular		Trapezoid		Angular	
	no.	%	no.	%	no.	%	no.	%	no.	%	no.	%
♂	25	33.0	3	4.0	39	51.3	8	10.5	1	1.3	—	—
♀	11	34.0	3	9.4	11	34.4	5	15.6	1	3.1	1	3.1
juv.	—	—	1	—	1	—	—	—	—	—	—	—
inf.	3	—	6	—	2	—	2	—	—	—	—	—
Total frequencies	39	31.7	13	10.6	53	43.1	15	12.2	2	1.6	1	0.8
	Cowichan deformation											
♂	21	25.9	10	12.4	27	33.3	17	21.0	5	6.2	1	1.2
♀	9	37.5	4	16.7	6	25.0	3	12.5	2	8.3	—	—
juv.	1	—	—	—	—	—	1	—	—	—	—	—
inf.	—	—	2	—	1	—	2	—	—	—	—	—
Total frequencies	31	27.7	16	14.3	34	30.4	23	20.5	7	6.3	1	0.8
	Chinook deformation											
♂	8	13.8	8	13.8	28	48.3	11	19.0	—	—	3	5.1
♀	4	17.4	5	21.7	6	26.1	7	30.4	1	4.4	—	—
juv.	1	—	—	—	1	—	—	—	—	—	1	—
inf.	3	—	2	—	1	—	—	—	—	—	—	—
Total frequencies	16	17.8	15	16.7	36	40.0	18	20.0	1	1.1	4	4.4
	Koskimo deformation											
♂	26	25.8	16	15.8	27	26.7	27	26.7	4	4.0	1	1.0
♀	6	19.3	5	16.1	10	32.3	7	22.6	3	9.7	—	—
juv.	2	—	—	—	—	—	—	—	—	—	—	—
inf.	—	—	2	—	2	—	1	—	2	—	—	—
Total frequencies	34	24.1	23	16.3	39	27.6	35	24.9	9	6.4	1	0.7

e. Nasion.

The nasion, dependent upon the relative development of the supraorbital forepart, the length of the pars nasalis of the frontal bone, and the relative degree of projection of the nasal bridge, is either mildly or not at all pronounced in the American Indian as in other mongolid varieties.

f. Spina nasalis anterior.

The crista nasalis which originates in the median-sagittal plane line at the floor of the nasal cavity by the union of the processus palatini of the maxillary bone. It terminates anteriorly in a more or less sharp process, the spina nasalis anterior. Phylogenetically, its degree of development results from the naso-alveolar flexion and the forward growth of the soft nose which latter as a racial character may bear correlation to the size of the spina. Thus, although one may recognize an average behavior in a racial group there is nevertheless a certain amount of variability to be dealt with in a given series. Using *Macalister*'s [179] terms for the sharp, blunt and cryptic behavior of the spina nasalis anterior, *summary 162* is divided into three columns under the captions oxyacanthic, lophacanthic and kryptacanthic. The greatest frequency in all our divisions, i. e., frequencies above the half-hundred, are assembled under lophacanthy, which is in accord with *Macalister*'s identification of this type as mongolid. The moderate size of the spina nasalis anterior in the Indian skull as compared to that of the Whites is also pointed out by *Hrdlička* in several of his writings, while *Lüthy* [180] finds that "die spina nasalis ist bei den Mongoloiden oft in ganz exzessiver Weise ausgebildet". The pronounced tendency toward kryptacanthy, however, obtaining in the Mongolids, is confirmed by its high percentages in our series, $40.0^\circ/_\circ$ to $45.0^\circ/_\circ$ in the Undeformed, and the Cowichan and Chinook deformations, but only $23.1^\circ/_\circ$ in the Koskimo. Oxyacanthy, as might have been expected, attains only small percentages, of which that for the Koskimo at $11.0^\circ/_\circ$ is the highest, and that for the Cowichan at $1.8^\circ/_\circ$ the lowest. These small percentages, however, help to prove the variability of this otherwise pronounced racial characteristic.

How great the individual variation may be within a given group may be seen from fig. 71, where *Macalister*'s three types of spina nasalis anterior are shown as occurring in the Chinook. It will be noticed that in the last tracing of fig. 71 there exists, besides a strongly developed spina, a marked degree of alveolar prognathy. A cursory observation has shown the present writer that in the Europeans a well developed spina is combined as a rule with

---

[179] *Macalister, A.*, 1898. The apertura pyriformis. Journ. Anat. Physiol. (London), v. XXXII, pp. 223–230.
[180] *Lüthy, A.*, 1912. Die vertikale Gesichtsprofilierung und das Problem der Schädelhorizontalen. Arch. Anthrop., N. F., v. XI, pp. 1–87 (44).

Summary 162.

Spina nasalis anterior: actual and percental frequency.

Sex and Age	Spina nasalis anterior					
	Undeformed					
	Oxyacanthic		Lophacanthic		Kryptacanthic	
	no.	%	no.	%	no.	%
♂	2	3.2	33	53.2	27	43.6
♀	1	3.6	18	64.3	9	32.1
juv.	—	—	—	—	1	—
inf.	4	—	5	—	5	—
Total frequencies	7	6.7	56	53.5	42	40.0
	Cowichan deformation					
♂	2	2.5	40	50.6	37	46.9
♀	—	—	16	80.0	4	20.0
juv.	—	—	4	—	—	—
inf.	—	—	2	—	5	—
Total frequencies	2	1.8	62	56.4	46	41.8
	Chinook deformation					
♂	1	2.0	20	40.8	28	57.2
♀	2	9.5	13	61.9	6	28.6
juv.	—	—	3	—	1	—
inf.	—	—	5	—	1	—
Total frequencies	3	3.7	41	51.3	36	45.0
	Koskimo deformation					
♂	7	8.3	55	65.5	22	26.2
♀	3	11.5	19	73.1	4	15.4
juv.	1	—	1	—	—	—
inf.	2	—	2	—	1	—
Total frequencies	13	11.1	77	65.8	27	23.1

relatively light alveolar prognathy, the different intensity of which is then a useful mark in racial study. As regards the individual development of the spina within a given group, *Klaatsch* [181] says that "in ganz jugendlichen.... Australiern finde ich die Spina auffällig stark entwickelt, während sie bei vielen erwachsenen Individuen Tendenz zur Reductionzeigt", and adds that *Turner* considers this the rule in Australians. A careful review of these conditions in our series shows the

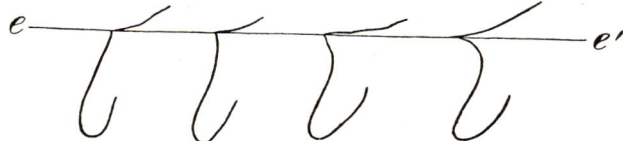

Fig. 71. Individual variation in the development of the spina nasalis anterior in Chinook skulls. Enumerative order of median-sagittal tracings: male 4446; female 4442; male 4448; female 4460. $e-e'$, parallel to ear-eye plane passing through points of spinae.

presence of oxyacanthy at slight percentages in the immatures, while the bulk follows the general trend of loph- and kryptacanthy. These observations then do not in fact demonstrate much more than the variability of a trait around an average condition.

g. Incisura piriformis inferior.

The terminology in connection with the apertura piriformis is somewhat confused. For instance, the term incisura nasalis of the maxillary bone indicating the medial curved edge of the corpus maxillare from the spina nasalis anterior to the point of union with the lateral border of the nasal bones is at times applied only to the lowermost portion of this incisure adjoining the spina nasalis, and again, as *Perna* [182] proposes, to the notch almost invariably found at the lower edge of the nasal bones, then again to the arch produced by the union of the distal edges of the nasal bones. Referring to the apertura piriformis as a formation of independent consideration, although resulting from configurating parts, the present writer proposes to retain *Perna*'s term of incisura nasalis of the nasal bones as one of ontogenetic significance, indicating their bipartite anlage, but to speak of incisura piriformis lateralis and inferior in connection with the apertura piriformis itself. If, however, the genetic point of view be considered, involving variation of morphologic significance, as listed in *summary 164*, he would prefer the term margo piriformis inferior.

The incisura piriformis inferior from the descriptive point of view shows variations with regard to its curvature in general and the difference of level of the two halves relative to the spina nasalis anterior. The curve in its

---

[181] *Klaatsch, Hermann*, 1908. Das Gesichtsskelett der Neandertalrasse und der Australier. Verh. Anat. Ges. 22. Vers. Berlin. pp. 1–51 (38).

[182] *Perna, Giovanni*, 1906. Die Nasenbeine. Eine embryologische und vergleichend-anatomische Untersuchung. Arch. Anat. Physiol. (Anat. Abt.), pp. 119–154.

totality may be (*a*) either on a level with, or drawn medially downward to the spina, or (*b*) the two halves on a level below the spina, or (*c*) the right lower than the left or (*d*) vice versa. These four conditions are accounted for in *summary 163*, where by far the greatest frequency in the Undeformed, and the Cowichan and Koskimo deformations lies with form *b*, while in the Chinook form *a* predomintes, which from the morphological point of view is very probably the more primitive. This same form occurs in the three first named divisions at moderate percentages of which the lowest is at 4.9% in the Koskimo division. Of the two irregular forms *d* considerably exceeds *c*, whose frequencies range from 1.6% to 8.3% in the four divisions.

The morphologic evaluation of these conditions giving preference to the forms *b*, *c* and *d* must be based on the phylogenetic changes which take place in this portion of the facial cranium and which will be remarked on in the following chapter.

h. Margo piriformis inferior.

The morphologic significance of the margo piriformis inferior as pointed out in the preceding chapter is the resultant of the naso-alveolar flexion of the higher forms. It is through this formation that two lines or ridges spring into relief at the inferior margin of the apertura piriformis, one of which being the continuation of the lateral margin of the apertura upon the alveolar process, and the other a line beginning at the spina nasalis anterior and turning, posteriorly of the former, toward the medial side of the nasal wall. These two lines are *v. Bonin*'s [183] cristae anterior and posterior, or *F. Sarasin*'s [184] margines nasoalveolaris and nasospinalis. Using these latter terms it is by their mutual behavior that varying combinations occur. The most primitive is the sulcus praenasalis ("Affenrinne") where, as characteristic of the Simiidae, a margo nasospinalis as a rule is only faintly indicated or not at all, while the margo nasoalveolaris is continued downward upon the alveolar process as a ridge or bulge, straight or slightly curved mesially. A formation brought about in man under similar premises, *Sergi*'s clivus nasoalveolaris, has a general occurrence of 5.6%, according to *Mingazzini*[185]. In our series, as may be gathered from *summary 164*, the sulcus praenasalis or *Macalister*'s [186] orygmocraspedotic (ὄρυγμα, sulcus; κράσπεδον, fold) form, attains a frequency of 1.8% in the Undeformed, 2.8% in the Cowichan and 4.4% in the Koskimo deformation, while no case was observed in the Chinook. Considerably less primitive, being, however, a condition somewhat primitive in man, is the fossa praenasalis,

---

[183] *Bonin, G. v.*, 1912. Zur Morphologie der Fossa praenasalis. Arch. Anthrop., N. F., v. XI, pp. 185-195.
[184] l. c., p. 207, (259).
[185] Quoted by *R. Martin* (Lehrbuch, 1914, 847).
[186] l. c., p. 301.

Summary 163.
Incisura piriformis inferior: actual and percental frequency.

Sex and Age	Incisura piriformis inferior							
	Undeformed							
	a		b			c			d
	Above or on level with spina nasalis ant.		On even level		Right lower		Left lower	
			Below spina nasalis ant.					
	no.	%	no.	%	no.	%	no.	%
♂	13	17.6	44	59.4	2	2.7	15	20.3
♀	2	6.1	26	78.8	—	—	5	15.2
juv.	—	—	1	—	—	—	—	—
inf.	5	—	8	—	—	—	1	—
Total frequencies	20	16.4	79	64.8	2	1.6	21	17.2
Cowichan deformation								
♂	12	15.6	45	58.4	5	6.5	15	19.5
♀	2	7.1	18	64.3	2	7.1	6	21.4
juv.	1	—	1	—	—	—	—	—
inf.	3	—	1	—	—	—	1	—
Total frequencies	18	16.1	65	58.0	7	6.3	22	19.6
Chinook deformation								
♂	28	50.0	15	26.8	3	5.3	10	17.9
♀	10	41.7	9	37.5	1	4.1	4	16.7
juv.	2	—	2	—	—	—	—	—
inf.	4	—	1	—	—	—	—	—
Total frequencies	44	49.5	27	30.3	4	4.5	14	15.7
Koskimo deformation								
♂	3	2.9	77	75.5	9	8.8	13	12.8
♀	1	2.8	26	74.3	3	8.6	5	14.3
juv.	1	—	1	—	—	—	—	—
inf.	2	—	3	—	—	—	—	—
Total frequencies	7	4.9	107	74.3	12	8.3	18	12.5

Summary 164.
Margo piriformis inferior: actual and percental frequency.

Sex and Age	Margo piriformis inferior							
	Undeformed							
	Amblykraspedotic		Bothrokraspedotic (fossa praenasalis)		Oxykraspedotic		Orygmokraspedotic (sulcus praenasalis)	
	no.	%	no.	%	no.	%	no.	%
♂	5	7.6	44	66.7	16	24.2	1	1.5
♀	4	12.5	20	62.5	7	21.9	1	3.1
juv.	—	—	1	—	—	—	—	—
inf.	12	—	1	—	1	—	—	—
Total frequencies	21	18.6	66	58.4	24	21.2	2	1.8
Cowichan deformation								
♂	11	15.1	36	49.3	24	32.9	2	2.7
♀	5	20.0	7	28.0	13	52.0	—	—
juv.	—	—	1	—	—	—	1	—
inf.	4	—	—	—	2	—	—	—
Total frequencies	20	18.9	44	45.5	39	36.8	3	2.8
Chinook deformation								
♂	6	10.3	29	50.0	23	39.7	—	—
♀	2	10.0	6	30.0	12	60.0	—	—
juv.	1	—	2	—	—	—	—	—
inf.	6	—	—	—	—	—	—	—
Total frequencies	15	17.2	37	42.6	35	40.2	—	—
Koskimo deformation								
♂	37	37.8	17	17.3	40	40.8	4	4.1
♀	13	43.4	1	3.3	15	50.0	1	3.3
juv.	—	—	—	—	1	—	1	—
inf.	4	—	—	—	2	—	—	—
Total frequencies	54	39.7	18	13.2	58	42.7	6	4.4

Macalister's bothrocraspedotic (βόθρος, groove) form, where the margo nasoalveolaris, reaching the spina nasalis anterior, and the margo nasospinalis, form between themselves a more or less wide, deep and extented groove. Occurring in Europeans, according to *R. Martin* (p. 846) in frequencies of 5.0 % to 12.0 %, the percentages rise to 18.7 % in Ural-Altaians and 42.8 % in Easter Islanders. This form assembles most of the cases in our series except the Koskimo who attain a frequency of only 13.2 % as against frequencies ranging from 42.6 % to 58.4 % in the other divisions. The small Koskimo frequency is compensated in this division by the highest occurrence of 42.7 % of the true anthropine form of the margo piriformis inferior where the two frequently mentioned margines nasospinalis and nasoalveolaris merge into a sharp edge which thus forms the inferior border of the nasal cavity. This is *Macalister*'s oxycraspedotic (ὀξύς, sharp) type, second in importance in our series. Appreciable percentages will also be noticed for the infantile form, the amblycraspedotic (ἀμβλύς, blunt) of *Macalister*, characterised by the weak continuation and early disappearance of the margo nasoalveolaris upon the alveolar process with only a mild attempt to reach the nasal spine. It will be readily noticed that with the exception of the Koskimo, the two principal types occurring at the inferior margin of the apertura piriformis are in enumerative order the fossa praenasalis and the oxycraspedotic. In the Koskimo the frequency of the infantile (amblycraspedotic) and the anthropine (oxycraspedotic) forms are strongly in evidence.

Regarding the naso-alveolar flexion from the racial point of view an observation by *Wetzel*[187] is of interest which states that in Tasmanians, Negroes and Bushmen the flexion takes place at the anterior, in Mongols and Europeans at the posterior margins.

5. Regio maxillaris.

a. Fossa canina.

The fossa canina, apparently a morphologically advanced character and correlative with the retraction of the upper jaw, shows its most pronounced development, i. e., its greatest depth, in the European varieties, and peculiarly enough also in Melanesians and Senoi, while the anterior surface of the maxillary bone in the Mongols and Mongolian varieties is either perfectly smooth or only very slightly depressed. The Neandertaloids also are devoid of this mark.

Our statistics in *summary 165* show that the shallow and medium deep fossae predominate in our series in such a way that the former state exceeds the latter quite considerably in the Undeformed, while the reverse is true of the deformed divisions where medium deep fossae occur

---

[187] *Wetzel, Georg*, 1922, Lehrbuch der Anatomie für Zahnärzte. 3 Ed. Jena. p. 180.

Summary 165.

Fossa canina: actual and percental frequency.

Sex and Age	Fossa canina Undeformed					
	Shallow		Medium		Deep	
	no.	%	no.	%	no.	%
♂	47	62.7	28	37.3	—	—
♀	17	54.9	13	41.9	1	3.2
juv.	1	—	—	—	—	—
inf.	12	—	2	—	—	—
Total frequencies	77	63.7	43	35.5	1	0.8
Cowichan deformation						
♂	23	28.8	50	62.5	7	8.7
♀	7	26.9	17	65.4	2	7.7
juv.	2	—	—	—	—	—
inf.	2	—	5	—	—	—
Total frequencies	34	29.6	72	62.6	9	7.8
Chinook deformation						
♂	23	41.1	28	50.0	5	8.9
♀	6	26.1	13	56.5	4	17.4
juv.	2	—	2	—	—	—
inf.	5	—	1	—	—	—
Total frequencies	36	40.5	44	49.4	9	10.1
Koskimo deformation						
♂	30	28.9	64	61.5	—	9.6
♀	11	32.4	22	64.7	1	2.9
juv.	—	—	2	—	—	—
inf.	2	—	5	—	—	—
Total frequencies	43	29.1	93	62.8	1	8.1

in 62.8% in the Koskimo. The high frequency of 63.7% of shallow fossae in the Undeformed is partly due to the fact that this division comprises groups like the Eskimo, Chukchee and Haida which have pronouncedly shallow fossae. The occurrence of the deep fossae is with 0.8% rather negligible in the Undeformed; it rises, however, to 10.1% in the Chinook, ranging slightly lower in the Cowichan and Koskimo.

It appeared on closer observation that a more shallow fossa canina, as seen in the Eskimo, Chukchee, Haida, rather favors the formation of a fossa praenasalis as well as a shallow crista infrazygomatica (see the following chapter), observations which may yield interesting results through a methodical investigation.

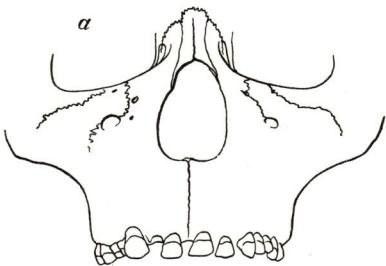

b. Crista infrazygomatica.

From the morphologic as well as the racial point of observation, the crista infrazygomatica [188] offers a number of interesting variations. In frontal aspect, its curvature may be either shallow, medium deep or deep, and with these three fundamental types certain other conditions appear to be correlated. Thus, the shallow curves combine as a rule with high alveolar processes and shallow or absent canine fossae. Increasing curvature, on the other hand, favors alveolar processes of diminishing height and deepening canine fossae. The three fundamental forms of the crista infrazygomatica, particularly with regard to their different degrees of curvature, are shown in fig. 72.

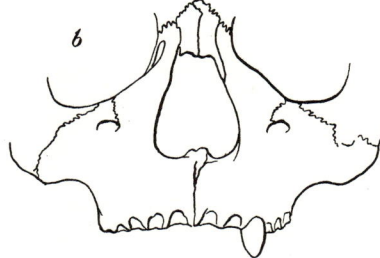

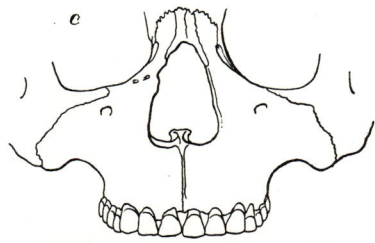

The actual and percental frequencies of these forms as listed in *summary 166* show most of the cases in the medium deep column, where all the frequencies attain percentages above the half-hundred mark, as high even as 79.3% in the Cowichan deformation. Shallow curves were noticed at their highest frequencies in the Undeformed and the Chinook at 38.2% and 22.2% respectively, and it is due in the former to the heterogeneous composition, as was the case regarding the high occurrence of canine fossae in the Undeformed groups of the Eskimo, Chukchee

Fig. 72. Three fundamental types of crista infrazygomatica representing in *a*, a shallow curve in a male Kwakiutl (4239); *b*, a moderately deep curve in a male Kwakiutl (3883), and *c*, a deep curve in a male Chukchee (3848). The three types with the increasing intensity of the curve show a decreasing height of the processus alveolaris. ²/₃.

---

[188] Crista infrazygomatica *Kopsch* (see *Rauber*'s Lehrbuch der Anatomie des Menschen, revised by *Fr. Kopsch*, 1919. v. II, p. 95), also called crista zygomaticoalveolaris *Wetzel*, l. c., p. 307 (174).

Summary 166.

Crista infrazygomatica: actual and percental frequency.

Sex and Age	Crista infrazygomatica					
	Undeformed					
	Shallow curve		Medium deep curve		Deep curve	
	no.	%	no.	%	no.	%
♂	32	42.1	37	48.7	7	9.2
♀	10	30.3	21	63.6	2	6.1
juv.	1	—	—	—	—	—
inf.	4	—	9	—	—	—
Total frequencies	47	38.2	67	54.5	9	7.3
	Cowichan deformation					
♂	11	13.4	63	76.8	8	9.8
♀	3	12.0	22	88.0	—	—
juv.	1	—	1	—	—	—
inf.	1	—	6	—	—	—
Total frequencies	16	13.8	92	79.3	8	6.9
	Chinook deformation					
♂	8	14.3	37	66.1	11	19.6
♀	6	25.0	17	70.8	1	4.2
juv.	3	—	—	—	1	—
inf.	3	—	2	—	1	—
Total frequencies	20	22.2	56	62.2	14	15.6
	Koskimo deformation					
♂	12	11.6	77	74.8	14	13.6
♀	7	20.6	24	70.6	3	8.8
juv.	—	—	1	—	—	—
inf.	3	—	5	—	—	—
Total frequencies	22	15.1	107	73.3	17	11.6

and Haida. The deeply curved crista infrazygomatica is most frequent in the Chinook and Koskimo deformations at 15.6%, and 11.6%, while the Undeformed and the Cowichan deformation attain frequencies of 7.3% and 6.9%.

Notwithstanding the fact that the medium deep curve is the predominant one in our series, noticeable even in the immatures, its tendency toward shallowness as expressed by appreciable frequencies strongly suggest its significance as a racial trait obtaining in the Mongolids. From the viewpoint of racial morphology of the jaw region, highly interesting observations by *Klaatsch*[189] throw light on the correlative behavior of the "Jugalwulst des Oberkiefers" (*Klaatsch*), i. e., the jugal bulge between the processus zygomatico-orbitalis (zygomaticomaxillaris) and the alveolar border, the edge of which is the crista infrazygomatica under discussion, and the first upper molar. *Klaatsch* recognized a primary human condition by the fixation of the posterior root of the first molar in the "Jugalwulst" of the Australian skull, a condition which the latter shared with the orang-utan and gorilla, and which to the author seemed suggestive of conditions existing in the common "Urform" of

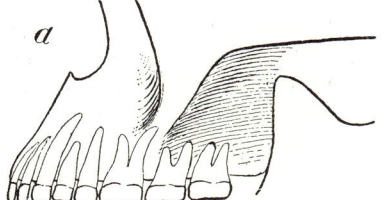 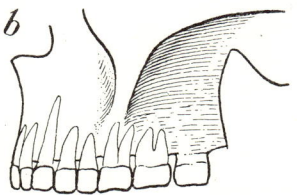

Fig. 73. Mutual relation between the "Jugalwulst" (*Klaatsch*) of the upper jaw and the roots of the first molar in *a*, Australian (*Klaatsch* K 72), and *b*, European (Anatomical Institute, Breslau). After *Klaatsch*, l. c., p. 9. (pp. 118, 117). About natural size.

the human and simian races. Identical correlations were observed by *Klaatsch* in the African Negro. Since, however, this correlation is missing in modern races, the Europeans frequently having the anterior root of the first molar anchored in the "Jugalwulst", he deems it justifiable to accept in this state a secondary adaptation i. e., a retraction of the alveolar process, all the more so since transitional stages were witnessed in the Malays and Mongolids. The present author in his own material has not followed up *Klaatsch*'s observations but found the latter interesting enough for representation in fig. 73.

c. Foramen and sutura infraorbitalis.

Considerable variability is found in regard to both, this foramen and suture. As regards the foramen infraorbitale for the nervus and arteria of the same name, there is normally one, rather large, on each side of the face

---

[189] l. c., p. 9 (116—118).

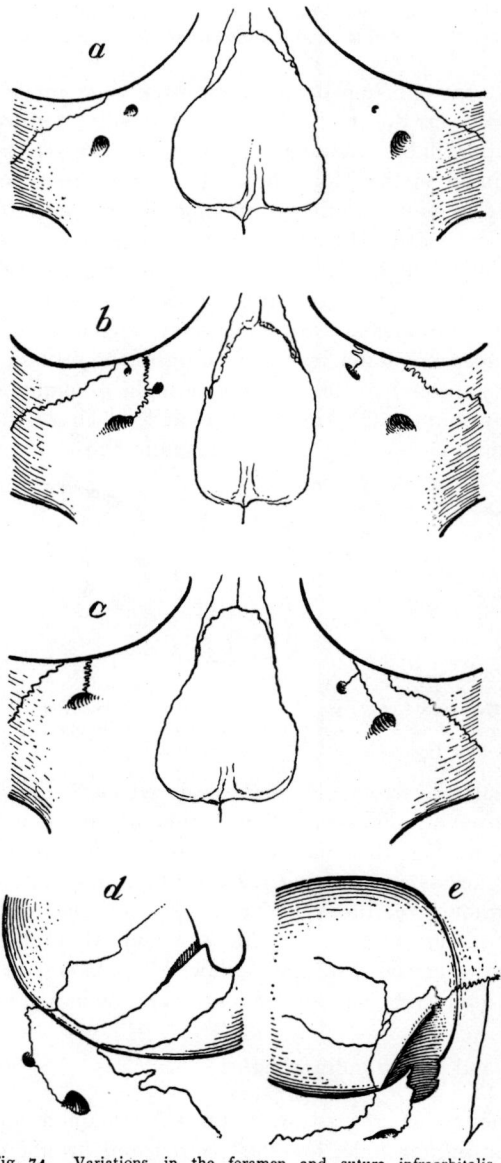

Fig. 74. Variations in the foramen and sutura infraorbitalis. *a*, multiple occurrence of the foramen, in a male Kwakiutl (4245); *b* and *c*, variations of the sutura in a male and female Kwakiutl (4239, 4242); *d*, variation in the orbital portion of the suture, in a female Haida (1611); *e*, irregular ossification of the orbital border at the inferomedial angle in a male Kwakiutl (1715). About natural size.

and well marked by size and appearance. Frequently, however, the number of foramina is augmented by one or more smaller ones, situated usually above, more rarely below, or sidewards of the larger ones, and the conditions may also differ as to right and left. A simple variation in this respect is that of fig. 74, *a*, where additional foramina will be noticed, one smaller on the right and one tiny one on the left side. The sutura infraorbitalis is more or less closely involved in the variability of the foramen in such a way that in cases of multiplicity of the latter, the sutura may begin its course at any of them and even connect the foramina among themselves. Such cases are illustrated in fig. 74, *b* and *c*. These conditions are complicated on the left side of *c*, by two sutures starting independently from the larger and the smaller foramen and joining just before reaching the lower orbital border at which junction a small Wormian ossicle is seen, and above which the suture pursues a single course. An interesting variation may be noticed in *d*, the two sutures of which run toward the sutura lacrimomaxillaris of each eye and then turning sharply toward the canalis infraorbitalis. A case of particular interest is that of *e*, where the sutura infraorbitalis is seen to enter a gap of the anterior lacrimal crest of the right orbit in front of the fossa sacci lacrimalis. This case may be due to irregular ossification, since according to *Le Double* [190], independent ossicles occur at times as "os de l'hamule" and "os surnuméraire" in this neighborhood. Other instances of sutura infraorbitalis may be seen in fig. 72.

Turning now to the statistical occurrence of the sutura infraorbitalis, it will be gained from *summary 167* that about half of our cases are devoid of a suture and that in the other half the typical double occurrence predominates, leaving only small percentages to one-sided, right or left, occurrence. It seems that the suture was first observed and described in Eskimo skulls and therefore taken for an Eskimo characteristic. Since then, however, its presence has been noticed in other varieties. In Europeans there is according to *R. Martin* (Lehrbuch, 1914, 825) a frequency of the facial portion of the suture of about 20% to 40%, and of the orbital portion of 40% to 60%.

---

[190] l. c., p. 211 (66, 193).

Summary 167.

Sutura infraorbitalis: actual and percental frequency.

Sex and Age	Sutura infraorbitalis									
	Undeformed									
	Absence		Both sides		Right only		Left only		Grand total	
	no.	%	no.	%	no.	%	no.	%	no.	%
♂	32	52.5	28	45.9	—	—	1	1.6	29	47.5
♀	8	27.6	19	65.5	—	—	2	6.9	21	72.4
juv.	—	—	—	—	—	—	—	—	—	—
inf.	7	—	7	—	—	—	—	—	7	—
Total frequencies	47	45.2	54	51.9	—	—	3	2.9	57	54.8
	Cowichan deformation									
♂	46	56.8	29	35.8	4	4.9	2	2.5	35	43.2
♀	11	39.3	17	60.7	—	—	—	—	11	60.7
juv.	2	—	—	—	—	—	—	—	—	—
inf.	2	—	2	—	1	—	—	—	3	—
Total frequencies	61	52.6	48	41.4	5	4.3	2	1.7	55	47.4
	Chinook deformation									
♂	32	59.3	19	35.2	1	1.9	2	3.7	22	40.7
♀	7	31.8	15	68.2	—	—	—	—	15	68.2
juv.	1	—	3	—	—	—	—	—	3	—
inf.	1	—	4	—	—	—	—	—	4	—
Total frequencies	41	48.2	41	48.2	1	1.2	2	2.4	44	51.8
	Koskimo deformation									
♂	51	48.1	50	47.2	2	1.9	3	2.8	55	51.9
♀	14	43.8	17	53.1	—	—	1	3.1	18	56.3
juv.	—	—	1	—	—	—	—	—	1	—
inf.	2	—	7	—	—	—	—	—	7	—
Total frequencies	67	45.3	75	50.7	2	1.3	4	2.7	81	54.7

NORMA OCCIPITALIS.

1. Occipital contour.

There is less morphological differentation to be observed in the norma occipitalis than in any other. With the vertical and lateral normae it shares the significance of outline which in reference to *Haberer* [191] one may distinguish as wedge, bomb and house form. The first named, with a tubera parietalia breadth exceeding the biauricular, is characteristic of the newborn, while the second, with its greatest breadth farther down between the tubera parietalia and squamae temporales, is typical of the immature skull, although it also occurs in the adult, particularly in the female skull. Between this form and the "house" the greatest breadth of which is to be found between the temporal squamae with more or less vertically oriented walls ("wall-sided") and a more or less rounded gable-shape roof, there exist a number of variations. *Haberer* adds the "tent" to his series of characteristic shapes, in which the greatest cranial breadth coincides with the biauricular breadth and which shape is characteristic of the adult ape, the young ape presenting a bomb shape occipital contour. The tent form is not accounted for in *summary 168*, while the three figure ontlines represented there are taken from *Haberer's* work (figs. 12, 13, 29).

In the normal, i. e., the undeformed skulls of our series, all the male specimens are assembled under the house form; one female belongs to the wedge form, where most of the immatures are likewise to be found. The bomb form is represented by three infantiles only. The house form then as the predominating one attains a frequency of 91.0%, the remaining percentages of 6.6% and 2.5% going to the wedge and bomb forms. The house form is also the prevailing one in the Cowichan and Koskimo divisions, and in even higher percentages than in the Undeformed. Their deformatory practices therefore have not altered the occipital aspect as it obtains in the normal skull from the North Pacific regions. The Chinook, however, differ in this respect, and the increase of the wedge shape of the occipital contour to 18.3% is entirely due to the conspicuous effects of their mode of deformation, resulting in the flattening of the skull and the compensatory lateral expansion so evident in occipital projection. The result is a drop to 81.7% of house shape contours.

The flattening of the contour just remarked upon obtains to a degree also in the deformed Salish skulls representing the Cowichan division, since the Cowichan mode of deformation resembles somewhat the Chinook without, however, producing analogous effects. But there are, on the other hand,

---

[191] *Haberer, K.*, 1898. Über die "norma occipitalis" bei Mensch und Affe. Munich.

Summary 168.
Occipital contour: actual and percental frequency.

Sex and Age	Occipital contour					
	Undeformed					
	Wedge		Bomb		House	
	no.	%	no.	%	no.	%
♂	—	—	—	—	77	100.0
♀	1	2.9	—	—	33	97.1
juv.	1	—	—	—	—	—
inf.	6	—	3	—	1	—
Total frequencies	8	6.6	3	2.5	111	91.0
	Cowichan deformation					
♂	—	—	—	—	82	100.0
♀	2	7.7	1	3.8	23	88.5
juv.	2	—	—	—	—	—
inf.	3	—	—	—	2	—
Total frequencies	7	6.1	1	0.9	107	93.0
	Chinook deformation					
♂	7	12.3	—	—	50	87.7
♀	5	19.2	—	—	21	80.8
juv.	1	—	—	—	3	—
inf.	4	—	—	—	2	—
Total frequencies	17	18.3	—	—	76	81.7
	Koskimo deformation					
♂	2	1.9	1	1.0	102	97.1
♀	—	—	—	—	36	100.0
juv.	—	—	—	—	2	—
inf.	3	—	3	—	2	—
Total frequencies	5	3.3	4	2.6	142	94.1

individual cases of strongly projecting tubera parietalia in the Undeformed with almost wedge-like appearance.

2. Relief of squama.

a. General remarks.

The external relief of the occipital squama throughout the entire series is of very moderate development. This refers to the inferior, superior and supreme lineae nuchae, the crista occipitalis externa, and the areas enclosed by them, and furthermore, the tuberculum linearum (*Merkel*), the protuberantia occipitalis externa and the torus occipitalis. Some of these characters will be discussed separately in the following chapters.

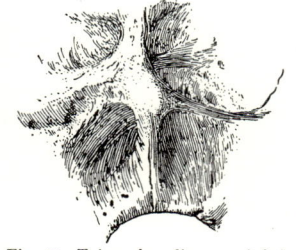

Fig. 75. Tuberculum linearum inferius, well defined in a male Haida (3755). Natural size.

The area between the posterior border of the foramen magnum and the lineae nuchae inferiores which might appropriately be called "*planum sub- or infralineare*", the main axes of which are sagittaly directed in contrast to the axes of the interlinear areae, are at times quite deep and complicated by sagittally directed ridges in indication of the insertions of mm. recti capitis posterior major and minor. Sometimes the orifices of channels are seen here which begin intracranially near the posterior border of the foramen magnum.

The *crista occipitalis externa* in many cases shows a better developed anterior portion, i. e., the portion between the posterior border of the foramen magnum and the point of union of the lineae nuchae inferiores, which point, in analogy to the *tuberculum linearum (Merkel)* of the lineae superiores, might be called *tuberculum linearum inferius*. That the latter can become quite prominent is shown in fig. 75, which is the case of a Haida male (3755). A somewhat irregular crista occipitalis, its middle portion bent over after a well defined superior course in continuation of the protuberantia occipitalis externa, is that of a Kwakiutl male (4236), depicted in fig. 76. In addition there may be seen an irregular number of vascular orifices on either side of the crista.

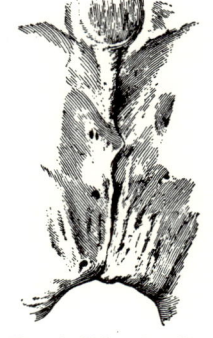

Fig. 76. Tuberculum linearum inferius, bent over in the course of a continuous crista occipitalis externa, in a Kwakiutl male (4236). Natural size.

With regard to the *lineae nuchae* it may be mentioned that quite frequently the ridge-shape lineae are replaced by irregular grooves, an appearance which, after a superficial examination of other human varieties, may also be seen there.

b. Protuberantia occipitalis externa.

The protuberantia occipitalis externa, as mentioned above, does not show excessively pronounced stages of development throughout our series; instead there are quite a number of variations to be noted. Resulting from a medial downward curvature of the lineae nuchae supremae, the area circumscribed by this inward curvature may represent extremely variable conditions from a mere tuberosity to a protuberance of appreciable size. Again, the latter as well as the shape may vary. Thus while in size the protuberance in cases merges with the tuberculum linearum (*Merkel*), in others it exceeds or does not reach it. The shape of the protuberance may be tongue-like, broad or narrow and short or long, and also run free of its base to assume a beak-shape, which latter, however, does not occur in our series. The narrow and broad tongue are shown in figs. 77 and 78, representing a Chukchee male (3843) and a Haida male (1606). It will also be noticed that the crista occipitalis externa in the former is well defined in its entirety and that it forms an almost uninterrupted ridge with the longstretched protuberantia.

Fig. 77. Protuberantia occipitalis externa: narrow tongue-shape in a male Chukchee (3843). Natural size.

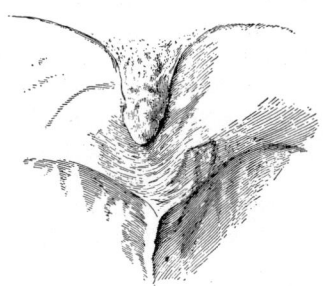

Fig. 78. Protuberantia occipitalis externa: broad tongue-shape, in a male Haida (1606). Natural size.

c. Torus occipitalis (*Ecker*).

The transverse elevation between the lineae nuchae superiores and supremae of each side, known as the torus occipitalis (*Ecker*), is to be considered an inferior morphological trait from which the more refined relief of nuchal lines and occipital protuberance must be derived. It is of typical occurrence in the Neandertaloids and marks here the flexion of the occiput. Its frequency therefore varies according to race. The torus, according to *R. Martin* (Lehrbuch, 1914, 735), is relatively rare in Europeans and Asiatics, and most frequent in Australians, Oceanians and Americans. Our own records confirm this statement.

In *summary 169* the torus has been classified as slight, medium and pronounced, the absences, in addition, being listed in column 1. It will readily be seen that most of the cases of torus formation are assembled in the column marked slight. This holds true for the Undeformed, and the Cowichan and Chinook deformations. The Koskimo have their greatest frequency in the medium column. The pronounced cases are very rare and limited to one male each in the Undeformed

Summary *169*.

Torus occipitalis: actual and percental frequency.

Sex and Age	Torus occipitalis								
	Undeformed								
	Absence		Slight		Medium		Pronounced		Total (♂; ♀)	Grand total
	no.	%	no.	%	no.	%	no.	%		
♂	13	16.7	43	55.1	21	26.9	1	1.3	83.3	
♀	11	35.5	16	51.6	4	12.9	—	—	64.5	69.7%
juv.	2	—	—	—	—	—	—	—	—	
inf.	11	—	—	—	—	—	—	—	—	
Total frequencies	37	30.3	59	48.4	25	20.5	1	0.8	—	
	Cowichan deformation								
♂	10	12.8	37	47.4	30	38.5	1	1.3	87.2	
♀	4	18.2	10	45.4	8	36.4	—	—	81.8	83.0%
juv.	1	—	1	—	—	—	—	—	—	
inf.	3	—	1	—	—	—	—	—	—	
Total frequencies	18	17.0	49	46.2	38	35.9	1	0.9	—	
	Chinook deformation								
♂	19	33.9	24	42.9	12	21.4	1	1.8	66.1	
♀	13	52.0	8	32.0	4	16.0	—	—	48.0	55.0%
juv.	3	—	1	—	—	—	—	—	—	
inf.	6	—	—	—	—	—	—	—	—	
Total frequencies	41	45.0	33	36.3	16	17.6	1	1.1	—	
	Koskimo deformation								
♂	7	6.6	34	32.1	63	59.4	2	1.9	93.4	
♀	6	16.6	15	41.7	15	41.7	—	—	83.3	86.7%
juv.	2	—	—	—	—	—	—	—	—	
inf.	5	—	1	—	—	—	—	—	—	
Total frequencies	20	13.3	50	33.3	78	52.0	2	1.4	—	

and the Cowichan and Chinook deformations, while there are two male cases in the Koskimo division. The frequency for the pronounced cases vacillates around $1°/_0$. The amount of absence of any torus formation is quite variable. Falling as low as $13.3°/_0$ and $17.0°/_0$ in the Koskimo and Cowichan divisions, the absence runs as high as $30.3°/_0$ and $45.0°/_0$ in the Undeformed and Chinook divisions. If all the cases of torus occipitalis from slight to pronounced are counted, markedly high frequencies are arrived at which range from $55°/_0$ in the Chinook division to $86°/_0$ in the Koskimo division.

If one considers that in this last division the greatest frequency of medium torus development occurs and two cases of strong as over against one in each of the other divisions, one may be tempted to consider artificial deformation as influential in the production of the torus. An examination of the inner relief, however, shows that the torus bulge is internally met by the concavities of the cranial fossae, and that a thickening of the bone here is not the rule. If one considers furthermore that the muscular insertions in the lineae nuchae superiores (mm. trapezius, occipitalis, splenius, sternocleidomastoideus) and supremae (galea aponeurotica) are frequently only slightly developed even in robust skulls, not to speak of the torus occipitalis, the assumption suggests itself that neither deformation nor muscular action is implicated in the torus production, but that a primitive morphological condition in connection with occipital flexion exists here which is preserved by morphologically more advanced varieties. The high frequency of moderate-sized tori may be considered as corroborating such a view.

In addition, it is rather significant that the external occipital relief, including the torus occipitalis, is scarcely developed, if at all, in infantile crania, a condition, remarked upon also by *Koganei* [192] with reference to the Koreans. Although this statement disposes of the direct transmission of a morphological character, its later appearance under functional strain nevertheless emphasizes the disposition towards it. In this connection it is the cerebral growth and particularly the posterior poles of the occipital brain lodging in, and perhaps pushing out the region in question, that are involved under the hereditary disposition.

f. Fossa supratoralis (*Klaatsch*).

This depression above the medial portion of the torus occipitalis was named so by *Klaatsch* in connection with the Krapina finds [193] It is not rare in recent skulls, and may occur without a torus as a tuberosity or a groove of rather undefined margins and different shape.

---

[192] *Koganei, Y.*, 1906. Über Schädel und Skelette der Koreaner. Zschr. Ethnol. v. XXXVIII, pp. 513—535 (525).
[193] *Klaatsch, H.*, l. c., p. 236 (393)
—— 1902, in: *Gorjanović-Kramberger, K.*, Der paläolithische Mensch und seine Zeitgenossen aus dem Diluvium von Krapina in Kroatien. Mitt. Anthrop. Ges. Wien, v. XXXII, 3. F., v. II, pp. 189—216 (*Klaatsch, H.*, pp. 194—201 [195]).

The examination of our series established a variety of fossa formations which are summarized in the classification as noted in *summary 170*. The absence at 42.5% in the Undeformed stands out against those of the other divisions, where the lowest absence is recorded at 3.2% in the Chinook. A tuberosity was noticed at fairly similar frequencies of 20% and slightly less in the Undeformed, and the Cowichan and Chinook deformations, while the Koskimo deformation attained only 3.2% of tuberosities. The other extreme, i.e., pronounced fossae, occurs with only low frequencies between 0.8% in the Undeformed and 4.4% in the Chinook. Between those two extremes fall the slight and medium grades at markedly higher figures in the former.

The shape of the fossa supratoralis proved to be quite variable; three

Figs. 79—81. Different shapes of Fossa supratoralis. Natural size.

Fig. 79. Oval (male Chinook, 4520).

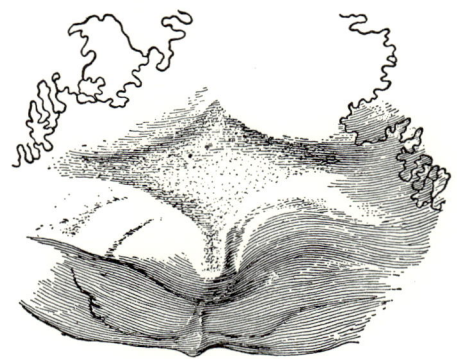

Fig. 80. Rhomboid (male Haida, 3747).

distinctly different types may be seen in figs. 79—81. The first represents a rather deep oval-shape fossa found in a Chinook male (4520). Fig. 80 is a well defined rhomboid with slightly concave sides, while fig. 81 is sombrero-like.

The fossa supratoralis on the whole seems to be more conservative than the torus, since our records list quite a number of infantile and juvenile cases for the tuberosity as well as the mild development of the fossa. However, there are no medium or pronounced cases of fossa supratoralis in the immatures.

Fig. 81. Sombrero-shape (male Eskimo, 3709).

The causation of this depression which in some cases is complicated by an inial canal, a good example of which is described by *A. W. Meyer* [194], seems to

---

[194] *Meyer, Arthur William*, 1917. Spolia anatomica, Addenda II: Inial fossae and canals. Anat. Rec., v. XII, pp. 43—94 (65—68).

Summary 170.

Fossa supratoralis: actual and percental frequency.

Sex and Age	Fossa supratoralis									
	Undeformed									
	Absence		Tuberosity		Slight		Medium		Pronounced	
	no.	%	no.	%	no.	%	no.	%	no.	%
♂	24	31.2	19	24.7	31	40.3	2	2.6	1	1.3
♀	16	53.4	3	10.0	10	33.3	1	3.3	—	—
juv.	2	—	—	—	2	—	—	—	—	—
inf.	9	—	—	—	—	—	—	—	—	—
Total frequencies	51	42.5	22	18.3	43	35.9	3	2.5	1	0.8
	Cowichan deformation									
♂	7	8.5	12	14.8	40	49.4	18	22.2	4	4.9
♀	—	—	5	22.7	15	68.2	2	9.1	—	—
juv.	—	—	—	—	2	—	—	—	—	—
inf.	1	—	2	—	1	—	—	—	—	—
Total frequencies	8	7.3	19	17.4	58	53.2	20	18.4	4	3.7
	Chinook deformation									
♂	2	3.5	11	19.3	21	36.8	20	35.1	3	5.3
♀	—	—	6	24.0	15	60.0	3	12.0	1	4.0
juv.	—	—	1	—	3	—	—	—	—	—
inf.	1	—	1	—	4	—	—	—	—	—
Total frequencies	3	3.2	19	20.7	43	46.7	23	25.0	4	4.4
	Koskimo deformation									
♂	17	16.1	2	1.9	49	46.2	35	33.0	3	2.8
♀	12	32.4	1	2.7	11	29.7	13	35.2	—	—
juv.	1	—	1	—	—	—	—	—	—	—
inf.	4	—	1	—	3	—	—	—	—	—
Total frequencies	34	22.2	5	3.2	63	41.2	48	31.4	3	2.0

be uncertain as yet. The assumption of an inial fontanel (*Maggi*, *Staurenghi*) or central fontanel (*Ranke*) between the upper and lower squama persistent in the adult, is quite plausible.

e. Os incae.

The terminology used for the variations in the ossification of the upper squamous portion of the os occipitale is somewhat confusing. The importance of the case may justify a brief recapitulation of the ontogenetic conditions supported by the schematic representation of fig. 82, which is *Ranke*'s conception of the ossification of the occipital squama. The Roman figures there indicate the centers of ossification, of which the I's belong to the cartilaginous lower squama (occipitale superius), and the others to the membranous upper, also called the interparietal. The homology with the mammalian os inter-

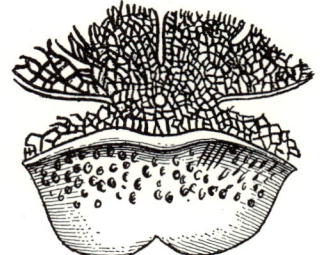 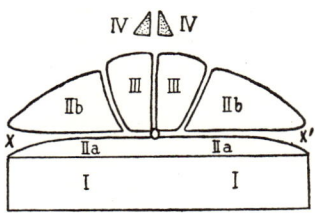

Fig. 82. Scheme of ossification of the occipital squama. After *Ranke*.
I—IV, centers of ossification; x, x', unossified embryonic matrix between upper and lower squama persisting in cases as sutura mendosa.

parietale, however, is not unequivocal, since in the human bone a strip of ossification extending from the inferior border of the upper squama coalesces with the superior marginal region of the lower squama. This strip designated as IIa in fig. 82, and joined to the lower squama is *Ranke*'s "Hautknochen-Ergänzungsstück der Unterschuppe". There is now between the ossific centers IIb and IIa on each side a zone which remains unossified for some time and which is known as sutura mendosa in the neonate skull, marked as x, x' in fig. 82. This gap then forms a zone of separation between the upper and lower squamae persisting sometimes either as a total transverse suture (*Virchow*'s "Sutura transversa foetalis squamae occipitalis), or as lateral indications of it, while as a rule it ossifies without leaving any traces. Above this gap there are, according to *Ranke* two more pairs of centers of ossification designated in our diagram as III and IV. The last of these will be referred to again below (p. 325). The upper row of paired osseous elements (IIb and III) is supposd to be separated in the uniform matrix by sutures (1) between this row and the lower squama (I) plus the additional portion of the upper squama (IIa), and (2) by sutures between the elements themselves of the upper squama, all of which cut through to a small circular unossified area of connective tissue, *Ranke*'s "Zentralloch" or "Zentralfontanelle".

The results of *Ranke*'s [195] conscientious studies were superseded by *Aichel* [196] who so far seems to have spoken the last word in regard to the process of ossification of the occipital squama. He showed that the normal ossification there arises from only two centers, that *Ranke*'s postulated four paired centers are of an atypical nature, and that only in this case complete division occurs between the parts of the atypical ossific "anlage". He showed furthermore that in the upper squama in the process of ossification, there occur typical incisures due to stress and tension as caused by the ossific growth of the adjoining bones likewise ossified in membrane, which as typical occurrences never cut through to *Ranke*'s circular area. *Aichel* therefore speaks of incisurae in this connection (transversa, sagittalis media, lateralis) which ossify in the course of growth. If, however, in the atypical "anlage", sutures are formed between the different osseous elements in the process of growth, such sutures may coincide, although not necessarily, with the typical incisures.

The persistence of the atypical sutures, first of all the transverse one, gives rise to varying combinations known as os incae and its variations [197]. It is well known that the total transverse division of the occipital squama was first observed in Peruvian skulls by *Rivero* and *v. Tschudi* [198], who applied to it the name of Inca bone or os incae, supposing that its occurrence was restricted to the Peruvian skulls under their observation. Subsequent investigations have demonstrated the contrary. Although noticed in quite a number of human varieties [199], it must be realized that frequencies in the Peruvians which in the works of different authors vary between $5.1°/_0$ and $23.4°/_0$ are slightly exceptional, and quite probably handed on as an atypical feature by isolation and inbreeding. *R. Martin*'s listings of os incae in non-Peruvian skulls contain frequencies of $1.2°/_0$ for Europeans, $2.3°/_0$ for Mongols, $2.6°/_0$ for Negroes, and an average of $4.8°/_0$ for North Americans. The figures for the last named rise to $5.7°/_0$ in the Ohio and Tennessee Indians, and to $6.5°/_0$ in the Florida tribes. Our own records as shown in *summary 171*, contain only small frequencies of $1.4°/_0$ and $1.7°/_0$ in the Cowichan and Undeformed, none in the Chinook and only $0.7°/_0$ in the Koskimo.

A particularly fine case of complete separation of the upper and lower

---

[195] l. c., p. 223.

[196] *Aichel, Otto*, 1915. Die normale Entwickelung der Schuppe des Hinterhauptbeines, die Entstehung der "Inkabein" genannten Anomalie der Schuppe und die kausale Grundlage für die typischen Einschnitte an der Schuppe. Arch. Anthrop., v. XIII, pp. 130—168.

[197] These may be found listed in a lucid way in: *Bartels, P.*, l. c., p. 276.

[198] *Rivero, M. E. y Tschudi S. J. de*, 1851. Antigüedades Peruanas. Vienna.

[199] *Martin, R.*, Lehrbuch 1914, (731, 732).

squamae, i. e., an os incae verum s. proprium is that in a Kwakiutl infant (4246) as shown in fig. 83. The slightly oscillating transverse occipital suture is evident from side to side and becomes somewhat livelier just before meeting the lambdoid suture in the asterion point.

Although quite a number of different combinations of osseous elements of the upper squama, as suggested by the study of fig. 82, may be possible, the one pictured by *Cameron* (1923, p. 30c; pl. VIII) and presenting only the independent parts II*b*, while the III's remain undistinguished, appears to be rather uncommon. Although that author describes his case as "showing two large Wormian bones possibly representing portions of the interparietal bone", there is no doubt that we have to deal here with a variation of os incae. It may be stated, however, that the independent elements of os incae share the characteristics of true Wormian or sutural bones in that they represent independent osseous elements separated by sutures from adjoining parts or bones.

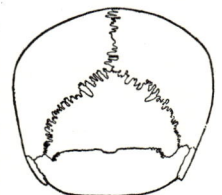

Fig. 83. Os incae verum s. proprium in a Kwakiutl inf. II (4246). 1/3.

f. Os apicis.

The fourth pair of ossification centers, marked IV in fig. 82, and accessory in its nature, gives rise at times to an independent bone generally of triangular shape embedded in the angle formed by the two halves of the lambdoid suture. Terminology as well as the views on derivation of this bone, like those on the os incae, are quite varied. Thus, while various names besides os apicis are in use, such as os praeinterparietale, os fonticuli posterioris, etc., the derivation is assumed to be connected either with the ossification of the upper squama or that of the occipital fontanel as indicated by the terminology. The underlying ontogenetic facts apparently provide, under the given abnormal conditions, for the independent ossification of both the fontanellar gap and the infralambdoid triangular space. Although *R. Martin* (Lehrbuch, 1914, 729) says that "dieser Spitzenknochen ist in seiner Lage durchaus durch die Fontanelle bedingt, daher ein reiner Fontanellknochen..... und seine Deutung als selbständiges Praeinterparietale hat daher wenig Wahrscheinlichkeit für sich", it is nevertheless to be considered that certain sutural conditions directly suggest the independent formation of an os apicis. The present writer sees his assumption shared by a statement of *Schlaginhaufen*[200] who asserts

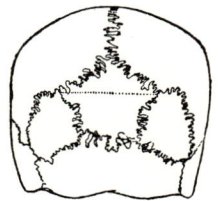

Fig. 84. Os incae tripartitum, the transverse interrupted line indicating a possible separation of an upper triangular portion of the os duplex medium ftom the rest of the medial portion of the os incae.

Modified after *Martin*.

---

[200] l. c., p. 245 (478).

"dass eine gewisse Tendenz zur Bildung des os apicis vorhanden ist, mag auch aus dem zuweilen auftretenden eigenartigen Verlauf der Sutura lambdoidea hervorgehen". Conscious of the simplicity of the pars lambdoidea of the lambdoid suture as against the livelier serration of its pars media, the present writer in the course of his methodical cranioscopic investigation soon noticed in the majority of cases a peculiar behavior of the two partes lambdoidea to the extent that by their more or less angular digression from the partes mediae and subsequent individual curvation toward the lambda they

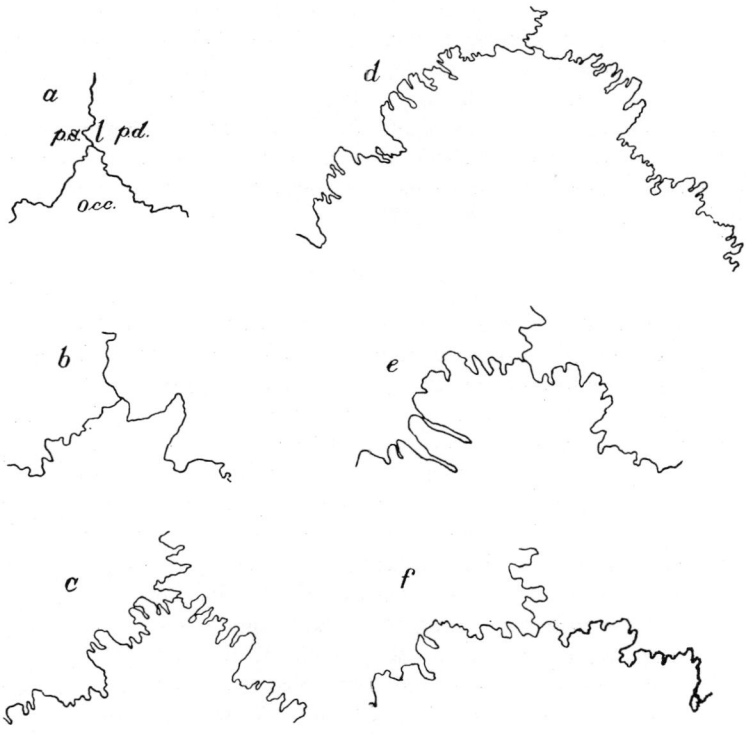

Fig. 85. The lambdoid portions of the lambdoid suture suggesting fontanel bones (ossa lambdoidea s. apicis) in skulls of: *a*, inf. II Chukchee (3847); *b*, male Nimkish (1666); *c* and *d*, male Chinook (4514, 4464), and *e* and *f*, inf. II and male Nimkish (1643, 1664). About natural size.
l, lambda; *p. s.*, *p. d.*, left and right parietal; *occ.*, occipital.

seem to enclose a separate bone incomplete only for the wanting transverse suture between the two points of angular digression. These enclosed areas, when of limited extension, encroaching upon the interparietal region proper and situated in advance of what might represent the lambda point under normal conditions, is suggestive of a true fontanel bone in contradistinction to an independent bone formation of triangular shape whose upper angle is the lambda and its base the transverse suture just mentioned. The latter, under such consideration, would then separate a triangular cap from what under given circumstances might have developed into the central portion of an os incae tripartitum and derived from the centers III of fig. 82. An illustration of such a case may be seen in fig. 84, which modified after *R. Martin* (Lehrbuch, 1914, 730) shows by the accessory interrupted line the frequently mentioned transverse suture between the two points of division of the lambdoid and medial portions of the lambdoid suture.

The sutural conditions indicative of the osseous formations discussed in the preceding paragraph are shown in fig. 85, where *a*, *b* and *c* in their complete states may quite probably have produced a fontanel bone proper, and *d*, *e* and *f*, the os apicis which as such would represent a true os praeinterparietale. Figs. 86, *a–d*, and 87, *a–c* exemplify such complete cases, the former, various forms of a fontanel bone complicated in two instances by sutural bones, and the latter, the os apicis, of which fig. 87, *b* is distinguished by a transverse and *c* by a longitudinal division.

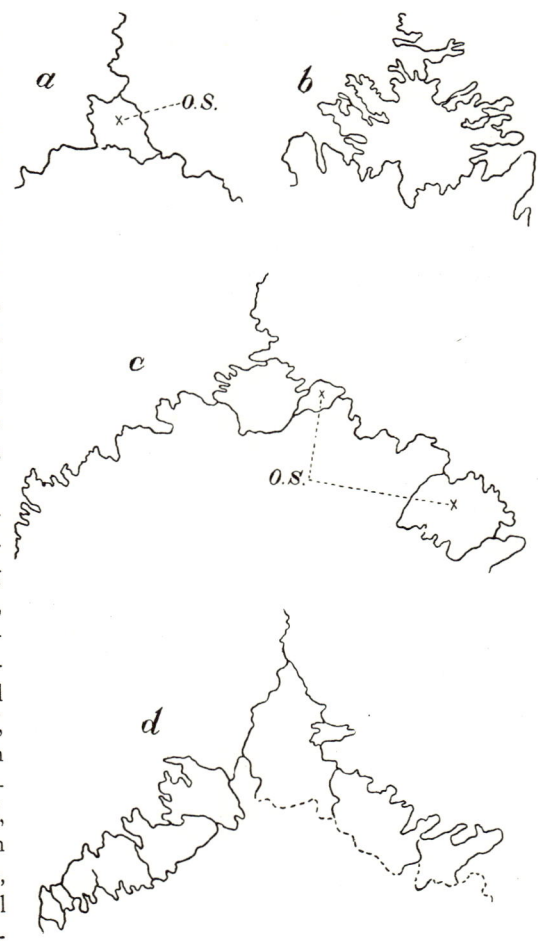

Fig. 86. Os lambdoideum, in *a*, inf. II Haida (1615); *b*, male Kwakiutl (3878), and *c* and *d*, male Chinook (4465, 4482). There are also Wormian bones (*o. s.* os suturarum) in *c* and *d*. About natural size.

The complexity of the conditions of ossification in the occipital squama will have to be based, first of all, on ontogenetic investigations as *R. Virchow*, *J. Ranke*, *H. Stieda*, *O. Aichel* and the Italian anthropologists have successfully carried on. From the conditions in the adult, however, it seems to the present writer that a definite nomenclature should be adopted, naming the fontanel bone os lambdoideum in analogy to the bones in the other fonticuli,

Summary 171.

Os incae: actual and percental frequency.

Tribe		Os incae	
		no.	%
Undeformed		2 (♂; ♀)	1.7
Cowichan	deformation	2 (♂)	1.4
Chinook		—	—
Koskimo		1 (inf)	0.7

Summary 172.

Os apicis: actual and percental frequency.

Os apicis	
no.	%
9 (4 ♂; 3 ♀; 2 inf)	7.8
18 (10 ♂; 8 ♀)	17.3
8 (5 ♂; 1 ♀; 2 inf)	9.8
20 (14 ♂; 2 ♀; 4 inf)	13.4

for instance, os bregmaticum and os epiptericum, and the other one under discussion os apicis, which in fact is an os praeinterparietale of accessory origin and merged in most cases with the upper medial border of the upper squama. The frequency of the latter in our series as revealed in *summary 172*, is higher in the deformed divisions as compared to the Undeformed, and

Fig. 87. Os apicis, in *a*, female Salish (1537); *b*, male Kwakiutl (3896); *c*, inf. II Clayoquot (1601). The os apicis is transversely divided in *b*, and sagittally in *c*. About natural size.

may be due to deformatory influences which also cause the abundance of Wormian bones as will be shown later on.

3. Regio mastoidea.
a. Foramen mastoideum.

The variability in size and number of the foramen mastoideum, observed also by other anthropologists (*Hrdlička, Hooton*, et al.) in Indian crania from various sections, holds likewise true for our series. Transmitting the ramus

Summary 173.

Foramen mastoideum: actual and percental frequency.

Sex and Age	Foramen mastoideum													
	Undeformed													
	Absence		Small		Medium		Large		r>1		r<1		Irregular occurrence	
	no.	%	no.	%	no.	%	no.	%	no.	%	no.	%	no.	%
♂	8	10.8	22	29.7	16	21.6	—	—	4	5.4	2	2.7	22	29.7
♀	3	10.0	7	23.3	7	23.3	—	—	2	6.7	3	10.0	8	26.7
juv.	—	—	—	—	—	—	1	—	—	—	—	—	—	—
inf.	4	—	—	—	2	—	—	—	—	—	1	—	4	—
Total frequencies	15	12.9	29	25.0	25	21.6	1	0.8	6	5.2	6	5.2	34	29.3
	Cowichan deformation													
♂	7	8.4	13	15.7	21	25.3	—	—	3	3.6	7	8.4	32	38.6
♀	4	17.4	4	17.4	5	21.7	—	—	—	—	2	8.7	8	34.8
juv.	—	—	—	—	—	—	—	—	—	—	1	—	1	—
inf.	—	—	—	—	—	—	—	—	—	—	—	—	4	—
Total frequencies	11	9.8	17	15.2	26	23.2	—	—	3	2.6	10	8.9	45	40.2
	Chinook deformation													
♂	10	17.5	13	22.8	7	12.3	2	3.5	3	5.3	2	3.5	20	35.1
♀	1	4.6	6	27.3	3	13.6	—	—	1	4.6	3	13.6	8	36.3
juv.	—	—	1	—	—	—	—	—	—	—	—	—	2	—
inf.	1	—	—	—	1	—	—	—	1	—	—	—	4	—
Total frequencies	12	13.5	20	22.5	11	12.4	2	2.2	5	5.6	5	5.6	34	38.2
	Koskimo deformation													
♂	10	9.8	7	6.9	34	33.3	—	—	9	8.8	2	2.0	40	39.2
♀	2	5.6	9	25.0	9	25.0	—	—	—	—	2	5.6	14	38.8
juv.	—	—	—	—	1	—	—	—	—	—	—	—	2	—
inf.	1	—	—	—	2	—	—	—	—	—	—	—	3	—
Total frequencies	13	8.8	16	10.9	46	31.3	—	—	9	6.1	4	2.7	59	40.2

mastoideus of the art. occipitalis and the emissarium mastoideum of the vena occipitalis, the foramen is typically situated in the occipitomastoid suture, but also frequently found on the pars mastoidea of the temporal bone. While absence, as listed in *summary 173*, occurs at appreciable percentages in the four divisions, multiplicity also in various combinations as regards right and left, is of no rare occurrence. Absence or singleness on one side may be combined with as many as three foramina on the other side. In special cases the diameters of almost circular foramina mastoidea may attain 5 mm. or more (Chinook juvenile 3734; Salish male 1581), while a number of cases have been recorded of merged foramina with still definable outlines (Kwakiutl male 3896; Chinook male 4526).

Summary 173 accounts for only a limited number of large-sized foramina, but for high frequencies, in fact the highest in each division, of irregular numerical occurrences. In normal occurrence, on the other hand, the small-sized foramina predominate in the Undeformed and Chinook with frequencies of $25.0°/_0$ and $22.5°/_0$ against $21.6°/_0$ and $12.4°/_0$ of medium-sized foramina as against the prevalence of medium-sized foramina in the Cowichan and Koskimo divisions at $23.2°/_0$ and $31.3°/_0$ against $15.2°/_0$ and $10.9°/_0$ of small foramina.

b. Asterion

There is likewise great variation to be noticed in the asterion region, the meeting point of sutt. lambdoidea, parietomastoidea and occipitomastoidea. The region is frequently transformed into a rugged, shrivelled area, or filled with Wormian bones. Statistics were not recorded.

MANDIBLE.

Corpus.

a. General remarks.

The cranioscopic examination of the lower jaw is concerned with the general appearance of the latter and the numerous morphologic details, quite a number of which are of phyletic importance. The anatomical description of the lower jaw has gained quite considerably in acuteness since in the course of recent years fossil finds have multiplied. The anatomical description likewise occasioned the revision and enrichment of the nomenclature as proposed and found in the specific works of *Klaatsch, Schoetensack, Gorjanović-Kramberger, Schwalbe, H. Virchow, Toldt, Walkhoff, M. v. Lenhossék, Gerrit S. Miller Jr., Pycraft*, et al., and which has been adopted by the present author. The following paragraphs treat of some of the more significant characters of the mandible. Quite a number of our skulls were devoid of their lower jaws — there are only five in the Chinook series — and although a number of stray mandibles could be united with the others, the total did not measure up to the number of skulls.

b. General appearance of lower jaw.

Characterized already in the metrical treatment as neither unusually large nor small, the lower jaw from the North Pacific regions exhibits no exaggerative conditions from the descriptive point of observation. Rather gracile in its general aspect the corpus, the ramus with its two processes, and the symphysial region are in no case bulky or massive as witnessed sometimes in the Eskimo mandible. Muscular marks are on the whole only mildly developed and that refers likewise to the striae platysmaticae *(H. Virchow)* on the anterior basal outside of the corpus, the digastric, masseteric and pterygoidal insertional areas, etc. Among the exceptions is a Haida male (3740) with well marked insertional ridges of the m. masseter and a peculiar thorn-like projection which has its basis at the basal border in the left incisura praeangularis (see under *c*) clasping the border and projecting upward on the external side of the corpus and closely merged with it for about 1 cm. The case seemed interesting enough for reproduction in fig. 88.

c. Incisura praemuscularis *(Klaatsch)*
s. praeangularis *(Frizzi)*; "Schaukelunterkiefer" *(Stahr)*.

With the exception of a few specimens in each division and of the immature mandibles in general where this concavity is quite pronounced, the basal outline of the corpus is straight or nearly so. The other extreme, total convexity of the basal border, giving rise to *Stahr*'s [201] „Schaukelunterkiefer" or rocker mandible and encountered by him at a high percentage in the Maori, occurs quite frequently in the Koskimo division of our series, namely in 8 out of 43 cases or $18.6°/_0$. Lesser frequencies were recorded for the Cowichan deformation and the Undeformed, the former comprising 3 among 80 cases or $3.8°/_0$, and the latter 1 among 65, or $1.5°/_0$. The Chinook mandibles, amounting only to five, were exempt from this particular shape.

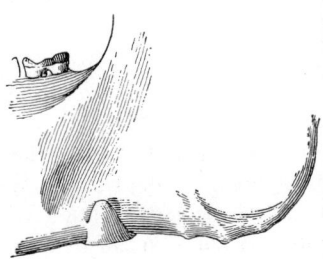

Fig. 88. Posterior end of corpus mandibulae of a male Haida (3740) with strong masseteric ridges and a clasp-like appendage in the incisura praeangularis. Natural size.

The three different appearances of the basal contour of the lower jaw as realized best in lateral projection are shown in fig. 89. They represent the mandibular outlines of a Nimkish inf. I (1669); a Haida male (3741); a Lillooet male (2618),

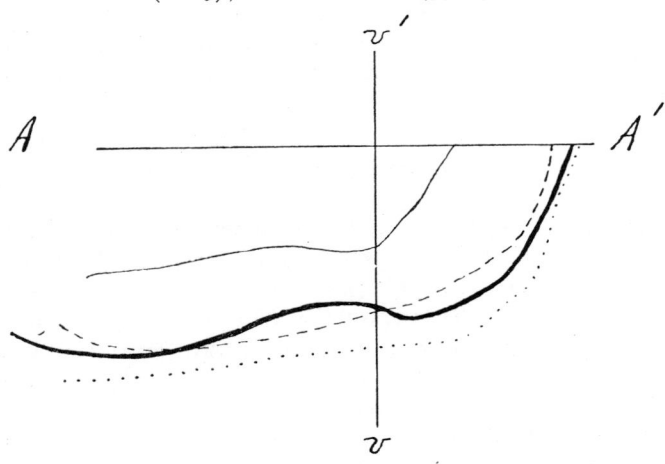

Fig. 89. Lower jaws in lateral projection and alveolar and post-m_2 vertical orientation, to show the different behavior of the basal border: incisura praemuscularis *(Klaatsch)* s. praeangularis *(Frizzi)* in —, inf. II Nimkish (1669), and —, male Haida (3741); ...., straight basal outline in a male Lillooet (2618), ---, „Schaukelunterkiefer" in a male Nimkish (1665). A-A', alveolar plane line; v-v', post-m_2 vertical. Natural size.

---

[201] *Stahr, H.*, 1906. Ueber den Maori-Unterkiefer und sein Vorkommen an Aegypterschädeln. Anat. Anz., v. XXIX, pp. 65—75.

and a Nimkish male (1665). In the first two outlines the praemuscular or praeangular incisure is well marked, while the third shows a perfectly straight basal border, and the fourth a fine case of "Schaukelunterkiefer."

d. Chin.

The medial ridge at the anterior or symphysial region of the lower jaw broadens out in its lower portion to a protuberantia mentalis. The more or less protruding and uniformly rounded prominence gives rise to the formation of a "median chin" *(Klaatsch)*[202]. In most of the cases and in proportion to its developmental stage, the latter is set off by the impressio subincisiva against the alveolar border proper. Sometimes a deep groove is noticed on either side of the symphysial ridge which as a fossa mentalis obtains in the fetus and the early infantile stages but in cases is preserved in the adult. A good case of fossa mentalis in a Chukchee inf. II (3847) is shown in fig. 90. From the condition of uniform roundness of chin, differentiations take their start which result in lateral prominences termed "lateral chin" by *Klaatsch*. Its causation must be seen in swellings at the basal border in the region of m. digastricus insertion. The lateral prominences just mentioned are the tubercula mentalia posteriora in contradistinction to the tuberculum mentale anterius situated between the two digastric fossae. Intermediate conditions between the median and lateral chins obtain in the Mongols.

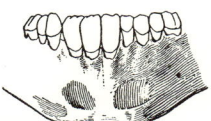

Fig. 90. Fossa mentalis in an inf. II Chukchee (3847). Natural size.

The chin, according to *Klaatsch*, may be either neutral, positive or negative. For the determination of those conditions a perpendicular is dropped from the alveolar plane in the prosthion inferius[203] or incision. If the incision vertical just touches the chin prominence forming with the alveolar plane line an angle of 90°; the chin is neutral. The negative chin falls short of the vertical and the positive exceeds it, the angle between a chin tangent and the alveolar plane dropping to 70° in the former (67° in Krapina H), and rising to 120° in the latter. Intermediate conditions here are offered by the Malays, Mongolids and Polynesians.

The designation of negative chin, however, is misleading for the reason first of all that the absence of a chin might be supposed and secondly that it is awkward if not impossible to indicate by a line a morphologic condition like the one in question. *R. Martin* (Lehrbuch, 1914, 871) remarks appro-

---

[202] l. c., p. 9 (109). The description of the morphologic detail of the lower jaw is to a great extent in accordance with that by *Klaatsch* in his paper just mentioned.

[203] The prosthion inferius of the lower jaw corresponds to the prosthion of the upper jaw. Other names for that mandibular point are incision *(Klaatsch)*; infradentale *(R. Martin)*; symphysion *(v. Török)*; catoprosthion *(H. Virchow)*.

priately that this method does not so much relate to the chin development as to the protrusion or recession of the entire corpus. *Frizzi*[204] therefore lays a correction vertical through the deepest point of the impressio subincisiva externa which is apt to disclose in the mandibulogram even the slightest indication of a mental prominence. The corrective vertical furthermore will claim as positive a goodly number, if not all, of neutral chins, while in doubtful cases the direct examination of specimens is given.

In fig. 91 the three conditions of chin prominence as defined by *Klaatsch* are shown by the lateral outlines of mandibles in alveolar orientation. The positive chin in *a* is that of a Lytton male (4308); the neutral chin of *b* was found in a Lillooet female (2622), and the negative of *c* in a Salish male mandible from Vancouver (1581 A). In the last of these *Frizzi's* corrective vertical is also drawn in by which the chin prominence is recognized as such.

Fig. 92 demonstrates three different forms of the chin by a system of horizontal curves, of which the solid one represents the basal curve, the interrupted one that of the impressio subincisiva externa and the dotted one that around the alveolar process. The types represent in *a*, a Tsimshian male (4588), the "median chin"; in *b*, a Lillooet male (2618), the "lateral chin" and in *c*, a Chukchee male (3849), a widely rounded almost semicircular chin. To each of these curve systems the mediansagittal symphysial outline is added, which shows each mandible provided with a positive chin, the most prominent of which is the square one of *b*.

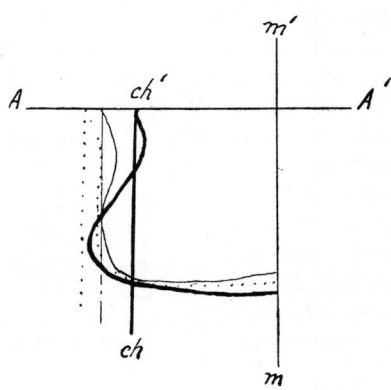

Fig. 91. Mandibular outlines in lateral projection and alveolar and post-m_1 vertical orientation showing *Klaatsch*'s three types of chin prominence, in —, the positive (male Lytton 4308); in —, the neutral (female Lillooet 2622), and in ...., the negative (male Salish 1581 A). A-A′, alveolar plane line; m-m′, post-m_1 vertical; ch-ch′, chin vertical through incision point; *Frizzi*'s corrective vertical coincides with the chin vertical for the male Salish (1581 A). Natural size.

It may be mentioned in this connection that *Frizzi*[205] does not approve of the term "lateral chin". He substitutes "round" and "abgekantet" (edged off) for median and lateral, claiming that both are medially situated and that the so-called "lateral chin" occurs only in exceptional cases.

Following *Klaatsch*'s terminology, however, the lateral chin appeared to be predominant in our series with 60.3°/₀ in the Undeformed, while 12.1°/₀ went to the median chin and 27.6°/₀ to the intermediate forms. Almost identical

---

[204] *Frizzi, Ernst,* 1910. Untersuchungen am menschlichen Unterkiefer mit spezieller Berücksichtigung der Regio mentalis. Arch. Anthrop., N. F., v. IX, pp. 252—286 (273).
[205] l. c., p. 334 (274).

proportions obtain in the other divisions, disclosing thus a pronounced tendency toward a squarish (lateral or edged-off) chin in the North Pacific tribes.

  e. Incisura submentalis and spina interdigastrica *(Klaatsch).*

It is to *Klaatsch's* credit to have called attention to the phyletic significance of a subsymphysial recess or incisure [206], which he observed in the gibbon,

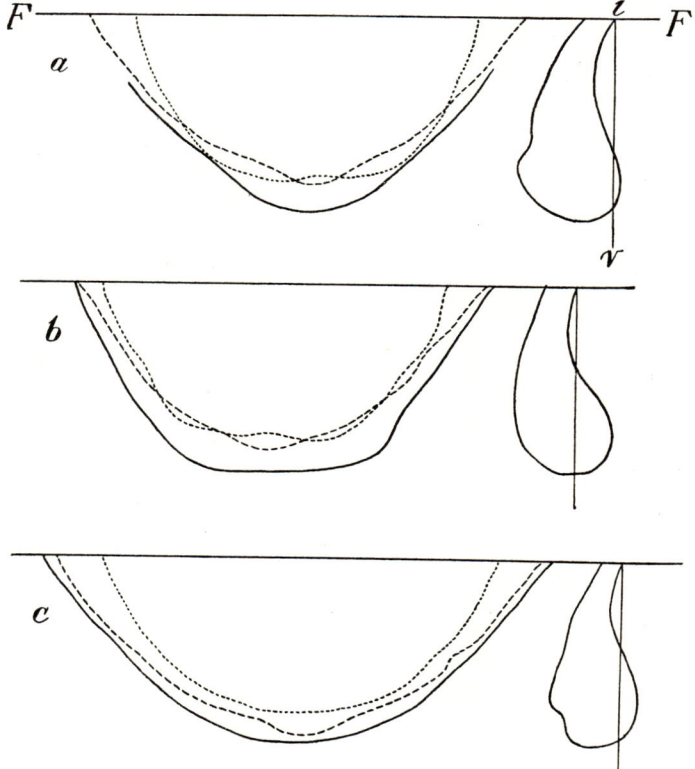

  Fig. 92. Horizontal curve system of *Klaatsch's* two chin types, *a*, the median (male Tsimshian 4588); *b*, the lateral (male Lillooet 2618). *c*, represents an exceedingly rounded, almost semi-circular chin (male Chukchee 3849). The median-sagittal symphysial outline is added to each curve system. 2/3. — basal curve; --- curve through deepest point of impressio subincisiva externa; ...... alveolar curve. F-F', frontal plane; *i-v*, incision vertical.

the old-diluvial fossils, in most of his Australians and indications thereof in recent human varieties. The fact that, as secondary adaptations, in the other

---

[206] l. c., p. 9 (110—111).

anthropoid forms the basal portion of the symphysial region is drawn out posteriorly into a basal plate under the simultaneous reduction of the digastric insertions, and the canine increase, is a further proof for the elimination of those forms from the human ancestral line. The more primitive, i. e., undifferentiated conditions in gibbon, replicas and vestiges of which are found in the human varieties, suggest, according to *Klaatsch*, a common gibbonoid ancestor.

The size of the incisura submentalis bears a commensurate relation to the lateral chin formation and to the size and position of the digastric fossae. These latter have, as is well known, a more basal situation in the fossils (Mauer, Krapina, Spy, etc.) as likewise in the morphologically more primitive human forms (Australians, Negroes, Eskimo, etc.), i. e., in forms where the incisura submentalis is frequently wide and deep. Its gradual disappearance was observed in many cases as correlated with the shifting of the digastric fossae to aft and upward, the condition encountered in the advanced human types.

In our series and in a number of cases, the fossae digastricae invariably occupy this higher position, ending medially in a ledge-like tuberosity sometimes assuming the shape of a spina interdigastrica. There were $26°/_0$ of pronounced spinae recorded in the Undeformed and slightly more in the Cowichan and Koskimo divisions. Regarding the incisura submentalis there were only indications of it to be noticed. They amounted to $57°/_0$ in the Undeformed, while $43°/_0$ represented total absence. The latter is even greater in the deformed divisions, attaining, for instance, $54.1^c/_0$ in the Cowichan series.

f. Foramen mentale.

The foramen mentale for a. and n. mentalis (r. mandibularis n. trigemini) in our series lies invariably on a level with the second premolar. Some variation may be noticed, however, in regard to its position within a small range, as it may fall in line with the anterior or posterior edge of that tooth, or in between the two. The position on the whole is more forward as compared with the conditions in the anthropoids and the older human fossils, where the foramen in most cases is found in the region of the first molar tooth. Phylogenetically therefore the foramen travels forward, while ontogenetically it moves backward from a position just behind the canine in fetal and early infantile ages to its definite position. It is during individual growth that "die Veränderung in der Form und Lage des Foramen mentale wird durch Verschiebung der oberflächlichen Knochenschichten bewirkt..."[207]. The foramen in general is of medium size, about 2 mm. or a little over in diameter.

---

[207] *Grunewald, Julius*, 1920. Über die Beanspruchung und den Aufbau des menschlichen Unterkiefers und die mechanische Bedeutung des Kinns. Arch. Anthrop., N. F., v. XVIII, pp. 100—113 (113).

Although the greatest frequency occurs in this size, there are cases of smaller and larger foramina which amount to 22.4% and 19.0% in the Undeformed, and in slightly varying percentages in the other divisions. Absence was not noticed, but there are a few cases with supernumerary foramina recorded which, as is known, are quite frequently encountered in the older fossils (Mauer, Krapina, etc.), and were also observed in the Santa Barbara mandibles B and E [208]. They are usually smaller than the principal foramina and situated in most cases above or in advance of the latter, more rarely behind and hardly ever below them. Of interest in this connection are supernumerary holes produced in oral surgery as observed and described by *Hooton* [209] in ancient Egyptian mandibles. They were characterized by their occurrence in sound tissue and their clean-cut edges in contradistinction to pathological perforations as caused by inflammatory absorption from within resulting in the thinning of the edges. In the other case, "the operator with considerable skill bored his holes in such a way as to avoid the roots of the teeth."

g. Spina mentalis interna.

The concrescence into one spinous projection of the four origins of mm. genioglossi and geniohyoidei seems to be altogether quite rare. The rule, on the contrary, is the individual formation of genioglossal and geniohyoidal grooves, tuberosities, spines, the latter either single or coalesced into a spina genioglossi and a spina geniohyoidei. Grooves and tuberosities seem to be the more primitive conditions as found in the genioglossal area in the anthropoids and the older diluvial human fossils. A groove is also of quite frequent occurrence in the Australians and typical in the young child. It seems to be very rare in the geniohyoidal area, where in fact a tuberosity marks the more primitive state while even a spina geniohyoidei is present in the Mauer mandible. In recent Hominidae, however, the better development of the spina genioglossi is the more prevalent condition.

The muscle marks in our series are quite variable and present themselves either as tuberosities, however rarely, or in various combinations expressible in symbols. Here the genioglossus marks are indicated above the fraction line and below it those of the geniohyoideus, the numbers standing for more or less developed spinae as: $\frac{1}{2}$; $\frac{tuberosity}{2}$; $\frac{2}{1}$; $\frac{2}{2}$; 2. Insertional tuberosities as mentioned before are exceedingly rare. There are two cases each in the Undeformed, and the Cowichan and Koskimo divisions, which cases comprise an infantile and an adult. The greatest frequency is attained in the two-to-two occur-

---

[208] See *Oetteking, Bruno*, 1925, p. 128.

[209] *Hooton E. A.*, 1917. Oral surgery in Egypt during the old Empire. Harvard African Studies, v. I, pp. 29—32 (30-31).

rence, amounting to 58.6%, in the Undeformed and almost identical figures in the other divisions. Next range the two-to-one muscle marks with 25% in the Undeformed, 16.2% in the Cowichan, and 20.4% in the Koskimo divisions. The other combinations as listed above are much less frequent.

A few interesting cases of muscle marks at the internal symphysial region are reproduced in figs. 93—95. Somewhat typical but not representing the greatest frequency is the case in fig. 93, of a Haida male (3740) with a muscle mark on either side of the middle line for the mm. genioglossi and a ridge twice as long as either of the former, below and between them for the

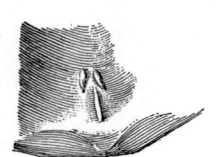 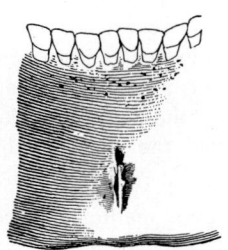 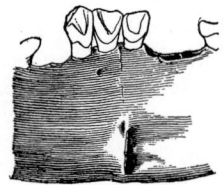

Fig. 93. Mm. genioglossus and geniohyoideus origins: $\frac{2}{1}$, in a male Haida (3740). Natural size.

Fig. 94. Mm. genioglossus and geniohyoideus origins: $\frac{1}{2}$, in a male Yakima (4334). Natural size.

Fig. 95. Mm. genioglossus and geniohyoideus origins: $\frac{\text{groove}}{1}$, in an inf. II. Yakima (4326). Natural size.

common origin of both mm. geniohyoidei. Lenhossék [210] has observed this condition in 42%, the greatest of the frequencies obtained by him. It is seen reversed in fig. 94, representing a Yakima male (4334). The size proportion between the muscle marks is likewise retained, i. e., the two geniohyoidal ridges are each double the size of a single and medially located genioglossal ridge. In fig. 95, the common origin of the geniohyoideus muscle is marked by the medial ridge while the genioglossus origin is indicated by a depression on the left and a smooth elevation on the right side. This is the case of a Yakima inf. II.

Ramus.

a. General proportions.

Supplementing the metrical investigation of the ramus as carried on in the first part of this work (pp. 117 ff.), the quantitative expression of proportion in connection with the superposed outlines in lateral projection has been resorted to for a representation of the two fundamentally diverging forms.

---

[210] *Lenhossék, M. v.*, 1922. Makroskopische Anatomie in: Handbuch der Zahnheilkunde by *Julius Scheff*, Wien-Leipzig. v. I, pp. 1—324 (34).

These are shown in alveolar orientation in fig. 96, where the rami of two male and two female mandibles of the Undeformed series may be seen superposed. The two postmolar points, i. e., the points in lateral projection where the linea obliqua intersects the alveolar plane, coincide. In *a*, the first pair of outlines of our figure, the high and narrow ramus is that of a Haida male (1610) with a ramus index of 47.7, while the lower and broader one of a Chukchee male (3846) has an index of 72.7. The female outlines under *b* repeat almost entirely these conditions in a Nicola Lake mandible (2609) with a ramus index of 50.9 and a Haida one (3742) at 68.5.

The ramus shape and proportions in the deformed series are fairly identical with those of the Undeformed. This refers not only to the high-narrow and low-broad extremes, but to all the intermediate forms which in fact represent the bulk, and center in an average Mongolid ramus of moderate height with a tendency toward a greater minimum breadth.

b. Incisurae subcoronoidea and subcondyloidea *(Klaatsch).*

The anterior and posterior borders of the vertical rami show concavities of varying dephts, named by *Klaatsch* incisurae subcondyloidea and subcoro-

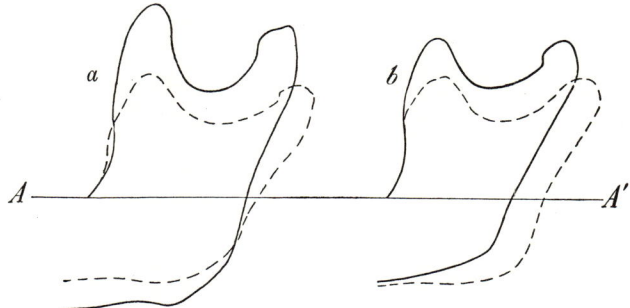

Fig. 96, *a. b.* Superposition of ramus outlines in alveolar and postmolar orientation representing height-breadth proportions as indicated in each case by the highest and lowest index. *a*, — male Haida (1610; ind. 47.7), - - - male Chukchee (3846; ind. 72.7). *b*, — female Nicola Lake (2609; ind. 50.9), - - - female Haida (3742; ind. 68.5). 2/3. A-A', alveolar plane.

noidea. The anterior border as a rule is the more concave in the human varieties and differs in this repect greatly from the conditions obtaining in the anthropoid apes where it is more or less straight in vertical orientation. The concavity of the posterior border, on the other hand, is conditioned both in man and ape, first by the behavior of the condyloid process, secondly by that of the posterior outline and thirdly in cases by the angulus mandibulae. Thus while the condyloid process in the apes is markedly curved backward — slightly less so in the gorilla mandible — coinciding with a more straightened

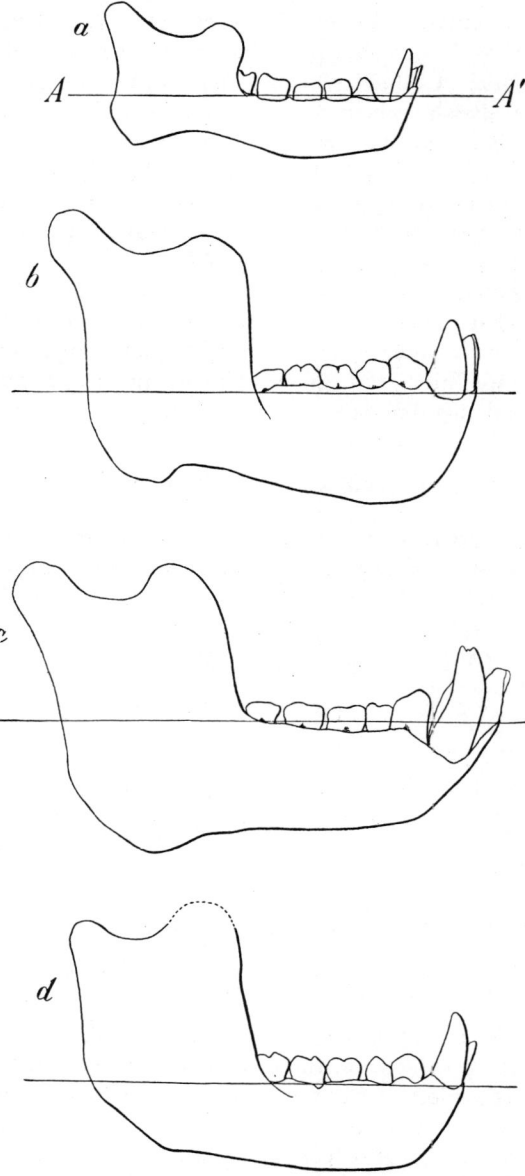

posterior border, the condyloid process in man is conspicuously erect with tendency toward forward curvature and the posterior border of the ramus curved from itself. The result is a concavity in which latter the entire posterior outline more or less intensively participates, while in apes the curve is shorter and situated higher, i. e., below the overhanging condyloid process. This is also the case in the Heidelberg (Mauer) jaw while the Neandertals seem to conform with more recent conditions. Hylobates likewise approximates human conditions in this respect. These variations may be studied from figs. 96 and 97, the former of which was used above for demonstration of varying sizes and proportions. The mandibular diagrams of fig. 97 are, *a*, of a Symphalangus syndactylus (Hylobates); *b*, of a Pongo pygmaeus (orang-utan); *c*, of a Pan calvus (chimpanzee) and *d*, of a gorilla [211] Attention may be called to the light form of a processus lemuriniscus s. Sandifortii *(Albrecht)* in *a* which as *R. Martin* (Lehrbuch 1914, 883) points out, occurs in Lemur and Hy-

Fig. 97. Outlines of anthropoid mandibles in lateral projection and alveolar orientation. *a*. Symphalangus syndactylus; *b*. Pongo pygmaeus; *c*. Pan calvus; *d*. Gorilla (After *D. G. Elliot* and *St. Oppenheim*). 2/3. A-A′, alveolar plane.

[211] *a*, *b* and *c* are after: *Elliot, Daniel Giraud*, 1912. A review of the primates., New York. v. III, pts. XXI, XXII, and XXXIV. *d* after *Oppenheim, Stefanie*, 1911. Zur Typologie des Primatencraniums. Zschr. Morph. Anthrop., v. XIV, pl. X.

lobates in posterior direction in opposition to man where in the rare cases of its occurrence it projects downward.

The statement made above regarding the greater curvature of the anterior mandibular border in man, where in fact the entire outline from the summit of the coronoid process (coronion) to the postmolar point is in cases divided into an upper convexity and a lower concavity, holds also true for our series. The posterior border, on the contrary, presents all the stages from almost complete straightness to total concavity.

c. Processus condyloideus and coronoideus.
Incisura mandibulae (condylocoronoidea).

The general appearance of the free end of the ramus is entirely dependent on the three factors named in the caption. The individual condition of the two processes on the other hand is implicated in the width and depth of the incisura mandibulae (condylocoronoidea). The latter, as is well known, tends to be shallow and wide in the anthropoid apes, the diluvial specimens, the infantile mandible and the more primitive varieties of mankind (Australians, Eskimo, Fuegians, etc.). Low and shallow incisurae are likewise to be observed in broad and low rami as a general occurrence in the human mandible, and particularly in our series, as against the deeper incisurae of higher and narrower rami[212]. Such differences may easily be read from the superposed mandibles of fig. 96[213]. *R. Martin* (Lehrbuch, 1914, 881) gives the incisura depth of the Mauer specimen at 7 mm., and a human range of 10—18 mm. which, however, is exceeded in a number of cases in our series even to 22 mm. in the Haida male of fig. 96.

The mutual behavior of the coronoid and condyloid processes may be estimated comparatively by the degree of deviation from a state of parallelism between the two. The coronoid processes on the whole are broad and bluntly pointed, and illustrate thus the conditions generally encountered in the American Indian and furthermore in the Mongolids. The condyles (capitulum mandibulae) are frequently somewhat worn down due probably to arthritic conditions, but on the whole rather elegantly shaped, sloping from without downward and inward, rarely in the opposite direction (Haida male 3753). Parallelism in direction of the two processes is more frequently found in man on account of the more erect position of the condyloid process as over against its backward tilt in the apes referred to above. The convergence, on the other hand, of the processes, i. e., the *intensive* deviation from the parallel state is rather

---

[212] The atrophic conditions of deep incisurae and high and thin coronoid processes are not directly comparable to the type conditions and therefore left out of consideration.

[213] See also illustration fig. 2 in: *Puccioni, Nello*, 1913. Ricerche sulla forma del mento e dell' incisura sigmoidea negli uomini e nelle scimmie. Arch. Antrop., v. XLIII, fasc. 1—2, pp. 1—39 (8).

apish, particularly gorilloid, and its occurrence in the human mandible may be expressed in that term. The *extensive* deviation, however, is more typically human, and it is here invariably the coronoid process which is the more variable, the condyloid process holding to a more conservative direction. It cannot be doubted that the dilation under discussion came about in correlation to the lengthening of the temporal fossa, the protrusion of the forehead and the consequent insertional spread of the temporal muscle. Fig. 98 after

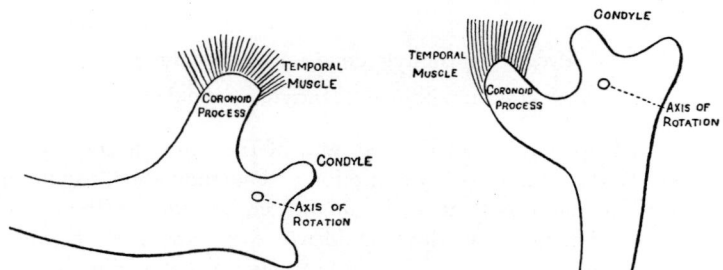

Fig. 98. Proc. coronoideus in a closed and open mandible of a carnivore to show the cause of coronoid recurvation. After *W. Wright*.

W. Wright[214] is quite instructive in this respect. The effect of the more posteriorly oriented center of muscular traction in a carnivore is lucidly shown by the recurved coronoid process. Centralized muscular traction is relieved and equalized with the upgrowth of the condyloid process in the higher forms, while reminiscences of the phylogenetically older conditions are at times encountered there. The superposed outlines of two rami in alveolar and condylocoronoid orientation, fig. 99, illustrate these conditions, the dilated form being that of a Chukchee male (3849), the more concentrated one with the slightly recurved coronoid process being observed in a Tsimshian male[215] (4588). For further comparison the ramus outline of a gorilla mandible has

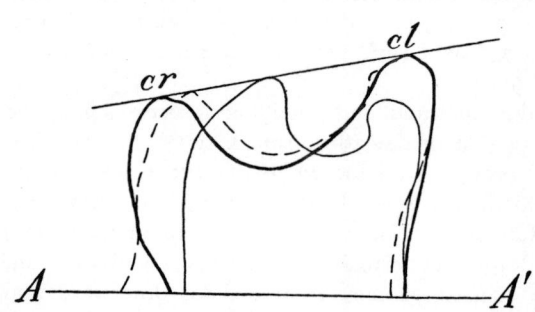

Fig. 99. Free ends of mandibular rami to show mutual behavior of condyloid and coronoid processes. —— male Chukchee (3849); —— male Tsimshian (4588); - - - Gorilla (the last v. *Lenhossék*, l. c., p. 338 (53). Our specimens in natural size. A-A', alveolar horizon. *cr*, coronion; *cl*, condylon.

---

[214] *Wright, W.*, 1913. The mandible of man from the morphological and anthropological points of view, in: Essays and studies presented to *W. Ridgeway*, Cambridge. pp. 1—13 (8).

[215] *M. v. Lenhossék*, l. c., p. 338 (53).

been added in fig. 99, demonstrating the contrast to the human conditions by the decidedly recurved coronoid process.

d. Trigonum postcoronoideum.

The two more or less distinct ridges which on the medial surface of the ramus descend from the condyloid and coronoid processes as cristae endocondyloidea and endocoronoidea (*v. Lenhossék*)[216] form between them with their angle of union as the apex and the condylocoronoid margin as a basis, a triangular depression which might be called trigonum postcoronoideum. It is of typical occurrence in the chimpanzee and was observed as of slight development in the Mauer mandible by *Schoetensack*[217] who named it fovea muscularis postcoronoidea. However it is peculiarly free of muscular insertions and of quite different causation as *v. Lenhossék* has shown whose planum triangulare (p. 51) marks the neutral space between several of the trajectorial slopes (transversum, basale, copulans) of the ascending ramus.

The trigonum postcoronoideum seems to be only weakly developed in the immatures. Its stronger appearance in the mandible of the adult must therefore be considered as of functional origin. It is quite variable in our series and by no means of regular occurrence. Deep and well specified trigona were observed in a Nimkish female (1675), a Salish male (1588), a Kwakiutl male (3990) and a number of others, amounting on the whole to about 25 %.

e. Fossa praecoronoidea and trigonum postmolare (*Klaatsch*).

These two features are of particular interest in the morphology of the lower jaw. The fossa praecoronoidea (*Klaatsch*) s. fovea coronoidea (*Waldeyer*) s. fovea retromolaris (*Bünte* and *Moral*) s. recessus mandibulae (*v. Lenhossék*), i.e. the vertical (longitudinal) groove between the anterior medial surface of the ramus, the crista endocoronoidea and the crista buccinatoria s. alveolo-marginalis (*Waldeyer*) of the trigonum postmolare, depends on the extent of deviation between the alveolar and the coronoid processes. It is to be noticed as of phylogenetic significance already in the anthropoids, but reaches its finest development in the human mandible. That function is also here active in its production may be assumed from the fact that the fossa praecoronoidea is only slightly developed, if at all, in the immature mandible, leaving, of course, out of consideration the first infantile stages.

Our records of the correlative occurrence of the depth and width of the fossa show the greatest frequencies for narrow-medium broad and shallow-medium deep fossae. Cases of extreme depth and width do not occur.

---

[216] L. c., p. 338 (51).
[217] *Schoetensack, O.*, 1908. Der Unterkiefer des Homo Heidelbergensis. Leipzig. p. 33.

The trigonum postmolare (*Klaatsch*) s. retromolare (*Brann*) s. area alveolaris (*Waldeyer*), the triangular tuberosity adjoining posteriorly the alveolus for m_3, is separated from the fossa praecoronoidea by the above named crista buccinatoria and medially marked off by the linea endoalveolaris. It is in varying stages of development of fair constancy in the human mandible, and its phylogenetic significance lies in the fact that it marks the place of origin of a fourth molar which is obsolete in man. *Klaatsch*[218] sees in the occasional enlargement of the regular third molar a concrescence with the rudiment of such a fourth molar tooth.

The posterior edge of the alveolus for m_3 forming the basis of the postmolar trigonum has its apex frequently drawn out into a ridge which appears as another proof of dental germ layer connection. The ridge, which has been seen even without the trigonum formation, reaches up in cases to a level with the foramen mandibulae and merges with the torus verticalis mandibulae (*v. Lenhossék*)[219], the unification of the same author's cristae endocondyloidea and endocoronoidea. Such a ridge is quite evident in the Mauer jaw and was recorded in about 33% of our series. The trigonum postmolare is present in fully 90% of our series in various stages of development. Its absence may be due to the process of progressive tooth reduction emphasized in single individuals.

f. Medial relief in general.

Muscle and ligament marks, and impressions caused by soft parts on the medial surfaces of corpus and ramus are in no case exaggerated in appearance. The lingula mandibulae for the insertion of the ligamentum sphenomandibulare, generally slightly to bluntly pointed, is in cases truncated, being sharply and broadly edged. Such a case is that of a N. Saanich male (2644 A) as illustrated in fig. 100. The sulcus mylohyoideus continuing forward and downward from the foramen mandibulare is somewhat variable in width and depth, and sometimes bridged singly or twofold due quite probably to the ossified insertion of the sphenomandibular ligament. A single bridging which occurs on the left ramus of a Haida male (3742) is shown in fig. 101 where a probe is run through the tunnel.

The torus mandibulae of *Fürst*, referred to above, was seen by *R. Virchow*[220] in mandibles from Santa Barbara and of the Koskimo and occurs quite

---

[218] l. c., p. 9 (108).
[219] l. c., p. 338 (50). This torus is not indentical with the horizontal torus mandibularis of *Fürst, Carl M.*, 1908. Der Torus mandibularis bei den Eskimos und anderen Rassen. Verh. Anat. Ges., pp. 295—296.
[220] *Virchow, R.*, l. c., p. 199 (28).

Virchow, R., 1889. Beiträge zur Craniologie der Insulaner der Westküste Nordamerikas. Zschr. Ethnol. (Verh.), v. XXI, pp. 382—403 (395; 401).

frequently in the Eskimo.[221] However, excepting slight reinforcements of the medial alveolar border, no true torus formation was noticed in our series. In regard to the causation of the torus *Ritchie*'s [222] statement that tortional stress rather than direct pressure on the teeth and alveoli are responsible for this formation, is of great interest.

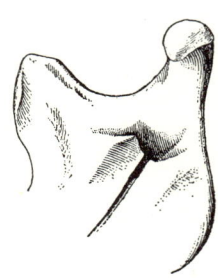
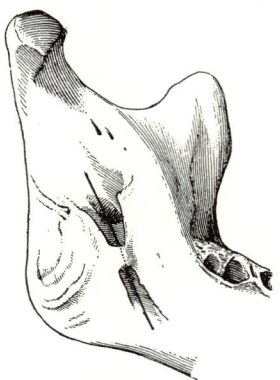

Fig. 100. Lingula mandibulae broadly truncated and sharply edged in a male Salish (2644 A). Slightly reduced.

Fig. 101. Sulcus mylohyoideus bridged with probe run through tunnel, in a female Haida (3742). Natural size.

The linea mylohyoidea and the impressions caused by the glandulae submaxillaris and sublingualis are also of moderate development.

---

[221] See here *Hooton, E. A.*, l. c., p. 255 (54).
[222] l. c., p. 193 (c 64—65 c).

SUTURES AND WORMIAN BONES.

Conditioned by the ontogenetic processes of cranial ossification, the principal sutures show the typical differences of conformation, the less serrated portions occupying the fonticular regions, and the more complicated ones the regions of most intensive thrive in diametrically opposite direction, of adjoining bones. Taking *Oppenheim*'s [223] sutural variations of four fundamental types of complexity as models, our records show an obvious tendency toward simple dentulation in the order of the relatively and generally more complex lambdoid suture, the sagittal and the coronal. The occasionally more extravagant patterns, particularly in the lambdoid suture, are not liable to mitigate this statement which characterizes the somewhat more primitive condition of the mongolid sutures as against the sutural complexity of the Whites. The sutural character in the Indian crania of the Pacific Northwest is thus seen to repeat the conditions of cranial series from other American provinces observed by various authors and recorded in their works (*Hrdlička*, *Hooton*, et al.), while *Mac Curdy* [224] notes in the Peruvians that "the sutures exhibit a wide range of

Summary 174.

Sutura coronalis: obliteration and Wormian bones: percental frequency.

Tribe	Sutura coronalis						Wormian bones
	pars bregmatica		pars complicata		pars temporalis		
	obliteration		obliteration		obliteration		
	total	part	total	part	total	part	
Undeformed	13.3%	5.5%	17.2%	3.1%	20.3%	10.2%	—
Cowichan (deformation)	3.5%	1.8%	2.6%	22.8%	3.5%	2.6%	6.1%
Chinook (deformation)	—	—	1.1	19.9%	—	—	13.2%
Koskimo (deformation)	—	—	—	13.7%	—	0.7	9.2%

[223] *Oppenheim, St.*, 1907. Die Suturen des menschlichen Schädels in ihrer anthropologischen Bedeutung. Korr.-Bl. Deut. Anthrop. Ges., v. XXXVIII, pp. 128—135.
[224] l. c., p. 15 (268).

variation from very simple to highly complex." Moderate serration was also recorded by *Koganei*[225] in Korean skulls.

The study of the principal cranial sutures involves two other factors, i.e., sutural obliteration and the occurrence of Wormian bones. The four

Summary 175.

Sutura sagittalis: obliteration and Wormian bones: percental frequency.

Tribe		Sutura sagittalis							
		pars bregmatica		pars verticis		pars obelica		pars postica		Wormian bones
		obliteration		obliteration		obliteration		obliteration		
		total	part	total	part	total	part	total	part	
Undeformed		10.3%	8.7%	13.4%	7.1%	12.6%	5.5%	15.0%	4.7%	0.8%
Cowichan	deformation	3.6%	2.7%	4.5%	14.3%	3.6%	7.1%	5.4%	11.6%	1.8%
Chinook		—	—	—	6.2%	—	2.1%	—	3.2%	—
Koskimo		—	—	—	4.0%	—	2.7%	—	4.0%	1.3%

Summary 176.

Sutura lambdoidea: obliteration and Wormian bones: percental frequency.

Tribe		Sutura lambdoidea						
		pars ·lambdoidea		pars media		pars asterica		Wormian bones
		obliteration		obliteration		obliteration		
		total	part	total	part	total	part	
Undeformed		8.7%	6.3%	11.0%	3.9%	6.3%	—	17.3%
Cowichan	deformation	2.7%	9.1%	2.7%	19.1%	0.9%	0.9%	20.0%
Chinook		—	8.8%	—	9.9%	—	2.2%	35.2%
Koskimo		—	10.1%	—	10.1%	—	—	27.5%

series of crania being fairly uniform in regard to composition, state of preservation and age stages, it seemed safe to treat them in direct comparative observation, the results of which are tabulated in *summaries 174—176*. In these, the natural divisions of the sutures as defined by *Oppenheim* (pp. 128—129)

---

[225] l. c., p. 320 (524).

are employed and the percental frequencies of total and partial obliteration recorded. We are first confronted by the outstanding observation that the decided excess of total obliteration in the three cranial sutures of the Undeformed as against those of the deformed divisions, reaches its highest percental figures in the coronal suture, while the sagittal and lambdoid sutures present somewhat diminishing frequencies. With all necessary caution, it may be inferred from this statistic statement that obliteration of the coronal suture, particularly its temporal and complicated parts precedes that of the sagittal suture where the partes postica and verticis present the highest percental frequencies. Third in successive order stands the lambdoid suture whose pars media exceeds its lambdoid and asteric parts in the percentage of total obliteration. This order of ektocranial obliteration of the "vault sutures" does not fully conform to the order of endocranial suture closure of *Todd*[226], where the sagittal obliteration procedes that of the coronal and lambdoid. It seems therefore not improbable that the time ratios between internal and external suture closure vary.

The most interesting feature, however, is recognized in turn not only in the decided gap between the sutural conditions in the Undeformed and those of the deformed divisions, but also between the latter themselves. Thus, while there still obtain small percental frequencies of obliteration in the Cowichan division, although, as stated, ranging widely below the Undeformed frequencies, there is practically no total obliteration to be noticed in the Chinook and Koskimo divisions. It is also here that part obliteration, perhaps with the exception of the pars complicata of the coronal suture, is almost negligible. It is thus clear that artificial head deformation must exercise a stimulating influence upon the sutural life in even proportion with the increasing deformatory strain, which furthermore seems to remain efficient here beyond the period of normal growth cessation of the bones, so that unmistakable obliteration is found in strenuously deformed heads only at a rather late age.

The conclusions of the preceding paragraph are in some degree corroborated by the occurrence of Wormian bones in the sutures. Although Wormian bones may originate without apparent mechanical stress, the lambdoid suture being particularly favored, the non-occurrence of supernumerary elements in the coronal suture of the Undeformed, and the increasing frequencies in the deformed divisions, point withal toward deformatory influences. This is not so clearly demonstrated by the sagittal suture where the percental occurrence of Wormian bones is fairly equally distributed, but all the more so by the lambdoid. The frequency here rises to $35.2°/_0$ in the Chinook and $27.5°/_0$ in the Koskimo, thus identifying the highest frequencies with the divisions of most strenuous deformation. The occurrence at all of Wormian bones in the

---

[226] *Todd, T. Wingate* and *Lyon, D. W., Jr.* 1924. Endocranial suture closure, its progress and age relationship. Am. Journ. Phys. Anthrop., v. VII, pp. 325—384 (381).

Undeformed skull is undoubtedly due to evolutional processes in connection with cerebral growth, processes which are mechanically intensified by deformatory means.

Wormian bones of different shape, size and number in the coronal suture

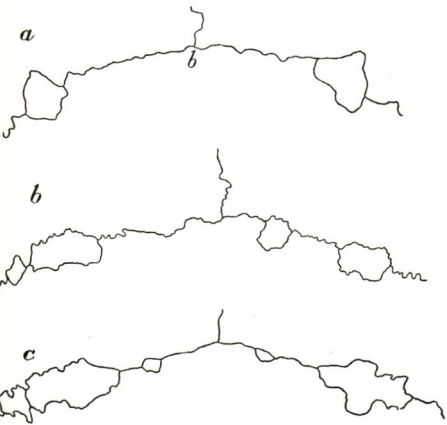
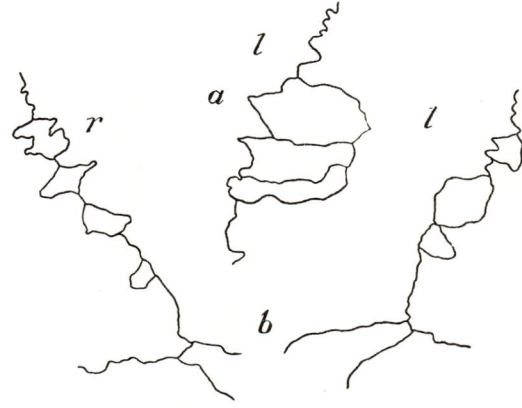

Fig. 102. Wormian bones, single and multiple, in the coronal sutures of *a*, male Koskimo (3837); *b* and *c*, male Chinooks (4444, 4459). *b*, bregma. About 2/3.

Fig. 103. Multiple Wormian bones in the partes complicatae of the coronal sutures of *a*, female Salish from "about Vancouver" (1821, left side only) and *b* Nanaimo (1627, right and left sides). About natural size.

are depicted in fig. 102, *a—c*. Such supplementary bones are particularly flourishing in the pars complicata as shown in lateral aspect in fig. 103, *a* and *b*; they are quite unusual in this region and *Giuffrida-Ruggeri*[227] designates a Wormian bone which he found in the coronal suture of a female Italian skull as "anomalia rarissima". Multiple occurrences here of sutural bones, in artificially deformed skulls, however, may be witnessed in connection with bregma bones in our fig. 23 (p. 166). An assemblage of Wormian bones in the lambdoid suture may be seen in fig. 86 (p. 327), where an os lambdoideum of fontanellar origin was shown. Sutural bones have been observed also in the lesser sutures of the cranium. They are relatively numerous in the sutura squamosa. A single case of a Wormian bone in the sutura internasalis in an inf. II Lillooet skull is depicted in fig. 104. It may not be superfluous in this connection to point out the uniform character of fontanel and Wormian bones, both being derived from independent ossific centers and, in completed state, separated by sutures from the adjoining osseous elements.

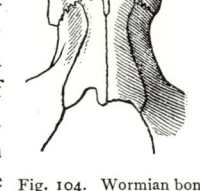

Fig. 104. Wormian bone in the sutura internasalis of an inf. II Lillooet (2629). Natural size.

---

[227] *Giuffrida-Ruggeri, V.*, 1911. Per una sistemazione del tipo di Cro-Magnon e una rara anomalia. Arch. Antrop., v. XLI, pp. 153—173 (172).

TEETH.

A metrical investigation of the teeth not being included in the plan of this work, our observations are principally statistical and odontoscopic. As to preservation, only a moderate percentage of dentures were found complete, in most of them post mortem losses had occurred, while intra vitam losses proved to be exceedingly rare. The completeness of eruption, referring only to the mature stages, was imperfect in one individual of the Cowichan division, as defined in *summary 177*, whose third molars were suppressed.

The teeth on the whole appeared neither especially large nor unusually small in size, but there are two conditions of marked constancy to be noticed, (1) wear and (2) lingual concaveness or shovel-shape of the incisors. The *attrition* of the teeth in general beginning at a relatively early age is rather pronounced and due, as frequently pointed out by anthropologists, to crude and primitively prepared food and to mechanical demands upon them. In quite a number of cases attrition had bared the pulp, and in connection therewith the destruction of the alveoli in varying degrees was noticeable, thus suggesting a causal relation between these two conditions. The lesions resulting from abscesses, periapical, periostitic and otherwise are indeed quite numerous and comprise all the forms described by *Leigh*[228] As in many other Indian tribes, caries on the other hand was exceedingly rare, although *Leigh* (p. 188) mentions 75%

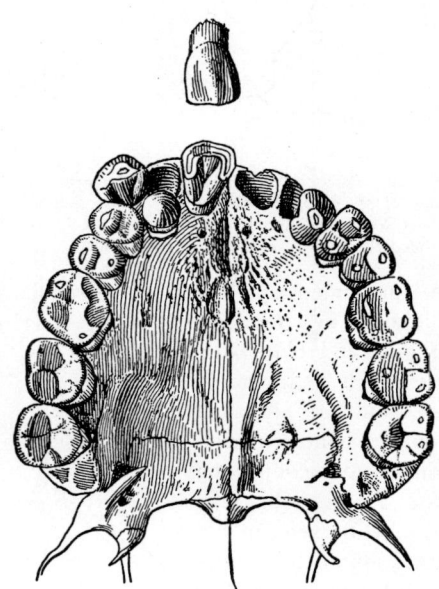

Fig. 105. Shovel-shape incisor with labial compensatory bulging (see isolated tooth), in a male Haida (1606). Between the second right incisor and the adjoining canine, on the lingual side, is a supernumerary tooth with an undifferentiated crown. About natural size.

---
[228] *Leigh, R. W.*, 1925. Dental pathology of Indian tribes of varied environmental and food conditions. Am. Journ. Phys. Anthrop., v. VIII, pp. 179—199.
Leigh, R. W., 1925. Dental pathology of the Eskimo. Dent. Cosmos, Sept., 16 pp.

[350]

Summary 177.

Dentes molares: actual and percental frequency.

Sex and Age	Dentes molares					
	Undeformed					
	$m_1 > m_2 > m_3$		$m_1 = m_2 = m_3$		m_3 non-erupted	
	no.	%	no.	%	no.	%
♂	38	90.5	4	9.5	—	—
♀	14	100.0	—	—	—	—
juv.	—	—	6	—	—	—
inf.	—	—	—	—	—	—
Total frequencies	52	83.9	10	16.1	—	—
	Cowichan deformation					
♂	48	88.5	3	5.8	1	1.9
♀	16	94.1	1	5.9	—	—
juv.	—	—	—	—	—	—
inf.	—	—	—	—	—	—
Total frequencies	64	92.8	4	5.8	1	1.4
	Chinook deformation					
♂	40	95.2	2	4.8	—	—
♀	19	100.0	—	—	—	—
juv.	1	—	—	—	—	—
inf.	—	—	—	—	—	—
Total frequencies	60	96.8	2	3.2	—	—
	Koskimo deformation					
♂	50	82.0	11	18.0	—	—
♀	11	100.0	—	—	—	—
juv.	2	—	—	—	—	—
inf.	—	—	—	—	—	—
Total frequencies	63	85.1	11	14.9	—	—

of it in the Zuni. Shovel-shape incisor teeth known as far back as 1844, and also observed in the Krapina finds by *Gorjanović-Kramberger*, were first extensively described in the American Indian by *Hrdlička* [229]. Of the three forms defined by him as trace, semi-shovel and shovel, the more pronounced concave forms occur as a rule in the upper medial incisors, the total frequency of the various degrees of concavity amounting in our series to about $80°/_0$. In a male Haida (1606) the lingual concavity of the right upper middle incisor was compensated by a distinct labial bulging. In fig. 105 the tooth in question is isolated to show the labial aspect. Another anomaly is seen here in a supernumerary cone-shape tooth behind the right lateral incisor. A crowding

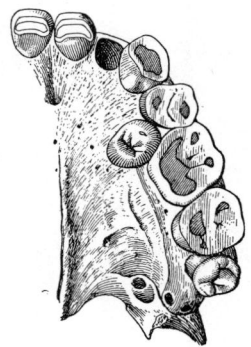
Fig. 106. Second left upper premolar crowded out lingually, in a male Kamloops (1284). Natural size.

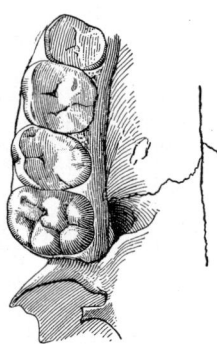
Fig. 107. Third right upper molar of extraordinary size, in a male Bellacoola (4546). Natural size.

out of the left upper second premolar is illustrated in fig. 106, representing that condition in a male Kamloops (1284). This tooth is perfectly intact, has a palatal position and shows naturally no signs of wear. In this jaw may also be noticed the extraordinarily small size of the third left molar the transverse and longitudinal diameters of which are 7 mm. each. Quite a number of third molars of still smaller size were seen in our series, illustrating the general assumption that "they are evidently decadent teeth which may eventually be entirely lost" [230]. In contrast to these conditions is a right upper third molar of considerable size with two or three accessory cusps in a male Bellacoola (4546) as illustrated in fig. 107. This case does not discredit the supposition of the phylogenetic trend of reduction in the molar sizes and their cusps [231]

---

[229] Among a number of his papers dealing with this phenomenon, the following, containing a consummate bibliography is of particular interest: *Hrdlička, Aleš*, 1921. Shovel-shaped teeth. Am. Journ. Phys. Anthrop., v. III, pp. 429—465.

[230] *Gregory, William K.*, 1921, l. c., p. 206 (174).

[231] *Sullivan, Louis R.*, 1920. Differences in the pattern of the second lower molar tooth. Am. Journ. Phys. Anthrop., v. III, pp. 255—257.

from fore to aft. It is, on the contrary, a true anomaly resulting quite probably from the concrescence of the anlage of a fourth molar with that of the third.

The number of molar cusps is smaller in the upper jaw where in the three molar teeth the typical conformations of 4–4–3, 4–4–2, and 4–3–3 are most numerous, while the predominant patterns of the lower jaw are 5–5–4, 5–4–4, and occasionally 5–4–3.

If then the progressive reduction of size is characteristic of the phylogenetic trend in the molars, the reverse is to be recognized as pithecoid [232] Only two such cases were witnessed in our series. Although there is a great constancy regarding the eruption of the third molar — only one case of non-eruption was recorded in our series and listed in *summary 177* — the bulk of the cases in each division manifests progressive reduction. Comparatively small percentages signify the equality of size of the three molars, reaching, however, 16.1% in the Undeformed, but only 3.2% in the Chinook.

---

[232] *Ritchie* observed a similar condition in the Western and Central Eskimo stating that: "This is particularly true in the molar series which unlike the civilized dentition, tends to revert to the generalized mammalian type where the molars increase in size in the anteroposterior direction". l. c., p. 193 (64c).

SUMMARY TO PART II: CRANIOSCOPY.

1. Facts and limitations.

Supplementing and condensing the general remarks on cranioscopic study (p. 157), it may be stated that the latter concerns itself with the investigation into the nature and frequency of morphologic distinctions with a view toward their possible recognition as racial characteristics. The systematic survey of the anatomic conditions in the five cranial normae was employed because it seemed to offer the most reliable and comprehensive mode of procedure. If, in respect to proper evaluation, the latter holds good for the normal, i. e. the non-deformed cranium, the results obtained from the artificially deformed cranium require an additional critical discernment. Although racial characteristics, if any, might be preserved in the deformed skull, changes brought about by deformation naturally lack significance as such and must be considered from the viewpoint of their causal origin, physiological adjustment and their quantitative occurrence.

Cranioscopic observations on the normal and deformed skulls are divisible (1) into those of racial pertinency, and (2) into those signifying morphologic variations, while (3) the latter may also be the results of deformatory strain in the deformed where, however, their specific appearance marks them as such in most of the cases, like the relatively long duration of openness of the principal cranial sutures.

Applying the descriptive and statistical methods to both our normal and deformed skull series, metrical sizing seemed to be indispensible in cases of abnormal occurrence of morphologic features in individual skulls, such as the os bregmaticum, the excessive size of vascular orifices, and so on. It may likewise be restated that "the range of personal estimation in evaluating minute differences in terms of relative magnitude" (p. 158) is liable to cause slight uncertainty as compared to the exact methods of metrical and mathematical inquiry.

In the following pages only the more important characteristics selected from the systematic array of anatomic features and their study in the five normae will be reviewed from the standpoint of their morphologic and racial significance. It may be stated in this connection that in all our series the male skull is somewhat cruder in structure and more pronounced in detail than the female, but that on the whole both the male and the female skulls represent a more refined cranial type as compared with the skulls of morphologically more inferior human varieties. Among the variety of types the Haida, among our material, represent a somewhat more robust type.

2. Norma verticalis.

Conforming with the mesobrachycranial conditions, the character of the *cranial outline* in norma verticalis in the Undeformed is somewhat variable in the character of the ovoid ground form. The Cowichan and Chinook deformations are prevailingly sphenoid in outline, while in the Koskimo the ovoides predominates with a leaning towards the ellipsoides in the Koskimo proper. The sphaeroides does not occur in any of the divisions. The influence of anteroposterior compression on the minimum frontal breadth in the Cowichan-Chinook series as a direct result, not as a compensatory one like the parietal expansion in those two series, serves slightly to modify the sphenoid cranial outline in vertical aspect.

A further distortion of the cranial outline so as to cause its bilateral occipital asymmetry under the descriptive caption of *plagiocephaly* is quite numerous in the Cowichan and Chinook and must be attributed here to their specific modes of deformation, while the Koskimo mode lends itself to a much lesser degree (5.3%) to that distortion. In the undeformed skulls, the most frequent cause of pathologic plagiocephaly, namely premature suture obliteration, was not observed. The frequency there of 11.5% of plagiocephaly is likewise due to mechanical influences, not, however, to intentional strain, but unintentional cradle-board pressure, or pressure from carriage on the mother's back.

Postorbital constriction, if judged by metrical determination of the minimum frontal breadth, is rather pronounced in the Undeformed crania and those deformed in the Koskimo fashion. It is slightly less marked in the Cowichan and Chinook series for reasons pointed out above. The actual condition of postorbital constriction is furthermore elucidated by the *phaenozygous* behavior of the arcus zygomaticus in vertical aspect, although allowance must be made for the degree of zygomatic extension in the skull of the American Indian, which, however, tends toward mitigation when compared with the conditions in the true Mongol and Eskimo. There are nevertheless appreciable frequencies of cryptozygy in the Undeformed and Chinook, while those of the Cowichan and Koskimo are considerably less in favor of high phaenozygous frequencies. Phaenozygy, on the whole appears to be a racial characteristic of the Indian skull.

The *foramina parietalia* present rather variable conditions regarding size, and regular or irregular occurrence. Excessive sizes do not occur, on the contrary, there is to be stated a general tendency toward the formation of small and diminutive foramina parietalia with the frequent occurrence of their entire absence in both the undeformed and deformed skulls. This is in agreement with the statements of other authors. The occurrence of the two foramina, one on each side of the sagittal suture in the obelion region is the typical condition, while the difference in size between the two is another noteworthy observation, as is the multiple occurrence of foramina on either the right or the left side. Quite regular is also the appearance of the obelion region as a roughened or knolled area on which the foramina occupy elevated positions. Although occurring in both the deformed and undeformed crania, there seemed to be a slight prevalence of this condition in the latter, due probably to deformatory strain. The same may be said of a tendency toward retarded closure of the principal cranial sutures which will be referred to again below (see chapter 8 of this summary).

3. Norma basilaris.

Commensurate with the moderate size of the northwestern cranium, the cranial base in general appears somewhat restricted, influenced by such component parts as the size and shape of the foramen magnum, the pars basilaris of the occipital bone, the palato-alveolar complex and numerous other morphologic details, more or less variable, at the cranial base.

Excessive deformation as in the Chinook is doubtless responsible for the bilateral *broadening of the cranial base* as demonstrated in a secondary way by the bicondylar breadth of the lower jaw (pp. 118, 136), and the increase of averages from the Undeformed conditions over the Cowichan to the Chinook deformation. It was likewise shown there that in the Koskimo deformation which causes narrowing of the skull, i. e. in contrast to the effects of anteroposterior deformation, the breadth of the cranial base is lessened, when judged by the same criterion. The foramen magnum, or rather its immediate circumference, appears depressed in quite a number of Chinook skulls, while the extreme portions of the partes laterales of the occipital bone are bulged out in a sagittal direction, in which they are joined across the occipitomastoid suture by the adjoining parts of the mastoid portions of the temporal bones. This, together with the cooperation of the *mastoid processes* of enlarged size, results in deep *incisurae mastoideae*, although large processes are not always correlated with deep incisurae.

Regarding certain primitive features at the cranial base, repeated attention has been called by *Hrdlička*[233] to the *relative depression of the petrous portions of the temporal bones* and in connection therewith the *small size of the foramen lacerum*. It appears that at a higher stage of brain development the parts of the cranial base which surround the pars petrosa are bulged out

---

[233] Extensively discussed: l. c., p. 14 (204—205) and l. c., p. 14 (46).

in consequence of the expansive power of the brain while the pars petrosa itself, being more conservative or resistive, retains its position which then appears more or less deeply sunk in the basal aspect. At the same time the foramen lacerum becomes larger. In our Indian skulls *Hrdlička's* observation of less advanced morphologic conditions indicated by a lesser degree of basal bulging and a stronger degree of flatness of the pars petrosa in the cranial base, as likewise the tendency toward the formation of smaller foramina lacera is to be corroborated. *Hrdlička* recognizes this condition as intermediate between the Negro and Caucasian. Of special interest in our case is the general depression of the cranial base in the Chinook, due quite probably to deformatory strain. The latter may also be responsible for the higher percentages of *processus paracondyloideus* in the deformed series, excepting however, the Koskimo. Processes of extreme size and cylindrical shape, however, may occur in any cranium without the stimulating influence of deformation, and has been described in this report in a Haida and Nootka skull (p. 191). The different forms of *ossification at the anterior border of the foramen magnum* are likewise more numerous in the deformed series. The *shape of the foramen magnum* proved to be somewhat variable, reserving the fact, however, that roundness is evident in the Chinook, and predominant in the Koskimo, Lillooet and Lytton, while the oval shape at appreciable percentages in all the groups predominates in the Haida, tending toward the elliptic in the Eskimo and Chukchee. Reference may here again be made to *MacCurdy's* statement (p. 133) of the deformatory influence on the size of the foramen magnum. Whether that influence is likewise noticeable in the shape of the foramen magnum will be difficult to judge, although its predominating roundness was observed in the Chinook who practiced anteroposterior deformation to an excessive degree. It is to be considered that relative roundness of the foramen magnum is a characteristic of the mongolid skull, a condition which quite probably is correlated with the brachymesocranial skull.

An interesting correlation was noted between the height of the *condylus occipitalis* and the degree of inclination of the foramen magnum plane referred to on p. 180. It seems that with an artificially depressed cranial base as in the Chinook the height of the condyles is likewise depressed while with a greater cranio-basal angle and particularly the higher position of the basion (minus condition of the foramen magnum plane) a higher condyle is implicated. If this observation is correct a functional change takes place in adjustment of the equilibrial conditions caused by the effects of artificial deformation.

Regarding the orifices in the neighborhood of the foramen magnum attention was called to the probable correlation of size between the *foramina condyloidea* and *jugularia* to the effect that a smaller condyloid foramen was compensated by a larger jugular, and vice versa. The size of the latter on the right side of the skull exceeded that on the left in the majority of cases as is usual in the human cranium. It is also in the larger right foramen jugulare that the greater frequency of division or semidivision occurs. No comparative data are available regarding this particular feature, but a superficial survey of other than Indian crania have assured the author of similar occurrences in other series.

Irregularities in the size or form of the *canalis hypoglossi* in our skulls do not exceed the conditions obtaining in any series of crania. They find their explanation in ontogenetic and phylogenetic conditions rather than in those of function and adaptation.

Correlations were observed between the depth of the *fossa mandibularis (glenoidalis)*, the height of the tuberculum articulare and vertical position of the anterior plate of the tympanic bone. A shallow fossa considered by some authors as a racial characteristic of the Eskimo was shown by others as not confined to them but of universal occurrence. Our own series did not show any outstanding characteristics in this respect. *Sullivan's* (p. 235) distinctions of deep and short; medium and short; shallow and elongated; flat and elongated, was also applicable without pronounced preference for one or the other.

A feature of special interest on the underside of the pars basilaris is the occurrence of a *fossa pharyngea* which *Sullivan* observed at quite a frequency in tribes of the Uto-Aztecan linguistic stock of southwestern United States and Mexico but not among the Pueblos (p. 198). The high frequencies of this feature in our series would add the North Pacific areas to the aforenamed morphologic province were it not for the uncertainty of the method of investigation. While, therefore, all the stages of a fossa from slight to pronounced yield high percental frequencies in our series, as high even as 55.7% in the Koskimo, thus greatly exceeding *Sullivan's* figures, the percentage of medium occurrence including a single pronounced case, conform rather to that author's average of 3.5% for the American Indian in general, our own range comprising the average values from 1.1% to 10.0%. Pending further systematic investigation the fossa pharyngea may, for the present, be designated as a group characteristic of intensified local occurrence and handed on there by inbreeding and inheritance, comparable to the slightly localized occurrence of the os incae and os malare s. zygomaticum bipartitum (japonicum s. ainonicum).

The pterygo-maxillary complex offers a number of morphologic details of racial and phyletic interest. There is first the *processus pterygoideus* whose two laminae are of an appearance characteristic of the mongolid skull, which is given by the marked prevalence of the lamina externa over the interna, and the well marked *fossa pterygoidea*. The larger development of the external lamina may have likewise to do with the tendency toward the formation of the *foramen pterygospinosum (Civinini)*. The tendency is particularly stressed here, since the true foramen is not too frequent, showing percentages, however, of from 4.4°/₀ to 7.7°/₀ in the four series. The latter is that for the Koskimo and as the next lower one, but still exceeding the undeformed frequency, is that for the Chinook, it is not improbable that artificial deformation is implicated with its origination. The foramen pterygospinosum is quite common in the apes and it was assumed (p. 204) following *von Brunn*'s opinion that it is rather of theromorphic significance which, however, throws little light on its causation. More stressed use of m. pterygoideus externus, attaching at the lamina externa also cannot be considered for the reason that it should hold true for the other more primitive human groups where, however, the foramen pterygospinosum, or the tendency towards its formation, is less outspoken.

Of primary phylogenetic import is the form of the *dental arch* which is paraboloid in the majority of our specimens, thus expressing an advanced morphologic condition. Quite interesting is the observation as gained from our *summary 123* that with the exception of the Cowichan the female paraboloid frequency exceeds the male, a proportion stated by *Ried* (see *Rudolf Martin*, Lehrbuch, 1914, 826) for the Bavarians of the foothills. The decidedly lower frequencies for the ellipsoid form shows, in our series, the opposite sex distribution. The occurrence of a *torus palatinus* appears to be a racial characteristic if judged by the high frequencies in our four series. Known as an Eskimoid feature it does not seem improbable that northwestern Indian groups are experiencing similar environmental stimuli for the production of this formation. One may, however, also assume a closer genetic proximity of the two groups which doubtless does exist in the Northwest, and through which features like the one in question may find at least a general, i. e. statistical explanation. The high frequencies around 80°/₀ in our different series include all the degrees of intensity but will reduce them by excluding the cases of tori only indicated, not so, however, as to deprive the remaining percentages of their significance. The shape of the *spina nasalis posterior* and the number of *foramina palatina minora* was also found quite variable.

4. Norma lateralis.

The norma lateralis affords a rich field for morphologic observation in that it presents a view of the cranial structure in almost its entirety. A division, therefore, into anatomic regions for the purpose of systematic investigation seemed here even more practical and advantageous than in the other normae.

The *cranial contour* in norma lateralis, applying *G. Sergi*'s tassonomic criteria, corresponds to the ellipsoides cuneatus in the Undeformed males and to the ellipsoides rotundus in the females whose characteristics are set forth on p. 222. The skull of the immatures conforms more to the females not only with regard to the rounder occipital outline with its steeper inferior portion but also to the more erect frontal contour. Slight modifications in the general outline of this norma are commensurate with the greater or lesser degree of shortheadedness in the tribal groups of which the Lillooet represent the former, the Haida and Eskimo the latter. Noteworthy and fairly typical in the latter is the protrusion of the outline of the upper occipital squama which causes an incurvation of the lambdoid region as shown in fig. 45. The cranial outline in general portrays the orthohypsicranial tendency and the moderate degree of prognathism of the mongolid skull in the normal state while the deformed ones show the more or less decisive alterations as brought about by the different deformatory practices and which are assembled in pls. I, III—XI.

The *tubera parietalia* and *lineae temporales* are relatively weakly developed. In the Chinook and Koskimo the latter yield to the frontal strain and in a number of cases the crista temporalis of the frontal bone follows the occasional abrupt horizontal backward turn of the coronal suture to rise again on the parietal bone and then follow the usual course of the lineae temporales inferior and superior. In no case were they found to rise as high on the facies parietalis as frequently found in the eastern Eskimo, i. e. in close proximity of the sagittal suture. In the Undeformed the straight course of the crista temporalis into linea temporalis inferior is the rule. While the latter reaches the *crista supramastoidea* in a sweeping curve, the linea temporalis superior reaches out farther and frequently forms strong ridges on the occipital side of the lambdoid suture which may be laid to deformatory strain. The size of the crista supramastoidea may also be dependent on sush strain. Although there is likewise a high frequency of marked cristae found in the Undeformed, exceptional sizes occur mostly in the Cowichan and Chinook deformations while on the other hand their development is rather moderate in the Koskimo. Such in general is the case also in the female skull. Coinciding with the well developed crista supramastoidea in the Undeformed just pointed out, the *sulcus supramastoideus* appears more or less deep and is frequently bounded by the bulging *crista mastoidea (Klaatsch)* [234], caused by the insertions of mm. splenius and sternocleidomastoideus.

Regarding the yielding of the immature (membranous) bones of the brain-case to pressure, an observation in the chapter on deformation (p. 13) may again be referred to. It was stated there that in a number of immature skulls the parietal bones overlap the frontal or occipital, or were overlapped by the latter. Naturally some sort of an adjustment takes place in the living, but our cranial specimens with no organic matter filling in the space between the distorted margins afford instructive cases.

The *sutura squamosa* is more varied in the deformed series, particularly the Chinook where a number of interesting cases were recorded of which two

---

[234] l. c., p. 236 (403).

are illustrated in fig. 47. No distinct difference in the size of the *squama temporalis* was noticed although it appeared that that of the Eskimo was comparatively large. Differences in shape, however, were observed to influence the size of the *incisura parietalis*, in such a way that lower squamae produced larger incisurae, i. e. larger than a right angle according to our classification. This condition is preponderant in the deformed series resulting in the Chinook in absence of the incisura in 45.9%.

Two processes of the temporal squama, *processus parietalis* and *processus frontalis* are apparently of phylogenetic importance. The former was described by *Adachi* (p. 228) in Japanese skulls at a frequency of 50%, while our own frequencies do not exceed 9.7% in the Koskimo, in an order, however, which shows the deformed series to exceed the Undeformed which have only 6.1% In all our series there is a predominance of left occurrence over right, and of male over female. The frontal process, on the other hand, is of typical occurrence in the catarrhine apes and was pointed out as a "Merkmal niederer Menschenrassen" by *R. Virchow* (p. 235). Against frequencies (*R. Martin*, Lehrbuch, 1914, 778), for instance, of 12.4% in Negroes and 15.7% in Australians, our own of 3.2% to 8.5% in the four series are quite moderate. They rather conform to the mongolian frequency of 3.7% of *R. Martin*'s list which exceeds the European figure of 1.6%. In our series the relatively high frequency of 6.2% in the Undeformed as exceeded only by 8.5% of the Chinook and, in addition, the fairly equal occurrence in the sexes is of interest. These statements corroborate first of all *R. Virchow*'s evaluation of the feature under discussion as one morphologically inferior, occurring less frequently in the more advanced varieties, and secondly its inaffectibility regarding the deformatory pressure, providing no significance be attached to the higher frequency in the Chinook, that group of most intensive distortional strain. An assumption like this is finds justification in the occurrence of the *os epiptericum* which is seemingly related to the processus frontalis. In the series of anteroposterior deformation the frequency of its occurrence rises above those of the Undeformed and the Koskimo deformation. On the whole, however, our frequencies from 6.2% to 9.5% which consider only the true cases, are not high if compared with *R. Martin*'s list (p. 779) where Mongols are credited with 16.0%. A tendency is likewise revealed there toward high frequencies simultaneously in the most primitive and the most advanced groups, i. e. 28.4% in both the Australians and the Swiss. Whether in consideration of these high frequencies the only relatively high figures of our series of anteroposterior deformation may be estimated as results of that deformation, will be difficult to decide. In itself there is the probability that by means of deformation, stimulating stress is brought to bear on a region the ossificatory conditions of which are liable to be unstable anyhow, and that thus the formation of abnormal accessory independent bones be favored.

Two other features which might be brought out in connection with deformatory influence or effect in this region is the formation of a *sulcus sphenoparietalis* and *stenocrotaphy*. Regarding the former there is the high frequency of $24.0°/_0$ of well developed sulci in the Undeformed against which the frequency of $9.7°/_0$ in the Cowichan is rather low, and zero in the Koskimo. Thus while the Koskimo mode of deformation seems to exercise prohibitive influence, the high frequency of deep sulci in the anteroposteriorly depressed Chinook crania, $20.7°/_0$, would be rather persuasive, were it not for the still higher frequency of $24.9°/_0$ in the Undeformed. Thus, while a well formed sulcus is doubtless commensurate with the development of the frontoparietal and temporal lobes of the brain divided by the Sylvian fissure, it seems likewise probable that intensive pressure may influence the feature under discussion. This is indicated not so much by the condition of stenocrotaphy which, peculiarly enough, is relatively most pronounced in the Koskimo where deep fossae are absent altogether, as by the unusual behavior in many instances of the sutura sphenoparietalis. The latter appears curved upon the upper border of the ala magna so that the sphenoid angle of the parietal bone seems to encroach upon it. It is by such indications that one is led to the assumption of deformatory effects.

The tympano-mastoid complex of phyletic interest is likewise susceptible to functional and adaptive changes. The *processus mastoideus*, for instance, wanting in animals of horizontal, i. e. quadrupedal, orientation, does not spring into relief until the first stages of erect posture. It then appears there in response to muscular demand, chiefly of m. sternocleidomastoideus. The proof of this is seen in the fact that only in the full-grown does it reach its definite size, and which from the viewpoint of sex is smaller in the female throughout the human varieties. From the racial point of view it seems that the Bushmen, Hottentots and Eskimo, as pointed out by *R. Martin* (p. 784) have small processes only, as is also the case with the Neandertalids. There is in our series a tendency toward large-sized processes, particularly in the Chinook and likewise in the Koskimo, where in both series the percentages for the small mastoids is rather negligible. Since the conditions in the latter respects tend rather toward the reverse in the Undeformed and Cowichan, it may be concluded that the size of the mastoid process is influenced by deformation, i. e. by the intensified muscular action due to the equilibrial changes in the distorted head. This assumption is corroborated by the slightly slanting direction of the mastoids in the Chinook where it appears less steep as compared with the direction in the other series. On the average, the processus mastoideus is of medium size and thus represents the mongolid status in this respect.

The *os tympanicum* offers quite a number of interesting features of which the hyperostotic thickening of its margin around the porus acusticus externus is a typical occurrence in the mongolid skull, showing frequencies there up to 100%, which status obtains likewise in our series. Explanation for this peculiarity is rather scarce and insufficient. Located in a potential area of decided phylogenetic efficaciousness, the tympano-mastoid complex is likewise associated with the phenomena of function and adaptation. Thus it seems to the present writer that a close adaptive relation exists between the developing mastoid process and the obvious necessity of reinforcing the adjoining tympanic part since both of these come under the influence of muscular traction together with the masticatory, an additional accessory, action, although not to the same degree of intensity. To the employment of the latter considerable importance must be attributed since tympanic hyperostosis is mostly found in races who use their dental apparatus in the mastery of crude, i. e. preferably animal, food and also as tools for mechanical purposes as in the preparation of leather, etc. as is the case with the Eskimo and other mongolid groups. As is well known, tympanic hyperostosis obtains far less frequently in the black and white races than in the older fossils where it is the rule. If function appears thus to be implicated in the origination and definite appearance of the details in the tympano-mastoid complex, the influence of deformation seems doubtful, but it may obtain in a secondary way through adaptation to distributed equilibrial conditions. Also doubtful is the origination of true *auricular exostoses* which in the compact texture of their structure differ from the more diffuse osseous consistency of hyperostosis. Although occurring in undeformed as well as deformed skulls, it is nevertheless a noteworthy fact that no exostoses were recorded in the former series, but that in the latter the frequencies attain 23.4% in the Chinook.

Considering the morphogenetic intricacy of the region under discussion it is quite probable that the shape of the *porus acusticus externus* likewise is a response to deformatory influence. This is shown by the high frequencies of diagonally oriented elliptic pori in the Chinook and Koskimo, and in addition the constricted dumb-bell shaped pori in the former. Granted that the elliptic to some extent signifies primariness of shape like the circular, but so in a lesser degree, the high frequency of elliptic shapes in the Chinook, enlarged by the conspicuously high frequency of the dumb-bell shape as pointed out above, must figure as an unmistakable sign of deformatory influence under excessive strain. That this holds true also for the Koskimo mode is demonstrated by the latter's high frequency of ellipses which in fact is the highest of our four series. Assumptions like these may be justifiable in consideration of the markedly high frequencies of round pori in the Undeformed and Cowichan.

Of other morphologic details in this potential region responding to phylogenetic and functional demands like the *tuberculum articulare, fossa mandibularis* (p. 358), *spina suprameatum, the perforations in the floor of the auditory meatus*, were found to attain considerable frequencies in American skulls. This anomaly, obtaining in undeformed as well as in deformed series, may owe its origin to divers causes, for instance, the insufficiency of ossific matter in the tympanic plate when the reinforcement of the porus became imperative; or the functional stress in the temporo-mandibular joint which from the peculiar nature of this articulation, however, is of secondary importance only, while the primary cause must perhaps be sought in the phyletic changes in this important region. It is rather peculiar that in our series the conspicuously low frequency of perforations of $8.5°/_0$ obtains in the Chinook who have the most excessive anteroposterior compression, as against the three other series where the Undeformed attain the same high frequency as the Cowichan, while the Koskimo exceed them. This condition speaks rather for a stabilized and heritable characteristic, influenced at the same time by deformatory stress, providing the Koskimo status here has any meaning at all. It is rather an interesting observation, also recorded by other authors, that the females markedly exceed the males in tympanic perforation, which again is quite pronounced in the immatures.

There are two features of interest in the facial region which require special mention, one representing an adjustment in deformatory distortion, and the other signifying a primitive morphologic condition. The former is the *crista infraorbitalis* at the lower border of the orbital surface of the ala magna of the sphenoid bone, forming the upper border of the fissura orbitalis inferior. In a number of cases of which fig. 62 forms an example, this crista was found drawn out into a true lamina which as such seemed to fill in the fissura space widened by distortion. A condition like this was found only in skulls deformed in the Koskimo mode, and particularly in the Koskimo tribe proper who practiced the conical deformation to an excessive degree. It is quite probable that besides the distortion in question, the comparatively great orbital height, i. e. the hypsikonchic condition of the Koskimo orbit is the result of their specific mode of deformation as stated in the chapter on the orbit (pp. 109, 113). The second feature mentioned above concerns the relative position of the *angulus zygomaticotemporalis* (mihi) as formed by the processus frontosphenoidalis and temporalis of the zygomatic bone. The relatively low position of this angle, i. e. its position below the plane line of ear-eye orientation represents a morphologically inferior mark as found in apes and monkeys. Similar conditions have been observed in Bushmen and the fossil hominidae which one is accustomed to consider as morphologically inferior human varieties. Applying this criterion, the feature under discussion will have to be classified in an identical sense. The *arcus zygomatici* in our cases of angulus zygomaticotemporalis (fig. 65, *b* and *c*) do not differ from the average conditions of the series, *b*, an Eskimo, representing the typical mongolid shape, i. e. the slightly ascending arcus above the praetubercular (tuberculum articulare) restriction of the lower border and the subsequent relapse above the tuberculum, and *c*, a Chinook, the concave upper margin. The latter appears to be influenced by deformation.

The comparative degree of *prognathy* in the Indian skulls was treated in the craniometric part (pp. 87–91; 135; 140; 144; 145; 148; 153–154; 156; 360). The cranioscopic discussion of the nasal bridge will be found with that of the nasal skeleton in the norma frontalis (p. 367).

5. Norma frontalis.

The *facial aspect* of the cranium as observed in norma frontalis is governed by the chief dimensions of the facial height and breadth, the facial outline in frontal projection and the configurative ensemble of the anatomic detail. As shown in the craniometrical part (pp. 82–83, 139, 143), the *facial height* and *breadth* differed in our four series in such a way that when compared with the Undeformed, the faces of the Cowichan and Chinook were not so high while those of the Koskimo were higher; regarding the breadth, however, that of the Cowichan and Chinook exceeded the Undeformed, while that of the Koskimo, only slightly in excess, was about equivalent. These conditions were responsible for the lower and broader faces of the Cowichan-Chinook series, and for the higher and narrower ones of the Koskimo, differences which were assumed to be due to deformation On the whole, however, they emphasize the feature which distinguishes the mongolid face from that of other races, i. e. the prominent cheek bones. This in the Undeformed group is most pronounced in the Lillooet, slightly less so in the Salish and Haida and comparatively least in the Eskimo (West) who are leptenic on account of their relatively higher faces.

The *facial outline* in frontal projection again emphasizes the expanding zygomatic region, narrowing slightly in the frontal and mandibular regions, more so, however, in the former as indicated in the craniometrical part by the jugofrontal and jugomandibular indices (pp. 93, 94, and *summary 63*). There is a marked similarity in the four jugofrontal proportions, but divers proportions obtain in the jugomandibular due to the increasing facial breadth in the Cowichan-Chinook divisions. Only in a few cases are the mandibular angles everted and, on the average, do not disturb the facial outline.

Sex differences, as far as the facial proportions are concerned, are on the whole but little to be noticed. They manifest themselves in the female skull in the smoother relief conditions which *per se* are not decisively marked in the mongolid skull, and the more gracile outline and character of the morphologic detail (see also p. 354–355).

Included in the frontal or facial aspect is the *cranial outline* which gains in importance in the parietal expansions of the anteroposteriorly compressed Cowichan and Chinook skulls. In the facial complex it is naturally the large *cavities of the eye and nose*, the *interorbital septum*, the *fossa canina* and the height of the *alveolar process of the maxillary* which influence the configurative picture. The *orbit* was recognized as rather high in the Indian skull of our area of investigation, and it was assumed that it was augmented by deformation, particularly in the Koskimo. Among these, they dominate the facial complex in no small degree, while in the Haida and Lillooet the orbits are relatively low. Quite interesting in this connection is the apparent adjustment in the lower orbital fissure, by the *crista infraorbitalis* of the sphenoid bone, to mitigate the gap caused by the Koskimo deformation, already referred to (p. 364). Anteroposterior compression practised to an extreme does not seem to produce the same effect, at least no anomalous conditions were noticed in this respect. The *upper rim* is lightly curved in general and rather sharp on the average, while the relative height gives the orbit a somewhat regular roundish-squarish appearance accentuated by the *lower lateral angle* which in the majority of cases is not drawn out downward as is quite typically the case in the skull of the whites. In the well defined upper rim the morphologically superior *foramen supraorbitale* is more frequent than the incisura, and is likewise coincident with the weak development of the *superciliary eminences* which frequently are entirely absent in the female skull. The sex difference is also manifest in the development of the *glabella*. Artificial deformation again was active in the Chinook skull where in many instances the complete flattening of the glabella region was evident. While this condition enhanced the impression of facial breadth, the relative breadth of the *interorbital septum* referred to as anterior interorbital breadth in the chapter on the orbit and elsewhere (pp. 114, 140) corroborate that impression only in the Haida and Eskimo. The deformed series and the other groups of the Undeformed are distinguished rather by orbital septa tending toward narrowness, which in the phyletic sense signifies a more primitive condition. The *nasal aperture* dominating the central region of the face is not so suggestive of facial breadth because of its tendency toward narrowness in the Indian skull in general. This impression is modified, however, in the Haida and Lillooet whose greater nasal breadth is due to the coincident lesser nasal height, thus suggesting relatively broader noses in the facial complex. With the tendency toward narrower noses which is to be considered as of evolutional progressiveness, other advanced conditions are related like the predominance of the bothrokraspedotic *margo piriformis inferior (fossa praenasalis)* in the Undeformed, Cowichan and Chinook, and even the oxykraspedotic in the Koskimo, besides the occurrence of the oxyacanthic *spina nasalis anterior*. The latter, however, is not of regular occurrence in the adult where the typical condition is rather that of lophocryptacanthy. It is rather peculiar that oxyacanthy is found quite frequently in the immature skull, corresponding thus to conditions in the immature Australian as pointed out by *Klaatsch* and *Turner* (p. 303). The *incisura piriformis inferior* which for its shape and depth depends mostly on the relative height of the crista nasalis (incisiva) is either double-lobed (resembling the Greek letter ω), evenly bulged or dipped medially. The latter is prevalent in the Chinook and is influenced by the gradually descending borders of the incisura piriformis inferior. The double-lobed form shows its predominance in the other divisions and is varied here by the difference of level which concerns either the right or the left lobe. Although it may not be a racial characteristic it seems that the well defined double-lobe is an indication of advanced morphology while the flat bottom is considered primitive, occurring in the as yet undifferentiated infantile skull and in the fossils as a mark of inferiority. The dipped bulge of the Chinook is hardly to be regarded as an emphasis of the flat form, all the more so since the bothro- and oxykraspedotic conditions show a prevailing frequency. It is there rather a tribal character.

In addition to a number of less prominent characteristics of the nasal skeleton, like the *nasofrontal suture* which varies in shape in almost any series of skulls and the form of the *nasal bones* which are mostly constricted and narrowly or broadly wing-shaped, the *nasion* and the outline of the *nasal bridge* require attention. The former is in the vast majority of our cases only mildly depressed as a result of the likewise mildly developed supraorbital and supranasal eminences. More interesting is the behavior of the nasal bridge which in true mongolid fashion of total convexity recedes at its upper end behind the vertical projection of the nasion upon the ear-eye plane of orientation. Representing what might be called the true mongolid type, its behavior is nevertheless quite variable. Although there is hardly any exception from the recession behind the nasion vertical, the behavior in advance of that line varies considerably not only in regard to its actual projection but likewise to the amount of convexity attained there and which in numerous instances in the Chinook and Koskimo give rise to pronounced double curvatures of the whole outline. One is tempted to lay this behavior to protocaucasid influence, of which more will be said further on (see Final Summary).

The *maxillary complex* in front view is distinguished by several features of racial significance. There is first to be mentioned the depression of the anterior wall of the corpus, posterior of the canine ridge, the so-called *fossa canina* which is directed laterally in the anthropoids. Its shallowness and even absence is a characteristic of the mongolid skull and is more pronounced the closer the affinity to the mongolian stock. The frequency of shallowness therefore in our Undeformed series, which comprises the Eskimo, Chukchee and Haida, is rather high with $63.7°/_{0}$. Although considerable frequencies of shallowness are attained also in the deformed series, particularly the Chinook

($40.5°/_0$), the general condition there is medium shallowness. Deep fossae, almost absent in the Undeformed, occur at frequencies up to $10°/_0$ in the deformed skulls, and are generally correlated with deeply curved *cristae infrazygomaticae* and lack of high alveolar processes. The shallow, nearly straight crista infrazygomatica, on the other hand, is combined as a rule with high alveolar processes and shallow fossae caninae or flatness in general of the surface of the corpus maxillare (fig. 72), and as a cursory observation made it likewise appear, the tendency toward the formation of the bothrokraspedotic to amblykraspedotic incisura piriformis inferior. In such a condition one will have to recognize a primitive morphologic state as well as one pertaining to mongolid morphology in general, while the more refined conditions are characterized by a none too high anteriorly straight, i. e. more or less vertical alveolar process, a well defined fossa canina and more or less deeply curved crista infrazygomatica.

Another feature, the *sutura infraorbitalis* must not remain unmentioned. With its high frequency of about $50°/_0$ in the series under discussion, while almost invariably present in the Eskimo, it attains the significance of a racial characteristic; other human varieties, where it also occurs, show smaller frequencies. The suture is quite variable in appearance and complicated sometimes by additional smaller infraorbital foramina connected by branches with the principal foramen, instances of which are shown in fig. 74.

6. Norma occipitalis.

The orthohypsicranial trend of the skull of the Northwestern Indian is typified also in norma occipitalis by its "house"-shaped *contour* with its well rounded or slightly and broadly gabled roof which is the prevailing one in the four series. The strongly deformed Chinook with their increased biparietal breadth give rise to a relatively greater percentage of the "wedge" shape ($18.3°/_0$), artificial in this specific case, which in the normal, i. e. undeformed skull signifies the neonate state. A somewhat more rounded "house" is recognized in the cylindrically deformed Koskimo who of our four series show in fact the highest percentage of this outline, namely $94.1°/_0$.

Conforming to the conditions in general of the cranial relief that of the occipital region is likewise rather weak and undeveloped in our skulls. Nevertheless, an outstanding feature in the Indian skull from the North Pacific Coast is the tendency toward the forming of a *torus occipitalis* in various degrees of intensity with the exclusion, however, of pronounced cases of which in fact only one male was recorded in each division. Although the torus like the other cranial relief is hardly indicated in the skull of the young child and develops only as growth and function proceed, one will have to reckon, nevertheless, with its hereditary nature since it occurs at so high a frequency in such restricted ethnic varieties as the Australians, Oceanians and Americans. It may therefore be considered a racial characteristic occurring at total frequencies of from 55.0% to 86.7% in our four divisions. The lowest figure is found in the Chinook where also the absence of the torus is compensatorily the highest, while 86.7%, the highest in the Koskimo, is compensated by the lowest absence. Judging from these statistical data one is tempted also to consider deformatory influence, especially in the Koskimo, since the origination of the torus seems to be the result much more of mechanico-physiologic processes in connection with occipital flexure and brain expansion than external functional influence.

Not directly dependent on the occurrence of the torus occipitalis except in well developed cases, the *fossa supratoralis* is found as a tuberosity or slight depression of varying extension above the torus. Its nature is not quite clear and may be connected with the osteogenetic processes in the occipital bone at the region between the membranous and cartilaginous portions of its squama. It is on the other hand quite conceivable that muscular action (m. trapezius, ligamentum nuchae), particularly in a skull of crude texture and morphology may assist in bringing about the condition under discussion, and from this angle artificial deformation might likewise be considered. This is evident judging by the amount of absence in *summary 170*, from the high frequencies of the fossa supratoralis in the Cowichan and Chinook deformation. Although the Koskimo frequency is somewhat smaller, it is yet considerably higher than that of the Undeformed. In these only 57.5% show the fossa as over against 77.8% in the Koskimo and frequencies even above 90% in the Cowichan and Chinook.

The variations in the occipital squama known as *os incae* and *os apicis* have been exhaustively treated of on pp. 323–328. There their origin was traced to the osteogenetic processes in the occipital bone and particularly that of the *os apicis* to the posterior fontanel (fonticulus occipitalis). Our frequencies for the os incae are exceedingly small, markedly smaller even than those for Ohio, Tennessee and Florida tribes (see *summary 171* and p. 324) and likewise the Peruvians who, although not exclusively possessed of the formation in question, preserve nevertheless a relatively high frequency. The higher percentage of os apicis is due to the mode of enumeration followed in this work and which accounts for the osteogenetic derivation of this particular bone.

7. Mandible.

The mandible, of which there are not many specimens in our material, has already been characterized in a general way from a descriptive point of view (p. 381). It was pointed out there that its osseous relief, rather gracile in shape, is on the average only weakly developed, which is in accord with similar conditions in the entire cranial complex. Due to the non-massiveness of the corpus with its fairly straight basal outline; slight chin development; the more anterior position of the foramen mentale, mostly in line with pm_1; the ramus of moderate height and its tendency toward a greater minimum breadth [235], a well defined anterior outline whose upper portion is slightly convex, its lower concave in lateral aspect, while the posterior border presents very variable degrees of concavity; the iso- to chamaecoronic condition of the condylo-coronoid height relation [236]; the weak muscle markings including the spina mentalis interna, the masseteric, mylohyoid and pterygoid insertions; the Northwestern mandible, if compared with caucasid standards, shows a number of primitive as well as advanced morphologic features which in their entirety portray the mongolid lower jaw.

The broadening of the cranial base, progressively in the Cowichan-Chinook order by means of artificial deformation has doubtless produced a greater bicondylar extension in those series as a mechanical adaptation, reference to which was made on p. 356.

8. Sutures and Wormian bones.

The general character of the principal cranial sutures in our Undeformed series is one of relative simplicity, increasing in the order coronal, sagittal and lambdoid sutures. The natural process of increased osseous growth in the more centrally located parts of the membranous bones of the skull-cap, which results in the complication of the sutures, appears to be intensified by the strains of artificial deformation. Obliteration of the entire sutures is therefore much less frequent in the deformed series, although occasionally obliteration in part is more numerous here. The stimulating influence of mechanical stress is likewise shown by the greater occurrence of Wormian bones especially in the coronal and lambdoid sutures, the latter conspicuously exceding the former. As a natural reactive process in response to organic stimuli which are enhanced by those of mechanical stress, *Marelli*'s [237] statement is quite plausible that "la lambdoidea parece ser la mas sensible de todas las articulaciones". The greatest frequencies of Wormian bones, as recorded in

---

[235] The two extremes of height and breadth ratios are given in our series (p. 338) by lower broad and higher narrow rami with shallower incisurae mandibulae (condylocoronoideae) in the former and higher ones in the latter. The average type, as pointed out above, signifies a medium condition with a tendency toward refinement.

[236] Our iso- to chamaecoronic findings with regard to the condylo-coronoid height relation do not conform to *Puccioni*'s (Morphologie du maxillaire inférieur. Anthrop., 1914, v. XXV, pp. 291—321 [300]) statement of hypsicorony in the American Indian. It could likewise not be corroborated in the Santa Barbara remains (*Oetteking*, l. c., p. 279 [140; 145—146]).

[237] Marelli, Carlos A., 1909. La complicacion y sinostosis de las suturas del cráneo cerebral de los primitivos habitantes de la República Argentina. Riv. Mus. La Plata, v. XVI (2. ser., v. III), pp. 353—487 (379).

summaries 174—176, are attained therefore in the excessively deformed Chinook and Koskimo series. Identical conditions prevail also in other parts of the world. Thus *Chervin*[238] pictures skulls of Bolivian natives where the lambdoid suture is completely filled in by sutural bones. The cause for their existence must be seen in the analogous conditions which prevail in the infantile skull when in the fonticuli the ossificatory matter proves to be insufficient and the gap is completed by the familiar fontanel bones (os bregmaticum, epiptericum, apicis). The gaps caused in the sutural regions as well as the increased process of ossification there under the stimulating strain of deformation likewise require the formation of new ossicles from supplementary ossification centers when the original arrangement proves to be insufficient.

9. Teeth.

The teeth, on the whole, were observed as medium in size, exceedingly healthy and conforming to the general phylogenetic trend of size reduction backward. Regarding their state of healthiness the observation holds true that caries is quite rare, but that excessive attrition seems to be responsible for a number of pathologic resorptions in the alveoli which are rather numerous. The freedom from caries is thus compensated by the disadvantageous wearing of the teeth and in cases by the subsequent inflammation of the alveoli. The moderate size of the Indian teeth is further distinguished by the lingual concaveness of the incisors, particularly the upper which as an Indian characteristic attains a frequency of $80°/_0$ in our series.

---

[238] *Chervin, Dr.*, 1907. Conférence sur l'anthropologie bolivienne. C.-R. Ass. Franç. Av. Sci. (Congr. Rheims), 20 pp. (19).

CONCLUSIONS.

A summary study of the cranioscopic observations leads to the following conclusions which under certain collective aspects are divisible into general and specific characters. It lies in the nature of such a division that the latter group of characters represent the distinguishing race or group features, while the former depict the general status of the series from the cranioscopic angle, i. e. those more generalized features which are distinguished neither by excessive or diminutive size nor by their sporadic appearance; but even as such these latter may be recognized and admitted as features characteristic of a specific group or race. Furthermore, the influence of deformatory practices upon the cranial complex and its configurative detail had to be considered, as well as diagnostic evaluation of the morphologic traits from the racial viewpoint. The different collective aspects are in the order of their importance:

1. General appearance

The skulls under investigation were on the average medium in size and occasionally decidedly submedium in the females; generally gracile in form; non-robust, except the Haida to some extent, and moderate in development of muscle markings and of the cranial relief in general. The weight of the skulls conforms to the conditions described, i. e. neither unusually light nor excessively heavy.

Anteroposterior and cylindrical deformations have caused artificial brachy- and dolichocrany, the extent of which has been recorded in Part I: Craniometry. Changes (intensifications, modifications) in the morphologic characters found in the normae will be pointed out below.

2. Specific appearance

a. Racial characteristics [239]

Norma verticalis

cranial outline ovoid;
phaenozygy, favored by postorbital constriction;
smallness or absence of foramina parietalia.

---

[239] Under racial characteristic have been admitted such features which occur in at least 50% of the cases on record, or such features of a lesser percental frequency which from the comparative viewpoint signify nevertheless a certain predominance. In cases of doubt an interrogation mark has been added.

Norma basilaris
- partes petrosae on level with surrounding parts or only slightly depressed;
- roundish foramen magnum;
- irregular ossifications on its anterior border;
- fossa pharyngea (?);
- torus palatinus;
- foramen pterygospinosum (*Civinini*);
- lamina externa of processus pterygoideus exceeds lamina interna in size;
- dental arch paraboloid.

Norma lateralis
- cranial outline ellipsoides cuneatus in the male, ellipsoides rotundus in the female;
- postbregmatic elevation;
- lineae temporales weak;
- nasion depression slight;
- mongolid concavity of nasal bridge modified by more or less pronounced projection in lower half or three-quarters;
- spina nasalis anterior of moderate development (comprising, however, extremes of negative and positive formation);
- alveolar prognathy;
- basal outline of lower jaw fairly straight;
- chin projection slight (neutral *Klaatsch*);
- processus mastoideus medium-sized;
- crista supramastoidea;
- tympanic hyperostosis;
- porus acusticus externus roundish-to-elliptic;
- fossa temporalis spacious, with few anomalies;
- arcus zygomaticus mongolid.

Norma frontalis
- bizygomatic prominence;
- orbits tending to be high (extremes: relatively low in the Haida, exceedingly high in the Koskimo);
- lower lateral angle of orbit rounded;
- glabella and superciliary eminences weakly developed;
- interorbital septum moderately broad, tending toward narrowness;
- apertura piriformis tending toward narrowness;
- incisura piriformis double-lobed, medially dipped in the Chinook;
- fossa canina shallow, correlated with shallow crista infrazygomatica and high alveolar processes;
- more refined conditions correlate relatively deep fossa canina with deep incisura infrazygomatica and a less high processus alveolaris;
- sutura infraorbitalis.

Norma occipitalis
- "house"-shaped contour;
- torus occipitalis (but no pronounced cases recorded);
- fossa supratoralis;
- susceptible to occipital variations.

Sutures and Wormian bones
: sutural complication simple to moderate;
moderate occurrence of Wormian bones (see however under *b.* β).

Teeth
: medium in size;
incisors shovel-shaped;
phyletic reduction of molar sizes.

b. Deformatory effects [240]

    α. Direct changes (configurative)

Cowichan-Chinook anteroposterior compression: foreshortening with compensatory biparietal expansion; artificial plagiocrany; enlargement of minimum frontal breadth;
Koskimo conical compression: elongation with fore-shortened cranial breadth;
bilateral compression usually with occipital applanation (shell sheap skulls from Lower Fraser River).

    β. Indirect changes (morphologic, organic)

Norma verticalis
: retarded obliteration of main sutures and increasing tendency toward the formation of Wormian bones.

Norma basilaris
: broadened cranial base in the Cowichan and Chinook; lowness of occipital condyles, correlated with depression of cranial base (basion-nasion), e.g. Chinook;
relatively greater number of ossifications at anterior border of foramen magnum;
increased frequency of foramen *Civinini*.

Norma lateralis
: occasional horizontal flexure of coronoid suture in stephanion region;
sutura squamosa more varied;
increased frequency of processus parietalis, left over right, male over female;
crista supramastoidea (Cowichan and Chinook);
fossa temporalis variations (processus frontalis, epiptericum, sulcus sphenoparietalis, stenocrotaphy) more numerous;
mastoids enlarged in Chinook and Koskimo;
bilateral compression of porus acusticus externus;
tympanic hyperostosis;
auricular exostoses (?);
perforation of tympanic plate;
crista infraorbitalis of ala magna drawn out in Koskimo.

Norma frontalis
: increased bizygomatic prominence in Cowichan and Chinook;
glabella region flattened out in Chinook and Koskimo.

---

[240] Direct or indirect effects of deformation traceable only through the more intricate metrical practices are enumerated in the conclusions to Part I.

Norma occipitalis

    increasing tendency toward occipital variations;
    flattening of occipital relief.

Sutures and Wormian bones

    total obliteration less frequent in deformed skulls, in favor of more frequent obliteration in part;
    increased tendency toward the formation of Wormian bones in coronal and lambdoid suturus.

3. General morphologic evaluation
(according to caucasid standards).

a. inferior traits

    phaenozygy in connection with postorbital constriction;
    relatively narrow nasal process of frontal bone;
    torus occipitalis;
    crista supramastoidea;
    tympanic hyperostosis;
    relative levelness of petrous parts.

b. advanced traits

    in addition to those named under 4: smoothness of cranial relief;
    tendency toward facial narrowing.

4. Extraneous characteristics.

    projecting nasal bridge;
    refined margo piriformis inferior;
    marked fossa canina;
    deep incisura (crista) infrazygomatica.

In summing up it is to be stated in final conclusion that our study of the crania (craniometric and cranioscopic) from the North Pacific Coast has yielded a number of definite facts. These consist in the statement of morphologic similarities and dissimilarities when compared with such racial types as the Mongol and the Caucasian. Sufficient evidence has been accumulated, however, to show the close relationship of our specimens with the Mongol variety of mankind. Comparative differences, amongst others, were seen in the tendencies toward cranial elongation, height diminution, narrowing of the face and nose, and toward prognathy, particularly alveolar. These divergencies were recognized not only as extant between the relatively pure mongolian type and our material from a generalizing point of observation, but gave rise, likewise, to the recognition of subtypes identical with the various tribes of our area of investigation which may be denominated as mongoloid. Whether such physiognomic traits as the narrowing of the head and nose and especially the remarkable projection of the nose in certain Indian tribes could have come about per se under the condition of changed natural environment through migration, geographic change of habitat, etc., one is as yet unable to decide. In addition, however, to the conceivable alteration of definite cranial race characteristics pertaining to a definite human variety by means of variability and mutability, racial interbreeding must be considered. Of a number of crossproducts the narrowing of the face and nose have been recognized as progressive and would have to be attributed in our case to the blending with another morphologically different and, as it were, superior racial group, such as early caucasid elements. Affinities to *Dixon*'s (1923) abstractly used Caspian and Mediterranean types are doubtless to be noticed in our material [241]. A mixture with precaucasid racial elements may have occurred already on Asian soil before the invading hordes migrated to this continent where they phaenotyped into the multifarious array of Indian tribal differentiation. This is all the more probable since the peopling of America apparently occurred at a relatively late period [242] when the racial development of Asia had produced the substantial types which at some time or other followed the natural trend of expansion. Concurring thus with other authors (*Boas* 1911/12; *Hrdlička* 1912, 1926; *Holmes* 1921; *Kroeber* 1923; *Dixon* 1923; *Steinmann* 1924; *Jochelson* 1926, et al.) in the concept of the primary Asiatic migration into this part of the world, the present author is aware of the fact that his work can be only a small contribution to the physical history of the Indian of the North Pacific Coast and the North American Indian in general. The study of the Jesup material, greatly complicated by the high percentage of deformed skulls, could dispose of only small contingents from among quite a number of autonomous tribes. The differential results will have to be tested by more numerous and, if possible, purer material. Under such conditions it may then be possible also to apply and exploit *Wissler*'s (1926) distribution concept of somatic traits.

It was not intended by the author to draw into his study of a rather limited but at the same time all the more important anthropologic domain, the problem of Polynesian or other origin. From his present investigations, however, he derives the conviction of North Asiatic migration, the mongolian affinity, the premigratory cross-breeding with distant (precaucasid?) elements, and finally the phaenotypical differentiation of the American Indian upon American soil.

---

[241] The increase of prognathy, especially the alveolar in, as it were, a morphologically progressively altered mongolid skull does not lend itself to easy explanation. It may be that the disposition toward prognathy retained in racial blending experienced new stimulation through it, or that the well-known crude food habits in the area under investigation afford the functional clue.

[242] This is also *Haddon*'s (1925, 137) opinion when he says "The North-west Coast population on the whole belongs to a later and distinct migration from Asia."

BIBLIOGRAPHY.

Only works with a direct bearing on the anthropology of the area under investigation are cited here. For other literature the reader is referred to the general index and the footnotes.

Boas, Franz, 1889. Deformation of heads in British Columbia. Science, v. XIII, pp. 364, 365.
——, 1890a. Schädelformen von Vancouver Island. (Letter to *Rudolf Virchow*, 21. Dez. 1889). Zschr. Ethnol. (Verh.), v. XXII, pp. 29—31.
——, 1890b. First general report on the Indians of British Columbia. Rep. Brit. Ass. Adv. Sci. (50. Meet. Newcastle-upon-Tyne, 1889), pp. 801—893.
——, 1891. Deformed crania from the North Pacific Coast. Rep. Brit. Ass. Adv. Sci. (60. Meet. Leeds, 1890). 6. Rep., pp. 647—655.
——, 1898—1906. Publications of the Jesup North Pacific Expedition. Leiden and New York. 10 volumes.
——, 1911/12. The history of the American race. Ann. N. Y. Ac. Sci., v. XXI, pp. 177—183.
——, 1921. Ethnology of the Kwakiutl. 35. Ann. Rep. Bur. Am. Ethnol. (1913/14), part. I; XI.
——, 1929. Migration of Asiatic races and cultures to North America. Scient. Monthly, February, pp. 110—117.
Cameron, John, 1923. Osteology of the Western and Central Eskimo. Rep. Canad. Arct. Exp. 1913—1918), v. XII: The Copper Eskimos. Pt. C.
Dixon, Roland B., 1923. The racial history of man. New York.
Haddon, A. C., 1925. The races of man and their distribution. New York.
Handbook of American Indians North of Mexico. 1910/12. Two volumes, edited by *Frederick Webb Hodge.* Bull. 30. Bur. Am. Ethnol.
Holmes, W. H., 1921. On the race history and facial characteristics of the aboriginal Americans. Smithson. Rep. for 1919. pp. 427—432.
Hrdlička, Aleš, 1906. Contribution to the physical anthropology of California. Univ. California Pub. Am. Archeol. Ethnol., v. IV, n. 2, pp. 49—64.
——, 1907. Skeletal remains suggesting or attributed to early man in North America. Bull. 33. Bur. Am. Ethnol. (Smith. Inst.).
——, 1912. The derivation and probable place of origin of the North American Indian. Proc. XVIII. Internat. Congr. Am. (London). pp. 57—62.
——, 1924. Catalogue of human crania in the United States National Museum Collections: The Eskimo, Alaska and related Indians, North Eastern Asiatics. Proc. U. S. Nat. Mus., v. LXIII, art. 12, pp. 1—51.
——, 1925. The origin and antiquity of the American Indian. Smiths. Rep. 1923, pp. 481—494.
——, 1926. Alaska yields secrets of first Americans. New York Times, Nov. 28.
Jochelson, Waldemar, 1926. The ethnological problems of Bering Sea. Nat. Hist. v. XXVI, no. 1, pp. 90—95.

Kroeber, A. L., 1923. Anthropology. New York.

Martin, R., 1914. Lehrbuch der Anthropologie. Jena. (Second edition 1928).

Oetteking, Bruno, 1925. Skeletal remains from Santa Barbara, California. Part. I, Craniology. Ind. Notes Monogr., no. 39.

Reicher, Michael, 1913. Untersuchungen über die Schädelform der alpenländischen und mongolischen Brachycephalen. Zschr. Morph. Anthrop., v. XV, pp. 421—562; v. XVI, pp. 1—64.

Ritchie, Stephen G., 1923. The dentition of the Western and Central Eskimo. Rep. Canadian Arctic Exped. 1913—11. v. XII, pt. C, pp. c 59—66 c.

Smith, Harlan I., 1900—1908. Shell heaps of the Lower Fraser River. The Jesup North Pacific Expedition, v. II, pp. 133—191.

——, 1900—1908. Archaeology of the Gulf of Georgia and Puget Sound. The Jesup North Pacific Expedition. v. II, pp. 301—441.

Steinmann, G., 1924. Zur Urbesiedelung Amerikas. Proc. XXI. Internat. Congr. Am. (The Hague) pp. 63—70.

Teit, James, 1900—1908. The Lillooet Indians (edited by Franz Boas). The Jesup North Pacific Expedition, v. II, pp. 195—300.

——, 1900—1908. The Shuswap (edited by Franz Boas). The Jesup North Pacific Expediton, v. II, pp. 447—789.

Virchow, R., 1892. Crania ethnica americana. Suppl. Zschr. Ethnol., v. XXIV. Berlin.

Wissler, Clark, 1926. The relation of nature to man in aboriginal America. New York-Oxford University Press.

Woldt-Jacobsen, 1884. Kapitän Jacobsens Reise an der Nordwestküste Amerikas 1881—1883. Leipzig.

INDEX.

Adachi, B., 227, 287, 361.
Advanced traits. *See* Morphology, cranial.
Affenrinne. *See* Sulcus praenasalis.
Age stages, 156. *See* also Sex differences.
Aichel, Otto, 324, 327.
Aigner, D., 223, 224.
Albrecht. *See* Fossula vermiana (*Albrecht*), and Processus lemuriniscus s. Sandifortii (*Albrecht*).
Alveolar plane, 9–11, 117.
Amblycraspedotic (*Macalister*). *See* Nose: Margo piriformis inferior.
Angelotti, G., 255.
Angle basilaire (*Broca*), 81.
Angles (with ear-eye and alveolar plane lines if not otherwise indicated). Angle basilaire (*Broca*), 81; anterobasal (mihi), 122, 127; basion-bregma (ear-eye plane), 29; basion-bregma (glabella-lambda plane), 26–28, central angle (Zentralwinkel *Klaatsch*), 26–28, 135; condylocoronoid (mihi), 127–129, 350; cranial base angles (correlation), 81, 134; craniobasal, 73, 74, 133, 134, 138; craniofacial, 95–96, 135–136, 140; foramen magnum, 78–81, 133, 134, 139; frontal, 57–58, 133, 138; glabella-lambda and ear-eye plane lines, 25; interoccipital, 70–71, 133, 138; occipital, 66–70, 132, 133, 138; orbital (verticosagittal declination), 115–116, 135; parietal, 60, 61, 62–63, 133, 138; profile, *see* prognathy; prognathy: alveolar 90–91, 135, 140. *See* 143, 154, 156, 365, 373, 376, facial 87–88, 135, 140, 143–148, 153, 154, 156, ·365, midfacial 89–90, 135; ramus, 123–125, 136, 141.
Angulus mandibulae, 365.
Angulus zygomaticotemporalis (mihi), 267, 268, 270–271, 364, 387.
Anoprosthion (*H. Virchow*), 10.
Anterobasal angle (mihi), 122; depending upon chin height, 127.
Apertura piriformis. *See* Nose.
Arc. Frontal, 45–46, 54; impairment through fronto-occipital deformation, 44; mediansagittal: general, divisions and divisional participation, 44–50; occipital, 46–47, 64; parietal, 46, 59; percental ratio between frontal and parietal, 49–50.
Arcus süperciliaris. *See* Supraorbital prominences.
Arcus zygomaticus. Beugestelle (*Lebzelter*), 267; Henkelform (*P.* and *Fr. Sarasin*), 267; lateral aspect, 266–270, 364, 365, 373; vertical aspect, 167-169, 355, 372, 373, 375; Wellenform (*Fr. Sarasin*), 266.
Area alveolaris (*Waldeyer*). *See* Trigonum postmolare (*Klaatsch*).
Arteria meningea media, 227.
Asterion region, 330.
Atlas. Assimilation, 177–179; ankylosis, 179-180.

Baake, William, 3.
Bartels, G., 209, 276.
Base, cranial. Angle, 74, 81, 133; broadening, 356, 374; depression of petrous parts, 356–357, 373, 374, 375; length, 72–73, 133, 138, 140; relation to other cranial dimensions, 74–75, 134.
Bauer, M., 204, 208, 213, 215, 217, 219.
Baur, Erwin. *See* Baur-Fischer-Lenz.
Baur-Fischer-Lenz, 141, 156.
Bibliography, 2, 377–378.
Birkner, F., 80.
Black, D., 194, 195.
Boas Franz, 1, 14, 16, 17, 20, 21, 131, 376, 377.
Bolk, L., 24, 173, 175, 177.
Bonin, G. v. *See* Cristae anterior and posterior (*v. Bonin*).
Bothrocraspedotic (*Macalister*). *See* Nose: Margo piriformis inferior.
Brachystaphyliny. *See* Palatal index.
Brachyurany. *See* Maxilloalveolar index.
Brass, M., 12.
Braun. *See* Trigonum retromalare (*Braun*).
Breadth, cranial. *See* Diameters, cranial, and Deformation.
Broca, P. *See* Angle basilaire.
Broesike, W., 234.
Brunn, A. v., 204, 359.

Cameron, John, 73, 193, 202, 222, 283, 325, 377.
Canalis condyloideus. *See* Fossa (canalis) condyloideus.
Canalis hypoglossi, 185–186; irregularities, 186, 358.
Canalis nasolacrimalis, 290.
Capacity, cranial, 32–33; increase through deformation, 32, 133, 138, 142, 146, 148, 150, 156; technique, 9.
Catarrhiny (*R. Virchow*), 294.
Caucasid elements. *See* Racial affinities.

380 INDEX.

Central angle. *See* Zentralwinkel (*Klaatsch*).
Chamaecorony. *See* Mandible: Condylocoronoid height relation.
Charles, R. Havelock, 172, 185.
Cheek bones, prominence of. *See* Racial characteristics; Mongolid morphology.
Chervin, A., 371.
Chin, 333–337; development, 156; lateral (*Klaatsch*), 333, 334; median (*Klaatsch*), 333, 334; negative, neutral, positive (*Klaatsch*), 333, 334; round (*Frizzi*), 334; squarish (abgekantet, edged off *Frizzi*), 334, 335.
Civinini, F., 202; *see* also Foramen pterygospinosum (*Civinini*) and Spina Civinini.
Circummuscular zone (*Dalla Rosa*), 224.
Clivus nasoalveolaris (*Sergi*). *See* Nose: Margo piriformis inferior.
Coefficient of variation (v), 148, 154.
Comparative differential aspect (craniometrical final). Cranio-typological, 148, 154, 156; four series, 130–136; Lillooet affinities, 145; method (differential formula), 131; metrical results, 131–154; mongolo-mongoloid, 141–145; mongolo-mongoloideo-causid, 146–148, 156; nondeformed tribal elements, 136–141, 156.
Conclusions (final), 372–376.
Concrescence of molar *anlagen*. *See* Teeth.
Condyli occipitales, 180–181, 357, 374; doublefaceted, 180–181.
Condylocoronoid angle (mihi), 127–128, 350; correlation with ramus angle, 129; height relation, 370; increase of the negative angle through deformation, 128–129.
Condylus tertius, 172, 175.
Contours, cranial. In Norma basilaris: *see* Base, cranial; in Norma frontalis, 365–366; in Norma lateralis, 221–222, 359, 360, 373; in Norma occipitalis, 315–317, 368, 373, 375; in Norma verticalis, 159–160, 355, 372.
Corner, E. M., 189.
Corrective vertical (*Frizzi*), 334.
Cradles used in head deformation, 13.
Cranial base. *See* Base, cranial.
Cranial diameters. Breadth, 34, 35–36, 131, 133, 138, 141, 142, 145, 146; comparison of principal, 36–38; general, 156; height, 36, 131, 138, 142, 145, 146, 156; height least variable, 38, 41; length, 34–35, 131, 138, 140, 142, 146, 156.
Cranial elongation, 375.
Cranial outline. *See* Contours, cranial.
Craniofacial angle (*Falkenburger*), 92, 93, 94, 95–96, 135–136, 140.
Craniofacial ratios. Jugofrontal index, 93–94; jugomandibular index, 94–95; transverse craniofacial index, 92–93, 134, 139, 144, 145, 146.
Craniology of the Pacific Northwest, 1; craniometric and cranioscopic, 2; plan of investigation, 1.
Cranio-maxillo-palatal correlation, 102–104.
Cranioscopy. Conclusions, 372–375; general, 157–158, 354–371, 359; summary, 355–371.
Cribra orbitalia, 287, 290.
Crista(ae): anterior and posterior (*v. Bonin*), *see* Nose: Margo piriformis inferior; buccinatoria s. alveolomarginalis (*Waldeyer*), 343; endocondyloidea (*v. Lenhossék*), 343, 344; endocoronoidea (*v. Lenhossék*), 343, 344; infraorbitalis, 264–266, 364, 366, 374; infratemporalis, 262–264; infrazygomatica (*Rauber-Kopsch*), 309–311, 368, 373, 375; marginalis, 219; mastoidea (*Klaatsch*), 224, 239, 240, 360; nasalis, 367; occipitalis externa, 317, 318; sphenomaxillaris, 264; supramastoidea, 222, 224, 232, 233–234, 240, 360, 373, 374, 375; temporalis ossis frontis (mihi), 222, 223, 360.
Crossbreeding on Asian soil. *See* Racial affinities.
Cryptozygy. *See* Arcus zygomaticus: Vertical aspect.
Cunningham, D. J., 282.

Dacryon, 109.
Davis, Joseph Barnard, 17.
Deformation, cranial. Since the effects of artificial deformation are noticeable in a great many features and configurative formations, as well as in the metrical conditions, the pages also on which references to such effects have been made, are listed with the other references under the various captions of this index. Adjustments, 14, 150–151; bilateral, 14, 21, 155, 372; compensatory and mechanical changes, 13, 14, 155, 356, 372; deleterious effects, 15; direct and indirect effects, 131, 155, 354, 360, 361, 372, 374; evaluation by tribes, 16; fallacy to identify tribes by deformation, 17–18; frequency in the sexes, 15; identical fashions in North and South America, 13, 17; intentional and unintentional, 12–13, 155, 355; methods, 1, 155; modification through growth, 16; quantitative treatment, 130–131; retention of deformatory effects, 130; reversion toward the normal, 130; types, two fundamental, 130, 155; type analysis: differential 154, perigraphical 18–23; type series, three principal (Cowichan, Chinook, Koskimo), 16, 17, 18–23; 155; time duration of application, 16 (and footnote); yielding to strain, 130.
Dehiscence (*Hyrtl*), spontaneous. *See* Spontaneous dehiscence (*Hyrtl*).

INDEX.

Dental arch, 204–208, 359, 373; correlations, 102–104, 206, 207, 208.
Differences, comparative and morphological, 375–376; sex, 354, 362, 365, 366, 375–376; size, 356; structural, 354; type, 355; western and eastern Eskimo, 142, 144, 156.
Differential treatment. *See* Comparative differential aspect.
Dillenius, A. J., 14, 223, 224.
Dixon, R. B., 376, 377.
Dolichurany. *See* Maxilloalveolar index.
Dwight, Th., 179.

Ear-eye plane, 9, 25, 29.
Easton, George F., 15.
Ecker, A. See Torus occipitalis (*Ecker*).
Elliot, G. D., 340.
Environmental changes, 376.
Epiptericum. *See* Os epiptericum.
Eskimo. Cranial characteristics of eastern, 156; type differences between western and eastern, 142, 144, 156.
Exostoses auriculares, 249–253, 374.
Extensive deviation (ramus mandibulae), 342.
Extraneous characteristics, 375.

Face. Bizygomatic breadth, 83, 134, 139, 140, 142, 145, 146, 365, 373, 374; height, upper facial, 82, 134, 138, 139, 142, 146, 156, 365; index, upper facial, 84, 134, 139, 144, 154; length, 85, 134, 139, 141; narrowing, 375; outline in frontal aspect, 365; profile angles. *see* Profilation Angles, Prognathy; triangle, facial, 86–87.
Facial triangle. *See* Face.
Faesebeck, J., 204.
Falkenburger, Fritz, 28, 95, 135, 140.
Fischer, E. See Baur-Fischer-Lenz.
Fissura: cerebri lateralis (*Sylvii*), 255; orbitalis inferior, 364; petrotympanica (*Glaseri*), 253; tympanicomastoidea, 248.
Fonticulus occipitalis, 369.
Foramen(ina): condyloideum, *see* Fossa(canalis) condyloideus; incisivum, 213; infraorbitale, 311–314, 368, 373; jugulare 186–189, correlations 185, 186, 357; divided 189, 358, size differences 357; lacerum 356; magnum: angle 78–81, 133, 134, 139, anterior border 7, 172–173, 357, 373, 374, correlations 80–81, deformatory influences 133, 357, index 77–78, length 76, 133, 138, 141, manifestation of occipital vertebra 175–177, 185, posterior border 173–175, shape 170–172, 356, 357, 373, size 356; mandibulare, 344; mastoideum, 328–330; mentale, 336–337, 370; palatina majora and minora, 219–220, 359; parietalia, 163–166, 355–356, 372; pterygospinosum (*Civinini*) 202–204, 358, general frequency 204, 373, 374; supraorbitale, *see* Incisura (foramen) supraorbitale.
Form in general, cranial, 372.
Fossa(ae): alaris, *see* Sulcus sphenoparietalis; canina 307–309, 367–368, 373, 375, correlations 373; (canalis) condyloideus 181–185, absence 185, bridging 357; digastricae, 336; glenoidalis, *see* Fossa mandibularis; mandibularis 193–194, 253, 255, 363, correlations 358; mastoidea s. foveola suprameatum (*Pensa*), 245; pharyngea, 198–201, 358, 373; praecoronoidea (*Klaatsch*) s. coronoidea (*Waldeyer*) s. fovea retromalaris (*Bünte and Moral*) s. recessus mandibulae (*v. Lenhossék*), 343, 344; praenasalis, *see* Margo piriformis inferior; pterygoidea, *see* Processus pterygoideus; scaphoidea, *see* Processus pterygoideus; supratoralis (*Klaatsch*), 320–323, 369, 373; temporalis, 255–262, 373, 374.
Fossula vermiana (*Albrecht*), 94, 195.
Fovea: coronoidea (*Waldeyer*), *see* Fossa praecoronoidea (*Klaatsch*); muscularis postcoronoidea (*Schoetensaek*), 343; retromalaris (*Bünte and Moral*) *see* Fossa praecoronoidea (*Klaatsch*); (spina) trochlearis, 287.
Foveola suprameatum (*Pensa*). *See* Fossa mastoidea.
Frédéric, J., 209, 213.
Frizzi, E., 334.
Frontal: angle smaller in normal and artificial longheads, 58, 133; breadth: maximum more variable in deformation 52, minimum smaller in females 51, 133, 138; outline, 55–57; skull type (*Manouvrier, Pittard*), 52, 53.
Fronton (*Bolk*), 24.
Froriep, A., 175, 185.
Fürst, C. M. See Torus mandibulae (*Fürst*).

General appearance of skulls, 372.
Giuffrida-Ruggeri, V., 349.
Glabella-lambda plane, 25, 26–31.
Glabellar development, 281–282, 366, 373, 374.
Glandula: sublingualis, 345; submaxillaris, 345.
Glaseri. See Fissura petrotympanica (*Glaseri*).
Gnathogram, 125, 390.
Goethe. See Sutura incisiva *Goethei*.
Gorjanović-Kramberger, K., 270, 271, 320, 331, 352.
Gosse, L. A., 17.
Gregory, W. K., 206, 208, 352.
Grosse, U., 204.
Gruber, W., 163.
Grunewald, J., 336.

Haberer, O., 315.
Haddon, A. C., 376, 377.
Haferland, R., 242.
Hamy, E. T., 25.
Hautknochenergänzungsstück (*Ranke*), 323.
Height, cranial. *See* Cranial diameters; Deformation.
Height diminution, 375.
Hermann, P., 9.
Heye, George G., 150.
Hyperostosis. *See* Os tympanicum.
Hypsicorony. *See* Mandible: Condylocoronoid height relation.
Hodge, F. W., 377.
Holmes, W. H., 376, 377.
Hooton, E. A., 151, 170, 222, 243, 252, 255, 328, 337, 345, 346.
Hrdlička, A., 12, 14, 15, 73, 131, 142, 150, 167, 172, 173, 179, 181, 186, 206, 215, 252, 301, 328, 346, 352, 356, 357, 376, 377.
Hunt, George, 16.
Hyrtl, J., 224, 248.

Imbelloni, J., 12, 15.
Incision (*Klaatsch*), 333.
Incisura: condylocoronoidea, *see* Incisura mandibulae; (foramen) frontalis, 285; infrazygomatica, *see* Crista infrazygomatica; mandibulae (condylocoronoidea), 341; marginalis posterior (*Toldt*), 173; mastoidea, 193, 356; occipitalis posterior (*Bolk*), 173; parietalis, 227–232, 361; piriformis inferior, *see* Nose; praeangularis (*Frizzi*), 331, 332; praemuscularis (*Klaatsch*), 332; subcondyloidea (*Klaatsch*), 339; submentalis, (*Klaatsch*), 335, 336; (foramen) supraorbitalis, 285, 287, 366.
Indices: cranial breadth-height, 42–43, 133, 138; cranial length-breadth, 38–40, 133, 138, 142, 145, 150, 156; cranial length-height, 41–42, 133, 138, 142, 145, 146, 151, 156; facial, upper, 83, 134, 140, 144, 146, 151, 154, 156; foramen magnum, 77–78; jugofrontal, 93–94, 365; jugomandibular, 94–95, 365; mandibular: breadth 119, ramus 121–122; maxilloalveolar, 98 –100, 135, 153, 154, 156; nasal, 106–108, 140, 144, 145, 148, 152, 154, 156; orbital: lacrimale 113–114, 143, 144, 145, 147, 148, maxillofrontale 112–113, 139–140, 149, 152, 154, 156; palatal, 101–102; sagittal: frontal 55–56, occipital 65, parietal 60–62; transverse: craniofacial 92–93, 132, 133, 134, 137, 139, 143, 144, 145, 146, 147, frontal 52–53, frontoparietal 53–54, 132–133, 137–138.
Inferior traits. *See* Morphology, cranial.
Infradentale (*R. Martin*), 333.

Infranasion (mihi), 279.
Instruments used, 9.
Intensive deviation (Ramus mandibulae), 341–342.
Interbreeding. *See* Racial interbreeding.
Interorbital breadth, 114–115.
Interorbital septum. *See* Orbit: Anterior interorbital breadth.
Intracranial correlations, 135–136, 140. *See* also Central angle (*Klaatsch*) and Craniofacial angle (*Falkenburger*).
Investigation, plan and scope. *See* Introduction; Summaries (craniometric and cranioscopic); Table of contents.
Isocorony. *See* Mandible: Condylocoronoid height relation.

Jacobsen, Adrian, 15.
Jochelson, W., 376, 377.
Jugalwulst des Oberkiefers (*Klaatsch*). *See* Crista infrazygomatica

Katoprosthion (*H. Virchow*), 10, 333.
Keith, Arthur, 24.
Kerckingii. *See* Os(siculum) *Kerckringii* s. manubrium squamae occipitalis (*R. Virchow*).
Killermann, S., 209.
Klaatsch, H., 9, 10, 25, 26, 27, 117, 135, 140, 191, 236, 239, 240, 267, 268, 303, 311, 320, 331, 333, 334, 336, 339, 344, 360, 367.
Kleiweg de Zwaan, J. P., 249, 259.
Knowles, F. H. S., 193.
Koganei, Y., 320, 347.
Kollmann, J., 175, 177, 179, 185, 189.
Koumaris, Jean H., 167, 172,
Kroeber, A. L., 376, 377,
Kryptacanthy. *See* Spina nasalis anterior.
Kunike, Hugo, 130.
Kupffer, C. v., 215.

Lacrimale, 9, 109.
Lambda, 26.
Lang, Herbert, 13.
Lebzelter, V., 267, 268, 270, 271.
Le Double, A. F., 194, 195, 209, 240, 253. 276, 287, 294, 313.
Leigh, R. W., 350.
Length, cranial. *See* Cranial diameters; Deformation.
Lenhossék, M. v., 331, 338, 342, 343, 344.
Lenz, Fritz. See Baur-Fischer-Lenz.
Leptostaphyliny. *See* Palatal index.
Ligamentum sphenomandibulare, 344.
Lillooet. Tribal position, 145, 156.
Linea(ae): mylohyoidea, 345; nuchae, 317, 320; temporales, 222–224, 360, 373.

INDEX. 383

Lingula mandibulae, 344.
Lophacanthy. *See* Spina nasalis anterior.
Loth, E., 227.
Lower jaw. *See* Mandible.
Lüthy, A., 301.

Macalister, A., 301, 304, 307.
Maciesza, A., 163.
MacCurdy, George Grant, 15, 133, 135, 240, 346, 357.
Maggi, L., 323.
Mair, Rud., 276.
Mandible. Angles: anterobasal 122, 127, condylocoronoid 127–129, 350, posterobasal 125–127, ramus 123–125, 136, 141; bicondylar breadth, 118; breadth index, 119; chin: height 122–123, morphology 127, 333–337, 370, 373; condylocoronoid height relation, 370; corpus, 331–338; general appearance, 331, 369–370; medial relief, 344–345, 370; outline: basal 332, 370, 373, ramus anterior and posterior 370, superior 370 (footnote); ramus: breadth 120–121, 370, height 119–120, 370, index 121–122, morphology 338–345; Schaukelunterkiefer (*Stahr*), 332, 333.
Mandibulogram. *See* Gnathogram.
Manouvrier, L., 52.
Mantegazza, P., 271.
Manubrium sqamae occipitalis (*R. Virchow*). *See* Os(siculum) *Kerckringii*.
Marelli, C. S., 370.
Margo(gines): nasoalveolaris and nasospinalis (*Fr. Sarasin*), *see* Margo piriformis inferior; piriformis inferior, *see* Nose: Morphology.
Martin, Rudolf, 9, 16, 34, 73, 82, 83, 105, 106, 109, 114, 119, 120, 122, 148, 154, 157, 167, 195, 204, 215, 217, 233, 234, 259, 267, 276, 279, 282, 283, 290, 294, 295, 296, 299, 304, 307, 313, 318, 324, 325, 327, 333, 340, 341, 359, 361, 362, 377.
Mason, Otis T., 13.
Material. See Skeletal material.
Maxillary bone. *See* Maxilloalveolar measurements; Palatal measurements.
Maxillary complex, 367, 373.
Maxilloalveolar measurements. Breadth, length, index: 97–100, 103, 104, 132, 135, 137, 140, 141, 149, 153.
Maxillo-cranial correlations, 102–104, 206.
Maxillofrontale, 9, 109.
Maxillonasofrontale (mihi), 279.
Meatonasion line, 25.
Merkel, F. See Tuberculum linearum (*Merkel*).
Mesostaphyliny. *See* Palatal index.

Mesurany. *See* Maxilloalveolar index.
Metrical designations, 25 (footnote 30*a*).
Metrical procedures (in general), 130.
Meyer, A. W., 321.
Migration, primary Asiatic, 376.
Miller, Gerrit S., Jr., 331.
Mingazzini, G., 276, 304.
Minimum frontal breadth. *See* Postorbital constriction.
Module, cranial, 142, 143, 146, 147, 148, 149, 150.
Mollison, Th., 281.
Mongol stock. Characteristics and affinities (metrical), 142, 144, 145, 146, 148, 156.
Mongolian affinity. *See* Racial affinities.
Mongolian and mongoloid, 375, 376.
Mongoloid morphology, 365, 368, 370, 371, 373.
Mongolid type, 367; relationship, 375.
Mongolo-mongoloid typology (metrical), 141–145, 156.
Mongolo-mongoloideo-caucasid typology, 146–148, 156.
Morphology, cranial, 375, 376.

Narrowing of face, 375.
Narrowing of head, 376.
Narrowing of nose, 375, 376.
Nasion, 301, 367, 373.
Nasoalveolar flexion, 307.
Nehring, A., 162, 163.
Norma: basilaris, 170–220, 356–359, 373, 374; frontalis, 275–313, 365–368, 373, 374; lateralis, 221–274, 359–365, 373, 374; occipitalis, 315–380, 363–369, 373, 375; verticalis, 157–169, 355–356, 372, 374.
Nose. Apertura piriformis, 366, 373; breadth, *see* width; bridge, 294–295, 365, 367, 373, 375; foramina nasalia, 295–296; incisura piriformis inferior, 303–304, 305, 367, 368, 373; margo piriformis inferior, 304, 306–307, 366–375; measurements: height, width, index, 105–108, 132, 134, 137, 139, 143, 144, 145, 147, 148, 149, 152–153, 156; nasal bones, 290, 293–294, 367; nasion, 367; projection, 376; sex difference, 107; spina nasalis anterior, 301–303, 366, 373; sutura internasalis, 296, 298–299; tendency toward leptorrhiny, 107, 143, 145, 148, 152.

Occipital variations, 373, 375.
Occipital vertebra. *See* Foramen magnum.
Occipiton (*Bolk*), 24.
Oetteking, Bruno, 73, 74, 142, 146, 147, 175, 179, 249, 337, 370, 378.
Oppenheim, St., 340, 346, 347.
Orbit. Angle (verticosagittal), 115–116, 132, 135,

137, 140; anterior interorbital breadth, 114–115, 140, 366, 373; measurements: height, width, index, 109–111, 113–114, 132, 134–135, 137, 139, 143, 144, 145, 147, 148, 149, 152, 156, 366, 373; morphology: general appearance 238, 285, 366, 373, lower lateral angle 366, 373, upper rim 366.

Orientation. Angular relations, 26–31; cranial planes, 24–25.

Orthogonal tracings, 9.

Orthozygy. *See* Arcus zygomaticus: Vertical aspect.

Orygmocraspedotic (*Macalister*). *See* Nose: Margo piriformis inferior.

Os(sa): apicis, 325–328, 371; aionicum, *see* Os japonicum s. aionicum; bregmaticum. 163, 166–167, 328, 354, 371; de l'hamule (*Le Double*), 313; epiptericum, 259–262, 328, 361, 371, 374; fonticuli posterioris, *see* Os apicis; incae 323–325, verum s. proprium 325, 328, 357, 369; incisivum, *see* Os intermaxillare s. incisivum s. praemaxillare; intermaxillare s. incisivum s. praemaxillare, 206, 211; japonicum s aionicum, *see* Os malare bipartitum; (ossiculum) *Kerckringii* s. manubrium squamae occipitalis (*R. Virchow*), 173, 175; malare s. zygomaticum bipartitum (japonicum s. aionicum, 358; maxillo-nasolacrimo-frontale (*Le Double*), 294; nasalia, *see* Nose; Praeinterparietale, *see* Os apicis; praemaxillare, *see* Os intermaxillare s. incisivum s. praemaxillare.

Os frontale. Angle, 57–58, 133, 138; indices: sagittal 55–57, transverse frontal 52–53, transverse frontoparietal 53–54; maximum breadth, 51–52; mediansagittal chord, 54–55; minimum breadth, 51, 133, 355, 374; outline, 359; pars nasalis, 279–281, 375; vaulting, 55–57.

Os occipitale. Angle, 66–70, 133; arc, 46, 64; interoccipital angle, 70–71, 133; mediansagittal chord, 64, 65; outline, 359, 375; pars basilaris, 356; protrusion of upper squama, 222, 360; relief, 357; sagittal index, 65; variation, 375.

Os parietale. Angle, 60, 61, 62–63, 133; arc, 46, 59; mediansagittal chord, 59–60; sagittal index, 60; vaulting, 61–62.

Os tympanicum. Correlations, 358; hyperostosis, 245–248, 249, 250, 362, 373, 374, 375; perforation, 248–249, 363–364, 374.

Oxyacanthy. *See* Spina nasalis anterior.

Oxycraspedotic (*Macalister*). *See* Margo piriformis inferior.

Palatal measurements. Length, 100; index, 101–102; width, 100–101.

Palatoalveolar complex, 356.

Pars lambdoidea. *See* Sutura lambdoidea.
Pars media. *See* Sutura lambdoidea.
Pars nasalis ossis frontis, 279–281.
Pathological skull forms, 160–162, 355.
Pensa, A., 245.
Perna, G., 294, 303.
Phaenotypical differentiation upon American soil, 376.
Phaenozygy. *See* Arcus zygomaticus: Vertical aspect.
Physical history of American Indians, 376.
Pittard, Eugène, 52.
Plagiocephaly (crany), Organic and artificial causes, 160–161, 355, 374.
Planes, cranial. *See* Orientation.
Planum sub- or infralineare (mihi), 317.
Planum triangulare (*v. Lenhossék*), 343.
Plenk, L., 163.
Polynesian origin, 376.
Porus acusticus externus, 243–245, 363, 373, 374.
Positive Entwicklungstendenz (*Bolk*), 175, 177.
Posnansky, Arthur, 13, 15.
Postbregmatic elevation, 373.
Posterobasal angle (mihi), 123, 125–126.
Postorbital constriction, 162–163; morphological significance, 162, 355, 372, 375.
Precondylar tubercles, 175.
Precaucasid racial elements. *See* Racial affinities.
Premigratory crossbreeding. *See* Racial affinities.
Primitive morphology, 368.
Processus: asteriacus (*Haferland*), 242; condyloideus, 341; coronoideus, 341; frontalis (squamae temporalis), 235–236, 374; origination of processus frontalis, 235 (footnote), 260, 361; frontosphenoidalis, 266, 270; lemuriniscus s. Sandifortii (*Albrecht*), 340; marginalis, 271–273; mastoideus, 236–239, 356, 362, 373, 374; paracondyloideus, 179, 189–192, 357; paramastoideus, *see* Processus paracondyloideus; parietalis, 227–228, 361, 374; paroccipitalis, *see* Processus paracondyloideus; postglenoidalis (s. tuberculum articulare posterius s. tuberculum tympanicum), 253–255; pterygoideus, 201–202, 358, 373; retromastoideus (*Waldeyer*), 194; temporalis, 266, 270.
Profilation, cranial. *See* Face, Angles, Prognathy.
Prognathy, 135, 140, 144, 145, 148, 153, 154, 156, 360, 365, 373, 375, 376. *See* also Profilation, cranial.
Progressive morphology. *See* Morphology, cranial.
Prosthion inferius, 333.
Protocaucasid influence. *See* Racial affinities.
Protuberantia occipitalis externa, 317, 318.
Pterygomaxillary complex, 358.
Puccioni, N., 341, 370.

INDEX.

Pycraft, W. P., 25, 331.

Quotations, method of, 2–3.
Quotient of σ, 131.

Racial affinities. Caspian and mediterranean, 376; caucasid, 376; crossbreeding on Asian soil, 376; mongolian, 376; protocaucasid influence, 367.
Racial characteristics, 355, 368, 372–374; cheek bones (prominence), 365; prognathy, 375, 376; size, 356; torus occipitalis, 369.
Racial interbreeding, 376.
Racial similarities and dissimilarities, 375.
Ramus angle. *See* Angles, Mandible.
Range of variation in deformed and undeformed skulls, 130.
Ranke, J., 223, 259, 323, 324, 327.
Rauber, (A.)-Kopsch, (Fr.), 309.
Recessus mandibulae (*v. Lenhossék*). See Fossa praecoronoidea (*Klaatsch*).
Reicher, M., 142, 378.
Relief, cranial, 372, 375.
Ridgeway, W., 342.
Ried, H. A., 173, 185.
Ritchie, S. G., 193, 345, 353, 378.
Rivero, M. E., y *S. J. de Tschudi*, 324.
Rüdinger, N., 15.
Russell, Frank, 167, 189, 195, 215, 252.

Sandifortii. See Processus lemurinicus s. Sandifortii (*Albrecht*).
Sanduhrform (*Fr.* and *P. Sarasin*) of nasal bones, 294.
Sarasin, Fr., 206, 266, 267, 281, 304.
Sarasin, Fr. and *P.*, 267, 281, 294.
Schaukelunterkiefer (*Stahr*). *See* Mandible.
Schlaginhaufen, O., 172, 173, 245, 325.
Schoetensack, O., 331, 343.
Schultz, Adolph H., 74, 167.
Schwalbe, Gustav, 48, 162, 163, 276, 282, 331.
Schwerz, Franz, 72.
Sergi, G., 157, 159, 221, 304, 359.
Sex differences. *See* Differences.
Sex differences, cranial, 148, 150, 156. *See* also Differences.
Shapiro, H. L., 387.
Shortheadedness in infantiles, 40.
Shovel-shape incisors. *See* Teeth.
Simon, Th., 163.
Size, 372. *See* also Differences, Capacity, Cranial diameters.
Skeletal material, 1; classification and survey, 4–8; heterogeneity, 2; nature of, 1, 130; serial arrangement, 2, 130; state of preservation, 8; Total number, 7.
Smith, E. Barclay, 166.
Smith, G. Elliot, 179.
Smith, Harlan I., 14, 378.
Spina: Civinini, *see* Foramen pterygospinosum (*Civinini*); geniohyoidei, *see* Spina mentalis interna; interdigastrica (*Klaatsch*), 335, 336; mentalis interna, 337–338, 370; nasalis anterior, *see* Nose; nasalis posterior, 217–219, 359; suprameatum, 245, 363, 364; trochlearis, *see* Fovea (spina) trochlearis.
Spontaneous dehiscence (*Hyrtl*), 248.
Sqama: occipitalis, 317, 360; temporalis 225–236, form and size, 225, 361.
Stahr, H., 332.
Staurenghi, C., 323.
Steinmann, G., 376, 378.
Stenocrotaphy, 257–259, 362, 374.
Stieda, L., 208, 215, 327.
Strecker, C., 180.
Striae platysmaticae (*H. Virchow*), 331.
Structure difference. See Differences.
Subtypes, 375.
Sulcus: arteriae temporalis mediae, 227; mastoideus (*Waldeyer*), 224; mylohyoideus 344, bridging 344; praenasalis (Affenrinne), 304; sphenoparietalis, 235, 255–257, 362, 374; supramastoideus (*Waldeyer*), 240, 241, 360.
Sullivan, Louis R., 158, 193, 194, 195, 198, 206, 352, 358.
Summary, conclusive, to Part I: Craniometry, 130–154, 155–156; to Part II: Cranioscopy, 354–371.
Superciliary eminences. *See* Supraorbital prominences.
Supraorbital prominences, 282–283, 366, 367, 373.
Sutura: coronalis, 223, 360, 374; epiptericoparietalis, 260; epiptericosphenoidalis, 259; frontalis s. metopica, 275; incisiva (*Goethei*), 211–213; infraorbitalis, 311–313; internasalis, see Nose; lambdoidea, 326; mastoideosquamosa, 239–241; metopica, *see* Sutura frontalis; nasofrontalis, 270, 299–300, 367; palatina media, 208; palatina transversa, 208–210; sagittalis, 348, 360; sphenoparietalis, 257–259, 362; sphenosquamosa, 234–235, 262; squamosa, 226, 227, 360, 374; transversa foetalis squamae occipitalis (*R. Virchow*), 323; transversozygomatica, 273–274; zygomaticomaxillaris, 273; zygomaticotemporalis, 267, 273.
Sutural bones. *See Wormian* bones.
Sutures, 346–348; obliteration, 347-348, 354–355, 356, 370, 373, 374, 375.

Swjetschnikow, S., 175, 177.
Sylvii. See Fissura cerebri lateralis (*Sylvii*).
Symphysion (*v. Török*), 333.

Tassonomic method (*G. Sergi*), 157, 221, 357.
Technique, craniometric and cranioscopic, 9–11.
Teeth, 350–353, 371, 373, 374; attrition, 350, 371; concrescence of molar anlagen, 353; lesions, 351, 352, 371; phylogenetic molar reduction (size), 352, 353, 371, 374; shovel-shape, 350, 352, 371, 374; size, 350, 374.
Teit, James, 16.
Todd, T. Wingate, and *D. W. Lyon, Jr.*, 348.
Török, A. v., 333.
Toldt, K., 173, 331.
Torus: mandibulae (*C. M. Fürst*), 344–345; occipitalis (*A. Ecker*), 317, 318–320, 368–369, 373, 375; palatinus, 208, 213–217, 359, 373; sagittalis ossis frontis (*G. Bartels*), 276, 278–279; supraorbitalis, *see* Supraorbital prominences; verticalis mandibulae (*v. Lenhossék*), 344.
Triangle. *See* Facial triangle.
Tribal differentiations, 376.
Trigonum: postcoronoideum (mihi), 343; postmolare (*Klaatsch*) s. retromolare (*Braun*) s. area alveolaris (*Waldeyer*), 343, 344; retromalare (*Braun*), *see* Trigonum postmolare (*Klaatsch*).
Tschudi, S. J. de, 17. *See also Rivero, M. E. y S. J. de Tschudi.*
Tubera: frontalia, 275; parietalia, 360.
Tuberculum(a): articulare, 253, 267, 363; correlations, 358; articulare posterius, *see* Processus postglenoidalis; basilaria, 175; linearum (*F. Merkel*), 317, 318; linearum inferius (mihi), 317; pharyngeum, 195–197; spinosum, 262–264; supramastoideum anterius (*Waldeyer*), 234, 240, 242; supramastoideum posterius (*Waldeyer*),

240–241; tympanicum, *see* Processus postglenoidalis.
Tympanomastoid complex, 362–364.
Type difference. *See* Differences.
Typology, cranial, 148–154, 156.

Uhde, C. F. W., 189.
Upper jaw. See Maxilloalveolar and Palatal measurements.

Variability, 154.
Verga, A., 287.
Virchow, H., 10, 11, 224, 279, 281, 331.
Virchow, R., 12, 150, 160, 162, 173, 235, 252, 258, 294, 323, 327, 344, 361, 378.

Waldeyer, W., 194, 195, 201, 202, 209, 217, 234, 240, 242.
Walkhoff, O., 331.
Weber, Rudolf, 3.
Weigner, K., 176.
Weight, cranial, 372.
Weinert, Hans, 24.
Welcker, H., 148, 276, 287.
Wetzel, G., 307, 309.
Wissler, C., 376, 378.
Woldt, 15.
Woldt-Jacobsen, 378.
Wormian bones, 230, 260, 325, 327, 228, 347, 348–349, 361, 370–371, 373, 374, 375; origination identical with that of fontanel bones, 349.
Wright, W., 342.

Zentralfontanelle (*Ranke*), 323, 324.
Zentralloch (*Ranke*). *See* Zentralfontanelle (*Ranke*).
Zentralwinkel (*Klaatsch*), 26–28, 135–136, 140.
Zuckerkandl, E., 281.

ADDENDA

p. 151, continuing first paragraph:
>A noteworthy attempt toward the correction of distorted skull proportions by means of statistical methods was recently made by *Shapiro*. [51a]
>
>>[51a] *Shapiro, H. L.*, 1928. A correction for artificial deformation of skulls. Anthrop. Pap. Am. Mus. Nat. Hist., v. III, n°. 1, pp. 1—38.

p. 313, continuing last text line:
>and *Hooton* [190a] found it in half of the Tenerife skulls.
>
>>[190a] l. c., p. 222 (143).

p. 375, add to list of inferior traits:
>angulus zygomaticotemporalis falling below ear-eye plane.

p. 376, add on line 20 to
>*Boas*: 1929; to *Hrdlička*: 1925. *See* also Bibliography.

p. 379, add to *Boas*, following figure 377, page reference 387.
p. 382, add to *Hooton*, following figure 346, page reference 387.
p. 382, add to *Hrdlička*, following figure 377, page reference 378.

Insert between "Mandible" and "Manouvrier" on p. 383, the following:
>Mandibulogram, 125, 390.

Insert between "*Glaseri*" and "*Goethe*" on p. 381, the following:
>Gnathogram. *See* Mandibulogram.

Page numbers quoted in the present study from the first edition of *R. Martin*'s Lehrbuch der Anthropologie (1914) and changed to those of the second edition (1928):

The present study	*R. Martin*, 1914	*R. Martin*, 1928, v. II
p. 16	p. 641	p. 744
„ 34	„ 661	„ 764
„ 73	„ 485	„ 588
„ 82	„ 790	„ 895
„ 83	„ 790—791	„ 895—896
„ 105	„ 833	„ 937
„ 106	„ 833	„ 938
„ 109	„ 857	„ 959
„ 114	„ 865	„ 967

The present study	R. Martin, 1914	R. Martin, 1928, v. II
„ 119	„ 517	„ 622
„ 120	„ 822	„ 983
„ 122	„ 822	„ 983
„ 154	„ 810	„ 914
„ 157	„ 587	„ 690
„ 167	„ 757	„ 865
p. 195	p. 737	p. 846
„ 204	„ 788	„ 893
„ 215	„ 832	„ 936
„ 217	„ 829	„ 934
„ 233	„ 781	„ 887
„ 234	„ 781	„ 887
„ 267	„ 782	„ 888
„ 276	„ 755	„ 862
„ 279	„ 758	„ 865
„ 282	„ 770	„ 876
„ 283	„ 863	„ 965
„ 290	„ 868	„ 970
„ 294	„ 840	„ 944
„ 295	„ 814	„ 920
„ 296	„ 843	„ 947
„ 299	„ 843	„ 947
„ 304	„ 847	„ 950
„ 307	„ 846	„ 950
„ 313	„ 825	„ 929
„ 318	„ 735	„ 844
„ 324	„ 731, 732	„ 840, 841
„ 325	„ 729	„ 838
„ 327	„ 730	„ 839
„ 333	„ 871	„ 972
„ 340	„ 883	„ 983
„ 341	„ 881	„ 982
„ 359	„ 826	„ 931
„ 361	„ 779	„ 884
„ 362	„ 784	„ 889

ERRATA

PLACE	INSTEAD OF	READ
Page 1, line 4	Musum	Museum
,, 2, ,, 8	divisons	divisions
,, 6, Summary 2, heading 7 . .	(single	(single)
do, vertical heading . . .	Salis	Salish
,, 14, line 5 (text) from below . .	part two	Part II
,, 16, line 8 (text) from below. .	slave-llke	slave-like
,, 19, legend to fig. 1.	$2/3$	$3/5$
,, 24, line 12.	morphological	phylogenetic
,, 24, ,, 21.	coincide	coincides
,, 26, ,, 13 from below	figures	values
,, 28, ,, 7	upon	of
,, 29, ,, 17 from below	reach ... up to ... values	attain figures
,, 32, Summary 9		
line 1 (Cowichan)	1365.3	1360.3
,, ,, (Koskimo)	1635	1630
,, 3 (Koskimo)	1350	1360
,, 4 (Cowichan)	1085	1080
,, 4 (Koskimo)	1010.0	1310.0
,, 33, ,, 9	12096	1209.6
,, 35, ,, 16	the nearly uniform figures in the Chinook	the figures for the Chinook
,, 37, Summary 15	female symbol ☿	♀
,, 39, ,, 17, column Range	75.0—74.9	75.0—79.9
,, 40, line 19 from below	groups or	groups of
,, 41, Summary 19, last column .	♂ + ☿	♂ + ♀
,, 44, line 8 from below	male	males
,, 49, Summary 27, column 1 . .	♂	♀
do	Juv.	juv.
do (last column)	62.0	62.5
,, 54, line 2 from below	naturälly	naturally
,, ,, ,, 1 ,, ,, ...	the a high	the high
do	113.8 mm.	113.8 mm.,
,, 56, last line of legend to fig. 8	The elevation	The greatest elevation
,, 57, line 7	segment	segmented
,, ,, ,, 5 from below	49.0° to 40.0°	48.0° to 49.0°
,, ,, Summary 34, Undeformed inf. range . .	—	49—57

ERRATA

PLACE	INSTEAD OF	READ
Page 62, line 1	cords	chords
„ 64, line 5 from below	6 3	6.3
„ 65, *Summary 39*, column 1. .	☿	♀
do „ 7. .	88 1	88.1
„ 68, legend to fig. 13.	Chinook ♀	Chinook ♂
do	„ ♂	„ ♀
„ 73, line 17	length 100.9 mm.	length of 100.9 mm.
„ 78, title of section 4	foraman	foramen
„ 85, line 2 from below	those of	of those
„ 87, line 19	inserted	enclosed
„ 90, „ 4	9%	8.6%
„ „ *Summarary 58*, Undeformed male range .	61—68	61—86
„ 95, *Summary 63*, last column .	76 5	76.5
„ 102, line 13 from below. . . .	rellated	correlated
„ 105, *Summary 74*, line 4 (Koskimo).	51.4	43.0
„ 109, *Summary 78*, line 4 (Koskimo).	9 31—41 27.0	8 31—40 34.4
„ 114, line 4 of section 4	interorbit	interorbital
„ 123, *Summary 95*, Koskimo female average	27.6	72.6
„ 125, line 15	mandibulogram	gnathogram
„ 127, „ 11 from below. . . .	infanriles	infantiles
„ 130, „ 11	cranio-metrical	craniometrical
„ 132, cranial length for Cowichan	— 8.2	— 6.2
do	— 1.2	— .9
„ 135, line 22 from below. . . .	ear-eye plane and glabella-lambda line	basion-bregma and glabella-lambda lines
„ 136, „ 10	former of the due	of the former, due
„ 137, cranial length for Lillooet	— 8.7	— 8.5
„ „ measurement 26	nasa	nasal
„ 139, line 19 from below. . . .	Liliooet	Lillooet
„ 145, „ 12	ortho-to hypsicranial	ortho-to-hypsicranial
„ 161, „ 16	cranical	cranial
„ 167, „ 27	crancrivorus	cancrivorus
„ 177, „ 20	light.	light,
„ „ „ 10 from below. . . .	28.0%	26.1%
„ „ „ 8 „ „	14.8%	13.7%
„ 178, *Summary 110*, Grand total for Undeformed	14.8%	13.7%
do, Koskimo.	28.0%	26.1%
„ 203, fig. 39		Reverse figure
„ 204, line 5 (text) from below .	theremorphic	theromorphic

ERRATA

PLACE	INSTEAD OF	READ
Page 207, *Summary 123*, Total frequency (paraboloid) for Undeformed	86	87
„ 223, footnote 132.	*Dalla Rosa L.*	*Dalla Rosa, L.*
„ 242, line 4	figurative	configurative
„ 245, footnote 148	*Schlagenhaufen*	*Schlaginhaufen*
„ 249, line 5	hyper	hyper-
„ 267, „ 6 from below . . .	732	782
„ 271, „ 19 „ „ . . .	or	of
„ 315, „ 13	rounded	pronounced
„ 344, footnote 219.	indentical	identical
„ „ „ 220.	199	160
„ 361, line 15 from below . . .	like this is finds	like this finds
„ 369, „ 1 „ „ . . .	381	331
TABLES OF MEASUREMENTS On even pages (table pagination) from p. 2 to p. 46, the heavy vertical line on the extreme right should be removed two columns to the left, in order to set off the cranial from the facial measurements.		
Page 3, caption of first two columns	Heigth	Height
„ 14, male average under caption Occipital Chord	96 2	96.2
„ „ column 5, line 9 from below	498.1	498.7
„ 15, column 4, line 9 from below	107.1	107.7
„ 19, column 2, line 16 from below	15.0	125.0
„ 26, column 3, line 1 from below	170.0	150.0
„ 43, column 15, line 16	12	22
„ 48, first line below captions of columns	ccm. and mm. symbols	(°)

DIAGRAMS AND PLATES

PART II — CRANIOSCOPY

TABLES OF MEASUREMENTS

TABLES OF

Tribal divisions and subdivisions / Catalogue Nos. / Sex and stages of life / Number of cases / Averages and ranges	Capacity	Length	Breadth	Height (ba-b)	Circumference (horizontal)	SKULL Median-sagittal Arc			SKULL Median-sagittal Chord			Cranial base (length n-ba)	Foramen magnum		Frontal bone		Length	
						Total (n-o)	Frontal	Parietal	Occipital	Frontal	Parietal	Occipital		Length	Width	Breadth (minimum)	Breadth (maximum)	Length (ba pr)	Inferior length (ba-gn)
	ccm.	mm.	mm.	mm.	mm.	mm.	mm.	mm.	mm.	mm.	mm.	mm.	mm.	mm.	mm.	mm.	mm.	mm.	mm.
UNDEFORMED																			
Athapascan																			
1551 ♂ ad	1340	184	147	143	526	365	131	114	120	116	105	92	102	37	30	95	118	102?	—
4337 ♂ mat	1350	180	135	136	511	368	126	128	114	110	112	94	105	32	28	98	116	100	110
4338 ♂ mat	1240	177	131	139	491	365	127	123	115	113	109	98	102	32	29	89	108	97	111
4339 ♂ ad-mat	1270	181	134	127	509	367	129	122	116	112	109	93	98	38	33	98	111	98	105
4340 inf. I—II	—	—	—	—	474?	—	124	—	—	106	—	—	—	36	28	90	107	—	—
4341 ♂ mat	1300	178	144	133	515	355	121	122	112	107	109	94	106	32	29	100	121	104	—
4342 ♀ ad-mat	1130	176	126	134	485	342	116	113	113	104	103	95	105	36	28	86	102	102	107
4343 ♂ ad	1180	175	130	132	491	358	125	122	122	109	109	92	96	36	29	91	105	103	114
♂ cases	6	6	6	6	6	6	6	6	6	6	6	6	6	6	6	6	6	6	4
range	1180–1350	175–184	130–147	127–143	491–526	355–368	121–131	114–128	111–120	107–116	105–112	92–98	96–106	32–38	28–33	86–106	105–121	97–104	105–114
average	1280.0	179.2	136.8	135.0	507.2	363.0	126.5	121.8	114.7	111.6	108.8	94.0	101.5	34.5	29.7	95.2	113.2	100.7	110.0
♀, 1 case	1130	176.0	126.0	134.0	485.0	342.0	116.0	113.0	113.0	104.0	103.0	95.0	105.0	36.0	28.0	86.0	102.0	102.0	107.0
inf. 1 case	—	—	—	—	474.0	—	124.0	—	—	106.0	—	—	—	36.0	28.0	90.0	107.0	—	—
Haida																			
1605 inf. II	1540?	161	157	—	495	366	139	116	111	115	103	96	—	—	—	90	122	—	—
1606 ♂ ad-mat	1320	177	137	136	506	364	129	122	113	113	109	96	103	35	31	90	110	106	—
1607 inf. II	1330	166	142	119	481	346	118	122	106	102	108	88	82	38	30	87	110	79	—
1608 ♀ ad	1180	171	134	135	489	356	127	120	109	112	107	90	98	33	29	94	111	100	105
1609 ♀ ad-mat	1290	173	145	132	502	352	117	115	120	104	104	97	101	32	29	90	117	102	104
1610 ♂ ad-mat	1450	187	147	136	533	379	132	127	120	114	114	94	101	35	27	102	127	102	125
1611 ♀ ad (lower jaw?)	1260	173	137	130	497	348	123	116	109	108	102	92	101	36	31	101	115	100	—
1613 ♂ mat	—	—	—	—	—	—	—	—	—	—	—	—	—	—	—	—	—	—	—
1614 ♂ mat	1440	192	144	135	532	385	132	113	140	114	103?	113?	104	35	29	89	118	101	—
1615 inf II	1440	173	137	128	490	358	126	124	108	108	109	91	84	41	29	95	114	86	94
1616 ♀ ad	1220	174	134	125	490	354	118	120	116	104	107	95	94	34	28	89	109	95	—
1617 ♂ mat	1240	179	143	135	512	354	121	103	130	107	94	104	107	34	30	99	115	111	—
3707 ♂ mat	1340	184	142	134	524	364	129	117	118	114	105	98	107	38	—	96	116	—	—
3733 ♂ ad	1500	179	149	140	517	365	129	109	127	116	99	105	104	38	29	93	121	—	—
3734 juv	1350	170	142	133	496	344	122	110	112	104	101	94	98	37	25	97	115	94?	—
3735 ♀? ad	1620	183	146	141	524	373	130	131	112	115	115	95	104	35	32	103	125	98	—
3736 ♂ mat	1500	191	144	136	540	392	132	127	133	115	114	103	99	37	27	97	120	107	—
3738 ♂ mat	1500	189	141	142	510	389	145	130	114	130	108	104	103	32	34!	90	119	100	116
3739? inf. II	1430	178	142	127	503	362	131	113	118	110	103	96	93	41	29	96	115	85	88
3740 ♂ mat	1320	183	148	132	529	361	120	107	134	109	99	108	108	34	29	97	117	107	118
3741 ♂ mat	1560	188	146	145	532	383	132	122	129	117	112	104	105	38	30	97	119	108	118
3742 ♀ ad	1260	165	137	134	485	347	117	115	115	105	101	94	99	34	27	92	110	97	104
3743 ♂ mat	1450	184	145	143	526	371	135	126	110	118	111	96	110	38	35	97	118	105	112
3745 ♂ mat	1450	192	136	135	535	370	129	129	112	114	116	93	110	38	30	99	115	109	—
3747 ♂ ad-mat	1640	192	150	143	547	395	140	134	121	119	120	101	104	38	38	99	127	102	122
3748 ♀ mat	1400	171	140	140	499	364	133	125	106	114	108	94	99	36	31	93	114?	101	106

MEASUREMENTS

FACE AND MANDIBLE

Heigth		Breadth						Orbit			Nose		Nasal bones		Maxillo-alveolar		Palatal		Mandible				
																			Breadth		Height		
Upper height (n-pr)	Total height (n-gn)	Bizygomatic	Upper facial (fmt-fmt)	Mid-facial (zm-zm)	Biorbital (ek-ek)	Ant. interorb. (mf-mf)	Post. interorb. (la-la)	Width (mf-ek)	Width (la-ek)	Height	Width	Height	Breadth (minimum)	Breadth (maximum)	Length	Breadth	Length	Width	Bicondylar	Bigonial	Ramus	Ramus	Chin
mm.	mm.	mm.	mm.	mm.	mm.	mm.	mm.	mm.	mm.	mm	mm.	mm.	mm.	mm.	mm.	mm.	mm.	mm.	mm.	mm.	mm.	mm.	mm.
73?	—	—	107	—	101	19	25?	44	40	35	25	53	8	16	—	—	—	—	—	—	—	—	—
76	120	133	108	96	100	18	21	45	40	36	21	55	10	15	55	63	48	44?	117	103	33	57	41
71	117	125	104	98	100	17	21	46	42	36	22	48	8	14	49	63	43	41	111	91	31	60	38
76	127	127	107	96	102	19	24	45	40	38	24	52	9	17	55	63	44	37	108	102	34	56	41
63	—	108?	92	78	87	18	22	39	36	34	20	43	8	15	—	—	35	30	103?	85?	28	45	27
76	—	143	111	104	102	21	25	44	40	36	24	53	12	15	52	66	43	42	—	—	—	—	—
64	104	117	—	—	—	18	21	—	—	—	24?	48	8	17	50	63	45	42?	106?	98?	33	51	33
70	115	126	105	96	100	17	21	44	40	33	25	49	5	16	55	65	49	42	115	97	36	59	35
6	4	5	6	5	6	6	6	6	6	6	6	6	6	6	5	5	5	5	4	4	4	4	4
70–76	115–127	125–143	104–111	96–104	100–102	17–21	21–25	44–46	40–42	33–38	21–25	48–55	5–12	14–17	49–55	63–66	43–49	37–44	108–117	91–103	31–36	56–60	35–41
73.7	119.8	130.8	107.0	98.0	100.8	18.5	22.8	44.7	40.3	35.7	23.5	51.7	8.7	15.5	53.2	64.0	45.4	41.2	112.8	98.3	33.5	58.0	38.8
64.0	104.0	117.0	—	—	87.0	18.0	21.0	—	36.0	—	24.0	48.0	8.0	17.0	50.0	63.0	45.0	42.0	106.0	98.0	33.0	51.0	33.0
63.0	—	108.0	92.0	78.0	—	18.0	22.0	39.0	—	34.0	20.0	43.0	8.0	15.0	—	—	35.0	30.0	103.0	85.0	28.0	45.0	27.0
60	—	109	90	77	86	17	20	37	34	34	19	40	9	14	36	56	35	29	—	—	—	—	—
70	—	137	108	100	102	19	25	42	38	35	26	47	7	16	56	66	49	44	—	—	—	—	—
52	—	111	88	77	83	15	19	37	34?r	32r	18	37	8	16	38	56	35	27	—	—	—	—	—
72	122	133	103	103	97	22	25	39	36	36	28	50	9	21	56	66	47	42	120	99	32	52	36
72	114	137	108	99	104	22	26	43	40	38	27	49	9	16	51	63	44	41	127	106	38	60	30?
73?	125	144	114	104	104	19	24	46	42	39	25	50	12	19?	55	64	49	43	128	110	38	78	40
78	—	138	108	95	102	18	23	43	39	38	24	50	9	17	53	63	49	43	110	98	36	56	30
—	—	—	—	—	—	—	—	—	—	—	—	—	—	—	—	—	—	—	124	108?	44	66	35
78	—	138	108	105	100	16	21	45	40	36	23	52	7	17	55	64	45	42	—	—	—	—	—
64	102	114	95	84	89	18	22	39	35	34	21	45	8	17	38	57	35	32	95	97	30	49	28?
70	—	127	102	96	96	17	21	41	39	34	24	45	8	16	52	61	45	38	—	—	—	—	—
74	—	138	114	105	107	18	24	48	43	34	26	49	10	19	55	66	47	46	—	—	—	—	—
—	—	—	107	—	—	17?	22?	—	—	—	—	—	7	—	—	—	—	—	—	—	—	—	—
64	—	132	101	—	98	18	21	42	40r	32r	21	46	6	14	—	—	—	—	—	—	—	—	—
70	—	140	111	101	105	21	25	44	40	35	23	50	9	16	54	69	44	43	—	—	—	—	—
77	—	144	112	106	105	20	25	45	43	33	27	51	7	19	59	73	49	46	—	—	—	—	—
82	130	137	107	100	101	19	23	44	40	38	22	57	8	15	57	62	49	40	127	115	36	65	38
63	101	120	99	87	92	17	21	39	36	37	21	43	9	16	39	59	37	33	109?	81?	31	40	26
76	123	148	118	110	110	21	26	47	43	37	27	55	10	20	59	71	51	45	127	112	42	64	36
78	133	146	112	110	104	19	25	45	40	36	29	53	8	20	58	71	48	44	127	111	41	68	41
67	112?	133	108	94	100	19	23	42	38	35	24	49	8	17	50	61	45	39	114	93	37	54	30
75	116	142	114	105	106	20	23	46	42	37	26	51	6	15	55	69	48	46	131	101	39	62	31
78	—	141	115	102	112	19	25	50	45	35	29	51	7	20	60	68?	52	40?	—	—	—	—	—
75	121	152	112	104	105	20	24	45	40	37	25	53	5	15	55	66	47	42	134	103	40	61	36
79	127	130	103	95	97	16	20	43	39	35	24	52	7	17	57	66	47	38	120	98	36	66	36

Tribal divisions and subdivisions / Catalogue No. / Sex and stages of life / Number of cases / Averages and ranges	Capacity	Length	Breadth	Height (ba-b)	Circumference (horizontal)	SKULL Median-sagittal Arc Total (n-o)	Frontal	Parietal	Occipital	Median-sagittal Chord Frontal	Parietal	Occipital	Cranial base (length n-ba)	Foramen magnum Length	Width	Frontal bone Breadth (minimum)	Breadth (maximum)	Length (ba-pr)	Inferior length (ba-gn)
	ccm.	mm.	mm.	mm.	mm.	mm.	mm.	mm.	mm.	mm.	mm.	mm.	mm.	mm.	mm.	mm.	mm.	mm.	mm.
UNDEFORMED																			
3749 ♀ ad	1290	166	143	130	496	348	125	116	107	110	102	94	96	34	31	88	115	105	113
3750 ♂ ad	1540	175	150	145	511	396	133	128	108	116	112	92	103	35	29	98	124	103	—
3751 ♂ mat	1390	196	139	139	549	378	127	125	126	112	114	102	113	36	31	97	115	110	127
3752 inf. I	1250	164	134	—	469	346	121	120	105	101	105	88	—	—	—	86	110	—	—
3753 ♂ mat	1220	176	140	133	508	355	118	111	126	105	102	101	98	35	30	92	112	97	107
3754 ♂ ad-mat	1240	177	141	127	511	354	121	119	114	109	107	93	99	36	27	99	120	101	—
3755 ♂ mat	1140	179	138	138	504	354	124	108	122	109	99	98	103	31	26	90	107	103	—
3759 ♂ mat	—	—	—	—	—	—	—	—	—	—	—	—	—	—	—	—	—	—	—
3760 ♂ sen	—	—	—	—	—	—	—	—	—	—	—	—	—	—	—	—	—	—	—
3761 ♂ ad-mat	—	—	—	—	—	—	—	—	—	—	—	—	—	—	—	—	—	—	—
3762 ♂ mat-sen	—	—	—	—	—	—	—	—	—	—	—	—	—	—	—	—	—	—	—
3763 ♂ mat-sen	—	—	—	—	—	—	—	—	—	—	—	—	—	—	—	—	—	—	—
♂ cases	18	18	18	18	18	18	18	18	18	18	18	18	18	18	17	18	18	16	8
range	1140–1640	175–196	136–150	127–145	504–549	354–395	118–145	103–134	108–140	105–130	94–120	92–113	98–113	31–38	26–38	89–102	107–127	97–111	107–127
average	1402.2	184.4	143.3	137.4	523.7	371.2	129.3	119.6	122.0	113.8	107.7	100.2	104.5	35.7	30.1	94.1	117.8	104.5	118.1
♀ cases	8	8	8	8	8	8	8	8	8	8	8	8	8	8	8	8	8	8	5
range	1180–1620	165–183	134–165	125–141	485–524	347–373	117–123	115–131	106–120	104–115	101–115	90–97	94–104	32–36	27–32	88–103	109–125	95–105	104–113
average	1315.0	172.0	142.7	133.4	497.8	355.2	123.7	119.8	111.7	109.0	105.8	93.9	99.0	34.1	29.8	93.8	114.5	99.8	106.4
juv. 1 case	1350.0	170.0	142.0	133.0	496.0	344.0	122.0	110.0	112.0	104.0	101.0	94.0	98.0	37.0	25.0	97.0	115.0	94.0	—
inf. cases	5	5	5	3	5	5	5	5	5	5	5	5	3	3	3	5	5	3	2
range	1250–1540	161–178	134–157	119–128	469–503	346–366	118–139	113–124	105–118	101–115	103–109	88–96	88–94	32–41	29–30	86–95	110–122	79–86	88;94
average	1398	168.8	142.4	124.7	487.6	355.6	127.0	119.0	109.6	107.2	105.6	90.8	89.7	39.3	29.3	90.8	114.0	83.3	91.0
Lillooet																			
2614 inf. I	—	156	136?	—	458?	332	116	121	95	99	93	80	—	—	—	87	111?	—	—
2615 inf. I	1020	145	139	—	445	308	102	104	102	87	93	84	—	—	—	83	106?	—	—
2618 ♂ ad-mat	1120	165	149	116	497	317	109	88	120	101	82	98	99	34	30	93	119	105	123
2619 inf. II	1030	157	144	—	462	332	114	93	125	99	86	97	—	—	—	86	108	—	—
2620 inf. II	1290	154	149	118	473	335	118	116	101	101	101	88	82	32	30	90	113	80	87
2621 ♂ mat	1260	164	152	126	507	334	118	108	108	106	99	87	96	34	29	93	120	90?	—
2622 ♀ ad	1180	165	146	124	490	335	115	116	104	102	104	81	91	33	26	91	117	95	99
2623 inf. I	—	—	—	—	—	—	—	—	—	—	—	—	—	—	—	—	—	—	—
2624 ♀ ad-mat (lower jaw doubtful)	1250	167	143	129	501	354	120	124	110	105	112	92	97	32	31	96	119	98	—
2629 inf. II	—	153	137	112	450	310	109	91	110	101	80	92	83	32	29	89	106?	87	95
♂ cases	2	2	2	2	2	2	2	2	2	2	2	2	2	2	2	2	2	2	1
range	1120–1260	164;165	149;152	110;126	497;507	317;334	109;118	88;108	108;120	101;106	82;99	87;98	96;99	34;34	29;30	93;93	119;120	90;105	—
average	1190.0	164.5	150.5	118.0	502.0	325.5	113.5	98.0	114.0	103.5	95.0	92.5	97.5	34.0	29.5	93.0	119.5	97.5	123.0

FACE AND MANDIBLE

Height		Breadth						Orbit			Nose		Nasal bones		Maxillo-alveolar		Palatal		Mandible				
																			Breadth		Height		
Upper height (n-pr)	Total height (n-gn)	Bizygomatic	Upper facial (fmt-fmt)	Mid-facial (zm-zm)	Biorbital (ek-ek)	Ant. interorb. (mf-mf)	Post. interorb. (la-la)	Width (mf-ek)	Width (la-ek)	Height	Width	Height	Breadth (minimum)	Breadth (maximum)	Length	Breadth	Length	Width	Bicondylar	Bigonial	Ramus	Ramus	Chin
mm.	mm.	mm.	mm.	mm.	mm.	mm.	mm.	mm.	mm.	mm.	mm.	mm.	mm.	mm.	mm.	mm.	mm.	mm.	mm.	mm.	mm.	mm.	mm.
69	118?	131	104	93	98	16	19	42	39	32	24	45	7	16	55	67	50	45	116	94	34	63	33
74	—	136	106	96	100	20	22	42	40r	34r	24	51	9	16	55	63	47	40	—	—	—	—	—
78	129	147	116	109	109	23	28	47	43	34	26	53	10	18	55	68	46	47	131	111	43	67	38
51	84?	104?	88	76	84	16	19?	38	35	34	20	36	10?	14?	33	52	32	36	88	74	23	37	23
75	124	134	108	100	102	18	23	43	39	37	28	53	7	15	52	67	45	49	128	114	41	66	35
74?	—	141	114	103	106	21	27	45	41	35	27	50	10	17	54?	70	—	—	—	—	—	—	—
70?	—	128	105	102	101	18	23	45	41	34	26	51	5	16	55	68	47	45	—	—	—	—	—
—	—	—	—	—	—	—	—	—	—	—	—	—	—	—	—	—	—	—	122	111	40	75	39
—	—	—	—	—	—	—	—	—	—	—	—	—	—	—	—	—	—	—	—	39	63?	—	—
—	—	—	—	—	—	—	—	—	—	—	—	—	—	—	—	—	—	—	125	106	38	64	37?
—	—	—	—	—	—	—	—	—	—	—	—	—	—	—	—	—	—	—	133	111	39	58	36?
—	—	—	—	—	—	—	—	—	—	—	—	—	—	—	—	—	—	—	116	105	39	58	34?
16	8	16	18	16	16	17	17	16	16	16	16	16	17	16	16	16	15	15	13	13	14	14	13
70–82	105–130	128–152	105–118	96–110	100–112	16–23	21–28	42–50	38–45	33–39	22–29	47–56	5–12	15–20	52–60	61–71	45–52	40–49	116–134	101–115	36–43	61–78	31–41
75.4	120.9	140.8	110.8	103.8	104.7	19.2	24.1	45.3	41.3	35.7	26.0	51.7	7.9	17.3	56.0	66.5	47.9	43.9	127.3	109.0	39.6	65.4	36.6
8	5	8	8	8	8	8	8	8	8	8	8	8	8	8	8	8	8	8	6	6	6	6	6
67– 79	112– 127	127– 140	102– 111	93– 103	96– 105	16– 22	19– 26	39– 44	36– 40	32– 38	23– 28	45– 52	7–9	16– 21	50– 57	61– 69	44– 50	38– 45	100– 127	93– 106	32– 38	52– 66	30– 36
72.3	118.6	133.6	105.9	97.0	99.9	18.6	22.8	42.1	38.8	35.4	27.8	48.8	8.3	17.0	53.5	64.5	46.4	41.0	119.5	98.0	35.5	58.5	32.5
64.0	—	132.0	101.0	—	98.0	18.0	21.0	42.0	40.0	32.0	21.0	46.0	6.0	14.0	—	—	—	—	—	—	—	—	—
5	3	5	5	5	5	5	5	5	5	5	5	5	5	5	5	5	5	5	2	3	3	3	3
51– 64	84– 101	104– 120	88– 99	76– 87	83– 93	15– 18	19– 22	37– 38	34– 36	32– 37	18– 21	36– 45	8–10	14– 17	33– 39	52– 59	32– 37	27– 36	88– 109	74– 97	23– 31	37– 49	23– 28
58.0	95.7	111.6	92.0	80.2	86.8	16.6	20.2	38.0	34.8	34.2	19.8	40.2	8.8	15.4	36.8	55.8	34.8	31.4	97.3	84.0	28.0	42.0	25.7
47	—	106?	85	76	80	15	19	34	32	32	20	35	—	—	33	53	31	36	—	—	—	—	—
46	—	110?	86	73	84	17	19	36	33	31	20	33	—	19	32	50	29	30	—	—	—	—	—
72	114	142	109	105	106	20	28	46	39	34	28	49	11	19	53	66	46	42	128	117	38	63	35
56	93	112?	91?	80?	85?	14	17	37	35?	33	22	39	7	12	37	58	35	35	97	80	26	47	27
64?	94	109	92	80	85	16	20	37	34	33	20	39	7	14	38?	56	34	29	93	85	28	45	25?
69?	—	145	106	106	101	17	20	46	42	40	27	55	8	18	47?	64	—	—	136	115	36	61	36
70	114	133	102	92	96	18	25	41	36	35	22	47	9	16	51	60	45	37	120	110	33	58	35
67?	—	132	106	94	97	17	22	43	38	32	25	47	5	15	53?	63	—	—	83	70	23	35	20
																			121	101	36	55	37
59	99	115	93	84	89	14	—	41r	—	31r	21	42	6	14	44	58	39	33	96	84	30	44	26
2	1	2	2	2	2	2	—	2	—	2	2	2	2	2	2	2	1	1	2	2	2	2	2
69; 72	—;	142; 145	106; 109	105; 106	101; 106	17; 20	20; 28	46; 46	39; 42	34; 40	27; 28	49; 55	8; 11	18; 19	47; 53	64; 66	—	—	128; 136	115; 117	36; 38	61; 63	35; 36
70.5	114.0	143.5	107.5	105.5	103.5	18.5	24.0	46.0	40.5	37.0	27.5	52.0	9.5	18.5	50.0	65.0	46.0	42.0	132.0	116.0	37.0	62.0	35.5

Tribal divisions and subdivisions — Catalogue No. — Sex and stages of life — Number of cases — Averages and ranges	Capacity	Length	Breadth	Height (ba-b)	Circumference (horizontal)	SKULL							Cranial base (length n-ba)	Foramen magnum		Frontal bone		Length	
						Total (n-o)	Median-sagittal Arc			Chord				Length	Width	Breadth (minimum)	Breadth (maximum)	Length (ba-pr)	Inferior length (ba-gn)
							Frontal	Parietal	Occipital	Frontal	Parietal	Occipital							
	ccm.	mm.	mm.	mm.	mm.	mm.	mm.	mm.	mm.	mm.	mm.	mm.	mm.	mm.	mm.	mm.	mm.	mm.	mm.
UNDEFORMED																			
♀ cases	2	2	2	2	2	2	2	2	2	2	2	2	2	2	2	2	2	2	1
range	1180; 1250	165; 167	143; 146	124; 129	490; 501	335; 354	115; 120	115; 124	104; 110	102; 105	104; 112	81; 92	91; 97	32; 33	26; 31	91; 96	117; 119	95; 98	—
average	1215.0	166.0	144.5	126.5	495.6	344.5	117.5	120.0	107.0	103.5	108.0	86.5	94.0	32.5	28.5	93.5	118.0	96.5	99.0
inf. cases	3	5	5	2	5	5	5	5	5	5	5	5	2	2	2	5	5	2	2
range	1020–1290	145–157	136–144	112; 118	445–473	308–335	102–118	91–121	95–125	87–101	80–101	88–97	82; 83	32; 32	29; 30	83–90	106–113	80; 87	87; 95
average	1133.0	153.0	140.0	115.0	457.6	323.4	111.8	105.0	106.6	95.4	90.6	88.2	82.5	32.0	29.5	87.0	108.8	83.5	91.0
Nicola																			
2606 ♂ mat	—	—	—	—	—	—	—	—	—	—	—	—	—	—	—	—	—	—	—
2607 ♀ ad	1100	165	135	117	447	325	116	111	98	102	100	81	96	33	28	90	112	97	—
2609 ♀ ad	—	—	—	—	—	—	—	—	—	—	—	—	—	—	—	—	—	—	—
2610 ♂ mat	1530	185	148	125	533	357	122	105	130	120	94	101	105	37	30	93	118	98	116
2611 ♂ ad	1370	182	143	130	527	363	123	127	113	108	112	85	103	32	29	93	122	102	113
2612 ♀ mat	1170	166	135	125	476	342	122	114	106	111?	97?	87	97	32	28	82	107	96?	—
2613 ♂ ad-mat	1370	173	148	124	510	345	120	106	119	119	95	98	101	36	29	94	117	100	118
♂ cases	3	3	3	3	3	3	3	3	3	3	3	3	3	3	3	3	3	3	3
range	1370–1530	173–185	143–148	124–130	510–533	345–363	120–123	105–127	113–130	108–120	94–112	85–101	101–105	32–37	29–30	93–94	117–122	98–102	113–118
average	1423.3	180.0	146.3	126.3	523.3	355.0	121.7	112.7	120.7	115.7	100.3	94.7	103.0	35.0	29.3	93.3	119.0	100.0	115.7
♀ cases	2	2	2	2	2	2	2	2	2	2	2	2	2	2	2	2	2	2	
range	1100; 1170	165; 166	135; 135	117; 125	476; 477	325; 342	116; 122	111; 114	98; 106	102; 111	97; 100	81; 87	96; 97	32; 33	28; 28	82; 90	107; 112	96; 97	
average	1135.0	165.5	135.0	121.0	476.6	333.5	119.0	112.5	102.0	106.5	98.5	84.0	96.5	32.5	28.0	86.0	109.5	96.5	
Lytton																			
1057 ♂ mat	1600	179	146	143	523	374	132	123	119	115	108	98	105	39	33	99	120	107	—
1058 ♀ mat-sen	1250	173	134	136	489	354	121	115	118	110	102	100	102	33	26	104	—	99?	—
1060 ♂ mat	—	172	129	—	—	—	—	—	—	—	—	—	—	—	—	—	—	—	—
1062 ♀ ad-mat	—	172	136	131	489?	349	121?	120?	108	105	106	93	102	33	27	98	111	—	—
1086 ♂ ad	—	—	—	—	—	116?	—	—	107?	—	—	—	—	—	—	—	—	—	—
1087 ♂ ad	—	—	—	—	—	—	—	—	—	—	—	—	—	—	—	—	—	—	—
1167 ♀? mat	—	180	145	—	525	357	122	115	120	111	104	100	—	—	—	98	120	—	—
1185 ♂ mat	1190	166	134	129	480	347	125	106	116	110	94	98	94	35	26	85	109	—	—
1223 ♀? mat																			
1555 ♀ mat	—	—	—	—	—	—	—	—	—	—	—	—	—	—	—	—	—	—	—
1563 inf. I—II	—	—	—	—	—	—	—	—	—	—	—	—	—	—	—	—	—	—	—
4307 ♂ juv-ad	—	174	136	135	—	355	123	118	114	109	108	94	100	36	31	92	—	101	107
4308 ♂ mat	1430	175	143	136	508	356	118	112	126	104	102	107	104	36	31	88	114	101?	113
4309 ♂ ad-mat	1280	183	130	133	510	—	126	122	103	111	112	83	103	37	29	91	113	—	—
4310 inf. II	1050	153	130	118	442	320	111	104	105	98	97	91	83	34	28	83	102	80	85
4311 ♂ juv-ad	—	170	134	129?	473	343	112	120	111	101	109	99	103	36	29	88	109	—	—

FACE AND MANDIBLE

Height		Breadth						Orbit			Nose		Nasal bones		Maxillo-alveolar		Palatal		Mandible				
																			Breadth		Height		
Upper height (n-pr)	Total height (n-gn)	Bizygomatic	Upper facial (fmt-fmt)	Mid-facial (zm-zm)	Biorbital (ek-ek)	Ant. interorb. (mf-mf)	Post. interorb. (la-la)	Width (mf-ek)	Width (la-ek)	Height	Width	Height	Breadth (minimum)	Breadth (maximum)	Length	Breadth	Length	Width	Bicondylar	Bigonial	Ramus	Ramus	Chin
mm.	mm.	mm.	mm.	mm.	mm.	mm.	mm.	mm.	mm.	mm.	mm.	mm.	mm.	mm.	mm.	mm.	mm.	mm.	mm.	mm.	mm.	mm.	mm.
2	1	2	2	2	2	2	2	2	2	2	2	2	2	2	2	2	1	1	2	2	2	2	2
67; 70	—	132; 133	102; 106	92; 94	96; 97	17; 18	22; 25	41; 43	36; 38	32; 35	22; 25	47; 47	5; 9	15; 16	51; 53	60; 63	—	—	120; 121	101; 110	33; 36	55; 58	35; 37
68.5	114.0	132.5	104.0	93.0	96.5	17.5	23.5	42.0	37.0	33.5	23.5	47.0	7.0	15.5	52.0	61.5	45.0	37.0	120.5	105.5	34.5	56.5	36.0
5	3	5	5	—	5	5	4	5	4	5	5	3	3	5	5	5	5	5	4	1	4	4	4
46–64	93–99	106–115	85–93	—	80–89	14–17	17–20	34–41	32–34	31–33	20–22	15–42	6–7	12–14	32–44	50–58	29–39	29–36	83–97	—	23–30	35–47	20–27
54.4	95.3	110.4	89.4	—	84.6	15.2	18.8	37.0	33.5	32.0	20.6	34.0	6.7	13.3	36.8	55.0	33.6	32.6	92.3	70.0	26.8	42.8	24.5
																			116	101	35	63	30
64	105	128?	104	96	94	19	23	41	37	32	27	48	6	18	50	62	43	42	123	102	33	54	32
																	—	—	113	92	30	59	30
77	129	146	109	101	98	19	23	42	38	36	26	57	8	16	52	69	45	47	121?	103?	37	65	33
76	125	141	111	101	104	21	25	45	41r	35	28	55	11?	—	56	68	48	44	121	101	36	57	38
63	—	123	96	91	91	18	20	38	35	32	25	47	7	17	45?	56	42	40	—	—	—	—	—
71	125	—	106	104	99	18	23	42	38	39	26	54	11	17	51	67	48	42	—	—	36	58	31
3	3	2	3	3	3	3	3	3	3	3	3	3	3	2	3	3	3	3	3	3	4	4	4
71–77	125–129	141; 146	106–111	101–104	98–104	18–21	23–25	42–45	38–41	35–39	26–28	54–57	8–11	16; 17	52–56	67–69	45–48	42–47	116–121	101–103	35–37	57–65	30–38
74.7	126.3	143.5	108.7	102.0	100.3	19.3	23.7	43.0	39.0	36.7	26.7	55.3	10.0	16.5	53.0	68.0	47.0	44.3	119.3	101.7	36.0	60.8	33.0
2	1	2	2	2	2	2	2	2	2	2	2	2	2	2	2	2	2	2	2	2	2	2	2
63; 64	—	123; 128	96; 104	91; 96	91; 94	18; 19	20; 23	38; 41	35; 37	32; 32	25; 27	47; 48	6; 7	17; 18	45; 50	56; 62	42; 43	40; 42	113; 123	92; 102	30; 33	54; 59	30; 32
63.5	105.0	125.5	100.0	93.5	92.5	18.5	21.5	39.5	36.0	32.0	26.0	47.5	6.5	17.5	47.5	59.0	42.5	41.0	118.0	97.0	31.5	56.5	31.0
77?	—	143	107	—	—	19?	—	44	40r	35r	—	50?	—	—	—	—	—	—	—	—	—	—	—
75?	—	123?	102	92?	93?	16	20?	41	37?	33	22	51	10	15	53?	58?	47?	38?	—	—	—	—	—
—	—	—	—	—	—	—	—	45r	—	37r	—	—	8	16	—	—	—	—	—	—	—	—	—
—	—	123?	104	—	—	18?	24?	41	36?	34	—	—	7	—	—	—	—	—	—	—	—	—	—
65	—	—	—	—	—	18	22	40	37r	32r	23	51	10	15?	50	62	45	38	—	—	—	—	—
73	—	—	—	—	—	19	23	45	41	35	28	55	10	18	58	68	48	43	—	—	—	—	—
67	—	—	102	89	98	19	23	42	39	34	26	46	8	—	54	62	47	38	—	—	—	—	—
—	—	—	—	108	—	—	—	—	—	—	—	—	—	—	—	—	—	—	—	—	—	—	—
—	—	127	98	—	—	—	—	40	38?	—	—	—	—	—	—	—	—	—	—	—	—	—	—
—	—	—	—	—	—	—	—	—	—	—	—	—	—	—	—	—	—	—	105	92	35	55	33
—	—	—	—	—	—	—	—	—	—	—	—	—	—	—	—	—	—	—	—	25	36	—	22
69	112	130	101	90	93	18	20?	40	37	37	23	48	9	17	52	66	48	38	121	94	37	55	34
67	109	143	103	100	97	16	19	43	39	35	23	48	7	12	52?	64	45?	39?	134	113	37	59	35
76	—	141?	107	—	—	15	24?	45	41?r	35	23	53	4	14	53?	65	49	40	—	—	37	66	40
58	96	111	90	83	84	14	20	37	32	33	20	42	8	13	39	55	34	36	104	85	29	49	26
—	—	—	92	—	—	19	—	—	—	—	—	—	10	—	—	—	—	—	—	—	—	—	—

7

Tribal divisions and subdivisions / Catalogue No. / Sex and stages of life / Number of cases / Averages and ranges	SKULL																		
	Capacity	Length	Breadth	Height (ba-b)	Circumference (horizontal)	Median-sagittal							Cranial base (length n-ba)	Foramen magnum		Frontal bone		Length	
						Arc				Chord									
						Total (n-o)	Frontal	Parietal	Occipital	Frontal	Parietal	Occipital		Length	Width	Breadth (minimum)	Breadth (maximum)	Length (ba-pr)	Inferior length (ba-gn)
	ccm.	mm.	mm.	mm.	mm.	mm.	mm.	mm.	mm.	mm.	mm.	mm.	mm.	mm.	mm.	mm.	mm.	mm.	mm.
UNDEFORMED																			
4313 ♀ ad	1150	165	136	125	479	336	113	110	113	100	96	91	96	41	30	86	108	101	—
♂ cases	3	7	7	5	5	5	7	6	6	7	6	6	5	5	5	6	5	3	2
range	1280–1600	170–183	129–146	129–143	473–525	343–374	112–132	112–123	103–126	101–115	102–112	83–107	100–105	36–39	29–33	88–99	109–120	101–107	107; 113
average	1436.7	176.1	137.6	135.2	507.8	357.0	121.3	118.3	115.5	108.3	107.2	96.8	103.0	36.8	30.6	92.7	115.2	103.0	110.0
♀ cases	3	4	4	4	4	4	4	4	4	4	4	4	4	4	4	4	3	2	—
range	1150–1250	165–173	134–146	125–136	479–489	336–354	113–125	106–120	108–118	100–110	94–106	91–100	94–102	31–35	26–30	85–104	108–111	99; 101	—
average	1196.7	169.0	135.0	130.2	484.3	346.5	120.0	112.7	113.7	106.3	99.3	95.5	98.5	33.0	27.3	93.3	109.3	100.0	—
inf. cases	1	1	1	1	1	1	1	1	1	1	1	1	1	1	1	1	1	1	—
range	—	—	—	—	—	—	—	—	—	—	—	—	—	—	—	—	—	—	—
average	1050.0	153.0	130.0	118.0	442.0	320.0	111.0	104.0	105.0	98.0	97.0	91.0	83.0	34.0	28.0	83.0	—	80.0	—
Spences Bridge																			
98 ♀ ad-mat	1160	162	132	124	470	330	116	112	102	103	101	86	95	35	28	91	108	91	100
99 ♂ mat	1460	192	147	133?	537	365	128	110	127	115	101	102	112?	37	30	102	119	105	126
1641 ♂ ad	1180	167	130	129	475	338	121	111	106	106	98	86	96	33	27	89	105	93	—
♂ 1 case	1460.0	192.0	147.0	133.0	537.0	365.0	128.0	110.0	127.0	115.0	101.0	102.0	99.0	37.0	30.0	102.0	119.0	105.0	126.0
♀ cases	2	2	2	2	2	2	2	2	2	2	2	2	2	2	2	2	2	2	1
range	1170; 1180	162; 167	130; 132	124; 129	470; 475	330; 338	116; 121	111; 112	102; 106	103; 106	98; 101	86; 86	95; 96	33; 35	27; 28	89; 91	105; 108	91; 93	—
average	1170.0	164.5	131.0	126.5	472.5	334.0	118.5	111.5	104.0	104.5	99.5	86.0	95.5	34.0	27.5	90.0	106.5	92.0	100.0
Kamloops																			
1284 ♂ ad-mat	1330	176	145	131	502	347	117	114	116	106	104	97	100	38	30	95	115	91	112
1286 ♂ juv-ad	—	—	—	—	—	—	—	—	—	—	—	—	—	—	—	—	—	—	—
1290 ♀ ad	—	162?	133?	127	—	—	125	105	—	108	95	—	95	—	—	89	114?	97	—
1291 ♀ ad	—	—	—	—	—	—	—	—	—	—	—	—	—	—	—	—	—	—	—
1292 ♀ mat	—	—	—	—	—	—	—	—	—	—	—	—	—	—	—	—	—	—	—
1293 inf. II	—	—	—	—	—	—	—	—	—	—	—	—	—	—	—	—	—	—	—
1295 inf. I	—	—	—	—	—	—	—	—	—	—	—	—	—	—	—	—	—	—	—
1410 ♀ ad	1220	166	138	115	478	334	116	102	116	103	93	96	93	33	28	89	113	88	100
1411 ♂ mat	—	179	137?	136	—	357	128	118	111	113	105	92	109	33	29	86?	—	99	—
1412 ♂? ad-mat	1250	173	140	—	501	347	122	99	126	107	92	100	—	—	—	93	114	—	—
1413 ♂ ad-mat	—	180	138?	135	511	355	125	112	118?	113	100	94?	109	—	—	91	114	106	—
1430 ♂ ad-mat	—	—	—	—	—	—	124	—	—	111	—	—	105	—	—	—	—	105	—
2602 ♂ mat	1280	169	139	132	492	340	126	96	118	113	89	99	101	34	32	83	109	103?	113
♂ cases	3	5	5	4	3	5	6	5	5	6	5	5	5	3	3	5	4	5	2
range	1250–1330	169–180	137–145	131–136	492–502	340–357	117–128	96–118	111–126	106–113	89–105	92–100	100–109	33–38	29–32	83–95	109–115	91–106	112; 113
average	1286.7	175.4	139.8	133.5	498.3	349.2	123.7	107.8	117.8	110.5	98.0	96.4	104.8	35.0	30.3	89.6	113.0	100.8	112.5

FACE AND MANDIBLE

Height		Breadth						Orbit			Nose		Nasal bones		Maxillo-alveolar		Palatal		Mandible				
																			Breadth		Height		
Upper height (n-pr)	Total height (n-gn)	Bizygomatic	Upper facial (fmt-fmt)	Mid-facial (zm-zm)	Biorbital (ek-ek)	Ant. interorb. (mf-mf)	Post. interorb. (la-la)	Width (mf-ek)	Width (la-ek)	Height	Width	Height	Breadth (minimum)	Breadth (maximum)	Length	Breadth	Length	Width	Bicondylar	Bigonial	Ramus	Ramus	Chin
mm.	mm.	mm.	mm.	mm.	mm.	mm.	mm.	mm.	mm.	mm.	mm.	mm.	mm.	mm.	mm.	mm.	mm.	mm.	mm.	mm.	mm.	mm.	mm.
71	117	132	102	99	96	18	21	42	38	33	24	50	10	15	50	61	49	40	110	94	40	63	36
6	2	4	6	2	2	7	5	7	6	7	5	6	7	6	5	5	5	5	2	2	3	3	3
65–77	109;112	130–143	92–108	90;100	93;97	15–19	19–24	40–45	37–41	32–37	23–28	48–55	4–10	12–18	50–58	62–68	45–49	38–43	121;134	94;113	37–37	55–66	34–40
71.0	110.5	139.3	103.0	95.0	95.0	17.7	21.6	43.1	39.2	35.1	24.0	50.8	8.3	15.3	53.0	65.0	47.0	39.6	127.5	103.5	37.0	60.0	36.3
3	1	4	5	3	3	4	4	5	5	4	3	3	4	2	3	3	3	3	2	2	2	2	2
67–75	—	123–132	98–104	89;99	93–98	16–19	20–24	40–42	36–39	33–34	22–26	46–51	7–10	15;15	50–54	58–62	47–49	38–40	105;110	92;94	35;40	59;63	33;36
71.0	117.0	126.3	101.6	93.3	95.7	17.8	22.0	41.2	37.6	33.5	24.0	49.0	8.8	15.0	52.3	60.3	47.7	38.7	107.5	93.0	37.5	59.0	34.5
1	1	1	1	1	1	1	1	1	1	1	1	1	1	1	1	1	1	1	1	—	2	2	2
—	—	—	—	—	—	—	—	—	—	—	—	—	—	—	—	—	—	—	—	—	25;29	36;49	22;26
58.0	96.0	111.0	90.0	—	84.0	14.0	20.0	37.0	32.0	33.0	20.0	33.0	8.0	13.0	39.0	55.0	34.0	36.0	104.0	—	27.0	42.5	24.0
61	98	123!	98	90	92	17	20	39	35?	32	23	46	7	13	49	57	43	37	103	94	29	51	26
73?	125?	152	115	105	103	19	23	45	41?	38	25	55	7	18	51?	67	48?	43?	130	110	44	66	37
65	—	125	96	87	88	15	18	40	36	35	22	49	8	12	47	53	42	34	—	—	—	—	—
73.0	125.0	152.0	115.0	105.5	93.0	19.0	23.0	45.0	41.0	38.0	25.0	55.0	7.0	18.0	51.0	67.0	48.0	43.0	130.0	99.0	44.0	66.0	37.0
2	1	2	2	2	2	2	2	2	2	2	2	2	2	2	2	2	2	2	1	1	1	1	1
61; 65	—	123; 125	96; 98	87; 90	88; 92	15; 17	18; 20	39; 40	35; 36	32; 35	22; 23	46; 49	7; 8	12; 13	47; 49	53; 57	43; 43	34; 37	—	—	—	—	—
63.0	98.0	124.0	97.0	88.5	90.0	16.0	19.0	39.5	35.5	33.5	22.5	47.5	7.5	12.5	48.0	55.0	43.5	35.5	103.0	98.0	29.0	51.0	26.0
75	—	135	107	91	99	18	23	43	39	35	21	55	9	13	49	63	44	40	—	—	—	—	32
—	—	—	—	—	—	—	—	—	—	—	—	—	—	—	—	—	—	—	97	85	29	48	28
65?	—	124?	98	89	91	17	22	39	35	35	23	48	10	16?	50	62	45	40	—	—	33	58	31
—	—	—	—	—	—	—	—	—	—	—	—	—	—	—	—	—	—	—	127?	96?	36	56	37
—	—	—	—	—	—	—	—	—	—	—	—	—	—	—	—	—	—	—	92	76	27	40	23
—	—	—	—	—	—	—	—	—	—	—	—	—	—	—	—	—	—	—	80	72	21	30	19
63	105	120	95	85	88	16	20	39	35	33	21	46	10	14	47	59	42	37	106	86	30	46	30
70	—	—	—	—	—	—	—	40	38?	35	—	48	—	—	—	—	—	—	—	—	—	—	—
65?	—	129	102	90	94	17	20	41	38	35	23	47	8	15	49?	55?	45?	36?	—	—	—	—	—
71	—	—	108	106	99	19	22	41	37	32	24	50	9	17	53?	63?	48	38	—	—	—	—	—
70	—	—	—	99	—	16	21	45	42r	35r	24	54	8	13?	53	67	44	43	—	—	—	—	—
74?	119?	139	103	98	98	18	20	42	38	33	23	55	10	14	—	—	—	—	125	110	38	54	33
6	1	3	4	5	4	5	5	6	6	6	5	6	5	5	4	4	4	4	2	2	2	2	2
65; 75	—	129–139	102–108	90–94	94–99	16–19	20–23	40–45	37–42	32–35	21–24	47–55	8–10	13–17	49–53	55–67	44–48	36–43	97; 125	85; 110	29; 38	48; 54	28; 33
70.8	119.0	134.3	105.0	96.8	97.0	17.6	21.2	42.0	38.3	34.2	23.0	51.5	8.8	14.4	51.0	62.0	45.3	39.3	111.0	97.5	33.5	51.0	31.0

Tribal divisions and subdivisions / Catalogue No. / Sex and stages of life / Number of cases / Averages and ranges	Capacity	Length	Breadth	Height (ba-b)	Circumference (horizontal)	SKULL Median-sagittal Arc Total (n-o)	Frontal	Parietal	Occipital	Median-sagittal Chord Frontal	Parietal	Occipital	Cranial base (length n-ba)	Foramen magnum Length	Width	Frontal bone Breadth (minimum)	Breadth (maximum)	Length Length (ba-pr)	Inferior length (ba-gn)
	ccm.	mm.	mm.	mm.	mm.	mm.	mm.	mm.	mm.	mm.	mm.	mm.	mm.	mm.	mm.	mm.	mm.	mm.	mm.
UNDEFORMED																			
♀ cases	1	2	2	2	1	1	2	2	1	2	2	1	2	1	1	2	2	2	1
range	—	162; 166	133; 138	115; 127	—	—	116; 125	102; 105	—	103; 108	93; 95	—	93; 95	—	—	89; 89	113; 114	88; 97	—
average	1220.0	164.0	135.5	121.0	478.0	334.0	120.5	103.5	116.0	105.5	94.0	96.0	94.0	33.0	28.0	89.0	113.5	92.5	100.0
inf. cases																			
range	—	—	—	—	—	—	—	—	—	—	—	—	—	—	—	—	—	—	—
average	—	—	—	—	—	—	—	—	—	—	—	—	—	—	—	—	—	—	—
Eskimo																			
3709 ♂ mat	1340	192	144	125?	540	379	145	116	118	128	106	97	96?	38	28	97	122	95?	—
3710 ♀ mat	1180	166	133	137	478	359	135	110	114	117	98	101	97	36	30	84	115	91	—
3711 ♂ ad	1180	177	133	128	500	367	132	120	115	114	107	94	96	34	27	94	113	98	—
3712 ♂ ad	1310	179	139	140	508	362	135	116	111	119	104	93	104	40	27	90	114	101	—
3713 ♀ ad	1170	173	133	—	486	351	122	119	110	109	103	95	—	—	—	85	110	—	—
3714 ♂ ad	1360	175	143	138	517	347	121	117	109	109	103	94	105	44	32	95	115	106	—
3715 ♂ mat	1450	184	147	137	529	392	139	139	114	120	113	94	98	33	29	98	120	95	—
3716 ♂ ad	1340	177	141	132	507	354	128	113	113	112	101	96	102	35	29	90	117	99	—
3717 ♂ ad	1300	175	135	139	508	369	130	117	122	112	103	103	95	35	27	96	115	105	—
3718 ♀ ad	1240	177	138	131	506	363	124	121	118	107	109	98	102	35	27	96	116	96	—
3719 ♂ ad	1340	188	140	139	529	378	130	117	131	115	107	110	100	40	30	91	117	101	—
3720 ♂ ad	1240	178	142	132	509	354	126	118	110	112	106	94	103	36	29	92	113	98	—
3721 ♂ ad	1170	178	130	126	495	358	118	127	113	106	110	95	97	34	31	89	107	99	—
3764 ♂ mat	1250	181	140	139	504	371	126	120	125	114	110	105	99	35	27	83	106	88	—
3765 ♂ ad	1550	189	140	132	533	370	137	122	111	119	110	91	107	37	31	101	118	104	—
3766 ♂ ad-mat	1440	188	142	135	534	378	135	130	113	117	117	95	112	38	28	100	115	99?	—
3767 ♂ ad	1170	176	135	127	502	355	123	119	113	109	106	94	96	35	27	88	112	94?	—
3768 ♂ ad	1270	177	140	136	506	361	128	118	115	115	106	99	107	34	30	95	110	109	—
3769 ♂ ad-mat	1280	180	140	129	507	351	123	107	121	110	98	99	104	38	29	90	109	101	106
3770 ♀ ad	1170	172	130	131	489	357	124	113	120	111	100	100	94	35	32	85	110	92	—
3771 ♂ ad-mat	1340	176	137	140	501	367	133	129	105	117	115	91	101	37	27	90	117	103	—
3772 ♂ ad-mat	1300	182	139	133	518	376	139	121	116	119	110	97	100	36	30	91	118	95	—
3773 ♂ ad	1110	167	132	131	482	349	122	117	110	107	103	86	97	37	32	93	108	99	—
3774 ♂ ad	1370	185	140	134	515	372	134	132	106	118	116	91	104	43	27	85	113	—	—
3775 ♂ ad	1210	184	135	134	512	373	126	125	122	113	113	101	102	35	28	93	112	102	—
3776 ♂ ad	1370	178	134	134	514	354	121	126	107	108	110	94	104	38	32	99	118	102	—
3777 ♂ ad	1450	182	144	139	524	368	127	128	113	111	111	95	106	37	31	102	116	105	—
3778 ♀ ad	1250	176	134	130	499	352	122	114	116	107	102	90	105	36	28	94	113	101	—
3779 ♀ ad	1320	179	136	131	508	380	128	131	121	110	115	101	101	33	29	95	110	96	—
3780 ♀ ad	1270	168	138	134	487	356	127	117	112	112	103	98	98	34	28	90	114	96	—
3781 ♀ ad	1240	174	139	125	498	339	121	111	107	109	99	88	100	37	26	89	115	100	—

| Height | | Breadth | | | | | | Orbit | | Nose | | Nasal bones | | Maxillo-alveolar | | Palatal | | Mandible | | | | |
																		Breadth		Height		
Upper height (n-pr)	Total height (v-gn)	Bizygomatic	Upper facial (fmt-fmt)	Mid-facial (zm-zm)	Biorbital (ek-ek)	Ant. interorb. (mf-mf)	Post. interorb. (la-la)	Width (mf-ek)	Width (la-ek)	Height	Width	Height	Breadth (minimum)	Breadth (maximum)	Length	Breadth	Length	Width	Bicondylar	Bigonial	Ramus	Ramus	Chin
mm.	mm.	mm.	mm.	mm.	mm.	mm.	mm.	mm.	mm.	mm.	mm.	mm.	mm.	mm.	mm.	mm.	mm.	mm.	mm.	mm.	mm.	mm.	mm.
2	1	2	2	2	2	2	2	2	2	2	2	2	2	2	2	2	2	2	2	2	3	3	3
63; 65	—	120; 124	95; 98	85; 89	88; 91	16; 17	20; 22	39; 39	35; 35	33; 35	21; 23	46; 48	10; 10	14; 16	47; 50	59; 62	42; 45	37; 40	106; 127	86; 96	30–36	46–58	30–37
64.0	105.0	122.0	96.5	87.0	89.5	16.5	21.0	39.0	35.0	34.0	22.0	47.0	10.0	15.0	48.5	60.5	43.5	38.5	116.5	91.0	33.0	53.3	32.7
—	—	—	—	—	—	—	—	—	—	—	—	—	—	—	—	—	—	—	2	2	2	2	2
—	—	—	—	—	—	—	—	—	—	—	—	—	—	—	—	—	—	—	80; 92	72; 76	21; 27	30; 40	19; 23
—	—	—	—	—	—	—	—	—	—	—	—	—	—	—	—	—	—	—	86.0	74.0	24.0	35.0	21.0
77?	—	141?	112	103	103	15	—	46	43	35	26	55	6	16?	—	—	—	—	—	—	—	—	—
70	—	124	98	100	95	16	21	41	37	37	26	52	7	18	49	61	39?	39	—	—	—	—	—
73	—	130?	109	102	102	19	23	43	40	34	24	52	7	12?	53	64	46	37	—	—	—	—	—
73	—	137	108	99	101	15	24	44	39	34	26	51	5	13	54	67	48	39	—	—	—	—	—
74	—	127	99	98	95	14	—	42	—	35	25	54	5	15?	48	61	44	42?	—	—	—	—	—
77	—	137	106	99	100	13	—	45	40?	38	22	55	7?	11?	52	69	48	43	—	—	—	—	—
73?	—	145	113	103	105	16	23?	46	41	38	23	53	5	15?	52?	61?	48	—	—	—	—	—	—
73	—	133	102	102	94	15	20	41	38	38	19	51	4	9?	50	63	43	39	—	—	—	—	—
74	—	138	108	102	101	13	22	45	41?	37	24	54	2	11?	54	65	44	43	—	—	—	—	—
71	—	131	105	98	99	18	22	42	40?r	36r	24	51	6	12?	—	—	—	—	—	—	—	—	—
85	—	144	110	109	101	14	—	43	40?	39	23	63	6	10	56	69	48	38	—	—	—	—	—
77	—	136	107	104	99	18	24	44	38	36	24	54	6	14	54	69	44	45	—	—	—	—	—
73	—	132	105	99	97	14	20	43	40	34	25	53	5	8	53	62	46?	40	—	—	—	—	—
70?	—	128	103	95	98	15	20?	42	38	36	25	49	4	12	—	—	—	—	—	—	—	—	—
84	—	144	112	96?	106	17	22	45	42	40	23	60	6	11?	49	68	39	45	—	—	—	—	—
80?	—	144	117	105	110	15	23	49	45	41	26	55	7	15	—	—	—	—	—	—	—	—	—
68?	—	130	103	88	95	15	22	43	38?	36	19	49	6	14	—	—	—	—	—	—	—	—	—
71	—	137	109	103	102	16	22	44	40	35	26	49	8	16	55	66	50	41	—	—	—	—	—
84	134	136	106	104	98	17	22	43	39	37	23	57	10	14	54	69	46	43	126	109	39	61	39
76	—	128	102	94	96	15	—	42	—	41	21	53	3?	10?	49	56	41?	36	—	—	—	—	—
76	—	133	105	98	98	17	20	42	38?	36	24	55	5	11	53	65	41	43	—	—	—	—	—
77	—	136	109	99	101	20	24	42	38	37	25	56	5	14?	52	66	45	42	—	—	—	—	—
77	—	128?	107	98?	100	20	23	42	38	35	26	54	9	16	50	59	45	40	—	—	—	—	—
—	—	129	100	—	—	16	19	43	39r	37r	—	—	6	12	—	—	—	—	—	—	—	—	—
76	—	130?	107?	97	99?	18	23	43	39	33r	22	53	8	15?	56	63	52	39	—	—	—	—	—
81	—	142	113	106	101	17	21	43	39	39	23	58	7	16	57	70	50	43	—	—	—	—	—
76	—	148	113	105	105	17	22	46	42	38	24	56	7	16	57	68	47	44	—	—	—	—	—
71	—	131	105	94	96	16	21?	42	39?	35	22	52	4	9?	49	64	42	38	—	—	—	—	—
72	—	130	103	99	96	13	19	42	38	33	21	50	4	12	55	64	46	39	—	—	—	—	—
70	—	132	104	94	96	14	18	43	39r	35r	26	51	6	15	50	—	—	—	—	—	—	—	—
75	—	139	103	96	97	15	19	43	39	35	24	55	4	10?	52	66	45	43?	—	—	—	—	—

Tribal divisions and subdivisions / Catalogue No. / Sex and stages of life / Number of cases / Averages and ranges	SKULL																	
	Capacity	Length	Breadth	Height (ba-b)	Circumference (horizontal)	Median-sagittal						Craniat base (length n-ba)	Foramen magnum		Frontal bone		Length	Inferior length (ba-gn)
						Arc				Chord								
						Total (n-o)	Frontal	Parietal	Occipital	Frontal	Parietal	Occipital		Length	Width	Breadth (minimum)	Breadth (maximum)	Length (ba-pr)	
	ccm.	mm.	mm.	mm.	mm.	mm.	mm.	mm.	mm.	mm.	mm.	mm.	mm.	mm.	mm.	mm.	mm.	mm.	mm.
UNDEFORMED																			
3782 ♂ ad	1300	179	139	132	507	335	127	112	116	113	100	95	103	35	28	97	115	100	—
3783 ♂ ad	1390	179	146	137	521	364	126	124	114	109	112	99	101	36	29	100	121	106	—
3784 ♂ mat	1390	189	146	140	543	373	127	120	126	113	110	101	111	39	30	103	120	104?	—
3785 ♀ ad	1350	168	140	139	487	351	124	114	113	112	103	100	99	36	30	95	114	96	—
3786 ♂ mat	1300	188	135	136	522	369	130	126	113	114	111	100	109	39	33	95	113	105	—
3787 ♂ ad	1540	184	143	142	523	381	130	126	125	114	112	104	103	38	31	93	118	103	—
3788 ♀ ad	1240	178	133	129	500	366	124	119	123	110	107	103	99	34	27	90	113	104	—
3789 ♂ ad-mat	1310	186	132	—	521	379	130	112	137	115	104	109	—	—	—	91	112?	—	—
3790 ♂ ad	1390	189	150	135	537	362	125	127	110	111	112	92	107	40	31	99	118	105	—
3791 ♀ ad-mat	1240	174	133	129	499	349	123	120	106	109	108	90	97	40	30	94	110	100	—
3792 ♂ mat	1600	191	147	148	544	393	139	125	129	118	112	106	105	39	29	97	120	99?	—
3793 ♂ mat	1350	189	144	139	534	371	133	122	116	118	111	98	109	37	29	99	115	105	—
3794 ♀ ad	1340	174	142	134	499	362	123	124	115	109	109	97	98	35	28	87	112	102	—
3795 ♂ ad-mat	1360	180	145	128	522	358	121	122	115	108	108	97	100	36	30	94	117	104	—
♂ cases	33	33	33	32	33	33	33	33	33	33	33	33	32	32	33	33	31	1	
range	1100–1600	167–192	130–150	125–148	482–544	335–393	118–145	107–139	105–137	106–128	98–117	86–110	95–112	33–44	27–33	83–103	106–122	88–109	—
average	1335.4	181.9	140.0	134.9	517.2	366.4	129.3	121.5	116.2	113.8	108.4	97.2	102.6	37.1	29.3	94.5	115.0	100.9	106.0
♀ cases	12	12	12	11	12	12	11	12	12	12	12	12	11	11	12	12	11		
range	1170–1350	166–179	130–142	125–139	478–508	339–380	121–135	110–131	106–123	107–117	98–115	88–103	90–105	33–40	26–32	84–96	110–116	91–104	—
average	1250.8	173.2	136.1	131.8	494.7	356.6	124.7	117.7	114.4	110.2	104.7	96.8	98.1	35.5	28.6	90.3	112.7	97.6	—
Chukchee																			
3843 ♂ mat	1410	178	139	132	515	365	123	126	116	110	112	96	95	40	28	100	115	94	—
3844 ♀ ad-mat	1290	169	133	136	490	352	125	109	118	106	99	101	98	37	28	97	119	96	100
3845 inf. I–II	1270	164	134	121	469	351	122	125	104	104	108	87	85	34	28	90	110	79	—
3846 ♂ mat-sen	1270	180	137	134	509	362	130	116	116	111	106	96	103	35	28	90	111	107	120
3847 inf. I–II	1300	165	137	125	477	353	124	109	120	107	98	100	86	37	30	91	112	82	90
3848 ♂ mat	1190	169	140	124	494	345	120	120	105	107	105	86	94	35	28	84	108	94	—
3849 ♂ mat	1370	188	140	127	528	388	133	135	120	118	118	97	98	34	29	98	114	102	107
♂ cases	4	4	4	4	4	4	4	4	4	4	4	4	4	4	4	4	4	4	2
range	1190–1410	169–188	137–140	124–134	494–528	345–388	120–133	116–135	105–120	107–118	105–118	86–97	94–103	34–40	28–29	84–100	108–115	94–107	107; 120
average	1310.0	176.2	139.0	129.2	511.5	360.0	126.5	114.2	114.2	111.5	110.3	93.8	97.5	36.0	28.3	93.0	112.0	99.3	113.5
♀ 1 case	1290.0	169.0	133.0	136.0	490.0	352.0	125.0	109.0	118.0	106.0	99.0	101.0	98.0	37.0	28.0	97.0	119.0	96.0	100.0
inf. cases	2	2	2	2	2	2	2	2	2	2	2	2	2	2	2	2	2	2	1
range	1270; 1300	164; 165	134; 137	121; 125	469; 477	351; 353	122; 124	109; 125	104; 120	104; 107	89; 108	87; 100	85; 86	34; 37	28; 30	90; 91	110; 112	79; 82	—
average	1285.0	164.5	135.5	123.0	473.0	352.0	123.0	117.0	112.0	105.5	103.0	93.5	85.5	35.5	29.0	90.5	111.0	80.5	90.0

							FACE AND MANDIBLE												Mandible			
Height		Breadth						Orbit			Nose		Nasal bones		Maxillo-alveolar		Palatal		Breadth		Height		
Upper height (n-pr)	Total height (n-gn)	Bizygomatic	Upper facial (inf-fmt)	Mid-facial (zm-zm)	Bizefrontal (ck-ek)	Ant. interorb. (mf-mf)	Post. interorb. (la-la)	Width (mf-ek)	Width (la-ek)	Height	Width	Height	Breadth (minimum)	Breadth (maximum)	Length	Breadth	Length	Width	Bicondylar	Bigonial	Ramus	Ramus	Chin
mm.	mm.	mm.	mm.	mm.	mm.	mm.	mm.	mm.	mm.	mm.	mm.	mm.	mm.	mm.	mm.	mm.	mm.	mm.	mm.	mm.	mm.	mm.	mm.
79	—	138	111	107	101	16	21	44	40	38	24	58	6	15	53	69	45	45	—	—	—	—	—
80	—	143	110	107	103	20	26?	42	37	37	24	55	7	14	55	69	50	43	—	—	—	—	—
82?	—	156	120	109	111	18	24	50	46	42	27	60	8	15	—	—	—	—	—	—	—	—	—
77	—	132	106	93	97	15	21	42	38	38	21	56	5	13	52	63	43	36	—	—	—	—	—
77	—	135	107	99	102	15	20	47	42	36	26	55	3	13?	—	—	—	—	—	—	—	—	—
81	—	138	106	102	101	17	22	44	41	39	25	55	6	15	50	63?	46	41	—	—	—	—	—
65	—	130	102	97	97	15	20	43	39	36	28	49	5	16?	—	—	—	—	—	—	—	—	—
76	—	136?	107	—	103	18	22?	44	40	36	27	53	10	17	—	—	—	—	—	—	—	—	—
82	—	149	115	105	105	16	24	46	41	36	29	58	8	18	54	63	49	45?	—	—	—	—	—
74	—	138	109	100	102	16	22	44	40	36	26	52	6	15	53	60	42	39	—	—	—	—	—
77?	—	144	110	102	103	18	22	44	41	37	26	57	6	14	—	—	—	—	—	—	—	—	—
80?	—	145	110	103	104	18	22?	45	41	37	24	58	7	15	—	—	—	—	—	—	—	—	—
75	—	130	104	96	98	16	21?	43	39	36	24	53	7	14	55	65	46	43	—	—	—	—	—
83	—	144	106	110	102	17	23	45	41	39	21	56	6	12	—	—	—	—	—	—	—	—	—
32	1	33	33	31	32	33	30	33	33	33	32	32	33	33	22	22	22	21	1	1	1	1	1
68–	—	128–	100–	88–	94–	13–	19–	41–	37–	33–	19–	49–	2–10	8–18	49–	59–	39–	37–	—	—	—	—	—
85	—	156	120	110	111	20	26	50	46	42	29	63			57	70	52	45					
77.3	134.0	138.4	105.6	101.9	101.6	16.5	24.2	44.3	40.2	36.9	24.2	54.9	6.3	13.6	53.3	65.8	46.1	41.8	126.0	109.0	39.0	61.0	39.0
12	—	12	12	12	12	12	10	12	10	12	12	12	12	12	10	9	9	9	—	—	—	—	—
65–	—	124–	98–	93–	95–	13–	18–	41–	37–	33–	21–	49–	3–7	9–18	48–	56–	39–	36–	—	—	—	—	—
77		139	109	100	102	18	22	44	40	41	28	56			55	66	46	43					
72.5		131.0	103.8	96.6	97.0	15.3	20.4	42.4	38.8	36.1	24.0	52.3	5.2	13.3	51.2	62.2	43.1	39.4					
70	—	132?	108	100?	103	16	24	45	41	36	26	50	9	16	50	57?	—	—	—	—	—	—	—
74	115	134?	107	102	98	16	21	42	38	35	23	52	3	11	50	65	43	40	116	109	34	58	34
55	—	111	93	85	85	18	21	35	32	31	21	40	8	15	36	56	35	34	—	—	—	—	—
70	108	137	105	101	101	19	24	44	39	34	27	51	5	18	55	—	50	—	129	111	40	55	30?
58	96	112	92	96	86	15	18	36	35	33	20	41	7	15	39	59	34	33	100	88	27	46	26
70	—	138	103	94	94	17	22	41	37	34	23	48	5	14	51	57	46	34	—	—	—	—	—
79	124	136	112	104	102	18	23	44	41	36	25	56	8	18	57	69	50	45	126	111	37	63	34
4	2	4	4	4	4	4	4	4	4	4	4	4	4	4	4	3	3	2	2	2	2	2	2
70–	108;	132–	103–	94–	94–	16–	22–	41–	37–	34–	23–	48–	5–9	14–	50–	57–	46–	34;	116;	111;	37;	55;	30;
79	124	138	112	104	103	19	24	45	41	36	27	56		18	57	69	50	45	129	111	40	63	34
72.3	116.0	135.8	107.0	99.8	100.0	17.5	23.3	43.5	39.5	35.0	25.3	51.3	6.8	16.5	53.3	61.0	48.7	39.5	127.5	111.0	38.5	59.0	32.0
74.0	115.0	134.0	107.0	102.0	98.0	16.0	21.0	42.0	38.0	35.0	23.0	52.0	3.0	11.0	50.0	65.0	43.0	40.0	116.0	109.0	34.0	58.0	34.0
2	1	2	2	2	2	2	2	2	2	2	2	2	2	2	2	2	2	2	1	1	1	1	1
55;	—	112	92;	84;	85,	15;	18;	35;	32;	31;	20;	40;	7; 8	15;	36;	56;	34;	33;	—	—	—	—	—
58			93	85	86	18	21	36	35	33	21	41		15	39	59	35	34					
56.5	96.0	111.5	92.5	84.5	85.5	16.5	19.5	35.5	35.5	32.0	20.5	40.5	7.5	15.0	37.5	57.5	34.5	33.5	100.0	88.0	27.0	46.0	26.0

Tribal divisions and subdivisions / Catalogue No. / Sex and stages of life / Number of cases / Averages and ranges	Capacity	Length	Breadth	Height (ba-b)	Circumference (horizontal)	SKULL Median-sagittal Arc Total (n-o)	Frontal	Parietal	Occipital	Chord Frontal	Parietal	Occipital	Cranial base (length n-ba)	Foramen magnum Length	Width	Frontal bone Breadth (minimum)	Breadth (maximum)	Length Length (ba-pr)	Inferior length (ba-gn)
	ccm.	mm.	mm.	mm.	mm.	mm.	mm.	mm.	mm.	mm.	mm.	mm.	mm.	mm.	mm.	mm.	mm.	mm.	mm.
UNDEFORMED																			
divisional total																			
♂ cases	73	79	79	75	75	77	80	78	78	80	78	78	76	74	73	78	76	71	24
range	1100–1640	164–196	129–152	110–148	473–549	317–395	109–145	88–139	103–140	101–130	82–120	83–113	94–113	31–44	26–28	83–106	105–127	88–111	105–127
average	1349.5	175.6	140.8	134.2	516.3	363.6	127.2	119.0	117.6	112.6	106.7	96.2	102.7	36.2	29.6	94.1	115.5	101.6	115.0
♀ cases	32	34	34	33	33	32	34	34	33	34	34	33	32	32	32	34	33	31	10
range	1100–1620	162–183	130–150	115–141	470–524	325–380	113–135	102–131	98–123	100–117	93–115	81–113	90–105	31–40	26–32	82–104	102–125	88–105	99–113
average	1243.8	170.3	136.5	130.2	484.4	350.1	122.3	115.9	112.0	107.9	103.0	93.6	97.3	34.4	28.6	91.4	112.5	97.6	103.8
juv. 1 case	1350.0	170.0	142.0	133.0	496.0	344.0	122.0	110.0	112.0	104.0	101.0	94.0	98.0	37.0	25.0	97.0	115.0	94.0	—
inf. cases	11	13	13	8	14	13	14	13	13	14	13	14	8	9	9	12	13	8	5
range	1020–1540	145–178	130–157	112–128	445–503	308–366	111–139	104–125	95–115	87–115	80–109	80–97	82–94	32–41	28–30	83–95	106–122	79–87	87–95
average	1268.2	160.9	139.5	121.0	470.0	339.9	119.2	112.2	108.5	102.0	98.8	91.0	86.1	35.9	29.0	88.5	111.0	82.3	90.8
COWICHAN																			
Tsimshian																			
4585 ♂ ad	1260	168	138	132	489	349	121	113	115	105	101	95	97	35	29	91	112	99	111
4586 ♂ ad	1270	170	140	142	499	336	126	106	104	113	93	89	108	35	31	95	115	100	—
4587 ♀ juv-ad	1180	166	137	128	477	339	122	101	116	109	91	98	95	33	28	90	113	89	—
4588 ♂ ad-mat	—	—	—	—	—	—	—	—	—	—	—	—	—	—	—	—	—	—	—
4645 ♂ ad	1270	158	151	124	488	333	118	113	102	110	95	84	87	36	31	92	115	97	—
4646 ♂ ad-mat	1120	159	144	127	479	328	108	107	113	101	91	92	95	32	29	94	118	103	—
4647 ♂ mat	1400	173	145	143	507	365	130	113	122	115	100	96	100	32	30	89	118	103	—
4648 ♂ mat	1300	172	144	139	502	351	130	109	112	118	97	97	105	33	32	98	116	102	—
4649 ♂ mat	1370	185	148	138	527	366	135	104	127	122	95	101	104	32	26	99	117	108	—
♂ cases	7	7	7	7	7	7	7	7	7	7	7	7	7	7	7	7	7	7	1
range	1120–1400	158–185	138–151	124–143	479–527	328–366	108–135	104–113	102–127	101–122	91–101	84–101	87–108	32–36	26–32	89–99	112–118	97–108	—
average	1284.3	169.3	144.2	135.0	498.1	346.8	124.0	109.3	113.6	112.0	96.0	93.3	99.4	33.7	29.7	94.0	115.9	101.7	111.0
♀ 1 case	1180.0	166.0	137.0	128.0	477.0	339.0	122.0	101.0	116.0	109.0	91.0	98.0	95.0	33.0	28.0	90.0	113.0	89.0	—
Yakima																			
4314 ♂ mat	1460	174	151	130	523	350	126	106	118	112	97	95	100	33	30	96	121	99	97
4318 ♂ ad	1440	175	153	129	522	345	118	98	129	110	91	106	103	37	34	87	117	108	—
4319 juv.	1250	162	149	123	482	329	115	110	104	104	93	92	91	31	26	89	117	89	101
4320 ♂ ad	—	—	—	—	—	—	—	—	—	—	—	—	—	—	—	—	—	—	—
4321 inf. II	1080?	144	134?	118	486	313	109	107	97	98	90	87	82	29	26	84	103	80	80
4323 ♂ ad	1210	—	—	—	—	—	—	115	108	106	86	—	—	—	—	88	117	—	—
4325 ♂ ad	—	158	148	129	—	337	121	107	109	110	93	91	94	33	29	—	117?	105	109

FACE AND MANDIBLE

Height		Breadth						Orbit			Nose		Nasal bones		Maxillo-alveolar		Palatal		Mandible Breadth			Mandible Height	
Upper height (n-pr)	Total height (n-gn)	Bizygomatic	Upper facial (zm-fm)	Mid facial (zm-zm)	Biorbital (ek-ek)	Ant. interorb. (mf-mf)	Post. interorb. (la-la)	Width (mf-ek)	Width (fu-ek)	Height	Width	Height	Breadth (minimum)	Breadth (maximum)	Length	Breadth	Length	Width	Bicondylar	Bigonial	Ramus	Ramus	Chin
mm.	mm.	mm.	mm.	mm.	mm.	mm.	mm.	mm.	mm.	mm.	mm.	mm.	mm.	mm.	mm.	mm.	mm.	mm.	mm.	mm.	mm.	mm.	mm.
76	23	70	77	69	70	78	73	78	77	78	74	76	78	75	62	61	59	57	30	30	33	33	32
65–85	105–130	125–156	92–120	88–110	93–112	13–23	19–28	40–50	37–46	32–42	19–29	47–63	2–12	8–20	47–60	55–71	39–52	34–49	97–136	85–117	29–44	48–78	28–41
75.0	121.2	138.5	107.1	101.5	101.6	17.7	23.6	44.2	40.1	35.9	24.7	53.1	7.4	16.5	53.7	65.4	46.7	42.0	123.9	106.0	37.7	61.9	35.7
33	12	34	34	32	32	34	32	34	32	33	33	33	34	32	31	30	29	29	17	17	18	18	18
63–79	105–127	117–140	95–111	87–103	13–105	13–22	18–26	38–44	35–40	32–41	21–28	45–56	3–10	9–21	45–57	53–69	39–50	36–45	103–127	86–110	29–40	46–66	26–37
70.2	11.8	129.6	102.9	95.0	96.4	16.9	24.4	41.6	37.9	34.9	24.0	51.4	6.9	14.8	51.3	61.9	44.6	39.6	115.7	98.0	34.2	56.4	32.7
64.0	—	132.0	101.0	—	98.0	18.0	21.0	42.0	40.0	32.0	21.0	46.0	6.0	14.0	—	—	—	—	12	8	13	13	13
14	8	14	14	8	14	14	13	14	13	13	14	14	12	12	13	13	14	14	12	8	13	13	13
46–64	84–101	104–120	85–99	76–87	83–92	14–18	17–22	34–41	32–36	31–37	18–22	15–45	6–10	14–17	32–44	50–59	29–39	27–36	80–109	72–97	21–31	30–49	19–28
56.9	95.6	110.9	91.0	81.0	85.6	16.0	19.8	37.3	34.1	33.0	20.2	37.7	7.9	14.6	37.1	55.7	34.3	32.4	95.0	80.4	26.8	41.8	24.5
72	116	135	102	100	97	16	21	43	39	33	26	51	7	15	57	69	49	42	113	95	38	62	35
75	—	145	110	105	102	17	20	46	42	38	24	55	6	15	50	63	43	41	—	—	—	—	—
66	—	—	100?	102?	95?	18	21	41	39r	38r	22	48	8	14	45	58	43	35	—	—	—	—	—
—	—	—	—	—	—	—	—	—	—	—	—	—	—	—	—	—	—	—	119	103	41	62	40
72	—	138	108	101	99	16	20	42	39	38	24	49	9	14	53	64	45	39	—	—	—	—	—
74	—	139	107	102	98	20	23	40	37	35	24	49	10	16	53	50	46	38	—	—	—	—	—
74	—	144	105	105	103	19	24	43	40	34	23	50	8	16	58	68	50	40	—	—	—	—	—
75?	—	151	108	106	103	18	21	45	42	37	25	55	10	18	55	67	48	41	—	—	—	—	—
86	—	147	114	110	106	21	26	45	41	37	26	57	7	18	60	70	54	43	—	—	—	—	—
7	1	7	7	7	7	7	7	7	7	7	7	7	7	5	7	7	2	2	2	2	2	2	
72–86	—	135–151	102–114	100–110	97–106	16–21	20–26	40–46	37–42	33–38	23–26	49–57	7	14–18	50–60	60–70	43–54	38–43	113; 119	95; 103	38; 41	62; 62	35; 40
75.4	116.0	142.7	107.1	104.1	101.1	18.1	22.1	43.4	40.0	36.0	24.6	52.3	8.1	16.0	55.1	65.9	47.9	40.6	116.0	99.0	39.5	62.0	37.5
66.0	—	—	100.0	102.0	95.0	18.0	21.0	41.0	39.0	38.0	22.0	48.0	8.0	14.0	45.0	58.0	43.0	35.0	—	—	—	—	—
69	110	147	104	100?	99	20	23	43	39	33	24	52	9	16	51	67	44?	44	129	103	37	57	33?
72	—	138	102	100	98?	18	21	42	38	36	23	50	6	13	54	66	48	42	—	—	—	—	—
64	103	129	99	90	92	19	23	40	36	34	21	49	9	15	46	59	41	39	—	—	32	51	27
—	—	—	—	—	—	15	23?	44	40	33	20	48	2!	11	53	60	48	37	112	96	36	63	38
52	84	106	86	75	80	16	20	35	31	31	21	39	8	14	36	52	34	31	95?	81	27	39	24
65	107?	130	100	97	93	16	21	40	36	30	20	48	9	14	51	65	43	40	113	82	27	50	32
69	107?	135	—	94	—	18	20	40	37	31	25	48	7	15?	57	63	47	43	115	91	33	56	34

Tribal divisions and subdivisions — Catalogue No. — Sex and stages of life — Number of cases — Averages and ranges	Capacity	Length	Breadth	Height (ba-b)	Circumference (horizontal)	SKULL						Cranial base (length n-ba)	Foramen magnum		Frontal bone		Length	
						Total (n-o)	Median-sagittal Arc			Median-sagittal Chord								
							Frontal	Parietal	Occipital	Frontal	Parietal	Occipital		Length	Width	Breadth (minimum)	Breadth (maximum)	Length (na-pr)	Inferior length (ba-gn)
	ccm.	mm.	mm.	mm.	mm.	mm.	mm.	mm.	mm.	mm.	mm.	mm.	mm.	mm.	mm.	mm.	mm.	mm.	mm.
COWICHAN																			
4326 inf. II	—	—	—	—	—	110	—	—	98	—	—	—	32	27	92	120	—	—
4328 juv.	1160	151	139	121	462	320	115	104	101	104	90	89	36	31	87	115	89	96
4329 inf. I	—	—	—	—	—	—	—	—	—	—	—	—	—	—	—	—	—	—
4332 inf. I	—	—	—	—	—	—	—	—	—	—	—	—	—	—	—	—	—	—
4333 ♀ mat	980	157	133	121	462	317	114	104	99	103	91	89	30	23	78	110	94	—
4334 ♂ ad-mat	1220	174	146	120	512	339	127	115	97	114	100	81	29	26	91	119	103	113
4335 ♂ ad	1260	165	148	130	498	341	122	108	111	113	94	93	98	36	28	90	116	99	117
4336 ♀ mat	1220	144?	152	134	473	326	120	99	107	112	86	96	91	30	29	98	119	94	97
♂ cases	5	5	5	5	4	5	6	6	5	6	6	5	5	5	5	5	6	5	4
range	1210– 1460	158– 175	146– 153	120– 130	495– 523	337– 350	115– 127	98– 115	97– 129	106– 114	86– 100	81– 106	94– 103	29– 37	26– 34	87– 96	116– 121	99– 108	97– 117
average	1318.0	168.4	149.6	127.6	513.0	342.4	121.5	107.0	112.8	110.8	93.5	93.2	99.4	33.6	29.5	90.4	117.8	102.8	109.0
♀ cases	2	2	2	2	2	2	2	2	2	2	2	2	2	2	2	2	2	2	1
range	980; 1220	144; 157	133; 152	121; 134	462; 473	317; 326	114; 120	99; 104	99; 107	103; 112	86; 91	86; 96	91; 92	30; 30	23; 29	78; 98	110; 119	94; 94	97;
average	1100.0	150.5	142.5	127.5	467.5	321.5	117.0	101.5	103.0	107.5	88.5	92.5	91.5	30.0	26.0	88.0	114.5	94.0	97.0
juv. case	2	2	2	2	2	2	2	2	2	1	2	2	2	2	2	2	2	2	2
range	1160; 1250	151; 162	139; 149	121; 123	462; 482	320; 329	115; 115	101; 104	101; 104	—	90; 93	89; 92	89; 91	31; 36	26; 31	87; 89	115; 117	89; 89	96; 101
average	1205.0	156.5	144.0	122.0	472.0	324.5	115.0	102.5	102.5	104.0	91.5	90.5	90.0	33.5	28.5	88.0	116.0	89.0	98.5
inf. cases	1	1	1	1	1	1	2	1	1	1	1	1	2	2	2	2	1	1	
range	—	—	—	—	—	—	109; 110	—	—	—	—	—	—	29; 32	26; 27	84; 92	103; 120	—	—
average	1080.0	114.0	149.0	118.0	486.0	313.0	109.5	107.0	97.0	98.0	90.0	87.0	82.0	30.5	26.5	88.0	111.5	80.0	80.0
Bella Bella																			
4635 ♂ ad	1440	172	158	127	528	349	120	112	117	112	96	95	97	34	32	93	126	98	—
4636 ♂ mat	1360	168	153	130	503	346	123	110	113	113	92	91	96	33	26	94	117	102	—
4637 ♂? ad	1280	159	141	131	475	342	120	114	108	107	99	86	88	35	25	92	115	94	—
4638 ♂ mat	1330	171	144	140	500	353	130	109	114	117	101	89	98	33	29	98	117	93	—
4639 ♂ mat	1330	173	141	137	505	345	125	105	115	114	94	95	105	40	31	89	112	101	—
4640 ♂ ad	1230	166	144	120	490	329	114	105	110	106	93	90	97	31	24	91	114	105	—
4641 ♂ mat	1360	179	147	139	518	368	128	106	134	115	98	105	100	33	27	103	119	102	—
4642 ♀ ad-mat	1250	166	138	134	487	341	116	100?	125	106	90	95	94	34	29	95	116	98	—
4643 ♂ mat	1440	180	150	125	524	357	121	120	116	108	105	91	99	34	34	87	116?	102	—
4644 ♂ sen	1510	175	157	137	525	366	127	115	124	116	102	96	103	34	33	100	122?	—	—
♂ cases	9	9	9	9	9	9	9	9	9	9	9	9	9	9	9	9	9	8	
range	1230– 1510	159– 197	141– 158	120– 140	490– 528	329– 368	114– 130	105– 120	108– 134	106– 117	92– 105	86– 105	96– 105	31– 40	24– 34	87– 103	112– 126	93– 105	—
average	1394.4	173.4	148.3	131.8	510.1	350.5	123.1	110.7	116.8	112.0	97.8	93.1	99.2	34.0	29.0	94.1	117.6	99.6	—
♀ 1 case	1250.0	166.0	138.0	134.0	487.0	341.0	116.0	100.0	125.0	106.0	90.0	95.0	94.0	34.0	29.0	95.0	116.0	98.0	—

								FACE AND MANDIBLE															
Height		Breadth						Orbit			Nose		Nasal bones		Maxillo-alveolar		Palatal		Mandible				
																			Breadth		Height		
Upper height (n-pr)	Total height (n-gn)	Bizygomatic	Upper facial (fmt-fmt)	Mid-facial (zm-zm)	Biorbital (ek-ek)	Ant. interorb. (mf-mf)	Post. interorb. (la-la)	Width (mf-ek)	Width (h-ek)	Height	Width	Height	Breadth (minimum)	Breadth (maximum)	Length	Breadth	Length	Width	Bicondylar	Bigonial	Ramus	Ramus	Chin
mm.	mm.	mm.	mm.	mm.	mm.	mm.	mm.	mm.	mm.	mm.	mm.	mm.	mm.	mm.	mm.	mm.	mm.	mm.	mm.	mm.	mm.	mm.	mm.
53	—	—	94	—	88	17	22	39	35	32	20	39	8	16	41	56	36	31	86	83	28	39	26
62	96	120	94	90	87	18	21	36	33	32	22	42	9	18	46	59	39	34	113	92	34	44	28
—	—	—	—	—	—	—	—	—	—	—	—	—	—	—	—	—	—	—	85	69	22	36	22
—	—	—	—	—	—	—	—	—	—	—	—	—	—	—	—	—	—	—	—	—	26	37	23
67	—	—	—	—	—	15	17	—	—	—	25	47	7	12	48	57?	45	—	—	—	33	56	33
74	121	136	107	99	97	18	23	41	37	37	24	54	9	17	52	63	45	40	121	105	37	60	38
66?	112	137	106	98?	98	18	24	42	38	34	24	46	8	15?	48	63	43	42	117	95	40	62	33
65	102	136	104	95	95	16	20	42	37	35	24	46	8	14	50	58?	45	53	119	98	30	47	30
7	6	6	5	4	6	5	7	7	7	7	7	7	7	7	7	7	7	7	6	6	6	6	6
65–	107–	130	100–	94–	93–	15–	20–	40–	36–	30	20–	46–	2–9	11–	48–	60–	43–	37–	112–	82	33–	50–	32–
74	124	147	107	100	99	20	24	44	40	37	25	54		17	57	67	48	44	129	105	40	63	38
69.3	113.5	137.2	103.8	98.0	97.0	17.6	21.1	41.7	37.9	33.4	22.9	49.4	7.1	14.4	52.3	63.9	45.4	41.7	117.8	95.3	36.7	58.0	34.7
2	1	1	1	1	1	2	2	1	1	1	1	2	2	2	2	2	2	1	1	1	2	2	2
65 ;	—	—	—	—	15 ;	17 ;	—	—	—	46 ;	7 ; 8	12 ;	48 ;	57 ;	45 ;	—	—	—	30 ;	47 ;	30 ;		
67					16	20					47		14	50	58	45					33	56	33
66.0	102.0	136.0	104.0	95.0	95.0	15.5	18.5	42.0	37.0	35.0	24.0	46.5	7.5	13.0	49.0	57.5	45.0	43.0	119.0	98.0	31.5	51.5	31.5
2	2	2	2	2	2	2	2	2	2	2	2	2	2	2	2	2	2	2	1	1	2	2	2
62 ;	96 ;	120 ;	94 ;	90 ;	87 ;	18 ;	21 ;	36 ;	33 ;	32 ;	21 ;	39 ;	9 ; 9	14 ;	46 ;	59 ;	39 ;	34 ;			32 ;	44 ;	27 ;
64	103	128	99	90	92	19	23	40	36	34	22	39		16	46	59	41	39			34	51	28
63.0	99.5	124.0	96.5	90.0	89.5	18.5	22.0	38.0	34.5	33.0	21.5	39.0	9.0	15.0	46.0	59.0	40.0	36.5	113.0	92.0	33.0	47.5	27.5
2	1	1	2	1	2	2	2	2	2	2	2	2	2	2	2	2	2	2	3	3	4	4	4
52 ;	—	—	86 ;	—	80 ;	16 ;	20 ;	35 ;	31 ;	31 ;	20 ;	42 ;	8 ; 8	15 ;	36 ;	52 ;	34 ;	31 ;	85–	69–	22–	36–	22–
53			94		88	17	22	39	35	32	21	49		18	41	56	36	31	95	83	28	39	26
52.5	84.0	106.0	90.0	75.0	84.0	16.5	21.0	37.0	33.0	31.5	20.5	45.3	8.0	16.5	38.5	54.0	35.0	31.0	88.7	77.7	25.8	37.8	23.8
76	—	152	108	107	101	18	23	44	40	37	22	55	8	13	53	68	45	42	—	—	—	—	—
72	—	137	109	101	103	18	24	45	41	35	23	50	8	15	53	67	45	41	—	—	—	—	—
68	—	125	99	91	94	16	22	40	37	35	23	48	8	15	50	61	45	37	—	—	—	—	—
72	—	143	106	99	98	16	21	43	39	36	24	52	8	15	52	64	43	40	—	—	—	—	—
72	—	147	105	102	102	18	22	44	40	38	27	52	10	16	54	64	45	40	—	—	—	—	—
66	—	136	105	99	99	16	21	43	39	35	21	43	6	15	54	63	46	41	—	—	—	—	—
78	—	139	112	103	106	20	26	45	40	37	23	54	10	17	56	71	48	43	—	—	—	—	—
78	—	137	105	97?	99	—	18	42	—	38	24	52	8	14	55	64	47	40	—	—	—	—	—
78	—	146	108	104	104	16	23	46	42	38	23	55	8	15	55	67	48	40	—	—	—	—	—
—	—	155	—	—	—	21	24	47	43	36	25	55	8	14	—	—	—	—	—	—	—	—	—
8	—	9	8	8	8	9	9	9	9	9	9	9	9	9	8	8	8	8					
66–	—	125–	99–	99–	94–	16–	21–	40–	37–	35–	21–	43–	6–10	13–	50–	61–	43–	37–	—	—	—	—	—
78		155	112	107	106	21	26	47	43	38	27	55		17	55	71	48	43					
72.7	—	142.2	103.1	100.8	100.9	17.7	22.9	44.1	40.1	36.3	23.4	51.5	8.2	15.0	53.3	65.6	45.6	40.5	—	—	—	—	—
78.0	—	137.0	105.0	97.0	99.0	—	18.0	42.0	—	38.0	24.0	52.0	8.0	14.0	55.0	64.0	47.0	40.0	—	—	—	—	—

Tribal divisions and subdivisions / Catalogue No. / Sex and stages of life / Number of cases / Averages and ranges	Capacity	Length	Breadth	Height (ba-b)	Circumference (horizontal)	SKULL Median-sagittal Arc Total (n-o)	Frontal	Parietal	Occipital	Chord Frontal	Parietal	Occipital	Cranial base (length n-ba)	Foramen magnum Length	Width	Frontal bone Breadth (minimum)	Breadth (maximum)	Length Length (ba-pr)	Inferior length (ba-gn)
	ccm.	mm.	mm.	mm.	mm.	mm.	mm.	mm.	mm.	mm.	mm.	mm.	mm.	mm.	mm.	mm.	mm.	mm.	mm.
COWICHAN																			
Bella Coola																			
4542 ♂ ad-mat	1290	167	152	130	500	346	121	117	108	109	102	88	97	32	28	97	115	101	—
4543 ♂ ad-mat	—	—	—	127	—	—	115	—	—	106	—	—	93	33	30	89	113	96	—
4544 ♂ ad-mat	1280	169	144	131	501	351	123	125	123	112	94	97	98	32	28	106	120	104	—
4545 ♀ ad	1210	164	145	130	480	349	120	120	119	109	106	90	91	32	27	85	110	94	—
4546 ♂ ad-mat	1420	169	160	137	519	347	124	109	114	115	96	96	100	38	31	100	118	104	—
4547 ♂ mat	1460	178	149	138	517	360	126	109	125	113	98	102	102	36	31	96	119	101	—
4548A ♂ ad-mat	—	—	—	—	—	—	—	—	—	—	—	—	—	—	—	97	—	—	—
4549 ♂ ad-mat	—	—	—	—	—	—	—	—	—	—	—	—	—	—	—	97	—	—	—
4551 inf. II	1210	162	142	120	475	328	117	90	121	103	84	98	85	35	27	92	113	80	—
4552 inf. I	—	—	—	—	—	—	100	—	—	92	—	—	—	—	—	90	107	—	—
4625 ♂ juv-ad	1480	162	152	132	493	351	122	109	120	109	97	100	90	37	31	96	121	90	—
4626 ♂ ad-mat	1400	175	147	133	517	349	122	117	110	108	104	89	99	38	31	101	118	99	—
4627 ♂ mat	1590	185	157	140	545	368	131	113	124	118	102	100	110	43	35	104	124	112	—
4628 ♀ ad-mat	1190	161	142	128	478	333	108	105	120	101	92	97	92	33	27	88	113	—	—
4629 ♂ ? mat	1270	166	148	131	498	336	111	105	120	106	93	101	100	—	—	—	116	102	—
4630 ♂ ad-mat	1340	169	152	130	505	333	125	110	108	114	96	90	97	36	28	98	118	97	—
4631 ♂ mat	1340	166	153	133	499	354	122	99	133	111	86	103	93	33	26	97	122	94	—
4632 ♂ ad-mat (def?)	1530	178	153	137	519	350	125	89	136	116	82	108	106	38	31	94	120	101	—
4633 ♂ mat	1360	170	150	130	501	337	114	103	120	107	91	92	96	36	31	90	115	103	114
4634 ♂ mat (def?)	1280	164	147	—	497	337	117	108	112	110	96	91	—	—	—	95	116	—	—
♂ cases	13	13	13	13	13	13	14	13	13	14	13	13	12	13	13	15	14	13	1
range	1270–1590	162–185	144–160	127–140	493–545	333–368	111–131	89–117	108–136	106–116	82–112	88–108	90–110	32–43	26–35	89–106	113–124	90–112	
average	1387.7	170.6	151.1	133.0	508.5	347.6	121.3	107.1	119.5	111.0	95.9	96.7	98.6	35.9	29.5	97.1	118.2	100.3	114.1
♀ cases	2	2	2	2	2	2	2	2	2	2	2	2	2	2	2	2	2	1	
range	1190;1210	161;164	142;145	128;130	478;480	333;349	108;120	105;120	119;120	101;109	92;106	90;97	91;92	33;33	27;27	85;88	110;113	—	—
average	1200.0	162.5	143.5	129.0	479.0	341.0	114.0	112.5	119.5	105.0	99.0	94.5	91.5	33.0	27.0	86.5	111.5	94.0	—
inf. cases	1	1	1	1	1	1	2	1	1	2	1	1	1	1	1	2	2	1	—
range	—	—	—	—	—	—	100;117	—	—	92;103	—	—	—	—	—	90;92	107;113	—	—
average	1210.0	162.0	142.0	120.0	475.0	328.0	108.5	90.0	121.0	97.5	84.0	98.0	85.0	35.0	27.0	91.0	110.0	80.0	—
About Vancouver																			
1537 ♀ ad-mat (def)	1130	158	141	122	471	325	118	90	117	110	79	100	94	35	31	90	109	101	109
1539 ♂ ad	—	—	—	—	—	—	116	—	—	109	—	—	—	—	—	96	108	—	—
1544 ♂ ad	1240	162	131	140	474	358	116	132	110	106	106	97	99	33	27	87	103	108	—
1549 ♂ ad	1330	175	137	134	493	353	119	121	113	111	106	100	103	36	30	91	110	—	—
1567 ♂ mat	—	176	144	133	509?	344	114	113	117	104	101	97	104	36	30	—	120	—	—
1568 ♂ ad	—	174	138	124	505?	342	115	117	110	107	104	91	96	37	29	88	—	94	—
1570 ♂ mat	—	—	—	—	—	—	—	—	—	—	—	—	—	—	—	—	—	—	—
1574 ♀ ad-mat	1240	163	144	—	488	—	112	107	—	102	94	—	—	—	—	98	116	—	—

18

FACE AND MANDIBLE

Height		Breadth						Orbit			Nose		Nasal bones		Maxillo-alveolar		Palatal		Mandible Breadth		Mandible Height		
Upper height (n-pr)	Total height (n-gn)	Bizygomatic	Upper facial (fmt-fmt)	Mid-facial (zm-zm)	Biorbital (ek-ek)	Ant. interorb. (mf-mf)	Post. interorb. (la-la)	Width (mf-ek)	Width (la-ek)	Height	Width	Height	Breadth (minimum)	Breadth (maximum)	Length	Breadth	Length	Width	Bicondylar	Bigonial	Ramus	Ramus	Chin
mm.	mm.	mm.	mm.	mm.	mm.	mm.	mm.	mm.	mm.	mm.	mm.	mm.	mm.	mm.	mm.	mm.	mm.	mm.	mm.	mm.	mm.	mm.	mm.
71	—	138	108	102	101	18	23	43	40	34	22	50	9	16	55	62	49	40	—	—	—	—	—
77	—	128	106	98	99	17	22	45	39	36	23	54	6	16	55	64	47	41	—	—	—	—	—
77	—	143	114	106	105	16	23	48	42	34	23	53	8	16	56	63	52	41	—	—	—	—	—
66	—	133	99	100	93	15	19	40	37	35	23	48	7	14	51	64	46	43	—	—	—	—	—
77	—	148	111	99	101	16	21	44	40	36	22	50	8	15	59	65	52	40	—	—	—	—	—
76	—	148	109	108	101	19	25	43	37	35	26	56	9	17	52	65	48	42	—	—	—	—	—
71	—	—	120	109	111	—	—	45	40	36	24	50	10	—	53	70	44	42	—	—	—	—	—
—	—	—	—	—	—	—	—	44	39	37	23?	53?	—	—	—	—	—	—	—	—	—	—	—
59?	—	—	96	—	—	18	20	39	36r	34r	—	41	—	—	—	—	—	—	—	—	—	—	—
52	—	—	91	77	85	17	20	36	34	31	19	35	7	15	35	53	32	29	—	—	—	—	—
71	—	128	103	94	96	15	21	43	40	37	22	49	8	15	49	63	43	38	—	—	—	—	—
68	—	145	111	100	102	19	23	43	40	37	26	48	9	16	55	64?	48	40	—	—	—	—	—
84	—	163	115	113	105	20	25	43	40	39	27	59	12	18	57	69	51	43	—	—	—	—	—
—	—	130	100	93	95	14	20?	43	38?	36	22	50	6	13?	—	—	—	—	—	—	—	—	—
76	—	138	109	99	101	19	22	42	39	34	25	54	13	17	54	60	45	39	—	—	—	—	—
73	—	141	112	100	102	18	22	43	40	37	21	50	7	15	51	69	45	42	—	—	—	—	—
71	—	142	108	101	98	20	26	42	38	36	25	53	10	15	51	66	46	41	—	—	—	—	—
75	—	148	109	102	102	18	22	43	40	35	26	58	10	17	55	64	47	38	—	—	—	—	—
83	125	147	106	108	98	16	20	42	39	38	25	60	11	18	54	60?	46	34?	117	107	38	67	36
75	—	141?	112	106	105	20	23	45	40	35	25	53	10	17	57	64	52	41	—	—	—	—	—
15	1	14	15	15	15	14	14	16	16	16	16	16	15	14	15	15	15	15	1	1	1	1	1
68–84	—	128–163	103–120	94–113	96–111	15–20	20–26	42–48	37–42	34–39	21–27	48–60	6–13	15–18	49–59	60–70	43–52	34–43	—	—	—	—	—
75.0	15.0	142.7	110.2	103.0	101.8	17.9	22.7	43.6	39.6	36.0	24.1	53.1	9.3	16.3	54.2	64.5	47.7	40.1	117.0	107.0	38.0	67.0	36.0
1	—	2	2	2	2	2	2	2	2	2	2	2	2	2	1	1	1	1	—	—	—	—	—
—	—	130; 133	99; 100	—	93; 95	14; 15	19; 20	40; 43	37; 38	35; 36	22; 23	48; 50	6; 7	13; 14	—	—	—	—	—	—	—	—	—
66.0	—	131.5	99.5	100.0	93.5	14.5	19.5	41.5	37.5	35.5	22.5	49.0	6.5	13.5	51.0	64.0	46.0	43.0	—	—	—	—	—
2	—	—	2	1	1	2	2	2	2	2	1	2	1	1	1	1	1	1	—	—	—	—	—
52; 59	—	—	91; 96	—	—	17; 18	20; 20	36; 39	34; 36	31; 34	—	35; 41	—	—	—	—	—	—	—	—	—	—	—
55.5	—	—	93.5	77.0	85.0	17.5	20.0	37.5	35.0	32.5	19.0	38.0	7.0	15.0	35.0	53.0	32.0	29.0	—	—	—	—	—
72	115	133	103	—	—	17	23	42	38	36	26	50	6	16	52	63	46	39	120	90	35	61	35
62	—	—	102	88	94	16	22	43	39	34	24	45	8	16?	53	60	47	35	—	—	—	—	—
72	—	129	98	92	90	16	18	39	36	33	20	49	8	14	57	59	52	36	—	—	—	—	—
—	—	139?	100	—	—	18?	21?	—	—	—	—	—	—	—	—	—	—	—	—	—	—	—	—
—	—	—	—	—	—	16?	—	—	—	—	—	—	—	—	—	—	—	—	126?	105	39	61?	38
74?	—	—	97	—	—	15	18	43	37	37	22	52	7	11	52	61	47	38	—	—	—	—	—
—	—	—	—	—	—	—	—	—	—	—	—	—	—	—	—	—	—	—	128?	113	38	57	37?
69?	—	127	105	96	98	18	24	43	39?	38	23	46	8	16	55	63	48	40	—	—	—	—	—

Tribal divisions and subdivisions						SKULL												
							Median-sagittal							Foramen magnum		Frontal bone		Length	
Catalogue No.	Capacity	Length	Breadth	Height (ba-b)	Circumference (horizontal)		Arc			Chord			Cranial base (length n-ba)						
Sex and stages of life						Total (n-o)	Frontal	Parietal	Occipital	Frontal	Parietal	Occipital		Length	Width	Breadth (minimum)	Breadth (maximum)	Length (ba-pr)	Inferior length (ba-gn)
Number of cases																			
Averages and ranges																			
COWICHAN	ccm.	mm.	mm.	mm.	mm.	mm.	mm.	mm.	mm.	mm.	mm.	mm.	mm.	mm.	mm.	mm.	mm.	mm.	mm.
1579 ♂ mat	1380	171	146	134	508	347	124	113	105	110	104	88	102	—	—	—	—	101	—
1581 ♂ mat	1500	179	148	132	526	366	123	125	117	111	108	99	103	34	27	103	125	—	—
1581A ♂ mat	—	—	—	—	—	—	—	—	—	—	—	—	—	—	—	—	—	—	—
1583 ♂ mat	1460	177	157	133	534	356	122	115	119	108	98	96	107	33	31	106	127	108?	—
1586 ♀ ad	1200	164	140	125	477	—	118	112	—	105	100	—	88	—	—	—	—	85	—
1587 inf. I	—	—	—	—	—	—	—	—	—	—	—	—	—	—	—	—	—	—	—
1588 ♂ mat	—	—	—	—	—	—	—	—	—	—	—	—	—	—	—	—	—	—	—
1596 ♂ ad-mat	1430	180	146	132	520	366	125	111	130	114	99	111	102	35	27?	100	117	96	—
1749 ♂ ad-mat	—	—	—	—	—	—	119	129	—	110	107	—	—	—	—	91	126	—	—
1752 ♀ mat	1270	166	137	131	480	359	122	124	113	108	104	95	92	34	29	90	106	96	—
1754A ♂ ad-mat	—	—	—	—	—	—	—	—	—	—	—	—	—	—	—	—	—	—	—
1754B ♂ mat	—	—	—	—	—	—	—	—	—	—	—	—	—	—	—	—	—	—	—
1756 ♂ mat	—	168	147	—	495	—	124	123?	—	115	107	—	—	—	—	89	113	—	—
1757 ♂ ad (def.)	1300	153	159	126	484	329	123	100	106	111	84	89	91	31	27	87	118	95	110
1761 ♂ ad	—	—	—	—	—	—	—	—	—	—	—	—	—	—	—	—	—	—	—
1762 ♂ ad	1420	169	145	134	497	360	128	104	128	115	93	105	91	37	30	94	122?	97?	106
1763 ♂ ad	—	—	—	—	—	—	—	—	—	—	—	—	—	—	—	—	—	—	—
1764 ♀ mat	1250	169	139	135	490	347	120	122	105	108	108	89	95	38	30	88	113	—	—
1766 ♂ mat	—	—	—	—	—	—	124	—	—	111	—	—	—	—	—	103	131	—	—
1767 ♂ mat	—	—	—	—	—	—	—	—	—	—	—	—	—	—	—	—	—	—	—
1768 inf. I	—	—	—	—	—	—	—	—	—	—	—	—	—	—	—	—	—	—	—
1770 ♀ mat	1250	164	147	126	488	349	124	115	110	113	100	91	92	33	28	98	115	97	106
1777 ♂ mat	—	—	—	—	—	—	—	—	—	—	—	—	—	—	—	—	—	—	—
1780 ♂ mat (def.)	1340	156	157	—	499	334	116	109	109	108	91	94	—	—	—	98	123	—	—
1781 ♂ ad-mat	—	—	—	—	—	—	—	—	—	—	—	—	—	—	—	—	—	—	—
1782 ♂ ad-mat	—	160	146	125	—	—	113	115	—	103	97	—	95	—	—	85	116	98	—
1784 ♀ ad-mat (def.)	1230	146	161	127	471	322	113	111	98	106	90	87	89	31	27	92	119	87	—
1787 ♂? mat	—	163	138	133	480	345	114	124	107	103	105	87	97	32	30	95	112	—	—
1788 ♂ ad	1520	170	158	142	519	—	129	118	118	116	103	93	101	35	30	100	125	102	117
1790 ♂ ad	—	—	—	—	—	—	—	—	—	—	—	—	—	—	—	—	—	—	—
1792 ♂ mat (def.)	—	157	160	—	494	—	116	—	—	107	—	—	—	—	—	98	122	—	—
1796 ♂ mat	—	178	150	—	520	376	127	128	121	114	111	98	—	—	—	100	122?	—	—
1799 ♀ mat (def.)	1110	153	144	126	469	314	118	87	109	108	77	95	97	34	27	89	115?	101	—
1800 ♂ ad	—	—	—	—	—	—	—	—	—	—	—	—	—	—	—	—	—	—	—
1807 ♂ mat	—	156	144	—	—	—	119	102	—	112	87	—	—	—	—	83	110	—	—
1810 ♂ mat	—	—	—	—	—	—	—	—	—	—	—	—	—	—	—	—	—	—	—
1811 ♂ mat	—	—	—	—	—	—	—	—	—	—	—	—	—	—	—	89	—	—	—
1812 ♂? mat	—	182	139	—	516	383	131	124	128	116	109	109	—	—	—	96	—	—	—
1813 ♂? mat	—	171	140	—	501	369	133	110	126	116	97	106	—	—	—	95	122	—	—
1817 ♀ mat	—	—	—	—	—	—	—	—	—	—	—	—	—	—	—	—	—	—	—
1818 ♂ mat	—	—	—	—	—	—	—	—	—	—	—	—	—	—	—	—	—	—	—

FACE AND MANDIBLE

Height		Breadth						Orbit			Nose		Nasal bones		Maxillo-alveolar		Palatal		Mandible				
																			Breadth		Height		
Upper height (n-pr)	Total height (n-gn)	Bizygomatic	Upper facial (fmt-fmt)	Mid-facial (zm-zm)	Biorbital (ek-ek)	Ant. interorb. (mf-mf)	Post. interorb. (la-la)	Width (mf-ek)	Width (la-ek)	Height	Width	Height	Breadth (minimum)	Breadth (maximum)	Length	Breadth	Length	Width	Bicondylar	Bigonial	Ramus	Ramus	Chin
mm.	mm.	mm.	mm.	mm.	mm	mm.	mm.	mm.	mm.	mm.	mm.	mm.	mm.	mm.	mm.	mm.	mm.	mm.	mm.	mm.	mm.	mm.	mm.
77?	—	142	109	—	—	18	—	44	41	36	22	50	12	—	54	60	45	35	—	—	—	—	—
—	—	—	111	—	101	20	25	43	38	36	—	—	7	15	—	—	—	—	112	92	34	55	34
75?	—	—	112	106	103	20	25	44	40	39	26	51?	9	17	59	68	56	43	—	—	—	—	—
63	—	—	98	88	93	18	19	40	37	35	22	47	9	15	46	56	39	34	—	—	—	—	—
—	—	—	—	—	—	—	—	—	—	—	—	—	—	—	—	—	—	—	101	81	28	38	26
—	—	—	—	—	—	—	—	—	—	—	—	—	—	—	—	—	—	—	133?	108	37	74	40
73?	—	—	109	103	103	19	—	43	—	38	25	55	7	13	52	69	48	45	—	—	—	—	—
71?	—	—	108	93?	100	15	22	46	42r	37	23	54	6	10	51?	58	47	39	—	—	—	—	—
64	—	—	95	86	88	14	17	41	38	35	22	47	6	14	54	59	48	37	—	—	—	—	—
—	—	—	—	—	—	—	—	—	—	—	—	—	—	—	—	—	—	—	110?	104	34	57	32
—	—	—	—	—	—	—	—	—	—	—	—	—	—	—	—	—	—	—	140	120	37	64	40
69	—	—	102	—	—	16	19	42	39	35	—	—	8	13	—	—	—	—	—	—	—	—	—
68	112	130	97	89?	90	14	18?	40	36	37	25	46	7	12?	52	57	48	36	115	98	37	52	33
—	—	—	—	—	—	—	—	—	—	—	—	—	—	—	—	—	—	—	123?	95?	39	62	36
69	119	—	—	—	—	15	19	42	39	35	22	49	6	13?	53	59	47	38	116?	93?	37	63	36
—	—	—	—	—	—	—	—	—	—	—	—	—	—	—	—	—	—	—	117?	105	37	58	38
—	—	—	101?	—	—	14?	—	—	—	—	—	—	—	—	—	—	—	—	—	—	—	—	35
73	—	—	108	103	101	18	23	45	41	35	26	54	8	—	53	64	47	42	—	—	37	—	34
—	—	—	—	—	—	—	—	—	—	—	—	—	—	—	—	—	—	—	127?	104?	40	60	35
—	—	—	—	—	—	—	—	—	—	—	—	—	—	—	—	—	—	—	98	80	24	40	26?
66?	106?	133	106	87	96	16	21?	45	41	35	25	44	8	15	51?	59	49?	40	121	94?	36	59	33
—	—	—	—	—	—	—	—	—	—	—	—	—	—	—	—	—	—	—	129?	92?	37	57	35
78?	—	—	107	102?	102?	16	22?	47	41	40	23	53	8	15?	51	70 (!)	48	45	—	—	—	—	—
—	—	—	—	—	—	—	—	—	—	—	—	—	—	—	—	—	—	—	—	—	35	59	36
69	—	—	102	90	95	15	21	41	38	34	25	47	6	16	47	61	44	40	—	—	—	—	—
63?	—	—	96	—	89	15	20	39	36	35	22	47	8	—	43	57	42	34?	—	—	—	—	—
—	—	—	101	—	—	—	—	—	—	—	—	—	8	—	—	—	—	—	—	—	—	—	—
77	126	—	104	—	94	18	22	41	37	39	24	56	9	—	56	63	53	42	—	—	42	64	37
—	—	—	—	—	—	—	—	—	—	—	—	—	—	—	—	—	—	—	127	108	37	60	37
80	—	144	105	99	100?	19	—	46	40	37	22	53	7	—	58	61	49	37	—	—	—	—	—
70	—	128?	99	89	94	16	19	40	38	39	22	52	7	14?	55	59	49	38	—	—	—	—	—
—	—	—	—	—	—	—	—	—	—	—	—	—	—	—	—	—	—	—	120?	98	38	58	32
70	—	136	99	96	95	16	22	43	39	36	21	52	6	13	61	56	53	33	—	—	—	—	—
—	—	—	—	—	—	—	—	—	—	—	—	—	—	—	—	—	—	—	—	—	37	54	35?
68	—	—	—	—	—	17	21?	40	37	34	23	50	7	14?	—	—	—	—	122	108	43r	52r	35
—	—	—	101	—	—	—	—	—	—	—	—	—	—	—	—	—	—	—	126	114	37	58	37?
—	—	—	—	—	—	—	—	—	—	—	—	—	—	—	—	—	—	—	—	—	36r	50r	35
—	—	—	—	—	—	—	—	—	—	—	—	—	—	—	—	—	—	—	—	—	37	61	34r

Tribal divisions and subdivisions / Catalogue No. / Sex and stages of life / Number of cases / Averages and ranges	Capacity	Length	Breadth	Height (ba-b)	Circumference (horizontal)	SKULL Median-sagittal Arc Total (n-o)	Frontal	Parietal	Occipital	Chord Frontal	Parietal	Occipital	Cranial base (length n-ba)	Foramen magnum Length	Width	Frontal bone Breadth (minimum)	Breadth (maximum)	Length Length (ba-pr)	Inferior length (ba-gn)
	ccm.	mm.	mm.	mm.	mm.	mm.	mm.	mm.	mm.	mm.	mm.	mm.	mm.	mm.	mm.	mm.	mm.	mm.	mm.
COWICHAN																			
1819 ♀ ad	—	—	—	—	—	—	—	—	—	—	—	—	—	—	—	—	—	—	—
1821 ♀ ad (def.)	1260	155	149	—	476	326	123	113	100	110	95	89	—	—	—	87	115	—	3
♂ cases	10	18	18	13	17	15	23	20	16	23	20	16	13	11	11	20	18	9	3
range	1240–1520	153–182	131–161	124–142	474–534	329–383	113–133	110–132	105–130	104–116	84–109	91–111	91–107	31–37	27–31	85–106	103–131	94–108	106–117
average	1392.0	169.5	146.6	132.5	504.6	355.2	121.3	116.9	116.5	110.3	100.9	98.1	99.3	34.5	28.9	95.1	119.4	99.9	111.0
♀ cases	9	9	9	7	9	7	9	9	7	9	9	7	7	6	6	8	8	6	2
range	1110–1270	146–169	137–161	122–135	469–490	314–359	112–124	87–124	98–117	102–113	77–108	87–100	88–97	31–38	27–31	87–98	106–119	85–101	106; 109
average	1215.5	159.8	144.4	127.4	478.9	334.6	118.7	109.0	107.4	107.8	94.1	92.3	92.4	34.2	28.7	91.5	113.5	94.5	107.5
inf. cases	—	—	—	—	—	—	—	—	—	—	—	—	—	—	—	—	—	—	—
range	—	—	—	—	—	—	—	—	—	—	—	—	—	—	—	—	—	—	—
average	—	—	—	—	—	—	—	—	—	—	—	—	—	—	—	—	—	—	—
Comox																			
2291 ♀ ad	—	—	—	134	—	—	123	103	—	114	86	—	88	32	28	89	—	94	101?
♀ 1 case	—	—	—	134.0	—	—	123.0	103.0	—	114.0	86.0	—	88.0	32.0	28.0	89.0	—	94.0	101.0
N. Saanich																			
1698 ♂ ad-mat (def.)	1260	160	147	141	481	359	124	108	127	115	91	111	96	30	28	85	113?	93	104?
1699 ♂ mat (def.)	—	168	147	135	497	355	125	100	130	115?	85?	111?	102	—	—	86	—	106	104
1701 ♂ mat (def.)	1480	173	149	139	512	333	113	115	105	120	98	95	106	35	30	102	124	104	114
1702 ♂ mat (def.)	—	172	155	117	512	339	115	122	102	105	101	97	101	31	29	97	121	106?	—
1703 ♀ ad	—	—	—	—	—	122	—	—	—	—	—	—	—	—	—	100	—	—	—
1706 ♂ ad-mat (def.)	1400	178	153	126	521	347	122	115	110	111	100	92	105	35	30	100	125	110	120
1707 ♂ mat (def.)	1340	159	157	123	490	333	114	101	118	105	85	102	93	32	34!	101	123?	101	—
1710 ♂ mat	—	174?	149?	—	—	—	126	113	—	118	99	—	—	31	30	93	—	—	—
2637 ♂ ad-mat	—	—	—	—	—	—	—	—	—	—	—	—	—	—	—	—	—	—	—
2644A ♂ mat	1570	178	159	137	537	356	131	110	115	119	95	99	105	40	29	99	127	106	117
2644B ♂ mat (def.)	1530	170	162	133	513	343	128	110	105	119	92	99?	105	35	30	97	130	117	120
2646 ♂ mat	—	167	—	—	—	—	111	115	—	104	100	—	—	—	—	—	—	—	—
2661 ♂ ad-mat (def.)	1350	169	159	133	515	340	121	117	102	112	98	87	108	30	30	101	128	113	—
2666 ♂ mat	1310	174	149	123	507	353	117	125	111	106	109	92	96	32	28	98	119	103	108
♂ cases	8	12	11	10	10	10	12	12	10	12	12	10	10	10	10	11	9	9	8
range	1260–1570	159–187	147–162	117–141	481–537	333–359	111–128	100–125	105–130	105–120	85–120	87–111	93–108	30–40	28–34	85–102	113–130	93–117	104–120
average	1417.5	170.3	153.3	130.7	508.5	345.8	120.6	111.7	116.0	112.4	112.4	98.5	101.7	33.1	29.8	96.2	123.3	105.9	111.6
♀ 1 case	—	—	—	—	—	—	122.0	—	—	115.0	—	—	—	—	—	100.0	—	—	—
Nanaimo																			
1618 ♂ mat (def.)	1560	172	167	133	528	356	119	106	111	111	95	95	105	36	31	102	130	104?	—
1619 ♀ juv-ad (def.)	1130	154	143	128	462	309	100	97	112	91	87	94	91	36	32	95	110	—	—

22

							FACE AND MANDIBLE													
Height		Breadth						Orbit			Nose		Nasal bones		Maxillo-alveolar		Palatal		Mandible			
																			Breadth		Height	
Upper height (n-pr)	Total height (n-gn)	Bizygomatic	Upper facial (fmt-fmt)	Mid-facial (zm-zm)	Biorbital (ek-ek)	Ant. interorb. (mf-mf)	Post. interorb. (la-la)	Width (mf-ek)	Width (la-ek)	Height	Width	Height	Breadth (minimum)	Breadth (maximum)	Length	Breadth	Length	Width	Bicondylar	Bigonial	Ramus	Ramus	Chin
mm.	mm.	mm.	mm.	mm.	mm.	mm.	mm.	mm.	mm.	mm.	mm.	mm.	mm.	mm.	mm.	mm.	mm.	mm.	mm.	mm.	mm.	mm.	mm.
—	—	—	—	—	—	—	—	—	—	—	—	—	—	—	—	—	—	—	122?	91?	35	47	30?
70	114	135	98	91	93?	15	18	40	38	36	22	49	7?	—	53	61	49	41	113	102	38	55	34
16	3	6	16	11	13	18	14	16	15	16	15	15	19	14	15	15	15	15	16	15	21	20	20
62–80	112–126	129–144	97–112	88–106	90–103	14–20	18–25	39–47	36–42	33–40	20–27	45–56	6–12	10–17	47–61	56–70	44–56	33–45	110–140	92–120	34–42	52–74	32–40
72.3	119.0	136.7	104.6	96.5	97.5	16.9	23.0	42.9	38.8	36.3	23.8	50.9	7.6	13.7	53.9	61.7	48.7	38.9	125.0	103.7	37.7	59.3	35.7
8	3	5	9	6	7	9	8	8	8	8	8	8	8	6	8	8	8	8	4	4	5	5	6
63–72	106–115	127–135	95–106	86–96	88–98	14–18	17–24	39–45	36–41	35–39	22–26	44–52	6–9	14–16	43–55	56–63	39–49	34–41	113–122	90–102	35–38	47–61	30–35
67.1	111.7	131.2	100.1	89.5	93.0	15.8	20.1	41.3	38.3	36.1	23.0	47.8	7.4	15.0	51.1	59.6	46.3	37.9	119.0	94.3	36.0	54.4	33.7
—	—	—	—	—	—	—	—	—	—	—	—	—	—	—	—	—	—	—	2	2	2	2	2
—	—	—	—	—	—	—	—	—	—	—	—	—	—	—	—	—	98 ; 101	80 ; 81	24 ; 28	38 ; 40	26 ; 26
—	—	—	—	—	—	—	—	—	—	—	—	—	—	—	—	—	—	—	99.5	80.5	26.0	39.0	26.0
70	110?	129?	100	95	96	17	23	42	38	33	21	49	8	15?	53	56	48	46	112	92	37	54	33
70.0	110.0	129.0	100.0	95.0	96.0	17.0	23.0	42.0	38.0	33.0	21.0	49.0	8.0	15.0	53.0	56.0	48.0	46.0	112.0	92.0	37.0	54.0	33.0
66	101	134	98	93	92	17	20?	41	39	36	26	49	9	12	47	59	—	—	—	—	46	58	31
67	105	—	106	97	98	17	20	43	40?	36	24	50	10	16	54	64	49	43	—	—	40	57	31
70?	111	—	106	102	97	18	24	42	38	35	26	53	9	14	54	67	47	41	132	104	37	60	32
73?	—	—	—	94	—	21	24?	45	40?	38	26	52	10	16	54?	62?	50?	37?	—	—	—	—	—
64	104	—	101	86	94	24	28	41	37	35	22	50	11	15	47	57	43	34	110	82	29	50	26
73	121	147	111	105	104	16	22	48	43	35	27	52	8	15?	59	73	53	47	134	108	35	70	37
67	—	135	108	97	100	19	22	44	40?	37	25	46	10	—	49	61	47	40	—	—	—	—	—
68	112	—	107	96	100	18	23	43	39	36	23	49	7	17	53	61	44	38	117	93	38	54	36
—	—	—	—	—	—	—	—	—	—	—	—	—	—	—	—	—	—	—	117	97	34	58	32
75	121	152	110	101	102	19	22	44	40	37	24	57	9	11	57	63	50	40	134	111	46!	63	34
71	114	148	110	103	102	20	23	43	38	37	25	51	3	14	61	65	54	40	132	110	37	64	36
—	—	—	—	—	—	17	24	47	40	41	21	52	7	12?	—	—	—	—	—	—	35	72	—
73	—	151?	110	101	105	22	28	45	41?	35	26	57	10	18	56	62	50	42	—	—	—	—	—
73	115	149	106	95	100	18	23	45	41	37	29	52	12	18	57	59?	51	40	116	97	31	51	34
11	8	7	10	11	9	11	11	12	12	12	12	12	10	11	11	11	11	4	7	10	10	9
66–75	101–121	134–152	98–111	93–105	92–105	16–22	20–28	41–48	38–43	35–41	21–29	46–57	3–12	10–18	47–61	59–73	43–54	34–47	116–134	93–111	31–46	51–72	31–37
70.5	112.5	146.6	107.2	98.5	100.0	18.5	22.9	44.2	39.1	36.8	25.2	51.7	8.8	16.2	54.6	63.3	48.9	40.2	126.4	102.7	37.9	60.7	38.7
64.0	104.0	—	101.0	86.0	94.0	24.0	28.0	41.0	37.0	35.0	22.0	50.0	10.0	16.0	47.0	57.0	—	—	110.0	82.0	29.0	55.0	26.0
72	—	152	111	104	100	18	25	46	40	37	25	54	8	13	56?	60	54	—	—	—	—	—	—
—	—	—	101?	—	—	23?	—	—	—	—	—	—	—	—	—	—	—	—	—	—	—	—	—

Tribal divisions and subdivisions	SKULL																
Catalogue No.							Median-sagittal						Foramen magnum		Frontal bone		Length
Sex and stages of life							Arc			Chord							
Number of cases	Capacity	Length	Breadth	Height (ba-b)	Circumference (horizontal)	Total (n-o)	Frontal	Parietal	Occipital	Frontal	Parietal	Occipital	Cranial base (length n-ba)	Length	Width	Breadth (minimum)	Breadth (maximum)	Length (ba-pr)	Inferior length (ba-gn)
Averages and ranges	ccm.	mm.	mm.	mm.	mm.	mm.	mm.	mm.	mm.	mm.	mm.	mm.	mm.	mm.	mm.	mm.	mm.	mm.
COWICHAN																		
1620 ♂ ad-mat (def.)	1490	170	162	127	518	347	114	103	130	108	92	108	98	34	32	97	124	107	119
1621 inf. I	—	—	—	—	—	—	—	—	—	—	—	—	—	—	—	—	—	—	—
1622 inf. II (def.)	1400	154	159	116	485	324	109	104	111	102	91	94	82	35	29	98	127	81	84
1623 ♀ ad-mat. (def.)	1190	154	155	115	485	305	110	87	108	104	76	94	98	31	28	88	123	105	112
1624 ♂ mat (def.)	1390	155	160!	128	495	325	111	105	105	105	93	91	94	34	33	92	131	98	107
1625 ♀ mat	1170	164	137	125	473	330	116	96	118	107	86	99	97	35	30	89	107	93?	—
1626 ♀ ad	1330	180	132	125	500	350	123	103	124	109	93	106	100	36	32	91	108	102	—
1627 ♀? ad	1240	171	134	129	482	342	124	98	120	111	90	102	96	32	29	88	110	98	103
1628 ♂ mat (def.)	1400	168	163	141	519	332	117	103	111	108	90	95	111	38	31	98	124	106	122
1629 ♂ mat (def.)	1500	173	172	134	532	352	111	113	128	108	99	104	103	31	31	101	134	102?	117
1631 ♂ mat (def.)	1490	164	174!	124	519	334	120	103	111	112	88	88	94	33	33	83	132	93	—
♂ cases	6	6	6	6	6	6	6	6	6	6	6	6	6	6	6	6	6	6	4
range	1390–1560	145–173	160–174	124–140	495–532	325–352	111–120	103–113	105–130	105–112	88–99	88–108	91–111	31–38	31–33	83–102	124–134	93–107	107–122
average	1471.7	165.3	166.3	131.0	518.5	337.7	115.3	106.2	116.0	108.7	92.8	96.8	100.8	34.3	31.8	95.5	129.2	101.7	116.3
♀ cases	5	5	5	5	5	5	5	5	5	5	5	5	5	5	5	5	5	4	2
range	1130–1330	154–180	132–155	115–129	462–500	305–350	100–124	87–103	108–124	104–111	76–93	94–106	91–100	31–36	28–32	88–95	107–123	93–105	103 ; 112
average	1212.0	164.6	140.2	124.4	480.4	326.6	114.6	96.2	118.4	103.4	86.4	99.0	96.4	34.0	30.2	90.2	111.6	99.5	107.5
inf. cases	1	1	—	1	1	1	1	1	1	1	1	1	1	1	1	1	1	1	1
range	—	—	—	—	—	—	—	—	—	—	—	—	—	—	—	—	—	—	—
average	1400.0	154.0	—	116.0	485.0	324.0	109.0	104.0	111.0	102.0	91.0	94.0	82.0	35.0	29.0	98.0	127.0	81.0	84.0
Point Roberts																		
1907A ♂ mat (def.)	1480	174	152	131	497	364	125	125	114	117	104	101	96	32	28	92	118	103	—
1908 ♀ mat	—	—	—	—	—	—	—	—	—	—	—	—	—	—	—	—	—	—	—
♂ 1 case	1480.0	174.0	152.0	131.0	497.0	364.0	125.0	125.0	114.0	117.0	104.0	101.0	96.0	32.0	28.0	92.0	118.0	103.0	—
♀ 1 case	—	—	—	—	—	—	—	—	—	—	—	—	—	—	—	—	—	—	—
Stanwood																		
2685 ♀ mat (def.)	—	168	152	—	—	343	118	112	113	112	96	103	—	—	—	—	—	—	—
2687 ♂ mat (def.)	1570	176	158	140	523	367	132	107	128	120	92	110	105	37	32	98	132	106	113
2688 ♂ ad (def.)	1460	165	167	126	525	334	122	111	101	110	94	88	105	35	33	105	141	108	—
2691 ♀? ad-mat (def.)	—	167	150	133	—	348	128	95	125	119	84	110	98	32	27	85	117	103	107
♂ cases	2	2	2	2	2	2	2	2	2	2	2	2	2	2	2	2	2	2	1
range	1460 ; 1570	165 ; 176	158 ; 167	126 ; 140	523 ; 525	334 ; 367	122 ; 132	107 ; 111	101 ; 128	110 ; 120	92 ; 94	88 ; 110	105	35 ; 37	32 ; 33	98 ; 105	132 ; 141	106 ; 108	—
average	1515.0	170.5	162.5	133.0	524.0	350.5	127.0	109.0	114.5	115.0	93.0	99.0	105.0	36.0	32.5	101.5	136.5	107.0	113.0
♀ cases	—	2	2	1	—	2	2	2	2	2	2	2	1	1	1	1	1	1	1
range	—	167 ; 168	150 ; 152	—	—	343 ; 348	118 ; 128	95 ; 112	113 ; 125	112 ; 119	84 ; 96	103 ; 110	—	—	—	—	—	—	—
average	—	167.5	151.0	133.0	—	345.5	123.0	103.5	119.0	115.0	85.0	106.5	98.0	32.0	27.0	85.0	117.0	103.0	107.0

FACE AND MANDIBLE

Height		Breadth						Orbit			Nose		Nasal bones		Maxillo-alveolar		Palatal		Mandible				
																			Breadth		Height		
Upper height (n-pr)	Total height (n-gn)	Bizygomatic	Upper facial (zm-fmt)	Mid-facial (zm-zm)	Biorbital (ek-ek)	Ant. interorb. (mf-mf)	Post. interorb. (la-la)	Width (mf-ek)	Width (la-ek)	Height	Width	Height	Breadth (minimum)	Breadth (maximum)	Length	Breadth	Length	Width	Bicondylar	Bigonial	Ramus	Ramus	Chin
mm.	mm.	mm.	mm.	mm.	mm.	mm.	mm.	mm.	mm.	mm.	mm.	mm.	mm.	mm.	mm.	mm.	mm.	mm.	mm.	mm.	mm.	mm.	mm.
70	113	142	111	105	104	19	25	44	40	33	27	48	9	18	58	65	53	42	125	101	36	61	33
—	—	—	—	—	—	—	—	—	—	—	—	—	—	—	—	—	—	—	92	79	23	37	22
63	97	120	98	82	91	14	18	40	37?	33	21	46	7	12	39	58	37	34	105	82	29	44	26
73?	114	134	104	98	97	16	18	43	—	38	25	54	8	16	54?	61	52	40	120	99	39	55	32
67	111	151	108	65	104	17	21	47	43	35	24	49	5	8	58	63	46	40	129	113	33	62	31
62?	—	134	102	96	96	15	17	43	40	38	24	50	5	13	52?	59	46	39	—	—	—	—	—
74	—	128	105	91	100	18	23	44	40	36	23	50	7	15	53	59	47	37	—	—	—	—	—
74	120	127	103	92	94	15	21	42	37	37	23	50	5	16	51	62	47	37	105	101	33	56	34
83?	127	159	114	107	102	15	21	46	41	40	26	62	7	14	54	69	49	47	140	118	40	70	33
75?	116?	154	111	106	101	22	27	42	38	34	24	57	13	19	54	71	50	40	140	112	40	61	33
70?	—	153	110	104	105	15	21	46	41	38	26	53	6	17	50	65	45	46	—	—	—	—	—
6	4	6	6	6	6	6	6	6	6	6	6	6	6	6	6	6	6	5	4	4	4	4	4
67–83	111–127	142–159	108–114	95–107	100–105	15–22	21–27	42?–47	38–43	33–40	24–27	48–62	5–13	8–19	50–58	60–71	45–54	40–47	125–140	101–118	33–40	61–70	31–33
72.8	116.8	151.8	110.8	98.5	102.7	17.7	23.2	45.2	40.5	36.2	25.3	53.8	8.0	14.8	55.0	65.5	49.5	43.0	133.5	111.0	37.3	63.5	32.5
4	2	3	5	4	4	5	4	4	3	4	4	4	4	4	4	4	4	4	2	2	2	2	2
62–74	114; 120	127–134	110–105	91–98	94–100	15–23	17–23	42–44	37–40	36–38	23–25	50–54	5–8	13–16	51–54	59–62	46–52	37–40	105; 120	99; 101	33; 39	55; 56	32; 34
70.8	117.0	129.7	103.0	94.3	96.3	17.4	16.8	43.0	39.0	37.3	23.8	51.0	6.3	15.0	52.5	60.8	48.0	38.3	112.5	100.0	36.0	55.5	33.0
1	1	1	1	1	—	1	1	1	1	1	1	1	1	1	1	1	1	1	2	2	2	2	2
—	—	—	—	—	—	—	—	—	—	—	—	—	—	—	—	—	—	—	92; 105	79; 82	23; 29	37; 44	22; 26
63.0	97.0	120.0	98.0	82.0	—	14.0	18.0	40.0	37.0	33.0	21.0	46.0	7.0	12.0	39.0	58.0	37.0	34.0	98.5	80.5	26.0	40.5	24.0
73	—	133	102	93	98	14	18	45	40	39	25	56	8	15	56?	58?	50?	42?	—	—	—	—	—
—	—	—	—	—	—	—	—	—	—	—	—	—	—	—	—	—	—	—	—	96	33	51	—
73.0	—	133.0	102.0	93.0	98.0	14.0	18.0	45.0	40.0	39.0	25.0	56.0	8.0	15.0	56.0	58.0	50.0	42.0	—	96.0	33.0	51.0	—
69	107	—	—	95	—	18	21	41	37	35	27	50	10	17	51	64	46	42	129	101	33	51	29
81	130	151?	112	114	104	22	26	44	40	38	27	55	11	—	58	68?	—	—	136	118	41	63	38
74?	—	152	119	110	110	24	29	46	43?	38	29	53	10	19	56	67	50	40	—	—	—	—	—
68	109	—	85	95	95	16	22	41	38?	34	25	47	9	18	54	63	48	39	—	—	35	49	34
2	1	2	2	2	2	2	2	2	2	2	2	2	1	2	2	2	1	1	1	1	1	1	1
74; 81	—	151; 152	112; 119	110; 114	104; 110	22; 24	26; 29	44; 46	40; 43	38; 38	27; 29	53; 55	10; 11	—	56; 58	67; 68	—	—	—	—	—	—	—
77.5	130.0	151.5	115.5	112.0	107.0	23.0	27.5	45.0	41.5	38.0	28.0	54.0	10.5	19.0	57.0	67.5	50.0	40.0	136.0	118.0	41.0	63.0	38.0
2	2	2	1	2	2	2	2	2	2	2	2	2	2	2	2	2	1	1	2	2	2	2	2
68; 69	107; 109	—	—	95; 95	—	16; 18	21; 22	41; 41	37; 38	34; 35	25; 27	47; 50	9; 10	17; 18	51; 52	63; 64	46; 48	39; 42	—	—	33; 35	49; 51	29; 34
68.5	108.0	—	85.0	95.0	95.0	17.0	21.5	41.0	37.5	34.5	26.0	48.5	9.5	17.5	52.5	63.5	47.0	40.5	129.0	101.0	34.0	50.0	31.5

Tribal divisions and subdivisions / Catalogue No. / Sex and stages of life / Number of cases / Averages and ranges	Capacity	Length	Breadth	Height (ba-b)	SKULL Circumference (horizontal)	Median-sagittal Arc Total (n-o)	Frontal	Parietal	Occipital	Chord Frontal	Parietal	Occipital	Cranial base (length n-ba)	Foramen magnum Length	Width	Frontal bone Breadth (minimum)	Breadth (maximum)	Length Length (lu pr)	Inferior length (ba-gn)
COWICHAN	ccm.	mm.	mm.	mm.	mm.	mm.	mm.	mm.	mm.	mm.	mm.	mm.	mm.	mm.	mm.	mm.	mm.	mm.	mm.
San Juan de Fuca																			
2682A ♀? ad-mat	—	—	—	—	—	120	—	—	111	—	—	—	—	—	—	92	112	—	—
2682B ♂ mat	1340	173	143	133	501	364	117	123	124	108	106	103	97	33	27	94	112	98?	110
2682C ♂ mat	—	—	—	—	—	—	—	—	—	—	—	—	—	—	—	—	—	—	—
2683 ♂ ad (def.)	1320	165	148	135	490	351	128	114	109	115	96	96	96	34	31	96	122	99	—
♂ cases	2	2	2	2	2	2	2	2	2	2	2	2	2	2	2	2	2	2	1
range	1320 ; 1340	165 ; 173	143 ; 148	133 ; 135	490 ; 501	351 ; 364	117 ; 128	114 ; 123	109 ; 124	108 ; 115	96 ; 106	96 ; 103	96 ; 97	33 ; 34	27 ; 31	94 ; 96	112 ; 122	98 ; 99	
average	1330.0	169.0	145.5	134.0	495.5	357.5	122.5	118.5	116.5	111.5	101.0	99.5	96.5	33.5	29.0	95.0	117.0	98.5	110.0
♀ 1 case	—	—	—	—	—	120.0	—	—	111.0	—	—	—	—	—	—	92.0	112.0	—	—
Port Williams																			
3045 ♂ mat (def.)	1370	163	162	126	508	325	113	100	112	107	90	94	99	32	29	99	125	105	112?
♂ 1 case	1370.0	163.0	162.0	126.0	508.0	325.0	113.0	100.0	112.0	107.0	90.0	94.0	99.0	32.0	29.0	99.0	125.0	105.0	112.0
Dungeness																			
2715 ♀? ad (def.)	1390	164	157	121	504	323	107	93	123	99	82	103	100	35	30	97	122	106	—
2719 ♀? mat (def.)	1120	155	149	118	483	308	109	91	108	102	82	97	96	35	29	96	119	107	—
2723 ♂ mat	1390	176	152	133	511	345	121	92	132	112	86	104	103	36	28	98	120	102	—
2724 ♀ mat	1340	170	146	128	503	336	115	109	112	105	100	95	99	35	30	96	116	101?	—
2725 ♂ mat	1320	167	152	125	504	328	113	110	105	107	96	89	97	36	30	90?	120?	101	—
2727 ♂ mat (def.)	1350	164	167	125	518	319	113	99	107	105	88	98	98	36	31	102	128	97	106?
2728 ♀? mat	1220	161	147	121	494	324	112	106	106	103	92	89	97	36	33	90	118?	95	104
2730 inf. II	—	—	—	—	—	—	—	—	—	—	—	—	—	—	—	—	—	—	—
2731 ♀ mat (def.)	1140	164	148	117	486	328	116	96	116	106	86	97	90	30	27	90	—	—	—
2734A ♂ ad-mat (def.)	1280	162	155	118	492	325	115	108	102	107	93	89	93	31	28	99	121	101	108
2734B ♂ ad	—	—	—	—	—	—	—	—	—	—	—	—	—	—	—	—	—	—	—
2734C ♂ ad	—	—	—	—	—	—	—	—	—	—	—	—	—	—	—	—	—	—	—
2735 inf. II	1280	160	150	111	481	318	109	95	114	101	87	99	86	35	30	98	119	89	88
2736 inf. II	—	—	—	—	477	348	122	118	108	107	105	89	—	33	27	89	103	—	—
♂ cases	4	4	4	4	4	4	4	4	4	4	4	4	4	4	4	4	4	4	2
range	1280– 1320	162– 176	152– 167	118– 133	492– 518	319– 345	113– 121	92– 110	102– 132	105– 112	86– 96	89– 104	93– 103	31– 36	28– 31	90– 102	120– 128	97– 102	106 ; 108
average	1335.0	167.2	156.5	125.2	506.3	329.2	115.5	102.2	111.2	107.8	90.8	95.0	97.0	34.8	29.3	97.3	122.3	100.3	107.0
♀ cases	5	5	5	5	5	5	5	5	5	5	5	5	5	5	5	5	4	4	1
range	1120– 1390	155– 170	146– 157	117– 128	483– 504	308– 336	107– 116	91– 109	106– 123	101– 107	82– 100	89– 103	90– 100	30– 36	27– 33	90– 97	116– 122	95– 107	
average	1242.0	162.8	149.4	121.0	494.0	323.8	111.8	99.0	113.0	103.0	88.4	96.2	96.4	34.2	29.8	93.8	118.8	102.3	104.0
inf. cases	1	1	1	1	2	2	2	2	2	2	2	2	1	2	2	2	2	1	1
range	—	—	—	—	477 ; 481	318 ; 348	109 ; 122	95 ; 118	108 ; 114	101 ; 107	87 ; 105	89 ; 99	—	33 ; 35	27 ; 30	89 ; 98	103 ; 109	—	—
average	1280.0	160.0	170.0	111.0	479.0	333.0	115.5	106.5	111.0	104.0	96.0	94.0	86.0	34.0	28.5	93.5	111.0	89.0	88.0

FACE AND MANDIBLE

Height		Breadth						Orbit			Nose		Nasal bones		Maxillo-alveolar		Palatal		Mandible				
																			Breadth			Height	
Upper height (n-pr)	Total height (n-gn)	Bizygomatic	Upper facial (fmt-fmt)	Mid-facial (zm-zm)	Biorbital (ek-ek)	Ant. interorb. (mf-mf)	Post. interorb. (la-la)	Width (mf-ek)	Width (la-ek)	Height	Width	Height	Breadth (minimum)	Breadth (maximum)	Length	Breadth	Length	Width	Bicondylar	Bigonial	Ramus	Ramus	Chin
mm.	mm.	mm.	mm.	mm.	mm.	mm.	mm.	mm.	mm.	mm.	mm.	mm.	mm.	mm.	mm.	mm.	mm.	mm.	mm.	mm.	mm.	mm.	mm.
65	102	—	102	95	96	21	24	40	37	34	26	48	12	19	53	62	48	40	115	101	36	55	30
66?	112?	130	104	90?	100	20	25	43	40?	35	25	47	8	—	—	—	—	—	118	97	33	66	33
																				—	41	65	35
70	113	135	—	100	—	19	21	40	36	33	23	49	8	14	55	56	49	40	124	103	35	62	33
2	2	2	1	2	1	2	2	2	.2	2	2	2	2	1	1	1	1	1	2	2	3	3	3
66 ;	112 ;	130 ;	—	90 ;	—	19 ;	21 ;	40 ;	36 ;	33 ;	23 ;	47 ;	8 ; 8	—	—	—	—	—	118 ;	97 ;	33–	62–	33–
70	113	135		100		20	25	43	40	35	25	49							124	103	41	66	35
68.0	112.5	132.5	104.0	95.0	100.0	19.5	23.0	41.5	38.0	34.0	24.0	48.0	8.0	14.0	55.0	56.0	49.0	40.0	121.0	100.0	36.3	64.3	34.0
65.0	102.0	—	—	95.0	96.0	21.0	24.0	40.0	37.0	34.0	26.0	48.0	12.0	19.0	53.0	62.0	48.0	40.0	115.0	101.0	36.0	55.0	30.0
69	113?	150	112	99	104	17	22	45	40	38	25	49	8	15	57	62	47	41	142?	111?	36	62	35
69.0	113.0	150.0	112.0	99.0	104.0	17.0	22.0	45.0	40.0	38.0	25.0	49.0	8.0	15.0	57.0	62.0	47.0	41.0	142.0	111.0	36.0	62.0	35.0
69	—	146	112	100	106	21	25	45	41	37	27	50	8	—	57	67	49	42	—	—	—	—	—
71	—	135 ?	106	97	100	18	25	42	39	35	24	48	9	—	57	66	47	44	—	—	—	—	—
74	—	142	110	—	102	18	25	44	40	37	23	52	11	—	54	66	44	41	—	—	—	—	—
72	—	107	95	100	19	23	43	38	37	25	48	8	16	54	59?	—	—	—	—	—	—	—	—
69?	—	146?	108?	—	102?	20	24?	43	40	39	27	50	8	—	53	65	49	41	—	—	—	—	—
70	111?	147	109	97	98	20	25	41	37	34	24	49	10	16	52	65	46	41	121	102	32	61	32
75	123	140 ?	109	94	100	20	25	45	40	36	23	52	7	15	50	58?	46	36	135	115	33	62	39
—	—	—	—	—	—	—	—	—	—	—	—	—	—	—	—	—	—	—	93?	86?	28	49	27
—	—	125?	—	—	17	22	40	37?	36?	—	—	—	—	—	58	—	39	—	—	—	—	—	—
76	120	133	107	99	100	21	26	41	38	35	24	52	13	17	58	64	51	41	124	100	31	56	37
—	—	—	—	—	—	—	—	—	—	—	—	—	—	—	—	—	—	—	126	106	38	64	31
—	—	—	—	—	—	—	—	—	—	—	—	—	—	—	—	—	—	—	120	104	35	54	36
61	98	—	98	86	90	17	21	37	34	31	24	42	10	15	43	60	40	33	108	82	32	43	28
62	—	—	94	83	86	15	18	39	35	34	22	45	7	14?	44	60	40	37	—	—	—	—	—
4	2	4	4	4	4	4	4	4	4	4	4	4	4	4	4	4	4	4	4	4	4	4	4
69–	111 ;	133–	107–	97 ;	98–	18–	24–	41–	37–	34–	23–	49–	8–13	16 ;	52–	64–	44–	41–	120–	100–	31–	54–	31–
76	120	146	110	99	102	21	26	44	40	39	27	52		17	58	66	51	41	126	106	39	64	37
72.3	115.0	136.5	108.5	98.0	100.5	19.8	25.0	42.3	38.8	36.3	24.5	50.8	10.5	16.5	54.3	65.0	47.5	41.0	121.8	103.0	34.3	58.8	34.0
4	1	4	4	4	4	5	5	5	5	5	4	4	2	2	5	5	5	5	1	1	1	1	1
69–	—	133–	106–	94–	100–	17–	22–	40–	37–	35–	23–	48–	7–9	15 ;	50–	58–	46–	36–	—	—	—	—	—
75		147 ;	112	100	106	21	25	45	41	37	27	52		16	57	67	49	44					
72.2	123.0	142.0	108.5	96.5	101.5	19.0	24.0	43.0	39.0	36.2	24.8	49.2	8.0	15.5	54.5	61.6	47.3	42.5	135.0	115.0	33.0	62.0	39.0
2	1	—	2	2	2	2	2	2	2	2	2	2	2	2	2	2	2	2	2	2	2	2	2
61 ;	—	—	94 ;	83 ;	86 ;	15 ;	18 ;	37 ;	34 ;	31 ;	22 ;	42 ;	7 ; 10	14 ;	43 ;	60 ;	40 ;	33 ;	93 ;	82 ;	28 ;	43 ;	27 ;
62			98	86	90	17	21	39	35	31	24	45		15	44	60	40	37	108	86	32	49	28
61.5	98.0	—	96.0	84.5	88.0	16.0	19.5	38.0	34.5	31.0	23.0	43.5	8.5	14.5	43.5	60.0	40.0	35.0	100.5	84.0	30.0	46.0	27.5

Tribal divisions and subdivisions / Catalogue No. / Sex and stages of life / Number of cases / Averages and ranges	Capacity	Length	Breadth	Height (ba-b)	Circumference (horizontal)	SKULL Median-sagittal Arc Total (n-o)				Median-sagittal Chord			Cranial base (length n-ba)	Foramen magnum		Frontal bone		Length	
							Frontal	Parietal	Occipital	Frontal	Parietal	Occipital		Length	Width	Breadth (minimum)	Breadth (maximum)	Length (ha-pr)	Inferior length (ba-gn)
	ccm.	mm.	mm.	mm.	mm.	mm.	mm.	mm.	mm.	mm.	mm.	mm.	mm.	mm.	mm.	mm.	mm.	mm.	mm.
COWICHAN Markham																			
3049 ♂ ad (def.)	1390	167	160	130	517	342	122	110	110	113	88	96	97	33	27	98	126	97	—
♂ 1 case	1390.0	167.0	160.0	130.0	517.0	342.0	122.0	110.0	110.0	113.0	88.0	96.0	97.0	33.0	27.0	98.0	126.0	97.0	—
Divisional total																			
♂ cases	69	81	80	74	77	76	88	84	77	88	84	77	73	72	72	84	80	68	26
range	1120–1590	145–197	131–174	117–147	474–545	319–383	108–135	89–132	97–136	101–122	82–112	81–111	87–111	29–43	24–35	83–106	103–141	90–117	97–122
average	1360.3	169.8	151.2	131.6	507.9	347.2	121.1	112.2	115.5	111.1	96.7	96.9	99.6	33.4	29.6	95.5	120.4	101.6	111.6
♀ cases	25	27	27	25	25	25	30	28	25	29	28	25	25	24	24	28	25	21	8
range	980–1350	144–180	132–161	115–135	462–504	308–359	100–128	87–124	98–125	91–119	76–112	87–110	88–100	30–38	23–33	78–100	106–123	85–107	97–112
average	1209.6	161.8	144.4	126.4	481.6	331.6	117.0	103.4	113.3	107.0	90.5	95.8	94.1	33.5	28.8	91.1	114.4	97.1	104.9
juv. cases	2	2	1	2	2	2	1	2	2	1	2	1	2	2	2	2	2	2	2
range	1160; 1250	151; 162	—	109–127	462; 482	320; 329	—	101–104	101–104	—	90–93	—	89; 91	31; 36	26; 31	87; 89	115; 117	89; 89	96; 101
average	1205.0	156.5	149.0	122.0	472.0	324.5	115.0	102.5	102.5	104.0	91.5	87.0	90.0	33.5	28.5	88.0	116.0	89.0	98.5
inf. cases	4	4	4	4	5	7	5	5	6	5	6	4	6	6	6	7	7	4	3
range	1080–1400	144–162	134–150	110–128	475–486	313–348	100–117	90–118	97–121	92–107	84–105	81–94	82–86	29–37	26–30	84–98	103–127	80–89	80–88
average	1242.5	155.0	141.0	116.3	480.8	326.0	110.9	102.8	110.2	100.5	91.4	93.5	83.8	33.2	27.7	91.9	113.1	82.5	84.0
CHINOOK																			
3051 ♀ mat	1310	160	140	121	497	316	110	94	112	102	84	96	80	34	32	94	122	88	—
3051B ♀ mat	—	—	—	—	—	—	—	—	—	—	—	—	—	—	—	—	—	—	—
3052 ♀ ad-mat	1260?	164	148	—	495	—	113	106	—	105	97	—	—	—	—	97	116	—	—
3053 ♂ mat	1250	161	166	116	510	322	114	103	105	109	84	95	95	34	31	98	130?	104	114
3054 ♀ mat	1020	164	156	102	512	306	110	93	103	102	84	87	86	34	30	96	119?	99	—
3055 juv-ad	—	—	—	—	305	—	113	92	100	104	78	90	—	30	30	—	—	—	—
3056 ♂ ad	1250	167	148	120	504	327	119	103	105	110	89	91	94	37	33	94	122	97	—
3057 ♂ ad	1370	167	164	122	518	333	118	97	118	108	83	102	94	33	31	97	125	101	113
4441 ♂ ad	1270	165	143	125	486	330	124	99	107	112	87	86	99	35	31	89	112	105	—
4442 ♀ mat	1140	148	152	120	468	309	112	98	99	105	83	87	90	30	26	88	115	91	—
4443 ♂ ad	1270	166	146	122	502	335	118	110	107	107	93	94	95	38	28	93	118	101	—
4444 ♂ ad	1270	165	150	125	496	327	113	103	111	105	89	99	100	36	31	91	118	106	—
4445 ♂ ad	1320	168	152	125	506	336	117	109	110	110	93	100	95	33	30	91	116	99	—
4446 ♂ mat	1430	170	158	131	516	359	123	115	121	111	103	107	97	31	31	97	127	102	—
4447 ♂ mat	1250	168	153	135	510	342	120	114	108	111	98	96	104	34	31	98	118	103	—
4448 ♂ mat	1320	166	156	126	510	324	121	90	113	114	80	97	99	34	30	91	117	107	—
4449 ♂ ad-mat	1150	156	148	117	488	306	109	98	99	103	81?	93	94	37	32	89	115	102	—
4450 inf. II	1200	153	145	—	470	329	118	105	106	108	90	95	—	—	—	87	110	—	—

FACE AND MANDIBLE

Height		Breadth						Orbit		Nose		Nasal bones		Maxillo-alveolar		Palatal		Mandible				
																		Breadth		Height		
Upper height (n-pr)	Total height (n-gn)	Bizygomatic	Upper facial (fmt-fmt)	Mid-facial (zm-zm)	Biorbital (ek-ek)	Ant. interorb. (mf-mf)	Post. interorb. (la-la)	Width (mf-ek)	Width (la-ek)	Height	Width	Height	Breadth (minimum)	Breadth (maximum)	Length	Breadth	Length	Width	Bicondylar	Bigonial	Ramus	Ramus	Chin
mm.	mm.	mm.	mm.	mm.	mm.	mm.	mm.	mm.	mm.	mm.	mm.	mm.	mm.	mm.	mm.	mm.	mm.	mm.	mm.	mm.	mm.	mm.	mm.
82	—	143	107	96	98	—	—	42	—	38	25?	56	—	—	53	64	45	42	—	—	—	—	—
82.0	—	143.0	107.0	96.0	98.0	—	—	42.0	—	38.0	25.0	56.0	—	—	53.0	64.0	45.0	42.0	—	—	—	—	—
81	29	65	77	74	73	82	78	84	82	84	83	83	85	73	79	79	79	78	44	43	53	52	52
62– 86	101– 130	125– 163	97– 120	65– 113	90– 111	14– 24	18– 29	39– 48	36– 43	30– 41	20– 29	43– 62	2–13	8–19	47– 61	56– 73	43– 56	33– 47	110– 142	82– 120	31– 46	50– 74	31– 40
72.8	116.0	142.7	107.2	100.0	100.4	17.9	22.9	43.5	39.5	36.1	23.7	51.8	8.3	15.3	54.2	63.9	47.8	40.5	124.6	103.3	36.6	62.3	34.8
26	12	17	26	23	23	29	28	27	25	27	26	27	27	23	26	27	23	23	12	13	16	16	16
62– 78	102– 123	125– 146	85– 112	86– 102	88– 106	14– 24	17– 28	39– 45	36– 41	33– 39	21– 27	44– 54	5–12	2–19	43– 57	56– 67	39– 52	34– 44	105– 135	82– 102	29– 39	47– 62	26– 39
68.7	110.5	134.0	101.7	93.9	95.9	17.2	21.2	41.9	38.2	36.3	23.6	48.9	7.4	15.1	51.7	60.4	46.6	39.1	118.5	97.1	34.4	53.9	32.6
2	2	2	2	2	2	2	2	2	2	2	2	2	2	2	2	2	2	2	1	1	2	2	2
62; 64	96; 103	120; 128	94; 99	90; 90	87; 92	18; 19	21; 23	36; 40	33; 36	32; 34	21; 22	42; 49	9; 9	15; 18	46; 46	59; 59	39; 41	34; 39	—	—	32; 34	44; 51	27; 28
63.0	99.5	124.0	96.5	90.0	89.5	18.5	22.0	38.0	34.5	33.0	21.5	45.5	9.0	16.5	46.0	59.0	40.0	36.5	113.0	92.0	33.0	47.5	27.5
7	3	2	7	5	5	7	7	7	7	4	7	6	6	6	6	6	6	6	9	9	10	10	10
52– 63	84– 98	106; 120	86– 98	75– 86	80– 90	15– 18	18– 22	35– 39	31– 36	31– 34	19– 24	35– 45	7–10	12; 16	35– 44	52– 60	32– 37	29– 37	85– 108	79– 86	22– 32	36– 49	22– 28
57.4	93.0	113.0	93.9	80.6	85.8	16.3	19.9	37.9	34.6	31.6	20.3	41.0	7.8	14.3	39.7	56.5	36.5	32.5	95.9	80.3	26.7	40.2	25.0
71	—	139	107	100	102	19	25?	43	39	38	24	48	10	—	48	68	43	43	—	—	—	—	—
66	—	127	1C4?	92	98	18	23	43	38	36	25	44	9	15	50	60	40	39	118?	104	37	52	32
74	121	135	111	92	104	19	26	45	41	37	21	52	4	12?	58	61	51	42	123	101	34	56	36
73	—	138?	103	—	99	20	25	41	37	34	23	49	8	—	50	64	36	42	—	—	—	—	—
77	—	140	109	101	103	21	25	42	38	39	25	53	8	15	50	63	43	39	—	—	—	—	—
72	122?	147	110	101	102	20	25	44	41	37	23	56	4	16?	52	67	48	48	130	101	37	59	35?
68	—	135	101	100	92	16	21	40	37	35	23	54	7	14	58	66	50	40	—	—	—	—	—
68	—	131?	99	—	94	16	22	43	38r	37r	20	49	6	13	46	62	41	42	—	—	—	—	—
70	—	134	110	102	100	18	24	43	39	37	23	48	5	12	53	73	45	47	—	—	—	—	—
75	—	141	106	106	99	17	22	44	39	36	24	52	9	15	55	68	49	45	—	—	—	—	—
75	—	135	102	94	97	19	22	41	37	36	22	53	10	14?	54	68	45	45	—	—	—	—	—
71	—	140	107	100	101	18	24	45	40	33	23	51	8	14?	53	68?	—	—	—	—	—	—	—
71	—	140	109	101	101	20	24	42	39	34	23	51	7	13	54	68	48	42	—	—	—	—	—
69	—	139	104	101	100	18	23	44	40	36	22	51	7	18	55	63	50	42	—	—	—	—	—
70	—	138?	103	79	99	16	20	43	40	35	27	54	7	15	51	61	45	42	—	—	—	—	—
55	—	108	87	76	83	15	22	36	32	31	19	39	5	13	38?	59	35	33	—	—	—	—	—

29

Tribal divisions and subdivisions / Catalogue No. / Sex and stages of life / Number of cases / Averages and ranges	SKULL																	
	Capacity	Length	Breadth	Height (ba-b)	Circumference (horizontal)	Median-sagittal						Cranial base (length n-ba)	Foramen magnum		Frontal bone		Length	Inferior length (ba-gn)
						Total (n-o)	Arc			Chord								
							Frontal	Parietal	Occipital	Frontal	Parietal	Occipital		Length	Width	Breadth (minimum)	Breadth (maximum)	Length (ba-pr)	
	ccm.	mm.	mm.	mm.	mm.	mm.	mm.	mm.	mm.	mm.	mm.	mm.	mm.	mm.	mm.	mm.	mm.	mm.	mm.
CHINOOK																			
4451 ♂ mat	1360	159	158	127	493	333	115	107	111	107	91	101	92	33	31	95	122	94	—
4452 ♂ ad	1550	160	158	136	505	346	122	120	104	114	96	93	100	37	31	101	125	104	—
4453 ♂ ad	1300	168	148	126	506	338	122	103	113	110	89	98	99	35	30	92	117	93	—
4454 ♂ ad	1380	163	153	139	494	348	127	101	120	113	89	101	97	33	30	93	117	95	—
4455 ♂ mat	1390	168	157	124	510	339	119	99	121	111	86	106	94	35	29	100	120	95	—
4456 ♂ mat	1360	162	157	128	505	344	117	115	112	110	97	100	93	31	31	97	127	94	—
4457 ♀ ad-mat	1160	162	138	128	473	332	113	100	119	106	89	104	98	33	29	92	121	100	—
4458 ♂ mat	1370	179	146	131	510	362	129	117	116	118	103	101	102	34	27	93	122	102	—
4459 ♂ ad-mat	1430	157	170	134	509	340	127	107	106	118	86	94	97	35	34	103	131	101	—
4460 ♀ ad	1270	165	147	122	495	325	115	102	108	107	90	94	103	33	31	96	116	108	—
4461 ♂ ad	1420	171	145	131	502	342	120	112	110	112	107	100	104	35	33	92	112	104	—
4462 juf	1100	149	142	116	456?	303	110	99	94	102	83	88	85	33	28	87	112	93	—
4463 ♂ ad-mat	1490	163	156	136	503	337	119	113	105	110	95	93	106	36	31	99	127	109	—
4464 ♂ ad	1400	165	159	127	505	336	118	112	106	110	94	95	99	35	31	96	125	96	—
4465 ♂ mat	1400	167	158	127	512	347	120	102	125	111	88	106	102	33	29	99	123	—	—
4466 ♀ mat	1300	159	155	120	494	321	119	90	112	111	80	93	95	33	30	89	118	96	—
4467 juv	1460	169	152	122	514	337	113	105	119	104	93	105	97	34	28	98	119	95	—
4468 inf. II	1400	165	161	110	517	334	108	98	128	100	88	110	80	33	27	95	121	81	—
4469 ♂ ad-mat	1460	170	162	131	510	351	123	113	110	115	91	100	100	33	30	101	128	104	—
4470 ♂ mat	1360	169	148	128	506	334	119	103	112	112	92	97	104	33	33	94	121	111	—
4471 ♂ ad-mat	1550	175	167	133	530	350	130	110	110	120	89	101	103	31	27	98	129	112	—
4472 ♂ ad	1540	167	154	138	513	345	130	107	108	118	92	100	104	34	32	96	128	102	—
4473 ♀ juv-ad	1350	163	158	111	495?	318	110	109	99	104	87	95	85	35	31	100	123	94	—
4474 ♀ ad	1290	156	152	122	486	322	118	100	104	105	88	93	90	33	29	94	119	96	—
4475 ♂ mat	1450	165	163	123	522	332	121	110	101	113	94	89	101	35	32	99	121	109	115
4476 ♂ mat	1360	165	161	132	513	347	115	114	118	109	93	102	100	34	28	104	128	102	—
4477 ♂ mat	1510	164	160	136	508	343	124	110	109	117	93	99	101	36	31	102	130	100	—
4478 ♂ ad-mat	1370	174	155	125	516	337	129	97	111	119	85	99	101	35	30	94	129	102	—
4479 inf. II	1330	157	148	122	480	322	117	107	98	106	90	87	88	37	28	97	116	86?	—
4480 ♀ ad	1330	158	154	123	494	322	117	90	115	111	80	103	94	34	32	95	122	96	—
4481 ♀ mat	1330	160	161	135	508	331	120	103	108	114	90	100	102	33	30	102	125	95	—
4482 ♂ ad	1230	160	168	127	515	322	113	103	106	109	90	97	94	33	32	98	126	96	—
4483 ♂ ad-mat	1260	160	156	117	498	319	109	102	108	102	87	98	97	32	29	93	120	98	—
4484 juv	1280	149	154	127	467	335	112	119	104	105?	91?	95	85	35	31	94	120	85	—
4485 inf. II	1220	152	157	122	474	318	108	109	101	102	85	92	86	33	29	97	122	90	—
4486 ♀ ad	1320	163	150	125	489	331	121	108	102	111	91	93	94	34	30	93	120	97	—
4487 ♀ mat	1390	178	148	126	513	365	128	106	131	116	93	106	95	34	30	93	118?	99	—
4488 ♂ mat	1290	164	157	127?	516	345	113	118	114	103	101	98	94	31	29	94	123	88	—
4489 ♂ ad	1310	162	156	124	491	325	111	90	124	104	82	109	99	34	31	94	120	106	—
4490 ♂ mat	1240	169	153	118	511?	345	122	98	125	114	87	109	87	28	28	94	123	88?	—
4491 ♀ ad	1180	155	144	127	471	322	112	111	99	103	94	89	96	31	27	95	117	97	—

FACE AND MANDIBLE

Height		Breadth						Orbit		Nose		Nasal bones		Maxillo-alveolar		Palatal		Mandible				
																			Breadth		Height	
Upper height (n-pr)	Total height (n-gn)	Bizygomatic	Upper facial (fmt-fmt)	Mid-facial (zm-zm)	Biorbital (ek-ek)	Ant. interorb. (mf-mf)	Post. interorb. (la-la)	Width (mf-ek)	Width (la-ek)	Height	Width	Height	Breadth (minimum)	Breadth (maximum)	Length	Breadth	Length	Width	Bicondylar	Bigonial	Ramus	Ramus	Chin
mm.	mm.	mm.	mm.	mm.	mm.	mm.	mm.	mm.	mm.	mm.	mm.	mm.	mm.	mm.	mm.	mm.	mm.	mm.	mm.	mm.	mm.	mm.	mm.
75	—	138	106	99	100	19	23	43	39	36	24	53	10	14?	51	64	45	40	—	—	—	—	—
75	—	144	109	109	109	18	22	42	39	35	23	53	8	13	53	67	46	44	—	—	—	—	—
79	—	137	104	93	97	17	21	42	38	38	23	56	9	16	54	62	45	39	—	—	—	—	—
75	—	132	102	93	96	15	20	44	40	35	24	50	—	—	54	65	46	45	—	—	—	—	—
70	—	140	108	95	99	19	24	43	39	35	24	50	11	15?	53	61	45	41	—	—	—	—	—
70	—	138	106	95	99	20	25	42	37	35	25	51	11	17?	52	62	46	39	—	—	—	—	—
66	—	130	105	97	96	17	21	42	38	35	25	46	10	16	50	63	43	40	—	—	—	—	—
72	—	139	106	98	99	21	25	43	39	36	26	52	10	19	53	67	47	42	—	—	—	—	—
83	—	151	113	105	105	23	29	45	40	35	24	55	11	14	58	73	48?	45	—	—	—	—	—
72	—	129?	105	92	96	17	21	42	38	36	24	50	9	16	54	67	49	45	—	—	—	—	—
75	—	142	106	106	95	18	22	42	39	38	22	58	4	12	55	71	43	44	—	—	—	—	—
63	—	120	94	88	89	15	20	38	34	33	22	45	8	15	48	60	42	34	—	—	—	—	—
74	—	150	112	108	105	21	27	45	40	35	29	53	9	15?	56	70	49	47	—	—	—	—	—
73	—	135?	105	99	98	15	20	44	40	37	24	57	9	12?	49	67	44	42	—	—	—	—	—
—	—	139	106	101	101	18	23	43	41	36	29	50	11	15?	—	—	—	—	—	—	—	—	—
72	—	136	99	96	93	16	18	42	39	38	20	51	8	11	49	65	43	41	—	—	—	—	—
69?	—	126?	100	95	95	20?	24?	40	36r?	37r	23	48	—	—	43	66	40	38	—	—	—	—	—
59	—	119	97	89	90	17	20	39	36	36	19	42	8	15	39	59	36	38	—	—	—	—	—
77	—	147	111	108	102	19	24	44	40	36	23	55	7	12	55	71	47	42	—	—	—	—	—
80	—	147	109	100	101	18	23	45	41	36	21	58	8	13	60	65	50	43	—	—	—	—	—
70	—	149	113	106	103	19	27	45	39?	36	23	51	7	14	59	68	51	43	—	—	—	—	—
76	—	143	107	101	98	16	20	44	40	39	24	55	8	16	53	67	44	42	—	—	—	—	—
62	—	130	105	92	94	19	23	39	35	36	22	47	7	14	47	63	42	36	—	—	—	—	—
65	—	128	100	93	91	18	22	38	35	35	22	44	8	16	50	66	45	42	—	—	—	—	—
76	118	147	108	106	104	20	27	44	39	36	26	54	10	19	58	67	51	39	135	106	38	61	34
72	—	151	112	101	104	19	24	46	41	38	23	55	10	15?	54	64	49	42	—	—	—	—	—
70	—	145	110	103	101	18	21	45	41	35	24	57	7	15	52	65?	48	43?	—	—	—	—	—
77	—	142	107	108	99	17	24	42	38	34	26	54	7	16	53	64	46	42	—	—	—	—	—
57	—	120	97	83	90	17	22	38	35	33	19	44	—	—	40	59	36	32	—	—	—	—	—
70	—	135	105	94	95	17	21	43	39	39	22	50	10	15	52	60	43	38	—	—	—	—	—
78?	—	137	111	96	105	18	21	47	43	40	23	57	10	15	50	58	43	35	—	—	—	—	—
71	—	140	104	95	98	18	22	42	38	35	20	50	9	14	49	61	42	32	—	—	—	—	—
75	—	140	107	103	104	19	23	45	41	38	24	52	9	—	53	63	44	40	—	—	—	—	—
60?	—	122	100	90	95	18	23	42	38	31	23	45	8	14?	44	61	40	36	—	—	—	—	—
67	—	119	97	81	88	17	21	39	35	34	20	50	12	15	46	59	43	34	—	—	—	—	—
69	—	132?	104	97	97	19	25	41	38	37	22	52	8	13	52	62	44	39	—	—	—	—	—
67?	—	135?	105	—	112?	17	20	45	42	37	24	49	8	13	50	—	—	—	—	—	—	—	—
74	—	138	110	108	108	18	21	49	45	37	27	51	12	15?	52	—	—	—	—	—	—	—	—
68	—	137	107	105	103	21	27	44	40	35	27	48	12	19	56	69	51	45	—	—	—	—	—
70?	—	135	108	101	103	18	26	45	40	37	27	50	10	17?	—	—	—	—	—	—	—	—	—
68	—	129	105	92	100	20	25	43	39	32	21	46	10	15?	53	65	46	41	—	—	—	—	—

Tribal divisions and subdivisions / Catalogue No. / Sex and stages of life / Number of cases / Averages and ranges	Capacity	Length	Breadth	Height (ba-b)	SKULL Circumference (horizontal)	Median-sagittal Arc Total (n-o)	Frontal	Parietal	Occipital	Median-sagittal Chord Frontal	Parietal	Occipital	Cranial base (length n-ba)	Foramen magnum Length	Width	Frontal bone Breadth (minimum)	Breadth (maximum)	Length Length (ba-pr)	Inferior length (ba-gn)
	ccm.	mm.	mm.	mm.	mm.	mm.	mm.	mm.	mm.	mm.	mm.	mm.	mm.	mm.	mm.	mm.	mm.	mm.	mm.
CHINOOK																			
4492 ♂ ad	1190	164	146	115	485	324	112	92	120	106	81	102	92	33	27	99	117	97	—
4493 ♂ ad	1320	161	163	123	505	313	114	103	96	108	88	90	101	38	32	105	130	109	—
4494 ♀ ad	1340	169	144	125	495	348	126	110	112	112	94	98	93	34	30	94	118	92	—
4495 ♂ mat	1250	165	159	129	504	348	121	108	119	116	90	103	93	35	31	89	119	98	—
4496 ♂ ad	1500	173	152	134	500	354	125	115	114	118	93	102	101	32	30	95	124	104	—
4497 ♂ ad-mat	1480	170	162	127	506	336	124	98	114	116	82	103	102	35	28	109	126	99	—
4498 ♀? ad	1300	165	157	115	508	323	112	98	113	106	86	100	91	34	29	93	120	90	—
4499 ♀ ad	1090	153	138	118	493	322	114	98	110	105	87	101	84	30	26	86	109	91	—
4500 ♀ ad	1290	157	144	121	479	320	109	106	105	102	90	93	94	31	27	97	118	98	—
4501 ♂ mat	1490	166	157	145	512	357	128	116	113	118	101	100	107	36	35	102	130	111	—
4502 ♀ mat	1280	166	146	122	492?	328	110	89	129	105	80	115	94	36	32	87	118	101	—
4503 ♂ ad-mat	1450	165	156	128	514	341	117	101	123	111	88	107	96	35	29	98	124	100	—
4504 ♂ ad	1520	163	160	127	505	337	120	105	112	115	87	102	95	34	32	96	123	97	—
4505 ♂ ad-mat	1390	172	157	123	525	335	124	104	107	116	89	96	97	31	30	98	125	108	—
4506 ♂ mat	1350	164	153	132	499	339	128	92	119	118	83	106	95	32	29	96	121	95	—
4507 inf. II	1360	166	155	119	507	330	118	92	120	109	85	106	85	34	28	93	120	85?	—
4508 ♀ mat	1260	160	152	129?	482?	333	118	112	103	111	90	96	93	31	27	97	126	99	—
4509 juv	1070	149	145	108	465	299	103	92	104	96	80	95	87	30	27	90	113	92	—
4510 ♂ mat	—	171	161	—	521	—	120	110	—	113	93	—	—	—	—	97	122	—	—
4511 ♂ ad	1420	155	168	130	507	327	117	107	103	110	89	92	100	36	34	104	133	106	—
4512 ♂ mat	1550	170	166	124	526	339	122	95	122	112	83	104	96	40	32	96	126	98	—
4513 ♂ mat	1460	161	157	133	504	337	120	114	103	113	91	91	99	35	33	102	127	99	—
4514 ♂ mat	1330	158	154	138	495	339	118	108	113	111	92	102	103	32	27	95	121	112	—
4515 ♂? mat	1310	165	157	125	498	336	118	115	103	112	92	92	97	30	28	102	127	98	—
4516 ♀ mat	1210	158	157	134	493	329	124	101	104	113	90?	93?	98	33	30	98	120?	102	—
4517 ♂ ad-mat	1500	169	153	140	505	352	129	114	109	120	98	98	106	35	30	100	120	110	—
4518 ♂ ad	1630	182	153	137	533	372	133	118	121	121	103	98	105	36	32	101	128	105	—
4519 ♂ mat	1610	179	161	132	540	343	122	104	117	113	91	108	102	41	33	96	130	105	—
4520 ♂ mat	1570	176	153	137	515	372	122	130	120	113	111	98	98	36	30	94	120	100	—
4521 ♀ ad	1160	154	143	120	465	320	110	109	101	103	89	92	91	32	27	89	110	96	—
4522 ♀ ad	1170	160	149	120	488	320	110	103	107	105	89	94	94	33	28	95	113	107	—
4523 ♂ mat	1410	168	155	132	507	339	129	100	110	120	87	100	100	31	28	98	125	102	—
4524 inf. II	1300	151	153	124	474	321	107	90	124	101	81	111	85	30	28	95	118	89	—
4525 ♀ ad-mat	1280	166	155	112	505	319	118	90	111	111	81	100	92	31	26	94	117?	101	—
4526 ♂ ad	1420	170	152	125	502	336	118	105	113	110	94	101	99	32	27	93	117	103	—
♂ cases	56	56	56	56	57	56	57	57	56	57	57	56	56	56	57	57	55	3	
range	1150–1630	155–182	143–170	115–145	485–540	306–372	109–133	90–130	96–125	103–121	80–111	86–109	87–107	28–41	27–35	89–109	112–133	88–112	113–115
average	1389.6	166.4	156.3	128.7	508.1	339.4	117.0	104.7	111.8	112.8	91.0	97.3	98.6	34.3	30.4	98.6	123.3	101.6	114.0

FACE AND MANDIBLE

Height		Breadth						Orbit			Nose		Nasal bones		Maxillo-alveolar		Palatal		Mandible				
																			Breadth		Height		
Upper height (n-pr)	Total height (n-gn)	Bizygomatic	Upper facial (fmt-fmt)	Mid-facial (zm-zm)	Biorbital (ek-ek)	Ant. interorb. (mf-mf)	Post. interorb. (la-la)	Width (mf-ek)	Width (la-ek)	Height	Width	Height	Breadth (minimum)	Breadth (maximum)	Length	Breadth	Length	Width	Bicondylar	Bigonial	Ramus	Ramus	Chin
mm.	mm.	mm.	mm.	mm.	mm.	mm.	mm.	mm.	mm.	mm.	mm.	mm.	mm.	mm.	mm.	mm.	mm.	mm.	mm.	mm.	mm.	mm.	mm.
71	—	133	102	96	94	18	21	41	37	37	24	51	10	14	53	64	44	41	—	—	—	—	—
72	—	139?	110	101	105	22	27	44	40	37	24	52	10	16	57	69	51	41	—	—	—	—	—
66	—	129	98	93	90	16	20	40	37	33	22	47	9	16	50	63	44	39	—	—	—	—	—
76?	—	138	105	94	99	16	20	44	40	34	24	52	6	13?	54	65	49	42	—	—	—	—	—
76	—	141	107	99	99	18	22	43	38	38	25	55	9	18	54	70	47	42	—	—	—	—	—
77	—	151	114	109	108	20	27	47	42	38	25	56	14	16	52	72	45	46	—	—	—	—	—
67	—	134	103	93	95	18	22	41	38	36	21	49	8	14	46	63	42?	42	—	—	—	—	—
63	—	123	96	91	91	14	18	41	37	34	20	47	6	12?	49	60	42	39	—	—	—	—	—
66	—	129	100	92	93	18	21	40	37	36	20	52	7	13	47	61	44	39	—	—	—	—	—
78	—	147	111	110	104	24	29	43	38	35	27	57	11	18	58	69	49	43	—	—	—	—	—
69	—	—	103	99?	99	17	22	43	39	39	26	55	7	—	51	—	—	—	—	—	—	—	—
75	—	137	107	100	100	18	23	44	40	35	23	52	7	16	51	64	44	38?	—	—	—	—	—
71	—	134	103	95	96	18	23	42	37	35	22	55	8	11	51	67	43	43	—	—	—	—	—
77	—	145	108	108	99	20	23	42	39	38	26	57	9	15	58	69	49	46	—	—	—	—	—
73	—	140	103	97	97	15	20	44	39	37	22	53	7	12	52	66	47	41?	—	—	—	—	—
62?	—	118	94	86	91	17	21	39	36	35	21	43	7	17	42?	60	38	35	—	—	—	—	—
72	—	134	103	100	95	18	22	41	38	37	24	54	7	17	53	61	45	40	—	—	—	—	—
61	—	112	93	85	87	18	24	37	33	32	21	44	9	16?	44	58	41	36	—	—	—	—	—
—	—	—	106	—	—	18	23	—	—	—	—	—	—	—	—	—	—	—	—	—	—	—	—
70	—	148	110	105	102	22	26	44	39	35	24	53	11	15	56	70	47	45	—	—	—	—	—
76	—	145	108	103	103	20	25	46	41	37	23	55	10	18	52	62	44	38	—	—	—	—	—
76	—	143?	112	98	102	20	24	44	40	38	24	55	8	15?	—	—	—	—	—	—	—	—	—
71	—	137	107	102	101	16	19	44	41	37	22	49	10	16	59	67	50	44	—	—	—	—	—
68	—	145	107	98	98	21	25	41	37	35	24	51	8	13	50	62	44	40	—	—	—	—	—
72	—	139	103	97	98	16	21	44	39	35	25	49	9	18	55	61	51	37?	—	—	—	—	—
72	—	144	111	108	103	18	24	45	40	38	24	53	10	17	58	66	50	46	—	—	—	—	—
78	—	147?	112	106	103	16	24	46	42	36	27	60	8	15	56	68	49	45	—	—	—	—	—
81	—	147	113	107	108	19	24	48	43	40	25	58	10	16	—	—	—	—	—	—	—	—	—
72	—	144	107	101	98	18	20	44	40	35	26	54	6	15	55	68	49	46	—	—	—	—	—
71	—	125	101	95	93	17	20	41	38	36	22	52	8	15?	51	62	44	38	—	—	—	—	—
73	—	139	107	94	99	18	22	44	40	38	22	49	9	15	58	66	52	42	—	—	—	—	—
74	—	138?	106	101	99	18	21	44	40	40	25	54	7	16	56	66	49	42	—	—	—	—	—
60	—	117?	94	87	88	17	19	38	35	34	21	44	10	15	43	59	39	35	—	—	—	—	—
70	—	135	102	98	95	20	26	39	35	36	24	52	7	16	51	64	43	44	—	—	—	—	—
72	—	138	104	99	96	16	19	43	39	36	23	55	8	13	52	69	46	43	—	—	—	—	—
55	—	56	57	56	56	57	57	56	56	56	56	56	55	55	52	51	50	50	3	3	3	3	3
68–	—	133–	101–	79–	92–	15–	19–	40–	37–	33–	20–	48–	4–14	11–	49–	61–	42–	32–	123–	101–	34–	56–	34–
83	—	151	114	110	109	24	29	49	45	40	29	60		19	60	73	51	48	135	106	38	61	36
73.6	—	141.3	107.6	101.0	100.7	18.7	23.4	43.7	39.6	36.3	24.2	52.4	8.6	15.1	54.2	66.5	47.1	42.5	129.3	102.7	36.3	58.7	35.0

Tribal divisions and subdivisions / Catalogue No. / Sex and stages of life / Number of cases / Averages and ranges	Capacity	Length	Breadth	Height (ba-b)	Circumference (horizontal)	SKULL Median-sagittal Arc Total (n-o)				SKULL Median-sagittal Chord			Cranial base (length n-ba)	Foramen magnum		Frontal bone		Length	
							Frontal	Parietal	Occipital	Frontal	Parietal	Occipital		Length	Width	Breadth (minimum)	Breadth (maximum)	Length (ba-pr)	Inferior length (ba-gn)
	ccm.	mm.	mm.	mm.	mm.	mm.	mm.	mm.	mm.	mm.	mm.	mm.	mm.	mm.	mm.	mm.	mm.	mm.	mm.
CHINOOK																			
♀ cases	25	25	25	24	25	25	26	26	25	26	26	25	24	25	25	25	25	24	—
range	1020–1390	148–166	138–161	102–134	465–513	305–365	109–128	89–112	99–131	102–116	78–97	87–115	80–103	30–36	26–32	86–102	109–126	88–108	—
average	1251.6	160.7	149.8	121.4	491.2	324.2	115.0	100.8	108.6	107.0	87.3	96.4	89.5	32.7	29.1	93.9	118.4	97.1	—
juv. cases	4	4	4	4	4	4	4	4	4	4	4	4	4	4	4	4	4	4	—
range	1070–1460	144–169	142–154	109–127	456–514	299–337	103–113	92–119	94–119	96–105	80–91	88–105	85–97	30–35	27–31	87–98	112–120	85–95	—
average	1227.5	152.7	148.2	118.5	475.5	318.5	109.5	103.7	105.2	101.8	86.7	95.8	88.5	33.0	28.5	92.8	116.0	91.3	—
inf. cases	6	6	6	5	6	6	6	6	6	6	6	6	5	5	5	6	6	5	—
range	1200–1400	151–166	145–161	110–124	470–517	318–334	107–118	90–109	98–128	101–109	81–90	87–111	80–88	30–37	27–29	87–97	110–122	81–90	—
average	1301.7	157.2	153.2	119.4	487.0	325.7	112.7	100.2	112.8	104.7	86.5	100.3	84.8	33.4	28.0	94.0	117.8	86.2	—
Coupeville																			
2676 ♂ mat (def.)	1340	179	150	132	512?	—	127	110	113	122	91	106	99	34	29	99	119	104	122?
♂ 1 case	1340.0	179.0	150.0	132.0	512.0	—	127.0	110.0	113.0	122.0	91.0	106.0	99.0	34.0	29.0	99.0	119.0	104.0	122.0
Divisional total																			
♂ cases	57	57	57	57	57	56	57	58	57	58	58	57	57	57	57	58	58	56	4
range	1150–1630	155–182	143–170	115–145	485–540	306–372	109–133	90–130	95–125	103–121	80–111	86–109	87–107	28–41	27–35	89–109	112–133	88–112	113–122
average	1388.8	166.6	156.3	127.8	508.1	339.8	117.2	105.0	111.8	112.6	91.0	97.4	98.6	34.3	30.4	98.6	123.1	101.7	116.0
♀ cases	25	25	25	24	25	25	26	26	25	26	26	25	24	25	25	25	25	24	—
range	1020–1390	148–166	138–161	102–134	465–513	305–365	109–128	89–112	99–131	102–116	78–97	87–115	80–103	30–36	26–32	86–102	109–126	88–108	—
average	1251.6	160.7	149.8	121.4	491.1	324.2	115.0	100.8	108.6	107.0	87.4	96.4	89.5	32.7	29.1	93.9	118.4	97.2	—
juv. cases	4	4	4	4	4	4	4	4	4	4	4	4	4	4	4	4	4	4	—
range	1010–1460	144–169	142–154	109–127	456–514	299–337	103–113	92–119	94–119	96–105	80–91	88–105	85–97	30–35	27–31	87–98	112–120	85–95	—
average	1227.5	152.8	148.3	118.5	475.5	318.5	109.5	103.8	105.3	101.8	86.8	95.8	89.5	33.0	28.5	92.8	116.0	91.3	—
inf. cases	6	6	6	5	6	6	6	6	6	6	6	5	5	5	6	6	5	—	
range	1200–1400	151–166	145–161	110–124	470–517	318–334	107–118	90–109	98–128	101–109	81–90	87–111	80–88	30–37	27–29	87–97	110–122	81–90	—
average	1301.7	157.2	153.2	119.4	487.0	325.7	112.7	100.2	112.8	104.3	86.5	100.5	84.8	33.4	28.0	94.0	117.8	86.2	—
KOSKIMO Kwakiutl																			
101 ♀ mat	1340	179	133	125	497	364	124	121	119	110	107	99	96	30	27	87	111	102	112
103 ♂ ad-mat	1550	198	137	140	535	391	134	109	148	122	100	125	106	39	33	105	116	107	126
1715 ♂? ad	1300	171	136	124	493	343	123	114	106	110	100	90	97	35	29	98	114	105	113
1716 ♂ ad	1530	179	140	138	513	371	124	127	120	114	110	104	104	32	27	95	119	101	119

FACE AND MANDIBLE

Height Upper (n-pr)	Height Total (n-gn)	Breadth Bizygomatic	Breadth Upper facial (fmt-fmt)	Breadth Mid-facial (zm-zm)	Breadth Biorbital (ek-ek)	Breadth Ant. interorb. (mf-mf)	Breadth Post. interorb. (la-la)	Orbit Width (mf-ek)	Orbit Width (h-ek)	Orbit Height	Nose Width	Nose Height	Nasal bones Breadth (minimum)	Nasal bones Breadth (maximum)	Maxillo-alveolar Length	Maxillo-alveolar Breadth	Palatal Length	Palatal Width	Mandible Breadth Bicondylar	Mandible Breadth Bigonial	Mandible Height Ramus	Mandible Height Ramus	Mandible Chin
mm.	mm.	mm.	mm.	mm.	mm.	mm.	mm.	mm.	mm.	mm.	mm.	mm.	mm.	mm.	mm.	mm.	mm.	mm.	mm.	mm.	mm.	mm.	mm.
26	—	24	25	22	25	25	25	25	25	25	25	25	25	21	25	23	23	23	1	1	1	1	1
62–78	—	123–140	96–111	91–103	90–112	14–20	18–26	38–47	35–43	32–40	20–26	44–57	6–10	11–18	46–58	58–68	40–52	35–45	—	—	—	—	—
66.6	—	132.6	103.2	95.3	97.0	17.7	22.0	42.0	38.3	36.3	22.7	49.6	8.3	14.7	50.6	62.9	44.3	40.1	118.0	104.0	37.0	52.0	32.0
4	—	4	4	4	4	4	4	4	4	4	4	4	3	4	4	4	4	4	—	—	—	—	—
60–69	—	112–126	93–100	85–95	87–95	15–20	20–24	37–42	33–38	31–37	21–23	44–48	8–9	14–16	43–48	58–66	40–42	34–38	—	—	—	—	—
63.3	—	120.0	96.8	89.5	91.5	17.8	22.8	39.3	35.3	33.3	22.3	45.5	8.3	15.0	44.8	61.5	40.8	36.0	—	—	—	—	—
6	—	6	6	6	6	6	6	6	6	6	6	5	5	6	6	6	6	6	—	—	—	—	—
55–67	—	108–120	87–97	76–89	83–91	15–17	19–22	36–39	32–36	31–36	19–21	42–44	5–12	13–17	38–46	59–60	35–43	32–38	—	—	—	—	—
60.0	—	116.8	94.3	83.7	88.3	16.7	20.8	38.2	34.8	33.8	19.8	43.7	8.4	15.0	41.3	59.2	37.8	34.5	—	—	—	—	—
74?	127?	149	111	101	103	16	21	47	42	37	26	56	6	14	—	—	—	—	132	108	36	67	37
74.0	127.0	149.0	111.0	101.0	103.0	16.0	21.0	47.0	42.0	37.0	26.0	56.0	6.0	14.0	—	—	—	—	132.0	108.0	36.0	67.0	37.0
56	—	57	58	57	57	58	58	57	57	57	57	57	56	56	52	51	50	50	4	4	4	4	4
68–83	—	133–151	101–114	79–110	92–109	15–24	19–29	40–49	37–45	33–40	20–29	48–60	4–14	11–19	49–60	61–73	42–51	32–48	118–135	101–108	34–38	56–61	32–36
73.6	—	141.8	107.7	101.0	100.7	18.7	23.3	43.8	39.7	36.3	24.2	52.5	8.6	15.1	54.2	66.5	47.1	42.5	126.5	104.0	36.0	60.8	34.3
25	—	24	25	22	25	25	25	25	25	25	25	25	25	21	25	23	23	23	1	1	1	1	1
62–78	—	123–140	96–111	85–95	90–112	14–20	18–26	38–47	35–43	32–40	23–26	44–57	6–10	11–18	46–58	58–68	40–52	35–45	—	—	—	—	—
69.2	—	132.6	103.2	89.5	97.0	17.7	22.0	42.0	38.3	36.3	22.7	49.6	8.3	14.7	50.6	62.9	44.3	40.1	118.0	104.0	27.0	52.0	32.0
4	—	4	4	4	4	4	4	4	4	4	4	3	3	4	4	4	4	4	—	—	—	—	—
60–69	—	112–126	93–100	85–95	87–95	15–20	20–24	37–42	33–38	31–37	33	44–48	8–9	14–16	43–48	58–66	40–42	34–38	—	—	—	—	—
63.3	—	120.0	96.8	89.5	91.5	17.8	22.8	39.3	35.3	33.3	22.3	45.5	8.3	15.0	44.8	61.5	40.8	36.0	—	—	—	—	—
6	—	6	6	6	6	6	6	6	6	6	6	6	5	6	6	6	6	6	—	—	—	—	—
55–67	—	108–120	87–97	76–89	83–91	15–17	19–22	36–39	32–36	31–36	19–21	42–44	5–12	13–17	38–46	59–60	35–43	32–38	—	—	—	—	—
60.0	—	116.8	94.3	83.7	88.3	16.7	20.8	38.2	34.8	33.8	19.8	43.7	8.4	15.0	41.3	59.2	37.8	34.5	—	—	—	—	—
74	118	125	103	95	98	16	21	43	39	37	23	49	6	16	52	63	46	38	109	101	33	58	33
78	129	142	113	102	105	21	26	45	41	37	22	56	9	14	57	70	48	45	128	116	39	73	35
73	119	135	109	99	100	18	24	44	40	36	23	48	8	17	56	62	52	38	118	97	40	65	34
77	118	144	111	103	104	15	23	49	43	38	22	55	5	13	55	66	46	42	118	103	39	65	33

Tribal divisions and subdivisions / Catalogue No. / Sex and stages of life / Number of cases / Averages and ranges	Capacity	Length	Breadth	Height (ba-b)	Circumference (horizontal)	SKULL Median-sagittal Arc Total (n-o)	Frontal	Parietal	Occipital	Chord Frontal	Parietal	Occipital	Cranial base (length n-ba)	Foramen magnum Length	Width	Frontal bone Breadth (minimum)	Breadth (maximum)	Length (ba-pr)	Inferior length (ba-gn)
	ccm.	mm.	mm.	mm.	mm.	mm.	mm.	mm.	mm.	mm.	mm.	mm.	mm.	mm.	mm.	mm.	mm.	mm.	mm.
KOSKIMO																			
1717 ♂ mat	1520	184	149	136	527	379	127	121	131	115	107	111	98	34	30	93	119	98	106
1718 ♂? ad-mat	1350	181	137	124	509	365	123	134	108	112	111	96	94	33	29	96	113	103	—
1719 ♂ mat	1420	191	144	139	536	381	134	119	128	122	109	110	103	34	26	98	119	100	—
1720 ♀ mat	1380	181	134	132	495	376	122	135	119	110	110	109	96	31	30	98	118	93	102
1723 ♂ ad-mat	1530	187	147	138	529	386	136	115	135	121	105	105	99	31	28	95	118	108	—
1724 juv	1360	166	141	132	485	351	128	122	101	113	105	88	94	33	30	98	117	88	—
1725 ♂ mat	1470	185	146	128	527	363	125	125	113	116	107	96	100	35	31	97	122?	105	—
1726 ♂ ad-mat	1320	183	136	126	517	359	124	120	115	112	106	94	103	35	30	93	112	103	—
1729 ♂ ad-mat	1530	186	144	135	528	379	134	114	131	123	100	110	103	35	29	97	118	107	123
1730 ♂? mat	1300	181	134	128	511	354	123	119	112	113	104	95	100	36	29	89	108	105	116
1731 ♀ juv-ad	1350	171	145	121	498	343	119	113	111	109	98	98	92	35	26	95	111	95	—
1731A ♂ ad	—	—	—	—	—	—	—	—	—	—	—	—	—	—	—	—	—	—	—
1732 ♂ ad	1450	174	155	133	510	344	123	120	101	114	105	89	99	36	31	94	119	97	110
1736 ♂ mat	1450	188 (191)	139	132	532	389	132	117	140	116	103	103	101	34	28	99	117	97	—
1737 ♂ mat	1300	179	135	135	500	364	124	120	120	113	104	105	103	34	27	91	120?	102	—
1738 inf. II	—	153?	139	127	464?	343	112	105?	126?	100	94?	105?	81?	34	27	90	112	75	—
1739 ♂ mat	1580	190	145	136	526	383	134	119	130	120	105	103	98	36	30	93	117	88	—
1739A ♂ mat	—	—	—	—	—	—	—	—	—	—	—	—	—	—	—	—	—	—	—
1740 ♂ ad-mat	1440	182	143	129	515	381	139	106	136	126	98	111	93	32	30	94	114	97	118
1742 ♂ mat	1400	186	137	132	522	363	127	115	121	115	102	98	103	37	28	103	111	105	119
1744 ♀ mat	1390	175	134	129	494	364	128	117	119	115	102	104	99	30	30	96?	114	102	113
1911 ♀ mat	1180	175	130	127	484	346	113	122	111	104	106	99	96	35	32	87	104	97	—
1912 ♂? ad	1460	174	143	135	495	353	122	121	110	112	105	97	102	37	33	89	113	108	—
1913 ♂ mat	1340	182	136	132	505	368	130	124	114	119	105	103	104	34	31	93	109?	102	—
3878 ♂ ad	1490	187	140	135	522	379	133	116	130	120	104	108	100	38	29	98	117	103	—
3879 ♂ ad-mat	1540	197	141	130	533	384	134	132	118	118	118	110	104	34	30	97	119	105	—
3880 ♂ mat	1540	182	145	141	525	393	133	134	125	118	118	100	97	35	30	101	119	95	—
3881 ♀? mat	1190	175	137	135	497	363	124	125	114	113	109	97	100	33	28	91	114?	98	—
3882 ♂ ad	1570	184	150	141	525	370	125	117	128	115	105	108	104	39	33	98	118	106	—
3883 ♂ ad	—	181	149	140	521?	372	133	119	120	121	106	101	100	33	31	98	117	96	—
3884 ♂ mat	—	187	138?	137	—	378	144	121	113	127	106	94	101	34	27	98	115	101	—
3885 ♂ mat	1450	182	139	132	515	369	127	127	115	113	110	102	98	33	31	100	116	97	—
3886 ♂ ad-mat	1270	182	136	130	507	362	129	110	123	116	97	105	103	36	29	93	107	106	—
3887 ♂? ad	1350	178	135	129	494	357	125	122	110	115	106	94	101	33	30	92	110	105	—
3888 ♀ ad	—	167	130	—	—	—	118	120	—	105	103	—	—	—	—	89	107	—	—
3889 ♀ ad	—	175	133	—	491	—	126	130	—	114	110	—	—	—	—	93	107?	—	—
3890 ♂ mat	1440	189	139	132	528	373	120	110	143	112	101	111	108	32	33	91	111	105	—
3891 ♀ ad-mat	1170	175	128	127	481	344	125	108	111	114	95	96	100	30	24	97	109	101	—
3892 ♀ mat	1100	169	127	123?	472	351	119	115	117	107	97	98	96?	32?	—	87	104	90?	—

FACE AND MANDIBLE

Height		Breadth						Orbit			Nose		Nasal bones		Maxillo-alveolar		Palatal		Mandible Breadth			Mandible Height	
Upper height (n-pr)	Total height (n-gn)	Bizygomatic	Upper facial (fmt-fmt)	Mid-facial (zm-zm)	Biorbital (ek-ek)	Ant. interorb. (mf-mf)	Post. interorb. (la-la)	Width (mf-ek)	Width (la-ek)	Height	Width	Height	Breadth (minimum)	Breadth (maximum)	Length	Breadth	Length	Width	Bicondylar	Bigonial	Ramus	Ramus	Chin
mm.	mm.	mm.	mm.	mm.	mm.	mm.	mm.	mm.	mm.	mm.	mm.	mm.	mm.	mm.	mm.	mm.	mm.	mm.	mm.	mm.	mm.	mm.	mm.
81	139	142?	110	97	105	20	25	45	41	38	24	52	9	17	55	63	49	39?	129	105	35	64	42
83	—	130	107	97	99	17	23	43	38	40	24	54	7	16	55	66	49	43	—	—	—	—	—
78?	—	144	112	101	104	16	22	47	43	36	28	55	8	17	53	65	46	42	—	—.	—	—	—
77	125	132	108	97	102	15	21	46	42	42	23	53	5	13	51	63(65)	46	40	113?	100	34	63	34
79	—	137?	109	105	101	19	25	44	40r	39r	24	54	10	17	52	68	48	41	—	—	—	—	—
68	—	125	101	94	95	16	22	41	37	35	23	49	6	16	45	64	40	40	—	—	—	—	—
83	—	143	110	106	103	19	25	45	40	38	23	60	7	14	55	70	47	45	—	—	—	—	—
74	—	138	112	95	103	19	26	45	40	37	25	52	9	18	53	61	49	40	—	—	—	—	—
81	127	143	111	105	105	17	24	48	43	38	26	58	5	20	58	66	52	41	123	117	40	74	35
79	122	136	106	99	101	17	22	45	40	38	25	55	11	16	57	59	50	38	125	99	39	63	35
64	—	125?	103	95	99	19	23	42	38	36	23	46	10	14	45	62	40	41	—	—	—	—	—
—	—	—	—	—	—	—	—	—	—	—	—	—	—	—	—	—	—	—	126	111	37	59	34
82	133	142?	103	98	98	18	24	43	39	40	22	58	7	12	52	67	45	40	121	114	41r	60r	37
80	—	144	112	102	105	19	25	47	42	37	27	52	8	16	52	67	46	42	—	—	—	—	—
78	—	137	109	101	104	17	27	46	41	39	25	56	9	17	56	66	47	42	—	—	—	—	—
60	—	110	91	79	86	13	19?	38	34	35	20	42	6	12	37	55	35	33	—	—	—	—	—
73	—	137	103	90	94	14	18	44	40	38	20	52	5	13	49	57	41	37	—	—	—	—	—
—	—	—	—	—	—	—	—	—	—	—	—	—	—	—	—	—	—	—	115	96	42	63	36
77	124	134	107	98	99	16	24	45	40	36	22	53	7	15	52	66	44	42	109	88	38	69	33
77	124	144	111	104	105	18	25	46	42	39	26	56	11	17	57	67	51	43	114	107	39	60	33
70	113	127	106	94	100	19	24	43	39	36	26	48	9	17	52	59	45	38	111	98	41	60	34
77	—	—	—	96	95	19	22	42	39r?	39r?	23	53	9	17?	52	62	48	32	—	—	—	—	—
79	—	131	103	93	97	15	20	44	39	39	24	58	5	14	57	67	51	42	—	—	—	—	—
71	—	131	103	103	98	18	23	45	41	37	25	52	10	17	55	66	48	44	—	—	—	—	—
75	—	137	109	105	103	19	25	45	40	40	25	52	8	15?	55	73	48	47	—	—	—	—	—
79	—	142	109	100	103	18	23	45	41	40	24	56	7	17	54	62	47	41	—	—	—	—	—
78	—	146	108	100	100	16	22	45	40	38	27	55	7	17	52	63	43	40?	—	—	—	—	—
76	—	142	108	96	103	19	25	44	40	36	26	53	10	16	52	64	45	44	—	—	—	—	—
74	—	145	111	107	101	21	26	43	38	37	23	51	10	16	57	69	51	44	—	—	—	—	—
74	—	134	105	100	98	20	24	42	39	37	25	52	10	18	51	63	45	38	—	—	—	—	—
76	—	131	—	94	—	—	—	44	40	36	—	49	—	—	56	61	48	40?	—	—	—	—	—
77	—	137	108	102	102	19	23	45	40	40	25	56	7	16	53	63	45	41	—	—	—	—	—
78	—	128	105	95	98	20	22	41	38	36	23	52	9	15	55	66	46	43	—	—	—	—	—
75	—	128	103	94	95	15	19	43	39	37	21	50	4	16	56	64	48	40	—	—	—	—	—
—	—	115?	94	86	89	18	17?	39	35	36	21	47	—	—	47	55	42	33	—	—	—	—	—
85	—	145	111	101	105	18	23	48	43	38	22	58	6	14	58	70	46	43	—	—	—	—	—
76	—	128	111	94	102	17	26	46	40	38	21	52	8	15	52	58	46	35	—	—	—	—	—
72	—	120?	99	—	95	16	23	42	36	36	20	49	6	15	—	—	—	—	—	—	—	—	—

Tribal divisions and subdivisions — Catalogue No. — Sex and stages of life — Number of cases — Averages and ranges	SKULL																
	Capacity	Length	Breadth	Height (ba-b)	Circumference (horizontal)	Median-sagittal						Cranial base (length n-ba)	Foramen magnum		Frontal bone		Length	
						Arc			Chord									
						Total (n-o)	Frontal	Parietal	Occipital	Frontal	Parietal	Occipital		Length	Width	Breadth (minimum)	Breadth (maximum)	Length (ba-pr)	Inferior length (ba-gn)
	ccm.	mm.	mm.	mm.	mm.	mm.	mm.	mm.	mm.	mm.	mm.	mm.	mm.	mm.	mm.	mm.	mm.	mm.	mm.
KOSKIMO																			
3893 ♂ ad	1550	188	141	137	521	378	130	126	122	117	107	109	104	35	30	97	119	103	—
3894 ♂ ad	1360	177	143	134	513	362	133	121	108	117	105	88	103	35	27	90	115	102	—
3895 ♂ ? mat	1340	187	140	131	517	372	118	122	132	108	109	111	101	34	31	87	109	100	—
3896 ♂ ad	1600	186	148	147	530	370	128	120	134	118	108	114	110	40	32	101	123	105	—
3899 ♂ ? mat	—	—	—	—	—	—	—	—	—	—	—	—	—	—	—	—	—	—	—
3900 ♂ mat	—	—	—	—	—	—	—	—	—	—	—	—	—	—	—	—	—	—	—
4236 ♂ ad-mat	1410	189	139	132	531	380	130	125	125	116	108	98	103	33	28	101	118?	99	—
4237 ♀ mat	1260	180	135	130	499	362	126	109	127	116	99	109	99	32	25	93	113	96	—
4238 ♀ ad	1240	167	124	124	485	341	114	113	114	105	96	98	95	30	27	87	110	95	—
4239 ♂ mat	1280	182	138	137	510	366	132	119	115	119	105?	97?	102	34	29	92	111	106	—
4240 ♀ ? mat	1330	180	137	132	512	374	130	126	118	115	108	108	97	30	27	91	—	100	—
4241 ♀ ad	1220	169	137	123	486	339	120	123	116	108	94	98	96	33	30	95	109	101	—
4242 ♀ mat	1220	177	138	132	505	358	124	98	136	112	90?	108?	97	35	27	83	107	100	—
4243 ♀ ad	1290	165	141	124	481	336	115	114	107	105	98	96	99	32	32	99	112	105	—
4244 ♂ mat	1370	189	140	135	532	381	124	135	122	113	114	102	106	37	30	99	117	105	—
4245 ♂ mat	1430	183	141	132	512	370	132	125	113	119	106	100	100	33	28	86	109	99	—
4246 inf. II	1280	165	135	124	464	342	119	106	117	107	96	97	87	36	27	—	107	—	—
4247 ♀ ad	1250	172	137	120	489	342	115	117	110	102	101	91	97	34	27	89	107	91	—
4248 ♂ mat	1400	185	150	133	532	372	126	121	125	114	107	98	103	35	30	95	115?	102	—
4249 ♂ mat	1350	181	135	132	503	360	124	105	131	113	96	114	101	31	29	91	109	99	—
4250 ♀ mat	1160	177	137	124	497	342	122	98	122	108	91	103	99	35	29	91	110?	101	—
4251 ♀ mat	1230	177	133	122	485?	346	120	108	118	110	98	102	95	33	29	94	112?	100	—
4252 ♀ ad	1240	174	135	128	493	360	128	116	116	114	102	96	94	29	27	92	111	95	—
4253 inf. II	1250	171	142	128	493	364	118	132	114	105	116	93	83	38	27	93	116	78	—
4254 ♂ ad	1370	179	136	138	504	359	120	121	118	109	106	100	107	35	32	88	108	104	—
4256 ♂ ad	1580	188	147	140?	527	379	128	115	136	114	101	113	104	39	30?	103	117	101	—
4257 ♂ ? mat	1420	177	145	130	506	359	124	127	118	113	95	101	103	33	30	100	116?	105	—
4258 ♂ ? ad	1320	176	141	127	598	347	125	111	111	113	98	98	97	33	28	96	114	105	—
4259 ♂ ? mat	1370	182	139	125	503	380	130	113	127	118	108	110	91	31	28	89	120	95	—
4260 ♂ ad-mat	1300	176	140	132	498	355	118	118	119	108	103	99	100	35	32	87	110	97	—
4261 ♂ mat	1310	183	137	128	493	364	123	127	114	112	111	100	101	30	27	86	109	105	—
4262 ♂ ? mat	1370	182	136	132	512	366	130	113	123	115	102	106	100	32	27	91	111?	102	—
4263 ♂ mat	1310	183	137	133	516	372	130	101	141	115	95	115	102	32	31	98	113	100	—
4264 ♂ ad	—	171	—	130	497	348	121	115	112	108	100	95	100	35	30	90	—	96	—
4265 ♂ mat	1510	172	148	133	514	354	127	104	112	108	88	101	101	34	31	93	120	106	—
4266 ♂ mat	1460	184	148	135	528	376	125	131	120	111	114	102	101	33	29	93	117	98	—
4267 ♂ ad	1300	179	134	133	500	362	124	114	124	112	99	104	98	32	27	97	108	100	—
4268 ♀ mat	1250	166	137	138	490?	346	117	122	107	108	104	93	96	35	27	87	104	98	—
4269 ♂ ? mat	1500	188	157	132	526	374	128	114	132	114	102	111	103	33	31	83	109	100	—
4270 ♂ ? sen	—	178	135?	130	—	355	125	106	124	112	94	105	97	35	26	—	—	99	—

FACE AND MANDIBLE

Height		Breadth						Orbit			Nose		Nasal bones		Maxillo-alveolar		Palatal		Mandible				
																			Breadth		Height		
Upper height (n-pr)	Total height (n-gn)	Bizygomatic	Upper facial (fmt-fmt)	Mid-facial (zm-zm)	Biorbital (ek-ek)	Ant. interorb. (mf-mf)	Post. interorb. (la-la)	Width (mf-ek)	Width (la-ek)	Height	Width	Height	Breadth (minimum)	Breadth (maximum)	Length	Breadth	Length	Width	Bicondylar	Bigonial	Ramus	Ramus	Chin
mm.	mm.	mm.	mm.	mm.	mm.	mm.	mm.	mm.	mm.	mm.	mm.	mm.	mm.	mm.	mm.	mm.	mm.	mm.	mm.	mm.	mm.	mm.	mm.
75	—	143	107	98	98	21	24	41	38	37	21	54	7	15	55	65	49	41	—	—	—	—	—
77	—	138?	105	97	98	20	26	43	38	35	23	51	8	15	53	62	48	42	—	—	—	—	—
76	—	131	100	97	96	19	22	42	39	37	25	54	8	16	50	61?	46	40?	—	—	—	—	—
81	—	149	110	108	103	19	23	46	42	41	24	58	7	15	57	71	48	46	—	—	—	—	—
—	—	—	—	—	—	—	—	—	—	—	—	—	—	—	—	—	—	—	125	102	39	60	34
—	—	—	—	—	—	—	—	—	—	—	—	—	—	—	—	—	—	—	120	—	37	60	36
78	—	143	112	102	104	20	28	47	40	40	26	58	10	17	55	63	48	37	—	—	—	—	—
76	—	130	105	92?	98	16	23	44	39	38	23	54	8	16	49	58	44	—	—	—	—	—	—
69	—	129	99	96	95	18	23	41	37	36	24	50	8	17	48	63	42	40	—	—	—	—	—
74	—	140	106	106	98	16	23	43	38	36	23	57	6	16	59	69	50	42	—	—	—	—	—
75	—	130?	102	—	98	20	22	40	38	37	25	53	9	—	55	64	47	39	—	—	—	—	—
74	—	127	105	94	95	18	22	41	37	37	23	52	8	15	55	66	47	39	—	—	—	—	—
73	—	133	101	97	97	16	19	42	39	35	25	52	5	15	55	62	48	38	—	—	—	—	—
67	—	142	108	102	100	22	26	44	39	36	25	46	12	20	53	64	46	40	—	—	—	—	—
86	—	150	113	107	105	19	25	46	40	38	25	56	11	16	56	68	53	42?	—	—	—	—	—
78	—	140	107	98	104	19	22	45	41	37	29	53	9	16	52	66	45	—	—	—	—	—	—
—	—	110?	—	—	—	17	—	39r	—	34	21	42	—	15?	—	—	—	—	—	—	—	—	—
67	—	128	100	90	96	18	23	42	39	35	23	49	7	16	47	59	43	36	—	—	—	—	—
87	—	151	114	101	107	19	25	46	42	37	25	56	5	15	54	66	46	43	—	—	—	—	—
75	—	132	109	93	101	19	25	43	39	39	24	51	8	18	49	64	44	41	—	—	—	—	—
75	—	134	102	91	94	16	22	41	38	37	23	51	6	16	51	58	46	34	—	—	—	—	—
70	—	138?	104	94	100	20	24	43	39	36	24	49	10	16	49	61	45	41	—	—	—	—	—
70	—	131	106	95	97	19	24	41	37	36	23	47	8	17	51	60	44	39	—	—	—	—	—
58	—	117	95	83	89	17	19	38	35	36	19	42	5	14	36	55	32	34	—	—	—	—	—
76	—	141	105	100	101	17	22	44	40	36	22	53	7	14	55	63	50	39	—	—	—	—	—
85	—	153	110	112	103	20	23	45	41	39	24	61	9	20	57	68	48	47	—	—	—	—	—
80?	—	144	113	109	107	20	27	47	42	39	27	54	11	18	54	67	49	43	—	—	—	—	—
71	—	137	109	98	103	17	23	47	42	37	23	50	6	16	56	70	48	46	—	—	—	—	—
74	—	129	102	88	98	16	21	43	40	39	22	54	6	14	51	56	47	—	—	—	—	—	—
74	—	134	109	104	—	14	21	49r	44r	37r	22	52	5	14	52	62	46	40	—	—	—	—	—
79	—	134	103	93	100	19	23	42	39	35	24	52	8	17	52	—	45	—	—	—	—	—	—
70?	—	131	103	96	99	18	25	42	38	37	27	50	6	15?	52	—	46	—	—	—	—	—	—
76	—	134	109	107	102	19	23	45	41	40	24	52	8	14	51	62	44	41	—	—	—	—	—
70	—	132?	102	92	96	15	21	45	41	38	23	51	6	15	51	67	46	43	—	—	—	—	—
78	—	143	115	104	107	18	23	46	42	37	24	54	5	14	55	62	47	43	—	—	—	—	—
77	—	141	109	100	101	18	23	44	39	39	26	53	7	18	—	—	—	—	—	—	—	—	—
71	—	134	105	93	99	22	26	41	38	35	24	48	10	16	53	61	47	38	—	—	—	—	—
73	—	126?	—	93	96	13	—	45r	—	38r	23	51	5	13	55	62	46	39	—	—	—	—	—
77	—	137	99	95	95	20	14	44	38	38	24	58	4	14	54	63	—	—	—	—	—	—	—
73	—	—	—	102	97	--	16	43	—	37	25	51	7	—	—	—	—	—	—	—	—	—	—

Tribal divisions and subdivisions / Catalogue No. / Sex and stages of life / Number of cases / Averages and ranges	Capacity	Length	Breadth	Height (ba-b)	Circumference (horizontal)	SKULL Median-sagittal Arz			Chord			Cranial base (length n-ba)	Foramen magnum		Frontal bone		Length	
						Total (n-o)	Frontal	Parietal	Occipital	Frontal	Parietal	Occipital		Length	Width	Breadth (minimum)	Breadth (maximum)	Length (ba-pr)	Inferior length (ba-gn)
	ccm.	mm.	mm.	mm.	mm.	mm.	mm.	mm.	mm.	mm.	mm.	mm.	mm.	mm.	mm.	mm.	mm.	mm.	mm.
KOSIMO																			
♂ cases	50	54	53	54	52	54	54	54	54	54	54	54	54	54	53	52	54	9
range	1270–1600	171–198	134–157	124–147	493–536	343–393	118–144	101–136	101–148	108–127	94–118	88–125	91–110	30–40	26–33	83–105	107–123	88–108	106–126
average	1402.0	182.9	139.4	133.2	517.8	368.8	127.6	117.1	121.7	115.4	104.9	102.9	101.0	34.4	30.5	94.5	116.8	101.7	115.5
♀ cases	19	21	21	19	20	19	21	21	19	21	21	19	19	18	18	21	20	19	3
range	1100–1390	165–181	124–145	120–138	472–512	336–376	113–130	98–135	107–127	102–116	90–110	89–109	92–100	29–35	24–32	83–99	107–118	90–102	102–113
average	1252.1	173.7	134.4	127.1	491.6	352.5	121.4	110.3	116.4	109.7	100.9	99.6	96.8	32.3	28.0	91.5	109.7	97.9	109.0
juv. 1 case	1360.0	166.0	141.0	132.0	458.0	351.0	128.0	122.0	102.0	113.0	105.0	88.0	94.0	33.0	30.0	98.0	117.0	88.0	—
inf. cases	2	3	3	3	3	3	3	3	3	3	3	3	3	3	2	3		2	
range	1280–1520	153–171	135–142	124–128	464–493	342–364	112–119	105–132	114–126	100–107	94–116	95–103	81–87	34–38	27–27	90; 93	107–116	75; 78	—
average	1400.0	163.0	138.7	126.3	473.7	349.7	116.3	114.3	119.0	104.0	102.0	98.3	83.7	36.0	27.0	91.5	111.7	76.5	—
Nimkish																			
1642 ♂? ad-mat	1370	185	137	127	518	370	130	104	136	115	95	111	100	36	32	90	112	105	—
1643 inf. II	—	179	144	125?	507?	368	126	108	134	111	98	108	89?	34	27	100	116	83?	—
1644 ad	1210	174	132	125	488	346	116	112	118	103	98	99	96	31	26	89	109	92?	—
1645 ♂ ad-mat	1520	188	145	132	531	374	131	130	113	117	112	97	102	37	32	97	116	102	—
1646 ♂ mat	—	178	139	—	514	367	134	128	105	119	111	93	—	—	—	98	112?	—	—
1647 ♂? ad	—	184	136	—	509	—	132	125	—	118?	109	—	—	—	—	96	—	—	—
1648 ♂ ad-mat	1440	182	140	134	519	371	129	129	113	116	108	93	100	35	29	95	115	102	118
1649 ♂ mat	—	191	144	139	541	390	135	130	125	121	119	104	106	37	35	95	—	105	118
1650 ♂ mat	1350	185	134	132	514	369	127	130	112	113	110	99	104	35	30	94	113	96	109
1651 ♂? ad	1290	173	135	131	487	357	122	122	113	111	106	100	96	32	29	90	110	97	109
1652 ♂ ad-mat	1480	182	142	134	513	369	129	129	111	117	111	94	101	37	29	86	114	99	—
1653 ♀ mat	1270	173	136	128	486	364	118	129	117	107	109	96	97	30	27	90	102	97	—
1654 ♂ ad	1550	194	143	130	532	378	133	114	131	121	105	104	100	36	30	93	119	100	—
1655 ♂ juv-ad	1480	184	138	129	514	366	125	109	132	115	97	112	98	38	30	96	115	95	114
1656 ♂ mat	1560	185	146	141	530	394	141	119	134	125	104	109	98	32	29	100	118?	95	—
1657 ♂ ad-mat	1470	192	137	134	531	378	141	124	113	125	106	101	102	36	30	97	116?	97	—
1658 inf. II	—	171?	136	—	—	—	116	109	—	105	98	—	—	—	—	89	108	—	—
1659 ♂? mat	1420	176	140	135	507	365	121	131	113	108	110	101	102	33	28	96	112	99	—
1660 ♂ ad	—	179	139	125	512	359	120	134	105	109	112	91	92	39	32	—	121	—	—
1661 ♂ ad	1360	189	136	131	515?	372	130	106	136	115	99	108	100	31	26	97	111	—	—
1662A ♂ ad	1290	173	142	134	508	359	135	120	104	118	103	92	101	31	27	92	119	96	—
1662B ♂ mat	—	—	—	—	—	—	—	—	—	—	—	—	—	—	—	—	—	—	—
1663 ♀? ad	—	172	128?	133	478	355	121	122	112	110	102	102	98	32	30	82	105	100	110?
1664 ♂ ad-mat	1440	177	145	134	510	362	125	126	111	113	108	95	98	36.3	32	92	117	92	110?
1665 ♂ mat	1530	184	150	127	539	373	125	128	120	120	113	98	100	34	32	98	121?	99	112
1666 ♂ ad-mat	1360	184	138	136	511	375	137	123	115	123	105	101	99	35	27	92	112	95	109
1667 ♂ ad-mat	1380	181	137	139	505	371	132	126	113	119	107	102	101	33	27	92	111	97	115

Height		Breadth						Orbit			Nose		Nasal bones		Maxillo-alveolar		Palatal		Mandible				
																			Breadth		Height		
Upper height (n-pr)	Total height (n-gn)	Bizygomatic	Upper facial (fmt-fmt)	Mid-facial (zm-zm)	Biorbital (ek-ek)	Ant. interorb. (mf-mf)	Post. interorb. (la-la)	Width (mf-ek)	Width (la-ek)	Height	Width	Height	Breadth (minimum)	Breadth (maximum)	Length	Breadth	Length	Width	Bicondylar	Bigonial	Ramus	Ramus	Chin
mm.	mm.	mm.	mm.	mm.	mm.	mm.	mm.	mm.	mm.	mm.	mm.	mm.	mm.	mm.	mm.	mm.	mm.	mm.	mm.	mm.	mm.	mm.	mm.
54	9	53	52	54	52	52	53	54	53	54	53	54	53	52	52	50	51	47	12	12	12	12	13
70–	118–	128–	99–	88–	94–	14–	16–	41–	38–	35–	20–	48–	4–11	12–	49–	56–	41–	37–	109–	88–	35–	60–	33–
87	139	153	115	112	107	22	28	49	44	41	29	61		20	59	73	53	47	128	109	42	74	42
77.3	126.1	138.6	107.2	99.9	101.3	18.0	23.4	44.3	40.2	37.2	23.7	57.5	7.6	15.8	53.2	67.5	47.4	41.7	120.2	105.3	39.0	64.7	35.3
19	3	19	18	18	20	26	18	20	19	20	20	21	19	18	19	19	19	18	4	4	4	4	3
64–	113–	115–	94–	86–	89–	15–	19–	39–	35–	35–	20–	46–	5–12	13–	45–	55–	40–	32–	109–	98–	33–	58–	33–
77	125	142	111	102	103	20	26	46	42	42	26	54		20	55	66	48	44	126	111	41	63	34
72.4	118.7	129.5	103.5	94.3	97.5	17.7	22.9	42.5	38.4	36.8	23.3	50.2	7.8	15.6	51.6	61.2	45.1	38.1	114.8	102.5	36.3	60.0	33.8
68.0	—	125.0	101.0	94.0	95.0	16.0	22.0	41.0	37.0	35.0	23.0	49.0	6.0	16.0	45.0	64.0	40.0	40.0	—	—	—	—	—
2	—	3	3	2	2	3	2	3	2	3	3	3	3	3	2	2	2	2	—	—	—	—	—
58 ;	—	110–	82–	79 ;	86 ;	13–	19 ;	38–	34 ;	34–	19–	42–	5–6	12–	36 ;	55 ;	32 ;	32 ;	—	—	—	—	—
60	—	111	95	83	89	17	19	39	35	36	21	42		15	37	55	35	33	—	—	—	—	—
59.0	—	110.3	89.3	81.0	87.5	15.7	19.0	38.3	34.5	35.0	20.0	42.0	5.7	13.7	36.5	55.0	33.5	32.5	—	—	—	—	—
72	—	133	102	96	97	16	18	43	41	36	23	50	7 ?	—	53	65	48	41	—	—	—	—	—
—	—	—	—	—	—	—	—	41	38	35	—	—	—	—	—	—	—	—	—	—	—	—	—
65 ?	—	126 ?	99	86	94	17	22 ?	39	36 ?	36	24	47	7	14	43	57	39 ?	37	—	—	—	—	—
79	—	139	108	101	102	20	25	45	40	39	23	54	11	18	52	63	45	40	—	—	—	—	—
73	—	—	108	97	—	17	22	47 r	43 ?	35	24	52	8	15	54	64	48	43	—	—	—	—	—
—	—	—	—	—	—	—	—	—	—	—	—	—	—	—	—	—	—	—	—	—	—	—	—
78	125	146	107	101	101	19	25	43	38	39	25	56	7	13	57	67	47	42	127 ?	91	37	61	35
80	132	—	—	103 ?	—	18 ?	26 ?	48	43	36	25	57	7	17	57	74	48	45	121 ?	119 ?	38	57 ?	37
76	126	145	107	97	98	16	22	42	38	39	24	56	9	16	52	72	43	43	123	111	36	62	35
73	119	129	103	97	99	16	20	44	40	38	23	52	6	15	49	62	44	40	118	99	40	62	32
78	—	135	104	104	98	16	21	45	40	39	23	54	6	12	53	65	45	39	—	—	—	—	—
76	—	128	100	92	94	18	21	42	38	35	22	51	10	14	55	67	48	41	—	—	—	—	—
74	—	138	106	96	99	15	22	44	41	38	23	55	9	13	50	63	46	40	—	—	—	—	—
68 ?	116	132	106	91	101	18	25 ?	44	40 ?	37	22	48	8	17	46	64	41	38	113	100	37	59	30
77	—	152	110	102	105	16	20	47	44 r	37 r	26	52	8	17	55	71	47	46	—	—	—	—	—
89	—	138	109	105	102	17	23	46	42	41	25	59	9	13	50	63	44	38	—	—	—	—	—
59 ?	—	109	91	80 ?	83	15	19	37	34 r	32	21	43	6	13	43	57	39	34	—	—	—	—	—
77	—	133	108	96	104	19	24	45	40 ?	36	26	53	7	17 ?	55	64	45	41	—	—	—	—	—
—	—	—	—	—	—	18 ?	—	—	—	—	—	—	5	—	—	—	—	—	—	—	—	—	—
—	—	136	—	—	—	20 ?	25 ?	—	—	—	26 ?	54 ?	8	—	—	—	—	—	—	—	—	—	34
75	—	136	103	100	94	18	22 ?	39	36	38	22	54	6	—	50	62	42	41	—	—	—	—	—
—	—	—	—	—	—	—	—	—	—	—	—	—	—	—	—	—	—	—	109	105	41	58	38
72	115	126	98	93	92	18	23	39	36	35	22	50	8	15	53	64	44	42	105	97	36	54	31
78 ?	129	139	107	95	100	20	25	44	40	36	22	55	8	16	49 ?	65	44 ?	40	114	97	34	65	36
79	124	147	112	105	106	16	22	48	43	40	24	56	8	17	53	63	47	42	120	98	36	58	38
72	117	138	103	97	97	18	26	42	39	34	26	52	7	18	51	65	44	40	120	97	38	61	31
75	120	138	106	99	100	20	25	43	40	40	25	53	9	18	54	64	46	39	124	117	42	59	33

Tribal divisions and subdivisions / Catalogue No. / Sex and stages of life / Number of cases / Averages and ranges	Capacity	Length	Breadth	Height (ba-b)	Circumference (horizontal)	SKULL Median-sagittal Total (n-o)	Arc Frontal	Arc Parietal	Arc Occipital	Chord Frontal	Chord Parietal	Chord Occipital	Cranial base (length n-ia)	Foramen magnum Length	Foramen magnum Width	Frontal bone Breadth (minimum)	Frontal bone Breadth (maximum)	Length (ba-pr)	Inferior length (ba-gn)
KOSKIMO	ccm.	mm.	mm.	mm.	mm.	mm.	mm.	mm.	mm.	mm.	mm.	mm.	mm.	mm.	mm.	mm.	mm.	mm.	mm.
1668 ♀ mat	1150	172	129	127	487	340	115	114	111	105	101	98	102	36	30	91	107	101	—
1669 inf. I	—	158	130	—	450	332	117	115	100	101	97	88	—	—	—	81	100	—	—
1670A ♂ ad-mat	1310	185	132	129	509	362	129	108	125	117	96	104	99	38	31	96	108	104	114
1670B ♂ mat	—	—	—	—	—	—	—	—	—	—	—	—	—	—	—	—	—	—	—
1671 ♂ mat	1330	185	136	125	515	364	126	113	125	114	101	106	101	36	28	96	115?	98	113
1672A ♂ mat	1450	191	138	138	528	371	130	110	131	117	97	109	109	37	30	100	113	107	120
1672B ♂ ad-mat	—	—	—	—	—	—	—	—	—	—	—	—	—	—	—	—	—	—	—
1673 ♂ mat	1370	188	137	132	519	375	126	112	137	115	103	112	99	35	29	90	114	95	—
1674 ♀ mat	1260	173	133	123?	487	354	125	119	110	113	103	98	94	35	28	85	105	—	—
1675 ♀ mat	1360	175	137	132	490	359	125	93	141	114	87	112	99	31	27	91	109	103	107
1676 ♂? mat	1360	182	139	131	511	374	127	136	111	109	119	98	100	32	27	95	116	102	107
1677 ♂? mat	1180	188	130	121	505	363	123	120	120	110	106	99	99	34	25	93	109?	100	118
1678 ♀ mat	1190	168	133	126	477	347	119	100	128	107	92	108	92	33	27	90	101	90	104
1679 ♀ ad	1330	177	138	121	498	348	130	110	108	114	99	92	94	34	28	87	109	93	—
♂ cases	23	27	27	25	27	26	26	27	26	27	27	26	25	25	25	26	25	23	14
range	1180–1560	173–194	130–150	122–141	487–541	357–394	120–141	104–134	104–125	108–119	95–112	91–109	92–109	31–39	25–35	83–100	108–121	92–107	107–120
average	1403.9	184.2	138.9	132.0	516.6	370.0	129.4	121.7	119.4	116.3	106.4	101.3	100.3	35.0	29.4	94.1	114.8	99.2	113.2
♀ cases	7	8	8	8	8	8	8	8	8	8	8	8	8	8	8	8	8	7	3
range	1150–1360	168–177	129–138	121–133	477–498	340–376	115–130	93–129	108–141	103–114	87–109	92–112	92–102	30–36	26–30	82–91	101–109	90–103	104–110
average	1225.8	173.0	133.2	126.9	486.4	351.6	121.1	112.4	118.1	109.1	98.9	100.6	95.3	32.6	27.9	88.1	105.9	96.6	107.0
inf. cases	—	3	3	1	2	2	3	3	2	3	3	2	1	1	1	3	3	1	—
range	—	158–179	130–144	—	450; 507	333; 368	116–126	108–115	100; 134	101–111	97–98	88; 108	—	—	—	81–100	100–116	—	—
average	—	169.3	136.7	125.0	478.5	350.1	119.7	110 7	117.0	106.7	97.7	98.0	89.0	34.0	27.0	90.0	104.7	83.0	—
Koskimo																			
3642 ♂ mat	1520	207	133	140	555?	410	145	149	116	132	114	111	99	35	30	97	115?	104	—
3643 ♂ mat	1440	190	137	130	527	373	130	117	126	115	106	107	103	36	28	97	119	102	115
3644 ♂ mat	1410	196	139	125	531	375	125	12C	130	121	102	109	102	33	29	89	115	103	—
3645 inf. II	1370	179	122	—	515	368	120	134	114	109	104	110	—	—	—	101	112	—	—
3646 ♂ mat	1630	183	152	136	527	392	135	134	123	119	113	107	99	31	33!	99	120	103	—
3647 ♀ juv-ad	1270	190	127	129	495?	383	136	109	138	127	92	120	88	32	28	93	103	94	104
3648 ♂ mat	1570	189	142	130	527	383	130	128	125	118	110	107	105	34	33	96	118?	105	—
3649 ♀? mat	1320	190	136	130	523	371	135	125	111	120	107	102	105	36	29	101	118?	101	—
3650 ♂ ad	1290	182	132	125	506	363	124	118	121	109	99	104	98	36	30	90	114	102	—
3837 ♂ mat	1510	195	140	132	538	384	133	118	133	117	103	109	104	34	30	95	123?	99	—
3838 ♂ mat	1450	191	139	130	522	371	131	103	137	118	96	112	102	35	29	98	115	101	—
3839 ♀ mat	1250	173	132	122	495	343	124	112	107	108	100	92	98	33	29	96	114	103	108
3840 ♂ ad-mat	1330	184	136	131	516	360	126	112	122	112	100	98	104	37	32	94	117	101	110
3841 ♀? ad	1340	184	133	130	503	363	127	115	121	113	101	108	102	36	33	94	113	102	108

FACE AND MANDIBLE

Height		Breadth						Orbit			Nose		Nasal bones		Maxillo-alveolar		Palatal		Mandible				
																			Breadth		Height		
Upper height (n-pr)	Total height (n-gn)	Bizygomatic	Upper facial (fmt-fmt)	Mid-facial (zm-zm)	Biorbital (ek-ek)	Ant. interorb. (mf-mf)	Post. interorb. (la-la)	Width (mf-ek)	Width (la-ek)	Height	Width	Height	Breadth (minimum)	Breadth (maximum)	Length	Breadth	Length	Width	Bicondylar	Bigonial	Ramus	Ramus	Chin
mm.	mm.	mm.	mm.	mm.	mm.	mm.	mm.	mm.	mm.	mm.	mm.	mm.	mm.	mm.	mm.	mm.	mm.	mm.	mm.	mm.	mm.	mm.	mm.
80	—	131	108	100	106	19	25	47	42	38	25	57	10	19	51	65	44	42	—	—	—	—	—
55	—	—	82	—	—	13	16?	35	31?	32	—	—	—	—	—	—	—	—	85	75	23	43	24
83	128	135	110	103	101	16	21	46	41	42	22	56	7	16	56	67	49	41	114	111	36	65	37
—	—	—	—	—	—	—	—	—	—	—	—	—	—	—	—	—	—	—	111	88	40	62	35
70	118?	132	104	91	98	19	23	43	40	38	22	53	8	14	50	62	45	40	119	98	38	61	36
80	130	142	112	103	104	18	23	46	41	39	21	57	7	15	56	67	50	42	116	104	39	67	39
—	—	—	—	—	—	—	—	—	—	—	—	—	—	—	—	—	—	—	115	91	39	64	30
75	—	135	103	98	98	19	23	43	38	37	23	55	8	15	53?	60	45	41	—	—	—	—	—
—	—	130	99	—	96	17?	—	41	37?	33	—	—	—	—	—	—	—	—	—	—	—	—	—
77	121	137	103	100	97	17	21	42	39	38	25	51	10	16	56	64	51	40	118	110	40	58	38
78	120	133	108	103	102	17	24	45	40	36	25	54	10	17	53	63	47	37?	122	90	37	61	37
70?	110	134	104	99?	98	16	25	44	39	37	23	53	4	18	52	61	47	—	118	100	43	58	32
77	115?	128	100	90	96	15	19	43	39	33	21	46	8	12	48	57	43	35?	113	98	34	50	33
77	—	128	100	97	95	16	21	42	39	38	20	52	6	15	48	60	42	38	—	—	—	—	—
24	13	23	23	24	22	26	25	24	24	23	25	25	26	12	24	24	24	23	17	16	17	17	18
68–	110–	129–	102–	91–	94–	15–	18–	39–	36–	34–	21–	48–	4–11	12–	46–	56–	41–	37–	109–	88–	34–	57–	30–
89	132	152	112	105	106	20	26	48	44	42	26	59		18	57	74	50	46	127	119	43	67	39
76.2	122.6	137.6	106.9	99.1	100.2	17.7	23.1	44.3	40.3	36.7	23.7	54.0	7.8	15.8	52.6	64.4	45.8	40.8	117.8	101.4	38.3	61.2	34.7
7	3	8	8	7	8	8	7	8	7	8	7	7	7	7	7	7	7	7	3	3	3	3	3
65–	115–	126–	98–	86–	92–	15–	19–	39–	36–	33–	20–	46–	6–10	12–	43–	57–	39–	35–	105–	97–	34–	50–	31–
80	121	137	108	100	106	20	25	47	42	38	25	57		19	56	67	51	42	118	110	40	58	38
74.8	117.0	129.2	100.9	94.0	96.3	17.1	21.7	41.9	38.2	35.7	22.7	50.5	8.4	14.4	50.6	62.0	44.4	39.3	112.0	101.7	36.7	54.0	34.0
2		1	1	1	1	2	2	3	3	3	1	1	1	1	1	1	1	1	1	1	1	1	1
55;	—	—	—	—	—	13;	16;	35;	31–	32–	—	—	—	—	—	—	—	—	—	—	—	—	—
59						15	19	37	38	35													
57.0	—	109.1	91.0	80.0	83.0	14.0	17.5	36.0	34.3	33.0	21.0	43.0	6.0	13.0	43.0	57.0	39.0	34.0	85.0	75.0	23.0	43.0	24.0
87	—	133	109	100	101	18	24	45	41	42	25	58	8	15?	60	76	52	45?	—	—	—	—	—
82	137	142	112	107	105	17	23	46	41	39	24	57	7	18	60	76	49	43	123	106	36	58	42
83	—	142	109	100	102	19	23	44	39	39	24	60	6	15	59	70	49	41	—	—	—	—	—
67	—	109	98	79	93	18	26	40	36	40	19	47	10	14	39	58	38	31	—	—	—	—	—
76	—	142	108	102	102	19	26	44	40	38	26	54	5	16	55	69	47	46	—	—	—	—	—
71	115	123	104	92	98	16	24	42	37	38	21	51	8	15	49	63	44	40	111	91	31	56	32
76	—	142	110	103	105	18	23	48	44	38	22	54	7	15	56	68	49	41	—	—	—	—	—
72?	—	137	107	91	101	20	27	43	38	40	24	52	12	17	53	—	48	—	—	—	—	—	—
79	—	135	104	100	100	18	22	43	40	39	25	56	6	13	54	67	48	42	—	—	—	—	—
85	—	142	110	101	105	19	27	47	40	39	24	59	7	15	58	70	53	42	—	—	—	—	—
77	—	138	109	101	103	19	23	45	41	40	24	53	9	16	55	73	48	42?	—	—	—	—	—
79	125	132	104	99	98	16	19	44	41	40	24	52	7	17	58	69	47	40	121	103	32	65	36
80	122	141	107	103	100	18	23	44	39	39	23	55	8	15	56	64	48	39	124	110	37	65	36
74	106	133	106	92	99	17	22	44	40	37	20	52	6	14	57?	65	49	40	118	96	31	61	35

43

Tribal divisions and subdivisions / Catalogue No. / Sex and stages of life / Number of cases / Averages and ranges	SKULL																	
	Capacity	Length	Breadth	Height (ba-b)	Circumference (horizontal)	Median-sagittal Arc			Median-sagittal Chord			Cranial base (length n-ba)	Foramen magnum		Frontal bone		Length	
						Total (n-o)	Frontal	Parietal	Occipital	Frontal	Parietal	Occipital		Length	Width	Breadth (minimum)	Breadth (maximum)	Length (ba-pr)	Inferior length (ba-gn)
	ccm.	mm.	mm.	mm.	mm.	mm.	mm.	mm.	mm.	mm.	mm.	mm.	mm.	mm.	mm.	mm.	mm.	mm.	mm.
KOSKIMO																			
♂ cases	10	9	9	9	9	9	9	9	9	9	9	9	9	9	9	9	9	9	2
range	1290–1630	182–207	132–152	125–140	506–555	371–410	124–145	103–149	113–133	109–132	96–114	98–112	98–105	31–37	28–33	89–99	114–123	99–105	110; 115
average	1456.0	190.8	139.8	131.0	527.7	379.0	131.0	122.4	125.8	117.9	104.8	107.1	101.8	34.6	30.4	95.0	117.3	102.2	112.5
♀ cases	4	4	4	4	4	4	4	4	4	4	4	4	4	4	4	4	4	4	3
range	1250–1340	173–190	127–137	122–130	495–523	343–383	124–136	109–125	107–121	108–127	92–107	92–120	88–105	32–36	23–29	93–101	103–118	94–103	104–108
average	1295.0	184.2	133.2	127.7	504.0	365.0	130.5	115.2	119.2	117.0	100.0	105.4	98.3	34.3	27.3	96.0	112.0	100.0	106.7
inf. 1 case	1370.0	179.0	122.0	—	515.0	368.0	120.0	135.0	114.0	104.0	104.0	110.0	—	—	—	101.0	112.0	—	—
Nootka																			
4559 ♀ juv-ad	1230	169	133	122	479	347	128	114	105	115	99	92	90	33	28	91	115	—	—
4560 ♀ mat-sen	1110	163	138	125	478	338	124	107	107	110	92	90	95	30	28	92	107	—	—
4561 ♂ ad	1220	174	128	130	482	356	125	120	111	113	100	99	97	34	32	87	108	102	—
4562 ♂ ? ad	1280	178	132	122	499	356	122	127	107	108	109	93	94	35	32	87	115	93	—
4563 ♀ ? mat	1130	180	129	121	490	355	125	109	121	114	99	104	93	31	29	95	108	98	—
4564 ♂ mat	1170	174	128	134	488	362	117	125	120	106	110	102	98	33	29	88	108?	98?	—
4565 ♂ ad-mat	1420	166	146	128	502	351	124	121	106	107	100	89	92	35	32	95	125	93	—
4566 ♀ ad	1170	174	136	116	492	337	119	97	121	108	88	98	94	35	29	90	106	99	—
4567 ♂ mat	1340	184	135	127	512	351	130	109	112	116	98	95	105	35	32	92	113	112	—
4568 ♂ ? ad-mat	1320	180	132	125	496	360	123	122	115	114	104	103	91	32	30	92	110	96	—
4569 ♂ ad	1360	178	136	125	497	358	124	129	105	110	110	91	97	32	30	90	112	97	—
4570 ♂ ad-mat	1350	184	135	123	508	371	127	130	114	114	110	100	93	35	29	95?	115	92	—
4571 ♂ ad-mat	1380	186	141	128	516	371	129	124	118	118	109	101	102	36	31	94	117	107	—
4572 ♂ mat	1220	174	131	125	494	341	118	98	125	107	89	101	101	34	28	85	102	99	—
4574 ♂ ad	—	—	—	—	—	—	122	—	—	109	—	—	—	33	28	98	111	—	—
♂ cases	10	10	10	10	10	10	11	10	10	11	10	10	10	11	11	11	10	9	—
range	1170–1420	166–186	128–146	122–134	482–516	341–371	117–130	98–130	105–125	106–118	89–110	88–110	91–103	31–36	28–32	85–98	102–125	92–107	—
average	1306.0	177.8	134.4	126.7	499.4	357.7	123.7	120.5	113.3	111.1	103.9	97.3	97.0	34.0	30.2	91.1	112.3	97.4	—
♀ cases	4	4	4	4	4	4	4	4	4	4	4	4	4	4	4	4	4	2	—
range	1110–1230	177–183	129–138	116–125	487–492	337–374	119–129	97–114	105–122	108–115	88–99	90–104	90–95	30–35	28–29	90–95	106–115	98; 99	—
average	1160.0	180.5	134.0	121.0	484.8	351.0	124.0	106.7	113.5	111.8	94.5	96.0	93.0	32.3	28.5	92.0	109.0	98.5	—
Clayoquot																			
1597 ♀ ? mat	1180	172	135	125	484	347	125	102	120	112	92	100	96	33	29	92	108	102	109
1598 ♂ ad	1340	182	138	126	511	359	125	121	113	107	106	95	99	33	27	98	116	95	—
1599 ♀ ? ad	1410	180	133	131	505	365	126	131	108	114	113	97	93	36	30	97	113	90	—
1600 ♂ ad	1370	183	127	128	510	354	120	120	114	109	105	98	102	41	33	88	111	103	—
1601 inf. II	1270	164	133	—	470	337	113	98	126	102	92	105	—	—	—	91	110	—	—
1602 ♂ ad-mat	1370	180	135	129	505	361	123	113	125	110	103	103	98	34	28	95	122	106	—

FACE AND MANDIBLE

Height		Breadth						Orbit			Nose		Nasal bones		Maxillo-alveolar		Palatal		Mandible				
																			Breadth		Height		
Upper height (n-pr)	Total height (n-gn)	Bizygomatic	Upper facial (ml-ml)	Mid-facial (zm-zm)	Biorbital (ek-ek)	Ant. interorb. (mf-mf)	Post. interorb. (la-la)	Width (mf-ek)	Width (la-ek)	Height	Width	Height	Breadth (minimum)	Breadth (maximum)	Length	Breadth	Length	Width	Bicondylar	Bigonial	Ramus	Ramus	Chin
mm.	mm.	mm.	mm.	mm.	mm.	mm.	mm.	mm.	mm.	mm.	mm.	mm.	mm.	mm.	mm.	mm.	mm.	mm.	mm.	mm.	mm.	mm.	mm.
9	2	9	9	9	9	9	9	9	9	9	9	9	9	9	9	9	9	9	2	2	2	2	2
77–87	122; 137	135–143	104–112	100–108	100–105	17–19	22–27	43–48	39–44	39–42	22–26	53–60	5–9	13–18	54–60	64–76	47–53	39–46	123; 124	106; 110	36; 37	58; 65	36; 42
80.2	129.5	140.8	108.7	102.6	102.6	18.3	23.8	45.1	40.5	39.2	24.1	56.2	7.0	15.2	57.0	70.3	49.2	42.3	123.5	108.0	36.5	61.5	39.0
4	3	4	4	4	4	4	4	4	4	4	4	4	4	4	4	3	4	3	3	—	3	3	3
71–79	106–125	123–137	104–107	91–99	98–100	16–20	19–27	42–44	37–41	37–40	20–24	51–52	6–12	14–17	49–58	63–69	44–49	40	111–121	—	31–32	56–65	32–36
76.5	115.3	131.2	105.2	93.5	99.0	17.3	23.0	43.2	39.0	38.7	22.5	51.7	8.3	15.8	54.3	65.7	47.0	40.0	116.7	—	31.3	60.7	34.3
67.0	—	109.0	98.0	79.0	93.0	18.0	26.0	40.0	36.0	—	19.0	47.0	10.0	14.0	39.0	58.0	38.0	31.0	—	—	—	—	—
—	—	125	97	—	—	—	—	—	—	—	—	—	—	—	—	—	—	—	—	—	—	—	—
—	—	133	102	89	93	13	19?	43	39	34	23	48	5	13	—	—	—	—	—	—	—	—	—
68	—	131	101?	94?	—	16	20	41	39 r?	36 r	22	47	5	12	54	65	46	43	—	—	—	—	—
64	—	133	96	91	91	17	—	39	37?	38	21	47	6	14	50	60	43	39	—	—	—	—	—
70?	—	133?	103	96?	97	18	—	41	37	33	25	51	7	13	52	59?	45	40	—	—	—	—	—
72	—	129	101	95	96	18	20	41	38	34	26	50	7	16?	57?	68	50?	37	—	—	—	—	—
72	—	147	107	94	97	15	21	43	38	38	25	53	7	12	50	62	45	40	—	—	—	—	—
72	—	127	103	96	97	16	22	44	39	37	23	51	7	15?	52	64	47	41	—	—	—	—	—
77	—	151	112	106	111	18	24	49	44	38	28	55	5	13?	57	67	50	45	—	—	—	—	—
73	—	132	98	97	93	15	21	40	36	37	22	54	6	12	51	63	45	39	—	—	—	—	—
65	—	130	100	91	94	16	22	43	38 r	35	24	49	7	15?	53	60	43	38	—	—	—	—	—
68	—	137	110	99	102	18	25	46	42	34	24	53	8	15	61	65	41	43	—	—	—	—	—
78	—	147	108	102	102	18	24	45	41	35	26	57	7	15	58	68	51	45	—	—	—	—	—
69	—	137	101	89	95	15	21	42	38	35	23	51	8	14	54?	60?	49	41?	—	—	—	—	—
67	—	—	104	93	99	22	26	42	38	36	24	47	11	17	50	61	48	39	—	—	—	—	—
11	—	10	11	11	9	11	10	11	11	11	11	11	11	11	11	11	11	11	—	—	—	—	—
64–78	—	129–151	96–112	89–106	91–102	15–22	20–26	39–49	36–44	34–38	21–28	47–57	5–11	12–17	50–61	60–68	41–51	34–45	—	—	—	—	—
70.3	—	137.4	103.4	95.5	107.3	17.1	23.8	42.8	39.0	36.0	24.1	51.2	7.0	14.1	54.1	63.5	46.5	40.0	—	—	—	—	—
2	—	4	4	3	3	2	2	3	3	3	3	3	3	2	2	2	2	2	—	—	—	—	—
70; 72	—	125–133	97–103	89–96	93–97	16; 19; 18	—	41–44	37–39	33–37	23–25	48–51	5–7	13–15	52; 52	59; 64	45; 47	40; 41	—	—	—	—	—
71.0	—	129.5	100.5	93.7	95.7	17.0	20.5	42.7	38.3	35.0	23.7	50.0	7.0	13.7	52.0	61.5	46.0	40.5	—	—	—	—	—
75	120	133	102	102	94	18	21	39	37	35	24	49	8	16	58	64	47	40	112	100	39	56	37
67?	—	139	103	103?	97	18	24	41	38?	35	25	50	10	15	46?	59	42	41	—	—	—	—	—
74?	—	127	103	87	93	18	24?	41	—	38	.20	49	8	16	47	64	40	41	—	—	—	—	—
77	—	133	105	99	97	16	22	42	39	39	24	57	6	16	57	64	53	42	—	—	—	—	—
58	—	113	90	80	80	18	20	36	35	31	21	41	11	13	38	59	37	30	—	—	—	—	—
74	—	134	102	98	97	17	23	42	38	35	23	54	7	—	59	67	49	42	—	—	—	—	—

Tribal divisions and subdivisions / Catalogue No. / Sex and stages of life / Number of cases / Averages and ranges	Capacity	Length	Breadth	Height (ba-b)	Circumference (horizontal)	SKULL Median-sagittal Arc			Median-sagittal Chord			Cranial base (length n-ba)	Foramen magnum		Frontal bone		Length	
						Total (n-o)	Frontal	Parietal	Occipital	Frontal	Parietal	Occipital		Length	Width	Breadth (minimum)	Breadth (maximum)	Length (ba-pr)	Inferior length (ba-gn)
	ccm.	mm.	mm.	mm.	mm.	mm.	mm.	mm.	mm.	mm.	mm.	mm.	mm.	mm.	mm.	mm.	mm.	mm.	mm.
KOSKIMO																			
1603 juv	1320	169	131	124	479	352	120	123	109	107	104	93	89	34	29	96	112	94	—
1604 ♂ ad	1370	177	137	129	505	353	122	123	108	109	105	92	103	36	32	95	116	100	—
♂ cases	4	4	4	4	4	4	4	4	4	3	4	4	4	4	4	4	4	4	—
range	1340–1370	163–180	127–138	126–129	505–511	353–361	120–125	113–123	108–125	107–109	103–106	92–103	98–103	33–41	27–33	88–98	111–122	95–106	—
average	1380.0	171.1	134.2	128.0	506.3	356.2	122.5	119.2	115.0	108.3	104.8	97.0	100.5	36.0	30.0	94.0	116.8	101.0	—
♀ cases	2	2	2	2	2	2	2	2	2	2	2	2	2	2	2	2	2	2	1
range	1180;1410	163;180	133;135	125;131	484;505	347;365	125;126	102;131	108;120	112;114	92;113	97;100	93;96	33;36	29;30	92;97	108;113	90;102	
average	1295.0	176.0	134.0	128.0	494.5	356.0	125.5	116.5	114.0	113.0	102.5	98.5	94.5	34.5	29.5	94.5	110.5	96.0	109.0
juv. 1 cases	1320.0	169.0	131.0	—	479.0	352.0	120.0	123.0	109.0	107.0	104.0	93.0	89.0	34.0	29.0	96.0	112.0	94.0	—
inf. 1 case	1270.0	164.0	133.0	124.0	470.0	337.0	113.0	98.0	126.0	101.0	88.0	105.0	—	—	—	91.0	110.0	—	—
Divisional total																			
♂ cases	96	104	103	102	102	103	104	104	103	104	104	103	102	103	103	103	100	99	25
range	1170–1630	163–207	127–158	122–147	482–555	341–410	117–145	98–149	101–148	106–132	89–119	86–125	91–110	30–41	25–35	83–103	102–125	88–108	106–126
average	1396.3	183.0	138.7	131.9	516.1	368.0	127.8	119.2	120.3	114.2	105.2	102.1	100.5	34.5	30.4	94.1	115.9	100.7	114.4
♀ cases	36	39	39	37	38	37	39	39	37	39	39	37	37	36	36	39	38	34	10
range	1100–1410	165–190	124–145	116–138	472–523	336–383	113–136	93–135	105–141	102–127	87–113	89–120	86–105	29–36	24–32	82–101	101–118	90–103	102–113
average	1264.2	175.5	134.0	127.3	491.2	353.7	122.7	111.2	116.6	110.7	99.8	100.0	96.1	32.7	28.0	91.3	109.1	97.8	107.7
juv. cases	2	2	2	2	2	2	2	2	2	2	2	2	2	2	2	2	2	2	—
range	1320;1360	166;169	131;141	124;132	458;479	351;352	120;128	122;123	102;109	107;113	104;105	88;93	89;94	33;34	29;30	96;98	112;117	88;94	—
average	1340.0	167.5	136.0	128.0	468.5	351.5	124.0	122.5	105.5	110.0	104.5	90.5	91.5	33.5	29.5	97.0	114.5	91.0	—
inf. cases	4	8	8	4	7	7	8	8	7	9	8	7	4	4	4	7	8	3	—
range	1270–1400	153–179	122–144	124–128	450–515	333–368	112–126	98–135	100–134	100–111	88–116	88–110	81–89	·34–38	27–27	81–101	100–116	75–83	—
average	1310.0	167.5	135.1	126.0	480.4	357.1	117.6	113.5	118.7	108.4	98.9	100.9	85.0	35.5	27.0	92.1	108.9	78.7	—

FACE AND MANDIBLE

Height		Breadth						Orbit			Nose		Nasal bones		Maxillo-alveolar		Palatal		Mandible				
																			Breadth		Height		
Upper height (n-pr)	Total height (n-gn)	Bizygomatic	Upper facial (fmt-fmt)	Mid-facial (zm-zm)	Biorbital (ek-ek)	Ant. interorb. (mf-mf)	Post. interorb. (la-la)	Width (mf-ek)	Width (la-ek)	Height	Width	Height	Breadth (minimum)	Breadth (maximum)	Length	Breadth	Length	Width	Bicondylar	Bigonial	Ramus	Ramus	Chin
mm.	mm.	mm.	mm.	mm.	mm.	mm.	mm.	mm.	mm.	mm.	mm.	mm.	mm.	mm.	mm.	mm.	mm.	mm.	mm.	mm.	mm.	mm.	mm.
66	—	124	102	94	93	17	21	40	37	34	23	45	5	14	49	64	45	37	—	—	—	—	—
73	—	143	108	103	101	18	26	45	40	33	25	55	11	16	54	64	47	42	—	—	—	—	—
4	—	4	4	4	4	4	4	4	4	4	4	4	4	3	4	4	4	4	—	—	—	—	—
67–77	—	133–143	102–108	98–103	97–101	16–19	22–26	41–45	38–40	33–39	23–25	50–57	6–11	15–16	46–59	59–67	42–49	41–42	—	—	—	—	—
72.7	—	137.2	104.5	100.8	98.0	17.3	23.8	42.5	38.4	35.5	24.2	54.0	8.5	15.7	54.0	63.5	45.3	41.7	—	—	—	—	—
2	1	2	2	2	2	2	2	2	1	2	2	2	3	2	2	2	2	2	1	1	1	1	1
74; 75	—	127; 133	102; 103	87; 102	93; 94	18; 18	21; 24	39; 41	—	35; 38	20; 24	49; 49	5–7	16; 16	47; 58	64; 64	40; 47	40; 41					
74.5	120.0	130.0	102.5	94.5	93.5	18.0	22.5	40.0	37.0	37.0	22.0	49.0	7.0	16.0	52.5	64.0	43.5	40.5	112.0	100.0	39.0	56.0	37.0
66.0	—	124.0	102.0	94.0	93.0	17.0	21.0	40.0	37.0	34.0	23.0	45.0	5.0	14.0	39.0	64.0	45.0	37.0	—	—	—	—	—
58.0	—	113.0	90.0	80.0	84.0	18.0	20.0	36.0	35.0	31.0	21.0	41.0	11.0	13.0	38.0	59.0	37.0	30.0	—	—	—	—	—
102	24	99	99	99	96	102	101	102	101	101	102	103	103	97	100	98	99	94	31	30	31	31	33
64–89	110–139	128–153	96–115	88–112	91–107	14–22	16–28	39–49	36–44	34–42	20–29	47–61	4–11	12–20	46–61	56–76	41–47	34–47	109–128	88–119	34–43	57–74	30–42
76.0	124.5	138.4	106.7	99.3	101.6	17.8	23.3	44.2	40.1	37.1	23.8	53.8	7.5	15.6	53.5	66.2	47.0	41.4	119.1	103.4	38.7	62.6	35.2
34	10	37	36	34	37	37	37	35	35	36	37	35	34	34	34	33	34	32	10	11	11	11	10
64–80	106–125	115–142	94–111	81–102	89–106	15–20	19–27	39–47	35–42	33–42	20–26	46–57	5–12	12–20	43–58	55–69	39–51	32–44	105–126	91–111	31–41	50–65	31–38
73.1	117.3	129.7	102.8	94.1	97.0	17.4	22.5	42.4	38.4	36.7	23.1	50.4	7.9	15.2	51.8	62.0	45.1	38.8	112.7	100.5	34.6	58.2	34.3
2		2	2	2	2	2	2	2	2	2	2	2	2	2	2	2	2	2					
66; 68	—	124; 125	101; 102	94; 94	93; 95	16; 17	21; 24	40; 41	37; 37	34; 35	23; 23	45; 49	5; 6	14; 16	39; 45	64; 64	40; 45	37; 40	—	—	—	—	—
67.0	—	124.5	101.5	94.0	94.0	16.5	21.5	40.5	37.0	34.5	23.0	47.0	5.5	15.0	42.0	64.0	42.5	38.5					
6	—	6	6	5	5	7	6	8	7	8	6	5	6	5	5	5	5	5	1	1	1	1	1
55–67	—	110–117	82–98	79–83	80–93	13–18	16–26	35–41	31–38	31–40	19–21	41–47	5–11	12–15	36–43	55–59	32–39	30–34	—	—	—	—	—
60.0	—	111.3	89.5	80.2	86.2	15.9	19.8	38.0	34.4	34.4	20.2	43.0	7.3	13.5	38.6	56.8	36.2	32.0	85.0	75.0	23.0	43.0	24.0

Tribal divisions and subdivisions / Catalogue No. / Sex and stages of life / Number of cases / Averages and ranges	"Central angle" (*Klaatsch*)	Cranio-facial (*Fuldenburger*)	Interoccipital	ANGLES										Mandibulo-alveolar plane				Length-breadth
				To ear-eye plane														
				Glabella-lambda	Basion-bregma	Nasion-basion	Basion-opisthion	Nasion-bregma	Lambda-bregma	Opisthion-lambda	Prosthion-nasion	Nasospinale-nasion	Prosthion-nasospinale	Orbital height	Ramus tangent-alveolar plane	Ramus tangent-basal tangent	Chin vertical-basal-tangent	Condylo-coronoid tangent-alveolar plane	
	ccm.	mm.	mm.	mm.	mm.	mm.	mm.	mm.	mm.	mm.	mm.	mm.	mm.	mm.	mm.	mm.	mm.	mm.	mm.
UNDEFORMED																			
Athapascan																			
1551 ♂ ad	93	90	108	11	82	25	−4	50	29	115	87	88	83	88	—	—	—	—	79.9
4337 ♂ mat	90	86	122	5	85	32	+3	47	29	124	84	86	79	93	62	131	75	+8	75.0
4338 ♂ mat	92	86	130	4	88	34	−2	47	30	122	83	86	75	84	72	128	69	−18	74.0
4339 ♂ ad-mat	90	91	120	5	85	27	−16	47	31	121	85	89	76	89	77	122	73	+1	74.0
4340 inf. I—II	—	—	—	—	—	—	—	—	—	—	—	—	—	—	57	129	83	+13	—
4341 ♂ mat	89	87	128	9	80	29	−4	49	26	116	85?	92?	69?	95	—	—	—	—	80.9
4342 ♀ ad-mat	90	90	126	12	78	28	+11	52	19	110	83	86	72	93	63	127	78	−9	71.6
4343 ♂ ad	90	90	125	6	84	30	−3	50	29	121	75	76	72	84	72	122	75	−8	74.3
♂ cases	6	5	6	6	6	6	6	6	6	6	6	6	6	6	4	4	4	4	6
range	89–93	86–91	108–130	4–11	80–88	25–34	+3 to −16	47–50	23–31	115–124	75–87	76–92	69–83	84–95	62–77	122–131	69–75	−18 to +8	74.0–80.9
average	90.7	88.6	122.2	6.7	84.0	29.5	−4.3	48.3	27.3	119.8	83.2	86.2	75.7	88.8	70.8	125.8	73.0	−4.3	76.3
♀ 1 case	90.0	90.0	121.0	12.0	78.0	28.0	+11.0	52.0	19.0	110.0	83.0	86.0	72.0	93.0	63.0	127.0	78.0	−9.0	71.6
inf. 1 case	—	—	—	—	—	—	—	—	—	—	—	—	—	—	57.0	129.0	83.0	−13.0	—
Haida																			
1605 inf. II	—	—	136	8	—	—	—	50	31	124	73	73	73	92	—	—	—	—	97.5
1606 ♂ ad-mat	90	92	126	7	83	28	−8	49	29	118	78	85	63	87	—	—	—	—	77.4
1607 inf. II	90	89	110	5	85	30	−10	52	27	123	85	85	85	90	—	—	—	—	85.5
1608 ♀ ad	90	88	124	6	84	30	−7	50	32	119	81	84	72	89	63	133	74	+12	78.4
1609 ♀ ad-mat	90	89	125	10	80	29	−4	51	23	115	82	88	68	86	66	116	86	+5	83.8
1610 ♂ ad-mat	91	90	117	4	87	32	−3	46	31	126	79	88	61	96	71	114	85	+9	78.6
1611 ♀ ad (lower jaw doubtful)	90	90	126	6	84	30	−5	46	28	117	81	84	71	90	62	122	85	+2	79.2
1613 ♂ mat	—	—	—	—	—	—	—	—	—	—	—	—	—	—	62	117	84	−3	—
1614 ♂ mat	97	87	123	10	87	32	−9	47	22	117	85	86	80	95	—	—	—	—	75.0
1615 inf. II	90	85	130	7	83	28	−6	53	27	116	90	90	90	98	63	123	83	+15	79.2
1616 ♀ ad	90	89	121	5	85	31	−9	48	28	124	82	86	74	85	—	—	—	—	77.0
1617 ♂ mat	92	90	118	14	78	27	−3	51	20	105	80	84	70	89	—	—	—	—	79.9
3707 ♂ mat	92?	—	126	4?	88?	32?	−8?	44	31	120	—	—	—	—	—	—	—	—	77.2
3733 ♂ ad	94?	—	123	11?	83?	29?	−3?	50	25	112	—	—	—	—	—	—	—	—	83.2
3734 juv	92	88	126	10	82	31	+3	52	24	114	82	82	82	90	—	—	—	—	83.5
3735 ♀? ad	90	86	129	6	84	31	+2	50	30	121	86	87	80	94	—	—	—	—	79.8
3736 ♂ mat	92	90	116	10	82	26	−7	54	24	117	82	84	75	98	—	—	—	—	75.4
3738 ♂ mat (def.)	97	90	132	11	96	35	−11	40	38	131	82	86	72	88	78	114	79	−1	74.6
3739 inf. II?	95	88	120	9	86	29	−6	49	26	117	89	89	89	95	58	126	85	+28	79.8
3740 ♂ mat	93	90	117	10	83	30	−4	47	20	113	81	81	80	90	65	116	87	+3	80.9
3741 ♂ mat	94	87	118	10	84	31	0	51	27	117	80	85	69	89	69	118	83	−2	77.7
3742 ♀ ad	90	86	123	10	80	30	+5	54	24	113	81	81	81	92	64	120	84	0	83.0
3743 ♂ mat	90	89	134	4	86	32	−5	46	32	119	79	84	76	90	70	118	81	−4	77.8
3745 ♂ mat	88	91	121	7	81	27	−1	48	27	119	85	87	79	92	—	—	—	—	70.8

	Skull									Face and mandible										Cranio-facial			
Length-height	Breadth-height	Transverse frontal	Transverse fronto-parietal	Sagittal parieto-frontal (arcs)	Sagittal frontal	Sagittal parietal	Sagittal occipital	Foramen magnum	Facial	Upper facial	Orbital (mf)	Orbital (la)	Interorbital (mf-mf to ek-ek)	Nasal	Transverse nasal bone	Maxillo-alveolar	Palatal	Bicondylo-bigonial breadth (mandible)	Ramus (mandible)	Transverse cranio-facial	Fronto-biorbital (ft-ft to fmt-fmt)	Jugo-frontal	Jugo-mandibular
77.7	97.3	80.5	64.6	87.0	88.5	92.1	76.7	81.1	—	—	79.5	87.5	18.8	47.2	50.0	—	—	—	88.8	—	—		
75.6	100.7	84.5	72.6	101.6	87.3	87.5	82.5	87.5	90.2	57.1	80.0	90.0	18.0	38.0	66.7	114.5	91.7	88.0	57.9	98.5	90.7	73.7	77.4
78.5	106.1	82.4	67.9	96.8	89.0	88.6	85.2	90.6	93.6	56.8	78.3	85.7r	17.0	45.8	57.1	128.6	95.3	82.0	51.7	95.4	85.6	71.2	72.8
70.2	94.8	88.3	73.1	94.6	86.8	89.3	80.2	86.8	100.0	59.8	84.4	95.0	18.6	46.1	52.9	114.5	84.1	94.4	60.7	94.8	91.6	77.2	80.3
—	—	84.1	—	—	85.5	—	—	77.8	—	58.3	87.2	94.4r	20.7	46.5	53.3	—	85.7	82.5	62.2	—	97.8	83.3	78.7
74.7	92.4	82.6	69.4	100.8	88.4	89.3	83.9	90.6	—	53.1	81.8	90.0	20.6	45.3	80.0	126.9	97.7	—	—	99.3	90.1	69.9	—
76.1	106.3	84.3	68.2	97.4	89.7	91.1	84.1	77.8	88.9	54.7	—	—	—	50.0	47.1	126.0	93.3	92.4	64.7	92.9	—	73.5	83.8
75.4	101.5	86.7	70.0	97.6	87.2	89.3	82.9	80.6	91.3	55.6	75.0	82.5r	17.0	51.0	31.2	118.2	85.7	84.3	61.0	96.9	86.7	72.2	77.0
6	6	6	6	6	6	6	6	6	4	6	6	6	6	6	6	5	6	5	5	6	5	6	4
70.2–78.5	92.4–106.1	80.5–88.3	64.6–73.1	87.0–101.6	86.8–89.0	87.5–92.1	76.7–85.2	80.0–90.0	90.2–100.0	53.1–59.8	75.0–84.4	82.5–95.0	17.0–21.6	38.2–51.0	31.2–80.0	114.5–128.6	84.1–97.7	82.0–94.4	51.7–61.0	94.4–99.3	85.6–91.6	69.9–77.2	72.8–80.3
75.4	98.8	83.7	69.6	95.8	87.9	89.4	81.9	85.7	93.8	56.5	79.8	88.8	18.5	45.5	56.3	120.5	90.7	87.2	57.8	97.0	89.2	72.8	76.9
76.1	106.3	84.3	68.2	97.4	89.7	91.1	84.1	77.8	88.9	54.7	—	—	—	50.0	47.1	126.0	93.3	92.4	64.7	92.9	—	73.5	83.8
—	—	84.1	—	—	85.5	—	—	—	—	58.3	87.2	94.4	20.7	46.5	53.3	—	85.7	82.5	62.2	—	97.8	83.3	78.7
—	—	73.8	57.3	83.5	82.7	88.8	86.5	—	55.0	91.9	100.0r	19.8	47.5	64.3	155.5	82.9	—	—	69.4	100.0	82.6	—	
76.8	99.3	81.8	65.7	94.6	87.6	89.3	85.0	88.6	—	51.1	83.3	92.1	18.6	55.3	43.7	117.9	89.8	—	—	100.0	83.3	65.7	—
71.7	83.8	79.1	61.3	103.4	86.4	88.5	83.0	79.0	—	46.8	86.5	94.1r	18.1	48.6	50.0	142.1	77.1	—	—	78.2	98.9	78.4	—
77.9	100.7	84.7	70.1	94.5	88.2	89.2	82.6	87.9	91.7	54.1	92.3	100.0	22.7	56.0	42.9	117.9	89.4	82.5	61.5	99.2	91.3	70.7	74.4
76.3	91.0	76.9	62.1	98.3	89.0	90.4	80.8	90.6	83.2	52.5	88.4	95.0	21.1	55.1	56.2	123.5	93.2	83.5	63.3	94.5	83.3	65.7	77.4
72.7	92.5	80.3	69.4	96.2	86.4	89.8	78.3	77.1	86.8	50.7	84.8	92.9	17.9	50.0	63.2	116.4	87.8	85.9	48.7	98.0	89.5	70.7	76.4
75.1	94.9	87.8	73.7	94.3	87.8	87.9	84.4	80.6	—	56.5	88.4	97.4	17.6	48.0	52.9	118.9	87.8	89.1	64.3	100.7	93.5	73.2	71.0
																		87.1	60.6				
70.3	93.7	75.4	61.8	85.6	86.4	91.1	80.7	82.9	—	56.5	80.0	90.0	16.0	44.2	41.2	116.4	93.3	—	—	95.8	82.4	64.5	—
74.0	93.4	83.3	69.3	98.4	85.7	87.9	84.3	70.7	89.5	56.1	87.2	97.1r	20.2	46.7	47.1	150.0	91.4	102.1	61.2	83.2	100.0	83.3	85.1
71.8	93.3	81.6	66.4	101.7	88.1	89.2	81.9	82.4	—	55.1	82.9	87.2	17.7	53.3	50.0	117.3	84.4	—	—	94.8	87.2	70.1	—
75.4	94.4	86.1	69.2	85.1	88.4	91.2	80.0	82.2	—	52.8	70.8	79.1	16.8	53.1	52.6	120.0	97.9	—	—	96.5	86.8	71.7	—
72.8	94.4	82.8	67.6	90.7	88.4	89.7	83.0	—	—	—	—	—	—	—	—	—	—	—	—	—	89.7	—	—
78.2	94.0	76.9	62.4	84.5	89.9	90.8	82.7	76.3	—	—	—	—	—	—	—	—	—	—	—	—	86.9	—	—
78.2	93.7	84.3	68.3	90.2	85.2	91.8	83.9	67.6	—	48.5	76.2	80.0	18.4	45.6	42.9	—	—	—	—	93.0	96.0	73.5	—
77.0	96.6	82.4	70.5	100.8	88.5	87.8	84.8	91.4	—	50.0	79.5	87.5	20.0	46.0	56.2	127.8	97.7	—	—	95.9	92.8	73.6	—
71.2	94.6	80.8	67.4	96.2	87.1	89.8	77.4	73.0	—	53.5	73.3	76.7r	19.0	52.9	36.8	123.7	93.9	—	—	100.0	86.6	67.4	—
75.1	100.7	75.6	63.8	89.7	89.7	83.1	91.2	106.3	94.9	59.8	86.4	95.0	18.8	38.6	53.3	108.8	81.6	90.5	55.4	97.2	84.1	65.7	83.9
71.3	89.4	83.5	67.6	86.3	84.0	91.1	81.4	70.7	84.2	52.5	94.9	102.8	18.5	48.8	56.2	151.3	89.2	74.3	77.5	84.5	97.0	80.0	67.5
72.1	89.2	82.9	65.5	89.2	90.8	92.5	80.6	85.3	83.1	51.3	78.7	86.0	18.9	49.1	50.0	120.3	88.2	88.2	65.3	100.0	82.2	65.5	75.7
77.1	99.3	81.5	66.4	92.4	88.6	91.8	80.6	79.0	91.1	53.4	80.0	90.0	18.3	54.7	40.0	122.4	91.7	87.4	60.3	100.0	86.6	66.4	76.0
81.2	97.8	83.6	67.1	98.3	89.7	87.8	81.7	79.4	84.2	50.4	83.3	92.1	19.0	49.0	47.1	122.0	86.7	81.6	68.5	97.1	85.2	69.2	69.9
77.7	98.6	82.2	66.9	93.3	87.4	88.1	87.3	92.1	81.7	52.8	80.4	88.1	18.9	51.0	40.0	125.4	95.8	77.1	62.9	97.9	85.1	68.3	71.1
70.3	99.3	86.1	72.8	100.0	88.4	89.9	83.0	79.0	—	55.3	70.0	77.8	17.0	56.9	35.0	113.3	76.9	—	—	103.7	86.1	70.2	—

Tribal divisions and subdivisions / Catalogue No. / Sex and stages of life / Number of cases / Averages and ranges	"Central angle" (Klaatsch)	Cranio-facial (Fahlenburg)	Interoccipital	ANGLES - To ear-eye plane											Mandibulo-alveolar plane				Length-breadth
				Glabella-lambda	Basion-bregma	Nasion-basion	Basion-opisthion	Nasion-bregma	Lambda-bregma	Opisthion-lambda	Prosthion-nasion	Nasospinale-nasion	Prosthion-nasospinale	Orbital height	Ramus tangent-alveolar plane	Ramus tangent-basal tangent	Chin vertical-basal tangent	Condylo-coronoid tangent-alveolar plane	
	(°)	(°)	(°)	(°)	(°)	(°)	(°)	(°)	(°)	(°)	(°)	(°)	(°)	(°)	(°)	(°)	(°)	(°)	
UNDEFORMED																			
3747 ♂ ad-mat	90	87	121	4	86	31	−12	48	33	123	83	83	83	95	68	121	80	+3	78.1
3748 ♀ mat	93	86	133	7	86	34	0	50	33	120	80	83	72	90	68	117	85	−7	81.9
3749 ♀ ad	90	91	132	10	80	25	+3	54	24	114	77	81	69	94	62	125	81	+4	86.1
3750 ♂ ad	89	86	129	4	85	31	−8	51	35	117	80	80	80	84	—	—	—	—	85.7
3751 ♂ mat	88	89	117	10	78	27	−5	50	23	115	87	88	84	98	72	119	78	−2	70.9
3752 inf. I	—	—	—	6	—	—	—	53	28	—	89	89	89	93	46	140	83	+18	81.7
3753 ♂ mat	90	86	115	8	82	31	−7	53	25	113	83	85	76	88	68	115	85	+3	79.5
3754 ♂ ad-mat	90	92	123	6	84	30	−11	46	28	120	80	80	80	88	—	—	—	—	79.7
3755 ♂ mat	93	90	120	11	82	28	−4	49	23	115	83	83	83	89	—	—	—	—	77.1
3759 ♂ mat	—	—	—	—	—	—	—	—	—	—	—	—	—	—	79	100	89	−3	—
3760 ♂ sen	—	—	—	—	—	—	—	—	—	—	—	—	—	—	71	119	80	+4	—
3761 ♂ ad-mat	—	—	—	—	—	—	—	—	—	—	—	—	—	—	69	112	88	+5	—
3762 ♂ mat-sen	—	—	—	—	—	—	—	—	—	—	—	—	—	—	68	122	80	−3	—
3763 ♂ mat-sen	—	—	—	—	—	—	—	—	—	—	—	—	—	—	69	115	84	+1	—
♂ cases	18	16	18	18	18	18	18	18	18	18	16	14	15	16	14	14	14	14	18
range	88–97	86–92	115–134	1–14	78–96	26–35	0 to −12	40–54	20–38	105–131	78–87	81–88	61–84	84–98	65–79	100–122	78–89	−4 to +9	70.8–85.7
average	91.7	89.0	123.1	7.5	84.2	29.9	−6.5	43.6	27.4	117.6	81.7	84.9	75.5	90.0	70.3	115.7	83.1	+0.7	77.8
♀ cases	8	8	8	8	8	8	8	8	8	8	8	8	8	8	6	6	6	6	8
range	90–93	86–91	96–133	5–10	80–96	25–34	+5 to −9	46–54	23–33	113–124	77–86	81–88	68–81	85–94	62–68	116–133	74–86	−7 to +12	75.0–86.0
average	90.4	88.1	122.8	7.5	82.8	30.0	−2.6	50.4	27.8	117.9	81.3	84.3	73.4	90.0	64.3	122.2	82.5	+2.7	83.0
juv. 1 case	92.0	88.0	126.0	10.0	82.0	31.0	+3.0	52.0	24.0	114.0	82.0	—	—	90.0	—	—	—	—	83.5
inf. cases	3	3	4	5	3	3	3	5	5	4	5	5	5	5	3	3	3	3	5
range	90–95	85–89	110–130	5–9	83–86	28–30	−6 to −10	49–53	24–31	116–124	73–90	73–90	73–90	90–98	46–63	123–140	83–85	+15 to +28	79.2–97.5
average	91.7	87.3	124.0	7.0	84.7	29.0	−7.3	51.4	27.8	120.0	85.2	85.2	85.2	93.6	55.7	129.7	83.7	+20.3	84.7
Lillooet																			
2614 inf. I	—	—	—	—	—	—	—	—	—	—	—	—	—	—	—	—	—	—	87.2
2615 inf. I	—	—	—	—	—	—	—	—	—	—	—	—	—	—	—	—	—	—	95.9
2618 ♂ ad-mat	93	96	121	16	77	23	−14	49	18	101	83	85	76	93	67	118	84	+4	90.3
2619 inf. II	—	—	116	13	—	—	—	51	24	115	85	86	82	91	52	135	83	+12	91.7
2620 inf. II	90	91	127	10	80	23	−14	57	26	117	88	94	63	95	58	126	86	+8	96.7
2621 ♂ mat	90	—	121	8	82	28	−10	50	30	113	89	92	72	97	75	111	82	−5	92.7
2622 ♀ ad	89	89	115	7	82	29	−4	52	31	119	81	88	66	92	60	127	83	+2	88.5
2623 inf. I	—	—	—	—	—	—	—	—	—	—	—	—	—	—	51	135	83	+13	—
2624 ♀ ad-mat (lower jaw doubtful)	86	91	125	7	79	25	−17	54	29	119	84	86	70	92	70	121	77	−8	85.6
2929 inf. II	—	—	—	—	—	—	—	—	—	—	—	—	—	—	62	126	82	−7	89.5

							INDICES													
			Skull							Face and mandible								Cranio-facial		
Length-height	Breadth-height	Transverse frontal	Transverse frontoparietal	Sagittal parieto-frontal (arcs)	Sagittal frontal	Sagittal parietal	Sagittal occipital	Foramen magnum	Facial	Upper facial	Orbital (mf)	Orbital (la)	Interorbital (mf-mf to ek-ek)	Nasal	Transverse nasal bone	Maxillo-alveolar	Palatal	Bicondylo-bigonial breadth (mandible)	Ramus (mandible)	Transverse cranio-facial	Fronto-biorbital (ft-ft to fmt-fmt)	Jugo-frontal	Jugo-mandibular
74.5	95.3	77.9	66.0	95.7	85.0	89.5	83.5	100.0	79.6	42.8	82.2	92.5	19.0	47.2	33.3	120.0	89.4	76.9	65.6	101.3	88.4	65.1	67.8
81.9	100.0	81.6	66.4	94.0	85.7	86.4	88.7	86.1	97.7	60.8	81.4	89.7	16.5	46.1	41.2	115.8	80.8	81.7	54.5	92.9	90.3	71.5	75.4
78.3	90.9	76.5	61.5	92.8	88.0	87.9	87.8	91.2	90.1	52.7	76.2	82.0	16.3	53.3	43.7	121.8	90.0	81.0	54.0	91.6	84.6	67.2	71.8
82.9	96.7	79.0	65.3	96.2	87.2	87.5	85.2	82.9	—	54.4	80.9	85.0	20.0	47.1	56.2	114.5	85.1	—	—	90.7	92.4	72.1	—
70.9	100.0	84.3	69.8	98.4	88.2	91.2	80.9	86.1	87.8	53.1	72.3	79.1	21.1	49.1	55.6	123.6	102.2	84.7	64.2	105.8	83.6	66.0	75.5
—	—	78.2	64.2	99.2	83.5	87.5	83.8	—	80.7	49.0	89.5	97.1	19.0	55.6	71.4	157.6	112.5	84.1	62.2	77.6	97.7	82.7	71.1
75.6	95.0	82.1	65.7	94.1	89.0	91.9	80.2	85.7	92.5	56.0	86.0	94.9	17.6	52.8	46.7	128.9	108.9	89.1	62.1	95.7	85.2	68.7	85.1
71.7	90.1	78.3	66.7	88.3	90.1	89.9	81.6	75.0	—	52.5	77.8	85.4	19.8	54.0	58.8	129.6	—	—	—	100.0	82.5	66.7	—
77.1	100.0	84.1	65.2	87.1	87.9	91.7	80.3	83.9	—	54.7	75.6	82.9	17.8	51.0	31.2	123.6	95.7	—	—	92.7	85.7	70.3	—
—	—	—	—	—	—	—	—	—	—	—	—	—	—	—	—	—	—	91.0	53.3	—	—	—	—
—	—	—	—	—	—	—	—	—	—	—	—	—	—	—	—	—	—	—	61.9	—	—	—	—
—	—	—	—	—	—	—	—	—	—	—	—	—	—	—	—	—	—	84.8	59.4	—	—	—	—
—	—	—	—	—	—	—	—	—	—	—	—	—	—	—	—	—	—	83.5	67.2	—	—	—	—
—	—	—	—	—	—	—	—	—	—	—	—	—	—	—	—	—	—	90.5	67.2	—	—	—	—
18	18	18	18	18	18	18	18	17	8	16	16	16	16	16	16	16	15	13	14	16	18	16	8
70.3–	89.2–	75.4–	61.8–	84.5–	85.0–	83.1–	77.4–	73.0–	79.6–	42.8–	70.0–	76.7–	16.0–	38.6–	31.2–	108.8	76.9–	76.9–	48.7–	90.7–	82.2–	64.5–	67.8–
82.9	100.7	86.1	72.8	100.0	90.8	92.5	91.2	106.3	94.9	59.8	86.4	95.0	21.1	56.9	63.2	129.6	108.9	90.9	67.2	105.8	92.4	72.1	85.1
74.6	95.9	80.6	66.5	91.7	88.1	89.9	81.8	84.1	87.4	52.5	78.9	86.4	18.6	51.5	46.1	120.3	91.9	85.9	61.0	98.5	83.8	67.8	76.8
8	8	8	8	8	8	8	8	5	8	8	8	8	8	8	8	8	6	6	8	8	8	8	6
71.8–	90.9–	76.5–	61.5–	92.8–	85.7–	86.4–	80.8–	79.4–	83.2–	50.0–	76.2–	82.0–	16.3–	46.0–	41.2–	115.8	80.8–	81.0–	54.0–	91.6–	83.3–	65.7–	69.9–
81.9	100.7	87.8	73.7	101.7	89.7	90.4	88.7	91.4	97.7	60.8	92.3	100.0	22.7	56.0	56.2	127.8	107.5	89.1	68.5	100.7	93.5	73.6	77.4
77.6	95.7	81.3	67.2	96.3	88.1	88.1	84.1	85.8	89.4	54.0	84.1	91.1	19.0	50.9	48.8	120.6	88.8	83.2	61.0	96.0	88.5	70.2	73.3
78.2	93.7	84.0	68.3	90.2	85.2	91.8	83.9	67.6	—	48.5	76.2	80.0	18.0	45.6	42.9	—	—	—	—	93.0	95.1	73.5	—
3	3	5	5	4	5	5	5	3	5	5	5	5	5	5	5	5	3	3	5	5	5	5	3
71.3–	83.8–	73.8–	57.3–	83.5–	82.7–	87.0–	81.4–	70.7–	80.7–	46.8–	86.5–	94.1–	18.1–	46.7–	47.1–	142.1	77.1–	74.3–	61.2–	69.4–	97.0–	78.4–	67.5–
74.0	93.4	83.3	69.3	99.2	86.4	87.9	86.5	79.0	89.5	56.1	94.9	102.8	20.2	55.6	71.4	157.6	112.5	102.1	77.5	84.5	100.0	83.3	85.1
72.3	88.9	79.2	63.9	91.5	84.5	88.8	83.8	79.7	85.0	51.9	90.0	98.0	19.2	49.4	57.6	151.2	90.6	86.8	67.0	78.6	98.8	81.4	74.6
—	—	78.4	64.0	104.3	93.4	76.9	84.2	—	—	44.3	94.1	100.0	18.8	57.1	—	160.7	109.1	—	—	77.9	97.7	82.1	—
—	—	78.3	59.7	102.0	85.2	89.4	81.4	—	—	48.1	86.1	93.9	20.2	60.6	—	156.3	103.5	—	—	79.1	96.5	75.5	—
70.3	77.8	78.1	62.4	80.7	92.7	93.2	81.7	88.2	80.3	50.7	73.9	87.2r	18.9	57.1	57.9	124.5	91.3	91.4	60.3	95.3	85.3	65.5	82.4
—	—	79.6	59.7	81.6	86.8	92.5	77.6	—	83.0	50.0	91.7	94.3	16.5	56.4	58.3	156.8	100.0	82.5	61.9	77.8	94.5	76.8	71.4
76.6	—	79.7	60.4	87.1	85.6	87.1	93.8	86.2	58.7	89.2	97.1	18.8	51.3	50.0	147.4	85.3	91.4	62.2	73.2	97.8	82.6	78.0
76.8	82.9	77.5	61.2	91.5	89.8	91.7	80.6	85.3	—	47.6	87.0	95.2	16.8	49.1	44.4	136.2	—	84.6	59.0	95.4	87.7	64.1	79.3
75.1	84.9	77.8	62.3	100.0	88.7	89.7	77.9	78.8	85.7	52.6	85.4	97.2r	18.7	46.8	56.2	117.6	82.2	91.7	56.9	91.1	89.2	68.4	82.7
—	—	—	—	—	—	—	—	—	—	—	—	—	—	—	—	—	—	84.3	65.7	—	—	—	—
77.2	90.2	80.7	67.1	103.3	87.5	90.3	83.6	96.9	—	50.8	74.4	84.2r	17.5	53.2	33.3	118.9	—	83.5	65.4	92.3	90.6	72.7	76.5
73.2	—	84.0	65.0	83.5	92.7	87.9	83.6	90.6	86.1	51.3	75.6	—	15.7	50.0	42.9	131.8	84.6	87.5	68.1	84.9	95.7	77.4	73.0

Tribal divisions and subdivisions / Catalogue No. / Sex and stages of life / Number of cases / Averages and ranges	"Central angle" (Klaatsch)	Cranio-facial (Fahlenburger)	Interoccipital	ANGLES															Length-breadth
				To ear-eye plane										Mandibulo-alveolar plane					
				Glabella-lambda	Basion-bregma	Nasion-basion	Basion-opisthion	Nasion-bregma	Lambda-bregma	Opisthion-lambda	Prosthion-nasion	Nasospinale-nasion	Prosthion-nasospinale	Orbital height	Ramus tangent-alveolar plane	Ramus tangent-basal tangent	Chin vertical-basal tangent	Condylo-coronoid tangent-alveolar plane	
	(°)	(°)	(°)	(°)	(°)	(°)	(°)	(°)	(°)	(°)	(°)	(°)	(°)	(°)	(°)	(°)	(°)	(°)	
UNDEFORMED																			
♂ cases	2	1	2	2	2	2	2	2	2	2	2	2	2	2	2	2	2	2	2
range	90; 93	—	121; 121	8; 16	77; 82	23; 28	−10 to −14	49; 50	18; 30	101; 113	83; 89	85; 92	72; 76	93; 97	67; 75	111; 118	82; 84	−5; +4	90.3; 92.7
average	91.5	96.0	121.0	12.0	79.5	25.5	−12.0	49.5	24.0	107.0	86.0	88.5	74.0	95.0	71.0	114.5	83.0	−.5	91.5
♀ cases	2	2	2	2	2	2	2	2	2	2	2	2	2	2	2	2	2	2	2
range	86; 89	89; 91	125; 135	7; 7	79; 82	25; 29	−4 to −14	52; 54	29; 31	119; 119	81; 84	86; 88	66; 70	92; 92	60; 70	121; 127	77; 83	−8; +2	85.6; 88.5
average	87.5	90.0	130.0	7.0	80.5	27.0	−10.5	53.0	30.0	119.0	82.5	87.0	68.0	92.0	65.0	124.0	80.0	+5.0	87.0
inf. cases	1	1	2	2	1	1	1	2	2	2	2	2	2	2	4	4	4	4	5
range	—	—	116; 127	10; 13				51; 57	24; 26	115; 117	85; 88	86; 94	63; 82	91; 95	51−62	126−135	82−86	−7 to +13	87.2−96.7
average	90.0	91.0	121.5	11.5	80.0	23.0	−14.0	54.0	25.0	116.0	86.5	90.0	72.5	93.0	55.8	130.5	83.5	+6.5	92.2
Nicola																			
2606 ♂ mat	—	—	—	—	—	—	—	—	—	—	—	—	—	—	74	111	86	−13	—
2607 ♀ ad	88	93	124	7	81	25	−9	48	30	118	83	88	67	93	63	125	81	+6	81.8
2609 ♀ ad	—	—	—	—	—	—	—	—	—	—	—	—	—	—	64	126	80	+1	—
2610 ♂ mat	94	89	113	9	85	30	−11	42	24	114	86	86	86	96	70	113	86	−8	80.0
2611 ♂ ad	86	89	111	2	84	30	−3	47	31	125	84	87	72	93	67	123	80	−3	77.6
2612 ♀ mat	90	92	125	8	82	27	−8	49	29	115	84	85	81	90	—	—	—	—	81.3
2613 ♂ ad-mat	95	94	118	11	84	27	0	45	26	114	84	89	65	85	63	123	83	+6	85.5
♂ cases	3	3	3	3	3	3	3	3	3	3	3	3	3	3	4	4	4	4	3
range	86−95	89−94	111−118	2−11	84−85	27−30	−3 to −11	42−47	24−31	114−125	84−86	86−89	68−86	85−96	63−74	111−123	80−86	−13 to +6	78.6−85.5
average	91.7	90.7	114.0	7.3	84.3	29.0	−8.0	44.7	27.0	117.7	84.7	87.3	74.3	91.3	68.5	117.5	83.8	−4.5	81.4
♀ cases	2	2	2	2	2	2	2	2	2	2	2	2	2	2	2	2	2	2	2
range	88; 90	92; 93	124; 125	7; 8	81; 82	25; 27	−8 to −9	48; 49	29; 30	115; 118	83; 84	85; 89	67; 81	90; 93	63; 64	125; 125	80; 81	+1; +6	81.3; 81.8
average	89.0	92.5	124.5	7.5	81.5	26.0	−8.5	48.5	29.5	116.5	83.5	86.5	74.0	91.5	63.5	125.0	80.5	+3.5	81.5
Lytton																			
1057 ♂ mat	91	93	117	6	85	32	−3	50	30	114	79	82	73	95	—	—	—	—	81.6
1058 ♀ mat-sen	93	92	131	9	84	32	−5	48	27	116	82	83	79	90	—	—	—	—	77.5
1060 ♂ mat	—	—	—	—	—	—	—	—	—	—	—	—	—	—	—	—	—	—	75.0
1062 ♀ ad-mat	—	—	—	—	—	—	—	—	—	—	—	—	—	—	—	—	—	—	79.1
1086 ♂ ad	—	—	—	—	—	—	—	—	—	—	—	—	—	—	—	—	—	—	—
1087 ♂ ad	—	—	—	—	—	—	—	—	—	—	—	—	—	—	—	—	—	—	—
1167 ♀? mat	—	—	—	—	—	—	—	—	—	—	—	—	—	—	—	—	—	—	—
1185 ♂ mat	—	—	—	—	—	—	—	—	—	—	—	—	—	—	—	—	—	—	80.6
1223 ♀? mat	—	—	—	—	—	—	—	—	—	—	—	—	—	—	—	—	—	—	80.7
1555 ♀ mat	—	—	—	—	—	—	—	—	—	—	—	—	—	—	69	124	77	−12	—
1563 inf. I—II	—	—	—	—	—	—	—	—	—	—	—	—	—	—	56	126	86	+15	—
4307 juv-ad	89	91	122	7	82	28	−9	51	30	116	80	88	63	96	67	118	84	+7	78.2
4308 ♂ mat	91	94	124	13	78	30	−4	53	19	108	82	82	82	95	61	114	84	0	81.7

										INDICES											
		Skull									Face and mandible								Cranio-facial		
Length-height	Breadth-height	Transverse frontal	Transverse frontoparietal	Sagittal parieto-frontal (arcs)	Sagittal frontal	Sagittal parietal	Sagittal occipital	Foramen magnum	Facial	Upper facial	Orbital (mf)	Orbital (la)	Interorbital (mf-mf to ek-ek)	Nasal	Transverse nasal bone	Maxillo-alveolar	Palatal	Bicondylo-bigonial breadth (mandible)	Ramus (mandible)	Transverse cranio-facial	Fronto-biorbital (ft-ft to fmt-fmt)	Jugo-frontal	Jugo-mandibular
2	2	2	2	2	2	2	2	2	1	2	2	2	2	2	2	2	1	2	2	2	2	2	2
70.3; 76.8	77.8; 82.9	77.5; 78.1	61.2; 62.4	80.7; 91.5	89.8; 92.7	91.7; 93.2	80.6; 81.7	85.3; 88.2	—	47.6; 50.7	73.9; 87.0	87.2; 95.2	16.8; 18.9	49.1; 57.1	44.4; 57.9	124.5; 136.2	—	84.6; 91.4	59.0; 60.3	95.3; 95.4	85.3; 87.7	64.1; 65.5	79.3; 82.4
73.6	80.4	77.5	61.8	85.5	91.3	92.5	81.2	86.5	80.3	49.3	80.5	91.0	18.0	53.1	51.0	130.4	91.3	88.0	59.7	95.4	86.5	64.9	80.9
2	2	2	2	2	2	2	2	2	1	2	2	2	2	2	2	2	1	2	2	2	2	2	2
75.1; 77.2	84.9; 90.2	77.8; 80.7	62.3; 67.1	100.9; 103.3	87.5; 88.7	89.7; 90.3	77.9; 83.6	78.8; 96.9	—	50.8; 52.6	74.4; 85.4	84.2; 97.2	17.5; 18.7	46.8; 53.2	33.3; 56.2	117.6; 118.9	—	83.5; 91.7	56.9; 65.4	91.1; 92.3	89.2; 90.6	68.4; 72.7	76.5; 82.7
76.2	87.6	78.5	64.7	101.5	88.1	90.0	80.8	87.0	85.7	51.7	79.9	90.5	18.5	50.0	44.5	118.3	82.2	87.6	61.2	91.7	90.0	70.6	79.6
2	—	5	5	5	5	5	5	2	3	5	5	4	5	5	3	5	2	4	4	5	5	5	3
73.2; 76.6	—	78.3; 84.0	59.7; 65.0	81.6; 104.3	85.6; 93.4	76.9; 92.5	77.6; 87.1	90.6; 93.8	83.0; 86.2	41.8; 58.7	75.6; 94.0	93.9; 100.0	15.7; 20.2	50.0; 60.6	42.9; 58.3	131.8; 160.7	84.6; 109.1	82.5; 91.4	61.9; 68.2	73.2; 83.9	94.5; 97.8	75.5; 82.6	71.4; 78.0
74.9	—	79.6	61.8	91.2	88.7	86.7	82.8	91.5	85.0	49.3	87.1	96.0	18.0	55.1	50.3	150.6	96.5	86.4	64.5	78.3	96.8	78.8	74.1
																87.1	55.6						
70.9	86.7	80.4	66.7	95.7	87.9	90.1	82.6	81.8	82.0	50.0	78.0	86.5 r	20.2	56.2	33.3	124.0	97.7	82.9	61.1	94.8	86.5	70.3	79.7
																81.4	50.9						
67.6	84.5	78.8	62.8	86.1	98.4	89.5	77.7	81.1	88.4	52.7	85.7	94.7 r	19.4	45.6	50.0	132.7	104.4	85.1	56.9	98.6	85.3	63.7	70.5
71.4	90.9	76.2	65.0	103.2	87.8	88.2	75.2	90.6	88.6	53.9	77.8	85.4	20.2	50.9	—	121.4	91.7	83.5	63.2	98.6	83.8	66.0	71.6
75.3	92.6	76.6	60.7	93.4	91.0	85.1	82.1	87.5	—	51.2	84.2	91.4	19.8	52.3	41.2	124.4	95.2	—	—	91.1	85.4	66.7	—
71.7	83.8	80.3	63.5	88.3	99.2	89.6	82.3	80.6	—	—	92.9	102.6r	18.2	48.1	44.7	131.4	87.5	—	62.1	—	88.7	—	—
3	3	3	3	3	3	3	3	3	2	2	3	3	3	3	2	3	3	2	3	3	3	3	2
67.6–71.7	83.8–90.9	76.2–80.3	62.8–65.0	86.1–103.2	87.8–99.2	88.2–89.6	75.2–82.3	80.6–90.6	88.4; 88.6	52.7; 53.9	77.8–92.9	85.4–102.6r	18.2–20.2	45.6–50.9	50.0–64.7	121.4–132.7	87.5–104.4	83.5–87.1	55.6–63.2	98.6; 98.6	83.8–88.7	63.7; 66.0	70.5; 71.6
70.2	86.4	77.7	63.8	92.3	95.1	89.1	78.4	83.7	88.5	53.3	85.5	93.7	19.0	48.2	57.5	128.5	94.5	85.2	59.5	98.6	86.0	64.9	71.1
2	2	2	2	2	2	2	2	2	1	2	2	2	2	2	2	2	2	2	2	2	2	2	1
70.9; 75.3	86.7; 92.6	76.6; 80.4	66.7; 66.7	87.9; 95.7	85.1; 91.0	82.1; 90.1	81.8; 82.6	87.5; —	50.0; 51.2	84.2; 91.4	86.5; 88.5	19.8; 20.2	53.2; 56.2	33.3; 41.2	124.0; 124.4	95.2; 97.7	81.4; 82.9	50.9; 61.1	91.9; 94.8	85.4; 86.5	66.7; 70.0	—
73.1	89.7	78.0	63.7	94.0	90.0	87.6	82.4	84.0	82.0	50.6	81.6	88.5	20.0	54.7	37.0	124.2	96.5	82.2	56.0	93.0	86.0	68.5	79.7
79.9	97.9	82.5	67.8	93.2	87.1	87.8	82.3	84.6	—	53.1	79.5	87.5 r	—	—	—	—	—	—	—	97.9	92.5	69.2	—
78.6	101.5	—	77.6	95.0	90.9	88.7	84.7	78.8	—	61.0	80.5	89.2 r	17.2	43.1	66.7	109.4	80.8	—	—	91.8	102.0	84.5	—
—	—	—	—	—	—	—	—	—	—	—	82.2	—	—	—	50.0	—	—	—	—	—	—	—	—
76.2	96.3	88.3	72.1	99.2	86.8	88.3	86.1	81.8	—	—	82.9	94.4	—	—	—	—	—	—	—	90.4	94.2	79.7	—
—	—	—	—	—	92.2	—	—	—	—	—	80.0	86.5	—	45.1	66.7	124.0	84.4	—	—	—	—	—	—
—	—	—	—	—	—	—	—	—	—	—	77.8	85.4 r	—	50.9	55.6	117.2	89.6	—	—	—	—	—	—
—	—	—	—	—	—	—	—	—	—	—	80.9	87.2 r	19.4	56.5	—	114.8	80.8	—	—	—	—	—	—
—	—	81.7	67.6	94.3	91.0	90.4	83.3	—	—	—	—	—	—	—	—	—	—	—	—	—	—	90.7	—
77.7	96.3	78.0	63.4	84.8	88.0	88.7	84.5	74.3	—	—	—	—	—	—	—	—	—	—	—	94.8	86.7	66.9	—
—	—	—	—	—	—	—	—	—	—	—	—	—	—	—	—	—	—	87.6	63.6	—	—	—	—
																			69.4				
77.6	99.3	—	67.1	95.9	88.6	91.5	82.5	86.1	86.1	53.1	92.5	100.0r	19.3	47.9	52.9	126.9	79.2	77.7	67.3	95.6	91.1	70.8	72.3
77.7	95.1	77.2	61.5	94.9	88.1	91.1	84.9	86.1	76.2	46.8	81.4	89.7r	16.5	47.9	58.3	123.1	86.7	84.3	62.7	100.0	85.4	61.5	79.0

Tribal divisions and subdivisions / Catalogue No. / Sex and stages of life / Number of cases / Averages and ranges	"Central angle" (Klaatsch)	Cranio-facial (Fialdenburger)	Interoccipital	ANGLES											Mandibulo-alveolar plane				Length-breadth
				Glabella-lambda	Basion-bregma	Nasion-basion	Basion-opisthion	Nasion-bregma	Lambda-bregma	Opisthion-lambda	Prosthion-nasion	Nasospinale-nasion	Prosthion-nasospinale	Orbital height	Ramus tangent-alveolar plane	Ramus tangent-basal tangent	Chin vertical-basal tangent	Condylo-coronoid tangent-alveolar plane	
	(°)	(°)	(°)	(°)	(°)	(°)	(°)	(°)	(°)	(°)	(°)	(°)	(°)	(°)	(°)	(°)	(°)	(°)	(°)
UNDEFORMED																			
4309 ♂ ad-mat	87	93	122	2	85	30	−4	46	33	122	72	72	72	89	72	118	79	−1	71.0
4310 inf. II	92	87	129	7	85	30	−14	51	29	119	84	84	84	91	63	122	84	+10	85.0
4311 ♂ juv-ad	—	—	129	—	—	—	—	—	—	—	—	—	—	—	—	—	—	—	78.8
4313 ♀ ad	90	91	120	10	80	29	−8	51	27	113	79	82	68	86	64	121	84	−2	82.4
♂ cases	4	4	5	4	4	4	4	2	4	4	4	4	4	4	3	3	3	3	7
range	87–92	91–94	117–129	2–13	78–85	28–32	−3 to −9	46–53	19–33	108–122	72–82	72–88	63–82	89–96	67–72	114–118	79–84	−1 to +7	71.0–81.7
average	90.0	92.8	123.8	7.0	80.2	30.0	−5.0	50.0	30.5	115.0	78.3	81.0	74.0	93.8	70.0	116.6	82.3	+2.0	78.1
♀ cases	2	2	2	2	2	2	2	1	2	2	2	2	2	2	2	2	2	2	4
range	90; 95	91; 92	120; 131	9; 10	80; 84	29; 32	−5 to −8	—	27; 27	113; 116	79; 82	82; 83	68; 79	86; 90	64; 69	121; 124	77; 84	−12 to −2	77.5–82.4
average	92.5	91.5	125.5	9.5	82.0	30.5	−6.5	51.0	27.0	114.5	80.5	82.5	73.5	91.5	66.5	122.5	80.5	−7.0	79.9
inf. cases	1	1	1	1	1	1	1	1	1	1	1	1	1	1	2	2	2	2	1
range	—	—	—	—	—	—	—	—	—	—	—	—	—	—	56; 63	122; 126	84; 86	−10; −15	—
average	92.0	87.0	129.0	7.0	85.0	30.0	−14.0	51.0	29.0	119.0	84.0	84.0	84.0	91.0	59.5	124.0	85.0	−12.5	85.0
Spences Bridge																			
98 ♀ ad-mat	89	90	123	9	80	26	−5	52	27	114	86	89	71	94	67	130	73	−11	81.5
99 ♂ mat	91	92	117	10	81	25	−9	46	23	110	90	91	83	96	79	108	82	−8	76.6
1641 ♀ ad	91	89	123	5	86	32	−4	49	32	118	82	83	73	90	—	—	—	—	77.8
♂ 1 case	91.0	92.0	117.0	10.0	81.0	25.0	−9.0	46.0	23.0	110.0	90.0	91.0	83.0	96.0	79.0	108.0	82.0	−8.0	76.6
♀ cases	2	2	2	2	2	2	2	2	2	2	2	2	2	2	1	1	1	1	2
range	89; 91	89; 90	123; 123	5; 9	80; 86	26; 32	−4 to −5	49; 52	27; 32	114; 118	82; 86	83; 89	71; 73	90; 94	—	—	—	—	77.8; 81.5
average	90.0	89.5	123.0	7.0	83.0	29.0	−4.5	50.5	29.5	116.0	84.0	86.0	72.0	92.0	67.0	130.0	73.0	−11.0	79.6
Kamloops																			
1284 ♂ ad-mat	90	86	120	10	81	29	−4	50	25	113	91	93	81	95	62	121	86	+18	82.4
1286 ♂ juv-ad	—	—	—	—	—	—	—	—	—	—	—	—	—	—	55	137	76	−8	—
1290 ♀ ad	—	—	—	—	—	—	—	—	—	—	—	—	—	—	—	—	—	—	82.1
1291 ♀ ad	—	—	—	—	—	—	—	—	—	—	—	—	—	—	66	119	83	−7	—
1292 ♀ mat	—	—	—	—	—	—	—	—	—	—	—	—	—	—	66	131	72	−8	—
1293 inf. II	—	—	—	—	—	—	—	—	—	—	—	—	—	—	69	130	72	+19	—
1295 inf. I	—	—	—	—	—	—	—	—	—	—	—	—	—	—	49	134	86	+18	—
1410 ♀ ad	93	93	121	10	83	25	−17	47	23	115	88	91	76	92	57	129	82	+5	83.1
1411 ♂ mat	—	—	—	—	—	—	—	—	—	—	—	—	—	—	—	—	—	—	76.5
1412 ♂? ad-mat	—	—	116	9	—	—	—	44	24	117	81	81	81	89	—	—	—	—	80.9
1413 ♂ ad-mat	93	91	121	13	80	26	+6	49	25	103	86	92	72	98!	—	—	—	—	76.7
1430 ♂ ad-mat	—	—	—	—	—	—	—	—	—	—	—	—	—	—	—	—	—	—	—
2602 ♂ mat	96	90	119	8	88	33	−4	44	28	113	79	79	79	90	75	115	79	+4	82.2

		Skull							Face and mandible									Cranio-facial			
Length-height	Breadth-height	Transverse frontal	Transverse fronto-parietal	Sagittal parieto-frontal (arcs)	Sagittal frontal	Sagittal parietal	Sagittal occipital	Foramen magnum	Facial	Upper facial	Orbital (mf)	Orbital (lk)	Interorbital (mf-mf to ek-ek)	Nasal	Transverse nasal bone	Maxillo-alveolar	Palatal	Bicondylo-bigonial breadth (mandible)	Ramus (mandible)	Transverse cranio-facial	Fronto-biorbital (ft-ft to fmt-fmt)	Jugo-frontal	Jugo-mandibular
---	---	---	---	---	---	---	---	---	---	---	---	---	---	---	---	---	---	---	---	---	---	---	---
72.7	102.3	80.5	70.0	96.8	88.1	91.8	80.6	78.4	—	53.9	77.8	85.4	—	43.4	28.6	122.6	81.6	—	56.1	108.5	85.0	64.5	—
77.1	90.8	81.4	63.9	93.7	88.3	93.3	86.7	82.4	86.5	52.2	89.2	103.1	16.7	47.6	61.5	141.0	105.9	81.7	59.2	85.4	92.2	74.8	76.6
75.9	96.3	80.7	65.7	107.1	90.2	90.8	89.2	80.6	—	—	—	—	—	—	—	—	—	—	—	—	95.6	—	—
75.8	91.9	79.6	63.2	97.3	88.5	87.3	80.5	96.8	88.6	53.8	78.6	86.8r	18.7	48.0	66.7	122.0	81.6	85.4	63.5	97.1	84.3	65.1	71.2
5	5	5	6	6	7	6	6	5	2	4	7	6	2	5	6	5	5	2	3	4	6	4	2
72.7–	95.1–	77.2–	61.5–	93.2–	87.1–	87.8–	80.6–	78.4–	76.2 ;	46.8–	77.8–	85.4–	16.5 ;	43.3–	28.6–	117.2–	79.2–	77.7 ;	56.1–	95.6–	85.0–	61.5–	72.3 ;
79.9	102.3	82.5	70.0	107.1	92.2	91.8	82.2	86 1	86.1	53.9	92.5	100.0	19.3	50.9	66.7	126.9	89.6	84.3	67.3	108.5	95.6	70.8	79.0
76.8	98.2	80.0	66.7	95.0	89.3	90.6	83.8	82.8	81.2	51.7	81.6	88.7	18.0	47.0	52.2	122.8	84.3	81.0	62.3	100.5	90.2	66.5	75.7
4	4	3	4	4	4	4	4	4	1	2	4	4	2	3	2	3	3	2	2	4	4	4	1
75.8–	91.9–	78.0–	63.2–	84.8–	86.8–	87.3–	80.5–	74.3–	—	53.8 ;	78.6–	86.8–	17.2–	43.1–	46.7 ;	109.4–	80.8–	85.4 ;	63.5 ;	90.4–	84.3–	65.1–	—
78.6	101.5	88.3	77.6	99.2	90.9	88.7	86.1	96.8		61.0	82.9	94.4	19.4	56.5	66.7	122.0	81.6	87.6	63.6	97.1	102.0	84.5	
77.1	96.5	81.7	64.8	93.8	88.6	88.3	84.0	82.3	88.6	57.4	80.7	89.0	18.3	49.2	66.7	115.4	81.1	86.5	63.6	93.3	91.8	74.0	71.2
1	1	1	1	1	1	1	1	1	1	1	1	1	1	1	1	1	1	1	2	1	1	1	1
—	—	—	—	—	—	—	—	—	—	—	—	—	—	—	—	—	—	—	59.2 ; 69.4	—	—	—	—
77.1	90.8	81.4	63.9	93.7	88.3	93.1	86.7	82.4	86.5	52.2	89.2	103.1	16.7	47.6	61.5	141.0	105.9	81.7	64.3	85.4	92.2	74.8	76.6
76.5	93.9	84.3	68.9	96.5	88.8	90.2	84.3	80.0	79.7	49.6	82.0	91.4	18.5	50.0	53.8	116.3	86.0	91.3	56.9	93.2	92.8	74.0	76.4
69.3	90.5	85.7	69.4	85.9	89.8	91.8	80.3	81.1	82.2	41.4	84.4	92.7r	18.4	45.4	38.9	131.4	89.6	84.6	66.7	103.4	88.7	67.1	72.4
77.2	99.2	84.8	68.5	91.7	87.6	88.3	81.1	81.8	—	52.0	87.5	97.2r	17.0	44.9	66.7	112.8	80.9	—	—	96.1	92.7	71.2	—
69.3	90.5	85.7	69.4	85.9	98.8	91.8	80.3	81.1	82.2	41.4	84.4	92.7	18.4	45.4	38.9	131.4	89.6	84.6	66.7	103.4	88.7	67.1	72.4
2	2	2	2	2	2	2	2	2	1	2	2	2	2	2	2	2	2	1	1	2	2	2	1
76.5 ;	93.9 ;	84.3 ;	68.5 ;	91.7 ;	87.6 ;	88.3 ;	81.1 ;	80.0 ;	—	49.6 ;	82.0 ;	91.4 ;	17.0 ;	44.9 ;	53.8 ;	112.8 ;	80.9 ;	—	—	93.2 ;	92.7 ;	71.1 ;	—
77.2	99.2	84.8	68.9	96.5	88.8	90.2	84.3	81.8		52.0	87.5	97.2	18.5	50.0	66.7	116.3	86.0			96.1	92.8	74.0	
76.9	96.6	84.6	69.2	93.5	88.2	89.3	82.7	80.9	79.7	50.8	84.8	94.0	18.0	47.4	60.3	114.5	83.5	91.3	56.9	94.7	93.0	72.6	76.4
74.4	90.3	82.6	65.5	97.4	90.6	91.2	83.6	79.0	—	55.6	81.4	89.7r	18.2	38.2	69.2	128.6	90.9	—	—	93.1	88.8	70.4	—
—	—	—	—	—	—	—	—	—	—	—	—	—	—	—	—	—	—	86.0	60.4	—	—	—	—
78.4	95.5	78.1	66.9	84.0	86.4	90.5	—	—	—	52.4	89.7	100.0r	18.7	47.9	62.5	124.0	88.9	—	—	93.2	90.8	71.8	—
—	—	—	—	—	—	—	—	—	—	—	—	—	—	—	—	—	—	—	56.9	—	—	—	—
—	—	—	—	—	—	—	—	—	—	—	—	—	—	—	—	—	—	—	64.3	—	—	—	—
—	—	—	—	—	—	—	—	—	—	—	—	—	—	—	—	—	—	82.6	67.5	—	—	—	—
—	—	—	—	—	—	—	—	—	—	—	—	—	—	—	—	—	—	90.0	70.0	—	—	—	—
69.3	83.3	78.8	64.5	87.9	88.8	91.2	82.8	84.9	87.5	52.5	84.6	94.3r	18.2	45.6	71.4	125.5	88.1	81.1	65.2	87.0	93.7	74.2	71.1
76.0	99.3	—	62.8	92.2	88.3	89.0	82.9	87.9	—	—	87.5	92.1r	—	—	—	—	—	—	—	—	—	—	—
—	—	81.6	66.4	81.1	87.7	92.9	79.4	—	—	50.4	85.4	92.1r	18.1	48.9	53.3	112.2	80.0	—	—	92.1	91.2	72.1	—
75.0	97.8	79.8	65.9	89.6	90.4	89.3	79.7	—	—	78.0	86.5r	19.2	48.0	52.9	118.9	79.2	—	—	—	84.3	—	—	—
—	—	—	—	—	89.5	—	—	—	—	—	77.8	°87.5	—	44.4	61.5	126.4	97.7	—	—	—	—	—	—
78.1	95.0	76.1	59.7	76.2	89.7	92.7	83.9	94.1	85.6	53.2	78.6	86.8	18.7	41.8	71.4	—	—	88.0	70.4	100.0	80.6	59.7	79.1

Tribal divisions and subdivisions / Catalogue No. / Sex and stages of life / Number of cases / Averages and ranges	"Central angle" (Klaatsch)	Cranio-facial (Falkenburger)	Interoccipital	ANGLES										Mandibulo-alveolar plane				Length-breadth
				Glabella-lambda	Basion-bregma	Nasion-basion	Basion-opisthion	Nasion-bregma	Lambda-bregma	Opisthion-lambda	Prosthion-nasion	Nasospinale-nasion	Prosthion-nasospinale	Orbital height	Ramus tangent-alveolar plane	Ramus tangent-basal tangent	Chin vertical-basal tangent	Condylo-coronoid tangent-alveolar plane	
	(°)	(°)	(°)	(°)	(°)	(°)	(°)	(°)	(°)	(°)	(°)	(°)	(°)	(°)	(°)	(°)	(°)	(°)	
UNDEFORMED																			
♂ cases	3	3	4	4	3	3	3	4	4	4	4	4	4	4	3	3	3	3	5
range	90–96	86–91	116–121	8–13	80–88	26–33	+6 to −4	44–50	24–28	103–117	79–91	79–93	72–81	89–95	55–75	115–137	76–86	−8 to +18	76.7–82.2
average	93.0	89.0	119.0	10.0	83.0	29.3	−0.7	46.8	25.5	111.5	84.3	86.3	78.3	95.5	64.0	124.3	80.3	+4.7	79.7
♀ cases	1	1	1	1	1	1	1	1	1	1	1	1	1	1	3	3	3	3	2
range	—	—	—	—	—	—	—	—	—	—	—	—	—	—	57–66	119–131	72–83	−8 to +5	74.4; 83.3
average	93.0	93.0	121.0	10.0	83.0	25.0	−17.0	47.0	23.0	115.0	88.0	91.0	76.0	92.0	63.0	126.3	79.0	−3.3	79.0
inf. cases	—	—	—	—	—	—	—	—	—	—	—	—	—	—	1	2	2	2	—
range	—	—	—	—	—	—	—	—	—	—	—	—	—	—	—	130; 134	72; 86	+18; +19	—
average	—	—	—	—	—	—	—	—	—	—	—	—	—	—	49.0	132.0	79.0	+18.5	—
Eskimo																			
3709 ♂ mat	100	94	129	7	94	27	−10	42	31	128	92?	92?	92?	96	66	121	82	+8	75.0
3710 ♀ mat	96	88	138	5	92	35	−13	44	34	120	82	83	76	85	—	—	—	—	80.1
3711 ♂ ad	92	90	121	5	87	29	−11	46	30	123	83	87	68	86	—	—	—	—	75.1
3712 ♂ ad	93	90	125	7	86	29	−3	47	32	114	82	88	69	87	—	—	—	—	77.6
3713 ♀ ad	90?	—	138	8	82?	28?	−8?	47	28	117	88	91	74	91	—	—	—	—	76.9
3714 ♂ ad	92	86	133	8	84	33	+2	48	27	111	79	83	64	88	—	—	—	—	81.7
3715 ♂ mat	92	89	125	2	90	32	−9	45	36	129	83	86	77	92	—	—	—	—	79.9
3716 ♂ ad	93	90	131	7	86	31	+1	45	28	120	83	84	78	87	—	—	—	—	79.7
3717 ♂ ad	94	89	128	9	85	31	−1	52	26	117	74	74	74	88	—	—	—	—	77.1
3718 ♀ ad	90	88	124	7	83	31	−12	48	28	119	85	87	77	91	—	—	—	—	78.0
3719 ♂ ad	98	85	121	9	89	34	−3	46	25	120	81	81	81	85	—	—	—	—	74.5
3720 ♂ ad	92	89	128	8	84	29	0	47	28	119	86	86	86	85	—	—	—	—	79.8
3721 ♂ ad	90	90	129	6	84	29	−10	49	27	123	82	87	67	89	—	—	—	—	73.0
3764 ♂ mat	93	85	129	9	84	29	−11	51	27	119	91	93	86	91	—	—	—	—	77.3
3765 ♂ ad	90	91	120	2	88	30	−8	42	34	126	86	89	77	86	—	—	—	—	74.1
3766 ♂ ad-mat	90	—	124	1	3	87	30	−10	46	32	125	—	—	—	87	—	—	—	—	75.5
3767 ♂ ad	91	90	124	3	88	32	−15	45	33	123	81	81	81	84	—	—	—	—	76.7
3768 ♂ ad	90	92	128	10	80	26	−10	49	27	113	82	83	76	85	—	—	—	—	79.1
3769 ♂ ad-mat	95	88	121	8	87	32	−4	49	25	116	84	85	81	84	—	—	—	—	77.8
3770 ♀ ad	95	87	124	4	91	35	−14	43	33	122	81	82	78	82	—	—	—	—	75.6
3771 ♂ ad-mat	90	88	130	3	87	31	−5	48	35	123	80	83	71	88	—	—	—	—	77.8
3772 ♂ ad-mat	93	89	123	1	92	34	−12	42	37	127	83	84	80	85	—	—	—	—	76.4
3773 ♂ ad	90	87	131	6	84	30	0	51	30	115	80	81	78	82	—	—	—	—	79.0
3774 ♂ ad	90	—	133	0	90	33	−15	41	38	131	—	—	—	94	—	—	—	—	75.7
3775 ♂ ad	90	90	126	4	86	30	−19	46	31	121	81	85	73	82	—	—	—	—	73.4
3776 ♂ ad	90	86	132	1	89	37	−8	42	34	125	77	78	73	85	—	—	—	—	75.3
3777 ♂ ad	90	87	126	3	87	36	−4	45	33	122	77	78	73	85	—	—	—	—	79.1
3778 ♀ ad	90	90	128	8	82	30	−4	48	28	114	85	86	83	87	—	—	—	—	78.4

INDICES

	Skull									Face and mandible										Cranio-facial			
Length-height	Breadth-height	Transverse frontal	Transverse fronto-parietal	Sagittal parieto-frontal (arcs)	Sagittal frontal	Sagittal parietal	Sagittal occipital	Foramen magnum	Facial	Upper facial	Orbital (mf)	Orbital (la)	Interorbital (mf-mf to ek-ek)	Nasal	Transverse nasal bone	Maxillo-alveolar	Palatal	Bicondylo-bigonial breadth (mandible)	Ramus (mandible)	Transverse cranio-facial	Fronto-biorbital (ft-ft to fmt-fmt)	Jugo-frontal	Jugo-mandibular
4	4	4	5	5	6	5	5	3	1	3	6	6	4	5	4	4	4	2	2	3	4	3	1
74.4–	90.3–	76.1–	59.7–	76.2–	87.7–	89.3–	79.4–	79.0–	—	50.4–	77.8–	86.5–	18.1–	38.2–	53.3–	112.2–	79.2–	85.9;	60.4;	92.1–	80.6–	59.7–	—
78.1	99.3	82.6	66.4	97.4	90.6	92.9	83.9	94.1		55.6	87.5	92.1	19.2	48.9	71.4	128.6	97.7	88.0	70.4	100.0	91.2	72.1	
75.9	95.6	79.5	64.0	87.0	89.4	91.0	81.9	86.7	85.6	53.1	81.5	88.7	18.5	44.3	63.8	121.5	87.0	87.0	65.4	95.2	86.3	67.4	79.0
2	2	2	2	2	2	2	2	1	1	2	2	2	2	2	2	2	2	3	2	2	2	2	1
69.3;	83.3;	78.1;	64.5;	84.0;	86.4;	90.5;	—	—	—	52.4;	84.6;	94.3;	18.2;	45.6;	62.5;	124.0;	88.1;	67.5;	56.9;	87.0;	90.8;	71.8;	
78.4	95.5	78.8	66.9	87.9	88.8	91.2				52.5	89.7	100.0	18.7	47.9	71.4	125.5	88.9	81.1	65.2	93.2	93.7	74.2	
73.9	89.4	78.5	65.7	85.5	87.6	90.9	82.8	84.9	87.5	52.5	81.2	97.0	18.5	46.8	67.0	124.8	88.5	74.3	62.1	90.1	92.5	73.0	71.7
																		2	2				
—	—	—	—	—	—	—	—	—	—	—	—	—	—	—	—	—	—	82.6;	67.5;	—	—	—	—
																		90.0	70.0				
—	—	—	—	—	—	—	—	—	—	—	—	—	—	—	—	—	—	86.3	68.8	—	—	—	—
65.1	86.8	79.5	67.4	80.0	88.3	91.4	82.2	73.7	—	54.6	76.1	81.4 r	14.6	47.3	37.5	—	—	—	—	97.9	86.6	68.8	—
82.5	103.0	73.0	63.2	81.5	86.7	89.1	88.6	83.3	—	56.4	90.2	100.0	16.8	50.0	38.9	124.5	100.0	—	—	93.2	85.6	67.7	—
72.3	96.2	83.2	70.7	90.9	86.4	89.2	81.7	79.4	—	56.1	79.1	85.0 r	18.6	46.1	58.3	120.7	80.4	—	—	97.7	86.2	72.3	—
78.2	100.7	78.9	64.7	85.9	88.1	89.7	83.8	67.5	—	53.3	77.3	87.2 r	14.8	51.0	38.5	124.1	81.2	—	—	98.6	83.3	65.7	—
—	—	77.3	63.9	97.5	89.3	86.5	86.4	—	—	58.3	83.3	—	14.7	46.3	33.3	127.1	95.4	—	—	95.5	85.8	66.9	—
78.9	96.5	82.6	66.4	96.7	90.1	88.0	86.2	72.7	—	56.2	84.4	95.0 r	13.0	40.0	63.6	132.7	89.6	—	—	95.8	89.6	69.3	—
74.5	93.2	81.7	66.7	100.0	86.3	81.3	82.5	87.9	—	50.3	82.6	92.7 r	15.2	43.4	33.3	117.3	—	—	—	98.6	86.7	67.6	—
74.6	93.6	76.9	63.8	88.3	87.5	89.4	85.0	82.9	—	54.9	92.7	100.0 r	16.0	37.2	44.4	126.0	90.7	—	—	94.3	88.2	67.7	—
79.4	103.0	83.5	71.1	90.0	86.1	88.0	84.4	77.1	—	53.6	82.2	90.2 r	12.9	44.4	18.2	120.4	97.7	—	—	102.2	88.9	69.6	—
74.0	94.9	82.8	69.6	97.6	86.3	90.1	83.0	77.1	—	54.2	85.7	90.0	18.2	47.1	50.0	—	—	—	—	94.9	91.4	73.3	—
73.9	99.3	77.8	65.0	90.0	88.5	91.4	84.0	75.0	—	59.0	90.7	97.5 r	13.9	36.5	60.0	123.9	79.2	—	—	102.9	82.7	63.2	—
74.2	93.0	81.4	64.8	93.6	88.9	89.8	85.4	80.6	—	56.6	81.8	94.7 r	18.2	44.4	42.9	127.8	102.3	—	—	95.8	86.0	67.6	—
70.8	96.9	83.2	68.5	107.6	89.8	86.6	84.1	91.2	—	55.3	79.1	85.0 r	14.4	47.2	62.5	117.0	87.0	—	—	101.5	84.8	67.4	—
76.2	98.6	78.3	59.3	95.2	90.5	91.7	84.0	77.1	—	54.7	85.7	94.7	15.3	51.0	33.3	—	—	—	—	91.4	80.6	64.8	—
69.8	94.3	85.6	72.1	89.0	86.9	90.2	82.0	83.8	—	58.3	88.9	95.0	16.0	38.3	54.5	138.8	115.4	—	—	102.9	90.2	70.1	—
71.8	95.1	87.0	70.4	96.3	86.7	90.0	84.1	73.7	—	55.5	83.7	91.1 r	13.6	47.3	46.7	—	—	—	—	101.4	85.5	69.4	—
72.2	94.1	78.6	65.2	96.7	88.8	89.1	83.2	77.1	—	52.3	83.7	94.7 r	15.8	38.8	42.9	—	—	—	—	96.3	85.4	67.7	—
76.8	97.1	86.4	67.9	92.2	89.8	89.8	86.1	88.2	—	51.8	79.5	87.5 r	15.7	53.1	50.0	120.0	82.0	—	—	97.9	87.2	69.3	—
71.7	92.1	82.6	64.3	87.0	89.4	91.6	81.8	76.3	98.5	61.8	86.0	94.9	17.3	40.3	71.4	127.8	93.5	86.5	63.9	97.1	84.9	66.2	80.1
76.2	100.8	77.3	65.4	91.1	89.5	88.5	83.3	91.4	—	59.4	97.6	—	15.6	39.6	30.0	114.3	87.8	—	—	98.5	83.3	66.4	—
79.5	102.2	76.9	65.7	97.0	88.0	89.1	86.7	73.0	—	57.1	85.7	94.7	17.3	43.6	45.4	122.6	104.9	—	—	97.1	85.7	67.7	—
73.0	95.7	77.1	65.5	87.0	85.6	90.9	83.6	83.3	—	56.6	88.1	97.4 r	19.8	44.6	35.7	126.9	93.3	—	—	97.8	83.5	66.9	—
78.4	99.2	86.1	70.4	95.9	87.7	88.0	78.2	86.5	—	60.2	83.3	92.1	20.0	48.1	56.2	118.0	88.9	—	—	97.6	86.7	72.7	—
72.4	95.7	75.2	60.7	98.5	88.1	87.9	85.8	62.8	—	86.0	94.9 r	—	—	50.0	—	—	—	—	—	92.1	85.0	65.9	—
72.8	99.3	83.0	68.9	99.2	89.7	90.4	82.5	80.0	—	58.5	76.7	84.6 r	18.2	41.5	53.3	112.5	75.0	—	—	96.3	86.9	71.5	—
75.3	100.0	83.9	73.9	104.1	89.3	87.3	87.8	87.5	—	57.0	88.4	97.4	16.8	39.7	43.7	122.8	86.0	—	—	106.0	87.6	69.7	—
76.4	96.5	87.9	70.8	100.8	87.4	86.7	84.1	83.8	—	51.3	82.6	90.5	16.0	42.9	43.7	119.3	93.6	—	—	102.8	90.3	68.9	—
73.9	94.2	83.2	68.1	93.4	87.7	89.5	77.6	77.8	—	54.2	83.3	89.7 r	16.7	42.3	44.4	130.6	90.5	—	—	94.9	89.5	71.8	—

Tribal divisions and subdivisions / Catalogue No. / Sex and stages of life / Number of cases / Averages and ranges	"Central angle" (Klaatsch)	Cranio-facial (Falkenburger)	Interoccipital	\multicolumn{11}{c	}{ANGLES}					Length-breadth
				Glabella-lambda	Basion-bregma	Nasion-basion	Basion-opisthion	Nasion bregma	Lambda-bregma	Opisthion-lambda	Prosthion-nasion	Nasospinale-nasion	Prosthion-nasospinale	Orbital height	Ramus tangent-alveolar plane	Ramus tangent-basal tangent	Chin vertical-basal tangent	Condylo-coronoid tangent-alveolar plane	
	(°)	(°)	(°)	(°)	(°)	(°)	(°)	(°)	(°)	(°)	(°)	(°)	(°)	(°)	(°)	(°)	(°)	(°)	
UNDEFORMED																			
3779 ♀ ad	91	88	127	6	85	30	−10	52	29	126	82	86	61	89	—	—	—	—	76.0
3780 ♀ ad	93	88	136	8	85	30	−8	49	29	118	83	88	68	89	—	—	—	—	82.1
3781 ♀ ad	90	92	129	6	84	29	−5	49	29	115	83	84	79	86	—	—	—	—	79.9
3782 ♂ ad	93	88	123	3	90	35	−6	41	33	123	81	82	75	82	—	—	—	—	77.6
3783 ♂ ad	91	86	134	10	81	30	0	53	25	117	80	80	80	87	—	—	—	—	81.6
3784 ♂ mat	90	87	115	2	88	37	−11	42	32	120	81	82	72	85	—	—	—	—	77.2
3785 ♀ ad	95	85	140	8	87	34	−8	49	30	116	82	85	72	83	—	—	—	—	83.8
3786 ♂ mat	90	90	135	5	85	32	−5	44	27	119	82	83	77	90	—	—	—	—	71.8
3787 ♂ ad	91	86	123	5	86	33	−12	49	30	118	79	80	77	88	—	—	—	—	77.7
3788 ♀ ad	91	93	126	7	84	29	−20	48	28	118	77	78	67	86	—	—	—	—	74.7
3789 ♂ ad-mat	—	—	120	11	—	—	—	49	24	117	82	82	82	87	—	—	—	—	71.0
3790 ♂ ad	90	87	123	6	84	32	−3	46	30	120	83	84	77	92	—	—	—	—	79.4
3791 ♀ ad-mat	90	90	122	4	86	31	−9	48	31	120	79	82	67	83	—	—	—	—	76.4
3792 ♂ mat	93	83	121	5	88	36	−9	48	33	119	82	82	82	87	—	—	—	—	77.0
3793 ♂ mat	90	90	122	4	86	30	−8	45	31	120	83	83	83	87	—	—	—	—	76.2
3794 ♀ ad	93	89	128	10	83	30	−7	51	27	118	80	82	72	79	—	—	—	—	81.6
3795 ♀ ad-mat	90	89	126	5	85	30	−9	48	27	121	83	85	78	86	—	—	—	—	80.6
♂ cases	32	30	33	33	32	32	32	33	33	33	29	30	30	33	1	1	1	1	33
range	90–100	83–94	115–136	0–11	80–94	26–37	+2 to −19	41–53	24–38	111–131	74–92	74–93	64–86	82–96	—	—	—	—	71.0–81.7
average	91.8	88.5	127.9	5.4	86.6	31.6	−7.1	46.1	30.2	120.7	81.9	83.5	76.5	87.0	66.0	121.0	82.0	+8.0	77.0
♀ cases	12	11	12	12	12	12	12	12	12	12	12	12	12	12	—	—	—	—	12
range	90–96	85–93	119–140	4–10	82–92	28–35	−4 to −20	43–52	27–34	114–126	77–88	78–91	61–83	79–91	—	—	—	—	74.4–83.8
average	92.0	88.9	129.2	6.7	85.3	31.0	−9.8	46.1	29.5	118.6	82.3	83.6	73.0	85.9	—	—	—	—	79.0
Chukchee																			
3843 ♂ mat	91	88	123	8	82	27	−8	52	26	117	86	92	74	93	—	—	—	—	78.1
3844 ♀ ad-mat	95	84	132	11	83	32	+1	52	23	112	82	84	74	89	62	123	84	+1	78.7
3845 inf. I-II	90	90	129	6	84	26	−10	51	30	125	88	89	81	91	—	—	—	—	81.7
3846 ♂ mat-sen	91	91	122	9	82	28	−5	50	26	115	81	83	73	89	59	124	85	+5	76.1
3847 inf. I-II	95	88	124	13	83	26	−15	54	25	113	87	91	74	95	56	129	84	+10	83.0
3848 ♂ mat	90	90	121	4	86	30	−10	47	32	122	83	85	72	92	—	—	—	—	82.8
3849 ♂ mat	91	93	120	0	91	28	−19	42	34	134	81	85	70	88	57	127	85	+15	74.5
♂ cases	4	4	4	4	4	4	4	4	4	4	4	4	4	4	2	2	2	2	4
range	90–91	88–93	120–123	0–9	82–91	27–30	−5 to −19	42–52	26–34	115–134	81–86	83–92	70–81	88–93	57–59	124–127	85; 85	+5; +15	74.5–82.8
average	90.5	90.5	121.5	5.2	85.2	28.3	−9.3	47.8	29.5	122.0	82.8	86.3	72.3	90.5	58.0	125.5	85.0	+10.0	77.9
♀ 1 case	94.0	84.0	132.0	11.0	83.0	32.0	+1.0	52.0	23.0	122.0	82.0	84.0	74.0	89.0	62.0	123.0	84.0	+1.0	78.8
inf. cases	2	2	2	2	2	2	2	2	2	2	2	2	2	2	1	1	1	1	2
range	90; 96	90; 88	124; 129	6; 13	83; 84	26; 26	−10 to −15	51; 54	25; 30	113; 125	87; 85	85; 91	74; 81	91; 95	—	—	—	—	81.7; 83.0
average	93.0	89.0	126.5	9.5	83.5	26.0	−12.5	52.5	27.5	119.0	87.5	88.0	77.5	93.0	56.0	129.0	84.0	+10.0	82.3

INDICES

	Skull									Face and mandible											Cranio-facial			
Length-height	Breadth-height	Transverse frontal	Transverse fronto-parietal	Sagittal parieto-frontal (arcs)	Sagittal frontal	Sagittal parietal	Sagittal occipital	Foramen magnum	Facial	Upper facial	Orbital (mf)	Orbital (la)	Interorbital (mf-mf to ek-ek)	Nasal	Transverse nasal bone	Maxillo-alveolar	Palatal	Bicondylo-bigonial breadth (mandible)	Ramus (mandible)	Transverse cranio-facial	Fronto-biorbital (ft-ft to fmt-fmt)	Jugo-frontal	Jugo-mandibular
73.2	96.3	86.4	69.8	102.3	85.9	87.8	83.5	87.9	—	55.4	78.6	86.8	13.5	42.0	33.3	116.4	84.8	—	—	95.6	92.2	73.1	—
79.8	97.1	78.9	65.2	92.1	88.2	88.0	87.5	82.4	—	53.0	81.4	89.7 r	14.6	51.0	40.0	—	—	129.6	95.6	95.6	86.5	68.2	—
71.8	89.9	77.4	64.0	91.7	90.1	89.2	82.2	70.3	—	55.4	81.4	89.7	15.5	43.6	40.0	129.6	95.6	—	—	100.0	86.4	64.0	—
73.7	95.0	84.3	69.8	88.2	89.0	89.3	81.9	80.0	—	57.2	86.4	95.0 r	15.8	41.4	40.0	130.2	100.0	—	—	99.3	87.4	70.3	—
76.5	93.8	82.6	68.5	98.4	86.5	90.3	86.8	80.6	—	55.9	88.1	100.0 r	19.4	43.6	50.0	125.4	86.0	—	...	97.9	90.9	69.9	—
74.1	95.9	85.8	70.5	94.5	89.0	91.7	80.2	76.9	—	52.6	84.0	91.3 r	16.2	45.0	53.3	—	—	—	—	106.8	85.8	66.0	—
82.7	99.3	83.3	67.9	91.9	91.1	90.3	88.5	83.3	—	58.3	90.5	100.0	15.5	37.5	38.5	121.1	83.7	—	—	94.3	89.6	72.0	—
72.3	100.7	84.1	70.4	96.9	87.7	88.1	88.5	84.6	—	57.0	76.6	85.7	14.7	47.3	23.1	—	—	—	—	100.0	88.8	70.4	—
77.2	99.3	78.8	65.0	96.9	87.7	88.9	83.2	81.6	—	58.7	88.6	95.1 r	16.8	45.4	40.0	126.0	89.1	—	—	96.5	87.7	67.4	—
72.5	97.0	79.6	67.7	96.0	88.7	89.9	83.7	79.4	—	50.0	83.7	92.3 r	15.5	57.1	31.2	—	—	—	—	97.7	88.2	69.2	—
—	—	81.2	68.9	86.1	88.5	92.9	79.6	—	—	55.9	81.8	90.0	17.5	50.9	58.8	—	—	—	...	103.0	85.0	66.9	—
71.4	90.0	83.9	66.0	101.6	88.8	88.2	83.6	77.5	—	55.0	78.3	87.8 r	15.2	50.0	44.4	116.7	91.8	—	—	99.3	86.1	66.2	—
74.1	97.0	85.4	70.7	97.6	88.6	90.0	84.9	75.0	—	53.6	81.8	90.0	15.7	50.0	40.0	113.2	92.9	—	—	103.8	86.2	68.1	—
77.5	100.7	80.8	66.0	89.9	84.9	89.6	82.2	74.4	—	53.5	84.1	90.2 r	17.1	45.6	42.9	—	—	—	—	98.0	88.2	67.4	—
73.5	96.5	86.1	68.7	91.7	88.7	91.0	84.5	78.4	—	55.2	82.2	90.2 r	17.3	41.4	46.7	—	—	—	—	100.7	90.0	68.3	—
77.0	94.4	77.7	61.3	100.8	88.6	87.9	84.3	80.0	—	57.7	83.7	92.3	16.8	45.3	50.0	118.2	93.5	—	—	91.5	83.6	66.9	—
71.1	88.3	80.3	64.8	100.8	89.3	88.5	84.3	83.3	—	57.6	75.6	82.9 r	16.7	37.5	50.0	—	—	—	—	99.3	88.7	65.3	—
32	32	33	33	33	33	33	33	32	1	32	33	33	32	33	33	22	21	1	1	33	33	33	1
65.1–79.5	86.8–103.0	75.2–87.9	59.3–73.9	80.0–107.6	84.9–90.5	81.3–92.9	78.2–88.5	62.8–91.2	—	50.3–61.8	75.6–92.7	81.4–100.0	12.9–20.0	36.5–53.1	18.2–71.4	112.5–138.8	75.0–115.4	—	—	91.4–106.8	80.3–90.9	63.2–72.7	—
74.2	96.5	81.5	67.4	93.7	88.1	89.3	83.8	78.7	98.5	55.7	83.3	91.8	16.3	44.2	46.5	123.5	90.8	86.5	63.9	98.9	86.8	68.1	80,1
11	11	12	12	12	12	12	12	11	—	12	12	10	13	12	12	9	9	—	—	12	12	12	—
71.8–82.5	89.9–103.0	73.0–86.4	61.3–70.7	81.5–102.3	85.9–91.1	86.5–90.3	77.6–88.6	70.3–91.4	—	50.0–59.4	78.6–97.6	86.8–100.0	13.5–18.2	37.5–57.1	30.0–50.0	113.2–130.6	83.7–100.0	—	—	91.5–103.8	83.3–92.2	64.0–73.3	—
76.6	96.7	79.8	66.4	94.0	88.4	88.9	84.0	80.4	—	55.5	85.1	92.3	16.1	46.0	40.0	121.4	91.6	—	—	97.1	87.4	69.0	—
74.2	95.5	87.0	71.9	102.4	89.4	87.8	82.8	70.0	—	53.0	80.0	87.8 r	15.5	52.0	56.2	114.0	—	—	—	95.0	92.6	75.8	—
80.5	102.3	81.5	72.9	87.2	84.8	90.8	85.6	75.7	85.8	55.2	83.3	92.1 r	16.3	44.2	27.3	130.0	93.0	94.0	58.6	100.7	90.6	72.4	81.3
73.8	90.3	81.8	67.2	102.5	85.2	86.4	83.6	82.4	—	49.5	88.6	96.9 r	21.2	52.5	53.3	155.5	97.1	—	—	82.8	96.8	81.1	—
74.4	97.8	81.1	65.7	89.2	85.4	91.4	82.8	80.0	78.8	51.1	77.3	87.2 r	18.9	52.9	27.8	—	—	86.0	72.7	100.7	85.7	65.7	81.0
75.8	91.2	81.2	66.4	87.9	86.3	89.9	83.3	81.1	85.7	51.8	91.7	94.3 r	17.4	48.8	46.7	151.3	97.1	88.0	58.7	81.7	98.9	81.2	78.6
73.4	88.6	77.8	60.0	100.0	89.2	87.5	81.9	80.0	—	50.7	82.9	91.9 r	18.1	47.9	35.7	111.8	73.9	—	—	98.6	81.5	60.9	—
67.5	90.7	86.0	70.0	101.5	88.7	87.4	80.8	85.3	91.2	58.1	81.8	87.8 r	17.6	44.6	44.4	121.0	90.0	88.1	58.7	97.1	87.5	72.0	81.6
4	4	4	4	4	4	4	4	4	2	4	4	4	4	4	4	3	2	2	2	4	4	4	2
76.5–88.6–	88.6–97.8	77.8–87.0	66.4–71.9	87.9–102.4	85.4–89.4	87.8–91.4	80.8–85.6	70.0–85.3	78.8; 91.2	50.7–58.1	77.3–91.7	87.2–96.9	15.5–18.8	44.6–52.9	27.8–56.2	111.8–121.0	73.9; 90.0	86.0; 88.1	58.7; 72.7	95.0–100.0	81.5–92.6	60.9–75.2	81.0; 81.6
74.4	97.8	87.0	71.9	104.2	89.4	91.4	85.3	80.0	91.2	58.1	82.9	91.9	18.8	52.9	56.2	121.0	90.0	88.1	72.7	100.0	92.6	75.2	81.6
72.4	93.0	82.8	66.9	98.0	88.2	88.8	81.3	78.8	85.0	53.2	80.7	88.0	17.8	49.4	41.0	115.6	82.0	87.1	65.7	97.7	87.1	68.6	81.3
80.5	102.3	81.5	72.9	87.2	84.8	90.8	85.6	75.7	85.8	55.2	83.3	92.1	16.3	44.2	27.3	130.0	93.0	94.0	58.6	100.7	90.6	72.4	81.3
2																							1
73.8	90.3	66.4	67.2	87.9	85.2	86.6	83.3	81.1	—	45.9–51.8	88.6–91.7	94.3–96.9	17.4–21.2	48.8–52.5	46.7–53.3	151.3–155.5	—	—	—	81.7–82.8	96.8–98.9	81.1–81.2	—
75.8	91.2	81.8	67.2	102.5	86.3	89.9	83.6	82.4	—								—	88.0	58.7				
74.8	90.8	81.5	66.8	94.5	85.8	88.2	83.5	81.8	85.7	50.7	90.2	95.0	19.0	50.7	50.0	153.4	—	88.0	58.7	82.3	97.9	81.2	78.6

Tribal divisions and subdivisions / Catalogue No. / Sex and stages of life / Number of cases / Averages and ranges	"Central angle" (Klaatsch)	Cranio-facial (Falkenburger)	Interoccipital	ANGLES														Length-breadth
				To ear-eye plane										Mandibulo-alveolar plane				
				Glabella-lambda	Basion-bregma	Nasion-basion	Basion-opisthion	Nasion-bregma	Lambda-bregma	Opisthion-lambda	Prosthion-nasion	Nasospinale-nasion	Prosthion-nasospinale	Orbital height	Ramus tangent-alveolar plane	Ramus tangent-basal tangent	Chin vertical-basal tangent	Condylo-coronoid tangent-alveolar plane	
UNDEFORMED	(°)	(°)	(°)	(°)	(°)	(°)	(°)	(°)	(°)	(°)	(°)	(°)	(°)	(°)	(°)	(°)	(°)	(°)	(°)
Divisional total																			
♂ cases	74	67	76	76	74	74	74	75	75	75	69	68	69	73	34	34	34	34	79
range	86–100	83–96	108–136	0–16	77–96	23–37	+6 to −19	40–54	18–38	101–134	72–92	72–93	61–86	82–98	55–79	100–137	69–89	−18 to +18	70.8–92.7
average	91.6	89.3	124.3	6.7	84.8	30.2	−6.7	46.0	28.7	117.4	82.3	84.6	75.9	89.6	69.0	118.4	81.8	+0.4	78.0
♀ cases	30	30	31	30	30	30	29	30	31	31	31	31	31	31	18	18	13	18	34
range	86–96	84–93	96–140	4–10	79–96	25–35	+11 to −20	43–54	19–34	110–126	77–88	78–91	61–83	79–94	57–70	116–131	72–86	−12 to +12	71.6–88.5
average	90.9	89.2	126.2	7.5	83.4	29.9	−6.5	48.1	28.2	117.3	82.3	84.6	72.9	89.0	64.2	124.2	80.5	−1.4	80.0
juv. 1 case	92.0	88.0	126.0	10.0	82.0	31.0	+3.0	52.0	24.0	114.0	82.0	—	—	—	—	—	—	—	83.5
inf. cases	7	7	9	8	7	7	7	10	10	9	10	10	10	10	12	13	13	12	13
range	90–96	85–89	110–130	5–13	80–86	23–30	−6 to −15	49–57	24–31	113–125	73–90	73–94	63–90	90–98	46–63	122–140	72–86	−8 to +28	79.2–97.5
average	91.8	88.3	124.3	8.1	83.7	27.4	−10.7	52.1	27.3	118.8	85.8	86.6	81.0	93.1	55.9	129.3	83.1	+12.8	85.0
COWICHAN																			
Tsimshian																			
4585 ♂ ad	90	87	119	7	83	31	−3	51	28	115	76	81	72	90	79	106	85	−4	82.1
4586 ♂ ad	90	85	125	7	83	32	+10	43	33	107	86	87	82	100	—	—	—	—	82.3
4587 ♀ juv-ad (def)	98	89	131	10	88	32	+3	45	25	117	82	85	74	89	—	—	—	—	82.5
4588 ♂ ad-mat	—	—	—	—	—	—	—	—	—	—	—	—	—	—	80	106	83	−11	—
4645 ♂ ad (def)	94	92	120	6	88	29	−10	50	35	117	76	81	66	87	—	—	—	—	95.6
4646 ♂ ad-mat (def)	92	89	121	13	79	27	−1	53	25	108	79	80	73	82	—	—	—	—	90.6
4647 ♂ mat (def)	92	87	114	9	83	30	−3	54	31	111	79	86	67	93	—	—	—	—	83.8
4648 ♂ mat	94	90	131	9	85	30	−1	48	31	111	84	88	71	95	—	—	—	—	83.7
4649 ♂ mat	98	90	114	11	87	28	+3	46	29	116	84	86	78	91	—	—	—	—	80.0
♂ cases	7	7	7	7	7	7	7	7	7	7	7	7	7	7	2	2	2	2	7
range	90–98	85–92	114–131	6–13	79–88	27–32	+10 to −10	46–54	25–35	107–117	76–86	80–88	66–82	82–100	79;80	106;106	83;85	−11;−4	80.0–95.6
average	92.9	88.6	120.6	8.9	84.0	29.6	−0.7	50.0	30.3	112.1	80.7	84.1	72.7	91.1	89.5	106.0	84.0	−7.5	85.4
♀ 1 case	98.0	89.0	131.9	10.0	88.0	32.0	+3.0	46.0	25.0	117.0	82.0	85.0	74.0	89.0	—	—	—	—	82.5
Yakima																			
4314 ♂ mat	96	91	117	14	82	25	+1	50	25	113	86	88	76	95	68	114	86	+11	86.8
4318 ♂ ad	97	93	122	14	83	27	−5	47	18	107	80	82	73	83	—	—	—	—	87.4
4319 juv	97	89	143	11	86	31	+10	48	24	121	82	83	75	87	66	120	84	+5	92.0
4320 ♂ ad	—	—	—	—	—	—	—	—	—	—	—	—	—	—	66	119	83	+1	—
4321 inf. II	95	87	136	13	82	27	−2	55	26	114	86	87	83	92	55	130	85	+14	93.1
4323 ♂ ad	—	—	—	12	—	—	—	55	36	—	80	81	76	85	72	112	85	+5	—
4325 ♂ ad	93	92	123	15	78	23	−9	57	28	106	80	82	72	87	67	126	76	−12	93.7
4326 inf. II	—	—	—	—	—	—	—	—	—	—	—	—	—	—	56	126	82	+4	—
4328 juv	95	91	135	10	85	23	−8	50	29	112	81	84	74	90	65	125	79	−6	92.0

	Skull								INDICES Face and mandible										Cranio-facial			
Length-height	Breadth-height	Transverse frontal	Transverse frontoparietal	Sagittal parieto-frontal (arcs)	Sagittal frontal	Sagittal parietal	Sagittal occipital	Foramen magnum	Facial	Upper facial	Orbital (mf)	Orbital (la)	Interorbital (mf-mf to ek-ek)	Nasal	Transverse nasal bone	Maxillo-alveolar	Palatal	Bicondylo-bigonial breadth (mandible)	Ramus (mandible)	Transverse cranio-facial	Fronto-biorbital (ft-ft to fmt-fmt)	Jugo-frontal	Jugo-mandibular
75	75	76	78	78	80	78	78	73	22	69	78	77	71	74	74	61	57	30	33	70	77	70	23
65.1-	77.8-	75.2-	59.3-	76.2-	84.9-	81.3-	75.2-	62.8	76.2-	41.4-	70.0-	76.7-	12.9-	36.5-	18.2-	108.8-	73.9-	78.9-	48.7-	90.7-	80.6-	59.7-	67.8-
82.9	106.1	88.3	73.9	107.6	99.2	98.2	91.2	106.3	100.0	61.8	92.9	102.6	20.2	57.1	80.0	138.8	115.4	94.4	72.7	108.5	95.6	77.2	85.1
74.3	95.5	81.6	66.8	93.5	88.7	89.7	82.3	82.0	87.7	54.1	81.7	90.0	17.4	46.5	48.6	122.4	90.1	85.9	61.3	98.5	86.5	68.1	76.9
33	33	33	33	34	34	34	33	32	12	32	33	31	33	33	32	30	29	17	18	34	33	34	14
69.3-	83.3-	73.0-	60.7-	81.5-	94.8-	85.1-	77.6	70.3-	79.7-	49.6-	74.4-	82.0-	13.5-	37.5-	27.3-	109.4	80.3-	67.5-	50.9-	87.0-	83.3-	64.0-	69.9-
82.5	106.3	88.3	73.7	103.3	91.1	91.2	88.7	96.9	97.7	61.0	97.6	100.0	22.7	57.1	71.4	130.6	100.0	94.0	68.5	103.8	102.0	84.5	85.8
76.5	95.6	80.9	66.6	94.8	88.3	88.9	83.8	82.9	87.3	54.2	83.8	91.7	17.6	48.4	46.7	120.8	89.1	86.6	60.8	95.3	89.0	70.6	75.9
78.2	93.7	84.3	68.3	90.1	85.2	91.8	83.9	67.6	—	48.0	76.2	80.0	18.0	45.6	42.9	—	—	—	—	93.0	95.1	73.5	—
8	6	14	13	12	14	13	13	9	8	14	14	13	12	14	12	13	14	12	13	13	12	14	9
71.3-	83.8-	73.8-	57.3-	81.6-	82.7	76.9-	77.6-	70.7-	80.7-	41.8-	86.1-	93.9-	15.7-	46.5-	42.9-	131.8-	77.1-	74.3-	58.7-	69.4-	92.2-	74.8-	67.5-
77.1	93.4	84.0	69.3	104.3	93.4	92.5	87.1	93.8	89.5	58.7	94.9	103.1	21.2	60.6	71.4	160.7	112.5	102.1	77.5	85.4	100.0	83.3	85.1
74.2	89.8	87.7	63.5	92.5	86.6	88.2	83.6	83.2	85.3	51.0	88.8	97.3	18.7	51.2	54.5	150.6	94.1	85.8	65.1	79.6	97.3	80.7	75.6
78.6	95.6	81.2	65.9	93.4	86.8	89.4	82.6	82.9	85.9	53.3	76.7	84.6 r	16.5	51.0	46.7	121.0	85.7	84.1	61.3	97.8	89.2	67.4	70.4
83.5	101.4	82.6	67.9	84.1	89.7	87.7	85.6	88.6	—	51.7	82.6	90.5 r	16.7	43.6	40.0	126.0	95.3	—	—	103.6	86.4	65.5	—
77.1	93.4	79.6	65.7	82.8	89.3	90.1	84.5	84.9	—	—	92.7	97.4 r	18.9	45.8	57.1	128.9	81.4	—	—	—	90.0	—	—
—	—	—	—	—	—	—	—	—	—	—	—	—	—	—	—	—	—	86.5	66.1	—	—	—	—
78.5	82.1	80.0	60.9	95.8	93.2	84.1	82.3	86.1	—	52.2	90.5	97.4 r	16.2	49.0	64.3	120.7	86.7	—	—	91.4	85.2	66.7	—
79.9	88.2	79.7	65.3	99.1	93.5	85.0	81.4	90.6	—	53.2	87.5	94.6 r	20.4	49.0	52.5	113.2	82.6	—	—	96.5	87.8	67.6	—
82.7	98.6	75.4	61.4	86.9	88.5	88.5	78.7	93.8	—	51.4	79.1	85.0 r	18.4	46.0	50.0	117.2	80.0	—	—	99.3	84.8	61.8	—
80.8	96.5	84.5	68.1	83.8	90.8	89.0	86.6	97.0	—	49.7	82.2	88.1 r	17.5	45.4	55.6	121.8	85.4	—	—	104.9	90.7	64.9	—
74.6	93.2	84.6	66.9	77.0	90.4	91.3	79.5	81.3	—	58.5	82.2	90.2 r	19.8	45.6	38.9	116.7	79.6	—	—	99.3	86.8	67.3	—
7	8	7	7	7	5	7	7	7	1	7	7	7	7	7	7	7	7	2	2	7	7	7	1
74.6-	82.1-	75.4-	60.9-	77.0-	86.8-	84.1-	78.7-	81.3-	—	49.7-	76.7-	84.6-	16.2-	43.6-	38.9-	113.2-	79.6-	84.1;	61.3;	91.4-	84.8-	61.8-	—
83.5	101.4	84.6	68.1	99.1	93.5	91.3	86.6	97.0	—	58.5	90.5	97.4	20.4	51.0	64.3	126.0	95.3	86.5	66.1	104.9	90.7	67.6	—
79.8	93.6	80.7	65.9	88.1	90.5	87.9	82.7	88.1	85.9	52.9	83.0	89.7	18.0	47.1	51.3	119.5	85.0	85.3	63.7	99.0	87.3	65.9	70.4
77.1	93.4	79.6	65.7	82.8	89.3	90.1	84.5	84.9	—	92.9	97.4	18.9	45.8	57.1	128.9	81.4	—	—	—	90.0	—	—	
74.7	86.1	79.3	63.6	84.1	88.9	91.5	80.5	90.9	74.8	46.2	76.7	84.6 r	20.2	46.1	56.2	131.4	100.0	79.8	64.9	97.3	92.3	65.3	70.1
73.7	84.3	74.4	56.9	83.0	93.2	92.9	82.2	91.9	—.	52.2	85.7	94.7 r	18.4	46.0	46.1	122.2	87.5	—	—	90.2	85.3	63.0	—
75.9	82.5	76.1	59.7	95.6	90.4	84.5	88.5	83.9	79.	49.6	85.0	94.4 r	20.6	42.9	60.0	128.3	95.1	—	62.7	86.6	89.9	69.0	—
—	—	—	—	—	—	—	—	—	—	—	75.0	82.5 r	—	41.7	18.2	113.2	77.1	85.7	57.1	—	—	—	—
81.9	88.1	81.5	62.7	98.2	89.9	84.1	89.7	89.7	79.2	49.1	88.6	100.0 r	20.0	53.8	57.1	144.4	91.2	85.3	69.2	79.1	97.7	79.2	76.4
—	—	75.2	—	93.9	92.2	79.6	—	—	82.3	50.0	83.3 r	17.2	41.7	64.3	127.4	93.0	72.6	74.0	—	88.0	67.7	63.1	
81.6	87.2	—	—	88.4	86.9	86.9	83.5	87.9	79.3	51.1	77.5	83.8 r	—	52.1	46.7	110.5	91.5	79.1	58.9	91.2	—	—	67.4
—	—	76.7	—	—	89.1	—	—	84.4	—	—	82.0	91.4 r	19.3	51.3	50.0	136.6	86.1	96.5	71.8	—	97.9	—	—
80.1	87.0	85.6	62.6	90.4	90.4	86.5	88.1	86.1	80.0	51.7	88.9	97.0 r	20.7	52.4	50.0	128.3	87.2	81.4	77.3	86.3	92.5	72.5	76.7

Tribal divisions and subdivisions / Catalogue No. / Sex and stages of life / Number of cases / Averages and ranges	"Central angle" (*Klaatsch*)	Cranio-facial (*Falkenburger*)	Interoccipital	\multicolumn{12}{c	}{ANGLES}	Length-breadth
				\multicolumn{10}{c	}{To ear-eye plane}	\multicolumn{4}{c	}{Mandibulo-alveolar plane}	
				Glabella-lambda	Basion-bregma	Nasion-basion	Basion-opisthion	Nasion bregma	Lambda-bregma	Opisthion-lambda	Prosthion-nasion	Nasospinale-nasion	Prosthion-nasospinale	Orbital height	Ramus tangent-alveolar plane	Ramus tangent-basal tangent	Chin vertical-basal tangent	Condylo-coronoid tangent-alveolar plane	
	(°)	(°)	(°)	(°)	(°)	(°)	(°)	(°)	(°)	(°)	(°)	(°)	(°)	(°)	(°)	(°)	(°)	(°)	
COWICHAN																			
4329 inf. I	—	—	—	—	—	—	—	—	—	—	—	—	—	—	57	130	82	+15	—
4332 inf. II	—	—	—	—	—	—	—	—	—	—	—	—	—	—	62	122	84	+9	—
4333 ♀ mat	94	90	137	4	90	34	0	42	30	133	75	76	71	85	55	133	82	−2	84.7
4334 ♂ ad-mat	89	95	122	2	87	27	−12	42	37	125	85	85	85	90	70	115	83	+3	83.9
4335 ♂ ad	94	93	121	12	82	24	−4	52	27	109	85	87	74	87	68	111	89	−9	89.7
4336 ♀ mat	98	90	141	13	85	29	−6	53	31	109	79	80	77	88	65	125	78	+4	105.6
♂ cases	5	5	5	6	5	5	5	6	6	5	6	6	6	6	6	6	6	6	5
range	89–97	92–95	117–123	2–15	78–87	23–27	+1 to −12	42–57	18–37	106–125	80–86	81–88	72–85	83–95	66–72	111–126	76–89	−12 to +11	83.9–93.7
average	93.8	93.2	121.0	11.5	82.5	25.2	−5.8	50.5	28.5	112.0	82.0	84.2	76.0	87.8	68.5	116.2	83.7	−0.2	88.2
♀ cases	2	2	2	1	2	2	2	2	2	2	2	2	2	2	2	2	2	2	2
range	91;98	90;90	137;141	—	85;90	29;34	0 to −6	42;53	30;31	109;123	75;79	76;80	71;77	85;88	55;65	125;133	78;82	−2;+4	84.7;105.6
average	94.5	90.0	139.0	13.0	87.5	31.5	−3.0	47.5	30.5	116.0	77.0	78.0	74.0	86.5	60.0	129.0	80.0	+1.0	95.1
juv. cases	2	2	2	2	2	2	2	2	2	2	2	2	2	2	2	2	2	2	2
range	95;97	89;91	137;141	10;11	85;86	23;31	+10 to −8	48;50	24;29	112;121	81;82	83;84	74;75	87;90	65;66	120;125	79;84	−6;+5	92.0;92.0
average	96.0	90.0	139.0	10.5	85.5	27.0	+1.0	49.0	26.5	116.5	81.5	83.5	74.5	88.5	65.5	122.5	81.5	−0.5	92.0
inf. cases	1	1	1	1	1	1	1	1	1	1	1	1	1	1	4	4	4	4	1
range	—	—	—	—	—	—	—	—	—	—	—	—	—	—	55–62	122–130	82–85	+4 to +15	—
average	95.0	87.0	136.0	13.0	82.0	27.0	−2.0	55.0	26.0	114.0	86.0	87.0	83.0	92.0	57.5	127.0	85.3	+10.5	93.1
Bellabella																			
4635 ♂ ad	97	90	115	8	89	30	−3	45	29	120	82	83	80	90	—	—	—	—	91.9
4636 ♂ mat	96	92	117	7	89	28	+4	50	28	113	80	80	80	84	—	—	—	—	91.1
4637 ♂? ad	94	88	114	9	85	29	−2	54	33	114	79	85	64	88	—	—	—	—	88.7
4638 ♂ mat	90	86	112	8	82	28	+1	54	34	113	89	90	80	91	—	—	—	—	84.2
4639 ♂ mat	95	89	124	7	88	34	+3	45	30	113	79	81	72	88	—	—	—	—	81.5
4640 ♂ ad	93	96	117	12	81	24	−1	49	23	113	80	85	69	83	—	—	—	—	86.7
4641 ♂ mat	96	87	117	10	84	30	−3	50	26	113	84	88	73	96	—	—	—	—	82.1
4642 ♀ ad-mat	96	84	112	9	86	35	−2	50	31	113	76	76	76	89	—	—	—	—	83.1
4643 ♂ mat	91	90	111	6	85	29	−6	46	30	121	82	82	82	92	—	—	—	—	83.3
4644 ♂ sen	91	—	120	9	82	26	−11	52	31	110	—	—	—	98	—	—	—	—	89.7
♂ cases	9	8	9	9	9	9	9	9	9	9	8	7	8	9	—	—	—	—	9
range	90–97	86–96	111–124	6–12	81–89	24–34	+4 to −11	45–54	23–34	110–121	79–89	86–90	64–82	83–98	—	—	—	—	81.5–91.9
average	93.7	89.8	116.3	8.7	85.0	28.7	−2.0	49.4	29.3	114.4	81.9	84.9	75.0	90.0	—	—	—	—	86.6
♀ 1 case	96.0	84.0	112.0	9.0	86.0	35.0	−2.0	50.0	31.0	113.0	76.0	—	76.0	89.0	—	—	—	—	83.1
Bellacoola																			
4542 ♂ ad-mat	90	90	118	10	80	25	−2	53	28	113	83	86	65	88	—	—	—	—	91.0
4543 ♂ ad-mat	90?	89	—	5?	85	30	−12	48	—	—	82	86	70	88	—	—	—	—	—
4544 ♂ ad-mat	94	90	113	10	84	28	−7	49	28	113	80	87	63	87	—	—	—	—	85.2

INDICES

	Skull									Face and mandible											Cranio-facial			
Length-height	Breadth-height	Transverse frontal	Transverse frontoparietal	Sagittal parieto-frontal (arcs)	Sagittal frontal	Sagittal parietal	Sagittal occipital	Foramen magnum	Facial	Upper facial	Orbital (mf)	Orbital (la)	Interorbital (mf-mf to ek-ek)	Nasal	Transverse nasal bone	Maxillo-alveolar	Palatal	Bicondylo-bigonial breadth (mandible)	Ramus (mandible)	Transverse cranio-facial	Fronto-biorbital (ft-ft to fmt-fmt)	Jugo-frontal	Jugo-mandibular
—	—	—	—	—	—	—	—	—	—	—	—	—	—	—	—	—	—	81.2	61.1	—	—	—	—
—	—	—	—	—	—	—	—	—	—	—	—	—	—	—	—	—	—	—	70.3	—	—	—	—
77.1	91.0	70.9	58.6	91.2	90.3	87.5	89.9	76.7	—	—	—	—	—	53.2	58.3	118.7	—	—	58.9	—	—	—	—
69.0	82.2	76.5	62.3	90.5	89.8	87.0	83.5	89.7	89.0	54.4	90.2	100.0r	18.6	44.4	52.9	121.1	88.9	86.8	61.7	93.1	85.0	66.9	77.2
78.8	87.8	77.6	60.8	88.5	92.6	87.0	83.8	77.8	81.7	48.2	80.9	89.5 r	18.4	52.2	53.3	131.2	97.7	81.2	64.5	92.6	84.9	65.7	69.3
93.1	88.2	82.3	64.5	82.5	93.3	86.9	89.7	96.7	75.0	47.8	83.3 l	94.6 r	16.8	52.2	57.1	116.0	95.6	82.3	63.8	89.5	94.2	72.1	72.1
5	5	5	4	6	6	6	6	5	5	6	7	7	5	7	7	7	7	6	6	5	5	5	5
69.0– 81.6	82.2– 87.8	74.4– 79.3	56.9– 63.6	83.0– 93.9	88.9– 93.2	79.6– 92.9	80.5– 83.8	77.8– 91.9	74.8– 89.0	46.2– 54.4	75.0– 90.2	82.5– 100.0	17.2– 20.2	41.7– 52.2	18.2– 64.3	110.5– 131.4	77.1– 100.0	72.6– 86.8	57.1– 74.0	90.2– 97.8	84.9– 92.3	63.0– 67.7	63.1– 77.2
75.6	85.5	76.2	60.9	87.7	91.2	87.5	82.7	86.8	81.4	50.1	80.1	87.9	18.4	46.3	48.4	122.4	90.8	80.9	63.5	92.9	87.0	65.8	69.4
2	2	2	2	2	2	2	2	2	1	1	1	1	1	2	2	2	1	1	2	1	1	1	1
77.1; 93.1	88.2; 91.0	70.9; 82.3	58.6; 64.5	90.3; 91.2	86.9; 93.3	89.7; 87.5	76.7; 89.9	76.7; 96.7	—	—	—	—	—	52.2; 53.2	57.1; 58.3	116.0; 118.7	—	—	58.9; 63.8	—	—	—	—
85.1	89.6	75.1	61.6	86.5	91.8	86.8	89.8	86.0	75.0	47.8	83.3	94.6	16.8	52.7	57.5	117.4	95.6	82.3	61.4	89.5	94.2	72.1	72.1
2	2	2	2	2	2	2	2	2	2	2	2	2	2	2	2	2	2	2	2	2	2	2	2
75.9; 80.1	82.5; 87.0	76.1; 85.6	59.7; 62.6	90.4; 95.6	90.4; 90.4	84.5; 86.5	88.1; 88.5	83.9; 86.1	79.8; 80.0	49.6; 51.7	85.7; 88.9	94.4; 97.0	20.6; 20.7	42.9; 52.4	50.0; 60.0	128.3; 128.3	87.2; 95.1	—	62.7; 77.3	86.3; 86.6	89.9; 92.5	69.0; 72.5	—
78.0	84.8	80.5	61.2	93.0	90.4	85.5	88.3	84.5	79.9	50.7	87.0	95.5	21.0	47.7	55.0	128.3	91.2	81.4	70.0	86.5	91.5	70.8	76.7
1	1	1	1	1	1	1	1	1	1	2	2	2	2	2	2	2	2	3	4	1	1	1	1
—	—	76.7; 81.5	—	—	89.1; 89.9	—	—	84.4; 89.7	—	—	82.0; 88.6	91.4; 100.0	19.3; 20.0	51.3; 53.3	50.0; 57.1	136.6; 144.4	86.1; 91.2	81.2– 96.5	61.1– 71.8	—	97.7; 97.9	—	—
81.9	88.1	78.5	62.0	98.2	89.5	84.1	89.7	86.5	79.2	49.1	85.3	95.5	19.5	52.6	53.5	140.5	88.7	87.7	68.1	79.1	97.8	79.2	76.4
73.8	80.4	73.8	58.9	93.3	93.3	85.7	81.2	94.1	—	50.0	84.1	57.5	17.8	40.0	61.5	128.3	93.3	—	—	96.2	86.1	61.2	—
77.4	85.0	81.2	61.4	89.4	91.9	83.6	80.5	78.8	—	52.5	77.8	85.4	17.5	46.0	53.3	126.4	91.1	—	—	89.5	86.2	68.6	—
82.4	92.9	80.0	65.2	95.0	89.2	86.8	79.6	71.4	—	54.4	87.5	94.6	17.0	47.9	53.3	122.0	82.2	—	—	88.6	92.9	73.6	—
81.9	97.2	83.8	68.1	83.9	90.0	92.7	78.1	87.9	—	50.3	83.7	92.3	16.3	46.1	53.3	123.1	93.0	—	—	99.3	92.4	68.5	—
79.2	97.2	79.5	63.1	84.0	91.2	89.5	82.6	77.5	—	48.9	86.4	95.0	17.6	51.9	62.5	118.5	88.9	—	—	104.3	84.8	60.5	—
72.3	83.3	79.8	63.2	92.1	93.0	88.6	81.8	77.4	—	48.5	51.4	89.7	16.2	48.8	40.0	116.7	89.1	—	—	94.4	86.7	66.9	—
77.6	94.6	86.5	70.1	82.8	89.8	92.4	78.4	81.8	—	56.1	82.2	92.5	18.9	42.6	58.8	126.8	89.6	—	—	94.6	91.9	74.1	—
80.7	97.1	81.9	68.8	86.2	91.4	90.0	76.0	85.3	—	56.9	90.5	—	—	46.1	57.1	116.4	85.1	—	—	99.3	90.5	69.3	—
69.4	83.3	75.0	58.0	99.2	89.3	87.5	78.4	100.0	—	53.4	82.6	90.5	15.4	41.8	53.3	121.8	83.3	—	—	97.3	80.6	59.6	—
78.3	87.3	82.0	63.7	90.6	91.3	88.7	77.4	97.1	—	—	76.6	83.7	—	45.4	57.1	—	—	—	—	98.7	—	64.5	—
9	9	9	9	9	9	9	9	9	—	9	9	9	8	9	9	8	8	—	—	9	8	9	—
69.4– 82.4	80.4– 97.2	73.8– 86.5	58.0– 70.1	82.8– 99.2	89.8– 93.3	83.6– 92.7	77.4– 82.6	71.4– 100.0	—	48.5– 56.1	76.6– 87.5	83.7– 95.0	15.4– 18.9	40.0– 51.9	40.0– 62.5	116.7– 128.3	82.2– 93.3	—	—	88.6– 104.3	80.6– 92.9	59.6– 74.1	—
76.9	89.0	79.8	63.5	90.0	90.7	88.4	79.8	84.7	—	51.8	82.5	90.2	17.1	44.5	54.8	123.0	88.8	—	—	95.9	87.6	76.4	—
80.7	97.1	81.9	68.8	86.2	91.4	90.0	76.0	85.3	—	56.9	90.5	—	—	46.1	57.1	116.4	85.1	—	—	99.3	90.5	69.0	—
77.8	85.5	84.3	63.8	96.7	90.1	87.2	81.5	87.5	—	51.4	79.1	85.0	17.8	44.0	56.2	112.7	81.6	—	—	90.8	89.8	70.3	—
—	—	78.8	—	—	92.2	—	—	90.9	—	60.2	80.0	92.3 r	17.2	42.6	37.5	116.4	87.2	—	—	—	84.0	69.5	—
77.5	91.0	88.3	73.6	85.4	91.1	89.5	78.9	87.5	—	53.8	70.8	80.9 r	15.2	43.4	50.0	112.5	78.8	—	—	99.3	93.0	74.1	—

Tribal divisions and subdivisions / Catalogue No. / Sex and stages of life / Number of cases / Averages and ranges	"Central angle" (*Klaatsch*)	Cranio-facial (*Falkenburger*)	Interoccipital	ANGLES To ear-eye plane										Mandibulo-alveolar plane				Length-breadth
				Glabella-lambda	Basion-bregma	Nasion-basion	Basion-opisthion	Nasion-bregma	Lambda-bregma	Opisthion-lambda	Prosthion-nasion	Nasospinale-nasion	Prosthion-nasospinale	Orbital height	Ramus tangent-alveolar plane	Ramus tangent-basal tangent	Chin vertical-basal tangent	Condylo-coronoid tangent-alveolar plane	
	(°)	(°)	(°)	(°)	(°)	(°)	(°)	(°)	(°)	(°)	(°)	(°)	(°)	(°)	(°)	(°)	(°)	(°)	
COWICHAN																			
4545 ♀ ad	90	90	125	9	81	26	−3	54	27	118	83	88	68	89	—	—	—	—	88.4
4546 ♂ ad-mat	95	90	126	12	83	28	−4	50	28	109	82	88	68	91	—	—	—	—	94.7
4547 ♂ mat	95	87	118	14	81	28	+2	52	23	109	85	—	—	94	—	—	—	—	83.7
4548 A ♂ ad-mat	—	—	—	—	—	—	—	—	—	—	—	—	—	—	—	—	—	—	—
4549 ♂ ad-mat	—	—	—	—	—	—	—	—	—	—	—	—	—	—	—	—	—	—	—
4551 inf. II	101	92	120	14	87	29	−9	48	22	112	84	84	84	94	—	—	—	—	87.7
4552 inf. I	—	—	—	—	—	—	—	—	—	—	—	—	—	—	—	—	—	—	93.8
4625 ♂ juv.-ad	97	86	120	11	86	30	−10	51	29	114	82	84	77	90	—	—	—	—	84.0
4626 ♂ mat	89	90	117	5	84	31	−7	48	33	115	80	83	68	92	—	—	—	—	84.9
4627 ♂ mat	92	91	118	10	82	27	−4	47	28	107	84	84	79	88	—	—	—	—	88.2
4628 ♀ ad-mat	93	85	116	11	82	29	−4	53	24	110	87	90	75	91	—	—	—	—	89.2
4629 ♂? mat	95	87	124	16	79	27	+5	52	18	108	85	86	78	89	—	—	—	—	89.9
4630 ♂ ad-mat	95	90	126	8	87	30	−1	47	32	117	83	87	73	88	—	—	—	—	92.2
4631 ♂ mat	100	87	111	15	85	29	+1	52	23	109	84	85	77	94	—	—	—	—	86.0
4632 ♂ ad-mat	100	89	112	16	84	29	0	48	22	103	86	89	74	92	—	—	—	—	88.2
4633 ♂ mat	98	89	110	11	87	32	−5	46	28	110	77	77	77	85	72	115	82	−3	89.6
4634 ♂ mat	—	—	115	17	—	—	—	53	28	108	80	84	70	87	—	—	—	—	13
♂ cases	13	13	13	14	13	13	13	14	13	13	14	14	14	14	1	1	1	1	13
range	89–100	86–91	110–126	5–17	79–87	25–32	+5 to −12	46–53	18–33	103–117	77–86	77–89	63–85	85–94					83.7–94.7
average	94.6	88.8	117.5	11.4	83.6	28.8	−3.4	49.7	26.8	110.4	82.4	85.1	73.1	89.5	72.0	115.0	82.0	−3.0	88.6
♀ cases	2	2	2	2	2	2	2	2	2	2	2	2	2	2					2
range	90; 93	85; 90	116; 125	9; 11	81; 82	26; 29	−3 to −4	53. 54	24; 27	110; 118	83; 87	88; 90	68; 75	89; 91					83.8–94.7
average	91.5	87.5	123.0	10.0	81.5	27.5	−3.5	53.5	25.5	114.0	85.0	89.0	71.5	90.0	—	—	—	—	88.3
inf. cases	1	1	1	1	1	1	1	1	1	1	1	1	1	1					1
range	—	—	—	—	—	—	—	—	—	—	—	—	—	—	—	—	—	—	—
average	101.0	92.0	120.0	14.0	87.0	29.0	−9.0	48.0	22.0	112.0	84.0	—	84.0	94.0	—	—	—	—	87.6
about Vancouver																			
1537 ♀ ad-mat	—	—	—	—	—	—	—	—	—	—	—	—	—	—	73	121	75	−17	89.2
1539 ♂ ad	—	—	—	—	—	—	—	—	—	—	—	—	—	—	—	—	—	—	80.9
1544 ♂ ad	90	87	127	11	79	30	+3	56	25	111	75	76	72	88	—	—	—	—	78.3
1549 ♂ ad	90	—	133	10	80	26	−7	51	25	113	—	—	—	88	—	—	—	—	81.8
1567 ♂ mat	90	—	124	8	82	32	−4?	48	25	114	—	—	—	—	67	123	79	−10	79.3
1568 ♂ ad	92	89	127	2	90	28	−8	41	32	126	81	80	81	92	—	—	—	—	88.3
1570 ♂ mat	—	—	—	—	—	—	—	—	—	—	—	—	—	—	73	117	79	−11	85.4
1574 ♀ ad-mat	—	—	—	—	—	—	—	—	—	—	—	—	—	—	—	—	—	—	82.7
1579 ♂ mat	90	88	123	6	84	31	+2	49	31	117	85	88	77	91	—	—	—	—	
1581 ♂ ad-mat	91	—	120	10	81	26	0	50	24	118	—	—	—	87	—	—	—	—	
1581 A ♂ mat	—	—	—	—	—	—	—	—	—	—	—	—	—	—	73	117	79	−3	—

INDICES

	Skull								Face and mandible										Cranio-facial			
Length-height	Breadth-height	Transverse frontal	Transverse frontoparietal	Sagittal parieto-frontal (arcs)	Sagittal frontal	Sagittal parietal	Sagittal occipital	Foramen magnum	Facial	Upper facial	Orbital (mf)	Orbital (la)	Interorbital (mf-mf to ek-ek)	Nasal	Transverse nasal bone	Maxillo-alveolar	Palatal	Bicondylo-bigonial breadth (mandible)	Ramus (mandible)	Transverse cranio-facial	Fronto-biorbital (ft-ft to fmt-fmt)	Jugo-frontal	Jugo-mandibular
79.3	89.7	77.3	58.6	100.0	90.8	88.3	75.6	84.4	—	49.6	87.5	94.6	16.1	47.9	50.0	125.5	93.5	—	—	91.7	85.9	63.9	—
81.1	85.6	84.7	62.5	87.9	92.7	88.1	84.2	81.6	—	52.0	81.8	90.0	15.8	44.0	53.3	110.2	76.9	—	—	92.5	90.1	67.6	—
77.5	92.6	80.7	64.4	86.5	89.7	89.9	81.6	86.1	—	51.3	81.4	94.6	18.8	46.4	52.9	125.0	87.5	—	—	99.3	88.1	64.9	—
—	—	—	—	—	—	—	—	—	—	—	80.0	90.0	—	—	48.0	—	132.1	95.4	—	—	80.8	—	—
—	—	—	—	—	—	—	—	—	—	—	84.1	94.9	—	—	43.4	—	—	—	—	—	—	—	—
74.1	84.5	81.4	64.8	76.9	88.0	93.3	81.0	77.1	—	87.2	94.4	—	—	—	—	—	—	—	—	95.8	—	—	—
—	—	84.1	—	—	92.0	—	—	—	—	—	86.1	91.2	20.0	54.3	46.7	151.4	90.6	—	—	—	98.9	—	—
81.5	86.8	79.3	63.2	89.3	89.3	89.0	83.3	83.8	—	55.5	86.0	92.5	15.6	44.9	53.3	128.6	88.4	—	—	84.2	93.2	75.0	—
76.0	90.5	85.6	68.7	95.9	88.5	89.9	80.9	81.6	—	46.9	86.0	92.5	18.6	54.2	56.2	116.4	83.3	—	—	98.6	91.0	69.7	—
75.7	89.2	83.9	66.2	86.3	90.1	90.3	80.6	81.4	—	51.5	90.7	97.5	19.0	45.8	66.7	121.0	84.3	—	—	103.8	90.4	63.8	—
79.5	90.1	77.9	62.0	97.2	93.5	87.6	80.8	81.8	—	—	83.7	94.7 r	14.7	44.0	46.1	—	—	—	—	91.5	88.0	67.7	—
78.9	88.5	—	—	—	94.6	95.5	88.6	84.2	—	55.1	80.9	87.2	18.8	46.3	76.5	111.1	86.7	—	—	93.2	—	—	—
76.9	85.5	83.0	64.5	88.0	91.2	87.3	83.3	77.8	—	51.8	86.0	92.5	17.6	42.0	46.7	135.3	93.3	—	—	92.8	87.5	69.5	—
80.1	86.9	79.5	63.4	81.1	91.0	86.9	77.4	78.8	—	50.0	85.7	94.7	20.4	47.2	66.7	129.4	89.1	—	—	92.8	89.8	68.3	—
77.0	89.5	78.3	61.4	71.2	92.8	92.1	79.4	81.6	—	50.7	81.4	87.5	17.6	44.8	58.8	116.4	80.8	—	—	96.7	86.2	63.5	—
76.5	86.7	78.3	60.0	90.3	93.9	88.3	76.7	86.1	85.0	56.5	90.5	97.4	16.3	41.7	61.1	111.1	73.9	91.4	56.7	98.0	84.9	61.2	72.8
—	—	81.9	63.8	92.3	93.2	88.9	81.2	—	—	53.2	77.8	87.5	19.4	47.2	58.8	112.3	78.8	—	—	95.9	84.8	67.4	—
12	12	13	12	13	14	13	13	12	1	14	16	16	14	14	15	15	15	1	1	13	14	13	1
75.7–	85.6–	78.3–	60.0–	71.2–	88.5–	86.9–	76.7–	77.8–	—	46.9–	70.8–	80.9–	15.2–	41.7–	37.5–	110.2–	73.9–	—	—	84.2–	80.8–	61.2–	—
81.5	92.6	88.3	73.6	96.7	95.5	92.1	84.2	90.9	—	60.2	90.8	97.5	20.4	54.2	76.5	135.3	95.4	—	—	103.8	93.2	75.0	—
78.0	88.2	81.5	65.5	87.7	91.5	88.8	81.0	83.2	85.0	52.8	82.6	90.6	17.8	45.4	56.9	119.3	84.4	91.4	56.7	95.2	87.9	68.1	72.8
2	2	2	2	2	2	2	2	2	1	2	2	2	2	2	2	2	1	—	—	2	2	2	—
79.3;	89.7;	77.3;	58.6;	97.2;	90.8;	87.6;	75.6;	81.8;	—	83.7;	94.7;	14.7;	44.0;	46.1;	—	—	—	—	—	91.5;	85.9;	63.9;	—
79.5	90.1	77.9	62.0	100.0	93.5	88.3	80.8	84.4	—	87.5	94.7	16.1	47.9	50.0	—	—	—	—	—	91.7	83.0	67.7	—
79.4	89.9	77.6	60.3	98.5	92.1	88.0	78.2	82.5	—	49.6	86.1	94.7	15.4	46.0	48.5	125.5	93.3	—	—	91.6	87.0	65.8	—
—	1	1	2	1	2	1	1	1	—	—	2	2	1	1	1	1	1	—	—	—	2	—	—
—	—	81.4;	—	—	88.0;	—	—	—	—	—	86.1;	91.2;	—	—	—	—	—	—	—	—	95.8;	—	—
—	—	84.1	—	—	92.0	—	—	—	—	—	87.2	94.4	—	—	—	—	—	—	—	—	98.9	—	—
74.1	84.5	82.7	64.8	76.9	90.0	93.3	81.0	77.1	—	—	86.7	92.8	20.0	54.3	46.7	151.4	90.6	—	—	—	97.4	—	—
77.2	86.5	82.6	63.8	76.3	93.2	87.8	85.5	88.6	86.5	54.1	85.7	94.7	—	52.0	37.5	121.1	84.8	75.0	57.4	94.3	87.4	67.7	67.7
—	—	88.9	—	—	94.0	—	—	—	—	—	79.1	87.2 r	17.0	53.3	50.0	113.2	74.5	—	—	—	94.1	—	—
86.4	106.9	84.5	66.4	113.8	91.4	80.3	81.2	81.8	—	55.8	84.6	91.7 r	17.8	40.8	57.1	103.5	69.2	—	—	98.5	88.8	67.4	—
76.6	97.8	82.7	66.4	93.4	93.3	87.6	85.0	83.3	—	—	—	—	—	—	—	—	—	—	—	101.5	91.0	65.5	—
75.6	92.4	—	—	99.1	91.2	89.4	82.9	83.3	—	—	—	—	—	—	—	—	—	83.3	63.9	—	—	—	—
71.3	89.9	—	63.8	101.7	93.0	88.9	82.7	78.4	—	—	86.0	100.0 r	—	42.3	63.6	117.3	80.8	—	—	—	—	—	—
—	—	—	—	—	—	—	—	—	—	—	—	—	—	—	—	—	—	88.3	66.7	—	—	—	—
—	—	84.5	68.1	95.5	91.1	87.8	—	—	—	54.3	88.4	97.4	18.4	50.0	50.0	114.5	83.3	—	—	88.2	77.2	77.2	—
78.4	91.8	—	—	95.2	88.7	88.1	83.8	—	—	54.2	81.8	87.8	—	44.0	—	111.1	77.8	—	—	97.3	—	—	—
73.7	89.2	82.4	69.6	92.9	90.2	85.7	84.6	79.4	—	—	83.7	94.7 r	19.8	—	46.7	—	—	82.1	61.8	—	—	—	—

Tribal divisions and subdivisions — Catalogue No. — Sex and stages of life — Number of cases — Averages and ranges	"Central angle" (*Klaatsch*)	Cranio-facial (*Falkenburger*)	Interoccipital	ANGLES To ear-eye plane										Orbital height	Mandibulo-alveolar plane				Length-breadth
				Glabella-lambda	Basion-bregma	Nasion-basion	Basion-opisthion	Nasion-bregma	Lambda-bregma	Opisthion-lambda	Prosthion-nasion	Nasospinale-nasion	Prosthion-nasospinale		Ramus tangent-alveolar plane	Ramus tangent-basal tangent	Chin vertical-basal tangent	Condylo-coronoid tangent-alveolar plane	
COWICHAN	(°)	(°)	(°)	(°)	(°)	(°)	(°)	(°)	(°)	(°)	(°)	(°)	(°)	(°)	(°)	(°)	(°)	(°)	
1583 ♂ mat	89	90	117	8	81	29	−4	49	27	111	80	82	72	90	—	—	—	—	88.7
1586 ♀ ad	95	86	—	7	88	32	—	48	31	—	83	84	77	87	—	—	—	—	85.4
1587 inf. I	—	—	—	—	—	—	—	—	—	—	—	—	—	—	55	131	82	+13	—
1588 ♂ mat	—	—	—	—	—	—	—	—	—	—	—	—	—	—	76	106	87	−9	—
1596 ♂ ad-mat	97	90	123	11	86	30	−8	46	22	116	86	87	81	88	—	—	—	—	81.1
1749 ♂ ad-mat	—	—	—	—	—	—	—	—	—	—	—	—	—	—	—	—	—	—	—
1752 ♀ mat	92	90	122	10	82	28	−2	53	27	116	79	80	75	91	—	—	—	—	82.5
1754 A ♂ ad-mat	—	—	—	—	—	—	—	—	—	—	—	—	—	—	69	117	85	+9	—
1754 B ♂ mat	—	—	—	—	—	—	—	—	—	—	—	—	—	—	79	106	83	+5	—
1756 ♂ mat	—	—	—	—	—	—	—	—	—	—	—	—	—	—	—	—	—	—	87.5
1757 ♂ ad	95	91	124	12	83	24	−15	52	34	106	83	92	64	91	80	106	82	−8	103.9
1761 ♂ ad	—	—	—	—	—	—	—	—	—	—	—	—	—	—	74	108	86	+4	—
1762 ♂ ad	100	90	120	11	89	31	−11	48	29	115	76	77	74	90	66	119	84	+11	85.8
1763 ♂ ad	—	—	—	—	—	—	—	—	—	—	—	—	—	—	70	116	82	+11	—
1764 ♀ mat	89	—	130	—	—	—	—	—	—	—	—	—	—	—	—	—	—	—	82.2
1766 ♂ mat	—	—	—	—	—	—	—	—	—	—	—	—	—	—	—	—	—	—	—
1767 ♂ mat	—	—	—	—	—	—	—	—	—	—	—	—	—	—	70	111	88	+5	—
1768 inf. I	—	—	—	—	—	—	—	—	—	—	—	—	—	—	53	133	83	+10	—
1770 ♀ mat	95	93	124	7	88	28	−11	48	32	122	80	80	80	86	74	113	83	−17	89.6
1777 ♂ mat	—	—	—	—	—	—	—	—	—	—	—	—	—	—	71	113	84	+4	—
1780 ♂ mat	—	—	124	10	—	—	—	51	31	109	81	84	68	87	—	—	—	—	100.6
1781 ♂ ad-mat	—	—	—	—	—	—	—	—	—	—	—	—	—	—	76	112	81	−3	—
1782? ♂ ad-mat	90	89	—	8	82	29	—	50	31	—	83	85	76	88	—	—	—	—	91.2
1784 ♂ ad-mat	95	89	131	14	81	25	−3	55	30	107	88	91	75	97	—	—	—	—	110.3
1787 ♂? mat	86	—	119	2	—	—	—	55	—	—	—	—	—	—	—	—	—	—	84.7
1788 ♂ ad	93	86	114	7	86	32	−4	50	35	114	81	82	74	93	72	108	88	+8	92.9
1790 ♂ ad	—	—	—	—	—	—	—	—	—	—	—	—	—	—	69	112	88	+1	—
1792 ♂ mat	—	—	—	—	—	—	—	—	—	—	—	—	—	—	—	—	—	—	101.9
1796 ♂ mat	—	—	—	—	—	—	—	—	—	—	—	—	—	88	—	—	—	—	84.3
1799 ♀ mat	101	92	130	15	86	29	+1	47	26	103	79	80	73	—	—	—	—	—	94.1
1800 ♂ ad	—	—	—	—	—	—	—	—	—	—	—	—	—	—	66	112	91	+4	—
1807 ♂ mat	—	—	—	—	—	—	—	—	—	—	—	—	—	—	—	—	—	—	92.3
1810 ♂ mat	—	—	—	—	—	—	—	—	—	—	—	—	—	—	71	115	83	−2	—
1811 ♂ mat	—	—	—	—	—	—	—	—	—	—	—	—	—	—	68	116	85	−5	—
1812 ♂? mat	—	—	—	—	—	—	—	—	—	—	—	—	—	—	—	—	—	—	76.4
1813 ♂? mat	—	—	—	—	—	—	—	—	—	—	—	—	—	—	71	114	83	+5	81.9
1817 ♀ mat	—	—	—	—	—	—	—	—	—	—	—	—	—	—	67	121	82	−5	—
1818 ♂ mat	—	—	—	—	—	—	—	—	—	—	—	—	—	—	77	114	78	−2	—
1819 ♀ ad	—	—	—	—	—	—	—	—	—	—	—	—	—	—	63	123	82	−5	—
1821 ♀ ad	—	—	134	10	—	—	—	33	110	82	87	68	94	69	113	86	−4	96.1	

INDICES

		Skull							Face and mandible										Cranio-facial			
Length-height	Breadth-height	Transverse frontal	Transverse frontoparietal	Sagital parietofrontal (arcs)	Sagital frontal	Sagital parietal	Sagital occipital	Foramen magnum	Facial	Upper facial	Orbital (mf)	Orbital (la)	Interorbital (mf-mf to ek-ek)	Nasal	Transverse nasal bone	Maxillo-alveolar	Palatal	Bicondylo-bigonial breadth (mandible)	Ramus (mandible)	Transverse cranio-facial	Fronto-biorbital (fn-ft to fmt-fmt)	Jugo-frontal	Jugo-mandibular
75.1	84.7	83.5	67.5	94.3	88.5	85.2	80.7	93.9	—	—	88.6	97.5 r	19.4	51.0	52.9	115.2	76.8	—	—	—	94.6	—	—
76.2	98.3	—	—	94.9	89.0	89.3	—	—	—	—	87.5	94.6	19.3	46.8	60.0	121.7	87.2	—	—	—	—	—	—
—	—	—	—	—	—	—	—	—	—	—	—	—	—	—	—	—	—	80.2	73.7	—	—	—	—
—	—	—	—	—	—	—	—	—	—	—	—	—	—	—	—	—	—	81.2	54.1	—	—	—	—
73.3	90.4	85.5	68.5	88.8	91.2	89.2	85.4	77.1	—	—	88.4	—	18.4	45.4	53.8	132.7	93.7	—	—	—	91.7	—	—
—	—	72.2	—	108.4	92.4	82.9	—	—	—	—	80.4	88.1	15.0	42.6	60.0	113.7	83.0	—	—	—	84.3	—	—
78.9	95.6	84.9	65.7	101.6	88.5	83.9	84.1	85.3	—	—	85.4	92.1	15.9	46.8	42.9	109.3	77.1	—	—	—	94.7	—	—
—	—	—	—	—	—	—	—	—	—	—	—	—	—	—	—	—	—	94.6	59.7	—	—	—	—
—	—	—	—	—	—	—	—	—	—	—	—	—	—	—	—	—	—	85.7	57.8	—	—	—	—
—	—	78.8	60.5	99.2	92.7	87.0	—	—	—	—	83.3	89.7	—	—	61.5	—	—	—	—	—	87.3	—	—
82.3	79.2	73.7	54.7	81.3	90.2	84.0	84.0	87.1	86.1	52.3	92.5	102.8	15.6	54.3	58.3	109.6	75.0	85.2	71.1	81.8	89.7	66.9	75.4
—	—	—	—	—	—	—	—	—	—	—	—	—	—	—	—	—	—	77.2	62.9	—	—	—	—
79.3	92.4	70.0	64.8	81.2	89.8	89.4	82.0	81.1	—	—	83.3	89.7	—	44.9	46.1	111.3	80.8	80.2	58.7	—	—	—	—
—	—	—	—	—	—	—	—	—	—	—	—	—	—	—	—	—	—	89.7	63.8	—	—	—	—
79.9	97.1	77.9	63.3	101.7	90.0	88.5	48.8	79.0	—	—	—	—	—	—	—	—	—	—	—	—	87.1	—	—
—	—	78.6	—	—	89.5	—	—	—	—	—	77.8	85.4	17.8	48.1	—	120.7	89.4	—	—	—	95.4	—	—
—	—	—	—	—	—	—	—	—	—	—	—	—	—	—	—	—	—	81.9	66.7	—	—	—	—
—	—	—	—	—	—	—	—	—	—	—	—	—	—	—	—	—	—	81.6	60.0	—	—	—	—
76.8	85.7	85.2	66.7	92.7	91.1	87.0	82.7	84.9	79.7	49.6	77.8	85.4	16.7	56.8	53.3	115.7	81.6	77.7	61.0	90.5	92.4	73.7	70.7
—	—	—	—	—	—	—	—	—	—	—	—	—	—	—	—	137.2	—	71.3	64.9	—	—	—	—
—	—	79.7	62.4	94.0	93.1	83.5	86.2	—	—	—	85.1	97.6 r	15.7	43.4	53.3	—	93.7	—	—	—	91.6	—	—
—	—	—	—	—	—	—	—	—	—	—	—	—	—	—	—	129.8	—	—	59.3	—	—	—	—
78.1	85.6	73.3	58.2	101.8	91.1	84.3	—	—	—	—	82.9	89.5	15.8	53.2	37.5	—	90.9	—	—	—	83.3	—	—
87.0	78.9	77.3	57.1	98.2	93.8	81.1	88.8	87.1	—	—	89.7	97.2	16.8	46.8	—	132.5	80.9	—	—	—	95.8	—	—
81.6	96.4	84.8	68.8	108.8	90.3	84.7	81.3	93.8	—	—	—	—	—	—	—	—	—	—	—	—	94.0	—	—
83.5	89.9	80.0	63.3	91.5	89.9	87.3	78.8	85.7	—	—	95.1	105.4	19.1	42.9	—	112.5	79.2	—	65.6	—	96.1	—	—
—	—	—	—	—	—	—	—	—	—	—	—	—	—	—	—	—	—	85.0	61.7	—	—	—	—
—	—	80.3	61.2	—	92.2	—	—	—	55.5	80.4	92.5 r	19.0	41.5	—	105.2	75.5	—	—	90.0	93.3	68.1	—
—	—	82.0	66.7	100.8	89.8	86.7	81.0	—	—	—	—	—	—	—	—	—	—	—	—	—	—	—	—
82.3	87.5	77.4	61.8	73.7	91.5	88.5	87.2	79.4	—	54.7	97.5	102.6	17.0	42.3	50.0	107.3	75.5	—	—	88.9	89.9	69.5	—
—	—	—	—	—	—	—	—	—	—	—	—	—	—	—	—	—	—	81.7	65.5	—	—	—	—
—	—	75.5	57.6	85.7	94.1	85.3	—	—	—	51.5	83.7	100.0	16.8	40.4	46.2	91.8	62.3	—	—	94.4	83.8	61.0	—
—	—	—	—	—	—	—	—	—	—	—	—	—	—	—	—	—	—	68.5	—	—	—	—	—
—	—	—	—	—	—	—	—	—	—	—	85.0	100.0	—	46.0	50.0	—	—	88.5	82.7	—	—	—	—
—	—	69.1	—	94.7	88.5	87.9	85.2	—	—	—	—	—	—	—	—	—	—	—	—	—	—	—	—
—	—	77.9	67.9	82.7	87.2	88.2	84.1	—	—	—	—	—	—	—	—	—	—	90.5	63.8	—	94.0	—	—
—	—	—	—	—	—	—	—	—	—	—	—	—	—	—	—	—	—	—	72.0	—	—	—	—
—	—	—	—	—	—	—	—	—	—	—	—	—	—	—	—	—	—	74.6	74.9	—	—	—	—
—	—	75.6	58.4	91.9	89.4	84.1	89.0	—	84.4	51.8	90.0	94.7	16.1	44.9	—	115.1	83.7	90.3	69.1	90.6	88.8	64.4	75.6

Tribal divisions and subdivisions / Catalogue No. / Sex and stages of life / Number of cases / Averages and ranges	"Central angle" (Klaatsch)	Cranio-facial (Fulcrowerger)	Interoccipital	ANGLES To ear-eye plane										Mandibulo-alveolar plane				Length-breadth
				Glabella-lambda	Basion-bregma	Nasion-basion	Basion-opisthion	Nasion-bregma	Lambda-bregma	Opisthion-lambda	Prosthion-nasion	Nasospinale-nasion	Prosthion-nasospinale	Orbital height	Ramus tangent-alveolar plane	Ramus tangent-basal tangent	Chin vertical-basal tangent	Condylo-coronoid tangent-alveolar plane	
	(°)	(°)	(°)	(°)	(°)	(°)	(°)	(°)	(°)	(°)	(°)	(°)	(°)	(°)	(°)	(°)	(°)	(°)	
COWICHAN																			
♂ cases	13	9	12	13	12	12	11	14	13	12	10	10	10	12	20	20	20	20	20
range	86-100	86-91	114-133	2-12	79-90	24-32	+3 to -15	41-56	22-35	106-126	75-86	76-92	64-81	87-93	66-80	106-123	78-91	-11 to +11	76.4-103.9
average	91.8	88.9	122.8	8.8	83.6	29.0	-5.1	49.7	28.5	114.2	81.1	83.3	73.0	89.4	71.9	113.1	83.8	+0.7	87.1
♀ cases	6	5	5	6	5	5	3	6	6	6	6	6	6	6	4	5	5	5	9
range	89-101	86-91	122-134	7-15	81-88	25-32	+1 to -11	47-55	26-33	100-122	79-88	80-91	68-80	86-97	67-74	113-123	75-86	-17 to +4	82.2-110.3
average	94.5	90.0	128.0	10.5	85.0	28.4	-3.10	50.7	29.8	109.7	80.2	83.7	74.7	90.1	70.6	118.2	81.6	-9.6	90.8
inf. cases	—	—	—	—	—	—	—	—	—	—	—	—	—	—	2	2	2	2	—
range	—	—	—	—	—	—	—	—	—	—	—	—	—	—	53; 55	131; 133	82; 83	+10; +14	—
average	—	—	—	—	—	—	—	—	—	—	—	—	—	—	54.0	132.0	82.5	+12.0	—
Comox																			
2291 ♀ ad	—	—	—	—	—	—	—	—	—	—	—	—	—	—	66	119	86	-3	—
♀ 1 case	—	—	—	—	—	—	—	—	—	—	—	—	—	—	66.0	119.0	86.0	-3.0	—
N. Saanich																			
1698 ♂ ad-mat	100	86	131	18	82	28	-4	56	22	107	86	88	78	90	64	119	84	0	91.9
1699 ♂ mat	99	92	128	19	80	25	-8	53	20	103	81	84	69	90	73	115	81	+20	87.5
1701 ♂ mat	94	92	134	11	83	26	+8	51	28	114	86	87	79	89	83	104	83	-12	86.1
1702 ♂ mat	90	97	127	8	82	25	-10	44	25	118	81	83	73	90	—	—	—	—	90.1
1703 ♀ ad	—	—	—	—	—	—	—	—	—	—	—	—	—	—	58	124	86	+1	—
1706 ♂ ad-mat	92	95	124	9	83	27	+3	45	24	116	80	82	71	87	74	112	85	-8	86.0
1707 ♂ mat	97	93	129	14	83	26	-11	50	21	108	78	83	63	87	—	—	—	—	98.7
1710 ♂ mat	—	—	—	—	—	—	—	—	—	—	—	—	—	—	74	121	76	-1	85.6
2637 ♂ ad-mat	—	—	—	—	—	—	—	—	—	—	—	—	—	—	75	114	80	-12	—
2644 A ♂ mat	90	91	131	4	86	29	+1	48	34	117	82	83	79	92	79	100	89	-12	89.3
2644 B ♂ mat	95	97	139	11	84	27	+4	47	25	110	72	74	66	85	60	125	84	+3	95.3
2646 ♂ mat	—	—	—	—	—	—	—	—	—	—	—	—	—	—	76	109	83	-3	—
2661 ♂ ad-mat	89	94	123	10	79	25	-5	50	31	109	81	85	69	100	—	—	—	—	94.1
2666 ♂ mat	91	93	123	8	83	27	-5	48	25	123	80	89	58	93	59	131	79	+10	85.6
♂ cases	10	10	10	10	10	10	10	10	10	10	10	10	10	10	10	10	10	10	11
range	89-100	86-97	123-139	4-19	79-86	25-29	+8 to -11	44-56	20-34	103-123	72-86	74-89	58-79	85-100	59-83	110-131	76-89	-12 to +20	85.6-98.7
average	93.7	93.0	128.9	11.2	82.5	26.5	-2.7	49.2	25.5	112.5	80.7	83.8	70.5	90.3	71.7	115.0	82.4	-1.5	90.0
♀ 1 case	—	—	—	—	—	—	—	—	—	—	—	—	—	—	58.0	124.0	85.0	+1.0	—
Nanaimo																			
1618 ♂ mat	94	90	129	9	85	31	-2	45	28	112	82	83	78	88	—	—	—	—	97.1
1619 ♀ juv-ad	95?	—	123	16?	79?	28?	—	53	17	104	—	—	—	—	—	—	—	—	92.9
1620 ♂ ad-mat	95	94	118	14	81	25	-15	50	20	109	76	82	63	85	68	121	80	-4	95.3
1621 inf. I	—	—	—	—	—	—	—	—	—	—	—	—	—	—	49	137	83	+12	—
1622 inf. II	96	88	128	9	87	30	-13	48	25	117	85	85	85	88	54	131	83	+12	103.9

											INDICES										
				Skull								Face and mandible							Cranio-facial		
Length-height	Breadth-height	Transverse frontal	Transverse fronto-parietal	Sagittal parieto-frontal (arcs)	Sagittal frontal	Sagittal parietal	Sagittal occipital	Foramen magnum	Facial	Upper facial	Orbital (mf)	Orbital (la)	Interorbital (mf-mf to ek-ek)	Nasal	Transverse nasal bone	Maxillo-alveolar	Palatal	Bicondylo-bigonial breadth (mandible)	Ramus (mandible)	Transverse cranio-facial	Fronto-biorbital (ft-ft to fmt-fmt)	Jugo-frontal	Jugo-mandibular
13	13	18	18	20	23	20	16	11	1	5	18	17	13	16	14	15	14	16	20	6	17	5	1
71.3–	79.2–	72.2–	54.7–	82.7–	87.2–	80.3–	78.8–	77.1–	—	51.5–	77.8–	85.4–	15.0–	40.4–	37.5–	91.8–	62.3–	71.3–	54.1–	81.8–	83.8–	61.0–	—
86.4	106.9	88.9	69.8	113.8	94.1	89.4	88.2	93.9		55.8	95.1	105.4	19.8	54.3	63.6	137.2	93.7	94.6	82.7	101.5	96.1	68.1	
78.1	91.3	79.7	64.3	94.0	91.0	85.8	83.7	83.6	86.1	53.9	85.0	93.6	17.5	46.0	52.7	115.0	80.6	84.2	64.0	93.9	91.5	65.8	75.4
7	7	8	8	9	9	9	7	6	3	5	8	8	7	8	6	8	8	4	5	5	8	5	3
76.2–	78.9–	75.6–	57.1–	73.7–	88.5–	81.1–	82.7–	79.0–	79.7–	49.6–	77.8–	85.4–	15.9–	42.3–	37.5–	107.3–	77.1–	74.6–	57.4–	88.2–	87.1–	64.4–	67.7–
87.0	97.1	85.2	68.1	101.7	93.8	89.3	89.0	88.6	86.5	54.7	97.5	102.6	19.3	56.8	60.0	132.5	87.2	90.3	74.9	94.3	95.8	77.2	75.6
79.8	88.6	80.1	63.1	91.2	90.8	86.4	86.0	83.3	83.7	52.9	87.8	94.4	17.1	48.3	49.0	117.2	82.0	79.4	66.9	90.5	91.1	70.5	71.3
—	—	—	—	—	—	—	—	—	—	—	—	—	—	—	—	—	—	2	2	—	—	—	—
																		80.2;	60.0;				
																		81.6	73.7				
																		80.9	66.9				
—	—	—	—	83.7	92.7	83.5	—	87.5	85.3	54.3	78.6	86.8 r	17.7	42.9	53.3	105.7	95.8	82.1	68.5	—	89.0	69.0	71.3
				83.7	92.7	83.5		87.5	85.3	54.3	78.6	86.8	17.7	42.9	53.3	105.7	95.8	82.1	68.5		89.0	69.0	71.3
88.1	95.9	75.2	57.8	87.1	92.7	84.3	87.4	93.3	75.4	49.2	87.8	92.3 r	18.5	53.1	75.0	125.5	—	—	79.3	91.2	86.7	63.4	—
80.4	91.8	—	58.5	80.0	92.0	85.0	85.4	—	—	—	83.7	90.0	17.3	48.0	62.5	118.5	87.8	—	70.2	—	81.1	—	—
80.3	93.3	82.3	68.5	101.8	94.2	85.2	90.5	85.7	—	—	83.3	92.1	18.6	49.1	64.3	124.1	87.2	78.8	61.7	—	96.2	—	—
68.0	75.5	80.2	62.6	94.3	91.3	82.8	95.1	93.6	—	—	84.4	95.0	—	50.0	62.5	114.8	74.0	—	—	—	—	—	—
											85.4	94.6 r	25.5	40.0	—	73.3	121.3	79.1	—	74.5	58.0	—	99.0	—
70.8	82.3	80.0	65.4	94.3	91.0	87.0	83.6	85.7	82.3	49.7	72.9	81.4	15.4	51.9	53.3	123.7	88.7	80.6	50.0	96.1	90.1	68.0	73.5
77.4	78.3	82.1	64.3	87.2	92.1	84.2	86.4	106.3	—	49.6	84.1	92.5	19.0	54.3	—	124.5	85.1	—	—	—	86.0	93.3	74.8
—	—	—	62.4	89.7	93.6	87.6	—	96.8	—	—	83.7	92.3	18.0	46.9	41.2	115.1	86.4	79.5	70.4	—	86.9	—	—
																		82.9	58.6				
77.0	86.2	77.9	62.3	84.0	90.8	86.4	86.1	72.5	79.6	49.3	84.1	—	18.6	42.1	81.8	110.5	80.0	82.8	73.0	95.6	90.0	65.1	73.0
78.2	82.1	74.6	59.9	85.9	93.0	83.6	94.3	85.7	77.0	48.0	86.0	97.4	19.6	49.0	21.4	106.6	74.1	83.3	57.8	91.4	88.2	65.5	74.3
				103.6	93.7	87.0		—			87.2	102.5	—	40.4	58.3	—	—		48.6				
78.7	83.6	78.9	63.5	96.7	92.6	83.8	85.3	100.0	—	48.3	77.8	85.4	20.9	45.6	55.6	110.7	84.0	—	—	95.0	91.8	66.9	—
70.7	82.5	82.3	65.8	106.8	90.6	87.2	82.9	87.5	77.2	49.0	82.2	90.2	18.0	55.8	66.7	103.5	78.4	83.6	60.8	100.0	92.4	65.8	65.1
10	10	9	11	12	12	12	10	10	5	7	12	12	10	12	11	11	11	7	10	7	10	7	4
68.0–	75.5–	74.6–	57.8–	80.0–	90.8–	82.8–	82.9–	72.5–	75.4–	48.0–	72.9–	81.4–	15.4–	40.4–	21.4–	103.5–	74.0–	78.5–	48.6–	86.0–	81.1–	63.4–	65.1–
88.1	95.9	82.3	68.5	106.8	94.2	87.6	95.1	106.3	82.3	49.7	87.8	102.5	20.9	55.8	81.8	125.5	88.7	83.6	79.3	100.0	96.2	74.8	74.3
77.0	85.2	78.9	62.8	92.3	92.3	85.3	87.3	90.2	78.2	48.7	83.1	91.7	18.5	48.9	49.4	116.1	82.6	81.6	63.0	93.6	89.7	66.9	71.5
											85.4	94.6	25.5	44.0	73.3	121.3	79.1		74.5	58.0	—	99.0	—
77.3	79.6	78.5	61.1	89.1	93.3	99.1	85.6	86.1	—	47.4	80.4	92.5	18.0	46.3	61.5	107.1	—	—	91.0	91.9	67.1	—	—
83.1	89.5	86.4	66.4	92.0	91.0	89.7	83.9	88.9	—	—	—	—	—	—	—	—	—	—	—	—	94.0	—	—
74.7	78.4	78.2	59.9	90.3	94.7	89.3	83.1	94.1	79.6	49.3	75.0	82.5	18.3	56.1	50.0	112.1	79.2	80.8	59.0	87.6	87.4	68.3	71.1
																		85.9	62.2				
75.3	73.0	77.2	62.4	95.4	93.6	87.5	84.7	82.9	80.8	52.5	82.5	100.0	15.4	45.6	58.3	148.2	91.9	78.1	65.9	75.5	100.0	81.7	68.3

Tribal divisions and subdivisions / Catalogue No. / Sex and stages of life / Number of cases / Averages and ranges	"Central angle" (*Klaatsch*)	Cranio-facial (*Falkenburger*)	Interoccipital	ANGLES To ear-eye plane										Mandibulo-alveolar plane				Length-breadth
				Glabella-lambda	Basion-bregma	Nasion-basion	Basion-opisthion	Nasion-bregma	Lambda-bregma	Opisthion-lambda	Prosthion-nasion	Nasopinale-nasion	Prosthion-nasospinale	Orbital height	Ramus tangent-alveolar plane	Ramus tangent-basal tangent	Chin vertical-basal tangent	Condylo-coronoid tangent-alveolar plane	
	(°)	(°)	(°)	(°)	(°)	(°)	(°)	(c)	(°)	(°)	(°)	(°)	(°)	(°)	(°)	(°)	(°)	(°)	(°)
COWICHAN																			
1623 ♀ ad-mat	96	95	130	10	86	28	−7	42	24	126	80	84	69	82	68	120	80	+6	100.6
1624 ♂ mat	92	89	130	6	86	32	−14	48	33	113	76	77	70	85	70	112	88	+1	103.2
1625 ♀ mat	97	90	125	8	89	33	−9	44·	26	112	82	83	74	90	—	—	—	—	83.5
1626 ♀ ad	98	92	130	12	86	29	−4	44	19	115	81	87	69	88	—	—	—	—	73.3
1627 ♀? ad	99	90	127	9	90	32	+4	43	25	120	79	80	75	86	71	118	81	+5	78.4
1628 ♂ mat	92	84	125	7	85	36	+2	44	32	107	80	80	80	87	72	113	86	−5	97.0
1629 ♂ mat	94	88	120	14	80	28	−5	51	22	111	85	85	85	86	72	114	82	−3	99.4
1631 ♂ mat	95	92	115	6	89	29	−13	45	35	114	84	83	83	86	—	—	—	—	106.1
♂ cases	6	6	6	6	6	6	6	6	6	6	6	6	6	6	4	4	4	4	6
range	92–96	84–95	115–130	6–14	80–89	25–36	+2 to −15	44–51	20–35	107–114	76–85	77–85	63–85	85–88	68–72	112–121	80–88	−5 to +1	95.3–106.1
average	93.6	89.5	122.8	9.3	84.3	30.2	−7.8	47.2	28.3	111.0	80.5	81.7	76.5	86.2	70.5	117.5	84.0	+2.8	99.7
♀ cases	5	4	5	5	5	4	4	5	4	4	4	4	4	2	2	2	2	5
range	95–99	90–95	123–130	8–16	79–90	28–33	+3 to −9	42–44	17–26	104–120	79–82	80–87	69–75	82–90	68;71	118;120	80;81	+5;+6	73.3–100.6
average	97.0	91.8	127.0	11.0	86.0	30.0	−4.0	43.3	22.2	112.0	80.5	83.5	71.8	86.5	69.5	119.5	80.5	+5.5	85.7
inf. cases	1	1	1	1	1	1	1	1	1	1	1	1	1	2	2	2	2	1
range	—	—	—	—	—	—	—	—	—	—	—	—	—	—	49;54	131;137	83;83	+12;+12	—
average	96.0	88.0	128.0	9.0	87.0	30.0	−13.0	48.0	25.0	117.0	85.0	85.0	85.0	88.0	51.5	134.0	83.0	+12.0	103.9
Point Roberts																			
1907 A ♂ mat	96	92	140	11	85	26	−9	49	28	120	84	88	69	87	—	—	—	—	87.4
1908 ♀ mat	—	—	—	—	—	—	—	—	—	—	—	—	—	—	57	129	83	−6	—
♂ 1 case	96.0	92.0	140.0	11.0	85.0	26.0	−9.0	49.0	28.0	120.0	84.0	88.0	69.0	87.0	—	—	—	—	87.4
♀ 1 case	—	—	—	—	—	—	—	—	—	—	—	—	—	—	57.0	129.0	83.0	−6.0	—
Stanwood																			
2685 ♀ mat	—	—	143	15	—	—	—	51	22	114	80	80	80	84	65	128	78	+2	90.5
2687 ♂ mat	97	90	124	11	86	30	−10	47	28	109	82	86	70	88	63	124	81	+12	89.8
2688 ♂ ad	96	95	122	13	83	26	−5	44	24	107	82	83	79	90	—	—	—	—	101.2
2691 ♀? ad-mat	103	93	131	17	86	26	+3	49	19	110	81	85	71	90	65	127	78	+11	89.8
♂ cases	2	2	2	2	2	2	2	2	2	2	2	2	2	2	1	1	1	1	2
range	96;97	90;95	122;124	11;13	83;86	26;30	−5;−10	44;47	24;28	107;109	82;82	83;86	70;79	88;90	—	—	—	—	89.8;101.2
average	96.5	92.5	123.0	12.0	84.5	28.0	−7.0	45.5	26.0	108.0	82.0	84.5	74.5	89.0	63.0	124.0	81.0	+12.0	95.5
♀ cases	1	1	2	2	1	1	1	2	2	2	2	2	2	2	2	2	2	2	2
range	—	—	131;143	15;17	—	—	—	49;51	19;22	110;114	80;81	80;85	71;80	84;90	65;65	127;128	78;78	+2;+11	89.8;95.0
average	103.0	93.0	137.0	16.0	86.0	26.0	+3.0	50.0	20.5	112.0	80.5	82.5	75.5	87.0	65.0	127.5	78.0	+6.5	90.1
San Juan de Fuca																			
2682 A ♀? mat	—	—	—	—	—	—	—	—	—	—	—	—	—	—	64	120	85	−7	—
2682 B ♂ mat	93	88	123	8	85	32	−5	50	26	120	77	80	65	86	77	109	83	−18	82.7

INDICES

	Skull									Face and mandible											Cranio-facial			
Length-height	Breadth-height	Transverse frontal	Transverse frontoparietal	Sagittal parieto-frontal (arcs)	Sagittal frontal	Sagittal parietal	Sagittal occipital	Foramen magnum	Facial	Upper facial	Orbital (mf)	Orbital (la)	Interorbital (mf-mf to ek-ek)	Nasal	Transverse nasal bone	Maxillo-alveolar	Palatal	Bicondylo-bigonial breadth (mandible)	Ramus (mandible)	Transverse cranio-facial	Fronto-biorbital (ft-ft to fmt-fmt)	Jugo-frontal	Jugo-mandibular
74.7	74.2	71.5	56.8	79.1	94.5	87.4	73.0	90.3	85.1	54.5	88.4	—	16.5	46.3	50.0	113.0	76.9	82.5	70.9	86.4	84.6	65.7	73.9
88.3	80.0	70.2	57.5	98.2	94.6	85.3	86.7	97.1	73.5	44.4	74.5	81.4	16.3	49.0	62.5	108.6	87.0	87.6	53.2	94.4	85.2	60.9	74.8
76.2	91.2	83.2	65.0	82.8	92.2	89.6	83.9	85.7	—	46.3	88.4	95.0	15.6	48.0	38.5	113.5	84.8	—	—	97.8	87.2	66.4	—
69.4	94.7	84.3	68.9	83.7	88.6	90.3	85.5	88.9	—	57.8	81.8	90.0	17.1	46.0	46.7	111.3	78.7	—	—	97.0	86.7	71.1	—
75.4	96.3	80.0	65.7	79.0	89.5	91.8	85.0	90.6	94.5	58.3	88.1	100.0	16.0	46.0	31.2	121.6	78.7	96.2	58.9	94.8	85.4	69.3	79.5
83.9	86.5	79.0	60.1	88.0	92.3	87.4	85.6	81.6	79.9	52.2	87.0	97.6	14.7	41.9	50.0	127.8	95.9	84.3	57.1	97.5	86.0	61.6	74.2
77.5	77.9	75.4	58.7	101.8	97.3	87.6	81.2	100.0	75.3	48.7	80.9	89.5	22.0	42.1	68.4	131.5	80.0	80.0	65.6	89.5	91.0	65.6	72.7
75.6	71.3	62.9	47.7	85.8	93.3	85.4	79.3	100.0	—	45.7	82.6	92.7	14.3	49.1	35.3	130.0	102.2	—	—	87.9	75.4	54.2	—
6	6	6	6	6	6	6	6	6	4	6	6	6	6	6	6	6	6	5	4	4	6	6	4
74.7–	71.3–	62.9–	47.7–	85.8–	92.3–	85.4–	79.3–	81.6–	73.5–	44.4–	74.5–	81.4–	14.3–	41.9–	50.0–	107.1–	79.2–	80.8–	53.2–	87.6–	75.4–	54.2–	71.1–
88.3	86.5	79.0	61.1	101.8	97.3	99.1	86.7	100.0	79.9	52.2	87.0	97.6	22.0	56.2	68.4	131.5	102.2	87.6	65.6	97.5	91.9	68.3	74.8
79.6	79.0	73.7	57.5	91.8	94.3	89.0	83.5	93.0	77.3	48.0	80.2	88.5	17.2	47.4	57.7	119.5	88.9	83.2	58.7	91.3	86.0	63.0	73.2
5	5	5	5	5	5	5	5	5	2	4	4	3	4	4	4	4	4	2	2	4	5	4	2
69.4–	72.2–	71.5–	56.8–	79.0–	88.6–	87.4–	73.0–	85.7–	85.1;	46.3–	81.8–	90.0–	15.6–	46.0–	31.2–	111.3–	76.9–	82.5;	58.9;	86.4–	84.5–	65.7–	73.9;
83.1	96.3	86.4	68.9	97.0	94.5	91.8	85.5	90.6	94.5	58.3	88.4	100.0	17.1	48.0	50.0	121.6	84.8	96.2	70.9	97.8	94.0	71.1	79.5
75.8	89.2	81.2	64.6	84.0	91.2	89.8	82.3	88.2	90.0	54.2	86.7	95.0	16.7	46.6	41.8	114.9	79.8	89.4	64.9	94.0	87.6	68.1	76.7
I	I	I	I	I	I	I	I	I	I	I	I	I	I	I	I	I	I	2	2	I	I	I	I
—	—	—	—	—	—	—	—	—	—	—	—	—	—	—	—	—	—	78.1; 85.9	62.2; 65.9	—	—	—	—
75.3	73.0	77.2	62.4	95.4	93.6	87.5	84.7	82.9	80.8	52.5	82.5	100.0	15.4	45.6	58.3	148.7	91.9	82.0	64.5	75.5	100.0	81.7	68.3
75.3	86.2	78.0	60.5	100.0	93.6	83.2	88.6	87.5	—	54.9	86.7	97.5	14.3	44.6	53.3	103.6	84.0	—	—	86.8	90.9	69.2	—
																			64.7				
75.3	86.2	78.0	60.5	100.0	93.6	83.2	88.6	87.5	—	54.9	86.7	97.5	14.3	44.6	53.3	103.6	84.0	—	64.7	86.8	90.9	69.2	—
—	—	—	—	94.9	94.9	85.7	91.1	—	—	85.4	94.6	—	—	54.0	58.8	125.5	91.3	78.3	64.7	—	—	—	—
79.5	88.6	74.2	62.0	81.8	90.9	86.0	85.9	86.5	86.1	53.6	86.4	95.0	21.1	49.1	—	117.2	—	86.8	65.1	95.6	87.5	64.9	78.1
76.4	75.4	74.5	62.9	91.0	90.2	84.7	87.1	94.3	—	48.7	82.6	88.4	21.8	54.7	52.6	119.6	80.0	—	—	91.0	88.2	69.1	—
79.6	88.7	72.6	56.7	74.2	93.0	88.4	88.0	84.4	—	82.9	89.5	16.8	53.2	50.0	116.7	81.2	—	71.4	—	100.0	—		
2	2	2	2	2	2	2	2	2	I	2	2	2	2	2	2	2	I	I	I	2	2	2	I
76.4; 79.5	75.4; 88.6	74.2; 74.5	62.0; 62.9	81.1; 91.0	90.2; 90.9	86.0; 84.7	85.9; 87.1	86.5; 94.3	86.1	48.7; 53.6	82.6; 86.4	88.4; 95.0	21.1; 21.8	49.1; 54.7	—	117.2; 119.6	—	—	—	91.0; 95.6	87.5; 88.2	64.9; 69.1	78.1
78.0	82.0	74.4	62.5	86.0	90.6	85.4	86.5	90.4	86.1	51.2	84.5	91.5	21.5	51.9	52.6	118.4	80.0	86.8	65.1	93.3	88.0	67.0	78.1
I	I	I	I	2	2	2	2	2	I	—	2	2	2	2	2	2	I	I	I	2	I	—	I
—	—	—	—	74.2; 94.9	93.0; 94.9	85.7; 88.4	88.0; 91.1	—	—	—	82.9; 85.4	89.5; 94.6	—	53.2; 54.0	50.0; 58.8	116.7; 125.5	81.2; 91.3	—	64.7; 71.4	—	—	—	—
79.6	88.7	72.6	56.7	84.0	94.0	87.1	89.6	84.4	—	84.2	91.5	17.8	53.6	54.4	121.1	86.3	78.3	68.1	—	100.0	—		
—	—	82.1	—	—	92.5	—	—	—	—	85.0	91.9	21.9	54.2	63.2	117.0	83.3	87.8	65.4	—	90.9	—	—	
76.9	93.0	83.9	65.7	105.1	92.3	86.2	83.1	81.8	86.1	50.8	81.4	87.5	20.0	53.2	—	—	—	82.2	50.0	90.9	90.9	72.3	74.6

Tribal divisions and subdivisions / Catalogue No. / Sex and stages of life / Number of cases / Averages and ranges	"Central angle" (Klaatsch)	Cranio-facial (Falkenburger)	Interoccipital	ANGLES To ear-eye plane										Mandibulo-alveolar plane				Length-breadth
				Glabella-lambda	Basion-bregma	Nasion-bregma	Basion-opisthion	Nasion-bregma	Lambda-bregma	Opisthion-lambda	Prosthion-nasion	Nasospinale-nasion	Prosthion-nasospinale	Orbital height	Ramus tangent-alveolar plane	Ramus tangent-basal tangent	Chin vertical-basal tangent	Condylo-coronoid tangent-alveolar plane	
	(°)	(°)	(°)	(°)	(°)	(°)	(°)	(°)	(°)	(°)	(°)	(°)	(°)	(°)	(°)	(°)	(°)	(°)	
COWICHAN																			
2682 C ♂ mat	—	—	—	—	—	—	—	—	—	—	—	—	—	—	85	99	85	−16	—
2683 ♂ ad	96	90	135	9	87	30	0	49	30	116	80	82	70	88	62	124	83	0	89.7
♂ cases	2	2	2	2	2	2	2	2	2	2	2	2	2	2	3	3	3	3	2
range	93 ; 96	88 ; 90	123 ; 135	8 ; 9	85 ; 87	30 ; 32	0 ; −5	49 ; 50	26 ; 30	116 ; 120	77 ; 80	80 ; 82	65 ; 70	86 ; 88	62−82	99− 124	83−85	−18 to 0	82.7 ; 89.7
average	94.5	89.0	129.0	8.5	86.0	31.0	−2.5	49.5	28.0	118.0	78.5	81.0	67.5	87.0	74.7	110.7	83.7	−11.3	86.2
♀ 1 case	—	—	—	—	—	—	—	—	—	—	—	—	—	—	64.0	120.0	85.0	−7.0	—
Port Williams																			
3045 ♂ mat	95	93	122	13	82	27	−2	49	25	110	78	84	60	92	72	113	85	−9	99.4
♂ 1 case	95.0	93.0	122.0	13.0	82.0	27.0	−2.0	49.0	25.0	110.0	78.0	84.0	60.0	92.0	72.0	113.0	85.0	−9.0	99.4
Dungeness																			
2715 ♀? ad	96	93	120	12	84	32	−1	43	17	109	74	78	61	85	—	—	—	—	95.7
2719 ♀? mat	97	95	135	15	82	25	−4	48	19	105	76	82	64	84	—	—	—	—	96.1
2723 ♂ mat	99	90	116	15	84	30	+7	48	19	108	85	89	72	88	—	—	—	—	86.4
2724 ♀ mat	94	90	129	10	84	30	−5	47	25	115	80	82	72	92	—	—	—	—	85.9
2725 ♂ mat	95	93	126	12	83	32	0	44	28	117	76	79	64	81	—	—	—	—	91.0
2727 ♂ mat	97	90	116	10	87	31	−2	45	23	113	81	89	65	89	68	120	81	−8	101.8
2728 ♀? mat	94	88	127	10	83	28	0	47	24	113	88	89	83	94	82	121	87	+6	91.3
2730 inf. II	—	—	—	—	—	—	—	—	—	—	—	—	—	—	53	130	86	+20	90.2
2731 ♀ mat	98	86	131	11	87	28	−3	45	21	118	82	87	62	87	—	—	—	—	95.7
2734 A ♂ ad-mat	97	94	136	9	88	28	−5	44	27	120	80	81	76	87	72	119	80	+2	—
2734 B ♂ ad	—	—	—	—	—	—	—	—	—	—	—	—	—	—	74	110	86	−7	—
2734 C ♂ ad	—	—	—	—	—	—	—	—	—	—	—	—	—	—	69	123	77	+12	—
2735 inf. II	98	92	127	16	83	25	−6	50	16	110	86	86	86	90	58	132	79	+15	93.8
2736 inf. II																			
♂ cases	4	4	4	4	4	4	4	4	4	4	4	4	4	4	4	4	4	4	4
range	95−99	90−95	116−136	9−15	83−88	28−32	+7 to −5	44−48	19−28	108−120	76−85	79−89	64−76	81−89	68−74	110−123	77−86	−8 to +12	86.4−101.8
average	97.0	92.3	123.5	11.5	85.5	30.3	0	45.3	24.3	114.5	80.5	84.5	69.3	86.3	70.8	118.0	81.0	−0.3	93.7
♀ cases	5	5	5	5	5	5	5	5	5	5	5	5	5	5	1	1	1	1	5
range	94−98	86−93	120−135	10−15	82−87	25−32	0 to −5	43−48	17−25	105 ; 118	74−88	78−89	61−83	84−94	—	—	—	—	85.9−96.1
average	95.8	90.0	128.4	9.6	85.0	28.6	−2.6	46.0	21.2	112.0	80.0	83.6	68.4	88.4	62.0	121.0	87.0	+6.0	91.8
inf. cases	1	1	1	1	1	1	1	1	1	1	1	1	1	1	2	2	2	2	1
range	—	—	—	—	—	—	—	—	—	—	—	—	—	—	53 ; 58	130 ; 132	79 ; 86 82.5	+15 to +20	—
average	98.0	92.0	127.0	16.0	83.0	25.0	−6.0	50.0	16.0	110.0	86.0	86.0	86.0	90.0	55.5	131.0	—	+17.5	93.7
Markham																			
3049 ♂ ad	99	88	130	6	93	34	−3	42	31	118	82	87	69	90	—	—	—	—	95.8
♂ 1 case	99.0	88.0	130.0	6.0	93.0	34.0	−3.0	42.0	31.0	118.0	82.0	87.0	69.0	90.0	—	—	—	—	95.8

	INDICES																						
	Skull									Face and mandible											Cranio-facial			
Length-height	Breadth-height	Transverse frontal	Transverse frontoparietal	Sagittal parieto-frontal (arcs)	Sagittal frontal	Sagittal parietal	Sagittal occipital	Foramen magnum	Facial	Upper facial	Orbital (mf)	Orbital (la)	Interorbital (mf-mf to ek-ek)	Nasal	Transverse nasal bone	Maxillo-alveolar	Palatal	Bicondylo-bigonial breadth (mandible)	Ramus (mandible)	Transverse cranio-facial	Fronto-biorbital (ft-ft to fmt-fmt)	Jugo-frontal	Jugo-mandibular
81.8	91.2	78.7	64.9	89.1	89.8	84.2	88.1	91.2	83.7	51.8	82.5	91.7	—	46.9	57.1	101.8	81.6	83.1	63.1 56.4	91.2	—	71.1	76.3
2	2	2	2	2	2	2	2	2	2	2	2	2	1	2	1	1	1	1	3	2	1	2	2
77.9 ;	91.2 ;	78.7 ;	64.9 ;	89.1 ;	89.8 ;	84.2 ;	83.1 ;	81.8 ;	83.7 ;	50.8 ;	81.4 ;	87.5 ;	—	46.9 ;	—	—	—	82.2 ;	50.0 ;	90.9 ;	—	71.1 ,	74.6 ;
81.8	93.0	83.9	65.7	105.1	92.3	86.2	88.1	91.2	86.1	51.8	82.5	91.7		53.2				83.1	63.1	91.2		72.3	76.3
79.4	92.1	81.3	65.3	97.0	90.6	85.2	85.6	86.5	85.0	51.0	82.0	89 0	20.0	50.5	57.1	101.8	81.6	82.7	56.5	91.1	90.9	71.7	75.5
—	—	82.1	—	—	92.5	—	—	—	85.0	91.9			21.9	54.2	63.2	117.0	83.3	87.8	65.4		90.9	—	—
77.3	77.8	79.2	61.1	88.5	94.7	90.0	83.9	90.6	75.3	46.0	84.4	95.0	16.3	51.0	53.3	108.8	87.2	78.2	58.1	92.6	88.4	66.0	74.0
77.3	77.8	79.2	61.1	88.5	94.7	90.0	83.9	90.6	75.3	46.0	84.4	95.0	16.3	51.0	53.3	108.8	87.2	78.2	58.1	92.6	88.4	66.0	74.0
73.8	77.1	79 5	61.8	86.9	92.5	88.2	83.7	85.7	—	47.3	82.2	90.2	21.0	54.0	—	117.5	85.7	—	—	93.0	86.6	66.4	—
76.1	79.2	80.7	64.4	83.5	93.6	90.1	89.8	82.9	—	52.6	83.3	89.7	18.0	50.0	—	115.8	93.6	—	—	90.6	90.6	71.1	—
75.6	87.5	81.7	64.5	76.0	92.6	93.5	78.8	77.8	—	52.1	84.1	92.5	17.6	44.2	—	122.2	93.2	—	—	93.4	89.1	69.0	—
75.3	87.7	82.8	65.7	94.8	91.3	91 7	84.8	85.7	—	—	86.0	97.4	19.0	52.1	50.0	109.3	—	—	—	—	89.7	—	—
74.8	82.2	75.0	59.2	97.3	94.7	87.3	84.7	83.8	—	47.3	90.7	97.5	19.6	54.0	—	122.6	83.7	—	—	96.0	83.3	61.6	—
76.2	74.8	79.7	61.1	87.6	92.9	88.9	91.6	86.1	75.5	47.6	82.9	91.9	20.4	49.0	62.5	125.0	89.1	84.3	52.5	88.0	93.6	69.4	69.4
75.2	82.3	76.3	61.2	94.6	92.0	86.8	84.0	91.7	87.9	52.1	80.0	90.0	20.0	44.2	46.7	116.0	78.3	85.2	53.2	95.2	82.6	64.3	82.1
																		92.4	57.1				
71.3	79.0	—	60.8	82.8	91.4	89.6	83.6	90.0	—	—	90.0	97.3 1	—	—	—	—	—	—	—	84.5	—	72.0	—
72.8	76.1	81.8	63.9	93.9	93.0	86.1	87.2	90.3	90.2	57.1	85.4	92.1	21.0	46.1	76.5	110.3	80.4	80.6	55.4	85.8	92.5	74.4	75.2
																		84.1	59.4				
																		86.7	64.8				
69.4	74.0	82.4	65.3	87.2	92.7	91.6	86.8	85.7	—	—	83.7	91.2	18.9	57.1	66.7	139.5	—	75.9	74.4	—	100.0	—	—
—	—	86.4	—	—	96.7	87.7	89.0	82.4	81.8	—	87.1	97.1	17.4	48.9	50.0	136.4	—	—	—	—	94.7	—	—
4	4	4	4	4	4	4	4	4	2	4	4	4	4	4	4	4	4	4	4	4	4	4	2
72.8-	74.8-	75.0-	59.2-	76.0-	92.6-	86.1-	78.8-	77.8-	75.5 ;	47.3-	82.9-	91.9-	17.6-	44.2-	46.7-	110.3-	80.4-	80.6-	52.5-	85.8-	83.3-	61.6-	69.4 ;
76.2	87.5	81.8	64.5	97.3	94.7	91.6	90.3	91.6	90.2	57.1	90.7	97.5	21.0	54.0	76.5	125.0	93.2	86.7	64.8	96.0	93.6	74.4	75.2
74.9	80.2	79.0	62.2	88.3	93.3	89.0	85.6	84.0	83.0	50.8	85.8	93.8	19.8	48.3	62.3	112.0	86.6	83.9	58.0	90.8	89.8	68.6	72.3
5	5	4	5	5	5	5	5	5	1	3	5	5	4	4	1	4	3	1	1	4	4	4	1
71.3-	77.1-	76.3-	60.8-	82.8-	91.3-	83.7-	83.6-	82.9-	—	47.3-	82.0-	89.7-	18.0-	44.2-	—	109.3-	78.3-	—	—	84.5-	82.6-	64.3-	—
76.1	87.7	82.8	65.7	94.8	93.6	91.7	89.8	91.7		52.6	90.0	97.4	21.0	54.0		117.5	93.6			95.2	90.6	72.0	
74.3	81.1	79.3	62.8	87.8	92.1	89.3	85.2	86.6	87.9	50.7	85.0	92.6	19.5	50.1	50.0	114.7	85.9	85.2	53.2	90.8	87.8	68.3	82.1
1	1	2	1	2	2	2	2	2	—	2	2	2	2	2	2	2	2	2	2	2	2	2	
—	—	82.4 ;	—	87.2 ;	87.7 ;	89.0 ;	82.4 ;	81.8 ;	—	83.7 ;	91.2 ;	17.4 ;	48.9 ;	50.0 ;	136.4 ;	82.5 ;	75.9 ;	57.1 ;	—	—	94.7 ;	—	
		86.4		96.7	91.6	91.6	86.9	85.7		87.1	97.1	18.9	57.1	66.7	139.5	92.5	94.4	74.4			100.0		
69.4	74.0	84.4	65.3	90.0	90.2	85.3	84.6	83.0	—	85.4	94.0	18.2	53.0	58.5	138.0	87.5	84.2	65.8	—	—	97.5	—	
77.8	81.2	77.8	61.2	90.2	92.6	80.0	87.3	81.8	—	57.3	90.5	—	25.5	44.6	—	120.7	93.3	—	—	89.4	91.6	68.5	—
77.8	81.2	77.8	61.2	90.2	92.6	80.0	87.3	81.8	—	57.3	90.5	—	25.5	44.6	—	120.7	93.3	—	—	89.4	91.6	68 5	—

73

Tribal divisions and subdivisions / Catalogue No. / Sex and stages of life / Number of cases / Averages and ranges	"Central angle" (*Klaatsch*)	Cranio-facial (*Falkenburger*)	Interoccipital	ANGLES										Mandibulo-alveolar plane				Length-breadth
				Glabella-lambda	Basion-bregma	Nasion-basion	Basion-opisthion	Nasion-bregma	Lambda-bregma	Opisthion-lambda	Prosthion-nasion	Nasospinale-nasion	Prosthion-nasospinale	Orbital height	Ramus tangent-alveolar plane	Ramus tangent-basal tangent	Chin vertical-basal tangent	Condylo-coronoid tangent-alveolar plane	
	(°)	(°)	(°)	(°)	(°)	(°)	(°)	(°)	(°)	(°)	(°)	(°)	(°)	(°)	(°)	(°)	(°)	(°)	(°)
COWICHAN																			
Divisional total																			
♂ cases	75	69	73	76	73	73	72	77	75	73	72	71	72	75	52	52	52	52	81
range	86–100	84–97	110–140	2–19	78–90	23–36	+10 to –15	41–57	18–37	103–126	72–89	74–92	58–85	81–100	59–85	99–131	76–91	–18 to +20	76.4–110.3
average	93.9	90.3	123.5	10.1	83.9	28.6	–3.6	48.9	27.7	112.7	81.3	84.1	72.9	89.2	71.9	114.4	83.2	–1.2	89.4
♀ cases	23	21	23	23	22	22	20	24	24	24	23	22	23	23	16	16	16	16	27
range	89–103	84–92	112–143	7–17	79–90	25–35	+3 to –11	42–55	17–33	100–123	74–88	76–91	61–83	82–97	65–74	113–133	75–87	–17 to +11	73.3–110.3
average	95.6	89.9	128.6	10.9	85.1	29.4	–2.7	48.3	25.2	112.2	80.7	83.5	72.6	88.5	65.1	122.1	81.7	–1.9	90.9
juv. cases	2	2	2	2	2	2	2	2	2	2	2	2	2	2	2	2	2	2	2
range	95;97	89;91	137;141	10;11	85;86	23;31	+10;–8	42;55	24;29	112;121	81;82	83;84	74;75	87;90	65;66	120;125	79;84	–6;+5	92.0;92.0
average	96.0	90.0	139.0	10.5	85.5	27.0	+1.0	49.0	26.5	116.5	81.5	83.5	74.5	88.5	65.5	122.5	81.5	–0.5	92.0
inf. cases	4	4	4	4	4	4	4	4	4	4	3	4	4	4	10	10	10	10	4
range	95–101	87–92	120–136	8–18	82–87	25–30	–2 to –13	48–55	16–26	110–117	84–86	85–87	83–86	88–94	49–62	122–137	79–86	+4 to +20	87.6–103.9
average	97.5	89.3	127.8	13.0	84.2	27.8	–7.5	50.3	22.3	113.3	85.3	86.0	84.5	91.0	55.2	130.2	82.9	+12.5	94.6
CHINOOK																			
Chinook																			
3051 ♀ mat	100	88	127	9	91	35	+1	41	24	118	79	80	70	89	—	—	—	—	87.5
3051 B ♀ mat	—	—	—	—	—	—	—	—	—	—	—	—	—	—	77	115	77	–8	—
3052 ♀ ad-mat	—	—	—	11	—	—	—	49	24	—	81	86	68	88	—	—	—	—	90.2
3053 ♂ mat	100	96	140	15	85	24	+3	45	17	113	80	82	73	87	64	125	79	–10	103.1
3054 ♀ mat	102	99	128	11	91	27	+3	38	19	123	77	79	72	83	—	—	—	—	95.1
3055 ♀ juv.-ad	—	—	—	—	—	—	—	—	—	—	—	—	—	—	—	—	—	—	—
3056 ♂ ad	100	93	135	8	92	31	–2	40	26	120	80	80	80	84	—	—	—	—	88.6
3057 ♂ ad	102	94	126	16	86	27	+9	47	15	113	80	80	80	85	73	116	81	–5	98.2
4441 ♂ ad	98	96	138	12	86	27	0	46	23	108	79	81	66	85	—	—	—	—	86.7
4442 ♀ mat	98	92	136	8	90	31	0	44	29	117	80	82	73	83	—	—	—	—	102.7
4443 ♂ ad	95	94	137	8	87	29	0	45	23	116	77	79	71	85	—	—	—	—	87.9
4444 ♂ ad	95	92	140	9	86	31	–2	44	22	113	74	78	64	86	—	—	—	—	90.9
4445 ♂ ad	99	92	142	11	88	30	+8	45	20	120	79	80	74	83	—	—	—	—	90.5
4446 ♂ mat	97	92	133	15	82	25	–7	52	20	115	82	84	69	90	—	—	—	—	92.9
4447 ♂ mat	95	89	136	11	84	31	+3	48	28	115	81	81	81	89	—	—	—	—	91.1
4448 ♂ mat	103	97	131	14	89	28	+7	43	21	112	74	75	72	78	—	—	—	—	94.0
4449 ♂ ad-mat	100	94	143	11	89	31	+6	42	20	113	74	75	67	80	—	—	—	—	94.9
4450 inf. II	—	—	139	12	—	—	—	51	27	120	83	84	73	90	—	—	—	—	94.8
4451 ♂ mat	99	90	139	14	85	27	–3	50	22	113	83	85	76	90	—	—	—	—	99.4
4452 ♂ ad	95	90	135	12	83	28	+3	50	30	112	80	81	76	83	—	—	—	—	98.7
4453 ♂ ad	97	88	128	9	88	31	–3	45	26	115	86	86	86	92	—	—	—	—	88.1
4454 ♂ ad	98	85	125	12	86	31	–3	51	30	130	82	83	78	96	—	—	—	—	93.9
4455 ♂ mat	104	92	133	16	88	29	–2	46	17	112	82	84	74	90	—	—	—	—	93.4

INDICES

	Skull									Face and mandible											Cranio-facial			
	Length-height	Breadth-height	Transverse frontal	Transverse frontoparietal	Sagittal parieto-frontal (arcs)	Sagittal frontal	Sagittal parietal	Sagittal occipital	Foramen magnum	Facial	Upper facial	Orbital (mf)	Orbital (la)	Interorbital (mf-mf to ek-ek)	Nasal	Transverse nasal bone	Maxillo-alveolar	Palatal	Bicondylo-bigonial breadth (mandible)	Ramus (mandible)	Transverse cranio-facial	Fronto-biorbital (ft-ft to fmt-fmt)	Jugo-frontal	Jugo-mandibular
	73	74	78	78	84	88	84	77	71	23	64	86	84	73	84	75	79	75	44	52	64	77	63	22
	68.0–	71.3–	62.9–	47.4–	71.2–	86.8–	79.6–	76.7–	71.4–	73.5–	44.4–	70.8–	80.9–	14.3–	40.0–	18.2–	91.8–	62.3–	71.3–	48 6–	81.8–	75.4–	54.2–	63 1–
	88.3	106.9	88.9	73.6	113.8	97.3	92.9	95.1	106.3	90.2	60.2	95.1	105.4	25.5	56.2	81.8	137.2	102.2	94.6	82.7	104.9	96.2	75.0	78.1
	77.7	87.3	79.5	63.4	91.3	90.5	87.1	83 5	86.9	80.9	51.4	83.1	91.5	18.0	46.7	53.5	118.2	80.5	83.3	62.2	94.1	88.9	66.7	72.4
	24	24	25	25	28	29	28	25	24	8	16	27	25	23	26	22	26	24	12	16	17	26	18	8
	69.4–	74.2–	70.9–	56.8–	73.7–	88.5–	81.1–	73.0–	76.7–	75.0–	46.3–	77.8–	85.4–	14.7–	46.0–	31.2–	105.7–	76.9–	74.6–	53.2–	84.5–	82.6–	63.9–	67.7–
	93.1	97.1	86.4	63.1	101.7	94.9	91.8	91.1	96.7	94.5	58.5	97.5	102.6	25.5	56 8	73.3	132.5	95.8	96.2	74.9	99.3	100.0	77.2	82.1
	78.1	87.9	79.9	63.1	88.7	91.6	87.9	84.6	86.0	84 9	52.6	86.1	93.5	18.0	48.8	51.5	117.2	82.5	82.2	64.6	92.0	90.2	68.9	74.1
	2	2	2	2	2	2	2	2	2	2	2	2	2	2	2	2	2	2	—	2	2	2	2	1
	75.9;	82.5;	76.1;	59.7;	90.4;	90.4;	84.5;	88.1;	83.9;	79.8;	49.6;	85.0;	94.4;	20.6;	42.9;	50.0;	128.3;	87.2;	—	62.7;	86.3;	89.9;	69.0;	—
	80.1	87.0	85 6	62.6	95.6	90.4	86.5	88.5	86.1	80.0	51.7	88.9	97.0	20.7	52.4	60.0	128.3	95.1	—	77.3	86.6	92.5	72.5	—
	78.0	84 6	80.9	61.2	93.0	90.4	85.5	88.3	85.0	79.9	50.7	87.0	95.7	21.0	47.7	55.0	128.3	91.2	—	70.0	86.5	91.5	70.8	76.7
	4	4	7	4	5	7	5	5	6	2	2	7	7	5	6	6	6	6	9	10	2	7	2	2
	69.0–	73.0–	76.7–	62.4–	76.9–	87.7–	84.0–	81 0–	77.1–	79.2;	49.1;	82.0–	91.2–	15.4–	45.6–	46.7–	136.6–	82.5–	75.9–	57.1–	75.5;	94.7–	79.2;	76.7;
	81.9	88.1	86.4	65.3	98.2	93.6	93.3	89.7	89.7	80.8	52.5	88.6	100.0	20.0	57.1	66.7	151.4	92.5	96.5	74.4	79.1	100.0	81.7	86.3
	75.2	79.9	81.4	63.8	90.9	90.4	87.1	84.9	83.6	80.0	50.8	85.2	95.0	19.0	51.8	54.8	142.8	89.1	84.1	66.6	77.3	98.0	80.5	72.4
75.6	86.4	77.0	67.1	85.4	92.7	89.4	85.7	94.1	—	51.1	88.4	97.4	18.6	50.0	—	141.7	100.0	—	—	99.3	87.8	67.6	74.8
—	—	83.6	65.5	93.8	92.9	91.5	—	—	52.8	83.7	94.7	18.4	56.8	60.0	120.0	97.5	—	88.1	71.2	85.8	93.3	76.4	—
72.0	69.9	75.4	59.0	90.3	95.6	81.5	90.5	91.2	89.6	54.8	82.2	90.2	18.3	40.4	33.3	105.2	82.3	82.1	60.7	81.3	88.3	72.6	74.8
62.2	65.4	80.7	61.5	84.5	92.7	90.3	84.5	88.2	—	52.9	82.9	91.9	20.2	46.9	—	128.0	91.3	—	—	88.5	93.2	69.6	—
—	—	—	—	81.4	92.0	84.8	90.0	100.0	—	—	—	—	—	—	—	—	—	—	—	—	—	—	—
71.9	81.1	77.0	63.5	86.5	92.4	86.4	86.7	89.2	—	55.0	92.9	102.6	20.4	47.2	53.3	126.0	90.7	—	—	94.6	86.2	67.1	—
73.0	74.4	77.6	59.1	82.2	91.5	85.6	86.4	93.9	83.0	49.0	84.1	90.2	19.6	41.1	25.0	128.8	100.0	77.7	62.7	89.6	88.2	66.0	68.7
75.8	87.4	79.5	62.2	79.8	90.3	87.9	80.4	88.6	—	50.4	87.5	94.6	17.4	42.6	50.0	113.8	80.0	—	—	94.4	88.1	65.9	—
81.1	78.9	76.5	57.9	87.5	93.7	84.7	87.9	86.7	—	51.9	86.0	97.4	17.0	40.8	46.1	134.8	102.4	—	—	86.2	88.9	67.2	—
73.5	83.6	78.8	63.7	93.2	90.7	84.5	87.8	73.7	—	52.2	86.0	94.9	18.0	47.7	47.1	137.7	104.4	—	—	91.8	84.5	69.4	—
75.8	83.3	77.1	60.7	91.9	92.9	86.4	89.2	86.1	—	53.1	81.1	92.3	17.2	46.1	60.0	123.6	91.8	—	—	94.0	85.8	64.5	—
74.4	82.2	78.4	59.9	93.2	94.0	85.3	90.9	90.9	—	55.5	87.8	97.3	19.6	41.5	71.4	125.9	100.0	—	—	88.8	89.2	67.4	—
77.1	82.9	76.4	61.4	93.5	90.2	89.6	88.4	100.0	—	50.7	73.3	82.5	17.8	45.1	57.1	128.3	—	—	—	88.6	90.6	69.3	—
80.4	88.2	83.0	63.4	95.0	92.5	86.0	88.9	91.2	—	50.7	80.9	87.2	19.8	45.1	53.8	125.9	87.5	—	—	91.5	89.9	70.0	—
75.9	80.8	77.8	58.3	74.4	94.2	88.9	85.8	88.2	—	49.6	81.8	90.0	18.0	43.1	38.9	114.5	84.0	—	—	89.1	87.5	65.5	—
75.0	79.0	77.4	60.1	80.7	94.5	82.6	93.9	86.5	—	50.7	81.4	87.5	16.2	50.9	46 7	119.6	93.3	—	—	93.2	86.4	64.5	—
—	—	79.1	66.9	89.0	91.5	85.7	89.6	—	—	50.9	86.1	96.9	18.1	48.7	38.5	155.3	94.3	—	—	74.5	100.0	80.6	—
79.9	80.4	77.8	60.1	93.0	93.0	85.0	91.0	93.9	—	54.2	83.7	92.3	19.0	45.3	71.4	125.5	88.9	—	—	87.3	89.6	68.8	—
85.0	86.1	80.8	63.9	98.4	93.4	80.0	89.4	83.8	—	52.1	83.3	89.7	16.5	43.3	61.5	126.4	95.6	—	—	91.1	92.7	70.1	—
75.0	85.1	78.6	62.2	84.4	90.2	86.4	86.7	—	—	57.6	90.5	100.0	18.5	41.1	56.2	114.8	86.7	—	—	92.6	88.5	67.1	—
85.3	90.8	79.5	60.8	79.5	89.0	88.1	84.2	90.9	—	52.8	79.5	87.5	15.6	48.0	—	120.4	97.8	—	—	92.8	91.2	65.5	—
73.8	79.0	83.3	63.7	83.2	93.3	86.9	87.6	82.9	—	50.0	81.4	89.7	19.2	48.0	73.3	115.1	91.1	—	—	89.2	92.6	71.4	—

Tribal divisions and subdivisions / Catalogue No. / Sex and stages of life / Number of cases / Averages and ranges	"Central angle" (Klaatsch)	Cranio-facial (Falkenburger)	Interoccipital	ANGLES — To ear-eye plane — Glabella-lambda	Basion-bregma	Nasion-basion	Basion-opisthion	Nasion-bregma	Lambda-bregma	Opisthion-lambda	Prosthion-nasion	Nasospinale-nasion	Prosthion-nasospinale	Orbital height	Mandibulo-alveolar plane — Ramus tangent-alveolar plane	Ramus tangent-basal tangent	Chin vertical-basal tangent	Condylo-coronoid tangent-alveolar plane	Length-breadth
	(°)	(°)	(°)	(°)	(°)	(°)	(°)	(°)	(°)	(°)	(°)	(°)	(°)	(°)	(°)	(°)	(°)	(°)	
CHINOOK																			
4456 ♂ mat	97	90	134	10	87	30	−4	48	27	119	81	85	71	90	—	—	—	—	96.9
4457 ♀ ad-mat	98	91	132	19	79	25	+4	53	15	108	82	84	72	90	—	—	—	—	85.2
4458 ♂ mat	98	93	132	13	85	26	+8	48	21	119	86	89	75	89	—	—	—	—	81.6
4459 ♂ ad-mat	98	89	135	12	86	27	−4	49	33	109	85	87	81	90	—	—	—	···	108.3
4460 ♀ ad	96	95	132	13	83	27	+4	45	21	113	79	83	68	85	—	—	—	—	89.1
4461 ♂ ad	97	91	142	10	87	32	+4	43	24	117	80	82	74	87	—	—	—	···	84.8
4462 juv	100	93	152	10	90	31	+4	45	25	118	73	74	66	77	—	—	···	—	95.3
4463 ♂ ad-mat	93	89	132	15	78	26	+6	52	25	105	81	81	81	92	—	—	—	—	95.7
4464 ♂ ad	95	90	138	12	83	27	−2	47	25	114	87	88	82	90	—	—	—	—	96.4
4465 ♂ mat	97	—	125	14	83	27	−15	47	23	109	—	—	—	84	—	—	—	—	94.6
4466 ♀ ad	106	94	139	15	91	28	−5	45	20	102	84	85	81	84	—	—	—	—	97.5
4467 juv	99	90	140	15	84	29	+8	46	14	115	83	84	80	87	—	—	—	—	89.9
4468 inf. II	94	90	159	6	88	31	+4	48	27	133	81	81	77	88	—	—	—	—	97.6
4469 ♂ ad-mat	99	93	141	11	88	29	−5	45	27	115	82	85	84	87	—	—	—	—	95.3
4470 ♂ mat	94	93	130	8	86	30	−8	43	29	113	77	77	77	85	—	—	—	—	87.6
4471 ♂ ad-mat	102	96	141	15	87	26	+14	46	22	115	76	77	71	86	—	—	—	—	95.4
4472 ♂ ad	97	90	146	7	90	33	+1	45	30	116	80	82	77	88	—	—	—	—	92.2
4473 ♀ juv-ad	101	97	157	11	90	28	−2	44	20	120	76	76	76	84	—	—	—	—	96.9
4474 ♂ ad	99	93	138	12	87	30	−3	47	26	114	78	81	70	87	—	—	—	—	97.4
4475 ♂ mat	94	97	133	10	84	23	−7	46	27	113	81	83	75	88	69	119	82	−12	98.8
4476 ♂ mat	96	89	127	14	82	28	−1	50	22	109	81	82	76	88	—	—	—	—	97.6
4477 ♂ mat	96	90	137	13	83	27	−2	51	27	108	83	83	83	90	—	—	—	—	97.6
4478 ♂ ad-mat	101	93	145	12	89	29	+9	43	20	117	84	84	84	87	—	—	—	—	89.1
4479 inf. II	97	—	143	12	85	27	+7	51	24	114	—	—	—	92	—	—	—	—	94.3
4480 ♀ ad	103	93	138	11	92	32	−5	42	24	114	77	85	60	87	—	—	—	—	97.5
4481 ♀ mat	97	88	145	11	84	31	+7	45	27	113	86	88	77	91	—	—	—	—	100.6
4482 ♀ ad	100	89	139	15	85	29	+11	49	20	113	81	79	88	88	—	—	—	—	105.0
4483 ♀ ad-mat	95	91	137	11	84	30	−4	44	20	113	83	88	70	91	—	—	—	—	97.5
4484 juv	98	87	143	14	84	29	0	55	25	111	80	81	72	88	—	—	—	—	103.4
4485 inf. II	100	88	135	15	85	30	+4	52	24	112	77	80	67	89	—	—	—	—	103.3
4486 ♀ ad	97	92	138	10	87	28	+2	47	27	117	81	85	68	88	—	—	—	—	92.0
4487 ♀ mat	99	94	120	13	86	25	−9	48	23	115	82	84	72	90	—	—	—	—	83.1
4488 ♂ mat	93	84	127	11	82	30	−4	51	23	118	87	87	87	100	—	—	—	—	95.7
4489 ♂ ad	99	94	136	18	81	27	−4	48	13	105	75	80	65	85	—	—	—	—	96.3
4490 ♂ mat	105	95	131	16	89	24	−3	48	16	120	—	—	—	88	—	—	—	—	90.5
4491 ♀ ad	93	88	137	12	81	28	+6	51	25	112	83	83	83	89	—	—	—	—	92.9
4492 ♂ ad	103	95	130	13	90	29	−3	42	17	115	80	83	68	88	—	—	—	—	89.0
4493 ♂ ad	96	96	145	11	85	29	+5	43	24	112	76	76	76	84	—	—	—	—	101.2
4494 ♀ ad	97	92	136	12	85	27	−4	49	24	117	85	87	78	97	—	—	—	—	85.2
4495 ♂ mat	100	92	134	14	86	25	−8	49	22	112	84	86	79	97	—	—	—	—	96.4
4496 ♂ ad	100	92	136	15	85	28	+8	49	22	115	83	84	77	88	—	—	—	—	87.9

INDICES

Skull									Face and mandible											Cranio-facial			
Length-height	Breadth-height	Transverse frontal	Transverse fronto-parietal	Sagittal parieto-frontal (arcs)	Sagittal frontal	Sagittal parietal	Sagittal occipital	Foramen magnum	Facial	Upper facial	Orbital (mf)	Orbital (la)	Interorbital (mf-mf to ek-ek)	Nasal	Transverse nasal bone	Maxillo-alveolar	Palatal	Bicondylo-bigonial breadth (mandible)	Ramus (mandible)	Transverse cranio-facial	Fronto-biorbital (ft-ft to fmt-fmt)	Jugo-frontal	Jugo-mandibular
79.0	81.5	76.4	61.8	98.3	94.0	84.3	89.3	100.0	—	50.7	83.3	94.6	20.2	49.0	64.7	119.2	84.8	—	—	87.9	91.5	70.3	—
79.0	92.7	76.0	66.7	88.5	93.8	89.0	87.4	87.9	—	50.8	83.3	92.1	17.7	54.3	62.5	126.0	93.0	—	—	94.2	87.6	79.8	—
73.2	89.7	76.2	63.7	90.7	91.5	88.0	87.1	79.4	—	51.8	83.7	92.3	21.2	50.0	52.6	126.4	89.4	—	—	95.2	87.7	66.9	—
85.3	78.8	78.6	60.6	84.2	92.9	80.4	88.7	97.1	—	55.0	77.8	87.5	21.9	43.6	78.6	125.9	93.7	—	—	88.8	91.1	68.2	—
73.9	83.0	82.8	65.3	88.7	93.0	88.2	87.0	93.9	—	55.8	85.7	94.7	16.7	48.0	56.2	124.1	91.8	—	—	87.8	91.4	74.4	—
76.6	90.3	82.1	63.4	93.3	93.3	95.5	90.9	94.3	—	52.8	90.5	97.4	18.9	37.9	33.3	128.1	102.3	—	—	96.1	86.8	64.8	—
77.8	81.7	77.7	61.3	90.0	92.7	83.8	93.6	84.9	—	52.5	86.8	97.1	16.8	48.9	53.3	125.0	80.9	—	—	84.5	92.5	72.5	—
83.4	87.2	77.9	63.5	95.0	92.4	84.1	88.6	86.1	—	49.3	77.8	87.5	20.0	54.7	60.0	125.0	95.9	—	—	96.1	88.4	66.0	—
77.0	79.9	76.8	60.4	94.9	93.2	83.9	89.6	88.6	—	54.1	84.1	92.5	15.3	42.1	75.0	136.7	95.4	—	—	84.9	90.5	71.1	—
76.0	80.4	80.5	62.7	85.0	92.5	86.3	84.8	87.9	—	—	83.7	87.8	17.8	58.0	73.3	—	—	—	—	88.0	93.4	71.2	—
75.5	77.4	75.4	57.4	75.6	93.3	88.9	83.0	90.9	—	52.9	88.1	97.4	17.2	39.2	72.7	132.6	95.3	—	—	87.7	89.9	65.4	—
72.5	80.3	82.3	64.5	92.9	92.0	88.6	88.2	82.4	—	54.8	92.5	102.8	21.0	47.9	—	153.5	95.0	—	—	82.9	98.0	77.8	—
66.7	68.3	78.5	59.0	90.7	92.6	89.8	85.9	81.8	—	49.6	92.3	100.0	18.9	45.2	53.3	151.3	105.6	—	—	73.9	97.9	79.8	—
77.1	80.9	78.9	62.3	95.9	93.5	77.1	90.9	90.9	—	52.4	81.8	90.0	17.6	41.8	58.3	129.1	89.4	—	—	90.7	91.0	68.7	—
75.7	86.5	77.7	63.5	86.5	94.1	89.3	86.6	91.7	—	54.4	80.0	87.8	17.8	36.2	61.5	108.3	86.0	—	—	99.3	86.2	63.9	—
76.0	79.6	76.0	58.7	84.6	92.3	80.9	91.8	87.1	—	46.9	80.0	92.3	18.4	45.1	50.0	115.2	84.3	—	—	89.2	86.7	65.8	—
82.6	69.6	75.0	62.3	82.3	90.8	86.0	92.6	94.1	—	53.1	88.6	97.5	16.3	43.6	50.0	126.4	95.4	—	—	92.9	89.7	67.1	—
68.1	70.2	81.3	63.3	99.1	94.5	79.8	96.0	88.6	—	47.7	92.3	102.9	20.2	46.8	50.0	134.1	85.7	—	—	82.3	95.2	76.9	—
78.2	83.0	79.0	61.8	84.7	89.0	88.0	89.4	87.9	—	50.8	92.1	100.0	19.8	50.0	50.0	132.0	93.3	—	—	84.2	94.0	73.4	—
74.5	75.5	81.8	60.7	90.9	93.4	85.4	88.1	91.4	80.2	51.7	81.8	92.3	19.2	48.1	52.6	115.5	76.5	78.5	62.3	90.2	91.7	67.3	72.1
80.0	82.0	81.2	64.6	90.9	94.8	81.6	86.4	82.4	—	47.7	82.6	92.7	18.3	41.8	66.7	118.5	85.7	—	—	93.8	92.9	68.9	—
82.9	85.0	78.5	63.7	88.7	94.3	84.5	90.8	86.1	—	48.3	77.8	85.4	17.8	42.1	46.7	125.0	89.6	—	—	90.6	92.7	70.3	—
71.8	80.6	72.9	60.6	75.2	92.2	87.6	89.2	85.7	—	54.2	80.9	89.5	17.2	50.0	43.7	120.7	91.3	—	—	91.6	87.8	66.2	—
77.7	82.4	83.6	65.5	91.4	90.6	84.1	88.8	75.7	—	47.5	86.8	94.3	18.5	43.2	—	147.5	88.9	—	—	81.1	100.0	80.8	—
77.8	79.9	77.9	61.7	76.9	95.0	88.9	89.6	94.1	—	51.8	90.7	100.0	17.9	44.0	66.7	115.4	88.4	—	—	87.7	90.5	70.4	—
84.4	83.8	81.6	63.3	85.8	95.0	87.4	92.6	90.9	—	56.2	85.1	93.0	17.1	40.3	64.7	116.0	81.4	—	—	85.1	91.9	74.4	—
79.4	75.6	77.8	58.3	100.0	96.5	87.4	91.5	97.0	—	50.7	83.3	92.1	18.4	40.0	64.3	124.5	76.2	—	—	83.3	94.2	70.0	—
73.1	75.0	77.5	59.6	93.6	93.6	83.1	90.7	90.6	—	52.1	84.4	92.7	18.3	46.1	—	118.9	90.9	—	—	89.7	86.9	66.4	—
85.2	82.5	78.3	61.0	106.2	93.7	76.5	91.3	88.6	—	49.2	73.8	81.6	18.9	51.1	57.1	138.6	90.0	—	—	79.2	94.0	77.0	—
80.3	77.7	79.5	61.8	100.9	94.4	78.0	91.1	87.9	—	56.3	87.2	97.1	19.3	40.0	80.0	128.3	79.1	—	—	75.8	100.0	81.5	—
76.7	83.3	77.5	62.0	89.3	91.7	84.3	91.2	88.2	—	52.3	90.2	97.4	15.6	42.3	61.5	119.2	88.6	—	—	88.0	89.4	70.4	—
70.8	85.1	78.8	62.8	82.8	90.6	87.7	80.9	88.2	—	49.6	82.2	88.1	15.2	49.0	61.5	—	—	—	—	91.2	88.6	68.9	—
77.4	80.9	76.4	59.9	104.4	91.1	85.6	86.0	93.6	—	53.6	75.5	82.2	17.1	52.9	80.0	—	—	—	—	87.9	85.4	68.1	—
76.5	79.5	78.3	60.3	81.1	93.7	91.1	87.9	91.2	—	49.6	79.5	87.5	20.4	56.2	63.2	123.2	88.2	---	—	87.8	87.8	68.5	—
69.8	77.1	76.4	61.4	80.3	93.4	88.8	87.2	100.0	—	51.8	82.2	92.5	17.5	54.0	58.8	—	—	—	—	88.2	87.0	69.6	—
81.9	88.2	81.6	66.0	99.1	92.0	84.7	89.9	87.1	—	52.7	74.4	82.0	20.0	45.6	66.7	122.6	89.1	—	—	89.6	90.5	73.6	—
70.1	78.8	84.6	67.8	82.1	94.6	88.0	85.0	81.8	—	53.4	90.2	100.0	19.1	47.1	71.4	120.7	93.2	—	—	91.1	97.0	74.4	—
76.4	75.5	80.8	64.4	90.3	94.7	85.4	93.7	84.2	—	51.8	84.1	92.5	20.9	46.1	62.5	121.0	80.4	--	—	85.3	95.4	75.5	—
74.0	86.8	79.7	65.3	87.3	88.9	85.4	87.5	88.2	—	51.2	82.5	89.2	17.8	46.8	56.2	126.0	88.6	—	—	89.6	95.8	72.1	—
78.2	81.1	74.8	56.0	89.3	95.9	83.3	86.5	88.6	—	55.1	77.3	85.0	16.2	46.1	46.1	120.4	85.7	—	—	86.8	84.8	64.5	—
77.5	88.2	76.6	62.5	92.0	94.4	80.9	89.5	93.8	—	53.9	88.4	100.0	18.2	45.4	50.0	129.6	89.4	—	—	92.8	88.8	67.4	—

Tribal divisions and subdivisions / Catalogue No. / Sex and stages of life / Number of cases / Averages and ranges	"Central angle" (Klaatsch)	Cranio-facial (Fahlenberger)	Interoccipital	\multicolumn{11}{c	}{ANGLES}	Length-breadth
				Glabella-lambda	Basion-bregma	Nasion-basion	Basion-opisthion	Nasion bregma	Lambda-bregma	Opisthion-lambda	Prosthion-nasion	Nasospinale-nasion	Prosthion-nasospinale	Orbital height	Ramus tangent-alveolar plane	Ramus tangent-basal tangent	Chin vertical-basal tangent	Condylo-coronoid tangent-alveolar plane	
	(°)	(°)	(°)	(°)	(°)	(°)	(°)	(°)	(°)	(°)	(°)	(°)	(°)	(°)	(°)	(°)	(°)	(°)	
CHINOOK																			
4497 ♂ ad-mat	104	92	149	16	88	29	+12	43	18	113	86	88	77	88	—	—	—	—	95.3
4498 ♀? ad	101	94	134	8	93	33	−1	38	21	122	80	80	80	79	—	—	—··	—	95.8
4499 ♀ ad	100	93	142	12	88	28	−10	48	22	117	79	83	65	86	—	—	—	—	90.2
4500 ♀ ad	95	92	139	13	82	28	−4	49	23	114	79	81	65	89	—	—··	—	—	91.7
4501 ♂ mat	95	90	129	14	81	28	−1	53	28	107	80	78	82	91	—	—··	—	—	94.6
4502 ♀ mat	107	92	140	18	89	33	+1	43	10	110	72	76	56	85	—	—	—	—	87.9
4503 ♂ ad-mat	100	90	129	15	85	28	−3	49	19	110	83	81	85	87	—	—	—	—	94.5
4504 ♂ ad	100	92	134	15	85	25	−1	50	22	111	87	89	75	89	—	—	—	—	98.2
4505 ♂ ad-mat	100	97	142	10	90	28	+9	42	23	122	76	78	68	84	—	—	—	—	91.3
4506 ♂ mat	105	90	135	15	90	30	−3	45	28	114	81	81	81	89	—	—	—	—	93.3
4507 inf. II	108	93	139	19	89	28	+7	49	14	116	80	82	72	82	—	—	—	—	93.4
4508 ♀ mat	100	91	151	10	90	33	+4	45	29	121	73	73	73	83	—	—	—	—	95.0
4509 juv	97	95	142	17	80	24	0	49	12	110	82	84	71	87	—	—	—	—	97.3
4510 ♂ mat	—	—	—	—	—	—	—	—	—	—	—	—	—	—	—	—	—	—	94.1
4511 ♂ ad	96	83	129	12	84	28	−8	43	30	108	77	79	69	87	—	—	—	—	108.4
4512 ♂ mat	99	94	130	14	85	23	0	49	21	111	86	87	84	93	—	—	—	—	97.6
4513 ♂ mat	95	89	136	8	87	30	−4	47	32	112	83	83	83	92	—	—	—	—	97.5
4514 ♂ mat	96	92	139	15	81	28	+1	52	23	106	73	78	62	88	—	—	—	—	97.5
4515 ♂? mat	96	93	136	10	86	27	+5	48	27	117	83	83	83	85	—	—	—	—	95.1
4516 ♀ mat	97	90	132	11	86	30	+5	48	29	113	80	81	73	90	—	—	—	—	99.4
4517 ♂ ad-mat	96	93	133	11	85	28	+1	48	28	112	79	80	75	90	—	—	—	—	90.5
4518 ♂ ad	94	90	118	11	83	26	−2	49	27	114	86	89	73	97	—	—	—	—	84.1
4519 ♂ mat	104	91	143	12	92	35	+5	40	21	117	75	82	61	86	—	—	—	—	89.9
4520 ♂ mat	93	90	123	9	84	29	−12	51	30	119	81	84	71	94	—	—	—	—	86.9
4521 ♀ ad	96	91	139	13	83	27	−2	50	22	112	83	82	79	88	—	—	—	—	92.9
4522 ♀ ad	97	95	132	11	86	29	+3	45	22	118	71	76	59	80	—	—	—	—	93.1
4523 ♂ mat	102	94	147	10	92	32	+9	41	27	121	78	80	69	85	—	—	—	—	92.3
4524 inf. II	106	89	135	23	83	30	+4	55	11	107	78	79	73	87	—	—	—	—	101.3
4525 ♀ ad-mat	105	99	140	12	93	27	−3	39	20	121	77	78	72	85	—	—	—	—	93.4
4526 ♂ mat	98	94	138	13	85	27	+3	46	21	118	79	79	79	90	—	—	—	—	89.4
♂ cases	56	55	56	56	57	56	56	57	56	56	55	53	54	56	3	3	3	3	57
range	93–105	83–97	123–149	7–18	78–92	23–35	+14 to −15	40–55	13–33	105–130	73–87	74–89	61–88	78–100	64–73	116–125	79–82	−12 to −5	81.6–108.4
average	99.8	91.8	135.2	12.3	87.6	28.3	+0.5	46.3	23.6	114.1	80.7	83.9	75.8	88.2	68.7	120.0	80.7	−9.0	93.8
♀ cases	24	25	24	25	24	24	24	26	25	24	25	25	26	25	1	1	1	1	25
range	93–107	97–99	120–157	8–19	79–93	25–35	+7 to 10	38–53	10–29	102–123	71–86	73–88	56–83	79–97	—	—	—	—	83.1–102.7
average	99.2	92.3	137.1	12.0	87.2	29.2	−0.5	45.6	22.6	115.2	79.5	81.8	71.2	86.4	77.0	115.0	77.0	−8.0	93.2
juv. cases	4	4	4	4	4	4	4	4	4	4	4	4	3	4	—	—	—	—	4
range	97–100	90; 93	140–153	10–17	80–90	24–31	+8 to 0	45–55	12–15	110–118	73–83	74–84	66–80	77–88	—	—	—	—	88.9–103.4
average	98.5	91.5	146.8	14.0	84.5	28.3	+3.0	48.8	19.0	113.5	79.5	80.8	72.3	84.8	—	—	—	—	96.5

	INDICES																						
	Skull									Face and mandible											Cranio-facial			
Length-height	Breadth-height	Transverse frontal	Transverse frontoparietal	Sagittal parieto-frontal (arcs)	Sagittal frontal	Sagittal parietal	Sagittal occipital	Foramen magnum	Facial	Upper facial	Orbital (mf)	Orbital (la)	Interorbital (mf-mf to ek-ek)	Nasal	Transverse nasal bone	Maxillo-alveolar	Palatal	Bicondylo-bigonial breadth (mandible)	Ramus (mandible)	Transverse cranio-facial	Fronto-biorbital (ft-ft to fmt-fmt)	Jugo-frontal	Jugo-mandibular
74.7	78.4	86.5	67.3	79.0	93.5	83.7	90.3	80.0	—	51.0	80.8	90.5	18.5	44.6	87.5	138.5	102.2	—	—	93.2	95.6	72.2	—
69.7	73.2	77.5	59.2	87.5	94.6	87.8	88.5	85.3	—	50.0	87.8	94.7	18.9	42.9	57.1	137.0	100.0	—	—	85.3	90.3	69.4	—
77.1	85.5	78.9	62.3	86.0	92.1	88.8	91.8	86.7	—	51.2	82.9	91.9	15.4	42.5	50.0	122.4	92.9	—	—	89.1	89.6	69.9	—
77.1	84.0	82.2	67.4	97.2	93.6	84.9	88.6	87.1	—	51.2	90.0	97.3	18.9	38.5	53.8	129.8	88.6	—	—	89.6	97.0	75.2	—
87.3	92.4	78.5	65.0	90.6	92.2	87.1	88.5	97.2	—	53.1	81.4	92.1	23.1	47.4	61.1	119.8	87.8	—	—	93.6	91.9	69.4	—
73.5	83.6	73.7	59.6	80.9	95.4	89.9	89.1	88.9	—	—	90.7	100.0	17.2	47.3	—	—	—	—	—	—	84.5	—	—
77.8	82.0	79.0	62.8	86.3	94.9	87.1	87.0	82.9	—	54.7	79.5	87.5	18.0	44.2	43.7	125.5	86.4	—	—	87.8	91.6	71.5	—
77.9	79.4	78.0	60.0	87.5	95.8	82.9	91.1	94.1	—	53.0	83.3	94.6	18.7	40.0	72.7	131.4	100.0	—	—	83.7	93.2	71.6	—
71.5	78.3	78.4	62.4	83.9	93.5	85.6	89.7	96.8	—	53.1	90.5	97.4	20.2	47.4	60.0	119.0	93.9	—	—	92.4	90.7	67.6	—
80.5	86.3	79.3	62.7	71.9	92.2	90.2	89.1	90.6	—	50.7	84.1	94.9	15.5	41.5	58.3	126.9	87.2	—	—	91.5	93.2	68.6	—
71.7	76.8	77.5	60.0	78.0	92.4	88.3	82.4	—	—	52.5	89.7	97.2	18.7	48.8	41.2	142.8	92.1	—	—	76.1	98.9	78.8	—
80.6	84.9	77.0	63.8	94.9	94.1	80.4	93.2	87.1	—	53.7	90.2	97.4	18.9	44.4	41.2	115.1	88.9	—	—	88.2	94.2	72.4	—
72.5	74.5	79.6	62.1	89.3	93.2	87.0	91.3	90.0	—	54.5	86.5	97.0	20.7	47.7	56.2	131.8	87.8	—	—	77.2	96.8	80.4	—
—	—	79.5	60.2	91.7	94.2	84.5	—	—	—	—	—	—	—	—	—	—	—	—	—	—	91.5	—	—
83.9	77.4	78.2	61.9	91.4	94.0	83.2	89.3	94.4	—	47.3	79.5	89.7	21.6	45.3	73.3	125.0	95.7	—	—	88.1	94.5	70.3	—
72.9	74.7	76.2	57.8	77.9	91.8	87.4	85.2	80.0	—	52.4	80.4	90.2	19.4	41.8	55.6	119.2	86.4	—	—	87.3	88.9	66.2	—
82.6	84.7	80.3	65.0	95.0	94.2	79.8	88.3	94.3	—	53.1	86.4	95.0	19.6	43.6	53.3	—	53.3	—	—	91.1	91.1	71.3	—
87.3	89.6	78.5	61.7	91.5	94.1	85.2	90.3	84.4	—	51.8	84.1	90.2	15.8	44.9	62.5	113.6	88.0	—	—	89.0	88.8	69.3	—
75.8	79.6	80.3	65.0	97.5	94.9	80.0	89.3	93.3	—	46.8	85.4	94.6	21.4	47.1	61.5	124.0	90.9	—	—	92.4	95.3	70.3	—
84.8	85.3	81.7	62.4	81.4	91.1	89.1	89.4	90.9	—	51.8	79.5	89.7	16.3	51.0	50.0	110.9	72.5	—	—	88.5	95.1	70.5	—
82.8	91.5	83.3	65.4	88.4	93.0	86.0	89.9	85.6	—	50.0	84.4	95.0	17.5	45.3	58.8	117.2	92.0	—	—	94.0	90.1	69.4	—
75.3	89.5	78.9	66.0	88.7	91.0	87.3	81.0	88.9	—	53.1	78.3	85.7	15.5	45.0	53.3	121.4	91.8	—	—	96.1	92.0	68.7	—
73.7	82.0	73.8	59.6	85.2	96.6	87.5	92.3	80.5	—	55.1	83.3	93.0	17.6	43.1	62.5	—	—	—	—	91.3	85.0	65.3	—
77.8	89.5	78.8	61.4	106.6	93.5	85.4	81.7	83.3	—	50.0	79.5	87.5	18.4	48.1	40.0	123.6	93.9	—	—	94.1	87.8	65.3	—
77.9	83.9	80.9	62.2	99.1	93.6	81.6	91.1	84.4	—	56.8	87.8	94.7	18.3	42.3	53.3	121.6	86.4	—	—	87.4	88.1	71.2	—
75.0	80.5	84.1	63.8	93.6	95.4	86.4	87.8	84.9	—	52.5	86.4	95.0	18.2	44.9	60.0	113.8	80.8	—	—	93.3	88.8	68.3	—
78.6	85.2	78.4	63.2	77.5	93.0	87.0	90.9	90.3	—	53.6	90.9	100.0	17.2	46.3	43.7	117.9	85.7	—	—	89.0	92.4	71.0	—
82.1	81.0	80.5	62.1	84.1	94.4	90.0	89.5	93.3	—	51.3	89.5	97.1	19.3	47.7	66.7	137.2	89.7	—	—	76.5	101.1	81.2	—
67.5	72.3	80.3	60.6	76.3	94.1	90.0	90.1	83.9	—	51.8	92.3	102.9	21.0	46.1	43.7	125.5	102.3	—	—	87.1	92.1	69.6	—
73.5	82.2	79.5	61.2	89.0	93.2	89.5	89.4	84.4	—	52.2	83.7	92.3	16.7	41.8	61.5	132.7	93.5	—	—	90.8	89.4	67.4	—
56	56	57	57	58	57	56	56	47	4	55	56	56	58	56	51	50	3	3	56	58	56	3
69.8–	69.9–	72.9–	56.0–	71.9–	89.0–	77.1–	80.4–	73.7–	80.3–	46.8–	73.3–	82.2–	15.3–	36.2–	25.0–	105.2–	76.2–	77.7–	60.7–	81.3–	84.5–	63.9–	68.7–
87.3	92.4	86.5	67.8	106.6	96.6	91.1	93.9	100.0	89.6	57.6	92.9	102.6	23.1	58.0	87.5	138.5	104.4	82.1	62.7	99.3	97.0	75.5	74.8
77.4	82.5	78.1	62.0	88.6	93.2	85.5	88.5	88.7	84.5	52.0	83.6	91.4	18.4	45.5	57.5	126.0	90.4	79.4	61.9	90.6	90.0	68.5	71.9
24	24	25	25	26	26	26	25	25	—	24	25	25	25	25	21	23	23	1	1	24	25	24	1
62.2–	65.4–	73.7–	57.4–	75.6–	88.9–	79.8–	80.9–	83.9–	—	47.7–	74.4–	82.0–	15.2–	41.2–	110.9–	72.5–	—	—	—	82.3–	84.5–	65.4–	—
84.8	92.7	84.1	67.4	99.1	95.4	91.5	96.0	100.0	—	56.8	92.3	102.9	21.0	56.8	72.7	141.7	102.4	—	—	99.3	97.0	76.9	—
75.6	81.2	78.8	61.9	87.2	93.0	86.9	88.9	88.2	—	25.2	86.4	94.6	18.0	45.9	56.6	124.3	90.9	88.1	71.2	89.1	91.0	71.0	74.8
4	4	4	4	4	4	4	4	4	—	4	4	4	4	4	4	4	4	—	—	4	4	4	—
72.2–	74.5–	77.7–	61.0–	89.3–	92.7–	76.5–	88.2–	82.4–	—	49.2–	73.8–	81.6–	16.8–	47.7–	53.3–	125.0–	80.9–	—	—	79.2–	92.5–	72.5–	—
85.2	82.5	82.3	64.5	106.2	93.7	88.6	93.6	90.0	—	54.5	92.5	102.8	21.0	51.1	57.1	153.5	95.0	—	—	84.5	98.0	80.4	—
76.9	79.6	79.5	62.1	94.3	93.2	84.0	90.8	86.0	—	52.5	84.9	94.3	19.5	48.7	55.3	136.8	88.4	—	—	83.2	95.5	76.8	—

Tribal divisions and subdivisions / Catalogue No. / Sex and stages of life / Number of cases / Averages and ranges	"Central angle" (Klaatsch)	Cranio-facial (Falkenburger)	Interoccipital	ANGLES											Mandibulo-alveolar plane				Length-breadth
				To ear-eye plane															
				Glabella-lambda	Basion-bregma	Nasion-basion	Basion-opisthion	Nasion-bregma	Lambda-bregma	Opisthion-lambda	Prosthion-nasion	Nasospinale-nasion	Prosthion-nasospinale	Orbital height	Ramus tangent-alveolar plane	Ramus tangent-basal tangent	Chin vertical-basal tangent	Condylo-coronoid tangent-alveolar plane	
	(°)	(°)	(°)	(°)	(°)	(°)	(°)	(°)	(°)	(°)	(°)	(°)	(°)	(°)	(°)	(°)	(°)	(°)	
CHINOOK																			
inf. cases	5	4	6	6	5	5	5	6	6	6	5	5	5	6	—	—	—	—	6
range	94–108	88–93	135–174	6–23	83–89	27–31	+7 to +4	48–55	12–27	107–133	77–83	79–84	67–77	82–92					93.4–103.3
average	101.0	90.0	144.3	14.5	86.0	29.2	+5.2	51.2	21.3	117.0	79.8	81.4	72.4	88.0					97.4
Coupeville																			
2676 ♂ mat (def)	104	95	148	15	89	27	+7	45	21	118	81	81	81	84	68	118	83	–1	83.8
♂ 1 case	104.0	95.0	148.0	15.0	89.0	27.0	+7.0	45.0	21.0	118.0	81.0	81.0	81.0	84.0	68.0	118.0	83.0	–1.0	83.8
Divisional total																			
♂ cases	57	56	57	57	58	57	57	58	57	57	55	54	55	57	4	4	4	4	58
range	93–105	83–97	123–149	7–18	78–92	23–35	+14 to –15	40–55	13–33	105–130	73–87	74–89	61–88	78–100	64–73	116–125	79–83	–12 to –1	81.6–108.4
average	99.9	91.8	135.4	12.4	87.6	28.2	+0.6	46.2	23.6	114.2	80.7	83.8	75.9	88.1	68.5	119.5	81.2	–7.0	92.1
♀ cases	24	25	24	24	24	24	24	26	25	24	25	25	26	25	1	1	1	1	25
range	93–107	87–99	120–157	8–19	79–93	25–35	+7 to –10	38–53	10–29	102–123	71–86	73–88	56–83	79–97					83.1–102.7
average	99.2	92.3	137.1	12.0	87.2	29.2	–0.5	45.6	22.6	115.2	79.5	81.8	71.2	86.8	77.0	115.0	77.0	–8.0	93.2
juv. cases	4	2	4	4	4	4	4	4	5	4	4	4	3	4					4
range	97–100	90;93	140;153	10–17	80–90	24–31	+8 to 0	45–55	12–25	110–118	73–83	74–84	66–80	77–88					89.9–103.4
average	98.5	91.5	146.8	14.0	84.5	28.3	+3.0	48.8	19.5	113.5	79.5	80.8	72.3	84.8					96.5
inf. cases	5	4	6	6	5	5	5	6	6	6	5	5	5	6	—	—	—	—	6
range	94–108	88–93	135–174	6–23	83–89	27–31	+7 to +4	48–55	12–27	107–133	77–83	79–84	67–77	82–92					93.4–103.3
average	101.0	90.0	144.3	14.5	86.0	29.2	+5.2	51.2	21.3	117.0	79.8	81.4	72.4	88.0					97.5
KOSKIMO																			
Kwakiutl																			
101 ♀ mat	92	92	123	6	86	29	–15	46	29	125	79	80	75	84	69	121	78	–9	74.3
103 ♂ ad-mat	102	90	123	16	86	29	+3	47	13	113	82	86	71	91	77	112	79	–12	69.2
1715 ♂ ? ad	91	93	130	5	86	28	–7	46	30	120	78	78	78	83	79	109	80	–8	79.5
1716 ♂ ad	91	87	130	6	85	32	–3	48	28	122	82	84	75	88	80	111	78	–6	78.2
1717 ♂ mat	99	87	129	9	90	34	–2	46	26	124	81	83	75	87	70	117	80	–8	81.0
1718 ♂ ? ad-mat	95	91	134	6	89	30	+6	45	27	131	78	80	72	86	—	—	—	—	75.7
1719 ♂ mat	98	89	134	1	87	30	–1	46	25	122	85	88	77	97	—	—	—	—	75.4
1720 ♀ mat	95	86	144	4	91	36	–3	44	21	129	81	82	78	89	69	120	80	–7	74.0
1723 ♂ ad-mat	98	89	111	8	90	31	+4	46	28	124	84	86	77	89	—	—	—	—	78.6
1724 juv	93	86	134	7	86	30	–1	49	33	121	86	89	79	95	—	—	—	—	84.9
1725 ♂ mat	96	91	128	4	92	33	+5	41	29	130	79	80	71	82	—	—	—	—	78.9
1726 ♂ ad-mat	93	92	121	4	89	33	+1	39	28	126	79	81	73	89	—	—	—	—	80.8
1729 ♂ ad-mat	101	90	122	9	92	34	0	44	27	122	78	78	78	85	83	104	82	–24	77.4
1730 ♂ ? mat	94	91	125	2	92	35	–8	39	33	128	74	78	62	90	73	119	77	–7	74.0
1731 ♀ juv-ad	98	94	137	9	89	29	–8	44	26	123	80	82	73	87	—	—	—	—	84.8

	INDICES																				
	Skull								Face and mandible										Cranio-facial			
Length-height	Breadth-height	Transverse frontal	Transverse frontoparietal	Sagittal parieto-frontal (arcs)	Sagittal frontal	Sagittal parietal	Sagittal occipital	Foramen magnum	Facial	Upper facial	Orbital (mf)	Orbital (la)	Interorbital (mf-mf to ek-ek)	Nasal	Transverse nasal bone	Maxillo-alveolar	Palatal	Bicondylo-bigonial breadth (mandible)	Ramus (mandible)	Transverse cranio-facial	Fronto-biorbital (ft-ft to fmt-fmt)	Jugo-frontal	Jugo-mandibular
5	5	6	6	6	6	6	6	5	—	6	6	6	6	5	5	6	5	—	—	6	6	6	—
66.7–	66.7–	77.5–	59.0–	78.0–	90.6–	78.0–	85.9–	75.7–		47.5–	86.1–	94.3	18.1–	40.0–	38.5–	128.3–	79.1–			73.9–	97.9–	78.8–	
82.1	82.1	83.6	66.9	100.9	94.4	92.4	91.1	93.3		56.3	92.3	100.0	19.3	48.8	80.3	155.3	105.6			81.1	101.1	81.5	
75.7	75.1	79.3	62.6	89.2	92.7	86.6	88.3	83.6		51.4	88.6	96.8	18.8	45.1	56.0	143.3	92.1			76.3	99.7	80.5	
73.7	88.0	83.2	66.0	86.6	96.1	82.7	93.8	85.3	85.2	49.7	78.7	88.1	15.5	46.4	42.9		—	81.8	53.7	99.3	89.2	66.4	72.5
73.7	88.0	83.2	66.0	86.6	96.1	82.7	93.8	85.3	85.2	49.7	78.7	88.1	15.5	46.4	42.9		—	81.8	53.7	99.3	89.2	66.4	72.5
57	57	58	58	59	58	58	57	57	5	56	57	57	58	57	57	51	50	4	4	57	59	57	4
69.8–	69.9–	72.9–	56.0–	71.9–	89.0–	77.1–	80.4–	73.7–	80.3–	46.8–	73.3–	82.2–	15.3–	36.2–	25.0–	105.2–	76.2–	77.7–	58.1–	81.3–	84.5–	63.9–	68.7–
87.3	92.4	86.5	67.8	106.6	96.6	91.1	93.9	100.0	89.6	57.6	92.9	102.6	23.1	58.0	87.5	138.5	104.4	82.1	62.7	99.3	97.0	75.5	74.8
77.3	82.5	78.7	62.1	88.6	93.2	85.5	88.6	89.1	84.5	52.0	83.8	91.7	18.4	45.5	57.5	126.4	90.4	79.1	61.0	90.8	90.0	68.4	71.9
24	24	25	26	26	26	26	25	24		25	25	25	25	25	21	23	23	1	1	24	25	24	1
62.2–	65.4–	73.7–	57.4–	75.6–	88.9–	79.8–	80.9–	83.9–		47.7–	74.4–	82.0–	15.2–	38.5–	41.2–	110.9–	72.5–			82.3–	84.5–	65.4–	
84.8	92.7	84.1	67.4	99.1	95.4	91.5	96.0	100.0		56.8	92.3	102.9	21.0	56.8	72.7	141.7	102.4			99.3	97.0	76.9	
75.6	81.2	79.3	62.7	87.2	93.0	86.9	88.9	88.7		52.2	86.4	95.0	18.0	45.9	56.6	124.7	90 6	88.1	71.2	88.6	91.0	71 0	74.8
4	4	4	4	4	4	4	4	4		4	4	4	4	4	3	4	4			4	4	4	
72.2–	74.5–	77.7–	61.0–	89.3–	92.7–	76.5–	88.2–	82.4–		49.2–	73.8–	81.6–	16.8–	47.7–	53.3–	125.0–	80.9–			79.2–	92.5–	72.5–	
85.2	82.5	82.3	64.5	108 2	93.7	88.6	93.6	90.0		54.3	92 5	102.8	21.0	51.1	57.1	153.5	95.0			84.5	98.0	80.4	
76 9	79.6	79.5	63.3	94.3	93.2	84.0	90.9	86.5		52.5	84.9	94.6	19.5	48.9	55.3	137.2	88 4			80.9	95.5	76.8	—
5	5	6	6	6	6	6	6	5	—	6	6	6	6	5	5	6	5	—	—	6	6	6	—
66.7–	68.3–	77.5–	59.0–	78.0–	90.6–	78.0–	85.9–	75.7–		47.5–	86.1–	94.3–	18.1–	40.0–	38.5–	128.3–	79.1–			73.9–	97.9–	78.8–	
82.1	82.4	83.6	66.9	100.9	94.4	92.4	91.1	93.3		56.3	92.3	100.0	19.3	48.8	80.0	155.3	105.6			81.1	100.1	81.5	
75.7	77.2	79.7	62.6	89.2	92.7	86.6	88.9	84.2		51.4	88.6	97.1	18.8	45.6	56.0	143.7	92.1			76.3	99.7	80.5	—
69.8	94.0	78.4	65.4	97.6	88.7	88.4	83.2	90.0	94.4	59.2	86.0	94.9	16.3	46.9	37.5	121.1	82.6	92.7	56.9	94.0	84.5	69.6	80.8
70.7	102.2	90.5	76.6	81.3	91.0	91.7	84.5	84.6	90.8	54.9	82.2	90.2	20.0	39.3	64.3	122.8	93.7	90.6	53.4	103.6	92.9	73.9	81.7
72.5	91.2	86.0	72.1	92.7	89.4	87.7	84.9	82.9	88.1	54.1	81.8	90.0	18.0	47.9	47.1	110.7	73.1	82.2	61.5	99.3	89.9	72.6	71.8
77.1	98.6	79.8	67.9	102.4	91.9	86 6	86.7	84.4	81.9	53.5	77.5	88.4	14.4	40.0	38.5	120.0	91.3	87.3	60.0	102.8	85.6	65.9	71.5
73.9	91.3	78.1	62.4	95.3	90.5	88.4	84.7	88.2	97.9	57.0	84.4	92.7	19.0	46.1	52.9	114.5	79.6	81.4	54.7	95.3	84.5	65.5	73.9
68.5	95.9	85.0	70.1	108.4	91.1	82.8	88.9	87.9	—	63.8	93.0	105.3	17.2	44.4	43.8	120.0	87.8	—	—	94.9	89.7	73.8	—
72.8	96.5	82.3	68.1	88.8	91.0	91.6	85.9	76.5	—	54.2	76.6	83.7	15.4	50.9	47.1	122.6	91.3	—	—	100.0	87.5	68.1	—
72.9	98.5	83.0	73.1	110.7	90.2	81.5	91.6	96.8	94.7	58.3	91.3	100.0	14.7	43.4	38.5	123.5	86.9	88.5	54.0	98.5	90.7	74.2	75.8
73.8	93.9	80.5	64.6	84.6	89.0	91.3	77.8	90.3	—	57.7	88.6	97.5	18.8	44.4	58.8	130.8	85.4	—	—	93.2	87.2	69.3	—
79.5	93.6	83.8	69.5	95.3	88.3	86.1	87.1	90.9	—	54.4	85.4	94.6	16.8	46.9	37.5	142.2	100.0	—	—	84.4	97.0	78.4	—
69.2	87.1	79.5	66.4	100.0	85.5	85.0	88.6	—	—	58.0	84.4	95.0	18.4	38.3	50.0	127.3	95.7	—	—	97.9	88.2	67.8	—
68.8	92.6	83.0	68.4	96.8	90.3	88.3	81.7	85.7	—	53.6	82.2	92.5	18.4	48.1	50.0	115.1	81.6	—	—	101.5	83.0	67.4	—
72.6	93.7	82.2	67.4	85.1	99.2	87.4	86.1	85.0	88.8	56.6	79.2	88.4	16.2	44.8	25 0	113.8	78.8	95.1	54.1	99.3	87.4	67.8	81.8
70.7	95.5	82.4	66.4	96.8	91.9	87.4	84.8	80.6	89.7	58.1	84.4	95.0	16.8	45.4	68.8	103.5	76.0	79.2	61.9	101.5	83.9	65.4	72.8
70.8	83.4	85.6	65.5	95.0	91.6	86.7	88.3	74.3	—	51.2	85.7	94.7	19.2	50.0	71.4	137.8	102.5	—	—	86.2	92.2	76.0	88.8

Tribal divisions and subdivisions	"Central angle" (*Klaatsch*)	Cranio-facial (*Falkenberger*)	Interoccipital	ANGLES											Mandibulo-alveolar plane				Length-breadth
Catalogue No.				To ear-eye plane															
Sex and stages of life				Glabella-lambda	Basion-bregma	Nasion-basion	Basion-opisthion	Nasion-bregma	Lambda-bregma	Opisthion-lambda	Prosthion-nasion	Nasospinale-nasion	Prosthion-nasospinale	Orbital height	Ramus tangent-alveolar plane	Ramus tangent-basal tangent	Chin vertical-basal tangent	Condylo-coronoid tangent-alveolar plane	
Number of cases																			
Averages and ranges																			
KOSKIMO	(°)	(°)	(°)	(°)	(°)	(°)	(°)	(°)	(°)	(°)	(°)	(°)	(°)	(°)	(°)	(°)	(°)	(°)	
1731 A ♂ ad	—	—	—	—	—	—	—	—	—	—	—	—	—	—	74	112	82	−8	—
1732 ♂ ad	93	87	133	3	90	34	+6	44	32	125	84	84	84	89	—	—	—	—	89.1
1732 (r) ♂ ad	—	—	—	—	—	—	—	—	—	—	—	—	—	—	74	113	81	−9	—
1736 ♂ mat	95	89	106	10	85	28	−2	48	25	119	88	89	84	91	—	—	—	—	73.9
1737 ♂ mat	95	88	136	5	90	36	−2	43	27	124	78	80	71	85	—	—	—	—	75.4
1738 inf. II	99	80	121	18	82	30	−7	58	20	112	86	85	88	92	—	—	—	—	90.8
1739 ♂ mat	99	89	118	9	90	31	−3	45	26	121	88	92	77	92	—	—	—	—	76.3
1739 A ♂ mat	—	—	—	—	—	—	—	—	—	—	—	—	—	—	75	112	83	−9	—
1740 ♂ ad-mat	104	96	119	12	92	24	−5	45	23	124	86	87	82	88	81	104	82	+5	78.6
1742 ♂ mat	94	92	121	7	87	30	+4	44	26	121	79	80	75	91	74	116	79	−3	73.7
1744 ♀ mat	94	94	132	11	83	25	−13	49	24	118	81	85	72	88	76	110	83	−16	76.6
1911 ♀ mat	92	91	138	6	86	30	−4	48	24	121	79	80	75	86	—	—	—	—	74.3
1912 ♂? ad	93	90	134	6	87	32	+2	46	28	120	75	77	70	86	—	—	—	—	82.2
1913 ♂ mat	95	90	143	6	89	32	−1	44	28	123	80	83	68	87	—	—	—	—	74.7
3878 ♂ ad	98	91	126	7	91	31	−4	44	26	121	79	82	69	82	—	—	—	—	74.9
3879 ♂ ad-mat	94	93	134	7	87	27	+6	46	25	128	85	86	79	91	—	—	—	—	71.6
3880 ♂ mat	92	86	121	4	88	31	−10	50	33	125	84	86	78	90	—	—	—	—	79.7
3881 ♀? mat	93	88	128	9	84	28	−1	51	27	120	85	87	78	89	—	—	—	—	78.3
3882 ♂ ad	94	90	129	9	85	30	+1	50	26	118	79	83	67	90	—	—	—	—	81.5
3883 ♂ ad	98	89	124	10	88	31	+3	47	30	123	83	86	73	88	—	—	—	—	82.3
3884 ♂ mat	97	92	126	0	97	36	0	38	39	134	76	80	68	85	—	—	—	—	73.8
3885 ♂ mat	93	88	136	6	87	32	−5	46	28	126	83	83	83	90	—	—	—	—	76.4
3886 ♂ ad-mat	98	93	130	8	86	27	+3	46	20	117	82	84	79	92	—	—	—	—	74.7
3887 ♂? ad	93	93	128	6	87	28	−2	45	29	124	81	81	81	79	—	—	—	—	75.8
3888 ♀ ad	—	—	—	—	—	—	—	—	—	—	—	—	—	—	—	—	—	—	77.8
3889 ♀ ad	—	—	—	—	—	—	—	—	—	—	—	—	—	—	—	—	—	—	76.0
3890 ♂ mat	98	89	115	10	88	33	+5	42	18	119	83	84	78	87	—	—	—	—	73.5
3891 ♀ ad-mat	98	93	129	10	88	29	+7	44	26	122	83	86	74	86	—	—	—	—	73.1
3892 ♀ mat	98	90	128	10	88	28	−7	47	23	119	86	89	78	90	—	—	—	—	75.1
3893 ♂ ad	97	90	140	9	88	33	+4	44	23	124	79	79	79	83	—	—	—	—	75.0
3894 ♂ ad	91	91	122	5	86	29	+3	47	32	121	82	82	82	95	—	—	—	—	80.8
3895 ♂? mat	95	90	124	13	82	28	+1	49	17	119	83	93	62	90	—	—	—	—	74.9
3896 ♂ ad	95	86	126	10	85	33	+9	48	25	116	82	82	82	86	—	—	—	—	79.6
3899 ♂? mat	—	—	—	—	—	—	—	—	—	—	—	—	—	—	79	107	81	−5	—
3900 ♂ mat	—	—	—	—	—	—	—	—	—	—	—	—	—	—	67	115	86	−7	—
4236 ♂ ad-mat	93	90	112	4	89	32	−3	43	30	127	85	86	77	91	—	—	—	—	73.5
4237 ♀ mat	100	90	128	10	90	31	0	44	22	122	84	87	75	85	—	—	—	—	75.0
4238 ♀ ad	95	90	130	11	84	29	−3	47	24	119	83	86	74	89	—	—	—	—	74.2
4239 ♂ mat	97	90	124	8	89	32	+9	44	28	125	80	81	75	87	—	—	—	—	75.8
4240 ♀? mat	95	90	122	7	88	30	+5	46	29	128	80	81	75	86	—	—	—	—	76.7
4241 ♀ ad	95	92	125	6	89	32	−7	43	27	121	76	79	69	80	—	—	—	—	81.1

INDICES

	Skull									Face and mandible												Cranio-facial			
Length-height	Breadth-height	Transverse frontal	Transverse frontoparietal	Sagittal parieto-frontal (arcs)	Sagittal frontal	Sagittal parietal	Sagittal occipital	Foramen magnum	Facial	Upper facial	Orbital (mf)	Orbital (la)	Interorbital (mf-mf to ek-ek)	Nasal	Transverse nasal bone	Maxillo-alveolar	Palatal	Bicondylo-bigonial breadth (mandible)	Ramus (mandible)	Transverse cranio-facial	Fronto-biorbital (ft-ft to fmt-fmt)	Jugo-frontal	Jugo-mandibular
76.4	85.8	79.0	60.6	97.6	92.7	87.5	88.1	86.1	93.7	57.7	93.0	102.6	18.4	37.9	58.3	128.8	88.9	88.1	62.7	91.6	91.3	66.2	80.3
—	—	—	—	—	—	—	—	—	—	—	—	—	—	—	—	—	—	94.2	68.3	—	—	—	—
70.2	95.0	84.6	71.2	88.7	87.9	88.0	73.6	82.3	—	55.5	78.7	88.1	18.1	51.9	50.0	128.8	91.3	—	—	103.6	88.4	68.7	—
75.4	100.0	75.8	67.4	96.8	91.1	86.7	87.5	79.4	—	56.9	84.8	95.1	16.3	44.6	52.9	117.9	89.4	—	—	101.5	83.5	66.4	—
83.0	91.4	80.9	64.7	93.8	89.3	89.5	83.3	79.4	—	54.5	89.7	102.9	15.1	47.6	50.0	148.6	94.3	—	—	79.1	98.9	81.8	—
71.6	93.8	79.5	64.1	88.8	89.5	88.2	79.2	83.3	—	53.3	86.4	95.0	14.9	38.5	38.5	116.3	90.2	—	—	94.5	90.3	67.9	70.1
—	—	—	—	—	—	—	—	—	—	—	—	—	—	—	—	—	—	83.5	66.7	—	—	—	—
70.9	90.2	82.5	65.7	76.3	90.6	92.4	81.6	93.7	92.5	57.5	80.0	90.0	16.2	41.5	46.7	126.9	95.4	80.7	55.1	93.7	87.8	70.1	65.7
71.0	96.3	72.8	75.2	90.6	90.5	88.7	81.0	75.7	86.1	53.5	84.8	92.9	17.1	46.4	64.7	117.5	84.3	93.9	65.0	105.1	92.8	71.5	74.3
73.7	96.3	84.2	71.6	91.4	89.8	87.2	87.4	100.0	88.9	55.1	83.7	92.3	19.0	54.2	52.9	113.5	84.4	88.3	68.3	94.8	90.6	75.6	77.2
72.6	97.7	83.6	66.9	108.0	92.0	86.9	98.2	91.4	—	—	92.9	100.0	20.0	43.4	52.9	119.2	66.7	—	—	—	—	—	—
77.6	94.4	78.8	62.2	99.2	91.8	80.8	88.2	89.2	—	60.3	88.6	100.0	15.5	41.4	35.7	117.5	82.3	—	—	91.6	86.4	67.9	—
72.5	97.1	83.8	68.4	95.4	91.5	84.7	90.3	91.2	—	54.2	82.2	90.2	18.4	48.1	58.8	120.0	91.7	—	—	96.3	90.3	70.9	—
72.2	96.4	83.8	70.0	87.2	90.2	89.7	83.1	78.9	—	54.7	88.9	100.0	18.4	48.1	53.3	132.7	97.9	—	—	97.9	89.9	71.5	—
66.0	92.2	81.5	68.8	98.5	88.1	89.4	93.2	88.2	—	55.6	88.9	97.6	17.5	42.9	41.2	114.8	87.2	—	—	100.7	88.9	68.3	—
77.5	97.2	84.9	69.7	101.0	88.7	88.1	80.0	85.7	—	53.4	84.4	95.0	16.0	49.1	41.2	121.1	93.0	—	—	100.7	93.5	69.2	—
77.1	98.5	79.8	66.4	101.0	91.1	87.2	85.1	84.8	—	53.5	81.8	90.0	18.4	49.1	62.5	123.1	97.8	—	—	103.6	84.3	64.1	—
76.6	94.0	83.0	65.3	94.0	92.0	89.7	84.4	84.6	—	51.0	86.0	97.4	20.8	45.1	62.5	121.0	86.3	—	—	96.0	88.3	67.6	—
77.3	94.0	83.8	65.8	89.5	91.0	89.1	84.2	93.9	—	55.2	88.1	94.9	20.4	51.1	55.6	123.5	84.4	—	—	89.9	93.3	73.1	—
73.3	99.3	85.2	71.0	84.3	88.2	87.6	83.2	79.4	—	58.0	81.8	90.0	—	—	—	108.9	83.3	—	—	94.9	—	74.8	—
72.5	95.0	86.2	71.9	100.0	89.0	86.6	88.7	93.9	—	56.2	88.9	100.0	18.6	44.6	43.8	118.9	91.1	—	—	98.6	92.6	72.9	—
71.4	95.6	86.9	68.4	85.3	89.9	88.2	85.4	80.6	—	60.9	87.8	94.7	20.4	44.2	60.0	120.0	93.5	—	—	94.1	88.6	72.7	—
72.5	92.8	83.6	68.1	97.6	92.0	86.9	85.4	90.9	—	58.6	86.0	94.9	15.8	42.0	25.0	114.3	83.3	—	—	94.8	89.3	71.9	—
—	—	83.2	68.5	101.7	92.9	85.8	—	—	—	—	92.3	102.9	20.2	44.7	—	117.0	78.6	—	—	88.5	94.7	77.4	—
—	—	86.9	69.9	103.2	90.5	84.6	—	—	—	—	—	—	—	—	—	—	—	—	—	—	—	—	—
69.8	95.0	82.0	65.5	91.7	93.3	91.8	77.6	103.1	—	58.6	79.2	88.4	17.1	37.9	42.9	120.7	93.5	—	—	104.3	81.9	62.8	—
72.6	99.2	89.0	75.8	86.4	91.2	88.0	86.5	80.0	—	59.4	82.6	95.0	16.7	40.4	53.3	111.5	76.1	—	—	100.0	87.4	75.8	—
72.8	96.8	83.5	68.5	96.6	89.9	84.3	83.8	—	—	60.0	85.7	100.0	16.8	40.8	40.0	—	—	—	—	94.5	87.9	72.5	—
72.8	97.2	81.5	68.8	96.9	90.0	84.9	89.3	85.7	—	52.4	90.2	97.4	21.4	38.9	46.7	118.2	83.7	—	—	100.4	90.6	67.8	—
75.7	93.7	78.3	62.9	91.0	88.0	86.8	81.5	77.1	—	55.8	81.4	92.1	20.4	45.1	53.3	116.9	87.5	—	—	96.5	85.7	65.2	—
70.0	93.6	79.8	62.1	103.4	91.5	89.3	84.1	91.2	—	58.0	88.1	94.9	19.8	48.1	50.0	122.0	86.9	—	—	93.6	87.0	66.4	—
79.0	99.3	82.1	68.2	93.8	92.2	90.0	85.1	80.0	—	54.4	89.1	97.6	18.4	41.4	46.7	124.6	95.8	—	—	100.7	91.8	67.8	—
—	—	—	—	—	—	—	—	—	—	—	—	—	—	—	—	—	—	81.6	65.0	—	—	—	—
—	—	—	—	—	—	—	—	—	—	—	—	—	—	—	—	—	—	—	61.7	—	—	—	—
69.8	95.0	85.6	72.7	96.2	89.2	86.4	78.4	84.8	—	54.5	85.1	100.0	19.2	44.8	58.8	114.5	77.1	—	—	102.9	90.2	70.6	—
72.2	96.3	82.3	68.9	86.5	92.1	90.8	85.8	78.1	—	56.5	86.4	97.4	16.3	42.6	50.0	118.4	75.9	—	—	96.3	88.6	71.5	—
74.2	100.0	79.1	70.2	99.1	92.1	85.0	86.0	90.0	—	53.5	87.8	97.3	18.9	48.0	47.1	131.2	95.2	—	—	104.0	87.9	67.4	—
75.3	99.3	82.9	66.7	90.2	92.0	88.2	84.3	85.3	—	52.8	83.7	94.7	16.3	40.3	37.5	116.9	84.0	—	—	101.4	86.6	65.7	—
73.3	96.3	—	66.4	96.9	88.5	85.7	91.5	90.0	—	57.7	92.5	97.4	20.4	47.2	—	116.4	82.9	—	—	94.9	89.2	70.0	—
72.8	89.8	87.2	69.3	85.8	90.0	91.3	84.5	93.7	—	58.3	90.2	100.0	18.9	44.2	53.3	120.0	82.9	—	—	92.7	90.5	74.8	—

Tribal divisions and subdivisions / Catalogue No. / Sex and stages of life / Number of cases / Averages and ranges	"Central angle" (Klaatsch) (°)	Cranio-facial (Fulenburger) (°)	Interoccipital (°)	ANGLES To ear-eye plane										Mandibulo-alveolar plane				Length-breadth
				Glabella-lambda (°)	Basion-bregma (°)	Nasion-basion (°)	Basion-opisthion (°)	Nasion-bregma (°)	Lambda-bregma (°)	Opisthion-lambda (°)	Prosthion-nasion (°)	Nasospinale-nasion (°)	Prosthion-nasospinale (°)	Orbital height (°)	Ramus tangent-alveolar plane (°)	Ramus tangent-basal tangent (°)	Chin vertical-basal tangent (°)	Condylo-coronoid tangent-alveolar plane (°)	
KOSKIMO																		
4242 ♀ mat	102	90	118	15	87	30	−5	48	22	112	80	82	72	91	—	—	—	—	78.0
4243 ♀ ad	93	94	130	10	83	28	−3	48	25	116	76	78	70	85	—	—	—	—	85.4
4244 ♂ mat	92	89	122	5	87	33	−3	43	28	126	81	82	78	90	—	—	—	—	77.1
4245 ♂ mat	96	90	132	1	95	34	−7	40	33	130	79	79	79	94	—	—	—	—	77.0
4246 inf. II	98	—	122	10	88	30	−6	49	26	120	—	—	—	88	—	—	—	—	81.8
4247 ♀ ad	91	91	126	6	85	29	−8	44	27	122	85	87	79	87	—	—	—	—	79.6
4248 ♂ mat	92	90	116	8	84	29	−4	47	28	119	84	85	77	90	—	—	—	—	81.1
4249 ♂ mat	100	90	129	11	89	33	+5	44	19	121	80	80	80	88	—	—	—	—	74.6
4250 ♀ mat	98	92	130	11	87	30	−2	43	18	117	80	82	72	86	—	—	—	—	77.4
4251 ♀ mat	98	95	132	11	87	27	−3	46	20	120	80	84	69	85	—	—	—	—	75.1
4252 ♂ ad	96	92	124	5	91	31	−3	45	32	129	79	81	73	86	—	—	—	—	77.6
4253 inf. II	91	84	125	8	83	29	−9	56	29	123	87	88	80	95	—	—	—	—	83.0
4254 ♂ ad	91	86	127	6	85	34	−4	47	29	116	80	82	71	87	—	—	—	—	76.0
4256 ♂ ad	99	85	127	8	91	27	−7	41	25	119	82	83	77	86	—	—	—	—	78.2
4257 ♂ ? mat	98	92	128	10	88	31	+4	43	25	119	80	83	71	89	—	—	—	—	81.9
4258 ♂ ? ad	98	94	136	8	90	31	+5	44	27	124	74	76	68	85	—	—	—	—	80.1
4259 ♂ ? mat	105	94	135	11	94	30	+2	42	23	130	82	82	82	83	—	—	—	—	76.4
4270 ♂ ad-mat	94	87	130	5	89	35	+7	43	26	124	79	79	79	87	—	—	—	—	83.8
4261 ♂ mat	93	91	135	9	84	28	0	46	24	126	82	86	73	86	—	—	—	—	74.9
4262 ♂ ? mat	97	93	127	8	89	30	−6	45	26	122	78	82	64	83	—	—	—	—	74.7
4263 ♂ mat	100	90	124	10	90	33	−8	47	22	119	80	81	78	88	—	—	—	—	74.9
4264 ♂ ad	94	89	128	8	86	31	−2	46	28	118	83	84	79	96	—	—	—	—	—
4265 ♂ mat	89	90	123	8	81	27	−5	51	30	116	83	85	74	93	—	—	—	—	86.0
4266 ♂ mat	92	87	124	7	85	30	−5	48	26	124	85	86	81	91	—	—	—	—	80.4
4267 ♂ ad	98	90	119	15	83	28	+6	51	21	115	81	82	78	85	—	—	—	—	74.9
4268 ♀ mat	93	88	133	5	88	34	−5	45	31	122	78	82	65	84	—	—	—	—	82.5
4269 ♂ ? mat	98	90	126	9	89	33	−2	42	23	123	81	83	73	91	—	—	—	—	83.5
4270 ♂ ? sen	98	90	130	12	86	29	+6	47	19	116	82	82	82	86	—	—	—	—	75.8
♂ cases	55	55	55	55	55	55	55	55	55	54	53	55	50	13	13	13	13	53	
range	89–105	85–96	111–143	0–16	81–97	24–36	+9 to −10	38–51	13–39	113–134	74–88	76–93	62–84	79–97	67–83	104–119	77–86	−24 to +6	69.2–89.1
average	95.8	90.0	126.7	7.7	88.1	30.9	+0.1	45.0	26.9	122.4	81.0	82.8	74.5	87.9	75.8	111.6	80.8	−6.2	77.4
♀ cases	18	18	18	18	18	18	18	18	18	18	18	18	17	3	3	3	3	21	
range	91–102	86–95	118–144	4–15	83–91	25–36	+5 to −15	43–51	18–32	112–129	76–86	78–89	65–79	80–91	69–76	110–121	78–83	−16 to +7	73.1–85.4
average	95.4	91.1	129.3	8.3	87.0	29.7	−5.0	45.4	25.1	121.3	80.7	83.0	73.4	86.3	71.3	117.0	80.3	−10.3	77.4
juv. 1 case	93.0	86.0	134.0	7.0	86.0	30.0	−1.0	49.0	33.0	121.0	86.0	89.0	79.0	—	—	—	—	—	84.9
inf. case	3	2	3	3	3	3	3	3	3	3	3	3	2	3	—	—	—	—	3
range	91–100	80; 85	121–125	8–18	82–88	29–30	−6 to −9	49–58	20–29	112–123	86–88	85–92	80; 88	88–95	—	—	—	—	81.8–90.0
average	96.3	82.5	122.7	12.0	84.3	29.7	−7.3	54.3	25.0	118.3	87.0	88.3	84.0	91.7	—	—	—	—	85.2

INDICES

	Skull									Face and mandible											Cranio-facial			
	Length-height	Breadth-height	Transverse frontal	Transverse frontoparietal	Sagittal parieto-frontal (arc)	Sagittal frontal	Sagittal parietal	Sagittal occipital	Foramen magnum	Facial	Upper facial	Orbital (mf)	Orbital (la)	Interorbital (mf-mf to ek-ek)	Nasal	Transverse nasal bone	Maxillo-alveolar	Palatal	Bicondylo-bigonial breadth (mandible)	Ramus (mandible)	Transverse cranio-facial	Fronto-biorbital (ft-ft to fmt-fmt)	Jugo-frontal	Jugo-mandibular
74.6	95.6	77.6	60.1	79.0	90.3	91.8	79.4	77.1	—	54.9	83.3	89.7	16.5	48.1	33.3	112.7	79.2	—	—	76.4	82.2	62.4	—
75.1	87.9	88.4	70.2	99.1	91.3	86.0	89.7	100.0	—	47.2	81.8	92.3	22.0	54.3	60.0	120.7	86.9	—	—	100.7	91.7	69.7	—
71.4	96.4	84.6	70.7	108.9	91.1	84.4	83.6	81.1	—	57.3	82.6	95.0	18.1	44.6	68.8	121.4	79.2	—	—	107.1	87.6	66.0	—
72.1	93.6	78.9	61.0	94.7	90.1	84.8	88.5	84.8	—	56.4	82.2	90.2	18.3	54.7	56.3	126.9	68.2	—	—	99.3	80.4	61.4	—
75.1	91.8	—	89.1	89.9	90.6	82.9	75.0	—	—	—	89.5	—	—	50.0	40.0	—	—	—	—	81.5	—	—	—
69.8	87.6	83.2	65.0	100.9	88.7	86.3	82.7	79.4	—	52.3	83.3	89.7	18.7	46.9	43.8	125.5	83.7	—	—	93.4	89.0	69.5	—
71.9	88.7	82.6	63.3	96.0	94.2	88.4	78.4	85.7	—	57.6	80.4	88.1	17.7	44.6	33.3	122.2	93.5	—	—	100.7	83.3	62.9	—
72.9	97.8	83.5	67.4	84.7	91.1	91.4	87.0	93.5	—	56.8	90.7	100.0	18.8	47.1	44.4	130.6	93.2	—	—	97.8	83.5	68.9	—
70.1	90.5	82.7	66.4	80.3	88.5	92.9	84.4	82.9	—	55.9	90.2	97.4	17.0	45.1	37.5	113.7	73.9	—	—	97.8	89.2	67.9	—
68.9	91.7	83.9	70.7	90.0	91.7	90.7	86.4	87.9	—	50.7	83.7	92.3	20.0	49.0	62.5	124.5	91.1	—	—	103.8	90.4	68.1	—
73.6	94.8	82.9	68.1	90.6	89.1	87.9	82.8	93.1	—	53.4	87.8	97.3	19.6	48.9	47.1	117.6	88.6	—	—	97.0	76.8	70.2	—
74.8	90.1	80.2	65.5	110.2	89.0	87.9	81.6	71.0	—	49.6	94.7	102.9	19.1	34.5	35.7	152.8	106.2	—	—	82.4	97.9	79.5	—
77.1	101.5	81.5	64.7	100.8	90.8	87.6	84.7	91.4	—	53.9	81.8	90.0	16.8	41.5	50.0	114.5	78.0	—	—	103.7	83.8	62.4	—
74.5	95.2	88.0	70.1	89.8	89.1	87.8	83.1	76.9	—	55.6	86.7	95.1	19.4	39.3	45.0	119.3	97.9	—	—	104.1	93.6	67.3	—
73.4	89.7	86.2	69.0	94.4	91.1	81.2	85.6	93.7	—	55.5	83.0	92.9	18.7	50.0	61.1	124.1	87.8	—	—	99.3	88.5	69.4	—
72.2	90.1	84.2	68.1	88.8	90.4	88.3	88.3	84.8	—	51.8	78.7	88.1	16.5	46.0	37.5	125.0	95.8	—	—	97.2	88.1	70.1	—
68.7	89.9	74.2	64.0	86.9	90.8	95.6	86.6	90.3	—	57.4	90.7	97.5	16.3	40.7	42.9	109.8	—	—	—	92.8	87.2	68.9	—
75.0	94.3	79.1	62.1	100.0	91.5	87.3	83.2	91.4	—	55.2	75.5	84.1	—	42.3	35.7	119.2	86.9	—	—	95.7	79.8	64.9	—
69.9	93.4	78.9	61.9	103.3	91.1	87.4	87.7	90.0	—	59.0	83.3	89.7	19.0	46.1	47.1	—	—	—	—	97.8	83.5	64.2	—
72.5	97.1	82.0	66.9	86.9	88.5	90.3	86.2	84.4	—	53.4	88.1	97.4	18.2	54.0	40.0	—	—	—	—	96.3	88.5	69.4	—
72.7	97.7	86.7	70.5	77.7	88.5	94.1	81.6	96.9	—	56.7	88.9	97.6	18.6	46.1	57.1	121.6	93.2	—	—	97.8	89.9	73.1	—
76.0	—	—	95.0	89.3	87.0	84.8	85.7	—	—	53.0	84.4	92.7	15.6	45.1	40.0	131.4	93.5	—	—	—	88.2	68.2	—
77.3	89.9	77.5	62.8	103.3	91.1	85.0	84.6	91.2	—	54.5	80.4	88.1	16.8	44.4	35.7	112.7	91.5	—	—	96.6	80.9	65.0	—
73.4	91.2	79.5	62.8	104.8	88.8	87.0	85.0	87.9	—	54.6	88.6	100.0	17.8	49.1	38.9	—	—	—	—	95.3	85.3	65.9	—
74.3	99.2	89.8	72.4	91.9	90.3	86.8	83.9	84.4	—	53.0	85.4	92.1	22.2	50.0	62.5	115.1	80.8	—	—	100.7	92.4	71.8	—
83.1	100.7	83.6	63.5	104.3	92.3	85.2	86.9	77.1	—	57.9	84.4	—	13.5	45.1	38.5	112.7	84.8	—	—	92.0	—	69.0	—
70.2	84.1	76.1	52.9	89.1	89.1	89.5	84.1	93.9	—	56.2	86.4	100.0	14.7	41.4	28.6	116.7	—	—	—	87.3	83.8	60.6	—
73.0	96.3	—	—	84.8	89.6	88.7	84.7	74.3	—	—	86.0	—	—	—	49.0	—	—	—	—	—	—	—	—
54	53	52	52	53	54	54	54	54	9	53	54	53	51	53	52	50	48	11	12	52	52	53	10
66.0-	84.1-	72.8-	52.9-	76.3-	87.9-	81.2-	73.6-	74.3-	81.9-	51.0-	75.5-	83.7-	14.4-	37.9-	25.0-	103.5-	68.2-	79.2-	53.4-	87.3-	79.8-	60.6-	65.7-
79.0	102.2	90.5	76.6	108.9	99.2	95.6	93.2	103.1	97.9	63.8	93.0	105.3	22.2	54.7	68.8	132.7	97.9	95.1	68.3	107.1	93.6	74.8	81.8
72.4	94.3	81.7	67.0	93.1	90.6	88.1	86.6	85.8	90.1	55.8	84.7	93.7	17.8	44.8	48.1	120.6	87.4	86.3	60.6	98.2	87.5	68.2	74.4
19	19	20	21	21	21	21	19	18	3	18	20	19	20	20	17	19	19	4	4	19	18	19	4
68.9-	83.4-	77.8-	60.1-	79.0-	88.7-	81.5-	79.4-	74.3-	88.9-	47.2-	81.8-	98.7-	13.5-	40.4-	33.3-	111.5-	66.7-	88.1-	54.0-	86.3-	82.2-	62.4-	75.8-
83.1	100.0	89.8	75.8	110.7	92.9	92.9	91.6	100.0	94.7	60.0	92.9	102.9	22.0	54.3	71.4	137.8	102.5	92.7	68.3	104.0	94.7	77.4	88.8
73.2	94.5	83.0	68.1	94.9	90.3	87.3	86.1	86.7	92.7	55.3	86.7	95.5	18.2	46.6	52.0	120.3	83.7	89.4	60.4	96.3	88.8	70.8	80.7
79.5	93.6	83.8	65.9	95.3	88.3	86.1	87.1	90.9	—	54.4	85.0	94.6	16.8	46.9	37.5	142.2	100.0	—	—	84.4	97.0	78.4	—
3	3	2	2	3	3	3	3	3	—	2	3	2	3	2	2	2	2	—	—	3	2	2	—
74.8-	90.1-	80.2-	64.7-	89.1-	89.0-	87.9-	81.6-	71.0-	—	49.6-	89.5-	102.9-	15.1-	34.5-	35.7-	148.6-	94.3-	—	—	79.1-	97.9-	79.5-	—
83.0	101.8	80.9	65.5	110.2	89.9	90.6	83.3	79.4	—	54.5	94.7	102.9	19.1	50.0	—	152.3	106.2	—	—	82.4	98.9	81.8	—
77.6	91.1	80.6	65.1	97.3	89.1	89.3	82.6	75.0	—	52.1	91.3	102.9	17.0	44.0	42.0	150.0	100.3	—	—	81.0	98.5	80.7	—

Tribal divisions and subdivisions — Catalogue No. — Sex and stages of life — Number of cases — Averages and ranges	"Central angle" (*Klaatsch*)	Cranio-facial (*Faulenberger*)	Interoccipital	ANGLES											Mandibulo-alveolar plane				Length-breadth
				Glabella-lambda	Basion-bregma	Nasion-basion	Basion-opisthion	Nasion-bregma	Lambda-bregma	Opisthion-lambda	Prosthion-nasion	Nasospinale-nasion	Prosthion-nasospinale	Orbital height	Ramus tangent-alveolar plane	Ramus tangent-basal tangent	Chin vertical-basal tangent	Condylo-coronoid tangent-alveolar plane	
	(°)	(°)	(°)	(°)	(°)	(°)	(°)	(°)	(°)	(°)	(°)	(°)	(°)	(°)	(°)	(°)	(°)	(°)	
KOSKIMO																			
Nimkish																			
1642 ♂ ad-mat	100	94	119	10	90	30	−9	42	21	119	77	82	64	90	—	—	—	—	74.0
1643 inf II	99	—	123	13	86	28	−4	50	19	118	—	—	—	88	—	—	—	—	86.4
1644 ♀ ad	95	90	129	11	84	30	+3	47	21	119	84	88	72	86	—	—	—	—	75.9
1645 ♂ ad-mat	93	90	130	5	88	32	+3	45	29	128	81	82	78	83	—	—	—	—	77.1
1646 ♂ mat	91	87	134	5	86	—	—	49	32	121	83	83	83	96	—	—	—	—	78.1
1647 ♂ ? ad	—	—	—	—	—	—	—	—	—	—	—	—	—	—	—	—	—	—	73.9
1648 ♂ ad-mat	94	90	131	4	90	34	+2	44	33	128	78	82	67	90	—	—	—	—	76.9
1648 A ♂ (r) ad-mat	—	—	—	—	—	—	—	—	—	—	—	—	—	—	74	115	80	0	—
1649 ♂ mat	93	90	114	5	88	31	−3	44	30	124	83	83	83	88	82	101	85	−1	75.4
1650 ♂ mat	93	89	135	5	88	32	+4	43	26	127	85	86	81	90	80	107	81	−2	72.4
1651 ♂ ? ad	95	89	137	5	90	33	−2	45	28	126	79	82	71	83	74	115	80	−10	78.0
1652 ♂ ad-mat	93	89	127	3	90	32	−4	44	32	127	83	85	77	87	—	—	—	—	78.0
1653 ♀ mat	92	89	117	6	86	31	−4	47	30	127	81	86	72	88	—	—	—	—	78.6
1654 ♂ ad	99	94	119	6	93	31	+3	40	26	129	81	83	75	88	—	—	—	—	73.7
1655 ♂ juv-ad	102	92	131	11	91	33	−4	43	20	120	80	83	73	86	60	130	78	−4	75.0
1656 ♂ mat	99	89	119	8	91	31	−10	45	31	123	86	88	80	93	—	—	—	—	78.9
1657 ♂ ad-mat	92	89	134	2	90	35	+6	37	31	134	84	86	83	85	—	—	—	—	71.3
1658 inf II	—	—	—	—	—	—	—	—	—	—	—	—	—	—	—	—	—	—	79.5
1659 ♂ ? mat	90	86	137	5	85	33	−7	48	27	122	81	85	71	92	—	—	—	—	79.5
1660 ♂ ad	92	—	132	10	82	34	+5	52	22	122	—	—	—	104	—	—	—	—	77.6
1661 ♂ ad	99	90	119	9	90	33	+7?	42	23	125	82	82	82	—	—	—	—	—	72.0
1662 A ♂ ad	92	90	137	4	88	29	−5	47	33	122	87	87	87	94	—	—	—	—	82.1
1662 B ♂ (r) mat	—	—	—	—	—	—	—	—	—	—	—	—	—	—	77	114	76	−8	—
1663 ♀? ad	96	90	145	11	85	30	+2	49	24	119	81	83	75	90	68	124	76	−8	74.4
1664 ♂ ad-mat	94	86	129	5	89	33	+2	46	30	125	86	88	79	94	75	114	80	+1	81.9
1665 ♂ mat	91	90	121	1	90	33	−8	42	30	130	80	82	74	89	73	119	76	−10	81.5
1666 ♂ ad-mat	99	91	136	8	91	31	+2	43	31	126	84	90	68	92	80	110	79	−5	75.0
1667 ♂ ad-mat	96	87	136	5	91	35	−2	44	32	126	81	82	75	88	77	111	80	−2	75.7
1668 ♀ mat	94	89	134	4	90	35	0	41	25	122	78	78	78	77	—	—	—	—	75.0
1669 inf I	95	91	133	5	90	—	—	47	30	131	80	79	85	85	55	130	83	+26	82.3
1670 A ♂ ad-mat	101	92	125	7	94	33	+6	39	24	125	77	77	77	83	72	120	77	+8	71.3
1670 B ♂ mat	—	—	—	—	—	—	—	—	—	—	—	—	—	—	74	111	83	−10	—
1671 ♂ mat	99	93	126	11	88	30	+3	42	20	121	83	82	78	82	72	116	81	+4	73.5
1672 A ♂ mat	97	89	118	11	86	31	+3	44	22	113	81	83	75	92	79	108	83	−1	72.2
1672 B ♂ ad-mat	—	—	—	—	—	—	—	—	—	—	—	—	—	—	74	112	83	−17	—
1673 ♂ mat	101	89	125	14	87	30	+4	47	18	120	86	87	82	88	—	—	—	—	72.9
1674 ♀ mat	97	—	133	11	86	25	−6	48	25	120	—	—	—	82	—	—	—	—	76.9
1675 ♀ mat	104	90	120	16	88	30	+4	47	16	113	79	81	71	85	78	113	79	−7	78.3
1676 ♂? mat	92	89	136	7	85	29	−2	50	29	127	82	84	76	87	75	113	80	−7	76.4
1677 ♂? mat	93	95	130	7	86	28	−8	44	24	125	81	81	81	86	87	104	78	−15	69.1

INDICES

	Skull									Face and mandible											Cranio-facial			
Length-height	Breadth-height	Transverse frontal	Transverse frontoparietal	Sagittal parieto-frontal (arcs)	Sagittal frontal	Sagittal parietal	Sagittal occipital	Foramen magnum	Facial	Upper facial	Orbital (mf)	Orbital (la)	Interorbital (mf/mf to ek-ek)	Nasal	Transverse nasal bone	Maxillo-alveolar	Palatal	Bicondylo-bigonial breadth (mandible)	Ramus (mandible)	Transverse cranio-facial	Fronto-biorbital (ft-ft to fmt-fmt)	Jugo-frontal	Jugo-mandibular
68.6	92.7	80.4	65.7	80.0	88.5	91.3	81.6	88.9	—	54.1	83.7	87.8	16.5	46.0	—	122.6	85.4	—	—	97.1	88.2	67.7	—
69.8	86.8	86.2	69.4	85.7	88.1	90.7	80.6	79.4	—	—	85.4	92.1	—	—	—	—	—	—	—	—	—	—	—
71.8	94.7	81.6	67.4	96.6	88.8	87.5	83.9	83.9	—	51.6	92.3	100.0	18.1	51.1	50.0	132.5	94.9	—	—	95.4	89.9	70.6	—
70.2	91.0	83.6	66.9	99.2	89.3	86.1	85.8	86.5	—	56.8	86.7	97.5	19.6	42.6	61.1	121.1	88.9	—	—	95.9	89.8	69.8	—
—	—	87.5	70.5	95.5	88.8	86.7	88.6	—	—	—	74.5	81.4	—	46.1	53.3	118.5	89.6	—	—	—	90.7	—	—
—	—	—	70.6	94.7	89.4	87.2	—	—	—	—	—	—	—	—	—	—	—	—	—	—	—	—	—
73.6	95.7	82.6	67.9	100.0	89.9	83.7	82.3	82.9	85.6	53.4	90.7	102.6	18.8	44.6	53.9	117.5	89.4	—	—	104.3	88.8	65.1	62.3
72.8	96.5	—	66.0	96.3	89.6	91.5	83.2	94.6	—	—	75.0	83.7	—	43.9	41.2	129.8	93.7	98.4	66.7	—	—	—	—
71.3	98.5	83.2	70.1	102.4	89.0	84.6	88.4	85.7	86.9	52.4	92.9	102.6	16.3	42.9	56.3	138.5	100.0	90.2	58.0	108.3	87.8	64.8	76.5
75.7	97.0	81.8	66.7	100.0	91.0	86.9	88.5	90.6	92.2	56.6	86.4	95.0	16.2	44.2	40.0	126.5	90.9	83.9	64.5	95.6	87.4	69.8	76.7
73.6	94.4	75.4	60.6	100.0	90.7	86.0	84.7	78.4	—	57.8	86.7	97.5	16.3	42.6	50.0	122.6	86.7	—	—	95.1	82.7	63.7	—
74.0	94.1	88.2	66.2	109.3	90.7	84.5	82.0	90.0	—	59.4	83.3	92.1	19.1	43.1	71.4	121.8	85.4	—	—	94.1	90.0	70.3	—
67.0	90.9	78.1	65.0	85.7	91.0	92.1	79.4	83.3	—	53.6	86.4	92.7	15.1	41.8	69.2	126.0	86.9	—	—	96.5	87.7	67.4	—
70.1	93.5	83.5	69.6	87.2	92.0	89.0	84.8	78.9	87.9	51.5	84.1	92.5	17.8	45.8	47.1	139.1	92.7	88.5	62.7	95.6	90.6	72.7	75.8
76.2	96.6	84.7	68.5	84.4	88.6	87.4	81.3	90.6	—	50.6	78.7	84.1	15.2	50.0	47.1	129.9	97.9	—	—	104.1	90.9	65.8	—
69.8	97.8	83.6	70.8	77.9	88.6	85.5	89.4	83.3	—	64.5	89.1	97.6	16.7	42.4	69.2	126.0	86.4	—	—	100.7	88.9	70.3	—
—	—	82.4	65.4	94.0	90.5	89.9	—	—	—	54.1	86.5	97.0	18.1	48.8	46.2	132.5	87.2	—	—	80.1	97.8	81.6	—
76.7	96.4	85.3	68.6	108.3	89.3	84.0	89.4	84.8	—	57.9	80.0	90.0	18.3	49.1	41.2	116.4	91.1	—	—	95.0	88.9	72.2	—
69.8	89.9	—	—	117.7	90.8	83.6	86.7	82.0	—	—	—	—	—	—	—	—	—	—	—	—	—	—	—
69.3	96.3	87.4	71.3	81.5	88.5	93.4	85.7	83.9	—	—	—	—	—	48.1	—	—	—	—	—	100.0	—	71.3	—
77.4	94.4	77.3	64.8	89.0	87.4	85.8	88.5	87.1	—	55.1	97.4	105.6	18.9	40.7	—	124.0	97.6	—	—	95.8	89.3	67.6	—
—	—	—	—	—	—	—	—	—	—	—	—	—	—	—	—	—	—	96.3	70.7	—	—	—	—
77.3	103.9	71.8	64.6	100.8	90.9	83.6	91.1	93.7	91.3	57.1	89.7	97.2	19.6	44.0	53.3	120.7	95.4	92.4	66.7	98.4	83.7	65.1	76.9
75.7	92.4	78.6	63.4	100.8	90.9	85.7	85.6	88.9	92.8	56.1	81.8	90.0	20.0	40.0	50.0	132.6	90.9	85.1	52.3	95.9	85.9	66.2	69.8
69.0	84.7	81.0	65.3	102.4	88.9	88.3	81.7	94.1	84.3	53.7	83.3	93.0	15.1	42.9	47.1	118.9	89.4	81.7	62.1	98.0	87.5	66.7	66.7
73.9	98.5	82.1	66.7	89.8	89.8	85.4	87.8	77.1	84.8	52.2	80.9	87.2	18.6	50.0	38.9	127.4	90.9	80.8	62.3	100.0	89.3	66.7	70.3
76.8	101.5	82.9	67.1	95.5	90.1	84.9	90.3	81.8	87.0	54.3	93.0	100.0	20.0	47.2	50.0	118.5	84.8	94.4	71.2	100.7	86.8	66.7	84.8
73.8	98.4	85.0	70.5	91.3	88.6	88.3	83.3	—	—	61.1	80.8	87.2	17.9	43.9	52.6	127.4	95.4	—	—	101.5	84.3	69.5	—
—	—	81.0	62.3	98.3	86.3	84.3	88.0	—	—	—	91.4	103.2	—	—	—	—	—	88.2	53.5	—	98.8	—	—
69.7	97.7	88.9	72.7	83.7	90.7	88.9	83.2	81.6	94.8	61.5	91.3	102.4	15.8	39.3	43.8	119.6	83.7	97.4	55.4	102.3	87.3	71.1	82.2
—	—	—	—	—	—	—	—	—	—	—	—	—	—	—	—	—	—	79.3	64.5	—	—	—	—
67.6	91.9	83.5	70.6	89.7	90.5	89.4	84.8	77.8	89.4	53.0	88.4	95.0	19.4	41.5	57.1	124.0	88.9	82.4	62.3	97.1	92.3	72.7	74.2
72.2	100.0	88.5	72.5	84.6	90.0	88.2	83.2	81.1	91.5	56.3	84.8	95.1	17.3	36.8	46.7	119.6	84.0	89.7	58.2	102.9	89.3	70.4	73.2
—	—	—	—	—	—	—	—	—	—	—	—	—	—	—	—	—	—	79.1	60.9	—	—	—	—
70.2	96.3	78.9	65.7	89.0	91.3	92.0	81.7	82.9	—	55.6	86.0	97.4	19.4	41.8	53.3	113.2	91.1	—	—	98.5	87.4	66.7	—
71.1	92.5	82.1	63.9	95.2	90.4	86.5	89.1	80.0	—	—	80.5	89.2	—	—	—	—	—	—	—	97.7	85.9	65.4	—
75.4	96.3	83.5	66.4	74.4	91.2	93.5	79.4	87.1	88.3	56.2	90.5	97.4	17.5	49.0	62.5	114.3	78.4	93.2	69.0	100.0	88.3	66.4	80.3
72.0	94.2	81.9	68.3	107.1	85.8	87.5	88.3	84.4	90.2	58.6	80.0	90.0	16.7	46.3	58.8	118.9	78.7	73.8	60.7	95.7	87.9	71.4	67.7
64.4	93.1	76.1	63.8	97.6	89.4	88.3	82.5	73.5	82.1	52.2	84.1	94.9	16.3	43.4	22.2	117.3	—	84.8	74.1	103.1	79.8	61.9	74.6

Tribal divisions and subdivisions / Catalogue No. / Sex and stages of life / Number of cases / Averages and ranges	"Central angle" (*Klaatsch*)	Cranio-facial (*Falkenburger*)	Interoccipital	ANGLES To ear-eye plane											Mandibulo-alveolar plane				Length-breadth
				Glabella-lambda	Basion-bregma	Nasion-basion	Basion-opisthion	Nasion-bregma	Lambda-bregma	Opisthion-lambda	Prosthion-nasion	Nasospinale-nasion	Prosthion-nasospinale	Orbital height	Ramus tangent-alveolar plane	Ramus tangent-basal tangent	Chin vertical-basal tangent	Condylo-coronoid tangent-alveolar plane	
	(°)	(°)	(°)	(°)	(°)	(°)	(°)	(°)	(°)	(°)	(°)	(°)	(°)	(°)	(°)	(°)	(°)	(°)	(°)
KOSKIMO																			
1678 ♀ mat	98	88	126	11	87	32	-13	47	23	117	82	85	74	90	78	123	67	-7	79.2
1679 ♀ ad	98	93	133	1	97	34	0	37	33	134	81	84	75	80	—	—	—	—	78.0
♂ cases	26	25	26	26	26	25	25	26	26	26	25	24	25	25	17	17	17	17	27
range	90–102	86–95	114–137	1–14	82–94	28–35	+7 to -10	37–52	18–33	113–134	77–87	77–90	64–70	82–104	60–87	101–130	76–85	-17 to +8	69.1–82.1
average	99.1	90.0	128.7	6.6	88.6	31.8	-0.6	34.3	27.0	124.7	82.0	83.9	76.1	89.2	75.6	112.9	80.0	-4.6	75.7
♀ cases	8	7	8	8	8	8	8	8	8	8	7	7	7	8	3	3	3	3	8
range	92–104	88–93	117–145	1–16	84–97	25–35	+4 to -13	37–49	16–33	113–134	78–84	78–88	71–78	77–90	68–78	113–124	67–79	-8 to +7	74.4–79.2
average	96.7	89.9	128.3	8.9	87.9	30.9	1.8	45.4	24.6	121.4	80.6	83.6	73.9	84.8	74.7	120.0	74.0	-7.3	77.0
inf. cases	2	1	2	2	2	1	1	2	2	1	1			2	1		1	1	3
range	95;99	—	123;133	5;13	86;90	—	—	47;50	19;30	—	—			85;88	—		—	—	79.5–80.4
average	97.0	91.0	128.0	9.0	88.0	28.0	-0.4	48.5	24.5	118.0	80.0	79.0		86.5	55.0		83.0	+26.0	80.7
Koskimo																			
3642 ♂ mat	101	93	156	2	99	34	+1	38	32	138	78	82	69	84	—	—	—	—	64.2
3643 ♂ mat	96	89	130	5	91	33	-6	40	24	125	82	83	77	91	80	115	72	0	72.1
3644 ♂ mat	100	94	127	5	95	32	+3	37	22	130	82	83	78	94	—	—	—	—	70.9
3645 inf. II	—	—	—	—	—	—	—	—	—	—	—	—	—	—	—	—	—	—	68.2
3646 ♂ mat	92	91	125	6	86	28	-14	49	28	124	80	81	78	90	—	—	—	—	83.1
3647 ♂ juv-ad	110	96	138	12	98	30	-3	41	21	128	78	78	78	83	69	121	78	+9	66.8
3648 ♂ mat	94	93	128	10	84	26	-7	47	22	120	86	91	74	96	—	—	—	—	75.1
3649 ♀? mat	97	94	140	6	91	30	+12	42	25	127	83	85	75	93	—	—	—	—	71.6
3650 ♂ ad	100	90	131	10	90	34	+12	42	17	123	77	80	69	84	—	—	—	—	72.5
3837 ♂ mat	96	89	126	5	91	32	-7	41	26	125	85	88	77	92	—	—	—	—	71.8
3838 ♂ mat	103	92	130	12	91	31	+3	42	19	120	82	83	80	86	—	—	—	—	72.8
3839 ♀ mat	95	92	125	4	91	32	-2	40	30	127	76	78	74	84	73	119	77	-8	78.7
3840 ♂ ad·mat	95	90	122	3	92	36	-2	40	30	122	77	77	77	89	77	113	79	-1	73.9
3841 ♀? ad	97	91	140	7	90	34	+3	40	22	124	77	80	69	87	71	119	79	-12	72.3
♂ cases	9	9	9	9	9	9	9	9	9	9	9	9	9	9	2	2	2	2	9
range	94–103	89–94	122–156	2–12	84–99	26–36	+12 to -14	37–49	17–32	120–138	77–86	77–91	69–80	84–96	77;80	113;115	72;79	-1;0	64.2–83.1
average	97.4	91.2	135.6	6.4	91.0	31.8	-1.9	41.8	24.4	125.2	81.0	83.1	75.4	89.6	79.0	114.0	75.5	-0.5	72.9
♀ cases	4	4	4	4	4	4	4	4	4	4	4	4	4	4	3	3	3	3	4
range	95–110	91–94	125–138	4–12	90–98	30–34	+3 to -5	40–41	21–30	124–128	76–83	78–85	69–78	83–93	69–73	119–121	77–79	-12 to +9	66.8–78.7
average	99.7	93.3	135.8	7.2	92.5	31.5	-0.5	40.5	24.5	126.5	78.5	80.3	74.0	86.8	71.0	119.7	78.0	-3.3	72.3
inf. 1 case	—	—	—	—	—	—	—	—	—	—	—	—	—	—	—	—	—	—	68.2
Nootka																			
4559 ♀ juv-ad	—	—	—	—	—	—	—	—	—	—	—	—	—	—	—	—	—	—	78.7
4560 ♀ mat-sen	95	—	128	3	92	33	-14	41	36	121	—	—	—	88	—	—	—	—	84.7
4561 ♂ ad	97	92	144	8	89	31	0	46	28	123	76	80	67	86	—	—	—	—	73.6

									INDICES												
		Skull								Face and mandible									Cranio-facial		
Length-height	Breadth-height	Transverse frontal	Transverse frontoparietal	Sagittal parieto-frontal (arcs)	Sagittal frontal	Sagittal parietal	Sagittal occipital	Foramen magnum	Facial	Upper facial	Orbital (mf)	Orbital (la)	Interorbital (mf-mf to ek-ek)	Nasal	Transverse nasal bone	Maxillo-alveolar	Palatal	Bicondylo-bigonial breadth (mandible)	Ramus (mandible)	Transverse cranio-facial	Fronto-biorbital (ft-ft to fmt-fmt)	Jugo-frontal	Jugo-mandibular
75.0	94.7	89.1	67.7	84.0	89.9	92.0	84.4	81.8	89.8	60.2	76.7	84.6	15.6	45.6	66.7	118.7	81.4	86.7	68.0	96.2	90.0	70.3	76.6
68.4	87.7	79.8	63.0	84.6	87.7	90.0	85.2	82.3	—	60.2	90.5	97.4	16.8	38.5	40.0	125.0	90.5	—	—	92.7	87.0	67.9	—
25	25	23	26	28	27	27	26	25	13	21	24	24	22	25	22	24	23	17	17	23	23	23	12
66.4– 77.4	84.7– 101.5	75.4– 88.9	60.6– 72.7	80.0– 111.7	85.8– 92.0	83.7– 93.4	79.4– 90.3	73.5– 94.6	82.1– 94.8	50.6– 64.5	74.5– 97.4	81.4– 105.6	15.1– 20.0	36.8– 50.0	22.2– 69.2	113.2– 139.1	78.7– 100.0	71.7– 96.6	52.3– 74.1	95.9– 108.3	79.8– 92.3	61.9– 72.7	62.3– 84.8
72.5	94.9	81.6	67.7	93.0	89.6	87.5	85.3	83.6	88.5	55.5	85.2	93.6	17.4	44.0	49.8	123.7	90.0	85.7	62.8	99.1	88.1	68.2	73.3
8	8	8	8	8	8	8	8	7	3	7	8	8	8	7	7	5	7	3	3	8	8	8	2
68.4– 77.3	92.5– 103.9	71.8– 89.1	63.0– 70.5	74.4– 109.3	88.8– 91.3	83.6– 93.5	79.4– 90.3	81.8– 93.7	88.3– 91.3	51.6– 61.1	76.7– 92.3	84.6– 97.2	15.6– 19.6	38.5– 51.1	40.0– 71.4	114.3– 132.5	78.4– 95.4	86.7– 93.2	66.7– 68.0	92.7– 101.5	83.7– 90.0	65.1– 70.6	76.6; 80.3
73.4	96.5	82.0	66.2	92.6	90.1	88.3	85.4	85.6	89.7	58.0	85.5	93.3	18.0	45.0	56.7	122.9	88.8	90.8	67.2	97.1	87.4	68.2	78.9
1	1	3	3	3	3	3	3	2	1	3	3	3	1	1	1	1	1	1	1	1	2	1	—
—	—	81.0– 86.2	62.3– 69.4	85.7– 98.3	86.3– 90.5	84.3– 90.7	80.6 ; 88.0	—	—	85.4– 91.4	92.1– 103.2	—	—	—	—	—	—	—	—	97.8 ; 98.8	—	—	—
69.8	86.8	83.0	65.7	92.0	88.3	88.3	83.3	79.4	—	54.1	87.8	97.3	18.1	48.8	46.2	132.5	87.2	88.2	53.5	80.1	98.5	81.6	—
67.6	105.3	84.3	72.9	102.8	91.0	76.5	95.7	85.7	—	65.4	93.3	102.4	17.8	43.1	53.3	126.7	86.5	—	—	100.0	88.9	72.9	—
68.4	94.9	81.5	70.8	90.0	88.5	90.6	84.9	77.8	96.5	57.7	84.8	95.1	16.2	42.1	38.9	126.7	87.8	86.2	62.1	103.6	86.6	68.3	74.6
63.8	89.9	78.1	64.0	96.0	96.8	85.0	83.8	87.9	—	58.4	88.6	100.0	18.6	40.0	40.0	118.6	83.7	—	—	102.2	81.6	62.7	—
—	—	90	82.8	111.6	90.8	77.6	96.5	—	—	61.5	100.0	111.1	19.3	40.4	71.4	148.7	81.6	—	—	89.3	103.1	92.7	—
74.3	89.5	82.5	65.1	99.3	88.1	84.3	87.0	106.4	—	53.5	86.4	95.0	18.6	48.1	31.3	125.4	79.9	—	—	93.4	91.7	69.7	—
67.9	101.6	90.3	73.2	80.2	93.4	84.4	87.0	87.5	93.5	57.7	90.5	102.7	16.3	41.2	53.3	128.6	90.9	82.0	55.4	96.8	89.4	75.6	73.9
68.8	91.5	81.4	67.6	98.5	90.8	85.9	85.6	97.1	—	53.5	79.2	86.4	17.1	40.7	46.7	121.4	83.7	—	—	100.0	87.3	67.6	—
68.4	95.6	85.6	74.3	92.6	88.9	85.6	91.9	80.6	—	52.5	93.0	105.2	19.8	46.1	70.6	—	—	—	—	100.7	94.4	73.7	—
68.7	94.7	78.9	68.2	95.2	87.9	83.9	85.9	83.3	—	58.5	90.7	97.5	18.0	44.6	46.2	124.1	87.5	—	—	102.3	86.5	66.7	—
67.7	94.3	77.2	67.9	88.7	88.0	87.3	81.9	88.2	—	59.9	83.0	97.8	18.1	40.7	46.7	120.7	79.2	—	—	101.4	86.4	66.9	—
68.1	93.5	85.2	70.5	78.6	90.1	93.2	81.7	82.9	—	55.8	88.9	97.6	18.4	45.3	56.3	132.7	87.5	—	—	99.3	89.9	71.0	—
70.5	89.0	84.2	69.1	90.3	87.1	89.3	86.0	87.9	94.7	59.8	90.9	97.6	16.3	46.1	41.2	118.9	85.1	85.1	49.2	92.3	92.7	72.7	78.0
71.2	96.3	80.3	69.1	88.9	88.9	89.3	80.3	86.5	86.5	56.7	88.6	100.0	18.0	41.8	55.3	114.3	81.2	88.7	56.9	103.7	87.8	66.7	78.0
70.6	97.7	83.2	70.7	90.5	89.0	87.8	89.3	91.7	79.7	55.6	84.1	92.5	17.2	38.5	42.9	114.0	81.6	81.4	50.8	100.0	88.7	70.7	72.2
9	9	9	9	9	9	9	9	9	2	9	9	9	9	9	9	8	9	2	2	9	9	9	2
63.8– 74.3	89.9– 105.3	77.2– 85.2	64.0– 72.9	78.6– 102.8	87.9– 96.8	76.5– 93.2	80.3– 95.7	77.8– 106.4	86.5 ; 94.7	53.5– 65.4	79.2– 93.3	86.4– 102.4	16.2– 18.6	40.0– 48.1	31.3– 56.3	114.3– 132.7	79.2– 90.9	86.2 ; 88.7	56.9 ; 62.1	93.4– 103.7	81.6– 103.1	62.7– 92.7	74.6 ; 78.0
68.7	94.4	80.7	68.5	92.7	90.0	86.2	85.2	87.9	83.0	57.7	85.9	96.6	17.9	42.9	45.8	123.7	86.1	87.5	59.5	100.7	87.6	67.9	76.3
4	4	4	4	4	4	4	4	4	5	3	4	4	4	4	4	3	4	3	2	3	4	4	3
67.9– 70.6	89.0– 101.6	83.2– 90.3	69.1– 74.3	80.2– 92.6	87.1– 93.4	84.4– 89.3	86.0– 91.9	80.6– 91.7	79.7– 94.7	52.5– 59.8	84.1– 92.5	92.5– 105.3	16.3– 19.8	38.5– 46.1	41.2– 70.6	114.0– 128.6	81.6– 90.9	81.4– 85.1	49.2– 55.4	96.3– 100.7	88.7– 94.4	70.7– 75.6	72.2– 78.0
69.4	96.0	85.5	71.8	88.0	90.8	86.8	85.0	89.7	87.0	56.4	89.7	97.2	17.3	43.0	52.0	120.5	85.9	82.8	51.8	98.5	91.0	73.2	74.7
—	—	90.2	82.8	111.6	90.8	77.6	96.5	—	—	61.5	100.0	111.1	19.3	40.4	71.4	148.7	81.6	—	—	89.3	103.1	92.7	—
72.2	91.7	79.1	68.4	89.0	89.8	86.8	87.6	84.8	—	—	79.1	87.2	13.9	47.9	38.5	—	—	—	—	94.0	93.8	72.8	—
76.7	90.6	86.0	65.9	86.3	88.7	86.0	84.1	93.3	—	—	79.1	87.2	13.9	47.9	38.5	—	—	—	—	96.4	90.2	69.2	—
74.7	101.6	80.6	68.0	96.0	90.4	83.3	89.2	94.1	—	51.9	87.8	92.3	—	46.8	41.7	120.4	93.5	—	—	102.3	86.1	66.4	—

89

Tribal divisions and subdivisions / Catalogue No. / Sex and stages of life / Number of cases / Averages and ranges	"Central angle" (Klaatsch)	Cranio-facial (Feidhenberger)	Interoccipital	ANGLES — To ear-eye plane											Mandibulo-alveolar plane				Length-breadth
				Glabella-lambda	Basion-bregma	Nasion-basion	Basion-opisthion	Nasion-bregma	Lambda-bregma	Opisthion-lambda	Prosthion-nasion	Nasospinale-nasion	Prosthion-nasospinale	Orbital height	Ramus tangent-alveolar plane	Ramus tangent-basal tangent	Chin vertical-basal tangent	Condylo-coronoid tangent-alveolar plane	
	(°)	(°)	(°)	(°)	(°)	(°)	(°)	(°)	(°)	(°)	(°)	(°)	(°)	(°)	(°)	(°)	(°)	(°)	
KOSKIMO																			
4562 ♂ ? ad	92	93	130	2	90	30	−15	44	30	128	81	82	73	94	—	—	—	—	74.2
4563 ♀ ? mat	99	96	133	9	90	27	−8	44	23	124	81	85	67	92	—	—	—	—	71.7
4564 ♂ mat	92	88	130	8	84	31	−7	50	26	121	79	79	79	91	—	—	—	—	73.6
4565 ♂ ad-mat	94	88	126	4	90	35	−6	45	34	123	77	77	77	87	—	—	—	—	87.9
4566 ♀ ad	100	96	122	10	90	29	0	42	20	120	79	89	56!	84	—	—	—	—	78.2
4567 ♂ mat	95	96	125	5	90	31	−1	39	30	123	75	75	75	88	—	—	—	—	73.4
4568 ♂ ? ad-mat	99	93	142	5	94	33	−7	41	29	132	76	79	62	80	—	—	—	—	73.3
4569 ♂ ad	91	92	131	3	88	30	−6	45	31	129	80	81	73	90	—	—	—	—	76.4
4570 ♂ ad-mat	97	94	132	8	82	26	−3	46	25	129	85	89	70	93	—	—	—	—	73.4
4571 ♂ ad-mat	94	95	128	6	88	28	−16	43	29	125	80	85	63	89	—	—	—	—	75.8
4572 ♂ mat	97	92	116	11	86	30	−5	44	22	112	81	83	74	92	—	—	—	—	75.3
4574 ♂ ad	—	—	—	—	—	—	—	—	—	—	—	—	—	—	—	—	—	—	—
♂ cases	10	10	10	10	10	10	10	10	10	10	10	7	10	10	—	—	—	—	10
range	91–99	88–96	116–144	2–11	84–94	26–35	0 to −16	39–50	22–34	112–132	75–85	79–89	62–79	80–94	—	—	—	—	73.3–87.9
average	94.8	92.3	130.4	6,0	88.8	30.5	−6.6	44.3	28.4	124.5	79.0	82.7	71.3	89.3	—	—	—	—	75.7
♀ cases	3	2	3	3	3	3	3	3	3	2	2	2	2	3	—	—	—	—	4
range	95–100	96; 96	122–133	3–10	90–92	27–33	0 to −14	41–44	20–36	120; 124	79; 81	85; 89	56; 67	84–92	—	—	—	—	71.7–84.7
average	98.0	96.0	127.7	7.3	90.2	29.3	−7.3	42.3	26.3	121.7	80.0	87.0	61.5	88.0	—	—	—	—	78.3
Clayoquot																			
1597 ♀ ? mat	97	93	124	9	88	31	−6	44	24	119	76	77	72	87	75	114	81	−2	78.5
1598 ♂ ad	92	90	125	5	87	32	−5	45	29	125	83	83	83	93	—	—	—	—	75.8
1599 ♀ ? ad	95	88	138	4	91	34	−4	44	30	131	82	85	76	92	—	—	—	—	73.9
1600 ♂ ad	93	90	129	4	89	35	−6	41	27	121	78	80	75	90	—	—	—	—	69.4
1601 inf. II	90	—	127	13	77	—	−2	55	17	108	86	89	78	92	—	—	—	—	81.1
1602 ♂ ad-mat	95	91	123	9	86	30	−5	48	23	118	77	79	68	86	—	—	—	—	75.0
1603 juv	94	90	128	6	88	32	−6	47	30	125	76	78	68	87	—	—	—	—	77.5
1604 ♂ ad	91	90	129	5	86	32	−5	45	29	120	83	84	76	88	—	—	—	—	77.4
♂ cases	4	4	4	4	4	4	4	4	4	4	4	3	4	4	—	—	—	—	4
range	91–95	90–91	122–129	4–9	86–89	30–35	−5 to −6	41–48	23–39	118–125	77–83	79–84	68–83	86–92	—	—	—	—	69.4–77.4
average	92.7	90.3	126.3	5.7	87.0	32.5	−5.3	44.8	27.0	121.0	80,5	81.0	75.5	89.3	—	—	—	—	74.4
♀ cases	2	1	2	2	2	2	2	2	2	2	2	1	1	2	1	1	1	1	2
range	95; 97	—	124; 138	4; 9	88; 91	31; 34	−4 to −6	44; 44	24; 30	118; 131	76; 82	—	—	87; 92	—	—	—	—	73.9; 78.5
average	96.0	93.0	131.0	6.5	89.5	32.5	−5.0	44.0	27.0	124.5	79.0	77.0	72.0	89.5	75.0	114.0	81.0	−2.0	76.2
juv. 1 case	94.0	90.0	128.0	6.0	88.0	32.0	−6.0	47.0	30.0	125.0	76.0	79.0	68.0	87.0	—	—	—	—	77.5
inf. 1 case	90.0	—	127.0	13.0	77.0	—	−2.0	55.0	17.0	108.0	86.0	89.0	78.0	89.0	—	—	—	—	81.1

				Skull								Face and mandible										Cranio-facial			
										INDICES															
Length-height	Breadth-height	Transverse frontal	Transverse fronto-parietal	Sagittal parieto-frontal (arcs)	Sagittal frontal	Sagittal parietal	Sagittal occipital	Foramen magnum	Facial	Upper facial	Orbital (mf)	Orbital (la)	Interorbital (mf:mf to ek-ek)	Nasal	Transverse nasal bone	Maxillo-alveolar	Palatal	Bicondylo-bigonial breadth (mandible)	Ramus (mandible)	Transverse cranio-facial	Fronto-biorbital (ft:ft to fmt-fmt)	Jugo-frontal	Jugo-mandibular
68.5	92.4	75.6	65.9	104.1	88.5	85.8	86.9	91.4	—	48.1	97.4	102.7	18.7	44.7	42.9	120.0	90.7	—	—	100.8	90.6	65.4	—
67.2	93.8	88.0	73.6	87.2	91.2	90.8	85.9	93.5	—	52.6	80.5	89.2	18.6	49.0	53.9	113.5	88.9	—	—	95.7	92.2	71.4	—
77.0	104.7	81.5	68.7	106.8	90.6	88.0	85.0	97.9	—	55.8	82.9	89.5	18.7	52.0	43.8	119.3	74.0	—	—	100.8	97.1	68.2	—
77.1	87.7	76.0	65.1	97.6	86.3	82.6	84.0	91.4	—	48.9	88.4	100.0	15.5	47.2	58.3	124.0	88.9	—	—	100.7	88.8	64.6	—
66.7	85.3	84.9	66.2	81.5	90.8	90.7	81.0	82.9	—	56.7	84.1	94.9	16.5	45.1	46.7	123.1	87.2	—	—	93.4	87.4	70.9	—
69.0	94.1	81.4	68.1	83.9	89.2	89.9	84.8	91.4	—	50.9	77.5	86.4	16.2	50.9	38.5	117.5	90.0	—	—	111.7	82.1	60.9	—
69.4	94.7	83.6	69.7	99.2	92.7	85.2	89.6	93.7	—	55.3	92.5	102.8	16.1	40.7	50.0	123.5	86.7	—	—	100.0	93.9	69.7	—
70.2	91.9	80.4	65.2	104.1	88.7	85.3	86.7	93.7	—	50.0	81.4	92.1	17.0	49.0	46.7	113.2	88.4	—	—	95.6	90.0	69.2	—
66.8	91.1	82.6	70.4	102.4	89.8	84.6	87.7	82.9	—	49.6	73.9	80.9	17.6	45.3	53.3	106.6	104.9	—	—	101.5	86.4	69.3	—
68.8	90.8	80.3	66.7	96.1	91.5	87.9	85.6	86.1	—	53.1	77.8	85.4	17.6	45.6	46.7	117.2	88.2	—	—	104.3	87.0	63.9	—
71.8	95.4	83.3	64.9	83.1	90.7	90.8	80.8	82.3	—	50.4	83.3	92.1	15.8	45.1	57.1	111.1	83.7	—	—	104.6	84.2	62.0	—
—	—	88.3	—	—	89.3	—	—	84.8	—	—	85.7	94.7	22.2	51.1	64.7	122.0	81.2	—	—	—	89.9	—	—
10	10	11	10	10	11	10	10	11	—	10	11	11	12	11	11	11	11	—	—	10	11	10	—
66.8–	90.8–	75.6–	64.9–	83.1–	86.3–	82.6–	80.8–	82.3–	—	48.1–	73.9–	80.9–	15.5–	40.7–	38.5–	106.6–	74.0–	—	—	95.6–	82.1–	60.9–	—
77.1	104.7	88.3	70.4	106.8	92.7	90.8	89.6	94.1		55.8	97.4	102.8	22.2	52.0	64.7	124.0	104.9			111.7	93.9	69.7	
71.3	95.4	80.8	67.4	97.0	89.8	86.3	86.0	88.6	—	51.4	84.2	92.2	17.7	47.1	49.5	117.7	87.3	—	—	102.2	87.8	66.0	—
4	4	4	4	4	3	4	4	4	—	2	3	3	3	3	3	2	2	—	—	4	4	4	—
66.7–	85.3–	79.1–	65.9–	81.5–	88.7	86.8–	81.0–	82.9–	—	52.6;	79.1–	87.2–	13.9–	45.1–	38.5–	113.5;	87.2;	—	—	93.4–	87.4–	69.2–	—
76.7	93.8	88.0	73.6	89.1	91.2	90.8	87.6	93.5		56.4	84.1	94.9	18.6	49.0	53.9	123.1	88.9			96.4	93.8	72.8	
70.7	90.4	84.3	68.5	85.8	90.2	88.6	84.7	88.0	—	54.7	81.2	90.0	16.7	46.7	46.7	118.3	83.1	—	—	94.9	90.8	71.2	—
72.7	92.6	85.2	68.1	81.6	89.6	90.2	83.3	87.9	90.2	56.4	89.7	94.6	19.1	49.0	50.0	110.3	85.1	89.2	69.6	98.5	90.2	69.2	75.2
69.2	91.3	84.5	71.0	96.8	85.6	87.6	84.1	81.8	—	48.2	85.4	92.1	18.6	50.0	66.7	128.3	67.6	—	—	100.7	95.1	70.5	—
72.8	98.5	85.8	72.9	104.0	90.5	86.3	89.8	83.3	—	58.3	92.7	—	19.3	40.8	50.0	136.2	102.5	—	—	95.5	94.2	76.4	—
69.9	100.8	79.3	69.3	100.0	90.8	87.5	86.0	80.5	—	57.9	92.9	100.0	16.5	42.1	37.5	112.3	79.2	—	—	97.1	101.1	80.5	—
—	—	82.7	68.4	84.5	90.3	93.9	83.3	—	—	51.3	85.6	86.1	21.4	51.2	84.6	155.3	81.1	—	—	85.0	101.1	80.5	—
71.7	94.8	77.9	70.4	91.9	89.4	91.1	73.6	82.3	—	55.2	83.3	92.1	17.5	42.6	—	113.6	85.7	—	—	99.3	93.1	70.9	—
73.4	94.7	85.7	73.3	102.5	89.2	84.5	85.3	85.3	—	53.2	85.0	91.9	18.3	51.1	35.7	130.6	82.2	—	—	94.6	94.1	77.4	—
72.9	94.2	81.9	69.3	100.8	89.3	85.4	85.2	88.9	1	51.0	73.3	82.5	17.8	45.4	68.8	118.5	89.4	—	—	104.4	87.9	66.4	—
4	4	4	4	4	4	4	4	4	1	4	4	3	4	4	4	4	4	1	1	4	4	4	1
69.2–	91.3–	79.3–	69.3–	91.9–	85.6–	84.5–	73.6–	80.5–		48.2–	73.3–	82.5–	16.5–	42.1–	37.5–	112.3–	79.2–			97.1–	83.8–	66.2–	
72.9	100.8	84.5	72.0	100.8	90.8	91.1	86.0	88.9		57.9	92.9	100.0	20.5	45.4	68.8	128.3	97.6			104.4	95.1	70.9	
70.9	95.3	80.3	70.0	96.8	88.8	87.9	82.3	82.8	—	53.1	82.7	91.7	18.0	45.0	58.0	118.2	88.0	—	—	100.4	90.0	68.5	—
2	2	2	2	2	2	2	2	2	1	2	2	2	2	2	2	2	2	1	1	2	2	2	1
72.7;	92.6;	85.2;	68.1;	81.6	89.6;	86.3;	83.3;	83.3;	—	56.4;	89.7;	—	19.1;	49.0	50.0;	110.3;	85.1;	—	—	95.5;	90.2;	69.2;	—
72.8	98.5	85.7	72.9	104.0	90.5	90.2	89.8	87.9		58.3	92.7		19.3		50.0	136.2	102.5			98.5	94.2	76.4	
72.8	95.6	85.0	70.5	92.0	90.1	83.3	86.6	85.6	90.2	57.4	91.2	94.6	19.2	44.9	50.0	123.3	93.8	89.3	69.6	97.0	92.0	72.8	75.2
—	94.7	85.8	73.3	102.5	89.2	84.5	83.3	85.3	—	53.2	85.0	91.9	18.3	—	35.7	130.6	82.2	—	—	94.6	94.1	77.4	—
73.4		82.7	68.4	84.5	90.3	93.9	85.3			51.3	85.6	86.1	21.4	51.2	84.6	155.3	81.1			85.0	101.1	80.5	

Tribal divisions and subdivisions / Catalogue No. / Sex and stages of life / Number of cases / Averages and ranges	„Central angle" (*Klaatsch*)	Cranio-facial (*Falkenburger*)	Interoccipital	ANGLES															Length-breadth
				Glabella-lambda	Basion-bregma	Nasion-basion	Basion-opisthion	Nasion-bregma	Lambda-bregma	Opisthion-lambda	Prosthion-nasion	Nasospinale-nasion	Prosthion-nasospinale	Orbital height	Ramus tangent–alveolar plane	Ramus tangent–basal tangent	Chin vertical–basal tangent	Condylo–coronoid tangent–alveolar plane	
				To ear-eye plane											Mandibulo-alveolar plane				
	(°)	(°)	(°)	(°)	(°)	(°)	(°)	(°)	(°)	(°)	(°)	(°)	(°)	(°)	(°)	(°)	(°)	(°)	
KOSKIMO																			
Divisional total																			
♂ cases	104	103	104	104	104	103	103	104	104	104	102	96	103	98	32	32	32	32	103
range	89–106	85–96	111–144	0–16	81–99	24–36	+12 to −16	37–52	13–39	112–138	74–88	76–93	62–90	79–104	60–87	101–130	72–86	−24 to +8	64.2–89.1
average	96.6	90.4	127.9	7.1	88.5	31.3	−1.1	44.5	26.9	123.3	81.1	83.0	75.2	88.5	75.9	112.5	80.0	−5.2	76.3
♀ cases	35	32	35	35	35	35	35	35	35	35	33	32	32	34	10	10	10	10	39
range	91–110	86–96	117–145	1–16	83–98	25–36	+5 to −15	37–51	16–36	112–134	76–86	77–89	56–79	77–93	68–78	110–124	67–83	−16 to +9	66.8–85.4
average	96.5	91.4	129.8	8.2	88.3	30.4	−3.7	44.5	25.1	122.1	81.2	82.7	72.8	86.3	72.6	118.4	77.8	−6.6	76.9
juv. cases	2	2	2	2	2	2	2	2	2	2	2	2	2	2	—	—	—	—	2
range	93;94	86;90	128;134	6;7	86;88	30;32	−1 to −6	47;49	30;33	121;125	76;86	79;89	68;79	87;95					66.8;84.9
average	93.5	88.0	131.0	6.5	87.0	31.0	−3.5	48.0	31.5	123.0	81.0	84.0	73.5	91.0	—	—	—	—	81.2
inf. cases	6	3	6	6	6	4	5	6	6	5	5	5	3	6	1	1	1	1	8
range	90–100	80–91	121–133	5–18	77–90	28–30	−2 to −9	47–58	17–30	108–123	80–92	79–92	78–88	85–95					68.2–90.0
average	95.5	85.3	125.2	11.2	84.3	29.3	−5.6	52.5	25.2	116.2	85.4	86.6	82.0	89.5	55.0	130.0	83.0	+26.0	81.0

INDICES

	Skull									Face and mandible											Cranio-facial			
Length-height	Breadth-height	Transverse frontal	Transverse frontoparietal	Sagital parieto-frontal (arcs)	Sagital frontal	Sagital parietal	Sagital occipital	Foramen magnum	Facial	Upper facial	Orbital (mf)	Orbital (la)	Interorbital (mf-mf to dk-dk)	Nasal	Transverse nasal bone	Maxillo-alveolar	Palatal	Bicondylo-bigonial breadth (mandible)	Ramus (mandible)	Transverse cranio-facial	Fronto-biorbital (ft-ft to fmt-fmt)	Jugo-frontal	Jugo-mandibular
102	101	99	101	104	105	104	103	103	24	97	102	101	95	102	79	98	95	30	31	98	99	99	24
63.8– 79.0	84.1– 105.3	72.8– 90.5	52.9– 76.6	76.3– 111.7	85.6– 99.2	76.5– 95.6	73.6– 95.7	71.4– 106.4	81.9– 97.9	48.1– 65.4	73.9– 97.4	80.9– 105.6	14.4– 22.2	36.8– 54.7	22.2– 69.2	103.5– 139.1	68.2– 104.9	71.7– 98.6	52.3– 74.1	87.3– 111.7	79.8– 95.1	80.6– 74.8	62.3– 84.8
72.0	95.0	81.9	67.4	94.2	90.2	87.6	85.7	86.1	89.4	55.4	84.9	94.0	17.7	44.7	48.7	120.8	87.9	86.1	61.7	99.1	87.8	68.0	74.0
37	37	38	39	39	38	39	37	36	10	33	37	35	37	36	33	33	33	11	11	37	36	37	10
66.7– 83.1	83.4– 103.9	71.8– 90.3	60.1– 75.8	74.4– 110.7	87.1– 93.4	81.5– 93.5	79.4– 91.9	74.3– 100.0	79.7– 94.7	47.2– 61.1	76.7– 93.0	84.6– 105.3	13.5– 22.0	38.5– 54.3	33.3– 71.4	110.3– 137.8	66.7– 102.5	81.4– 93.2	49.2– 69.6	86.2– 104.0	82.2– 94.7	62.4– 77.4	72.2– 88.8
72.5	94.7	83.7	68.3	93.1	90.3	87.4	86.1	86.7	90.6	56.1	86.6	95.2	18.0	45.8	52.4	120.8	85.9	88.0	60.8	96.6	89.1	70.7	77.9
2	2	2	2	2	2	2	2	2	—	2	2	2	2	2	2	2	2	—	—	2	2	2	—
73.4 ; 83.0	93.6 ; 94.7	83.8 ; 85.7	69.5 ; 73.3	95.3 ; 102.5	88.3 ; 89.2	84.5 ; 86.1	85.3 ; 87.1	85.5 ; 90.9	—	53.2 ; 54.4	85.0 ; 85.1	91.9 ; 94.6	16.8 ; 18.3	46.9 ; 51.1	35.7 ; 37.5	130.6 ; 142.2	82.2 ; 100.0	—	—	84.4 ; 94.6	94.1 ; 97.0	77.4 ; 78.4	—
75.7	94.2	84.8	71.4	98.9	88.8	85.8	86.2	88.1	—	53.8	85.5	93.5	17.5	49.0	37.0	136.4	91.1	—	—	89.5	85.5	77.9	—
4	4	7	7	8	8	8	7	4	—	5	8	7	5	6	6	5	5	1	1	6	6	5	—
69.8– 83.0	86.8– 91.8	80.2– 90.2	64.7– 82.6	84.5– 111.6	86.3– 90.8	77.6– 93.9	80.6– 96.5	71.0– 79.4	—	49.6– 61.5	85.4– 100.0	86.1– 111.1	15.1– 21.4	34.5– 50.0	35.7– 84.6	132.5– 155.3	81.1– 106.2	—	—	79.1– 89.3	97.7– 103.1	79.5 ; 92.7	—
75.7	90.0	83.3	68.5	95.9	86.7	85.5	84.9	76.2	—	54.2	90.4	99.3	18.6	45.4	54.7	147.4	90.1	88.0	53.5	82.9	99.7	83.2	—

PLATE I

Superposition of mediansagittal diagrams of: ——, Kamloops ♂ (1284); ...., Chinook ♂ (4449); - - -, Koskimo ♂ (3642).

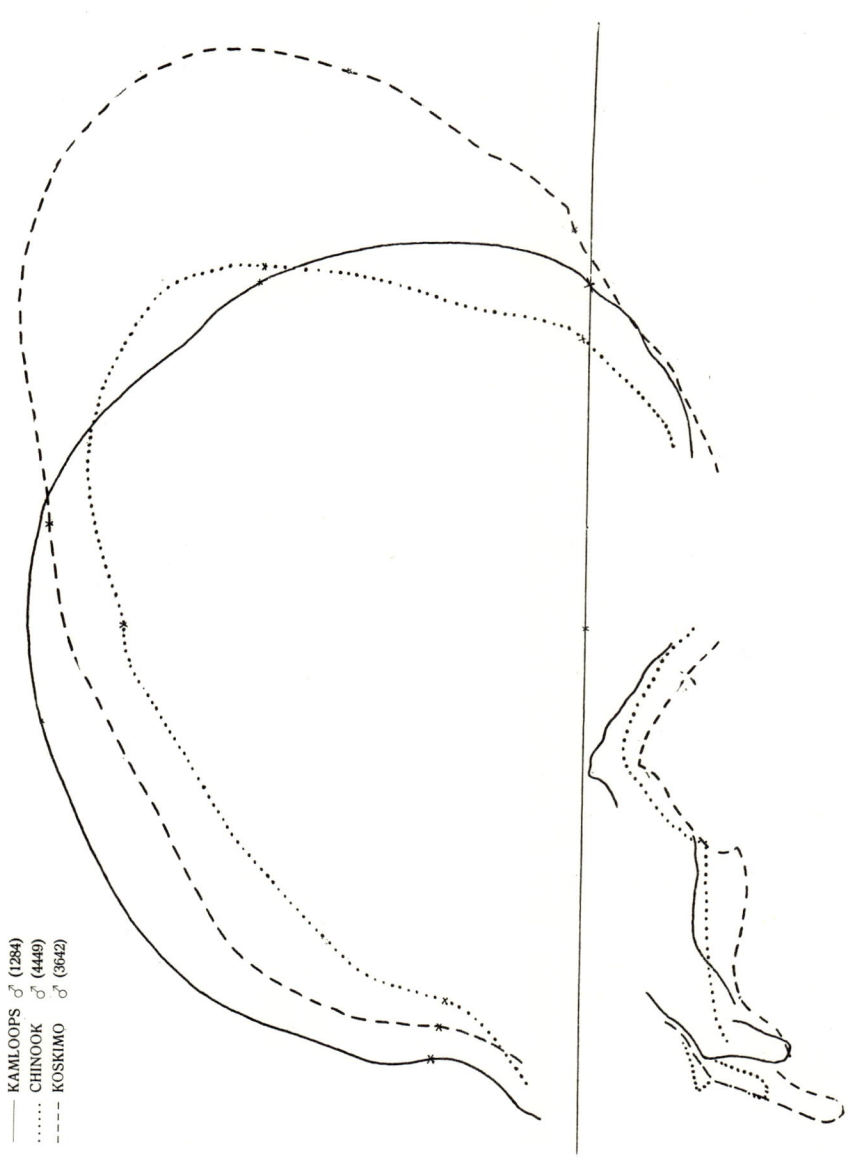

The North Pacific Coast.

PLATE II.

MEDIANSAGITTAL TRACINGS OF THE UNDEFORMED VARIETIES
(about one-sixth natural size):

---

1. Chukchee,   3846 ♂,   3844 ♀
2. Eskimo,   3712 ♂,   3710 ♀
3. Athapascan,   1551 ♂,   4339 ♀
4. Haida,   3747 ♂,   3742 ♀
5. Kamloops,   1284 ♂,   1410 ♀
6. Spences Bridge,   99 ♂,   1641 ♀
7. Nicola Lake,   2611 ♂,   2612 ♀
8. Lytton,   1057 ♂,   4313 ♀
9. Lillooet,   2621 ♂,   2622 ♀

Letters in connection with enumeration 1—9, comprising in each case a male and a female specimen, signify:

A. Superposition of male (———) and female (– – – –) outlines in ear-eye orientation, the poria coinciding.

B. Superposition of male outlines: ———, glabella ear-eye orientation; ········, glabella-opisthocranion orientation, the glabellae coinciding.

C. Superposition of female outlines, as under B.

Jesup North Pacific Expedition, Vol. XI.   Plate II.

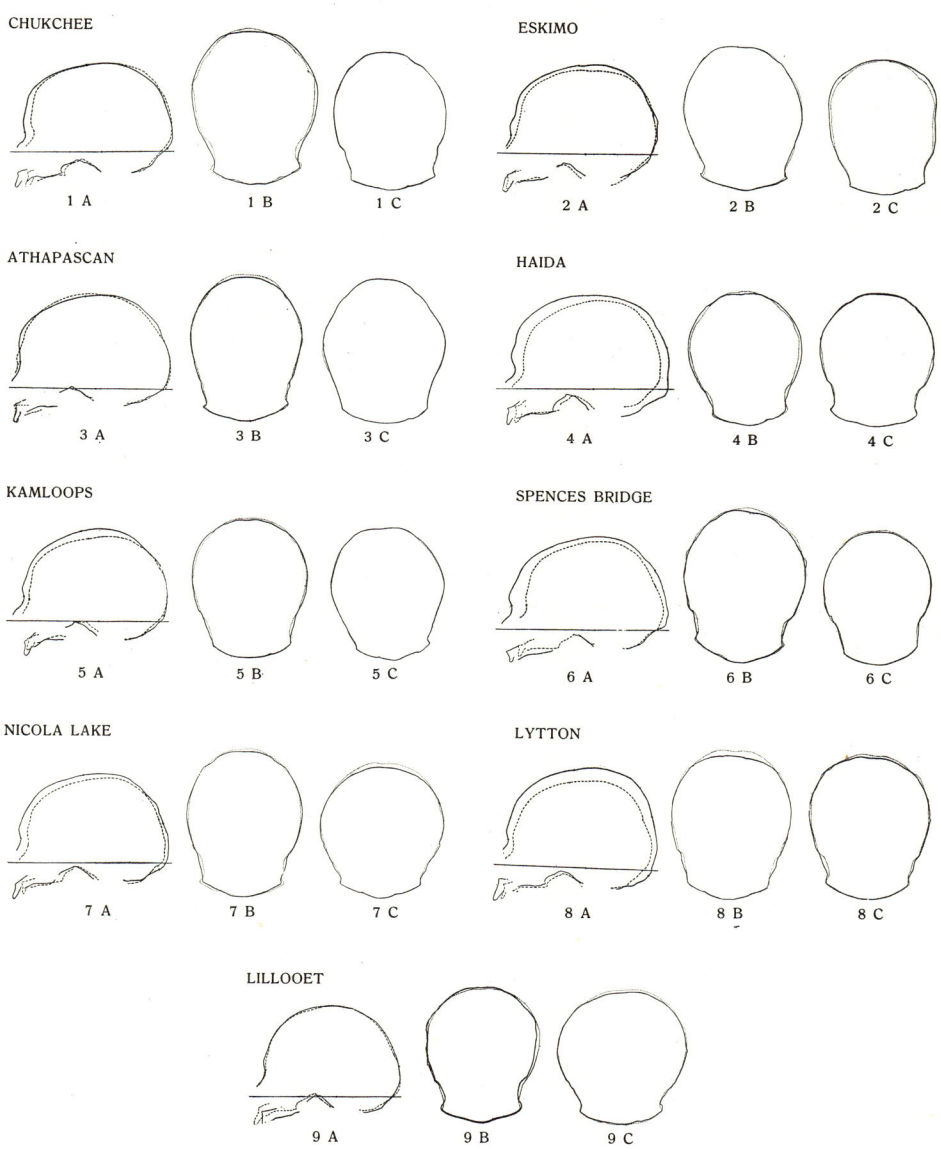

The North Pacific Coast.

PLATE III

Lillooet (2618 ♂) in the five cranial normae.

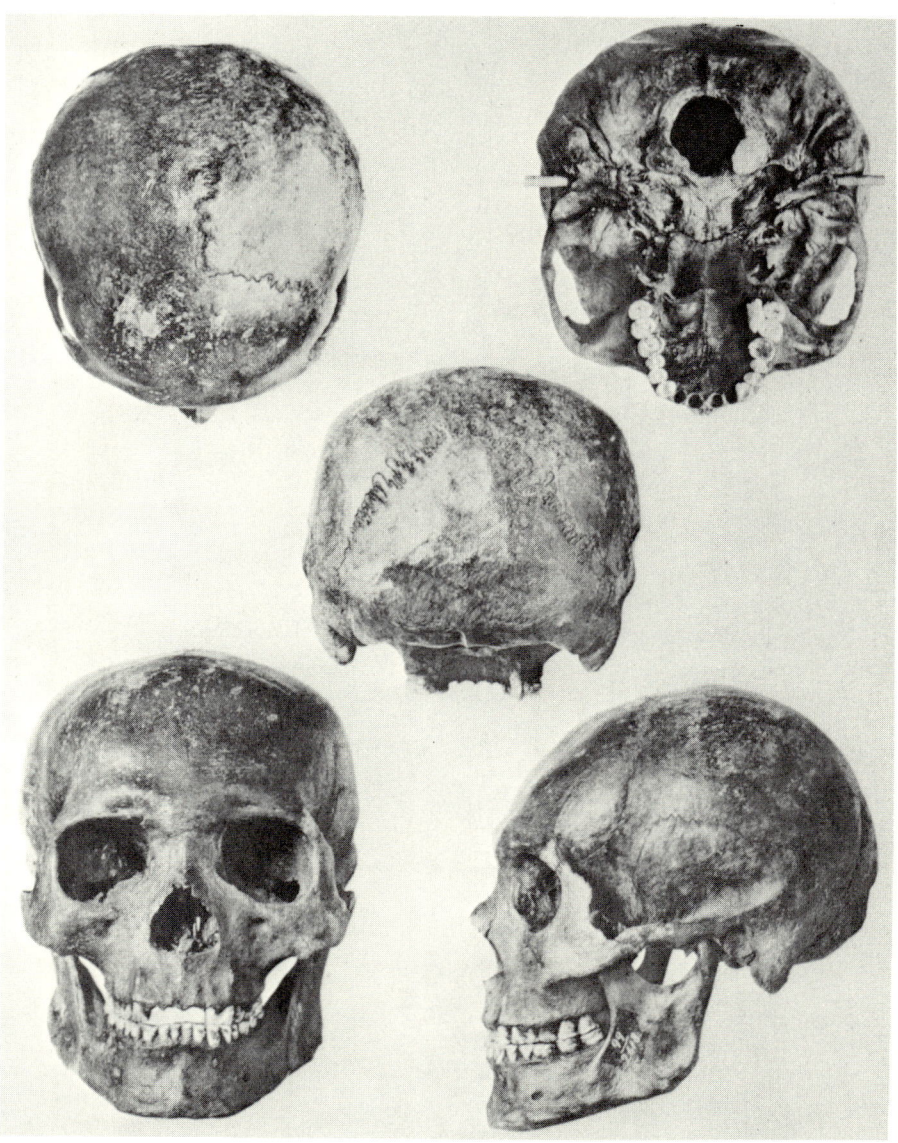

The North Pacific Coast.

PLATE IV

Kamloops (1410 ♀) in the five cranial normae.

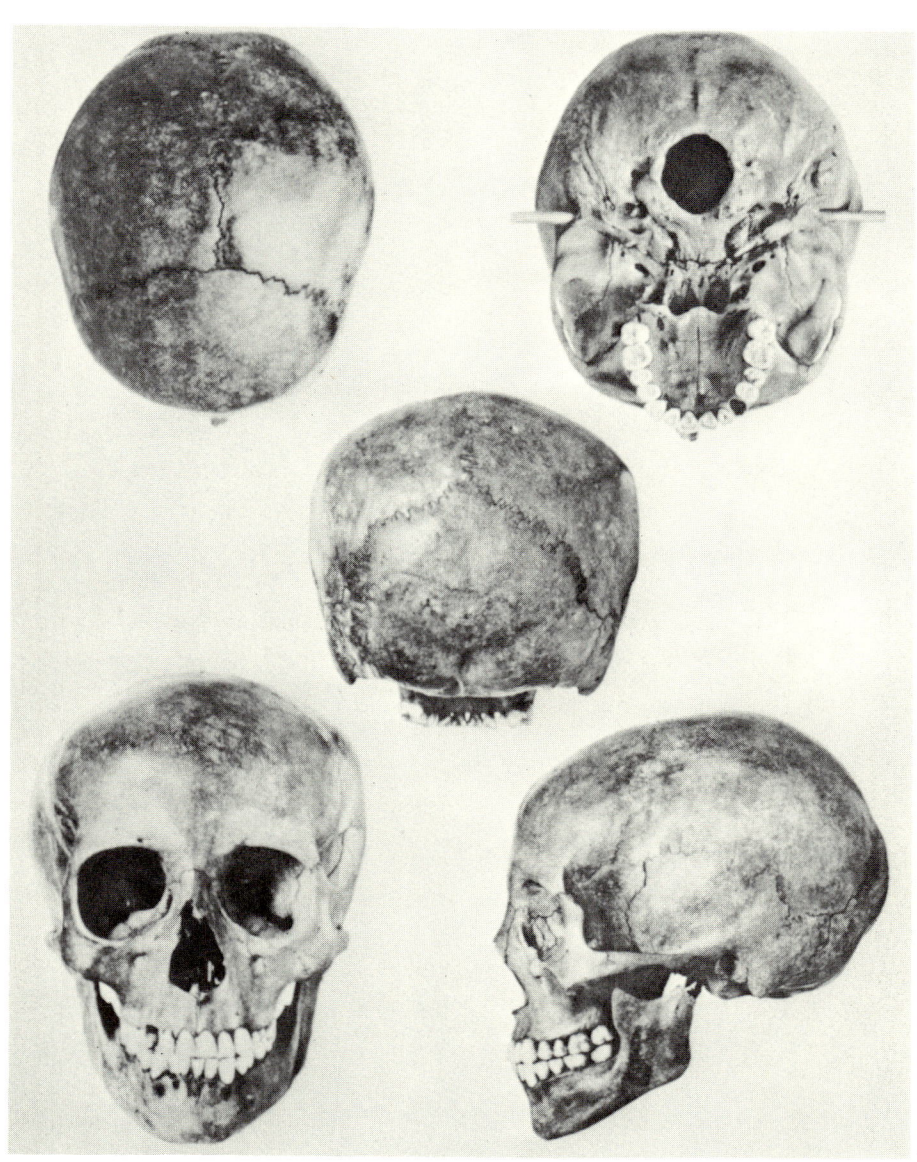

The North Pacific Coast.

PLATE V

Spences Bridge (99 ♂) in the five cranial normae.

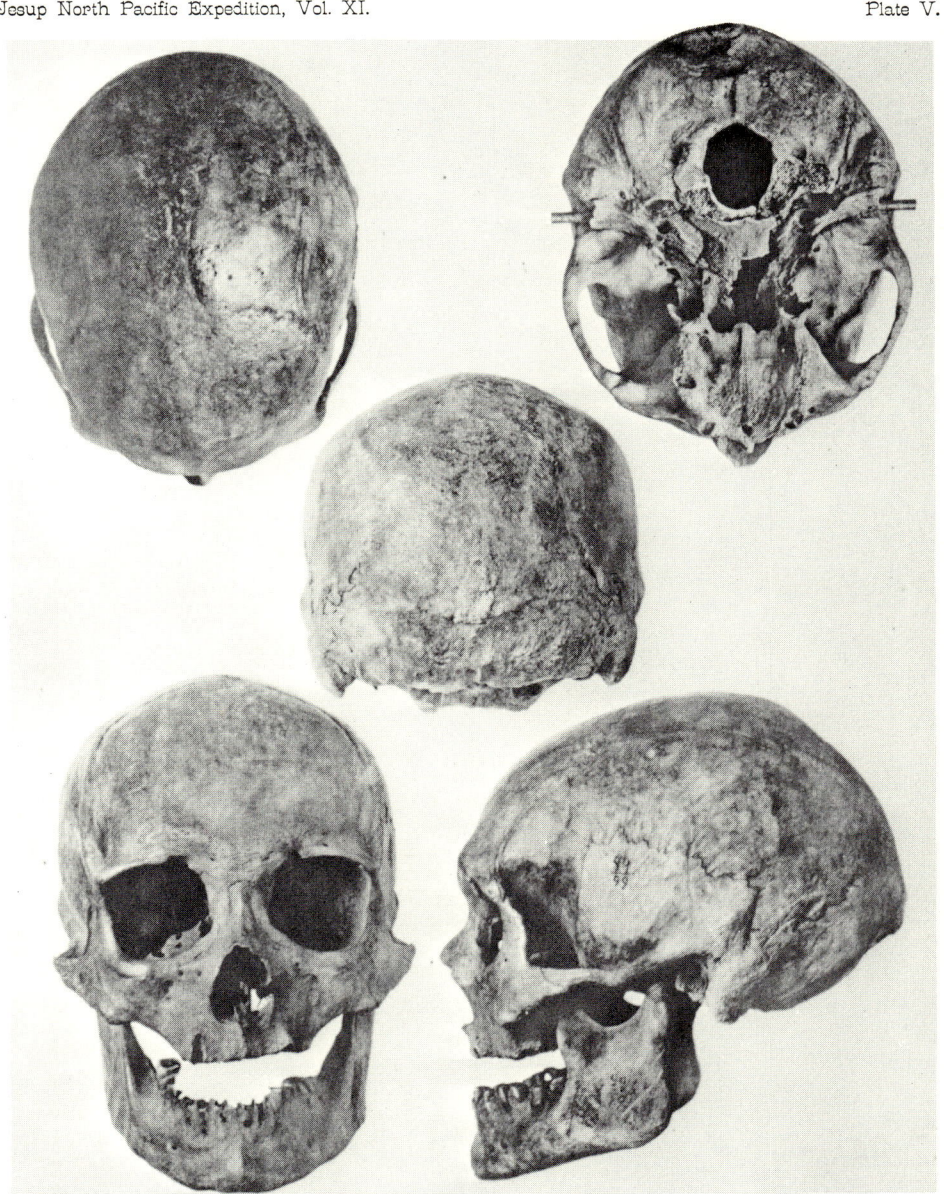

The North Pacific Coast.

PLATE VI

Haids (3751 ♂) in the five cranial normae.

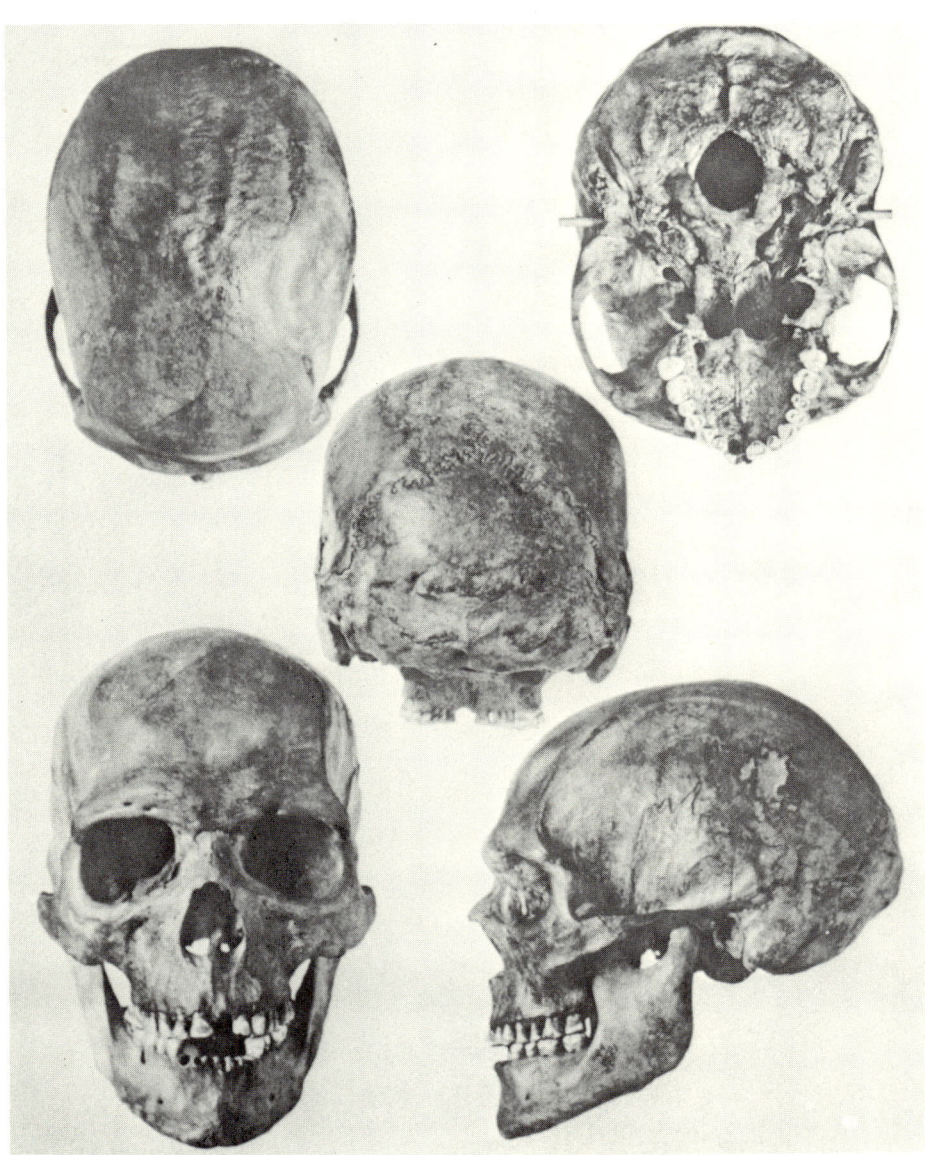

The North Pacific Coast.

PLATE VII

Eskimo from Indian Point, Siberia, (3776 ♂) in the five cranial normae.

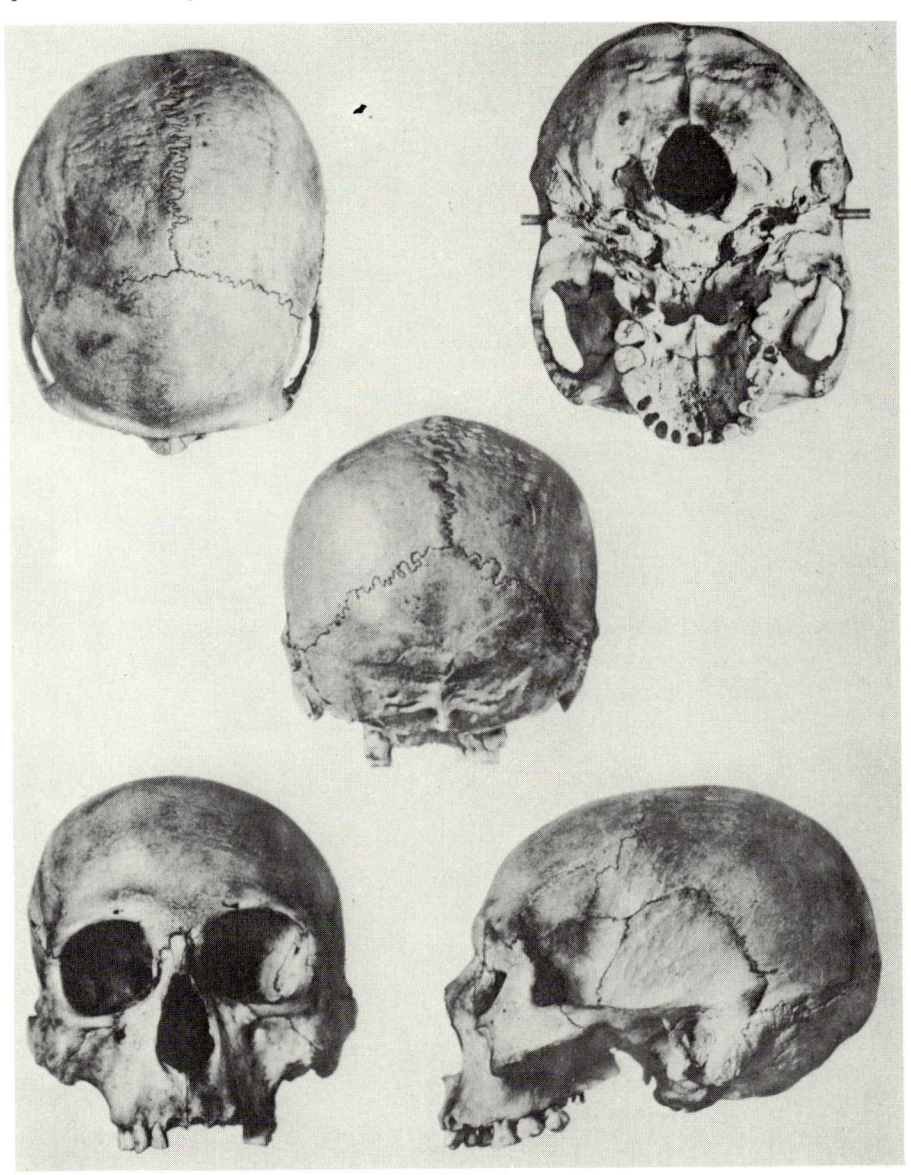

The North Pacific Coast.

PLATE VIII

Salish, North Saanich (2644 A ♂) in the five cranials normae.

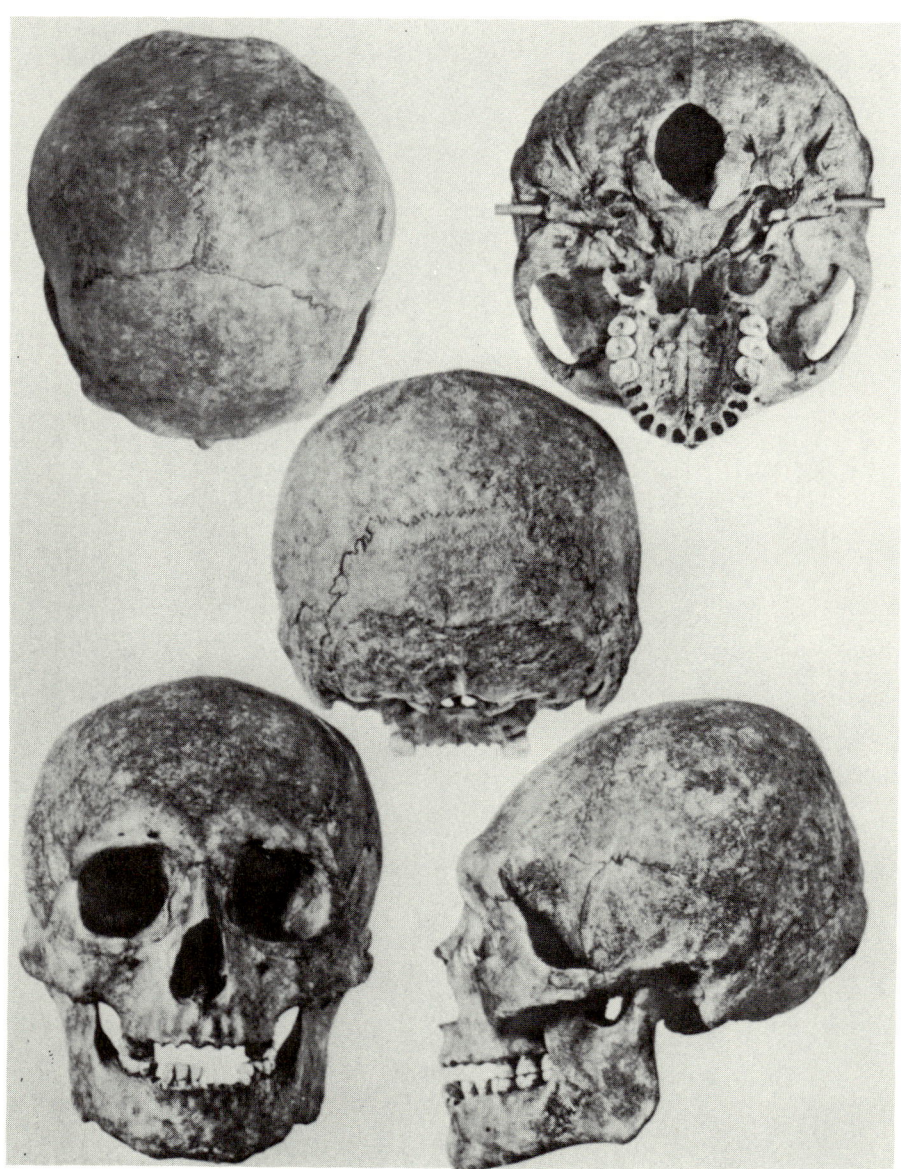

Plate VIII.

The North Pacific Coast.

PLATE IX

Chinook (2676 ♂) in the five cranial normae.

Jesup North Pacific Expedition, Vol. XI. Plate IX.

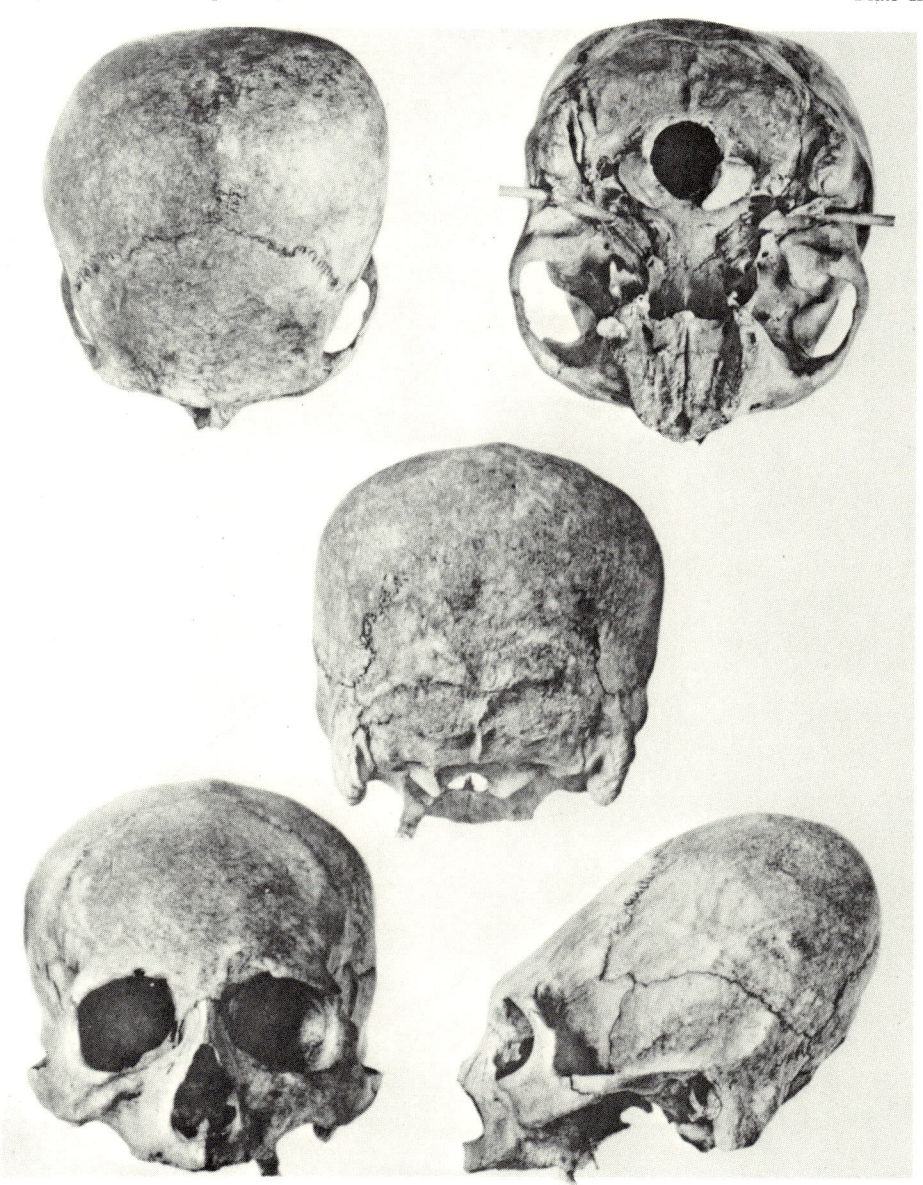

The North Pacific Coast.

PLATE X

Nimkish (1671 ♂) in the five cranial normae.

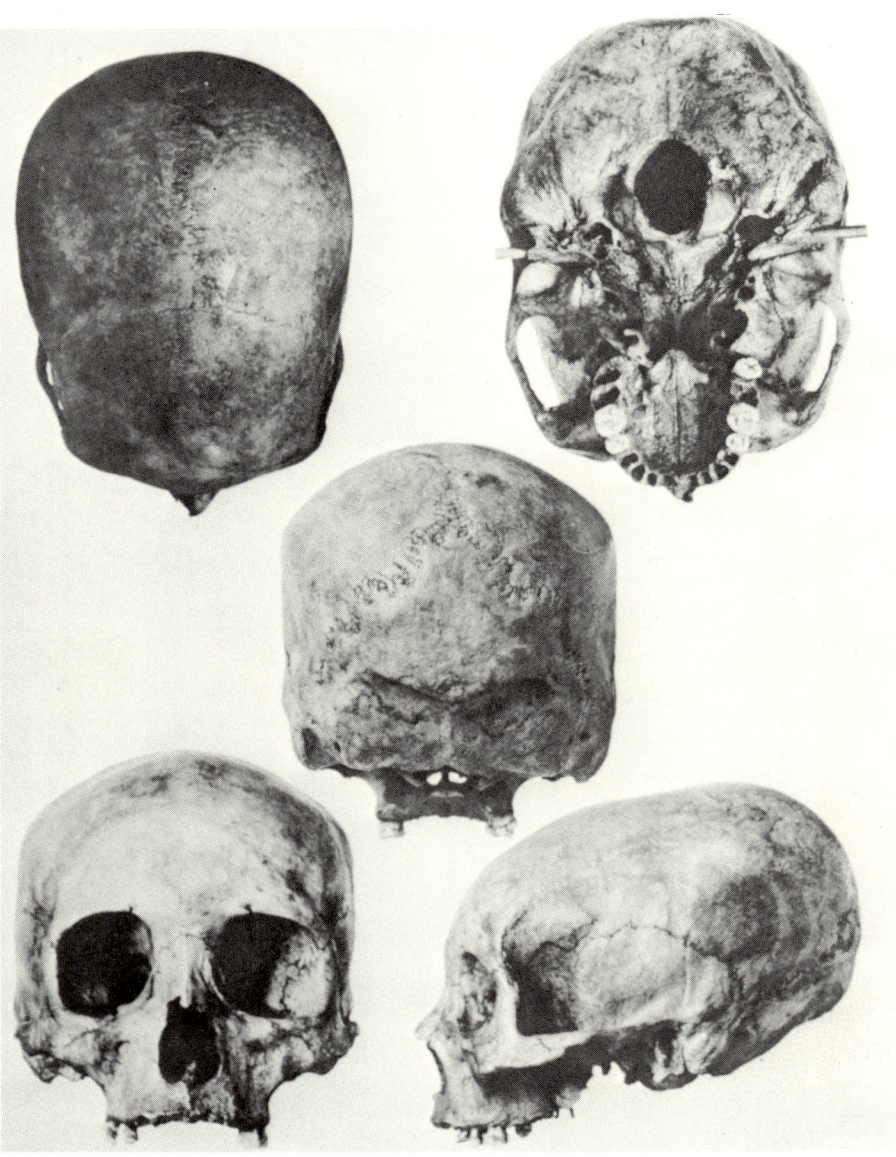

The North Pacific Coast.

PLATE XI

Koskimo (3642 ♂) in the five cranial normae.

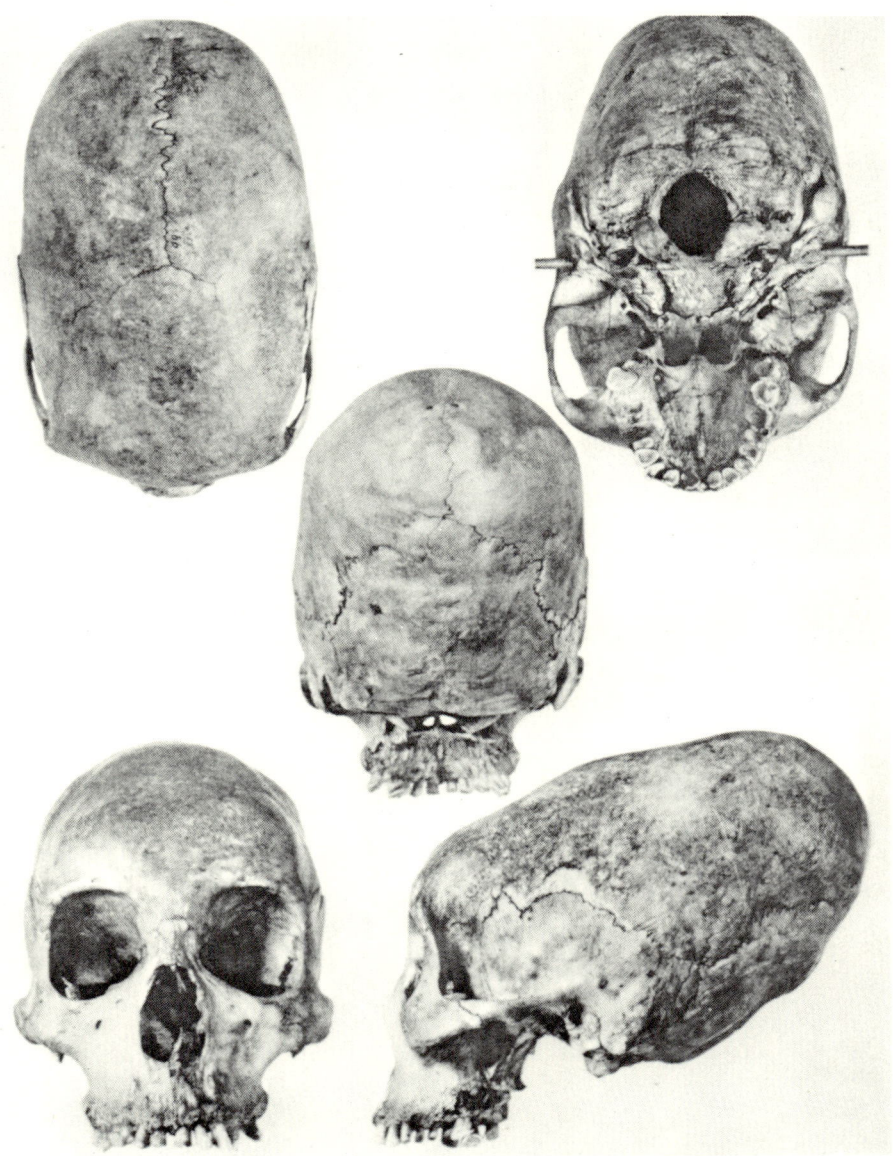

The North Pacific Coast.

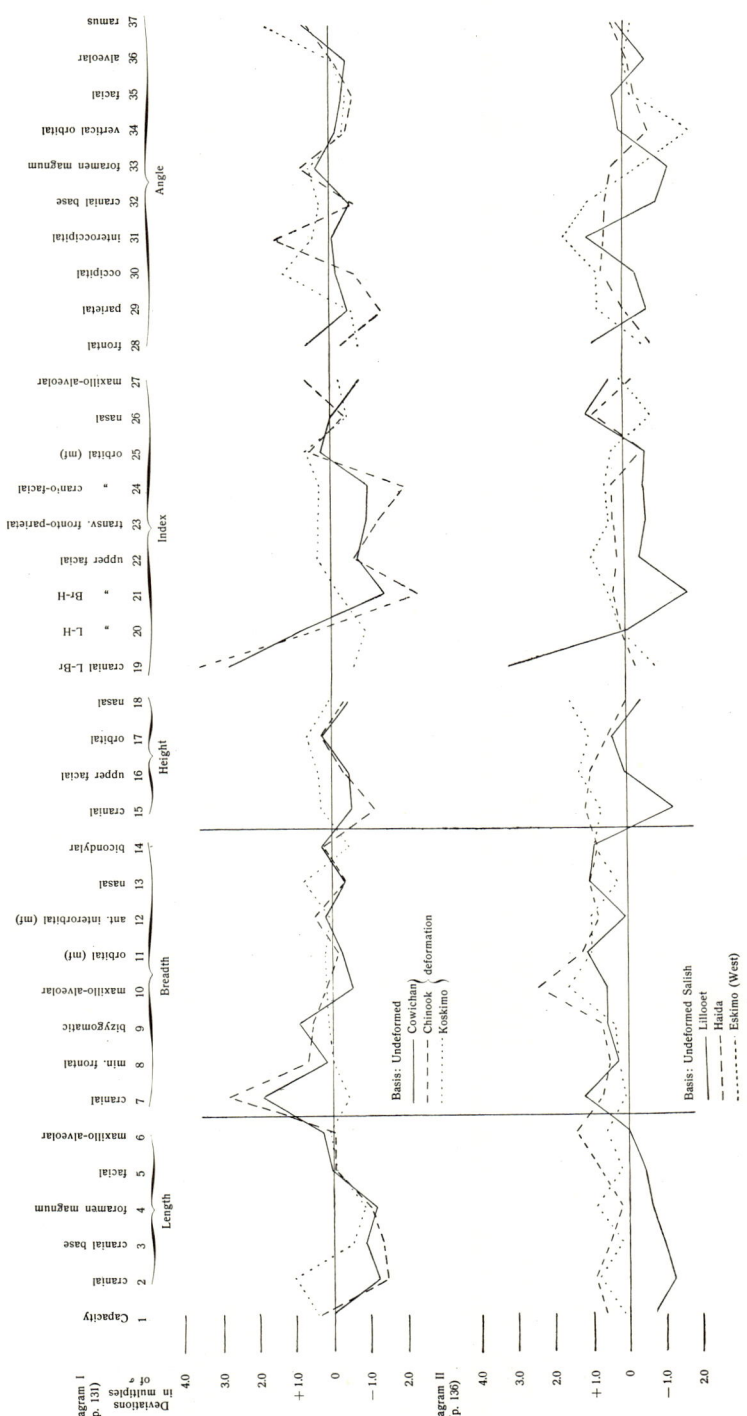

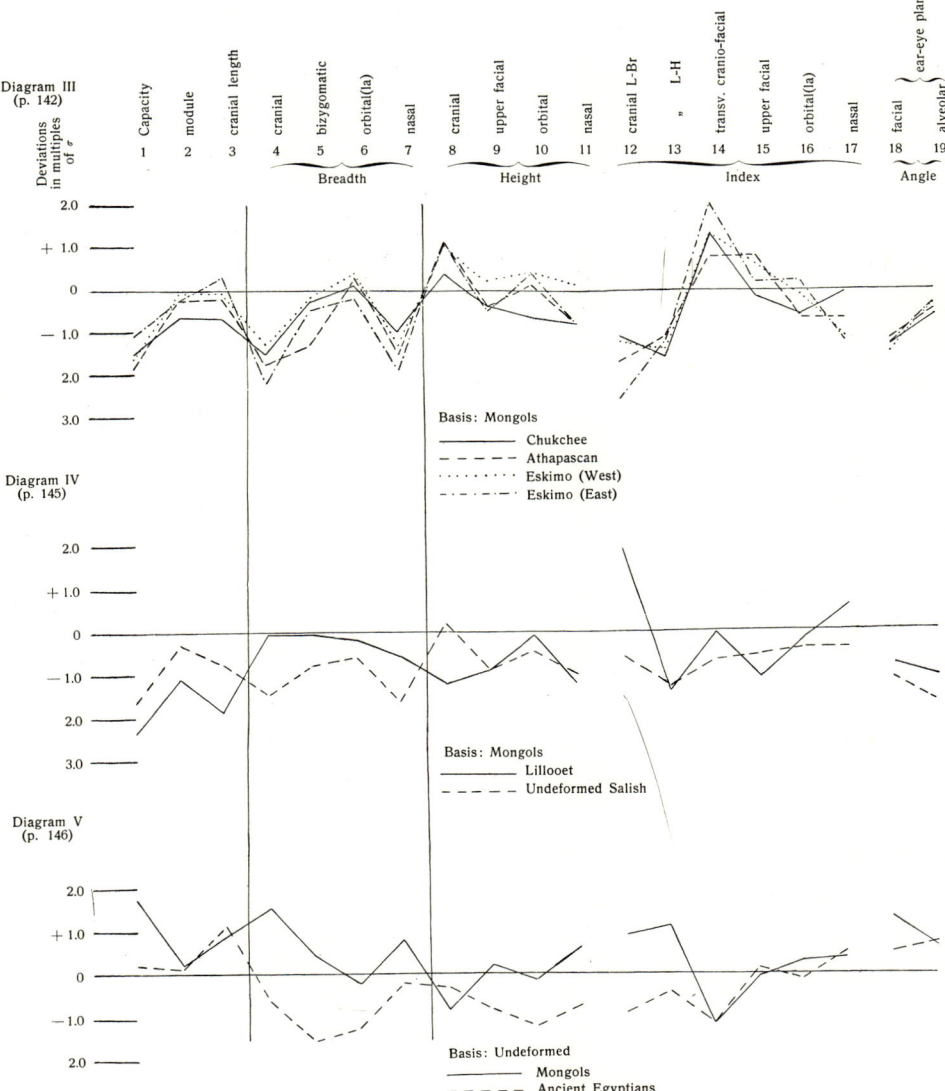